BUSINESS
WORLD

BUSINESS WORLD

LAWRENCE J. GITMAN
Wright State University

CARL McDANIEL, JR.
University of Texas at Arlington

JOHN WILEY & SONS
NEW YORK   CHICHESTER   BRISBANE   TORONTO   SINGAPORE

Acknowledgments for Cases and Career Appendixes
appear after Glossary.

Illustrator: John Balbalis
Designer: Rafael Hernandez
Photo Editor: Kathy Bendo
Depth Editor: Arthur Vergara
Senior Production Supervisor: Mary Halloran
Editorial Assistant: Susan Ahlstrom

Library of Congress Cataloging in Publication Data

Gitman, Lawrence J.
    Business world.

    Bibliography
    Includes index.
    1. Business.   2. Industrial management.   I. McDaniel,
Carl D.   II. Title.
HF5351.G5   1983   658   82-17577
ISBN 0-471-08165-5

Printed in the United States of America

10 9 8 7 6 5 4 3

To our children:
Zachary and Jessica;
and Mark, Shelly,
Kelcy, and Wendy

ABOUT THE AUTHORS

Lawrence J. Gitman is well-known as the author of *Principles of Managerial Finance*, 3d ed. (Harper & Row, 1982), *Personal Finance*, 2d ed. (Dryden Press, 1981), and numerous articles in such revered journals as *Financial Management, Journal of Economics and Business*, and *Journal of Financial Research*. He is a coauthor of *Fundamentals of Investing* (Harper & Row, 1981), *Financial Management: Cases* (West Publishing, 1978), *Porstrat: A Portfolio Strategy Simulation* (John Wiley & Sons, 1981), and the forthcoming *Managerial Finance* (Harper & Row, 1984). He has degrees from Purdue University, the University of Dayton, and the University of Cincinnati, where he earned his doctorate in Finance. Currently Professor of Finance at Wright State University, Dr. Gitman was a member of the faculties of San Diego State University and The University of Tulsa.

Carl McDaniel, Jr. is known to teachers and students of business studies as the author of *Marketing*, 2d ed. (Harper & Row, 1982), and many articles in such well-known journals as *Business Horizons, Journal of Marketing*, and *California Management Review*. He is a co-author of *Contemporary Marketing Research* (Harper & Row, 1983) and the editor of *Readings in Contemporary Marketing*, 2d ed. (Dryden Press, 1977). He has degrees from the University of Arkansas and Arizona State University, where he earned both his master's degree and a doctorate in Business Administration. Dr. McDaniel is chairman of the Department of Marketing at the University of Texas at Arlington and the co-owner of a large Dallas-based marketing research firm.

PREFACE

Business World has been developed to provide students with what may just possibly be the most lively, interesting, and stimulating textbook of their college careers. In the making of the book, equal importance has been given to the depth and the breadth of the topics covered. "Lively, interesting" shouldn't be translated as "superficial, shallow." Rather, extensive research ensures that the *right* material has been covered, and in sufficient detail to provide a solid foundation for the student. An in-depth model for the text and each chapter was used, based on a broad marketing research survey of over 400 introductory course instructors.

Because this is the only course in which students will be exposed to all areas of business, it's imperative that subjects aren't given a "quick once-over." On the contrary, we've created an intellectually sound text to meet the highest standards. It's a book conceived with both the student and the instructor in mind. Before each chapter was written, current research on the subject was thoroughly reviewed. Traditional concepts were updated with the latest findings and contemporary business practices. We also solicited and utilized the comments of over 90 reviewers.

A DELIGHTFUL AND ENJOYABLE BOOK TO READ

As a busy instructor, perhaps teaching over a hundred students and several different subjects, you recognize the importance of choosing the right textbook. The first criterion of such a book is that it hold the reader's interest. There's probably no greater hindrance to learning than a dull textbook. With this in mind, we've strived to make *Business World* a truly pleasurable and captivating reading experience. This has been accomplished by:

- **A state-of-the-art design program.** The business-magazine format of *Business World* creates a stimulating visual orientation. It's familiar to the student, businesslike and beautiful—but not watered down.
- **A creative, custom-designed art program.** We incorporate 110 original illustrations and many full-color photographs throughout *Business World* to illustrate concepts and drive home key points.
- **A lively, informal writing style developed over the years by two highly experienced and successful authors.** Careful attention to language, sentence structure, and the use of hundreds of "real-world" examples make *Business World* engrossing while at the same time easy to use.
- **Highlighting of real-world examples.** Not only is there a multitude of examples in the body of the text, but there's more in special, highlighted sections of *Business World*. Each chapter opens with a real-life vignette designed to stimulate the student to think about the topic to be covered and to want to know more about the subject. The *Talking Business* sections in each chapter offer anecdotes from the business world that help bring theoretical concepts to light so that students may see their practical applications. Each chapter also contains *On the Firing Line*—a contemporary, controversial issue that presents pros and cons yet lets the student draw his or her own conclusions.
- **Thorough coverage of small business.** Because many readers will enter the world of small business, *Business World* makes a special effort to meet their needs. We begin by devoting a full chapter to the subject in Part One. Each chapter also contains a *Perspective on Small Business* section. Real-world examples are used to illustrate how the material in a chapter is applied in the world of small-business management.
- **Special sections on career opportunities.** At the conclusion of each part of *Business World* a Ca-

reer Appendix is included. It begins with a general discussion of careers relevant to the material just completed (e.g. management, marketing, finance). Specific jobs are then previewed along with where the opportunities can be found, what skills are required, the employment outlook through 1990, and salary ranges. In addition, Chapter 25 offers a glimpse into the future of business and how to prepare for finding the right first job.

- **A unique chapter on real estate.** Because some students will select a career in real estate—and because everyone will hopefully have an opportunity to purchase his or her own property—*Business World* has a special chapter on real estate.

A PROFESSIONAL LEARNING TOOL

Creating a book that's a pleasure to read is an important step in developing an effective learning tool. Still, pedagogical devices are necessary to complete the task. *Business World* offers:

- Chapter learning objectives that challenge the student to explain, discuss, understand, and clarify the concepts to be presented.
- An opening vignette, full-color photos and illustrations, and special in-text sections to amplify and clarify text material.
- A comprehensive chapter summary.
- Key terms—bold-faced in the text and listed at the end of the chapter.
- Review questions, recalling key points in the chapter.
- Discussion questions—probing, thought-provoking questions designed to stimulate class discussion.
- Two case studies per chapter—short, real-world, written in a lively style to enhance student learning and enjoyment.
- A glossary, defining all key terms in the text.

A MODEL FOR THE TEXT

The model for chapter sequence and topical coverage in *Business World* was essentially developed by you, the instructor, based on our extensive marketing research study. It embodies a contemporary design to focus on today's business world. Part One begins with an overview of our business system, then explores the nature of the

social responsibilities of business. The stage is then set for a discussion of the forms of business organization. Part One concludes with a chapter on small business and its unique problems and opportunities.

The remainder of *Business World* follows in a logical sequence:

- Part Two   **Management**
- Part Three   **Marketing**
- Part Four   **Finance**
- Part Five   **Business Tools**

Part Six—**Further Dimensions and Opportunities**—presents chapters on the legal and tax environment of business, international business, and a concluding chapter on opportunities for the student in tomorrow's business world.

Each of the six parts of *Business World* has been designed to stand alone as a logical, highly teachable unit. Most importantly, every chapter was developed as a separate unit so that instructors can create their own unique sequence of material. For example, coverage of accounting prior to money and the financial system is easily accomplished without creating confusion for the student. Our "stand-alone" chapter design avoids the "building block" approach that can create gaps in understanding if the instructor departs from a rigid sequence of chapters.

AN INSTRUCTOR'S RESOURCE LIBRARY SECOND TO NONE

The key variables in creating a motivated and enthusiastic learning environment are: the textbook, the instructor's lectures, and supplemental material used to augment and reinforce the textbook. Because *Business World* reflects an awareness of the tremendous importance of the first course in business, we've created an instructor's resource library—**The Library**—to (1) minimize unnecessary classroom preparation time and (2) maximize the student's understanding and appreciation of the world of business and *Business World.* We want to thank Harold Gray at the University of Nebraska, Omaha for his contribution to the Instructor's Resource Manual, Student Study Guide, Test Bank, Course Index, and **The Library** Guide. We offer:

- *An Instructor's Resource Manual*—providing the most comprehensive resource for the instructor, including course and chapter outlines; suggested testing and grading procedures; topical outlines; teaching techniques; projects and answers to end-of-chapter cases; answers to review and discussion questions; quizzes; anecdotes to accompany each lecture; sample lectures to accompany each chapter; regional cases and issues; plus many more support items.

- *A Student Study Guide*—describing the objectives of the course, introducing the text, furnishing an outline of the highlights of the chapters in the text, providing self-tests, and offering future directions for study. We recommend the use of the Student Study Guide along with *Business World* as a formal part of the course; it acts as an effective learning and study aid.
- *A Test Bank*—containing over 2000 questions comprised of true/false as well as multiple-choice items. The Test Bank is available in printed as well as in computerized format.
- *Transparency Masters*—prepared by Jack Hill of the University of Nebraska, Omaha, and numbering over 200, supplementing and supporting the text material. The Transparency Masters are not repetitive of illustrations in the textbook; they were created especially to assist you in teaching the introductory course.
- *A Course Index and Package Guide*—prepared by Harold Gray, separately bound, and listing all of the supplements available to accompany *Business World*. It has suggested uses as well as material describing each supplement.
- *The World of Business Game*—developed by Harold Wilson and Ronald Hickman of Southern Illinois University, Carbondale, giving the student hands-on experience with decision making in the business environment. The game is easy to use, requiring only minutes' preparation time. The game is available upon request through the publisher, on computer tape or in card deck form.
- *Profiles of Business Leaders*—bound in one volume, and furnishing short biographies of key business leaders. The profiles can be used to illustrate key points within each chapter.
- *Business Forms*—a package of forms (sample invoice, stock certificate, mortgage, etc.) that intro-

duce students to the forms they'll be coming in contact with.

All items are separately bound and organized in *The Library* for easy access. *The Library* was designed to provide a helpful resource for storing and filing the many supplements that accompany *Business World*.

SLIDE LECTURE PROGRAM TO ACCOMPANY *BUSINESS WORLD*:

The *Business World* Slide Lecture Program was developed by Jerome Kinskey and Walter J. Bunnell of Sinclair Community College. It is designed to:

- Assist in condensing, illustrating, and reinforcing basic concepts and terms as part of classroom introduction-to-business lectures.
- Provide a method of instruction for self-directed and tutorial students.

The series is divided into four modules. The topics covered include:

- An Overview of the Business World
- Organization and Management
- Marketing
- Financial Management

The modules contain approximately 140 slides and are accompanied by a manual providing the instructor with a condensed easy-to-use format for covering business essentials quickly and conveniently. Topics were carefully selected for inclusion in this package and are arranged in a logical sequence. The slides and manual are related specifically to *Business World* and contain supplemental materials, examples, and illustrations. The slide and lecture program was developed from years of successful lectures in order to ensure a highly effective teaching aid. Lectures using these slides should help to hold the interest of students. The slide presentation can be used on an individualized basis to enhance classroom lectures. Students will be free to review the modules as often as needed in order to guarantee successful completion.

TO THE STUDENT

We wrote *Business World* for you. The study of the many exciting aspects of business described in this text should open the door to the wide, wide world of business. It may even motivate you to pursue further studies in this area as well as to take up a career in business—small or large. We urge you to open your mind, relax, and enjoy this text. Its magazine format, lively writing style, interesting illustrations, use of color, and the many learning aids included in each chapter should make your first exposure to the study of business pleasant as well as highly informative.

To help you understand the career opportunities that await you in the business world, we've included career sections at the end of each part of the text. These sections preview specific jobs and describe where the opportunities can be found, what skills are required, the employment outlook through 1990, and salary ranges. Also, the final chapter—"Opportunities for You in Tomorrow's World"—discusses the future of business and how to prepare for finding the right job. The glossary at the end of the text should help you to define key terms. For your convenience, the entries are keyed to the chapter in which they are first discussed.

The Student Study Guide for *Business World* is available for further enriching your first exposure to the world of business. It begins by presenting the course objectives and introducing the text. For each chapter the guide includes chapter outlines and highlights, self-tests with answers, and future directions for study. While the use of this guide may be optional, it should ease as well as augment your learning experience.

We applaud you for choosing to learn about the business world, and we're confident that this text and the study guide will greatly enhance your learning experience—and, as we've said, perhaps even help you to pursue further studies in business. Here's to you!

LAWRENCE J. GITMAN
CARL McDANIEL, JR.

ACKNOWLEDGMENTS

Special thanks go to a number of people who acted as subject-matter experts on several of the chapters of *Business World*. Allen Bludehorn, University of Missouri at Columbia; David Gray, University of Texas at Arlington; Ross A. Flaherty, Texas Weslyan University; Paul Lerman, Fairleigh Dickinson University for his contribution to Chapter 10; Arthur L. Schwartz, Jr., University of South Florida at St. Petersburg; and Bernard J. Winger, University of Dayton.

Thanks are also due Harold Gray, University of Nebraska at Omaha, for his outstanding contributions to the *Business World* Instructor's Resource Library as well as to the text. Hal's cooperation and perseverance are most appreciated and bear heavily on the success of the project.

Others who have made significant contributions to the text include free-lancers; Jo-Anne Naples, and her roster of talent associated with Naples Editing Services, including Judith Bleicher, Beverly Peavler, and Joyce Miller; Shirley Moore, who put together the glossary; and Sheila Ary, who compiled the index.

Special recognition goes to the team of professionals at John Wiley and Sons who made it all happen: Arthur Vergara, depth editor, for his outstanding work; Kathy Bendo, photo editor; David Smith, photo research assistant; John Balbalis, illustrator; Mary Halloran, senior production supervisor; Rafael Hernandez, designer; Dennis Sawicki, marketing manager; Rosanne McManus, marketing assistant; Bill Kellogg, supplements manager; and Susan Ahlstrom, editorial assistant, who kept the project on track.

The guiding and motivating force behind this enormous undertaking was our acquisition editor, Rick Leyh, without whose countless hours of devotion to the development, coordination, and marketing of this project it couldn't have achieved its high degree of teachability/learnability and been published in such timely fashion. We're deeply grateful to Rick for his almost unbelievable efforts. Special thanks are also due Serje Seminoff and other Wiley executives who were willing to make the sizable investment required for a project of this magnitude.

Our research assistants, Matthew T. Boone and Melanie Calahan, were invaluable in gathering countless materials in preparation of the first and subsequent drafts of the manuscript. We also owe a debt of gratitude to our secretaries and typists—Debbie Farmer, Ann Frazee, and Pat Kelly. A final word of thanks is due our families, who were most supportive during the nearly three years of intense work required to develop and produce this text.

The most important contributors to the text are the many reviewers and questionnaire respondents without whose input we couldn't have designed the text to satisfy the needs of those teaching introduction-to-business courses. In recognition of their important contributions, each of them along with his/her affiliation is listed below. We're most appreciative of their help.

Dick Adams
College of the Redwoods

Stanley R. Adamson
East Texas State University

Bertee Adkins
Eastern Kentucky University

Henry R. Adler
Michael J. Owens Technical
 College

Frank Aleman
Quinebaug Valley Community
 College

Carol A. Allen
California State University,
 Sacramento

Curtis Almlie
Mayville State College

James O. Armstrong III
John Tyler Community College

Doug Ashby
Lewis & Clark Community College

G. K. Barrett
Findlay College

Ray Bauer
Normandale Community College

Richard P. Baxter
Tennessee State University,
Nashville

Robert C. Bennett, Jr.
Delaware County Community
College

Daniel A. Bequette
Hartness College

Sidney M. Bernstein
The Loop College—Colleges of
Chicago

Donald Bertram
Lincoln Land Community College

Leonard S. Bethards
Miami-Dade Community College

Robert John Bielski
Indiana River Community College

Rex Bishop
Germanna Community College

Maurice H. Boutelle
Brenard Community College

John S. Bowdidge
Southwest Missouri State
University

Frank R. Bowen
Defiance College

James Bowman
Stephen F. Austin State University

Harvey S. Bronstein
Oakland Community College

Betty J. Brown
University of Tennessee, Knoxville

Howard Budner
Manhattan Community College

Bob S. Bulls
J. Sargeant Reynolds Community
College

Donald Cappa
Chabot College

James R. Carlson
Indian River Community College

Carmen Caruana
St. John's University

James Cathey
University of Arkansas–Monticello

Augusta Chadwick
Los Angeles Valley College

Ron Christy
Wichita State University

David J. Cirillo
Suffolk University

Herbert E. Clark
Shepard College

Jim Cockrell
Chemeketa Community College

Irving Cohen
Manhattan Community College

Charles W. Cole
University of Oregon, Eugene

Walter G. Connell
Montgomery County Community
College

Gerry Conner
Linn-Benton Community College

John L. Cook
Northeast Wisconsin Technical
Institute

John Coppola
Consumnes River College

Lucille Cordova
Community College of Denver,
Auraria

Helene A. Corley
Oxnard College

L. J. Cumbo, Jr.
Emory and Henry College

Cary E. Dermer
West Coast University

John E. Dittrich
University of Colorado, Colorado
Springs

G. A. Dod
Wayland Baptist College

Michael J. Dougherty
Milwaukee Area Technical College

Judy S. Edwards
University of Southwestern
Louisiana

Pat Ellebracht
Northeast Missouri State University

Howard Erdman
Southwest Texas Junior College

Leo A. Erlon
Rockland Community College

John Ernest
Los Angeles City College

S. J. Fader
Ramapo College of New Jersey

Tom Faranda
Inver Hills Community College

Wilson Fraker
College of San Mateo

Raymond Franz
Illinois Central College

Arthur Friedberg
Mohawk Valley Community College

William M. Friedman
Fontbonne College

Don C. Gaiser
Tyler Community College

Eduardo F. Garcia
Laredo Junior College

A. Gastineau
Valencia Community College

Carl Gates
Sauk Valley College

Marlin E. Gerber
Kalamazoo Valley Community College

Edwin Giermak
College of Du Page

Raymond Gilchrist
Longwood College

Bill Glover
Paris Junior College

Robert Goldberg
Northeastern University

David G. Goodman
University of Wisconsin-Whitewater

Phyllis K. Goodman
College of Du Page

W. G. Gordon
Bluefield College

C. Mallory Graves
Central Virginia Community College

Harold Gray
University of Nebraska, Omaha

Victor D. Green
San Joaquin Delta College

Maxine Gross
Gateway Technical Institute

Glenn G. Grothaus
St. Louis Community College at
    Meramec

Daryl Gruver
Mt. Vernon Nazarene College

James A. Guyor
St. Clair Community College

J. W. Hairston
South Carolina State College

Gene Hale
Iowa Western Community College

K. Hamide
Clark College

John W. Hamilton
Stephen F. Austin State University

Joseph C. Hecht
Montclair State College

Gale E. Heiman
Aims Community College

Larry Heldreth
Danville Community College

Arthur Hess
Brooklyn College

Charles Higgins
Loyola Marymount

Robert W. Higgins
Middlesex County College

Jack A. Hill
University of Nebraska-Omaha

Harald Hillmer
Riverside City College

Marie Hodge
Bowling Green State University

Y. Hoffer
Napa College

Judith S. Holding
Humboldt State University

Sally Japhet
McMurray College

William Jedlicka
Harper College

George F. Johnson
Norfolk State University

Thomas A. Johnson
Harper College

Francis L. Jones
Cypress College

Lanny A. Karns
State University of New York, Oswego

Bernard V. Katz
Oakton Community College

George A. Katz, Jr.
San Antonio College

Marvin S. Katzman
George Washington University

Lawrence L. Keen
Delaware Technical & Community
    College

Warren Keller
Grossmount College

David Kelmar
Santa Monica College

Lloyd I. Kenniston
State University of New York, Delhi

James C. Kerr
Phoenix College

Betty Ann Kirk
Tallahassee Community College

V. Wayne Klemin
Central Washington University

Craig S. Kuhns
City College of San Francisco

Alexander Langfelder
Middlesex County College

Keith F. Lawson
West Liberty State College

David Leese
Mount St. Mary's College

James A. Lentz
Moraine Valley College

George Leonard
St. Petersburg Junior College

Jim Lerner
Sullivan County Community College

Norbert F. Lindskog
The Loop College—Colleges of
    Chicago

Pam Little
North Harris County College

John W. Lloyd
Monroe Community College

E. J. Lodell
St. Mary's University

Paul James Londrigan
C. S. Mott Community College

Marvin P. Long
New River Community College

James R. McAnelly
Waubonsee Community College

R. McGinty
Eastern Washington University

Martin S. McKell
College of the Desert

F. R. MacKenize
Idaho State University

R. MacTeague
Moorpark College

Nick Maccione
Clark College

Charles S. Madden
Texas A & M University

Stuart L. Mandell
University of Lowell

Jack Mars
Mercer County College

Martin Marsh
Humboldt State University

John Martin
Mt. San Antonio College

Terry Mendenhall
Pittsburgh State University

James Meszaros
County College of Morris

Henry Metzner
University of Missouri–Rolla

Michael L. Miller
North Idaho College

Sandra Miller
Mineral Area College

Emerson N. Milligram
Carlow College

John D. Minch
Cabrillo College

Bernard A. Moreau
Indiana University of Pennsylvania

Jim Lee Morgan
West Los Angeles College

James Muck
Milwaukee Area Technical College

W. Gale Mueller
Spokane Community College

Robert J. Mullin
Orange County Community College

Mary K. Nelson
University of
    Minnesota—Minneapolis

Kathleen A. O'Brien
Alverno College

Eugene L. O'Connor
California Polytechnic State
    University

John Paxton
Wayne State College

Clifford C. Phifer
Tennessee Technological University

Bobby Phillips
Johnston Technical College

Joseph Plutts
Miami-Dade Community College

Joel Podell
Queensborough Community
    College

Robert L. Powell, Jr.
Gloucester County College

Dave Priddy
Piedmont Virginia Community
    College

Richard W. Przybyski
Mission College

Richard Randall
Nassau Community College

John H. Reed
Clarion State College

Robert Rednick
Lincoln Land Community College

Barbara Redmond
Briar Cliff College

James Reinemann
College of Lake County

Bill Reynolds
Three Rivers Community College

Bill Roberts
Cleveland State Community College

Walter R. Rooney
University of Houston

Ronald Rotter
Los Angeles Mission College

Charles S. Rygiel
Mohave Community College

Donald Sande
West Hills College

Phillip Schlarb
Trenton Junior College

John E. Seitz
Oakton Community College

George Sekul
Mississippi Gulf Coast Junior
    College

Paul J. Shinal
Cayuga Community College

Russell E. Skallerup
Henderson State University

James R. Snyder
College of Charleston

Carl Sonntag
Pikes Peak Community College

Robert F. Sroka
Milwaukee Area Technical College

Jeff Stauffer
Ventura College

Ronald Steele
Sacramento City College

Stanley Stein
Montgomery College

Robert T. Strager
Edison State College

Charles Strain
Ocean County College

Daniel Sullivan
College of San Mateo

L. William Sutherland
Suffolk University

R. E. Tansky
St. Clair Community College

Gerald R. Tapp
Western Wyoming College

Le Roy F. Thomas
Sacramento City College

John E. Tower
Oakland University

Robert Ulbrich
Parkland Community College

Pablo Ulloa
El Paso Community College

Dan Underwood
Inver Hills Community College

Ted Valvoda
Lakeland Community College

Robert H. Vaughn
Lakeland Community College

Robert Wagley
Wright State University

Arthur J. Walter
Suffolk County Community College

Carl Walters
Merritt College

John Warner
University of New Mexico

Peter Weiksner
Lehigh County Community College

William Weller
Modesto Junior College

Edward T. White
Danville Community College

Bern Wisner
Central Oregon Community College

Bennie Woods
Burlington County College

Heidi Vernon Wortzel
Northeastern University

Timothy W. Wright
Lakeland Community College

Gene C. Wunder
Ball State University

Bernard Yevin
Alma College

A. R. Yguado
Mission College

Adelle W. Zeimer
Lehigh County Community College

Joseph Zoric
University of Steubenville

CONTENTS

BUSINESS
WORLD

PART 1

THE BUSINESS
WORLD

CHAPTER 1

OUR BUSINESS SYSTEM

After studying this chapter you should be able to:

1 Understand practical definitions of business and the free-enterprise system.
2 Identify and recognize the importance and relationship of the six basic resources in our business system: people, money, machines, materials, methods, and markets.
3 Recognize the importance of profit, and the role profit plays in the free-enterprise system under capitalism.
4 Explain the role of government under capitalism, socialism, and communism.
5 Describe the interaction of supply, demand, and competition in the economic system.
6 Trace the historical development of U.S. business from 1776.
7 Discuss current trends and the future outlook for American business.

Walter S. Mack figures life was easier back in 1938, when he took Pepsi-Cola, then a syrup sold through candy stores, and in only three years turned it into the second largest selling soft drink. He's in the cola business once again, but with a greater challenge. "Back then I only had Coke to deal with," he recalls. "Now I have to fight both Coke and Pepsi."

At 85 Mack has left retirement behind to become chairman of King-Cola, a three-year-old New York company that expects to capture between 1.5% and 2% of the $12.5 billion cola market this year [1981] and between 7% and 10% by 1987. "I'm an ambitious fellow," Mack says.

To do battle with the big boys, Mack has surrounded himself with a group of former Pepsi executives who have a total of 188 years of soft drink experience. His vice-chairman is in his 70s and the man in charge of the secret formula is in his 60s.

Coke and Pepsi have around 1000 territorial bottlers between them. King-Cola has only 26 "kingdoms," covering 41 states, but these larger divisions, Mack claims, make his system more efficient. Unlike the giants, King-Cola delivers only to central warehouses, not to individual supermarkets. That slices into the largest cost of a bottle of pop: transportation. In most markets, Mack's cola is 20 to 30 cents cheaper—depending on the size of the purchase—than Coke or Pepsi.

Beating the competition with a pricing strategy is nothing new for Mack. Long before most of the Pepsi generation was born, he promoted Pepsi with a radio commercial that hit Coke in the pocket: "Twice as much for a nickel, too." Says Mack, "We wouldn't have started King-Cola unless our back cost was a dollar a case less than theirs. Coke and Pepsi can match our price sometimes, but they can't stay there and make money."

Source: Reprinted with permission of *INC.* Magazine. "Pepsi Veteran Pops Up Again with King-Cola," *INC.*, June 1981, p. 20. Copyright © 1981 by INC. Publishing Company, 38 Commercial Wharf, Boston, MA 02110.

Walter S. Mack, like many businesspeople, seems to possess an intuitive understanding of business, and he is also willing to take financial risks to achieve his goals, which makes him an **entrepreneur.** His main reason for competing with Pepsi and Coke is to make a profit—an important part of **free enterprise** (which means individuals rather than government determine what goods and services to produce, how to produce them, and who gets the rewards from their production). But in the process he's also making available to the consuming public an alternative cola at perhaps a lower price—and that's important to consumers. Because of Walter Mack and entrepreneurs like him, the United States has been the undisputed leader in providing consumption goods; but most of us give little thought to why we have such a broad range of goods and services from which to choose. The reason for those choices is the subject of this book: The American free-enterprise system and the thousands of business firms—large and small—that are a necessary part of it. Some people have contempt for business. Others worship it almost as a religion. Most of us are somewhere in between. But regardless of our philosophical perspective, it's important to understand how this system works and what's necessary to keep it working efficiently. Many students have also found it a fascinating subject to study.

TALKING BUSINESS

It's wonderful, of course, to read Shakespeare, look into Chinese history or essay the higher math. But why not get an early start on your basic Fear and Greed?

Courses at Yale College in corporate finance, capital markets, and investment theory and application have been swamped by student applicants, in some cases four times as many as the number of spots available. And one group of students is planning a stock-market plunge.

Yale traditionally has prided itself on lofty ideals of liberal education. The world of commerce beckons soon enough, it was thought. Six years ago, then-President Kingman Brewster admonished Yalies to beware of "grim pre-professionalism."

Times may have changed. Peggy Gries, one of the students interested in business—and also a history major writing a senior thesis about U.S. foreign policy toward Egypt—says, "I think the university is coming around to the fact that there is more need and desire among students for practical business courses."

Source: Excerpted from Steve Mufson, "Changing Times at Yale: Courses on Getting Rich Become Crowded," *Wall Street Journal*, 10 March 1982, p. 25. Reprinted by permission of The Wall Street Journal, © Dow Jones & Company, Inc., 1982. All rights reserved.

WHAT IS BUSINESS?

The term *business* means different things to different people. To some it means IBM, General Motors, Gulf Oil, and the many other very large organizations we hear of every day. To others *business* means a job. Still others think of it as the small family enterprise that's been their livelihood for many years. In its most far-reaching sense, **business** can be thought of as a social process involving the assembly and utilization of productive resources to produce products and services capable of satisfying society's needs and wants. In this sense business is as much a part of the social system of the Soviet Union or the People's Republic of China as it is of the United States. Regardless of a nation's political structure, economic goods and services must be produced and distributed. What distinguishes American business firms from Russian or Chinese firms is our almost complete reliance on individual decision making—guided by the **profit motive**—to determine the output of goods and services. In collectivist economies, central planning replaces private initiative to a very large extent.

All business firms—those run by individuals as well as those centrally planned—employ six basic resources: people, money, machines, materials, methods, and markets. These six resources are the basic inputs and outputs that are common to all productive activity.

Basic Inputs

Five of the six resources are inputs for the production of the goods and services business firms offer in the marketplace. The first is people. The human factor refers to the employment of men and women who perform the many tasks of manufacturing and selling the firm's products or services.

The second input to production is money. Money is the capital needed to maintain the flow of productive resources into the business firm. Money is needed to meet payroll, buy gasoline for delivery vehicles, pay for heat, light, and power to keep machinery running, and pay numerous other operating expenses needed to support production. Money also buys new machinery to expand production, replace worn-out equipment, and update production technology.

Machines are a third input to production. They

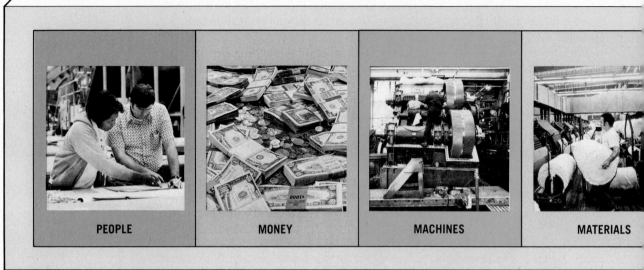

PEOPLE   MONEY   MACHINES   MATERIALS

embody the productive technology needed to convert labor and materials into products and services customers want. Machines may be technically complex devices, such as industrial robots, or they may be as simple as a good set of hand tools.

The fourth input to production is materials—the raw productive resources used to manufacture a product. For example, Exxon buys crude oil from a small producer in East Texas and moves it to a refinery in Houston. The crude oil is refined into gasoline, fuel oil, and many other products.

The fifth and final input to production is methods. Methods refers to techniques of production, such as making shoes by hand or by machine. While the long-run trend is toward machines, nevertheless in recent years there's been a growing interest in high-quality handcrafted items.

Basic Outputs

The final "M" of the basic resources—markets—symbolizes the output—products and services—of the enterprise. The basic inputs are utilized by the firm to produce the output demanded by customers. A **product** is a tangible good manufactured by the business firm. Understood broadly, the product is the good itself, its package, its brand name, its serviceability and its image. To General Motors, its products are more than cars, more than its Chevrolets and Buick Regals. GM maintains it is in the business of *personal transportation*—a Chevrolet, a Buick, or a GMC bus being only its tangible or outer form.

The other form of output is a **service.** Examples of services are functions performed by barbers, beauticians, dry cleaners, attorneys, and accountants. Many service firms are small enterprises, but there are also large service firms, such as Price-Waterhouse and Company (Certified Public Accountants, or CPAs), Holiday Inns (hotels), and Merrill Lynch (stockbrokers).

Rewards

We've already observed that the reward to a business firm for providing products and services that customers want (and are willing to buy) is economic profit. **Profit** is the amount remaining from sales revenues after all production and sell-

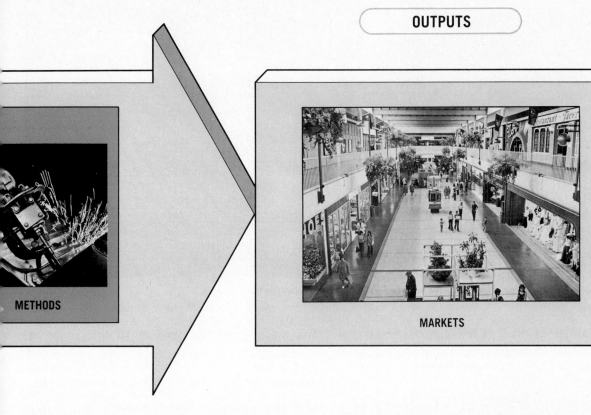

METHODS

MARKETS

ing costs are deducted. It's the return the business owner receives for assembling the productive resources and, more importantly, taking the risks of business ownership. Profit's also a way of measuring the success of a business from both an individual and a social point of view.

Profits tell us as individuals which firms and industries are attractive investment opportunities. We move our investment funds into those with superior profit performances and away from those with poor performances. Society, in turn, is improved to the extent that businesses meeting public demands are able to grow—whereas those that don't must contract.

THE FREE ENTERPRISE SYSTEM: CAPITALISM

We often take for granted what people in other parts of the world consider the real economic marvel of the United States—the ability to participate, either directly or indirectly, in business. Those willing to make the effort can usually acquire their own businesses, while those less ambitious can choose to purchase stocks and bonds of existing firms. Both are supplying capital, and

from this activity comes the term **capitalism.** In a capitalist economy such as ours, business and productive facilities are relatively free from government ownership.

The Role of Competition

Private citizens are free to enter and leave business as they desire. This freedom is considered a basic right of free enterprise and results in competition relative to prices, quality of products, diversity of choices, and economic efficiency. As higher potential rewards bring more firms into the marketplace, increased competition forces each firm to watch these factors more intently. For example, as more firms move into a given marketplace, prices are often reduced to maintain market positions. Naturally, the lower prices resulting from increased competition benefit the consumer by making products or services more affordable.

Impact on Availability Competition often leads firms to produce different products or else the same basic product in more styles, sizes, col-

Outputs of business can be products, such as wicker goods, or services, such as hairstyling.

ors, or other qualities. Each business seeks new market areas by responding to customers' needs not being satisfied by existing products.

Impetus toward Economic Efficiency A useful benefit of competition is the incentive it gives businesses to cultivate **efficiency** — that is, to produce their output at the lowest possible cost. Initially, lower costs allow the firm to enhance profits, but in a truly free-enterprise environment, a firm may find these extra profits sooner or later eroded away by increased competition. Conversely, a firm experiencing increasing costs may not be able to pass them on to its customers in the form of higher prices. It's got to become more efficient or else leave the industry. Few of us remember Dumont TV, although at one time it was a major manufacturer of TVs.

The Role of Government

The appropriate role of government in the American free-enterprise system has been a matter of long-standing controversy. While most Americans have traditionally felt that business should be relatively free from interference and regulation, nevertheless government involvement in business increased dramatically from 1930 to about the early 1970s. Since then there's been a trend toward reduction in intervention and regulation. Today most government regulation occurs in the

five major areas described in Table 1.1. Recognizing the social nature of many of our problems — such as pollution control — very few people advocate a total absence of government regulation.

Alternative Economic Systems

Two major alternative economic systems to capitalism exist in the world today — socialism and communism. These two economic ideologies represent different approaches to the problems of producing and distributing goods and services.

Socialism Under **socialism,** the basic industries are owned and operated by the government. The state owns or controls all transportation, communication, utilities, and large-scale industries. To varying degrees, government determines the goals of business, the prices and selection of goods, and the rights of workers. Socialism is the basic economic system in many Western European countries (see Figure 1.1). However some of these countries are more centrally controlled than others; and in nearly all the European Socialist countries (see Figure 1.1) many smaller businesses are still privately owned and operated.

Communism In the nineteenth century, Karl Marx, a German economist, developed a theory on which most of the doctrine of **communism** is based. Marx believed that a social revolution

TABLE 1–1

Key Areas of Government Regulation of Business

Occupational and Public Safety　Government plays an active role in seeking to make the workplace and the work environment safe for the worker. This relates to both physical safety and health safety. The passage of the Occupational Safety and Health Act (OSHA) in 1970 clearly put business on notice that the government was concerned with employee safety. Concerns for public safety have resulted in legislation dealing with such issues as children's toys, flammable fabrics, public smoking, packaging of poisonous products, safe drinking water, and highway speed limits.

Pollution Protection　The major environmental pollution acts, which began with the Air Pollution Control Act in 1962, are intended to eliminate pollution of the air, water, and land in the United States. These regulations have led to an increased awareness by the business community that the Environmental Protection Agency (EPA) is serious about ending useless and careless pollution of the environment. Many companies have taken steps, in cooperation with governmental agencies, to reduce pollution and clean up their operations. As a result of these activities, the EPA reported overall gains in air and water quality in the United States in the period 1975–79.

Fair Labor Practices　Legislation and regulations that prohibit discrimination in labor practices by business have been passed by Congress. These regulations were designed to reduce barriers to employment based on race, sex, age, national origin, and marital status.

Consumer Protection　The rise in consumerism has led to government regulation of business and its relationships with its customers. One such regulation is the Consumer Credit Protection Act of 1969, which requires that consumers be fully informed about the rates they are paying for borrowed money. Another is the Consumer Product Safety Act of 1972—a broad-based law that gives the government authority to examine, and to force a business to withdraw from sale, any product that it feels is hazardous to the consumer. An example of the application of this regulation was the required withdrawal of all hairdryers with asbestos insulation after it was determined that lab animals exposed to the asbestos had developed cancer.

Economic Protection　The economic security of the individual and of business is an issue the government has addressed. Provisions relating to retirement security and vocational rehabilitation were included in legislation passed in 1974. The government makes many low-cost loans and business assistance programs available to both businesses and individuals who have experienced economic and natural-disaster hardships.

would occur and eventually result in a classless society that would own all productive resources collectively rather than individually. Government would wither away since the productive resources would be operated for the good of society and no government control would be needed. Paramount to Marx's theory was that members of society would receive economic benefits based on their needs and that they would contribute to society according to their abilities.

In this respect, none of the Communist-bloc countries is the truly Communist economy described by Marx. These economies are characterized by full central planning of most business activity, almost complete government ownership of production resources, and strict control of prices, including the income levels of business and workers. The disruptions of work and the other protests in Poland in the early 1980s illustrate the widespread dissatisfaction of the Polish people with these strict economic controls.

Mixed Economies Systems characterized as **mixed economies** have both public ownership of some basic industries and private ownership of others. Examples are Canada, Great Britain, Sweden, and—to some extent—the United States. In Canada the communications, utilities, and public transportation industries, as well as some natural-resource industries, are government

SOCIALIST/COMMUNIST ECONOMIES: EUROPE 1982

FIGURE 1.1

owned. But most other productive activity is carried on by free enterprise. These mixed economies are often referred to as **social welfare economies.**

ECONOMICS OF FREE ENTERPRISE

To understand the complex mechanism of the free enterprise system it's necessary to examine some of its economic components. The role of competition, the interaction of supply and demand that arises from the needs of the economy, and the role this interaction plays in determining the prices of goods and services in the market-

place are all important in understanding business and its role in the free-enterprise system.

Pure Competition

Pure competition is viewed as a market structure consisting of so many buyers and sellers that no individual buyer or seller has any influence on either the price of the product or the amount traded over some period of time. Each seller's output is identical to all others, and both buyers and sellers can enter or leave the market easily; thus there are no barriers to competition. Within this framework the forces of supply and demand are

ON THE FIRING LINE

Regulation: How Much Is Too Much?

In a free-enterprise system, "the market is the thing." People are free to negotiate within the market to the best of their ability. They're free to acquire and trade property, to build businesses, and to expand—or go bankrupt. Whether they succeed or fail, in a free-enterprise system they don't have to fear government intervention.

Curiously, though, our government does intervene in the business world. Business leaders across the nation express despair in the face of the massive regulatory burden government has placed on them. Everywhere they turn, they say, they're restrained by regulations—on environmental pollution, on product and workplace safety, on hiring and firing, and on wages and employee benefits. Complying, they complain, costs both individual business people and the whole economy a great deal.

One direct business expense—the paperwork associated with regulations—is particularly burdensome, they say. Added personnel are required just to shuffle all the necessary papers. There are other direct costs. Often manufacturers must install new equipment or institute new processes in their plants to meet safety and pollution standards. Or costly features must be added to products. All the safety gear automakers must build into cars is just one of many examples.

We all feel the indirect costs of regulation, explain these same unhappy business people. Product prices go up to cover direct costs the corporate world must bear. Such price hikes, they say, are a "hidden tax" that consumers pay—and fuel for inflation as well.

As taxpayers, we also support the massive bureaucracies that do the regulating. But worse, maintain business leaders, is the fact that many of the bureaucrats responsible for regulation have no business know-how. As a result, the rules these agency bureaucrats devise and enforce often undermine rather than improve business.

Critics of the current level of regulation suggest letting the profit incentive take the place of regulation. It can be effective, they insist, and they offer an example: Suppose working conditions in a plant are unsafe. Trained workers will choose not to work there. Wages will have to be high if employees are to be found, and insurance costs will be high too. Profits will drop sharply; so to maintain or increase profits, employers must provide safe working conditions.

Many disagree with the view that there is too much regulation. Capitalism is not the only tradition basic to our government, they note. As a nation we have long struggled to ensure a minimum standard of living for all, they say. We have long acknowledged the need for regulation to achieve this goal. Moreover the Great Depression showed how disastrous uncontrolled free enterprise can be. It was to avoid further financial crises of that degree that regulations for stock market, banking, and financial operations were drawn up.

There is no free-market incentive, for instance, to control pollution. The costs of eliminating pollution add greatly to product prices and result in no increase in product value. Thus companies that do expend extra sums on pollution control cannot hope to compete with companies that don't. Consumers will buy the cheaper products.

The idea of cost-benefit analysis is ludicrous, say proregulation people. How much, in dollars, is a person's health or life worth? Who can decide? Even if someone presumed to decide, statistical analysis of costs and benefits of regulation would be unreliable. As a House of Representatives report on the analytic techniques involved notes, "It is easy to achieve virtually any desired conclusion."

But the ultimate irony of business's position against regulation, comment those who feel regulation is appropriate, is business's current *dependence* on regulation. This is clearest, they say, in foreign trade. The government protects many American businesses from healthy competition by taxing and/or limiting competing imports.

Is government regulation of business and industry a moral necessity? Is it an economic necessity? Can we hope to achieve a regulatory balance between concern for the well-being of individuals and for the well-being of the economy?

at their strongest in influencing the product's price and how much of it will be produced.

Supply is thought of as the relationship between quantity and price. It's assumed always to be positive; that is, sellers will offer more for sale at higher prices than they do at lower prices. Conversely, **demand** is always viewed as a negative relationship between quantity and price: more is demanded at low prices and less at high prices. When supply and demand are brought together in a market; a market price is determined that satisfies the intentions of both buyers and sellers. This is illustrated in Figure 1.2.

Here we see that sellers are selling 1,000,000 bushels of corn a day at a price of $3 a bushel; conversely, buyers are buying this amount at the same price. Naturally, each would like to do better; buyers would like a lower price, sellers would like a higher one. But a lower price would simply mean that sellers would offer less for sale while buyers would demand more, and price would be bid up. At a higher price, the reverse takes place and price would be bid down. Where will the bidding end in each case? When the price of $3 a bushel is reached. Supply and demand are very useful concepts; they will be explained in more detail in Chapter 15.

FIGURE 1.2

HYPOTHETICAL MARKET FOR CORN

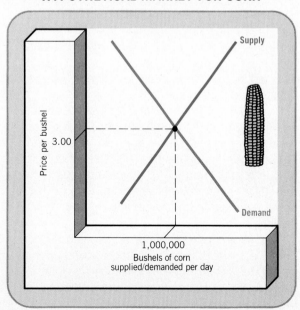

Price per bushel

Supply

Demand

3.00

1,000,000
Bushels of corn
supplied/demanded per day

Other Competitive Environments

Competition in the free-enterprise system is not always as free as might be desired. In fact, a purely competitive industry as we have just described it probably doesn't exist anywhere, even for corn. In order to describe the wide variety of competitive environments existing in the United States (or elsewhere), economists have devised three other general forms: **monopolistic competition, oligopoly,** and **monopoly.** These three, along with pure competition, are called *market structures.* They are described in Table 1.2.

Judged by the total number of firms, monopolistic competition would be the dominant market structure. But if total sales, payrolls, or other financial barometers are the criteria, oligopoly is by far the most important.

DEVELOPMENT OF THE U.S. ECONOMY

The growth of business in the United States closely parallels the growth of the nation itself. Business history and tradition have had a major influence on the nature of today's business environment. The colonial business was primarily a family enterprise. Self-sufficiency was the mainstay of most colonial families. As surplus production developed, it became common practice to sell or trade the excess with other families. Thus the commerce system started. As production processes became more efficient, more surplus goods became available for commercial activity. The **factory system** and the organized business system featuring work specialization began to develop more rapidly in the late 1800s.

Near the beginning of the nineteenth century the **Industrial Revolution** began in the United States. This period in American business history was characterized by major changes in production technology and the development of large-scale factories. New technologies emerged, such as Eli Whitney's production of Army rifles using interchangeable parts, the invention of the telegraph, the mechanization of agricultural production, and the increased mechanization of factory production. During the nineteenth century railroads and public transportation, new markets, and new industries began to emerge. Large urban

TABLE 1–2
Market Structures Other than Pure Competition

Monopolistic Competition   Product differentiation is the principal characteristic in monopolistic competition. In this environment a large number of sellers sell products that are generally the same but that are differentiated as a result of minor changes in product design, style, or technology. The business firm under conditions of monopolistic competition has enough influence on the marketplace to exert some control over its own prices. Monopolistic competition exists in many United States industries; the fast-food industry is a good example.

Oligopoly   An oligopoly is an industry that's controlled by a few large companies. The automobile industry is an oligopoly. Four companies—American Motors, Chrysler, Ford, and General Motors—make up the U.S. automobile industry. Each has a strong influence on product choice, price, and market structure within the industry. The oligopoly is characterized by few firms, many entry barriers, and strong control over price.

Monopoly   An industry with only one firm is a monopoly. Monopolies exist because of barriers to entry to other business firms. The monopoly is sustained by a market situation where there are no suitable substitute products. Since government antitrust legislation prohibits monopolistic activities, most monopolies in the U.S. exist under strong government regulation. Examples of monopolies are electric utilities, telephone companies, and cable TV companies.

areas with emphasis on commerce and employment of people in the urban economy became focal points of activity. The large financial institutions founded by people like J. P. Morgan were developed to finance these activities. The Industrial Revolution gave the economy the concepts of mass production, mass marketing, and concentrated financial resources.

The Captains of Industry (1865–1900)

In the latter part of the nineteenth century there emerged several individuals who were to have a profound effect on American business history. These "captains of industry" were instrumental in developing the largest and most powerful compa-

Self-sufficiency was the mainstay of most colonial families.

nies in America. John D. Rockefeller built Standard Oil. Andrew Carnegie founded U.S. Steel. Andrew Mellon started the Aluminum Company of America (ALCOA). These men utilized new technologies in building business firms. They were entrepreneurs in the truest sense of the word.

The role the entrepreneur played in shaping American industry cannot be overemphasized. Their willingness to take considerable risks in starting a business reflected a similar spirit throughout the young country. The adventurous attitude displayed by these men became the spirit that accelerated growth of the economy in the late 1800s.

Mass Production and Specialization (1900–1930)

The Industrial Revolution produced the concept of mass production, but industrialists of the early twentieth century perfected the system. In 1913 Henry Ford introduced the concept of the movable assembly. This innovation was destined to be a major breakthrough in production technology. By the use of the fixed work station, work specialization, and moving the work to the worker, Ford was able to implement substantial improvements in worker productivity. Because of his assembly-line technique, the cost of a Ford fell to under $200 while most other cars were well above $1000. Thus the automobile age started in America.

In 1776 Adam Smith, a Scottish economist, had written his famous *The Wealth of Nations*. In it he discussed the gains that could be achieved by allowing workers to focus all their efforts on one specific task rather than on several tasks. The concept of labor specialization became the hallmark of the mass-production era.

Maturity and Regulation (1930–Present)

In the five decades from 1930 to 1980, business underwent many changes. There were changes in consumers' buying habits and expectations. Government regulations were enacted in response to problems of the Great Depression. Labor unions became more powerful and influential. New technology and major production changes became commonplace in all industries. The rise of the nonowner management professional was an essential element to business growth. These management specialists began to apply work specialization to the job of the manager.

Consumer Preferences The emergence of a service economy occurred during this same time period. Consumers began hiring others to perform tasks that previously they'd done for themselves. So much have preferences shifted from products to services that today service industries are the fastest-growing segment of the economy.

Government Regulation The collapse of the economy in 1929 and the inability to recover

An early-1900s aircraft assembly line.

quickly led to many government regulations of business. The Securities and Exchange Acts (1933 and 1934) were passed to control speculation by investors. The Robinson-Patman Act of 1936 was enacted to control unwarranted pricing practices by business. Since then, many additional laws affecting business practices have been enacted. Consumer protection, worker protection, environmental protection, taxation, and energy administration are the areas of major focus by government regulators.

Labor Unions With the organization of the **Congress of Industrial Organizations (CIO)** by John L. Lewis in 1936, labor unions began to gain strength. Lewis had split away from the **American Federation of Labor (AFL)** in 1935. The AFL and the CIO created competing national labor movements, each trying to induce workers to join its ranks by seeking to win bigger concessions from business. This trend of labor union competition continued until the merger of the AFL and CIO in 1955. During this period labor unions were successful in gaining a major foothold in negotiations with business. They got wage and benefit increases and won better working conditions for their members. The labor union movement is more fully treated in Chapter 9.

Automation and Computerization International Business Machines Company (IBM), while not the first to introduce the electronic computer, almost single-handedly revolutionized production technology after World War II. IBM developed and introduced computer technology to almost every aspect of business operations. The major factor in IBM's marketing computers so widely was its ability to price its products so that many private companies—large or small—could afford them. Automation and computer applications are currently used in manufacturing processes, information systems, and reporting systems.

A recent development in computerization is the microcomputer. Steve Jobs and Steve Wozniak built the first Apple computer in Jobs' garage in 1976, and a new industry began. Since then, small computers have been introduced by other companies. Some of them are the Radio Shack TRS-80, Warner's Atari, and Commodore's Pert; they begin at prices as low as $250 and range upward to about $25,000. These small, relatively inexpensive units put computer power within the reach of many more businesses and individuals than ever before. Chapter 22 more fully discusses computers and their uses.

The Economy Today and Tomorrow

The economy of the 1980s is facing many problems. Double-digit inflation since the mid-1970s and almost double-digit unemployment in the early 1980s has strained fiscal and monetary management. Business firms have faced very high interest rates and frequent shortages of credit, which have severely hampered activity in the construction industry and small business sectors.

High unemployment coupled with inflation is referred to as **stagflation.** It's also characterized by stagnant economic growth, which has been a serious problem since 1980. In 1973 the economy awoke to another problem—an energy crisis. Long service-station lines, odd-even gasoline rationing, and the end of the 40¢ gallon of gasoline became realities. Despite these problems, today's economy is characterized by growing consumer affluence and expanding demand for services. Moreover consumers have begun to assert their rights in the marketplace, and "buyer beware" attitudes of sellers are no longer tolerated.

The Outlook for Business As American business moves toward the year 2000, what challenges does it face? One challenge will continue to be how to control inflation yet still stimulate growth of the economy. Success in controlling stagflation will depend in large part on the policies developed for managing the economy.

A second challenge to be faced by future businesses will be the changing work ethic and work expectations of the American worker. As the education level of the economy rises, workers will have higher expectations concerning their jobs and the nature of the work they perform. These expectations often involve bringing the worker into the decision-making process, particularly in the area of production.

Business will be called on to meet these increased demands for status. Illustrative of this was the auto industry in the early 1980s. Both Ford and GM insisted on major concessions from the United Auto Workers in an effort to regain competitiveness with Japanese automakers. As new auto sales literally fell apart in early 1982, no one in the industry or the UAW doubted for a moment

PERSPECTIVE ON SMALL BUSINESS

And now a sad tale of nitrates and nitrites, vigilant government and the darkest hour of buffalo jerky.

The setting is Jackson, Wyo., a little town known to most people for its Grand Teton mountains, but known to a discerning few for the buffalo products of Beck Sausage Inc. They include the Original Trapper Style Buffalo Jerky (which is dried, sliced buffalo meat), Smoked Buffalo Roast, Teton Wilderness Buffalo Salami (which is spiced with sage) and Jackson Hole Buffalo Salami (which isn't).

For years, those products have been cured with nitrates or nitrites as beef or pork might be. But last week [November 1981], a newly arrived government meat inspector notified the company that buffalo isn't beef or pork—or any other "domestic" animal. It is, instead, "wild game." Therefore, he said, under a tangle of federal regulations, it is against the law to use nitrates or nitrites in preserving buffalo.

And without nitrates or nitrites, it's goodnight for Beck Sausage.

"If this doesn't get resolved this week, we are out of business," says John Beck, 24, who runs the company, which his father heads and which got into the buffalo game about a year ago by buying out a local outfit that had been making the products for decades. "We can't wait any longer" he adds. "We will be bankrupt—it's that simple."

Without the additives, says Mr. Beck, there is no practical way of preserving the meat. And, with Christmas approaching, he has some 30,000 pounds of frozen buffalo meat lying around, and 20 live buffalo waiting for slaughter.

Mr. Beck has been "fighting like crazy" to get the ruling overturned. He finds the whole affair nitpicking and outrageous. The official involved—Robert E. Fetzner, a federal meat inspector on loan to Wyoming—warns that solving the problem won't be easy.

Buffalo, he says, would have to be reclassified as a domestic meat, something that "is going to take legislation to change." Meanwhile, he is only doing his job, and he isn't entirely unsympathetic to buffalo jerky.

"Just because we enforce these rules doesn't mean we think they are right," he says.

[Epilogue: Six months after this article appeared in the *Wall Street Journal*, Beck Sausage was still in business—tentatively. The commissioner of the Food and Drug Administration (FDA) allowed the company to conduct business as usual while the matter was being studied. John Beck, with the help of Wyoming Senator Malcolm Wallop, was still trying to find a way to have buffalo classified as a domestic animal. Meanwhile, said Mr. Beck, "We're in limbo."]

SOURCE: Eric Morgenthaler, "Want to Defy the Bureaucrats? Live on the Wild Side? Try Buffalo Jerky," *Wall Street Journal*, 3 November 1981, p. 25. Reprinted by permission of The Wall Street Journal, © Dow Jones & Company, Inc., 1981. All rights reserved.

---

the seriousness of the situation. Major segments of such industries as electronics, photography, clothing (in addition to many others) had been lost to Japan, and there was little reason to doubt that a similar fate awaited the auto industry—unless significant changes could be made.

Finally, the challenge of contending with resource shortages will have to be met in the last two decades of the twentieth century. High energy costs, shortages of traditional energy sources, shrinking natural resources, and increased nationalism worldwide will challenge the "Yankee ingenuity" to do more with less. American business must prepare to meet these dramatic technological requirements for alternative energy sources and improved management of the complex, highly intelligent organizations required to cope with the problems of future growth.

THE STUDY OF BUSINESS

The study of business attracts many people. Business and nonbusiness researchers alike seek answers to how businesses operate, allocate resources, and make decisions. And because business affects the life of every citizen, every American should try to understand as much about the U.S. business and economic environment as possible. Each person assumes several roles in our society—including those of consumer, worker, citizen—and each role requires an understanding of different elements of business.

As a consumer, it is useful to understand how a product is produced and moved to the marketplace, and how the price paid for it is determined. This understanding leads to better-informed purchase decisions and helps the consumer select the proper remedies when confronted with problems in the merchandise that's been bought. In order to understand one's rights as a consumer, one must first understand business.

Members of society form the labor force of the economy. In order to make career selections, to determine what price to ask for one's services, and to know what skills are needed to deal with advances in technology, an understanding of the business environment is essential.

Finally, business has a social responsibility, but what is it? Only the informed members of society—those who actually understand the role of business—can determine what its responsibility to society should be. Business neither caused all the social ills of the economy nor will it be able to cure all of them. By understanding the impact of business on society, we can make intelligent decisions about the proper role of business in finding solutions to society's problems.

How to Study Business

Unlike physics or zoology, most of us know something about business because we come in contact with it each day. This is an informal approach. Along with it, there is a formal study.

Informal Study Valuable knowledge of the business system can be gained from experience in various areas. By working in a particular industry, by reading business books, magazines, and newspapers, and by talking to other people at meetings and parties, much can be learned about the role of business and its operations. Information developed by this **informal study** of business can help us make better decisions as consumers, employees, and voters.

Formal Study **Formal study** of the business system may take many forms. The most common type is the degree program offered by community, junior, and four-year colleges and universities. Advanced degrees, such as the Master of Business Administration (MBA) and the Doctorate in Business Administration (DBA), are also offered. Business schools have grown as students discover the challenging nature of business.

Many business school programs combine the value of formal classroom instruction with the practical knowledge gained from actual work experience. Cooperative Education, internships with business firms, credit for summer work, and Small Business Institute programs are examples of work-experience programs. These programs try to bridge the gap between classroom theory and realities of the business world.

"GIVEN THE DOWNWARD SLOPE OF OUR DEMAND CURVE AND THE EASE WITH WHICH OTHER FIRMS CAN ENTER THE INDUSTRY, WE CAN STRENGTHEN OUR PROFIT POSITION ONLY BY EQUATING MARGINAL COST AND MARGINAL REVENUE. ORDER MORE JELLY BEANS."

TALKING BUSINESS

Despite its sputtering performance, the US shows no sign of losing its status as top global producer of goods and services—at least not right away.

If trends of the last 10 years are a guide, this country will widen its already commanding lead over other industrial nations by 1990, according to an analysis by the Economic Unit [of *U.S. News & World Report*]. At the end of this decade, the U.S. is expected to be outproducing its closest competitor—the nations of the European Common Market—by nearly 300 billion dollars a year, after adjustment for inflation.

The forecast is that the U.S. will hold on to its No. 1 slot even though Japan and the Soviet Union are expected to grow at faster rates. Still, Japan is given a chance of outstripping this country in total production within the next century if past growth trends continue—but that won't happen until around 2025.

Source: Excerpted from "Industrial Giants of 1990—Will the U.S. Still Be No. 1?" Reprinted from *U.S. News & World Report*, 9 February, 1981, pp. 58–59. Copyright 1981, U.S. News & World Report, Inc.

Objective of this Book

This book provides a formal overview of the business world. Not only is emphasis given to the overall structure of our business system, but each of the key functional areas of activity of the business manager is described. The importance, duties, and interrelationships of the functional activities are emphasized in order to provide an understanding of the principles and practices used to operate a business. The applicability of these principles and practices to both large and small, domestic and international, firms is made clear in each of the topical discussions. Regardless of whether subsequent study of business is pursued formally or informally, careful study of the materials presented throughout this text should provide a solid foundation on which to build your understanding of business.

SUMMARY

In the broadest sense, business can be thought of as a social process involving the assembly and utilization of productive resources to produce products and services capable of satisfying society's needs and wants. All business firms employ six basic resources: people, money, machines, materials, methods, and markets. The first five resources represent inputs for production; the final resource—markets—symbolizes the outputs, which can be either products or services. The reward to a business firm for providing products and services that customers want and are willing to buy is economic profit.

In a free-enterprise, or capitalistic, economy, business and productive facilities are relatively free from government ownership; and private citizens are free to enter and leave business as they want. This freedom results in competition, which affects prices, quality of products, diversity of choices, and economic efficiency. The appropriate role of government in the free-enterprise system has been a long-standing area of controversy. In the US, government involvement in business increased dramatically from 1930 to about the early 1970s. Since then, it has tended to decrease.

Two major alternatives to capitalism are socialism and communism. In addition, there are mixed economies, sometimes called social welfare economies, which feature both public and private ownership of basic industries. To some extent, the United States is a mixed economy.

To understand the complex mechanism of the free enterprise system, it's necessary to understand its economic components. In addition to competition, an important component is the interaction of supply and demand and the role of this interaction in determining the prices of goods and services in the marketplace.

Competition in a free-enterprise system is not totally free. In fact, pure competition probably does not exist anywhere. Market structures more commonly found in the free-enterprise environment are monopolistic competition, oligopoly, and monopoly.

The growth of business in the United States closely parallels the growth of the nation itself. The colonial business was primarily a family enterprise. Near the beginning of the nineteenth century, the Industrial Revolution began in the United States, giving the country the concepts of mass production, mass marketing, and concentrated financial resources. In the later part of the nineteenth century, an influential group of entrepreneurs—the "captains of industry"—emerged. Industrialists of the early twentieth century, such as Henry Ford, perfected the mass production system. From 1930 to 1980 business experienced many changes, including changes in consumers' buying habits and expectations, increases in government regulations, the growth of labor unions, and the introduction of automation and computerization. The rise of the nonowner management professional was an essential element in business growth in this period.

In the 1980s business faces many problems, such as stagflation and an energy crisis. Business must deal with these, as well as with problems presented by the changing work ethic and work expectations of the US worker and growing competition from foreign manufacturers.

Business affects the life of every US citizen; so everyone should try to understand as much about the US business and economic environment as possible, through both informal and formal study. This book provides a formal overview of the business system.

KEY TERMS

American Federation
    of Labor (AFL)
business
capitalism
communism
Congress of Industrial
    Organizations (CIO)
demand
efficiency
entrepreneur
factory system
formal study
free enterprise
Industrial Revolution
informal study
mixed economies
monopolistic
    competition
monopoly
oligopoly
product
profit
profit motive
pure competition
service
social welfare
    economies
socialism
stagflation
supply

REVIEW QUESTIONS

1. Define *business* and describe its function in our society.
2. What distinguishes American business firms from Russian or Chinese firms?
3. List the six basic resources that are the inputs and outputs used in all production of goods and services in American business enterprises.
4. Define *profit* and tell what it measures.
5. Describe the free-enterprise system and explain how it brings together the forces of supply and demand.
6. What is the role of government—or the state—in communism and socialism?
7. What is the role of government in the American free-enterprise system?

DISCUSSION QUESTIONS

1. What should be the role of government in the American free-enterprise system?
2. Explain the market structure of pure competition.

3. Describe the difference between oligopoly and monopoly.
4. Trace the Industrial Revolution in this country from the Civil War to the present.
5. What is the outlook for American business in the year 2000?

CASE: UNCLE SAM WILL TAKE CARE OF YOU

George Hill and Tom Acres were sitting in the reception room of the Student Placement Office waiting their turns at interviews with business executives. It was spring—recruiting season for the corporations who sent their representatives to campuses to recruit the best talent for their management development programs. George and Tom were pretty good students, with G.P.A.s of 3.5 and 3.8 respectively; but they weren't too certain of themselves and their prospects for employment in a market that seemed to be soft. The papers were full of articles on the rising unemployment rate, and the economy wasn't taking off the way it should.

Tom turned to George and said, "Did you hear the radio program this morning—where they were interviewing students who'd just graduated from high school somewhere in the east?" "No," said George, "I was busy studying for an exam. What did they have to say?" Tom went on to describe how one student was very bitter about not being able to jump right into a good-paying job. He'd just graduated from high school and was ready to go to work—but there didn't seem to be enough jobs to go around. As usual, teenagers throughout the country had the highest unemployment rate, and it seemed to be rising. Tom quoted the student as saying, "This high school diploma won't do me any good if I can't get a job!" The young man went on to say that the government had better do something about it or there was going to be trouble from a lot of high school graduates who couldn't find work. The radio announcer also talked about the great number of people who were unemployed, emphasizing the adult breadwinners who could not feed their children and had gone on relief.

George's reaction was "I don't see why this guy thinks the government owes him a job—that shouldn't be the responsibility of the government." But Tom countered, "I disagree—I think the government does owe jobs to young people who've worked hard to get through high school; and when I get my degree in June, I'll feel just like this kid. When there's high unemployment and the economy is in trouble, the government should provide jobs for people. That's what governments are for."

The two were off to a good discussion about the roles of government and private industry in providing jobs for people. From there they went on to argue about the responsibility of the Federal Government to provide loans for students to help them pay for their education. Millions of students had been afforded that opportunity after World War II. The G.I. Bill of Rights provided for subsidies for men and women in the armed services so that they could go back to school to continue their education and take their rightful place in society as wage-earners and tax-paying citizens.

1. What should be the role of the federal government in providing loans for students to continue their education?
2. In a depressed economy, what strategy should be used by students seeking employment if they get no help from the government?
3. How is unemployment handled in the Soviet Union?

CASE: SURVIVAL OF THE FITTEST

It may be trite to say "There's a real jungle out there in the business world," but it sometimes seems as though it could be true of the free-enterprise system. Pursuing this analogy from nature, we might turn to Charles Darwin's "theory of natural selection," which some have dubbed "the survival of the fittest." Darwin theorized that those forms which were able to survive were those which adapted best to the environment, thus resulting in a process of natural selection.

Whether or not you accept Darwin's theory, it does make some sense in tracing the survival of vigorous entrepreneurs and small-business enterprises—those that can meet competition directly, satisfy the needs of customers, charge a price that customers are willing to pay, and still come up with a surplus over expenses for a profit. This process describes survival of business—a very simple economic process but a business system that has given Americans the highest standard of living in the world.

Interestingly, Adam Smith's model for laissez-faire capitalism and Darwin's theories came at roughly the same time in history and could well be merged in a model of the American business system. Smith explained how business could really thrive if left alone, without government interference, and how small businesses could survive and flourish in a highly competitive environment. Those businesses that survived had to be vigorous and healthy, financially and economically, and they could continue as profitable enterprises for long business lives.

1. What do you think of Darwin's theory as applied to American business?
2. Can you give some examples of business enterprises that have survived in a highly competitive environment?

CHAPTER 2

MEETING SOCIAL
RESPONSIBILITIES

After studying this chapter you should be able to:

1 Explain the concept of social responsibility for a business.
2 Present arguments for and against social responsibility for a business.
3 Describe major social issues that have an impact on business.
4 Discuss the effect that consumerism has had on business.
5 Evaluate the importance of ethics in business.

Jackson Hole, Wyoming has got to be one of the most beautiful spots in the United States—a scenic slice of northwest Wyoming surrounded by Grand Teton National Park. The booming popularity of Jackson Hole has led the one airline that serves it—Frontier—to push for a bigger airport. Frontier's argument: its propeller-driven Convair aircraft were increasingly inefficient to operate.

So it was that in 1981 Frontier for the fourth straight year petitioned for scheduled service to Jackson Hole from Denver and Salt Lake City using Boeing 737 jets. Frontier asked the local airport authority to extend the 6305-foot runway by 1700 feet so that jets could land and take off at full capacity with room to spare.

However Jackson Hole possesses a unique distinction: it has the only U.S. commercial airport inside a national park. And many consider majestic, mountainous Grand Teton the crowning jewel of the entire national park system. Opponents of the runway expansion said that the noise and exhaust from scheduled jet travel could lead to a "substantial degradation of the park's environment."

On top of that, the Department of the Interior had its own concern: airport construction, said the department, could disrupt the nesting habits of the Western Sage Grouse. It seems that local denizens perform their mating dance over— you guessed it—the Jackson Hole airport runway. And the Grand Teton park superintendent chimed in that the airport already marred the view of the Teton range. He would prefer to see the whole landing strip bulldozed under. Others suggested moving the airport 65 miles southeast to the small town of Daniel.

Frontier Airlines for its part noted that the new jets would be only slightly noisier than propeller planes—and that even this difference was not likely to be noticeable, given the special noise abatement procedures mandated for the Jackson Hole operation. Numerous private jets had long since been using the airport, some of them very large craft. Frontier wanted to be a good neighbor to the community, which it had been serving since as far back as 1959, when it was flying DC-3s into Jackson Hole. Any "degradation of the park's environment" would sooner or later be reflected in a decline in Jackson Hole's popularity. And that would mean less business for Frontier.

A federal review of the situation—the Federal Aviation Administration reporting to the Department of Transportation—agreed with Frontier's position, and commercial jet service began in June 1981. At that point the conservationist Sierra Club jumped in, taking the government to court. Sierra's goal: getting Jackson Hole declared off limits to Frontier's jet fleet.

But what of the Western Sage Grouse? Not to be overlooked, they were last seen flying with the airlines, not the conservationists. Their population has actually grown with the increase in airport activity!

Based on George Getschow, "Proposal to Expand Airport at Jackson Hole Stirs Fight over National Park's Future," *Wall Street Journal*, 12 March 1981, p. 27. Used by permission of The Wall Street Journal, ©Dow Jones & Company, Inc., 1981. All rights reserved.

WHAT IS SOCIAL RESPONSIBILITY?

The Frontier Airlines story illustrates the difficulty many firms have in determining the scope of their social responsibilities. Here **social responsibility** is business concern for the welfare of society as a whole. It consists of those obligations that a corporation has to the larger society (than merely its stockholders) and that go beyond those provided for by law or union contracts. This definition has two important aspects. First, management's obligations should be adopted voluntarily. Managerial action that stems from federal legislation, such as cleaning up factories that are polluting air and water, cannot be credited as voluntary. Second, the obligations of social responsibility are very broad. They extend beyond the traditional accountability to shareholders, reaching to other societal groups, such as consumers, employees, suppliers, and neighboring communities.

Social responsibility is an obligation of every manager within a company. A businessperson may lead a model personal life yet continue to rationalize the organization's pollution of a river because no direct personal consequence is involved. Such a manager might consider the pollution a "public" problem, to be solved by society at large. However the concept of social responsibility obliges the manager to consider his or her acts in terms of society as a whole. Individuals must think beyond themselves and begin to build societal values into their actions.

The Case for Social Responsibility

The concept of social responsibility provides a logical argument for claiming that businesses should be socially responsible. There are a number of reasons often cited for social responsibility. One is that it is society, through its corporate laws and the privilege of owning private property, that has given business the right to exist. A corporation is a citizen of a country. It has rights and duties just like any other citizen. Society can change its expectations of business whenever it wishes. There seems to be a new social contract emerging between society and business that increasingly involves business in broader social roles. An acceptance of this new contract is implied by a statement made by the president of the Prudential Insurance Company of America: "Business belongs to the people. Business has, in effect, a franchise granted to it by society, and the franchise will be continued only as long as society is satisfied with the way it is handled."[1]

During the decade of the mid-1960s, we began to see major changes in attitudes toward business as key civil rights legislation was passed, including the law guaranteeing equal employment opportunity. America launched a war on poverty, and the federal government took important new steps in support of education and medical care for the elderly. At the same time, public opinion polls showed that confidence in our business institutions was declining.

The mid-1960s also brought dramatic opposition to the "technological imperative" (if you *can* do it, you *should* do it), focusing on the SST (supersonic transport) program. The defeat of the program in 1971 signaled a change in society's attitude toward technology. Big was no longer seen as necessarily better—a conclusion dramatically reinforced in the next decade by the fate of "gas-guzzlers" caught in the grips of the energy crunch. In fact by the beginning of the 1970s the consumer and environmental movements were in full

"BUT LET'S LOOK AT THE BRIGHT SIDE. WE DID NOT CREATE ONE — NOT ONE — HAZARDOUS WASTE."

bloom, and the desirability of economic growth for its own sake was sometimes questioned. Society was now saying, in effect, that business must do more than simply produce a product or service. Production goals must now share the spotlight with the goal of improving the quality of life.

Another argument for social responsibility is that it in fact creates a better environment for business. As the quality of life improves, conditions for business become more favorable. If, for example, labor is satisfied, it will be more efficient. If workers are receiving adequate wages, purchasing power will increase in society. As incomes grow, there will be greater demand for new

goods and services. Moreover labor strife will be minimal; turnover and absenteeism will decline. With social improvements, crime should decrease, and less taxes will have to be paid in support of police services. Moreover there will be less need for government regulation, and the government bureaucracy can be reduced. So the argument goes.

A socially responsible business will also improve its public image (see Figure 2.1). Companies such as Weyerhauser, Georgia Pacific, Storer Broadcasting, and International Harvester use advertising to promote their own awareness of their social responsibilities. In some cases consumer groups have boycotted a company's products and stock

FIGURE 2.1

SOUNDING HISPANIC FREEDOM

Hispanics in the United States number 18 million or more, 1 in 12 of all Americans. In some communities they are the majority.

Yet these numbers have not translated into proportionate civic and community participation. The result is inequity in job opportunities, education, fair treatment under the law and sharing of public funds.

This deprives the individuals of their full measure of freedom and the communities of their fullness of life.

Gannett newspapers and broadcast stations are working hard to do something about that.

The Nevada State Journal and Reno Evening Gazette described abuses in jobs, education and housing suffered by Northern Nevada's large,

but largely ignored Hispanic population. By focusing on the struggles of individual Hispanics pursuing their American dream, the series of articles clarified needed community remedies.

An El Paso Times series offered readers a close inspection of the problems Mexican-Americans face in their daily lives within the unique border community. And the newspaper continues to place major emphasis on news about the Hispanic community.

KBTV in Denver scheduled public service spot announcements in all parts of its broadcast day, urging Hispanics to cooperate fully with the 1980 census. Hispanics make up an estimated one-fourth of the Colorado population.

In San Bernardino, California, The Sun opened a news bureau in the heart of the Hispanic and Black West Side. A vibrant, active community is now better known to all area residents. The Sun also added a columnist who writes exclusively about Hispanic political activities.

KPNX-TV in Phoenix airs a weekly public-affairs program concentrating on Hispanic needs and events.

To better serve the entire community, the Tucson Citizen in Arizona offers free Spanish lessons to every staff member.

A third of the news staff has already signed up.

And Gannett and Michigan State University have launched a large-scale study of communication behavior and attitudes of Hispanic-Americans. The study will help newspaper and broadcast professionals serve the audience according to its needs and preferences.

In these ways and others, Gannett members strive to serve all segments of their communities, each according to its own special needs.

At Gannett, we have a commitment to freedom in every business we are in, whether it is newspaper, TV, radio, outdoor advertising, film production, magazine or public opinion research.

That freedom rings throughout Gannett, from Tucson to Tarrytown, from Salinas to Santa Fe, from Visalia to the Virgin Islands, in news coverage, in editorial opinions, in community service, each member serving its own audience in its own way.

GANNETT
A WORLD OF DIFFERENT VOICES
WHERE FREEDOM SPEAKS

when they felt that it wasn't socially responsible. At various times both U.S. Steel (pollution) and Safeway Stores (nonunion-picked produce) have been boycotted for a perceived lack of social responsibility. In turn, business itself has used economic leverage with other areas of industry to secure social responsibility. In 1981 Procter & Gamble, the nation's largest single television advertiser, withdrew sponsorship from dozens of programs that it felt were not sufficiently responsible in such matters as sex and violence.

Another more compelling argument for social responsibility is that it aids in avoiding further government regulation. Today the businessperson must cope with the Department of Labor's Occupational Safety and Health Administration (OSHA), the Environmental Protection Agency (EPA), the Consumer Product Safety Commission (CPSC), the Federal Trade Commission (FTC), the Equal Employment Opportunity Commission (EEOC), the Food and Drug Administration (FDA), and the Internal Revenue Service (IRS), to name some. When business abuses its social power, it can expect a steady increase in government regulation, for which we all must pay.

An argument for social responsibility that can be easily overlooked is that it often translates into money and jobs. The Harvard Business School reported that as of 1980 businesses involved in cleaning the environment totaled nearly $50 billion and were growing by 20 percent a year. True, the Environmental Protection Agency calculated that plant closings related to pollution control requirements affected 25,311 workers between 1971 and 1980. But the agency identified 36,000 new jobs in the pollution control manufacturing industry that were created in 1976 alone. Pollution control spending could reduce the unemployment rate by two-tenths of 1 percent yearly between 1982 and 1986. (Of course, this is only one side of the controversy over the effects on the economy of pollution control expenditures. Government economists expect the positive impact on productivity to reverse itself in coming years with the effects of declining productivity and higher inflation becoming more pronounced—should these turn out to be the case.)[2]

A final argument for social responsibility is that business has the resources—plant and equipment, capital resources, and managerial talent—that can be applied to social problems. Therefore society should use these resources. An example that applies to the human resource is the employment

of persons with almost no education. In this case a business organization provides incentive for workers to improve their basic reading, writing, and mathematics skills. Employing minorities and providing equal opportunities may give those who benefit from these policies the feeling that they are now fully participating members of our society.

The Case against Social Responsibility

The major argument against social responsibility centers on profit maximization. As Peter F. Drucker, a famous management scholar, has put it:

> Profit discharges a function essential to the success, if not the survival, of any industrial society. Profitability must be the criterion of all responsible business decisions, whether the society is organized along free enterprise, socialist, fascist, or communist lines.[3]

Economist Milton Friedman has also argued strongly that social responsibility is no longer appropriate for corporations. He asks:

> Have you ever heard anyone suggest that the "mom and pop" corner grocery store should sell food below cost to help the poor people who shop there? Well, that would obviously be absurd. Any corner grocery that operated that way would be out of business very soon. The same is true on the larger scale. Larger enterprise could have money to exercise social responsibility only if it has a monopoly position: if it is able to hire its employees at lower wages than their worth; if it is able to sell its product at a higher price than can otherwise be charged. If it is a monopoly, it ought to be prosecuted under the anti-trust laws. Any businessperson who boasts to the public that he or she has been using corporate funds to exercise social responsibility should be regarded as asking for an investigation by the anti-trust division of the Justice Department.[4]

Friedman goes on to say that a business is owned by stockholders and that it's the responsibility of management to make as much money as possible for them. Social responsibility initiatives, on the other hand, would reduce the return to the stockholders. Management would be spending their money for social goals. This in turn would raise prices to customers and perhaps lower the

PERSPECTIVE ON SMALL BUSINESS

How do the owners and managers of small business perceive their responsibility to society? One study suggests that many small-business people view socially responsible behavior mainly as behavior that increases profitability.

During the period 1976–1978, Professor Erika Wilson and some of her students at the California State University, Los Angeles, interviewed 180 owners or managers of businesses with fewer than twenty-five employees. Most were retail businesses that sold products or services; the rest were manufacturers, commercial suppliers, and professional firms. No preformulated responses were provided; the interviewers asked one basic question—"How do you see your responsibility to society?"

More than 10 percent said either that they felt no specific responsibility to society or that they did not know what was meant by the term. The specific statements of the others (541 statements in all) were grouped by Professor Wilson's team into five general areas of concern: consumers, employees, ethics, the community, and profits.

More than half the statements related to responsibility to customers, especially to customer satisfaction. It seems, though, that ensuring customer satisfaction was regarded mostly as a good way to encourage customers to come back and perhaps to recommend the business to others.

Many fewer statements—about 15 percent—dealt with responsibility to employees. Most of the people who made these statements believed they discharged this responsibility by providing good or fair wages, fringe benefits, and working conditions. Some, however, mentioned such things as providing employees with growth opportunities and providing jobs for members of minorities.

Ethics was mentioned in 13 percent of the statements. Honesty and fairness seemed the main concerns in this category. But at least some of the respondents equated ethical behavior with behavior that would create return business.

Another 13 percent of the statements mentioned responsibility to the community. Here again, though, many of the business people seemed to regard contributing time, effort, or money to community causes as a sort of public relations investment.

Finally, 12 percent of the statements specifically mentioned profit. Some respondents said profit was their only concern; but most professed an interest in making as much profit as possible while fulfilling some of the responsibilities described above.

SOURCE: Based on Erika Wilson, "Social Responsibility of Business: What are the Small Business Perspectives?" *Journal of Small Business Management* 18 (July 1980): 17–24. Used by permission.

---

wages of employees. The manager is not only spending the stockholders' money, then, but that of customers and employees as well.

Another argument is that managers are not trained to pursue social goals. If managers attempt to right social wrongs, there may be serious inefficiencies, inadequacies, and inequities. What do managers know about educating the illiterate? If a corporation decides to make a donation to the poor, how should it determine which cause or group is most worthy?

The answers to these and other questions are not very easy. Yet it seems that today many—if not most—major corporations have accepted social responsibility as a legitimate corporate function. Management must believe that the arguments *for* social responsibility outweigh the negative ones.

SOCIAL ISSUES THAT IMPACT ON BUSINESS

There are a number of social issues that are raised by the concept of social responsibility. Among them are environmental problems, consumerism, and employee relations.

Environmental Problems

Ecology is the interrelationship of living things and their environments, including the interaction between different kinds of living things. These interrelationships are complex, and the interrelationship between humans and their environment is no exception to this complexity. Each act that we take is intricately connected to other situations and events both in the chain of life and in the overall ecosystem—the ecological community and the environment taken together.

Sometimes even the best of intentions may have unforeseen and undesirable consequences. For example, the advent of the automobile brought us a faster means of transporting people and materials across great distances. But we were not aware of the resulting problems of air pollution, gasoline shortages, extensive use of raw materials to produce vehicles, deaths and injuries resulting from vehicular accidents, and a host of other problems. Irrigation of former desert land such as the high plains of Texas and areas of Arizona and California has produced a rich increase in agricultural production. But the water table in these areas has fallen drastically during the past 20 years, raising the prospect of a complete shutoff of the water supply. The use and reuse of the Colorado River for irrigation as it flows toward the sea raises the saltiness so much that by the time it reaches the Mexican border it's almost useless for crops.

The Concept of Responsible Consumption   If society prepares for future possibilities such as the deepening of the energy crisis or major water shortage, the ecological impact can perhaps be reduced. It's estimated that rising demand levels will strain the ability of technological advances and natural processes to support the expected growth of the world population by the year 2000.[5] This would mean that we need to reduce individual consumption of resources that are in scarce supply and substitute better forms of consumption in place of those that are ecologically damaging. **Responsible consumption,** then, is the rational and efficient use of resources by consumers and business with a view to the present and future condition of society.

Since about one third of all homes in the United States have two or more cars, and since the automobile is a major polluter, responsible consumption may in this respect mean reducing the number of vehicles per family. Reduction of the demand for automobiles—and so for gasoline—may mean that wilderness preserves and offshore waters can be maintained rather than opened up for mineral and petroleum exploration. And auto companies—as well as other sectors of industry—can be socially responsible by building greater durability and safety into their products.

Responsible consumption might also enable businesses to reduce their use of pesticides and heavy metals, such as mercury. And such byproducts as carbon dioxide, sulfur dioxide, and noise and heat pollution could also be decreased. Instead, firms would emphasize ecologically sound products such as biodegradable plastics and pesticides, bicycles, solar-powered vehicles, mass transit, mass communication rather than physical travel, multiple-family housing, and solid-waste incinerators for power.

Another way to enhance our ecology is through recycling. Progressive companies, such as Alcoa and Reynolds Aluminum, actively promote the recycling of aluminum cans. Society's long-term direction is toward extensive recovery and reuse of both metals and glass from solid waste. While the program for the separate recycling of aluminum has been very successful, it has still reached only a small fraction of the total aluminum container supply.

Pollution is the contamination of the environment with byproducts and effects of human activity. Pollutants include liquid and solid waste, gaseous and particulate discharges into the air, noise, heat, poison, and radiation. When air and water pollutants are discharges from a factory, they may have certain effects on the environment. Some, like arsenic, persist for a long time. Others, like cyanide, decompose rather quickly. Many pollutants, such as iron, have no effect on humans but can kill plant and fish life. Certain pollutants, like mercury and DDT, seem to concentrate in the food chain and thus tend to become more dangerous to life years after they were released. Some pollutants have one effect when released in large amounts for a short period and still

Getting to work in the Netherlands vs. Los Angeles.

other effects when continually released in small amounts. In concentrations of over 20 parts per million sulfur dioxide is associated with choking, tearing, and sneezing. In concentrations as low as 0.2 parts per million over a long period, it is supposed to contribute to lung disease.

Consumerism

Government tries to protect not only the environment but also the consumer. Like pollution control, consumerism is another major area where society has called on corporations to assume their social responsibilities. Specifically, **consumerism** is the organized effort by independent groups (and also by groups within government and business) to protect the consumer from undesirable effects resulting from the manufacture and the sale of goods and services.

Consumer protection can originate in three areas. The first is consumer oriented groups. These are concerned with increasing consumer awareness by providing information to improve purchase decision making. They also take a stand for the consumer on public issues. The second area is government, through the development of laws protecting consumers as well as through the adoption of consumer oriented regulations by government agencies. The third area is business itself, taking the initiative in meeting its social responsibilities.

ON THE FIRING LINE

Bottle Bill—Cure for the Nation's Litter Ills?

A national "bottle" bill was first proposed in Congress in the 1970s. Its purpose was to reduce the litter and solid waste pollution that result from disposable beverage containers—cans as well as bottles. The bill required consumers to pay a nickel deposit on all beer and soft-drink cans and bottles, returnable or not. It also banned flip top and pull tab openers on cans. The merits of a nickel deposit quickly became the subject of heated debate. The issues argued were several: (1) how best to reduce litter, (2) how best to save energy, (3) the bill's effect on prices, (4) the gain or loss of jobs, (5) problems for storeowners, and (6) the bill's effect on free market competition.

Litter

Those opposed to the bottle bill maintain it is not the way to solve our litter problem. Beverage bottles and cans, they say, make up only a small portion of all solid waste. The better approach would be to enact a comprehensive and tough anti-litter law. Such a law, they think, should place a small tax on *all* disposable containers and stiff fines on litterers. The revenues from the tax should fund added clean-up efforts and a program of public education.

Fines are unenforceable and therefore useless, reply bottle bill advocates. Who in authority ever sees a litterer in the act? No police force would be big enough to put an anti-litter law into effect. Taxes on all disposable containers would be grossly unfair. They would result in higher prices for all—litterers and nonlitterers alike. A bottle bill would cost only those more who did not use (or return for their deposit refund) returnable containers. In fact, in states where bottle bills have been passed, they have resulted in reduced litter overall. In Maine, for instance, roadside beverage container litter was cut by 78 percent and total litter by 32 percent.

Energy

Those against bottle laws point out that far more energy will be used to transport returnable containers back to the factories for refills. In Oregon, after a bottle bill was passed, fuel consumption doubled for the Pacific Coca-Cola Bottling Company. Additional energy will also be needed to run new equipment for bottle washing.

These costs are minor compared to the energy savings gained by recycling bottles and cans, say others. Bottles, of course, can be used several times. Though cans must be made anew out of returned cans, far less energy is involved in this process. For aluminum cans, recycling uses only 5 percent of the energy required to make new cans. Federal studies estimate that at least 33,000 and perhaps as many as 81,000 barrels of oil a day could be saved by enacting a bottle bill.

Jobs

A bottle bill would be an economic disaster in terms of jobs lost, argue those against such a law. In the steel, aluminum, and glass industries, quantities of jobs will disappear, they say. These industries and their employees will suffer, and so will the areas where they are concentrated. In fact, makers of cans have found that their markets have been cut by as much as one half in states with bottle bills. For states, higher unemployment means a loss in tax revenues.

The bill's advocates refute this view. The three federal studies done, they point out, estimate a *net* nationwide increase in jobs by anywhere from 29,000 to 53,000. The experience of the states with bottle bills appears to support these results. In Oregon, there was said to be an increase of around 365 jobs after passage of a bottle bill. These advocates do not deny that jobs in glass, steel, and aluminum will become fewer. But, they say, there will be far more jobs handling and transporting the recycled containers.

TALKING BUSINESS

Those who believe that consumerism is a purely modern phenomenon should note these excerpts dealing with prescriptions for marketplace behavior:

1. On selling wine.
    If a wine seller make the measure for drink smaller than the measure for corn, they shall call that wine seller into account and they shall throw her into the water.
    —The Code of Hammurabi (2100 B.C.)
2. On scales in the marketplace.
    You shall not pervert justice in measurement for length, weight, or quantity. You shall have true scales, true weights, true measures dry and liquid.
    —The Bible (Leviticus 19:35–36)
3. On selling bread.
    If any default be found in the bread of a baker of this city, the first time let him be drawn up a hurdle [sled], from the guild hall to his own house with the false loaf hanging from his neck; if a second time, he shall be found committing the same offense, he shall be placed in a pillory and there remain for at least an hour.
    —King John of England (1202)

Based on George Kentera, "Consumer Protection from Ancient Short-Changers," *Milwaukee Journal*, 14 October 1974, Greensheet, p. 1.

Growth of Consumerism   Consumerism is not of recent origin; its roots are in fact ancient. The first American consumer protection law, passed in 1872, made it a federal crime to defraud consumers through the mails. Another law, passed in 1883, prohibited the sale of unwholesome tea and barred the importation of spoiled food and drink.

In 1889 the Consumers' League was formed as a result of perceived consumer abuses. In 1906 Upton Sinclair wrote *The Jungle*, which exposed the filthy conditions of Chicago's meat-packing houses. The book created such an outcry that Congress passed the Meat Inspection Act in the same year and also set up the Food and Drug Administration (FDA). Consider this passage:

There would be meat stored in great piles in rooms; and the water from leaky roofs would drip over it, and thousands of rats would race about on it. It was too dark in these storage places to see well, but a man could run his hand over these piles of meat and sweep off handfuls of the dried dung of rats. These rats were nuisances, and the packers would put poisoned bread out for them; they would die, and then rats, bread, and meat would go into the hoppers together.[6]

In 1962 President John Kennedy, in a special message to Congress, outlined the rights of consumers. These included:

1. the right to safety—to be protected against goods that may be hazardous to health or life;
2. the right to be informed—to be protected against fraudulent, deceitful, or grossly misleading information, advertising, labeling, and other practices, and to be given the facts needed to make an informed choice;
3. the right to choose—to be assured of access to a variety of products and services at competitive prices;
4. the right to be heard—to be assured that consumer interests will receive full and

sympathetic consideration in the creation of government policy.

The president's consumer rights message set the stage for an outpouring of consumer legislation. The 1960s saw the passage of:

1. the Cigarette Labeling Act: required cigarette manufacturers to label cigarettes as hazardous to health;
2. the Fair Packaging and Labeling Act: declared that deceptive packaging for certain consumer products is illegal;
3. the Child Protection Act: allowed the Food and Drug Administration to remove dangerous children's products from the market;
4. the Truth in Lending Act: required full disclosure of financial charges and consumer credit agreements.

In 1972 the Consumer Products Safety Act was passed, which created the Consumer Product Safety Commission (CPSC). The act charged the commission with establishing safety standards to protect consumers from risk and injury. The CPSC can ban the sale of products and require manufacturers to perform safety tests and either repair or recall unsafe products. The commission also maintains a "hot line" for reporting hazardous products.

The early 1980s found consumerism returning to grass root issues such as truth in advertising and maintaining product quality. More importantly, consumer advocates have been appointed to a number of high government positions, such as the National Highway Traffic Safety Administration and the Federal Trade Commission. Consumerists now have a growing voice in Washington's bureaucracy.

Response to Consumerism by Business The response of the business community to consumerism during the 1960s and 1970s was by no means overwhelming. One study found that 63 percent of industrial firms polled—e.g. steel and chemical manufacturers—revealed that they had not been affected by consumerism.[7] And about half of the consumer goods companies—e.g. cosmetic and food manufacturers—claimed that consumerism had affected them.

A 1977 study showed some improvement in the attitude of businesses toward consumerism,[8] and the 1980s have witnessed a still more positive ap-

We who make and sell whiskey say "TONIGHT WHEN IT'S ONE FOR THE ROAD BE SURE IT'S COFFEE"

THE HOUSE OF SEAGRAM
FINE WHISKIES SINCE 1857

proach. Many firms now foresee potential consumer problem areas and try to take preventive action before problems arise; many are also trying to communicate better with their customers. Whirlpool Corporation, for example, has a 24-hour "cool line" that allows customers to call toll-free from anywhere in the country to ask a question about company products or to register a complaint. Nabisco Brands, Johnson & Johnson, and Pillsbury have also sped up their response to consumers' written inquiries or complaints. Litton Industries and Sears Roebuck provide more detailed instructions for use of their products as well as consumer safety tips.

A wide range of advertisers have more carefully prepared their advertising to avoid potentially misleading claims. Advertisers are "telling it like it is" and avoiding exaggerated claims that might lead to unrealistic expectations. The Adolph Coors Company has encouraged the EPA to go ahead with national legislation affecting beverage containers even though most of the beer industry opposes the law. Coors executives claim that they're realists and that they're helping to shape fair laws.

Procter & Gamble, Bristol-Myers, and others have developed programs of consumer education.

Bristol-Myers offers a "free consumer guide to information." Shell Oil has distributed millions of its *Shell Answer Man* booklets. Hunt-Wesson Foods has offered computerized menus to help homemakers budget food expenses.

There's no doubt that efforts by Shell Oil, Bristol-Myers, and thousands of other companies have improved the lot of the consumer. Business has made major strides in some areas, while other aspects still need improvement. As Figure 2.2 shows, business is doing a good job in developing new products yet often fails to communicate adequately with consumers.

Employee Relations

A third major area where businesses can exercise their social responsibility is in employee relations. Among the abuses in this area needing correction has been the thorny problem of discrimination.

Race, National Origin, Religion When people are treated unfairly because of their race, **racism** is said to take place. In recent years much ef-

fort has been made to overcome discrimination against minorities. Although blacks and other groups have made considerable progress in getting fair treatment, many feel that they've not yet truly achieved equal opportunity. According to Vernon Jordan, past president of the National Urban League,

> *There is widespread belief among blacks in managerial positions that there is a firm ceiling on their future prospects, that their white peers will move out of middle management and into upper levels while they remain behind.* [9]

Besides racism, another form of discrimination occurs when a particular group is treated unfairly because of its national origin or religion. The group most likely to be discriminated against varies widely from place to place, and even by type of industry. In New York City, for example, it's often Puerto Ricans who are discriminated against; in many Texas cities it can be Mexican Americans.

Sexism **Sexism** exists when people are treated unfairly merely because they are males or fe-

FIGURE 2.2

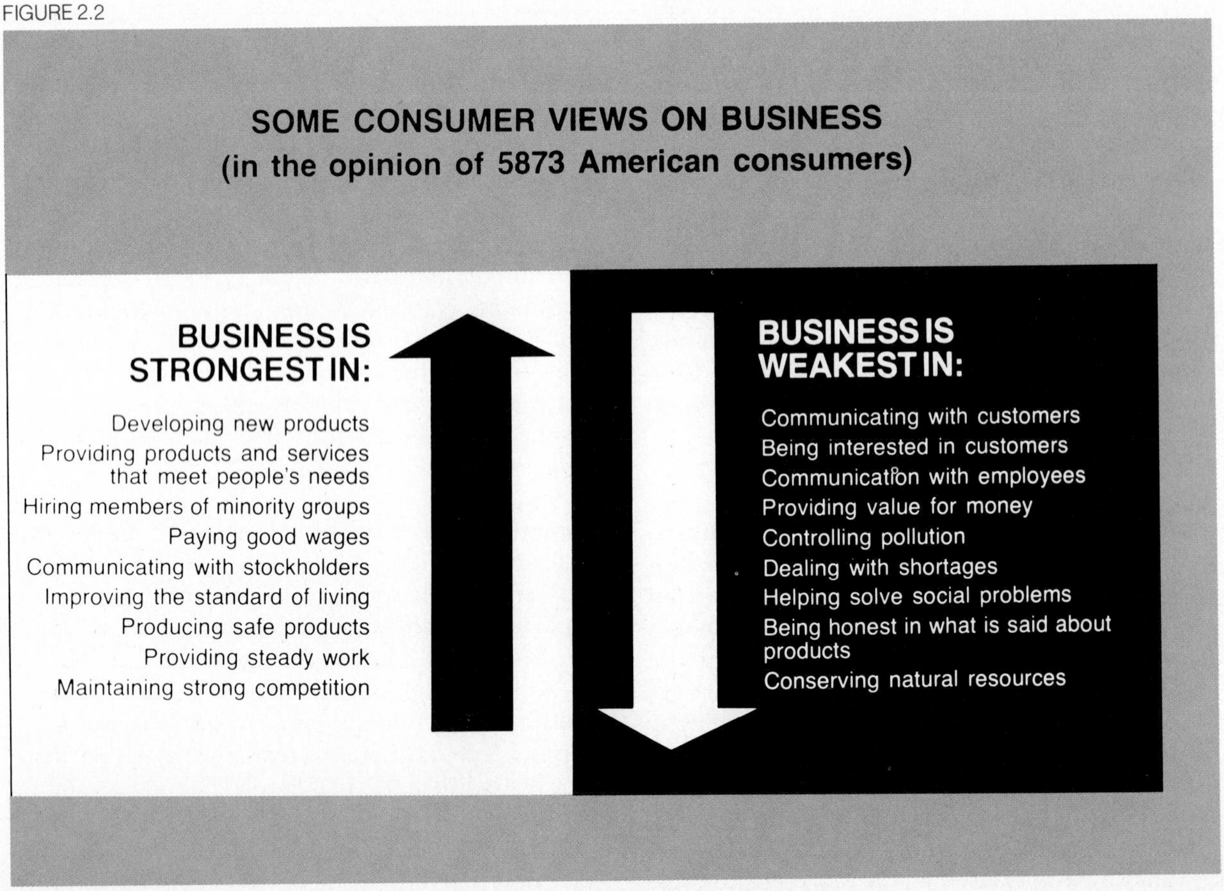

SOME CONSUMER VIEWS ON BUSINESS
(in the opinion of 5873 American consumers)

BUSINESS IS STRONGEST IN:

Developing new products
Providing products and services that meet people's needs
Hiring members of minority groups
Paying good wages
Communicating with stockholders
Improving the standard of living
Producing safe products
Providing steady work
Maintaining strong competition

BUSINESS IS WEAKEST IN:

Communicating with customers
Being interested in customers
Communication with employees
Providing value for money
Controlling pollution
Dealing with shortages
Helping solve social problems
Being honest in what is said about products
Conserving natural resources

Source: Reprinted from *U.S. News & World Report.* Copyright 1978 U.S. News & World Report, Inc.

An area where businesses are exercising social responsibility: the hiring of women and minorities.

males. The pattern of discrimination has especially been against women. In employment this occurs when it is believed that males and females should perform the same job for different levels of pay or when the sexes are segregated by type of activity, both on and off the job. About three fourths of America's 40 million working women are concentrated in stereotypically "female" occupations. These include secretary/stenographer, household worker, bookkeeper, elementary school teacher, and waitress. Only 6 percent of working women hold management or professional administrative jobs. But men are also victims of sexism. For example, airlines have traditionally preferred female to male flight attendants, and women are preferred as librarians, receptionists, and nurses.

Age Discrimination As the "aging of America" continues — that is, as more of us live longer — the problem of **ageism** may grow. This is the unfair treatment of individuals merely because of their age. The elderly have been especially affected. Even though federal legislation outlaws age discrimination prior to age 70, older workers still suffer discrimination. Nor is ageism limited to the elderly. Many large national companies won't hire anyone 35 years or older for entry-level management positions. The organizations claim that a person 35 + would be out of step with their promotion sequence.

Handicaps It's also true that people with mental and physical handicaps have been denied many job opportunities that they can handle just

as well as the nonhandicapped. Today progress is being made in reducing physical barriers to employing the handicapped, and employers' attitudes seem to be improving. One of the Bell System telephone companies has used a comprehensive employment program for the handicapped for a number of years. Bell often restructures a job in order to offer a wider range of disabled people meaningful employment.

Hiring and Training the Disadvantaged
There are many who fall into the category of the disadvantaged, sometimes called "unemployables" or the **"hard-core unemployed."** These people do not meet normal company selection standards for even the lowest-level jobs. Strictly speaking, they are not necessarily unemployable — or even unemployed — although they typically spend a great deal of time without work. Besides the handicapped, the disadvantaged include high school dropouts, young people under 22 years of age, older workers (over 55 years of age), the poor, minorities, persons with prison records, and those with drinking or drug problems.

Socially responsible companies hire and train the disadvantaged.

Recruiting the disadvantaged presents some unique problems. Many haven't applied for jobs for a number of years because they consider their chances of getting meaningful employment very slim. They also may not know how to fill out the complex array of applications and other forms that are required. The disadvantaged may live a long way from the employment offices of major firms in large cities or in suburbs and have no means of private transportation.

Employee Relations and the Law   The policies of Raytheon, Westinghouse, and many other companies in employing the disadvantaged are voluntary. However, a broad structure of federal legislation helps to wipe out discrimination and encourages employment of the disadvantaged. Among the important pieces of legislation are:

1. the Equal Pay Act (1963): employers are prohibited from paying unequal wages for equal work on account of sex;
2. Title VII of the Civil Rights Act of 1964 (Equal Employment Opportunity): prohibits discrimination because of race, color, religion, sex, or national origin in hiring, upgrading, and all other phases of employment; the act also created the Equal Employment Opportunity Commission to administer the law and investigate complaints about violations;
3. the Age Discrimination in Employment Act of 1967: employers of 25 or more persons cannot discriminate against a person between the ages of 40 and 65 in any area of employment because of age; the act was amended in 1978 and extended the mandatory age from 65 to 70;
4. the Vocational Rehabilitation Act of 1973: requires federal contractors and subcontractors to take affirmative action to seek out qualified handicapped people and fully utilize them; the act also requires the removal of architectural barriers to the handicapped: people in wheelchairs must have access to all parts of the building.

These laws show how society can force business to behave in a socially responsible manner. In the area of employee relations, for example, when society has deemed that business hasn't been responsible, it has acted through government to compel responsibility, as evidenced by the variety of federal laws.

BUSINESS ETHICS
Ethics Defined

Social responsibility and ethics are intertwined: the question of *social* responsibility for the firm may become an *ethical* question for the individual businessperson. A corporation is made up of individuals, and individuals are the ones who make the decisions about the nature and extent of social responsibility that will be acceptable by the firm.

Ethics refers to the set of criteria or standards for judging the rightness or wrongness of human conduct. A study of business ethics seeks to understand business practices, institutions, and actions in the light of some concept of human value. When a corporation is criticized for its failure to respond to environmental pressures by limiting the amount of pollutants it discharges, the firm is being evaluated on ethical grounds. On the other hand, when companies like International Harvester or Westinghouse are praised for hiring the disadvantaged, it is implied that their actions contribute directly to the sum total of human good.

Society expects businesspersons to act in an ethical manner. This means that their actions should not have unjust and harmful consequences, leading to social condemnation, loss of customer goodwill, disapproval of their peers, and/or court action. Business ethics tend to come from five sources: religion, philosophical systems, cultural experience, legal systems, and professional codes. Religion stresses the dignity of man under God and requires recognition of the rights of others and of one's own obligations. Philosophical systems, such as those originating with Aristotle, claim that reason produces valid ethical norms. Cultural experience provides values that society expects a business firm to uphold. Legal systems have traditionally tried to prevent only the worst violations of socially accepted ethical standards. Professional codes may be derived from a corporate philosophy, as in the example of ARMCO (see **Talking Business**). Most major corporations have written codes of ethics (see Figure 2.3).

Guides to Ethical Conduct

In addition to formal written statements on corporate ethics, there are a number of general guides for ethical behavior that are available to the businessperson. Perhaps the most popular and the one that says it best is the well-known Golden Rule: "Do unto others as you would have them do unto you." This is a generally accepted ethical standard for business; it was J. C. Penney's motto for his stores and in fact gave them their first name (Golden Rule Stores). He attributed his success to following this basic rule. Some people have modified versions of the Golden Rule to take into account people's differing values, such as "Don't do unto others as you'd have them do unto you, because their tastes may be different." Such restatements are in the spirit of the original idea. The basic concept of the Golden Rule has been translated in a number of ways into our business system. There are slogans such as "Share the United Way" and "A Mind Is a Terrible Thing to Waste" (United Negro College Fund).

Another guide to ethical conduct is to "do the greatest good for the greatest number"; it might be called the philosophical basis of a democracy. Applying this ethical guideline to the individual firm is not always easy, however. Consider a textile manufacturer with a heavily unionized work force located in a small New England community. The manufacturer has an opportunity to move to a southern state where the prospects for unionization are slight. Moreover the move will enable the manufacturer to install the latest technology and increase the productivity of the organization. What is the good for the greatest number? If we're speaking of the number of workers, then closing the plant will obviously harm all of its workers, with repercussions for the New England community. But if the number we're speaking of is the stockholders, then they'll be better served by closing the unionized, "outdated" plant.

Developing a Personal Code of Business Ethics The example of the threatened plant closing points up the difficulty of many ethical decisions: things are not always black or white, absolutely right or wrong. Still, the individual manager must reach a decision, guided by sound ethical principles incorporated into his or her own value system and behavior pattern. Table 2.1 lists a number of principles that should be an important part of a businessperson's ethics and values.

TABLE 2-1

Important Values for Businesspeople

1. *Justice.* Justice means fairness in the treatment of others. Inclusion of pregnancy as a compensated disability in company medical policies is considered a matter of justice.

2. *Truth.* The alternative to telling "the whole truth" is not always telling an *untruth.* Sometimes it is a question of *not telling all* or even of *not saying anything* (unless, of course, something is required by law or ethics). This is because telling the whole truth must be balanced with the effects of revealing that knowledge. One's right to private knowledge has to be established before one can assert a claim to know. For example, a person may not have the right to go into a corporation and examine in detail its books or demand to know how a secret production process works.

3. *Courage.* Courage includes the idea of standing up for what one believes in, e.g. refusing to go along with an ad campaign portraying women in an unfavorable light.

4. *Freedom.* Freedom refers to independent thinking and expression as well as being free from physical restraints. The right to some measure of one's own lifestyle when on the job (and entirely when off the job) is an example of personal freedom.

5. *Fairness.* Fairness means that there must be justice and impartiality in decision making and in the treatment of others. A manager should evaluate an employee solely on merit instead of on personal feelings.

6. *Sharing.* Sharing involves including others—workers, union leaders, etc.—in the power process. Inviting workers to help set the goals and standards by which they will be evaluated is an example of sharing.

SOURCE: Table (pp 86-87) based on "Ethical Consideration," by Grant W. Newton in *Organization and Behavior, including Ethical Considerations,* edited by Grant W. Newton, Copyright © 1978 by Grant W. Newton. Used by permission of Malibu Publishing Company. (Originally published by Harper & Row, Publishers, Inc.)

TALKING BUSINESS

Back in 1919, when steelmaker Armco, Inc. was known as The American Rolling Mill Co., an associate urged Founder George M. Verity to put down on paper the fundamental beliefs he had preached to employees since the company opened for business in 1900. The son of a circuit-riding Methodist minister in whom the Christian ethic ran strong, Verity thereupon composed *Policies*, which is believed to be the first corporate code of ethics ever published. Its tenets:

- To do business guided and governed by the highest standards of conduct so the end result of action taken makes a good reputation an invaluable and permanent asset.
- To insist on a square deal always. To make sure people are listened to and treated fairly, so that men and women really do right for right's sake and not just to achieve a desired result. For everyone to go beyond narrowness, littleness, selfishness in order to get the job done.
- To develop and maintain an efficient, loyal, aggressive organization, who believe in their company, to whom work is a challenge and to whom extraordinary accomplishment is a personal goal.
- To create and maintain good working conditions . . . to provide the best possible equipment and facilities . . . and plant and offices that are clean, orderly and safe.
- To adopt "Quality and Service" as an everyday practice. Quality will be the highest attainable in products, organization, plant, property and equipment. Service will be the best possible to customers, to shareholders, to city, state and nation.
- To employ people without regard to race, sex, religion or national origin. To encourage employees to improve their skills by participating in available educational or training programs. To provide every possible opportunity for advancement so that each individual may reach his or her highest potential.
- To provide not only fair remuneration, but the best compensation . . . it is possible to pay under the changing economic, commercial and other competitive conditions that exist from time to time. It is Armco's ambition to develop an organization . . . that can and will secure results which will make it possible for individual members to earn and receive better compensation than would be possible if performing a similar service in other fields of effort.
- To provide realistic and practical incentive as a means of encouraging the highest standard of individual performance and to assure increased quantity and quality of performance.
- To recognize cooperation as the medium through which great accomplishments are attained. Success depends more on a spirit of helpful cooperation than on any other one factor.
- To always consider what is right and best for the business as a whole, rather than what may be expedient in dealing with a single situation.
- To prohibit employees from becoming financially interested in any company with which Armco does business, if such financial interest might possibly influence decisions employees must make in their areas of responsibility. The above policy does not apply to ownership in publicly owned companies. This is not considered a conflict of interest but, rather, is encouraged as part of the free-enterprise system.

■ To create and maintain a working partnership between industry and community in this country and throughout the world. To support constructive agencies in communities where [Armco] people live and work in an effort to create civic conditions that respond to the highest needs of the citizens.

According to Armco Chairman C. William Verity Jr., grandson of the founder, these beliefs are still faithfully followed. "In a time during which traditional values have come under attack and challenge," he says, "Armco *Policies* have stood fast."

Reprinted from p. 58 of "Business's Big Morality Play" by Robert Levy with special permission of *Dun's Review*, August 1980. Copyright 1980, Dun and Bradstreet Publications Corporation.

FIGURE 2.3

TABLE 2–2
Topics Included in a Social Audit

EDUCATION
Direct financial aid to schools, including scholarships, grants and tuition refunds.
Support for increases in school budgets.
Donation of equipment and skilled personnel.
Assistance in curriculum development.
Aid in counseling and remedial education.
Establishment of new schools, running schools and school systems.

EMPLOYMENT AND TRAINING
Active recruitment of the disadvantaged.
Special functional training, remedial education and counseling.
Provision of day-care centers for children of working mothers.
Improvement of work/career opportunities.
Retraining of workers affected by automation or other causes of joblessness.
Establishment of company programs to remove the hazards of old age and sickness.
Supporting where needed and appropriate the extension of government accident, unemployment, health, and retirement systems.

CIVIL RIGHTS AND EQUAL OPPORTUNITY
Ensuring employment and advancement opportunities for minorities.
Facilitating equality of results by continued training and other special programs.
Supporting and aiding the improvement of black educational facilities, and special programs for blacks and other minorities in integrated institutions.
Encouraging adoption of open-housing ordinances.
Building plants and sales offices in the ghettos.
Providing financing and managerial assistance to minority enterprises, and participating with minorities in joint ventures.

POLLUTION ABATEMENT
Installation of modern equipment.
Engineering new facilities for minimum environmental effects.
Research and technological development.
Cooperating with municipalities in joint treatment facilities.
Cooperating with local, state, regional, and federal agencies in developing improved systems of environmental management.
Developing more effective programs for recycling and reusing disposable materials.

CONSERVATION AND RECREATION
Augmenting the supply of replenishable resources, such as trees, with more productive species.
Preserving animal life and the ecology of forests and comparable areas.
Providing recreational and aesthetic facilities for public use.
Restoring aesthetically depleted properties such as strip mines.
Improving the yield of scarce materials and recycling to conserve the supply.

CULTURE AND THE ARTS
Direct financial support to art institutions and the performing arts.
Development of indirect support as a business expense through gifts in kind, sponsoring artistic talent, and advertising.
Participation on boards to give advice on legal, labor, and financial management problems.
Helping secure government financial support for local or state arts councils and the National Endowment for the Arts.

SOURCE: Excerpted from John Corson, George Steiner, and Robert Meehan, *Measuring Business Social Performance: The Corporate Social Audit* (New York: Committee for Economic Development, 1974), pp. 27–29. Reprinted by permission.

Merging Ethics and Social Responsibility

Can a corporation be ethical and yet not have any social responsibilities? This question is still subject to a great deal of heated debate, yet the emerging answer seems to be *No.* Most business executives today feel that social responsibility is an ethical issue.[10] Responsibilities of both the individual and the corporation tend to be defined in terms of the social obligations that are at work in society at large (for example, the pledge to hire the disadvantaged). Ethics concerns the rules by which these responsibilities are carried out. Hiring the disadvantaged for jobs that management plans to abolish in the near future would be poor ethics. Thus it is extremely hard to separate the rules of the game from the game itself.

Organizing for Social Responsibility

In order to get a clear picture of the "game and the rules of the game," many companies have turned to the **social audit.** This is a systematic assessment of, and report on, company activities that have social impact. The concept of the social audit is relatively new, having been in use only since about 1970.

As the following examples illustrate, there's no "best" way to conduct a social audit. In one company the chief executive assigned the task of designing a social audit procedure to his public affairs group. This group, naturally enough, was primarily interested in increasing the company's role in community affairs. Consequently it designed an audit that would demonstrate a close link between social programs and long-range profitability. In another case a company president wanted to satisfy his conscience that the company was indeed behaving responsibly. Inevitably, the issues the firm selected for the audit were those that were important to him personally.

To offset the problems these examples point up, many large corporations have turned to outside social auditors. These are experts that can make an independent and impartial appraisal of company policies and actions from the social viewpoint. A list of some of the topics examined in a social audit is shown in Table 2.2.

In addition to social audits, many companies have established committees within their board of directors to decide which social programs the company should undertake. General Motors, for instance, created a public policy committee composed of five members of the GM board. The committee meets once a month to make recommendations to GM's top management. Other companies that use board members to guide social responsibility policies are Ford Motor, IBM, Kimberly-Clark (Kleenex), and Philip Morris.

Firms have also changed their organization structures so that social action programs are the responsibility of one person, an entire department, or a committee. The power and scope of these persons and groups vary, of course. The point is that the company has specifically assigned responsibility for social programs.

Social responsibility officers help ensure that the firm makes a social as well as an economic contribution to society. Quaker Oats expects the communities in which it locates new plants to offer equal opportunities comparable to those offered by Quaker Oats. The company was thinking of building a major food plant in Danville, Illinois. Quaker Oats advised the city's leaders that passage of an open housing ordinance would impress the company as an indication of the city's intent to work for social progress. The ordinance passed. Two days later Quaker Oats approved the location of a new plant in Danville.

SUMMARY

Social responsibility is the concern of business for the welfare of society as a whole. Among the reasons often cited for business to accept social responsibility are the following: (1) Society, through its laws, has given business the right to exist and can therefore change its expectations of business when it wishes. (2) When businesses assume social responsibility, the need for government regulation is decreased. (3) Social responsibility can translate into money and jobs; for example, many new jobs have been created by the movement to clean up the environment. (4) Finally, businesses have the resources to deal with social problems; thus society should expect business to use these resources for that purpose.

The most important argument against expecting business to accept social responsibility says that management's main responsibiity is to make as much money as possible for the firm's stockholders. Another argument says that managers are not trained to pursue social goals. However it appears that many major corporations today have accepted social responsibility as a legitimate corporate function.

Among the social issues involved in the corporation's exercise of social responsibility are environmental problems, consumerism, and employee relations. With regard to the environment, technological advances have led to problems of scarcity and overuse. The concept of responsible consumption advises rational and efficient use of resources with a view to the present and future condition of society. Pollution is another major environmental concern. Pollutants include liquid and solid waste, gaseous and particulate discharges into the air, noise, heat, poison, and radiation.

Consumer protection can originate in consumer activist groups, government, or business itself. In the United States, the 1960s saw the passage of a number of laws strengthening consumers' positions; and in 1972, the Consumer Product Safety Commission was created. Today, many consumerists hold government positions. The response of business to consumerism has grown more positive from the 1960s through the present.

Employee relations is mainly concerned with the problem of discrimination, which may be based on race, national origin, sex, age, or the existence of physical or mental handicaps. In addition, employment problems exist for the disadvantaged—people who, for various reasons, cannot meet normal company selection standards for even the lowest-level jobs. A broad structure of federal legislation has sought to eliminate discrimination and encourage the employment of the disadvantaged. Such legislation, like that aimed at environmental and consumer concerns, shows how society can force business to act in a socially responsible manner.

Most executives today believe that social responsibility is an ethical issue. Business ethics tend to come from five sources: religion, philosophical systems, cultural experience, legal systems, and professional codes. In addition, such general codes as the Golden Rule are often used as ethical guides.

Individual managers often feel pressured to compromise their personal ethics to achieve corporate goals. For this problem to be alleviated, ethical codes must be supported by top management.

A number of companies have begun to use the social audit to assess and report on company activities that have social impact. Further, some companies have established committees to determine which social programs to undertake; others have changed their organizational structures to make social programs the responsibility of an individual, a department, or a committee.

KEY TERMS

ageism
consumerism
ecology
ethics
"hard-core
    unemployed"
pollution
racism
responsible
    consumption
sexism
social audit
social responsibility

REVIEW QUESTIONS

1. What are the main arguments for and against social responsibility in business?
2. List what you feel are the five most important social issues that society thinks business should help solve.
3. Who should pay for pollution control?
4. What are the major areas of legislation that have come from the consumer movement?
5. Should a small business be exempt from pollution control requirements if it means a higher risk of failure to comply?
6. What are the major elements of a social audit for a business?
7. Do you think that business ethics can be taught?

DISCUSSION QUESTIONS

1. Does social responsibility in a business contribute to or detract from its profits?
2. Is it in the stockholders' interest for a major corporation, located in a large city, to spend

time and money on community and public affairs activities?

3. Are there limits to the social responsibilities of a business? What are they?

4. "Left to themselves businesses will solve pollution problems without government interference." Do you agree? Explain your answer.

5. In what way can a social audit benefit a business?

6. It has been said that it is difficult to make a profit in business and be ethical at the same time. Do you agree or disagree? Explain.

CASE: MUCH GRASS, JOHN M.!

During the last 20 years, New York City's South Bronx has undergone major changes in its ethnic makeup. Once a middle-class white area, it is now dominated by a Hispanic population, mostly from Puerto Rico. Many speak poor English and have trouble reading and writing the language. It doesn't seem a likely place to find a high-technology industry making precision parts used in defense equipment. Yet this is where Wellbuilt Electronics Die Corp. not only exists but thrives.

In 1971 John Mariotta obtained a loan for the firm from the Small Business Administration. After ten years of government support, Wellbuilt was ready to go it alone. Without that support, however, the company probably would have gone under, and an important small industry would have disappeared.

At the outset there was some doubt whether the enterprise would be a good investment. Wellbuilt's workers are Spanish-speaking, and the language barrier might have made it difficult to train them in high-technology work. Yet they needed the work and wanted to work, so Mariotta stuck it out. In late 1981 Wellbuilt landed several contracts to make jet parts and enlarged its engineering staff by hiring Russian engineers who had recently migrated to the US. They don't speak English, but they do know their technology!

John Mariotta is proud of the fact that he has been able to make a business flourish in the economically and socially deprived South Bronx.

1. How does this case fit in with your ideas of the social responsibilities of business?

2. Do you think that government should support businesses until they can make it themselves if they bring employment to economically deprived areas?

CASE: WHAT ABOUT SOCIAL RESPONSIBILITY FOR BUSINESS?

For years people have been pointing accusing fingers at business, demonstrating against business abuses of the environment—factories polluting the air and the water, toxic waste disposal, exploitation of natural resources, etc.

Auto companies have been hounded by champions of consumer causes, who have sought safer automobiles with more antipollution devices, while labor has cried out for guaranteed annual wages, desirable fringe benefits, early retirement incentives, pensions, and insurance.

Finally the tables turned, and business ran out of profits with which to finance all of these adopted social and economic obligations. In too many cases profits dried up like the fresh-water rivers in a drought, and bankruptcies mounted. The first part of 1982 posted the worst record of business failures since the Great Depression.

Suddenly there was a rising voice from the unemployed (over 9 million) crying for the federal government to come to the rescue. Some businesses joined in the plea, the first being American Motors, which asked for $200,000,000. But the big cry came from Chrysler with a tearful bid for federal loan guarantees of a billion and a half dollars to save the jobs of 150,000 workers in a business teetering on the edge of bankruptcy.

Ford Motor Company lost over a billion dollars for two years in a row; shouldn't the federal government help out Ford too? Who's responsible for the business as it struggles for survival? Maybe Peter Drucker is right: the primary responsibility of business is to make a product people can afford to buy at a price that will give business a profit for survival.

1. Should the federal government assume the responsibility for rescuing failing businesses? Or should it rescue only big corporations with huge labor forces? What can be done for the 6000 companies that failed during the first part of 1982?

2. Should the federal government come to the rescue before these businesses fail?

3. Should Darwin's theory—"survival of the fittest"—be applied to business?

C H A P T E R   3

FORMS OF
ORGANIZATION

After studying this chapter you should be able to:

1 Understand why an entrepreneur selects a particular organizational form for a business.
2 Compare the advantages and disadvantages of a sole proprietorship, a partnership, and a corporation.
3 Describe the ownership and organizational structure of a corporation and how it is managed.
4 Explain why "big business" is so closely identified with corporations.
5 Recognize how income and profits are earned and distributed in various forms of business.
6 Understand the nature of, and need for, quasi-public corporations and co-operatives.

47

Two and a half years ago, four of us started out on a great adventure together—our own consulting partnership. For six months, we struggled along with no clients. Then we hit the big time: a $1.3 million contract. But somehow our success at attracting clients was greater than our ability to work together harmoniously. This April, our original partnership broke up. The experience was one of the toughest I've ever gone through—but it taught me some valuable lessons about what makes a partnership succeed.

When it became apparent, after several attempted salvage operations, that there were irreconcilable differences in our partnership, we called in our attorney. "Splitting up a partnership," he said, "is just like a divorce without the kids." He meant to reassure us with the comment about kids, but I found that the dissolution of a partnership can be just as emotional as a divorce. Like ours, many partnerships consist of friends and former colleagues, and many other partnerships include relatives. Couple these personal relationships with the intense involvement required to run a small business, and you can see why a failing partnership creates misunderstandings, bruised egos, bitterness, hurt feelings, and anger. . . .

Of course, no one puts together a partnership thinking about the unpleasantness of breaking it up. The key is to recognize that a partnership arrangement is subject to some stresses that are not found in other corporate structures.

Source: Reprinted with permission of *INC.* Magazine. Stephen G. Thomas, "Why Partnerships Break Up," *INC.*, July 1981, pp. 67–70. Copyright © 1981 by INC. Publishing Company, 38 Commercial Wharf, Boston, MA 02110.

When you decide to accept the role of an entrepreneur and develop your own business enterprise, you come up against the need to make decisions, decisions, and then . . . more decisions. One of these—the choice of the form of business organization—has far-reaching consequences, as Stephen Thomas' experience makes clear. This single decision touches all phases and aspects of the firm's operations. What, then, are the choices? In today's business environment there are four major kinds of legal business organization: the sole proprietorship, the partnership, the corporation, and the cooperative. Each of these has its own particular set of advantages and disadvantages.

In choosing which structure to use, the business owner must first of all evaluate his or her own circumstances. It's essential to consider the many factors that will be faced in managing the firm, marketing its products and services, and financing its operations. The U.S. Small Business Administration suggests that the business owner look for answers to the questions you see in Table 3.1 before choosing a form of business organization. With the answers to these questions, the owner can then make a more informed decision about the kind of legal structure that's best for his or her business enterprise.

SOLE PROPRIETORSHIPS

As you might guess, the **sole proprietorship** is a business firm that is established, owned, financed, and operated by a single individual. In many cases, the owner of the sole proprietorship also works in the business and is, in this sense, an employee of the firm. Of course, he or she always has complete responsibility for all decisions required in operating the business. The proprietorship is the easiest of all businesses to establish. After securing any licenses and permits (if they're required—for many business they're not), the owner simply begins operations. The proprietorship is also the least expensive of business forms to

TABLE 3-1

Considerations in Choosing a Business Form

1. What is the size of the owner's liability for the debts and taxes of the business?
2. Would the firm continue if something happened to the owner?
3. What are the effects of the tax and regulatory laws on the business?
4. How easy will it be to raise more capital? To attract qualified employees?
5. What is the cost and procedure of starting a given form of business?
6. What are the enterprise goals, and what form contributes most to these purposes?
7. How much control of operations does the owner have?

SOURCE: Adapted from Antonio M. Olmi, *Selecting the Legal Structure for Your Firm* (Washington, D.C.: Small Business Administration, 1977), Management Aids, No. 231.

get off the ground. There are no agreements between parties (necessary in a partnership) or applications for a charter (required for a corporation). So time and money are conserved.

The proprietorship predominates in any census of the types of business organizations. Historically, about 80 percent of all firms in the United States have been sole proprietorships, accounting for only about 10 percent of the total receipts of American business firms. Most proprietorships are therefore extremely small in terms of business receipts.

The majority of sole proprietorships are found in agriculture, wholesale and retail trade, and services. Agricultural proprietorships account for 31 percent of all proprietorships. Wholesale and retail trade make up another 20 percent, and services account for 28 percent.

Advantages of Proprietorships

The proprietorship has several advantages contributing to its widespread use as a business form.

1. Easy Formation and Low Costs The sole proprietorship doesn't require formation under specific legal procedures. The prospective owner usually doesn't even have to hire an attorney to help with meeting the legal requirements. Applying for, and securing, the necessary permits and licenses can be done by contacting local govern-

ment directly. This procedure helps keep organization costs low.

For example, suppose that you're a stamp-, coin-, or comic book collector and you want to start a business trading in these popular collectibles. All you have to do is register the name of the business with the city or county, get a license to sell, obtain a state sales tax permit (if required), and use part or all of your collection as the original inventory of the business. That's exactly how many merchants dealing in these and other collectibles start their businesses.

2. All Profits to the Owner The owner of the sole proprietorship has claim to all the profits the business makes. He or she is free to use the profits as desired without having to account to anyone else. Of course, if the business is successful, the tax collector will be looking for a share of the profits.

3. Direct Control of the Business The proprietor is responsible for all decisions regarding the operation of the business; there are no co-owners to consult. This direct control allows the owner to be as secretive (within the law) about the business

A sole proprietor in front of her store.

PERSPECTIVE ON SMALL BUSINESS

Being their own boss is more important to some people than almost anything else. They tend to ask themselves questions like "Why am I working so hard for someone who is good at saying *yes* to his superiors and *no* to me?" From such discontent new businesses grow.

But chucking a steady paycheck for the uncertain returns of entrepreneurship is often traumatic. The shock is worsened by the slapdash way in which so many people go into business. It needn't be so, as some six dozen men and women learned at a recent seminar in Dallas, a hotbed of new enterprises where even the driver of a run-down cab talks of the $65,000 he's raised to begin wildcat drilling on land he knows is "gonna make me a rich man."

Still, some people shouldn't go it alone. You have to be cut out for entrepreneurship, says William McCrea, chairman of the Entrepreneurship Institute, sponsor of the two-day seminar. You have to like solving problems all the time; you have to be healthy and willing "to work your tail off." You also have to find some way to finance your way into a business, once you've found the business you want.

Fed up with being an employee, Kenneth Gjemre left a job in retailing about ten years ago to open a used-book store. Today, he owns the 16-store chain known as Half Price Books. His advice to the hopefuls at the seminar: "Get to know your banker on a first-name basis." Level with your banker as you would with few other people; "he's the only one you should undress in front of," says Gjemre.

But Clinton S. Hartmann needed more money than a banker would provide to get RF Monolithic Inc. into production of sophisticated radio components. Hartmann had developed the parts while a Texas Instruments Inc. employee. It took him 15 months to get nearly $3 million from a group of venture capital concerns.

His advice to venture capital seekers: "Don't be bashful. Tell your venture capital guy your dream. He wants to believe you're the next Apple Computer or Xerox." To get the money they needed, Hartmann and his cofounders had to give up more than 50% of the equity in RF Monolithic, but it was a deal he considers reasonable.

SOURCE: Excerpted from Sanford L. Jacobs, "Aspiring Entrepreneurs Learn Intricacies of Going It Alone," *Wall Street Journal*, 23 March 1981, p. 27. Reprinted by permission of The Wall Street Journal, © Dow Jones & Company, Inc., 1981. All rights reserved.

as he or she desires. Direct control also allows the owner to be flexible and make changes quickly in order to meet changing business conditions. Robert Townsend makes exactly this point in his well-known book *Up the Organization.* He says that owners can take more chances and develop better timing because they don't have to prove their case to anyone else (e.g. a board of directors) before they act.[1]

4. Maximum Freedom from Government Regulation   All business firms are subject to government control of their activity. The sole proprietorship has more freedom from government control since its formation is not controlled by law. The relative absence of government control lets the owner operate the business as he or she sees fit, reducing the problems and difficulties in dealing with the thousands of state, federal, and local regulations. This doesn't mean that a small, owner-operated business is exempt from all the regulations and instructions of regulatory agencies—as the owner of one small restaurant found out.

Robert Boose owned and operated a restaurant in Putnam, Illinois. An inspector from the local office of the Occuptional Safety and Health Agency (OSHA) told Mr. Boose that he had to remove a short electrical cord from an aisle in his restaurant in order to comply with OSHA standards—despite the fact that the cord was both concealed and well protected. At a cost of $240,

Boose complied with the inspector's orders. So even a fairly small business, such as a restaurant, is subject to some degree of regulation.

(Incidental intelligence: when Boose went to the OSHA office to report his compliance with the order, he was told that the inspector wouldn't be in for at least two weeks—he'd broken his collar bone in tripping over a typewriter cord in the OSHA office.)[2]

5. No Special Taxation Proprietorships are not subject to special franchise or organization taxes. Proprietorships aren't required to pay income taxes on the profits of their activities; instead business profits are taxed as personal income of the owner. (You'll find taxation of proprietorships discussed in more detail later in this chapter.)

6. Ease of Dissolution Since there are no co-owners or partners involved, the proprietor is free to withdraw from the business or to sell it at any time. Because of the ease of entry and withdrawal, proprietorship is the form often used by an owner to test new business ideas before forming a less flexible and more expensive corporation.

Disadvantages of Proprietorships

There are several disadvantages that commonly characterize the proprietorship.

1. Unlimited Liability The proprietorship isn't a separate legal entity; that is, the business isn't independent of its owner. This means that the owner is fully liable for all business debts of the proprietorship—even when they exceed the owner's business assets. In the event of a lawsuit or failure of the business, the owner can be held personally liable (to the extent of his or her personal assets) for all creditor claims against the business.

2. Difficulty in Raising Capital Because of full liability, the owner may have a hard time raising additional capital to help the business grow. Why? Lenders may be reluctant to advance money to a proprietorship because of the future possibility of creditors' claims against assets. Projects necessary for the growth of the business usually must be financed from business profits or loans from friends or relatives.

Other typical sources of financing available to the sole proprietor include borrowing on life insurance, taking a second mortgage on the house, withdrawing money from personal savings, and lowering one's standard of living to raise cash.

3. Limited Management Expertise The experience and expertise that can be focused on problems of the business are limited to the viewpoint of the owner. There's no one to look to for advice—unless the owner hires a consultant or outside adviser to help with business problems.

4. Unstable Business Life The business will last only as long as the owner desires or is able to operate it. The enterprise may be impaired or ended by the death or disability of the owner. The problem of estate taxes is a major reason for this—a subject we'll examine later in the chapter.

5. Difficulty in Attracting Qualified Employees The sole proprietorship may find it no easy matter to attract and keep qualified employees because of the limited incentives. Proprietorships, because they tend to remain small, usually have little potential for management development and promotion into top management positions.

6. All Losses to the Owner While all profits to the owner is an advantage of the sole proprietorship, unfortunately the owner must also absorb all losses. However by allowing the deduction of business losses from other personal income, the tax law softens the impact of losses—as we shall now see.

Taxation of Proprietorships

The proprietorship is neither a legal nor a taxable entity. The profits of the business must be reported on the owner's individual tax return. Revenues and expenses of the proprietorship are reported on Form 1040, Schedule C. Business income is combined with all other sources of income and is taxed according to personal income tax rates. The personal tax bracket ranges from 0 percent to a maximum of 50 percent.

There's tax advantage for the proprietorship that comes from this very requirement for reporting business income. Briefly stated: if the business suffers any losses, these may be combined with personal income and so reduce the taxes the owner is required to pay. If the losses should happen to exceed other sources of income, the owner may use the "operating loss carryback and carryforward" provision of the tax law. This allows the proprietor to apply losses to past and future years—something that can be very useful in trying to control a business that shows a highly unstable pattern of income or losses in its early years of operation.

PARTNERSHIPS

The Uniform Partnership Act, Section 6, defines a **partnership** as "an association of two or more persons to carry on as co-owners a business for profit." While the required agreement procedure is more formal than the machinery for setting up a sole proprietorship, the partnership is still quite easy to form. It simply requires that the co-owners agree to do business as partners and to secure any necessary permits and licenses before beginning operations.

The partnership enjoys limited popularity as a business form in the United States. There are many large partnerships with very recognizable names in the accounting and legal fields. Price, Waterhouse and Company, Arthur Young and Company, and Peat, Marwick and Mitchell are all partnerships, and each is recognized as one of the "Big Eight" accounting firms in the United States. Entire businesses themselves can form partnerships. Gulf Oil Corporation and Royal/

Dutch Shell not long ago ended a partnership they began in 1973 to build nuclear power plants. (The partnership was ended because no power plants were ever built, due to lack of demand.)[3]

Partnership Agreement

The Uniform Partnership Act doesn't require a written agreement, but written articles of partnership are usually developed. The **partnership agreement** generally specifies the contributions of the partners to the business, the roles each partner will play, and the major points of agreement among the partners.

Although not essential, it's usually advisable to have an attorney develop the partnership agreement. A properly executed agreement can prevent many of the problems that might later arise among the partners.

Types of Partnerships

Partnerships may take one of three basic types: the general partnership, the limited partnership, and the joint venture. Each kind of partnership has its own particular value and meets a different requirement, or set of requirements, of the owners of the business.

General Partnership   The **general partnership** is the standard form referred to by the Uniform

Congenial business partners in their sandwich shop.

TALKING BUSINESS

High production costs and interest rates have driven movie studios to seek alternatives to traditional financing. MGM hopes to interest investors in an unusual partnership venture that plans to finance up to half of all MGM Film productions over a five-year period.

The joint venture involves a newly formed limited partnership called SLM Entertainment Ltd. At the core of SLM Entertainment is SLM Inc., MGM's general partner in the venture. The four directors of SLM Inc. plan to invest at least $5 million of their own in the venture and in addition offer 10,000 limited partnership interests to the investing public at $5000 each.

Even for limited partners, investing in movies is risky; but even if the movie fails and no profits materialize, there are always tax benefits. "The tax-shelter benefits really make these deals go," says a securities analyst.

Source: Adapted from Stephen Sansweet, "MGM Film Gives Small Investors a Chance to Share in Rising Cost of Making Movies," *Wall Street Journal*, 13 August 1981, p. 19. Adapted by permission of The Wall Street Journal, © Dow Jones & Company, Inc., 1981. All rights reserved.

Partnership Act. In the general partnership all partners share in the management and profits, possess co-ownership of the business assets, and may act on behalf of the business firm. All partners in a general partnership are subject to unlimited liability for business debts and contracts.

The general partnership is easily established. The owners agree to the terms of the partnership agreement, sign the agreement, and, after compliance with local ordinances, begin their business operations. The general partnership might be viewed as the operation of several proprietorships in a single business firm. One of the best known American businesses (now a corporation) began as a general partnership. The men who started it were Richard Warren Sears and Alvah Curtis Roebuck.[4]

Limited Partnership Some states allow the formation of a partnership known as the **limited partnership**. This is an association of one or more general partners who have unlimited liability and one or more (usually many more) limited partners whose liability is limited to their capital contributions. Limited partnerships allow the owners to attract needed money for investment in the business by offering the limited partner the advantages of limited liability. And note: in return for this limited liability, the limited partner agrees to give up any participation in the management of the firm. The limited partnership isn't widely used as an operating business firm. It's more often used in real estate ventures, oil and gas drilling projects, agricultural operations, Broadway shows, and attracting investors for tax shelters. Generally, you should have a net worth of at least $100,000 and be in a 50 percent tax bracket before investing in most limited partnerships.

Joint Venture The **joint venture** is a special type of partnership that's established to undertake a specific project or to operate for a specific amount of time. Once the project is completed or the period has elapsed, the partnership is dissolved and the profits are distributed as agreed.

Joint ventures are quite common in the extractive industries, where the cost of exploring for oil and gas is extremely high. It isn't unusual to hear about large companies such as Exxon, Texaco, and Shell joining together to purchase and develop offshore oil and gas properties near the coasts of Texas, Louisiana, or California. In just this way Texaco, Pogo Producing, and Amax Petroleum produced a natural gas well 90 miles south of Houma, Louisiana. In the same state Texaco, Pogo, and Diamond Shamrock also produced a well 150 miles south of St. Charles.[5]

Advantages of Partnerships

The partnership reveals several advantages when compared with the other basic business forms.

1. Ease of Formation While not as easy to form as a proprietorship, the partnership still is less difficult to form than the corporation. The partners agree to do business together and draw up and sign the partnership agreement. There are no complex state laws regulating the establishment of the partnership.

2. More Capital Available The partnership has more capital available to it because it doesn't have to rely on a single individual as the source of its funds. The added financial strength of the partners increases the borrowing and equity base of the partnership.

3. More Diverse Skills and Expertise The partnership involves more people in the decision-making process. The *ideal* partnership will bring together partners who complement each other — not partners who have the same background and experience. Such a complementing process allows for more and better decisions about the business operations of the firm.

This advantage became clear in the partnership formed by two New York fashion designers, Barbara Dorio and Victor Whitehurst. The two formed a partnership and produced a small but very popular line of clothes. Although they fast proved themselves as designers, they had trouble managing the financial side of the business. Solution: bringing Gerrit van der Meer into the business as a third partner to act as the firm's business manager, because of his skills in precisely this area.[6]

4. Flexibility The partnership can quickly adapt to changes in the business environment because the owners are active in the routine management of the business. Their very closeness to the activities of the firm enables them to decide more quickly what changes are needed to meet the competition. Of course, this is also an advantage of the sole proprietorship.

5. Relative Freedom from Government Control The partnership, like the sole proprietorship, has fewer government controls over its activities.

Disadvantages of Partnerships

The most commonly cited disadvantages of the partnership are:

1. Unlimited Liability All general partners have unlimited liability for the debts of the business. In fact, depending on the financial position of the other partners, one partner can be held liable for all partnership debts. This occurs when the insolvency of the business leads to the insolvency of the partners as well.

2. All Partners Responsible for Acts of Each One partner may take an action that binds the firm to a contract and makes all the other partners responsible for the performance of that contract. This joint responsibility for the actions of each other may put significant strain on the partners' relationship.

3. Limited Life A partnership is automatically dissolved by the death or withdrawal of a partner. Under the Uniform Partnership Act, the partnership can continue to operate for a limited period of time under the right of survivorship, with the possible creation of a new partnership by the survivors. In connection with this, most partners enter into buy-sell agreements that enable a surviving partner to buy a deceased partner's interest from his or her estate. Very often life insurance is used to provide funds necessary for the buy-out. This is explained in greater detail in Chapter 19.

4. Sharing of Profits The partners must share the profits of the business with each other. However, profit sharing need not be on an equal basis.

5. Difficulty of Disposing of Partnership Interest The disposition of a partner's interest is difficult to accomplish without specific prearrangement in the written agreement or the other partners agreeing to the sale of the interest. But even if the procedure for sale is covered in the partnership agreement or the other partners agree, the existing partnership is terminated and a new one is formed.

Taxation of Partnerships

The partnership is a "quasi-taxable entity." This means that although the Internal Revenue Service requires the partnership to file a partnership tax return, nevertheless the partnership pays no income tax itself. The partnership income tax return is only an information return; it reports the amount of profit the partnership made and how the profit was divided among the partners.

The partnership profits are divided and reported on the individual partner's personal income tax return and are taxed at the individual tax rate of each partner. In the event of a partnership loss, each partner's proportionate share of the loss can be used to offset his or her other personal income in the same way as the sole proprietor uses the losses from the proprietorship.

CORPORATIONS

In *Trustees of Dartmouth College* v. *Woodward* (1819) Chief Justice John Marshall defined a corporation as "an artificial being, invisible, intangible, and existing only in contemplation of the law." Marshall's definition describes the corporation as an entity with an existence separate from its owners. More particularly, the **corporation** is a "legal person" established by the laws of the state in which it is formed. The state government issues the corporation a charter that specifies the corporation's business objectives and gives it the author-

ity to operate as a business. The corporation can buy and hold property; make, and be party to, contracts; sue and be sued. And it must pay taxes.

The Corporate Structure

The corporation has a very distinctive organizational structure with several important components. These components are the incorporators, the stockholders, the directors, and the operating managers. They're represented in Figure 3.1.

Incorporators The incorporators are the organizers of the corporation. Most states require at least three incorporators, who must sign the initial application for a corporate charter. The incorporators decide on the name of the corporation, its purpose, and the amount of initial shares of stock to be issued. Since these decisions are vital to the success of the business, it's advantageous for the incorporators to be stockholders in the new corporation. Many incorporators are people who started the business as a sole proprietorship or as a partnership.

Stockholders The stockholders are the owners of the corporation. After the certificate of incorporation is filed and the charter is granted by the state, the corporation sells and issues shares of stock to individuals who want to own an interest in the corporation's business operations.

Divisional offices of W. R. Grace & Co.

ORGANIZATIONAL STRUCTURE OF A CORPORATION

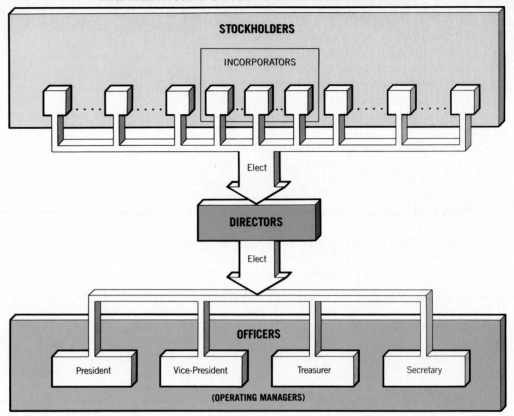

FIGURE 3.1

A stockholder possesses certain rights. He or she is entitled to vote at the annual meeting of stockholders, to vote for the directors of the corporation, to receive dividends when these are declared, and to sell or transfer ownership whenever he or she desires.

Directors   The board of directors is elected by the stockholders of the corporation. The directors are responsible to the stockholders for the overall management of the corporation. They set the major corporate policies, elect corporate officers, and generally oversee the operational and financial affairs of the corporation. In smaller and in some medium-sized corporations, the stockholders of the corporation may also be its directors.

Managers   The board of directors is responsible for electing the officers of the corporation. The number and titles of the officers is specified in the corporation's bylaws. The officers are responsible for the day-to-day operation of the business and are commonly referred to as the managers of the

corporation. They bear such titles as president and chief executive officer, vice-president, treasurer, and secretary. Lee Iacocca, Frank Sellinger, and Frank Borman are examples of corporate managers who are well known to the public. They're also very likely to be stockholders in their companies.

Advantages of Corporations

The corporation has several advantages over the proprietorship and the partnership. The most significant advantages are:

1. Limited Liability   The corporation is a legal person that exists separately from its owners. Because of this legal standing, the corporation affords its owners **limited liability** for the debts of the business firm. The stockholder's liability for corporate debts is limited to the actual amount invested in the corporation for the shares of stock

Corporate directors meeting to review and establish company policy.

the stockholder owns. Should the corporation go bankrupt, creditors can look only to the assets of the business for satisfaction of their claims. For example, if a firm such as Braniff Airlines goes under, stockholders will lose at most only the price they paid for their stock. They have no other liability. A special provision of the Federal Bankruptcy Act—Chapter 11—even allows a corporation facing bankruptcy to apply for special court-granted immunity from creditor lawsuits so that it can have extra time to work out ways to pay its debts. For example, Pathcom Inc., a manufacturer of two-way radios, received Chapter 11 protection in 1981 when it incurred heavy losses.[7]

2. Transferability of Ownership Stockholders are free to transfer their ownership of the corporation by selling or assigning their shares. The transfer of ownership doesn't cause the termination of a corporation, as it would with the proprietorship or partnership. It's this very transfer of ownership in corporations that keeps the New York and American stock exchanges, as well as the over-the-counter exchange (discussed in Chapter 17), so busy. Millions of shares of stock of the larger corporations are bought and sold on these exchanges every day.

It should be emphasized that, except for new stock issues, the trading of stock brings no new cash to the company. The buyer, through a broker, pays the selling price to an individual who owns the specific shares. These shares may have been traded dozens of times since they were originally sold by the corporation to raise cash.

3. Stability of Existence The life of the corporation is perpetual. Even when the corporation is required to have a specific number of years of life stated in the charter, there are provisions for continued renewal of the corporate charter. The corporation isn't affected by death, illness, or withdrawal of a stockholder, director, or officer. The corporation continues to exist and do business.

4. Relative Ease of Obtaining Additional Capital In order to raise additional funds, stock may be sold to people besides the founders who also have faith in the corporation's future growth and profit potential. This is referred to as "going public."

Banks and other lenders may also be more willing to lend money to small corporations if the shareholders will cosign the notes. Cosigning gives lenders more security by allowing them recourse to both corporate and shareholder assets. Of course, this takes away much of the limited-liability advantage of the corporate form.

Disadvantages of Corporations

The corporation might seem ideal as a business form, but it does have its disadvantages.

1. Double Taxation of Profits The corporation is a taxable entity and must pay tax on its profits. Dividends are paid from the after-tax profits of the corporation. The stockholder who receives the dividend must pay taxes on the dividends he receives. So because profits of corporations are taxed as corporate income, and dividends are taxed as personal income to the shareholder, the same income stream is taxed twice.

2. Cost and Complexity of Formation To form a corporation it's necessary to apply for a charter from the state in which the incorporators want to base the corporation. An attorney may be needed to prepare the articles of incorporation and make the proper filings. Incorporators are also required to pay filing fees and may have to pay license and registration fees. In some states, such as California and Texas, these fees may be as high as $500. In New York the cost may reach $1000.[8] Because of very lenient requirements, Delaware is a popular state to incorporate in.

3. More Government Restriction The corporation is subject to many restrictions from which the proprietorship and partnership are exempt. The corporation must register with each state in which it wants to do business. If it wants to sell stock to the public, it must register with the Securities and Exchange Commission. Of the three types of business forms, the corporation is the most closely regulated; and the reporting requirements of this regulation often result in increased operating costs. Antitrust actions such as the government's refusal in 1981 to let Mobil purchase Marathon Oil are only the more spectacular examples of this degree of regulation.[9] A more familiar example would be AT&T's efforts to raise the cost of the 10¢ pay call. The corporation succeeded, as of this writing, in 31 states after years of negotiation with regulators.[10]

Some companies find regulations so important an aspect of their dealings that they develop special programs to teach employees how to understand, apply, and comply with them. The A.H. Robins pharmaceutical firm has actually developed a board game to teach its employees about Food and Drug Administration rules. (Business savvy note: in addition to using it for training its own employees, Robins will be marketing the game to other pharmaceutical companies at a cost of $180 a set.)[11]

Taxation of Corporations

As we've noted, the corporation must pay income taxes on the profits it earns. The corporate tax rate is 15 percent on the first $25,000 of earnings, 18 percent on the next $25,000, 30 percent on the third $25,000, 40 percent on the next $25,000, and 46 percent on the balance of the corpora-

tion's earnings. So a corporation with taxable income of $200,000 would pay taxes of $71,750 [(.15 x $25,000) + (.18 x $25,000) + (.30 x $25,000) + (.40 x $25,000) + (.46 x $100,000)]. How does this compare with the rates applicable to a proprietorship or partnership? For these, on $200,000, the tax would be $91,318. Since the maximum personal tax rates go as high as 50 percent, the corporate tax structure offers many corporations an advantage.

The corporation must file a tax return and pay its income taxes within two-and-a-half months after the close of its fiscal year. Businesses select fiscal years to coincide with the seasonality of their operations—usually when inventories are low and easy to count. Obviously, a fiscal year may not coincide with the calendar year. The major revenue and expense components of corporate business operations are the same as those for all forms of business organization and are basically treated no differently.

A **Subchapter S corporation,** or tax-option corporation, was authorized by Subchapter S of the 1958 Internal Revenue Code. Under this part of the income tax law, a corporation's shareholders (if they total 25 or less) may elect to be taxed like a partnership.

Role of the Corporation in the U.S. Economy

The word *corporation* is often thought to imply bigness. The fact is, though, that more than 75 percent of all U.S. corporations take in less than $500,000 in annual gross receipts. Naturally, the "biggies" such as IBM, Texaco, Xerox, GM, and Safeway are more visible in our day-to-day activities.

While historically corporations have accounted for only about 15 percent of all business firms in the United States, they have usually generated more than 80 percent of the total of all business receipts. In 1981 the largest 500 industrial firms listed by *Fortune* magazine generated about 29 percent of total corporate revenues. If we include the second 500 largest, these 1000 firms account for nearly 32 percent—an increase of only 3 percent being attributable to these second firms. So after the largest and most visible firms are evaluated, the relative contribution to sales revenues drops quickly.

The 25 largest industrial corporations of the Fortune 500, 1982 (ranked by sales)

RANK '81	RANK '80	COMPANY	SALES ($000)	ASSETS ($000)	ASSETS RANK	NET INCOME ($000)	NET INCOME RANK
1	1	**Exxon** (New York)	108,107,688	62,931,055	1	5,567,481	1
2	2	**Mobil** (New York)	64,488,000	34,776,000	3	2,433,000	3
3	3	**General Motors** (Detroit)	62,698,500	38,991,200	2	333,400	57
4	4	**Texaco** (Harrison, N.Y.)	57,628,000	27,489,000	5	2,310,000	5
5	5	**Standard Oil of California** (San Francisco)	44,224,000	23,680,000	7	2,380,000	4
6	6	**Ford Motor** (Dearborn, Mich.)	38,247,100	23,021,400	8	(1,060,100)	490
7	9	**Standard Oil (Indiana)** (Chicago)	29,947,000	22,916,000	9	1,922,000	7
8	8	**International Business Machines** (Armonk, N.Y.)	29,070,000	29,586,000	4	3,308,000	2
9	7	**Gulf Oil** (Pittsburgh)	28,252,000*	20,429,000	11	1,231,000	14
10	11	**Atlantic Richfield** (Los Angeles)	27,797,436	19,732,539	13	1,671,290	9
11	10	**General Electric** (Fairfield, Conn.)	27,240,000	20,942,000	10	1,652,000	10
12	15	**E.I. du Pont de Nemours** (Wilmington, Del.)[1]	22,810,000	23,829,000	6	1,401,000	12
13	12	**Shell Oil** (Houston)	21,629,000	20,118,000	12	1,701,000	8
14	13	**International Telephone & Telegraph** (New York)	17,306,189	15,052,377	16	676,804	24
15	16	**Phillips Petroleum** (Bartlesville, Okla.)	15,966,000	11,264,000	20	879,000	17
16	17	**Tenneco** (Houston)[2]	15,462,000	16,808,000	14	813,000	19
17	18	**Sun** (Radnor, Pa.)	15,012,000	11,822,000	19	1,076,000	16
18	20	**Occidental Petroleum** (Los Angeles)[3]	14,707,543	8,074,543	28	722,216	22
19	19	**U.S. Steel** (Pittsburgh)	13,940,500	13,316,100	17	1,077,200	15
20	21	**United Technologies** (Hartford)	13,667,758	7,555,103	32	457,686	37
21	23	**Standard Oil (Ohio)** (Cleveland)[4]	13,457,091	15,743,296	15	1,946,898	6
22	22	**Western Electric** (New York)[5]	13,008,000	8,338,300	25	711,300	23
23	26	**Getty Oil** (Los Angeles)	12,887,360	9,536,356	22	856,865	18
24	25	**Dow Chemical** (Midland, Mich.)	11,873,000	12,496,000	18	564,000	31
25	24	**Procter & Gamble** (Cincinnati)[6]	11,416,000	6,961,000	35	593,000‡	29

Source: *Fortune* Magazine, "The 500 Largest Industrial Companies in the U.S." © 1982 Time, Inc.

It almost goes without saying that the largest corporations are huge by any standards. In 1981 the biggest corporation (by number of employees) in the Fortune 500 was General Motors, with almost 3/4 million employees—more than twice the population of Luxembourg. Measured by sales volume, the largest corporation was Exxon, with $100 billion in sales. This is more than the Gross National Products of Greece, Peru, Egypt, Kenya, and Portugal combined.[12] However supersized corporations like GM and Exxon are exceptional cases. They are very rare.

The revenue figures of U.S. business firms are clearly dominated by corporations—more particularly, by the larger corporations. It's this domination of revenues that gives these large corporations their visibility. And perhaps because of this visibility, we expect more of large corporations by way of community service and leadership in community affairs.

Chartering the Corporation

The corporation is organized under the laws of a particular state government. The majority of the state statutes governing the formation of corporations are based on the Model Business Corporation Act of the American Bar Association. The major steps in incorporating are:

1. Selecting a name for the business.
2. Completing the articles of incorporation and filing them with the appropriate state official, usually the secretary of state.
3. Paying the required fees and taxes.
4. Holding the organizational meeting.
5. Adopting bylaws and electing directors.

A word about the first two of these steps:

Unique Name The corporate name must not

ON THE FIRING LINE

Corporations in Politics: For Better or for Worse?

In 1971 a new law allowed corporations to use general funds for the first time to set up political action committees (PACs). The main purpose of these PACs was to collect money from stockholders and donate it to the election campaigns of favored candidates.

In 1974 when Congress put a $1000 lid on the amount that any individual could contribute to a candidate's campaign, business people who wanted to make sizable contributions had to resort to PACs. Corporate PACs began to spring up in numbers. There were only 89 in 1974, but by 1980 the number had grown to 1204.

Some have been alarmed by this development. Business and industry, they worry, can now buy legislation. PAC money plays a large role in getting candidates elected, they say. The legal limits on corporate PAC contributions have offered little restraint. So many corporations now have PACs that they can form coalitions and pour thousands of dollars into crucial campaigns. The less vocal and less well-to-do minority interest groups can never hope to combat the power of corporate PAC money. Government will soon be of, by, and for the corporate world, say corporate PAC opponents.

Letting the corporate world charge into the political arena will also drive up the cost of campaigns, critics charge. As corporate PACs spend more, other PACs—of labor and other associations and organizations—try their best to match them. Fewer and fewer persons without a sizable personal fortune or a PAC endowment can hope to win office, if this continues.

There are other concerns, too. Party politics may become a thing of the past. It may give way entirely to PACs—corporate and other. Candidates, some say, may find themselves tied to a confusing variety of special interests by campaign contributions. The principles expressed in party platforms may fail to have a role in law making. Instead, laws will be passed because they favor this or that special interest—to whom legislators are already indebted and from whom they hope to obtain future campaign funds. In this chaos, corporate PACs can form a controlling power bloc, their critics warn.

Many would disagree with these negative views of corporate PACs, however. Business, they maintain, has just as much right to take part in politics as any other group. In fact, they say, with PACs business can at last be labor's political equal. For years labor has had too much power. Even before PACs, highly organized unions were the most effective interest groups in getting out the votes for labor candidates. They expected and received favorable laws in return for their efforts. Now there are countless PACs of all kinds. They are run by environmentalists and consumerists, for instance, as well as by labor and corporations.

The belief that business buys legislators through PAC contributions is naive, insist corporate PAC backers. Everyone knows that legislators are most of all concerned with popular support. They cannot afford to lose the public trust. They want the people to keep voting them into office. Lawmakers therefore won't take the risk of selling out to the corporate world.

The view that corporate PACs are harmful because they cause campaign spending to spiral is equally misguided, many think. Right now the public gets little information about candidates—at any level. More money needs to be spent to inform voters, say PAC advocates. The floods of corporate PAC money now surging onto the political sands may help candidates reach voters. They will undoubtedly bring more money in from nonbusiness PACs. With more money, candidates will have more access to the media, and voters will learn more about them.

In addition, point out corporate PAC supporters, the party system seems to have gained—not lost—through PAC efforts. The Republican party was said to be on its last legs after the Watergate scandal. Yet in 1980 corporate PAC money ($7 million) added needed strength to the Reagan campaign and to the campaigns of key Republican challengers in congressional elections.

Will corporate political action committees help or harm our political system? It will be some time before we can tell. Meanwhile, legislators, lobbyists, and judges must together assess their impact and decide their proper role.

be similar enough to another corporation's name to be misleading. Most states also require that the name end in "company," "incorporated," "corporation," "limited," or the abbreviation of these. In this way the public is served notice that the liability of the owners is limited.

Articles of Incorporation   The articles of incorporation are completed and filed on a form authorized or supplied by the state corporation officials. The Model Act adopted by most states requires that the articles of incorporation cover the following points:

1. Name and address of the corporation.
2. Objectives of the corporation.
3. Classes of stock and number of shares of each class of stock to be issued.
4. Duration of the corporation.
5. Capital required at the time of incorporation.
6. Provisions for transfering shares.
7. Provisions for regulation of internal affairs.
8. Address of registered office.
9. Names and addresses of initial board of directors.
10. Names and addresses of incorporators.

The charter of the corporation is issued on the basis of the information supplied in the articles of incorporation. When the charter is issued, the organizational meeting is held. At this meeting the bylaws are adopted, the board of directors is elected, and the initial operating resolutions are passed.

A Say in Management

The shareholder of the corporation has an indirect vote in the management of the firm. As an owner of the corporation, the shareholder has the right to attend the annual meeting and vote for the board of directors. However that's where the shareholder's voice in managing the company begins and ends — unless he or she is either elected to the board of directors or elected an officer of the corporation by the board of directors.

Voting Rights   The shareholder is generally entitled to one vote for each share of stock owned. Voting rights apply to the election of directors,

"True, I'm head of Wheatex cereal, but that's only a product of Ascot Foods, which is a division of Allvale Industries, which is a member of the Interweld family . . . ."

special elections, and in other matters affecting the corporation as provided for in the charter and bylaws. As a rule, all common-stock owners have voting rights, but sometimes a special nonvoting class of common stock is issued. This class of stock is a device for raising additional money for investment without giving up control by the other classes of common stock.

Proxies   The shareholder may assign his/her vote to someone else, who then votes the share(s) for the shareholder. A **proxy** or proxy statement is the name of the document that when signed by the shareholder conveys this voting right. A proxy statement for Hammermill Paper Company is shown in Figure 3.2.

Management typically solicits shareholders' proxies in order to keep or strengthen control in voting matters. Proxies are also used in what is known as a proxy battle. A **proxy battle** is waged at the corporation's annual meeting when a group seeks to unseat existing management. This the group does by trying to get proxies from shareholders, which it then uses to vote for its proposals or slate of directors. Proxy battles often occur when one company tries to take over another. Or a group of dissatisfied stockholders may want to change the fortunes of a company by electing a new board of directors.

Holly Sugar Corporation's experience in 1981 illustrates many of the typical features of a proxy

TALKING BUSINESS

American Telephone & Telegraph Co. Now there's a name that says something. No mistaking AT&T's line of business. But what about Prodigy Systems Inc., Beehive International, Turf Paradise Inc., and Ultimate Corp.? What do they do?

There's a school of thought that says an ambiguous name is good for business. An artfully conceived corporate label can make a company with a mundane product line sound contemporary and up-beat. Goodyear Tire & Rubber Co., an $8.2 billion giant, makes tires. Acceleration Corp. of Columbus, Ohio, sells insurance. Which firm sounds racier?

A name that's properly abstract can help a firm discard a stodgy image (National Lead Co. is now NL Industries Inc.), or ease the pain of a merger (CSX Corp. is the new parent of two railroads: Seaboard Coast Line and the Chessie System).

A name that's vaguely scientific can attract investors turned on by such hot fields as genetics and computers. Genetech Inc. blazed this trail, and Cetus Corp. and ENS Bio Logicals Inc. followed. The idea also appealed to a New York race-horse breeder, Standard-Bred Pacers & Trotters Inc., which announced a new company name but ultimately withdrew it. The proposed name: Gen-Equus Inc.

Cheering from the sidelines are the marketing consultants who typically earn $50,000 to $200,000 for giving a company a name job. Lippincott & Margulies Inc., New York, lists these new identities in its credits: Amtrak, Tenneco Inc., Uniroyal Inc., Ambex Corp., and InterNorth Inc. "To come up with a useful name today is a super-colossal effort," says Walter Margulies, chairman. "And to find a name and to be able to protect it is some task because of all the preempted names."

For the record, Beehive International has nothing to do with honey. It manufactures video-display terminals. Turf Paradise, which sounds as if it sells sod, is a Phoenix race track. Prodigy Systems and Ultimate Corp. both make computers.

Not even AT&T is immune to the name-change fever. Two shareholder groups want Ma Bell to be formally known as American Telephone & Technology Inc. Management says there's no evidence that changing a name that's nearly 100 years old would strengthen the company's image.

The proposed name was put to an AT&T shareholder vote at the company's annual meeting April 15 [1981]. It was soundly defeated.

Source: John D. Williams, "To Shed Stodgy Corporate Images, Some Firms Just Get New Names," *Wall Street Journal*, 27 April 1981, p. 25. Reprinted by permission of The Wall Street Journal, © Dow Jones & Company, Inc., 1981. All rights reserved.

battle. Michael Buchsbaum began buying Holly stock in 1980 and then led a proxy fight to win control of the board of directors the following year. The battle became very bitter, with charges of incompetence hurled at management and claims of fraud and perjury made against Buchsbaum. Next came legal action involving Buchs- baum's rights to vote certain blocks of stock. When the election was held toward the end of 1981, Buchsbaum's faction won with 62 percent of outstanding stock voting in his favor compared to 12 percent in management's. Buchsbaum's motivation seemed to be a desire to make changes that would improve the company's profits, which

HAMMERMILL PAPER COMPANY

**HAMMERMILL
PAPER COMPANY**
Erie, PA. 16533

**Proxy
Solicited on
Behalf of
the Board of
Directors**

The undersigned hereby appoints A. F. Duval, D. S. Leslie, Jr. and R. J. Kilgore, or any of them, attorneys and proxies for the undersigned with full power of substitution, to represent and to vote in their discretion cumulatively, or for a substituted nominee if the nominees named below are unable or unwilling to serve, all shares of the undersigned as fully as the undersigned could do if personally present at the Annual Meeting of Stockholders of Hammermill Paper Company on Tuesday, May 11, 1982 at 9:30 a.m. or at any adjournment thereof as follows:

1. ELECTION OF DIRECTORS.
   Nominees: L. H. Roddis, Jr. and C. M. Williams for a term of 3 years.

   ☐ VOTE FOR all nominees as listed above, except vote withheld from following nominees (if any):

   _____

   ☐ VOTE WITHHELD from all nominees.

2. In their discretion on such other business which may properly come before the meeting.

**HAMMERMILL
PAPER COMPANY**

This proxy when properly executed will be voted in the manner directed herein by the undersigned stockholder.
If no direction is given this proxy will be voted as stated in the accompanying proxy statement.
IMPORTANT: Please sign exactly as name(s) appear below. When stock is in two or more names, all should sign. When signing as attorney, executor, administrator, trustee, guardian, etc., give full title. If a corporation, please sign in full corporate name by President or other authorized officer. If a partnership, please sign in partnership name by authorized person.

**P
R
O
X
Y**

Dated _____, 1982   _____

_____

Signature(s)

**PLEASE MARK, SIGN, DATE AND RETURN THIS PROXY PROMPTLY
IN THE ENCLOSED ENVELOPE.**

FIGURE 3.2
Proxy statement for Hammermill Paper Company.

didn't compare well with others in the same industry.[13]

OTHER BUSINESS ORGANIZATIONS

Although most businesses are organized as sole proprietorships, partnerships, or corporations, there are alternatives: quasi-public organizations and cooperatives. The principal difference between these forms and the traditional ones has to do with the profit motive or the distribution of profits. In the case of quasi-public organizations, the profit motive isn't always paramount; thus prices of output may be set in some way to reflect the common good rather than to maximize profits for the owners. While the profit motive exists in cooperatives, profits realized from operations are distributed usually on the basis of the amount of business done with the cooperative. To illustrate: a medium-sized dairy in Cincinnati (known to the public as French-Bauer) was organized many years ago as a cooperative by dairy-farmer suppliers of raw milk. To outsiders the dairy appears to be a typical corporation and in fact is operated as one. However the annual profits from dairy operations are distributed to the dairymen on the basis of how much milk they sell to the dairy during the year.

Quasi-Public Organizations

In **quasi-public organizations,** some level of government — state, local, or federal — has an active role in the operation of the business. This may range from total ownership and management, such as a turnpike authority, to a very distant oversight role. An example of the latter is the Federal National Mortgage Guaranty Corporation (FNM), which is in the residential lending business. Actually, FNM's stock is owned by the public and traded on the New York Stock Exchange.

Public involvement in FNM and all other quasi-public organizations usually derives from some aspect of the business that's unappealing to private investors. This might involve very high risk, as was true of the electrification program throughout the southeast in the 1930s (TVA). Or there might be substantial capital requirements that wouldn't be forthcoming without government intervention to ensure against total failure (such as with FNM). Another possibility is that the business might be expected to operate at a loss to serve the public interest (e.g. most art museums and other cultural activities, public radio and television, and most local transit systems). The government's role in each of these instances is analogous to that of a protector of the last resort; that is, if the enterprise doesn't generate sufficient revenues on its own to cover its costs, the government is expected to be the final underwriter. Naturally, the public interest is presumed to be sufficiently served by these organizations to warrant public involvement. However some critics argue that we have gone too far in this area and that these organizations should stand on their own feet or be eliminated.

Cooperatives

In contrast to quasi-public organizations, cooperatives have no government connection and so must be self-sufficient. Many not only meet this criterion but also are reasonably profitable. For example, you're probably familiar with Sunkist fruits but may not know that they're grown and marketed by a cooperative called the California Fruit Growers Exchange.

Cooperatives are set up to provide the opportunity for businesses or individuals with like products, services, or interests to act in concert in carrying out their business mission. A buying cooperative, for example, is formed to secure the best prices possible by buying in volume or bargaining from a position of strength by virtue of larger numbers. In recent years buying cooperatives have been formed by individuals who might wish to buy organic foods, whole certified milk, and other so-called "health foods." (You may have coops of this type on your campus.) With buying cooperatives, any profits generated during the year are usually distributed among the cooperators (the members of the cooperative) on the basis of how much they purchased during the year.

SUMMARY

The three major categories of business organization are the sole proprietorship, the partnership, and the corporation. The sole proprietorship is owned, financed, and operated by a single person. Most US firms are sole proprietorships; yet they account for only about 10 percent of total business receipts.

Advantages of the sole proprietorship include ease and low cost of formation, the owner's right to all profits, the owner's right to directly control the business, relative freedom from government regulation, absence of special taxation, and ease of dissolution. Disadvantages include the owner's unlimited liability for debts, difficulty in raising capital, limited management expertise, unstable business life, and difficulty in attracting qualified employees. Since the proprietorship is not a taxable entity, profits are reported on the owner's individual tax return.

A partnership—the least-used organizational form—is an "association of two or more persons to carry on as co-owners a business for profit." Though not required, written articles of partnership are usually developed. The partnership agreement generally specifies the contribution of each partner to the business, the partners' roles, and other major points of agreement. The three types of partnership are the general partnership, the limited partnership, and the joint venture.

Advantages of partnerships include ease of formation, availability of more capital, increased diversity of viewpoint, flexibility, and relative freedom from government control. Disadvantages include partners' unlimited liability for debts, responsibility of all partners for the acts of each, limited life of the business, necessity of sharing profits, and difficulty of disposing of a partnership interest. The partnership is a quasi-taxable entity; it must file a tax return to provide information on profits and how they were divided, but profits are reported on each partner's individual tax return.

A corporation is an entity with an existence separate from that of its owners. Components of the corporation's organizational structure are its incorporators, stockholders, directors, and managers.

Advantages of the corporation include its owners' limited liability for debts, transferability of ownership, stability of existence, and ease of obtaining additional capital. Disadvantages include double taxation of corporate profits, cost and difficulty of formation, and extensive government regulation. Corporations must pay taxes on their profits. The maximum tax rate for a corporation is 46 percent, compared with 50 percent for an individual.

Corporations comprise about 15 percent of US businesses but earn over 80 percent of business receipts. While 75 percent of corporations are relatively small, US business is dominated by the larger corporations.

The corporation is organized under the laws of a particular state. The major steps in incorporation are: to select a unique name for the business, to complete and file articles of incorporation with the appropriate state official, to pay the required fees and taxes, to hold the organizational meeting, and to adopt bylaws and elect directors. Shareholders are entitled to attend the annual meeting and vote for the board of directors as well as to vote in special elections and the like. This right to vote may be assigned to someone else—a proxy. A proxy battle occurs when a group tries to use proxies solicited from shareholders in order to force adoption of its proposals or its own slate of directors.

In addition to sole proprietorships, partnerships, and corporations, some businesses are organized differently; these are called quasi-public organizations or cooperatives. They differ from the traditional forms either in not being operated only for profit (quasi-public organizations) or in the way profits are distributed to owners (cooperatives).

KEY TERMS

cooperative
corporation
general partnership
joint venture
limited liability
limited partnership
partnership
partnership
  agreement
proxy
proxy battle
quasi-public
  organization
sole proprietorship
Subchapter S
  corporation

REVIEW QUESTIONS

1. What are the major forms of business organization?
2. Why are there so many sole proprietorships in the United States?
3. What form of business might be best for the farmer?
4. What are some inportant advantages of a sole proprietorship? State some disadvantages.
5. What causes most problems in partnerships?
6. What are two advantages of a corporate form? Are there disadvantages?
7. Which form of business may have a tax advantage? How might it also have a tax disadvantage?
8. Which form of business offers the most freedom to the owner?
9. How do quasi-public organizations and cooperatives differ from conventional organizational forms?

DISCUSSION QUESTIONS

1. What factors determine the form of business to be used by its organizers?
2. Discuss the comparison of a partnership with marriage and divorce.
3. Of the three major forms of business, which offers managers (who are not owners) the most control?
4. Which form of business has the best chance of raising capital funds to start the business?
5. Compare the owner's liability in the various forms of business.
6. In starting a new enterprise, which form of business will encounter the most "red tape"?
7. How are profits divided in the different forms of business? Be sure to include cooperatives in your answer.
8. Quasi-public organizations should be made either all public—and then supported by tax revenues—or all private—and then treated like any other corporation. Do you agree?

CASE: PIZZA—PIZZA— EVERYWHERE!

The Great Gatsby story has a midwestern counterpart in a young man who's captured a big share of the pizza market, with his star (and "dough") rising in Omaha, Nebraska and now shining brightly across America.

"Wild Willy" Theisen decided about nine years ago to follow his hunch and expand his partnership with a friend into a bigger operation. Willy had a bar, his friend a pizza parlor called "Godfather's." His partner was not as ambitious, so Willy bought him out and forged ahead, making a corporation of the business.

Godfather's business thrived, riding the crest of the popular movie of the same name, and Willy decided to sell franchises. Then his business really took off. Godfather's now boasts of near 500 franchises in 42 states, including Alaska.

Godfather's was started with a few thousand dollars from friends and relatives. It's already passed the $100 million annual sales figure, perhaps to the chagrin of bankers who were just a little reluctant to lend Willy any money when he really needed it.

It's understandable that Godfather's was a closely held corporation since after Willy shed the partnership; but still moving on, Willy decided to "go public" and put shares in Godfather's on the market.

1. What different forms of business did Willy Theisen go through to finance and operate his thriving pizza business?
2. Why would an entrepreneur with the controlling interest in a successful corporation want to offer his stock for sale to the public?
3. What would be your forecast for this business in light of the current state of the economy?

CASE: THE DRIPPING FAUCET

Joe Walters had a great idea for a new business. He had been a plumber for many years, and he knew the reputation that some plumbers have of overcharging customers, forgetting their tools, adding the trip back to the store on the cost of the job, and "featherbedding" the job—much to the chagrin of the vulnerable customer.

Joe wanted to do his part to change the "image" of the plumber and provide a worthwhile service to the many customers who need help with their plumbing sooner or later. With the high cost of living and the recession, many people were doing their own plumbing work—yet most of them still needed help.

Joe saw that these people could be given some "professional" help on a consultative basis and still do most of the small tasks themselves. They could get needed assistance by stopping at his shop and discussing the problem. For a fee, Joe could then tell them how the job ought to be done and with what tools, even supplying them with parts, equipment, or tools if needed—for an added fee.

Joe would call his shop "The Faucet Shop," which would be fitting, as many a plumbing job starts with a dripping faucet. His brother-in-law could help out in the business the way he had done for many years while Joe operated as a plumber, making "house calls" at all hours of the day and night. Joe also had a buddy, Harry Burke, who had been a plumber for many years but who retired early on the fat fees he had extracted from unsuspecting customers. Now he'd have an opportunity to give back some of this money in providing the kind of service Joe was proposing for the new business. Harry didn't really want anything that looked like work. He was enjoying life too much. But this venture sounded different—and easy.

So Joe had the business idea, the talent—plus help—and the money to start up this new business and make a good living for himself, his brother-in-law, and his buddy.

1. Does Joe have "what it takes" to start a business?

2. What would be the best form for this new business?

3. How can Joe protect himself against misunderstandings or conflicts of opinion, work scheduling problems, and profit-sharing splits, to satisfy his two sidekicks?

CHAPTER 4

SMALL BUSINESS

After studying this chapter you should be able to:

1 Understand what's meant by small business and identify its main advantages and disadvantages.
2 Recognize the typical characteristics of entrepreneurs and small business managers.
3 Anticipate some of the problems encountered in starting a small business.
4 Describe many of the qualities it takes to be a small-business manager and to make a profit in a business enterprise.
5 Understand the importance of management, marketing, finance, and accounting considerations in launching a new business, including a detailed business plan.
6 Identify what's important in managing the small business after it has had a successful start.
7 Recognize the advantages and disadvantages of franchising.
8 Understand the role that the Small Business Administration (SBA) plays in assisting small and minority-owned businesses.

69

The Sanskrit word *Maya* means "illusion," and for Charles Levitt, founder of Maya Video Products, Inc., it sometimes seemed that the wisdom of going into business for himself—the joy and the profit of it—was just that: an illusion. There seemed to be no joy. And there certainly wasn't any profit. Levitt was living almost a hand-to-mouth existence, bills seemed to defy payment, and capital there was none. With all of his skills in one basket—electronics technology—the business world was to Charles Levitt very much like a forest of factors—organization, marketing, finance, legal and tax considerations—through which he just didn't see his way.

It had all been easier in the days when Levitt was running a home-entertainment operation—sales, installation, and service of TVs, stereos, air conditioners. But his quick sense told him there was a huge market potential in territory left amazingly untouched: everywhere personal computers were burgeoning into use in businesses small, medium, and large. Yet no matter how big the organization, it was necessary for workers, analysts, staff, conference members and the like to huddle over the small computer screen and crane their necks to catch a glimpse of the read-out. Here, then, was the perfect market for a projector unit that could be easily hooked up to the computer and flash the read-out in crisp projection on a big screen, with ease of visibility for even a conference-roomful of people.

So the idea was right, and initial business contacts and responses confirmed it—and yet, working only with a single prototype and with almost no credit from the manufacturer (who meanwhile didn't know how much to produce and how far to go with him), Levitt was having a hard time. To make matters worse, he had to do everything himself: get orders (which he had trouble financing; the manufacturer would give him only a minimum credit line), try to raise financing and get credit extended, service the units he sold—and be there to answer the phone. The result was stagnation, due to the great difficulty in meeting bills and turning over sales. Little wonder that for Levitt, going into business was equatable with illusion.

At this point he was introduced to John A. Miller, a former vice-president, sales, for Barricini Candies and a crackerjack salesman all his long business life. It was a marriage which, if not exactly made in heaven, was almost made in a church, since the two met through a church affiliation. In fact, Levitt attributes his breakthrough above all to a religious faith. Overnight, everything changed for the better. Miller had the manner, and knew how best to knock on the corporate door—and batter it down when necessary. Sales began to climb; the manufacturer became impressed and eased the credit. Banks grew friendlier. And Levitt was more comfortably back at the administrative end, with a newly hired assistant, Jim Hardcastle, to help in the demonstration and service of units.

Maya Video was selling big to IBM, Sperry-Univac, Citicorp, Bankers Trust, Union Carbide, and Burroughs—to name a few—and was projecting yearly sales over $1 million before its fourth birthday. Levitt was meanwhile searching for employees, taking on a new line—computer display monitors—planning audio/visual total environments, and mapping a strategy of expansion from Maya's home base in New York City.

Levitt may not be about to change the name of the firm, but the name of the game has certainly changed for him: it's "success," not "illusion."

Small-business ownership is part of the Great American Dream. Each year about 250,000 new business are launched. Their owners start with high expectations, hopes, and ambitions; and being in business gives them the feeling of independence and freedom of choice that so many individuals dream of. Small businesses like Maya Video Products have played, and will continue to play, an important role in our economy. They provide a variety of goods and services that give consumers wider choices in the marketplace because small businesses function and survive in areas where large businesses could not afford to operate. For example, a "mom and pop" general store might do quite well in McDaniel, Maryland (pop. 150), but a Safeway supermarket would not have enough business to justify keeping its doors open. Small businesses fill voids in the modern mass-distribution system that's used in the United States.

WHAT IS A SMALL BUSINESS?

Small, like beauty, is in the eye of the beholder. A business that's small by one standard would be quite large by another. American Motors is a relatively small company in comparison to GM, Ford, and Chrysler. It's also small when compared with many of the well-known energy giants such as Exxon or Shell. On the other hand, if American Motors, with sales of $2.6 billion, is compared with Dr Pepper, which has sales of $333.2 million, it's a very large firm. In the 1981 *Fortune* listing of the 1000 largest industrial companies, American Motors was ranked 155 and Dr Pepper 598. Yet by most standards both of these companies would be considered large. What, then, is "small business"?

The Small Business Administration (SBA) defines a small business as "one which is independently owned and operated, not dominant in its field of operation, and meets certain standards of size in terms of employees or annual receipts." The key elements of the definition are: (1) independence, which refers to a lack of outside control; (2) enterprise, which means the owners accept risks inherent in the business; and (3) dominance, which means that the firm is not dominant in its field and has little if any influence on the activities of the industry as a whole.

By this definition then, about 97 percent of all nonfarm businesses are small. Some facts about these small businesses are given in Table 4.1.

TABLE 4–1
Facts About Small Business

1. There were 11.4 million nonfarm businesses producing $4,279.6 billion in receipts during 1977.
2. Regarding nonfarm businesses, 96.7 percent are considered "small" by the Small Business Administration's size standards.
3. The average number of new businesses started each year has been approximately 250,000.
4. New business incorporations increased by 13.7 percent in 1977 and 9.8 percent in 1979.
5. Of all the businesses in the U.S., 55 percent fail (go bankrupt or are discontinued) within their first five years of operation.
6. Of all of the business failures, 95 percent are a direct result of poor management.
7. Small business accounts for 43 percent of the Gross National Product and 48 percent of the Gross Business Product.
8. Small business provides livelihood, directly or indirectly, for over 100 million Americans.
9. One third of all small businesses are in the service industries and account for six of every ten dollars of small business receipts.
10. Small businesses account for nearly one fourth of the retail trade industry and account for 70 percent of sales made by wholesalers and retailers.

SOURCE: U.S. Small Business Administration, *Facts About Small Business and the U.S. Small Business Administration*; U.S. Department of Commerce, *Statistical Abstract of the United States*, 1980 edition.

Types of Small Businesses

Most statistical data classify small-business activity into four major categories—service, retail or wholesale, construction, and manufacturing. **Service businesses** are engaged in providing essential or special services to their customers. These services generally are activities that customers need but can't perform for themselves because they lack time, skill, or both. Service businesses provide such services as drycleaning, automotive repair, hairstyling, and legal aid.

Retail and wholesale businesses provide merchandising activities. These firms assist in the distribution of goods by moving them to points where they're needed. Examples of retailers include grocery stores, bookshops, bakeries, and department stores. Wholesalers are exemplified by businesses which sell primarily to other businesses.

Construction businesses build houses, office buildings, manufacturing plants, highways, and many other facilities needed by society for shelter, production, and convenience. A new type of construction firm that's recently emerged is the "rehab contractor." This contractor specializes in redesign and restoration of older buildings for both historical and economic reasons.

Manufacturing businesses are actively engaged in the conversion of raw materials and labor into products needed by society. The large investment required and volume of production needed for efficient operation cause manufacturing to be less attractive to small firms than are other types of small businesses. However the high profit potential often lures some entrepreneurs into this area.

Advantages of Small Business

Small business has several operating advantages over its larger counterparts. One is that small firms are able to react more quickly to changes in operations. They're usually owner-operated, and this feature allows them to try new products, new methods, and new ideas without requiring lengthy and elaborate approval before changes can be made. (Endless hours spent "in committee" are eliminated.) Small-business flexibility of operations has been instrumental in the flow of new products and inventions. Patent statistics indicate that nearly half of all new patents are issued to individuals or to small and medium-sized firms.

A second advantage of small business is its "personal touch" in handling customers. Fine restaurants, high-style boutiques, and custom jewelry stores are examples where the personal touch is needed—and most of these are small firms.

Still a third advantage is that when the market for goods and services is limited, a small business may be able to survive on the receipts generated by the limited market. Because of the large amount of overhead usually incurred by the operation of large-scale businesses some markets would go unserved were is not for small business. By its very nature, small business is uniquely fitted to fill this void and offer a better selection of products and services than would otherwise be available.

Also, it's often the vision of small-business pioneers that turns what starts out as a limited market into a major industry. A perfect example is Apple Computer. Its founders, Steve Jobs and Steve Wozniak, began developing their small personal computer in 1976 because computer-industry leaders felt that the market was too small. By 1982 Apple was selling 300,000 of its computers a year, and large firms such as IBM and Xerox had changed their minds and were aggressively competing for market shares in this new industry, estimated to grow at a 50 percent annual rate through most of the 1980s.

Disadvantages of Small Business

The smaller firm faces some definite disadvantages in the competitive arena. The most significant are limited managerial skill, inadequate capital-raising capacity, and excessive government regulation. The entrepreneur is usually adept at starting firms, but skills to manage them may be lacking. Even with partners or other stockholders, the pool of managerial skill is still limited. Also, small business is at a disadvantage in trying to hire qualified employees from the labor market. While it may be able to offer a salary and fringe benefit package that's attractive, it often lacks a suitable growth incentive or opportunity for advancement.

Since small businesses must compete with established firms with proven track records, obtaining adequate financing is often difficult. The small firm usually has limited equity capital invested in the business, yet a good equity base is a prerequisite for successfully borrowing money for expansion and operation. If the owner wants to maintain control of the company, the opportunity for raising additional equity is further limited, since selling additional shares means new owners are brought into the business.

A final disadvantage is that small business must cope with many government regulations. Much concern was voiced by the 1980 White House Conference on Small Business about the level of government regulation and the burden of compliance costs on small business. Linked to the elements of regulation and taxes is the problem of the paperwork required to report activities to the various regulatory agencies. The small firm can't afford a professional staff to deal with the paperwork. Since the owner is the only one who knows

Examples of basic types of small businesses: drycleaner (service); bookstore (retail); home building in California (construction); mocassin production by Oglala Indians in South Dakota (manufacturing).

what's needed, the burden of reporting falls on his or her shoulders. This added responsibility causes many owners to feel overworked or else to ignore the paperwork requirements. Beginning in 1981, there developed an increased awareness of these kinds of problems confronting the small business. One of the results of this was passage of the Equal Access to Justice Law, which enables a small business to recoup some of its legal expenses in challenging a government action. These expenses would include attorney fees, fees paid to expert witnesses, and any other reasonable cost incurred in the case.[1]

STARTING A SMALL BUSINESS

In starting a small business many factors must be considered, for it's easy to start, but can just

TALKING BUSINESS

Running a small business may lack some of the prestige associated with the stewardship of a big corporation, but the small business folks think they have more fun.

In a survey conducted by The Roper Organization, Inc., for Walter E. Heller International Corporation's Small Business Institute, 91 percent of small business chief executive officers polled said they are happier where they are than they would be if they held similar positions in larger companies. The survey covered a national sample of 1,200 CEO's from firms with 40 to 500 employees.

Although 73 percent of the executives think they work harder than their counterparts in large corporations, they also say they have greater job security (73 percent) and make more money (72 percent). An even larger majority, 88 percent, say they have more satisfactory day-to-day associations with co-workers and employees. About 85 percent think they also have a better chance to make a significant impact in their line of work.

Source: "Do Small-Firm CEO's Have More Fun?" p. 22, reprinted by permission from *Nation's Business*, March 1981, Copyright 1981 by Nation's Business, Chamber of Commerce of the United States.

about as easily fail. In fact, 55 percent of new businesses fail within the first five years of operation. The reasons for failure are many, but the most common are:

1. lack of business experience,
2. lack of financing,
3. lack of sufficient sales,
4. poor location,
5. lack of business records,
6. improper accounts receivable management,
7. insufficient stock turnover,
8. poor inventory control, and
9. improper markups.

Many of these causes of failure might have been avoided if proper steps had been taken when forming the business.

Assessing the Owners

The first step in starting a small business is to evaluate the business capability of the owner. Three things are required of any business owner. First is **experience**. The owner must have a working knowledge of the kinds of decisions that are needed in operating the business. The owner must also understand likely potential problems and what to do about them. The second requirement is **commitment**. The owner must be willing to stay with the business long enough for it to become successful. Finally, a business requires **sacrifice**. A small-business owner must be willing to "pay the price" for the business to be successful. Devoting enough time, money, and effort to make the business more than just survive—or just to survive—can weigh heavily on the person who isn't prepared for the rigors of business ownership.

The potential owner should spend a substantial amount of time finding out whether he or she can stand the inconveniences that can come with owning one's own business. The entrepreneur should ask such questions as:

- Am I the kind of person who can start and operate a successful business?
- Why do I *really* want my own business?
- Do I have the needed experience?
- Am I a good manager?
- Do I have the needed training?

The questionnaire shown in Table 4.2 is an example of some of the self-assessment forms that a potential business owner should use.

The Business Plan

Every business venture begins as someone's idea. The purpose of the business plan is to develop the business idea in writing. The business plan should be completed in sufficient detail so that it can serve as a blueprint for building the business. What's the value of the business plan? It gives the entrepreneur a chance fully to analyze and to think through the concept of the business. A venture that sounds good at the idea stage may prove to be inadvisable upon closer analysis.

The business plan is often used as the early operating plan for a new business. The owner will be so busy making sure the business operates smoothly that little time will be available for detailed planning. Some time spent in developing a good business plan before starting operations will aid in making decisions later on. A final use of the business plan is to inform potential investors about the company, its potential for growth, and the experience its management has. When the owner needs additional capital to start the business, the business plan is the primary method for allowing potential financial backers to assess the proposed business. For example, *Venture* magazine, which puts out a "Venture Capital Directory" (designed to bring together entrepreneurs and venture capitalists) indicates that venture capitalists have one preliminary, essential requirement of the entrepreneur: a detailed business plan.[2] The key sections normally included in the business plan are described in Table 4.3.

Organizational Form

The business must have an organization form, and the owner must decide whether to use a proprietorship, partnership, or corporation. The advantages and disadvantages of each form have already been considered in Chapter 3. The organizational form does not have to be permanent over the life of the business. For instance, an owner with sufficient capital and wishing to maintain complete ownership control may form a

TABLE 4–2

Self-Assessment Worksheet

ARE YOU A SELF-STARTER?

_____ I do things on my own. Nobody has to tell me to get going.

_____ If someone gets me started, I keep going all right.

_____ Easy does it. I don't put myself out until I have to.

HOW DO YOU FEEL ABOUT OTHER PEOPLE?

_____ I like people. I can get along with just about anybody.

_____ I have plenty of friends—I don't need anyone else.

_____ Most people irritate me.

CAN YOU LEAD OTHERS?

_____ I can get most people to go along when I start something.

_____ I can give the orders if someone tells me what we should do.

_____ I let someone else get things moving. Then I go along if I feel like it.

CAN YOU TAKE RESPONSIBILITY?

_____ I like to take charge of things and see them through.

_____ I'll take over if I have to, but I'd rather let someone else be responsible.

_____ There's always some eager beaver around wanting to show how smart he is. I say let him.

HOW GOOD AN ORGANIZER ARE YOU?

_____ I like to have a plan before I start. I'm usually the one to get things lined up when the group wants to do something.

_____ I do all right unless things get too confused. Then I quit.

_____ You get all set and then something comes along and presents too many problems. So I just take things as they come. **(continued)**

TABLE 4–2

Self-Assessment Worksheet (continued)

HOW GOOD A WORKER ARE YOU?

_____ I can keep going as long as I need to. I don't mind working hard for something I want.

_____ I'll work hard for a while, but when I've had enough, that's it.

_____ I can't see that hard work gets you anywhere.

CAN YOU MAKE DECISIONS?

_____ I can make up my mind in a hurry if I have to. It usually turns out OK, too.

_____ I can if I have plenty of time. If I have to make up my mind fast, I think later I should have decided the other way.

_____ I don't like to be the one who has to decide things.

CAN PEOPLE TRUST WHAT YOU SAY?

_____ You bet they can. I don't say things I don't mean.

_____ I try to be on the level most of the time, but sometimes I just say what's easiest.

_____ Why bother if the other fellow doesn't know the difference?

CAN YOU STICK WITH IT?

_____ If I make up my mind to do something, I don't let anything stop me.

_____ I usually finish what I start—if it goes well.

_____ If it doesn't go right away, I quit. Why beat your brains out?

HOW GOOD IS YOUR HEALTH?

_____ I *never* run down!

_____ I have enough energy for most things I want to do.

_____ I run out of energy sooner than most of my friends seem to.

NOTE: If most checks are beside the first answer, those individuals probably have what it takes to run a business. If not, they are likely to have more trouble than they can handle. If many checks are beside the third answer, not even a good partner will likely overcome the respondent's deficiencies.

SOURCE: U.S. Small Business Administration, *Checklist for Going Into Business*, Small Marketers Aid no. 71 (1977).

proprietorship. After operating for some time, the owner could decide that both the tax burden and personal risk would be reduced by incorporating. So a business can use different forms of organization as its needs change.

Management Considerations

The individual who starts a business has selected him- or herself to manage the operations of the enterprise. As manager, the owner must decide what resources are needed by the firm and how to use them in the most efficient manner.

Staffing Building a qualified, capable, and well-trained staff is a challenge for any business, but small-business owners face an even greater challenge because of the limited financial incentives and promotion opportunities they usually can offer. The need for hiring employees exists for several reasons. First, employees can release the owner from routine duties so that more time can be spent on planning and controlling the operations. Second, as the business expands, staff must also expand in order to maintain the volume and quality of customer service. Finally, employees must be relied on to operate the business when the owner is absent. A long-run aspect of this last reason is the development of management succession so that if the owner decides to retire or begin another venture, the company can continue to operate.

Companies have responded to the staffing problem in various ways. Some, like Lincoln Electric Company (a manufacturer of arc-welding equipment), employ a very generous profit-shar-

TABLE 4-3
Key Sections of a Business Plan

Description of the Products or Services   The description of the products or services should be complete and in simple terms so that the reader of the business plan can easily understand what the company plans to do.

Market Description   The analysis of the market should describe the state of the art in the marketplace, why a new company is needed, and what needs the new products or services offered by the company will satisfy.

Marketing Plans   This section of the business plan will describe the approach that the company will take to capture its market share. Plans regarding sales force, advertising, and promotional literature should be disclosed in this section.

Operating Plans   The description of how the products or services will be produced and how the company will be organized are described under operating plans. Sales forecasts, financial projections, and planned operating systems are examples of the contents of this section.

Owners' Qualifications   Details of the owners' objectives and qualifications for operating the new business are discussed in this section. Résumés of the owners which give details of experience and unique expertise for managing the company are included.

ing plan. All of Lincoln Electric's employees share in the profits of the company after allowances have been made for reasonable dividends and debt servicing. Others, such as Harris Hub Co. (a manufacturer of bed frames and other metal products) rely more on job security. Allan Harris, president of Harris Hub, says, "When you hire somebody, don't consider him an employee; consider him part of the family. You don't fire him or lay him off."[3]

Still another approach attempts to pass on ownership (all or a portion) of the business to key employees when the owner dies. This has the added advantage of establishing a concrete value of the business for estate tax purposes. (Very often in the absence of clear value the estate tax appraiser may attach a value—and a related tax—far higher than what the owners' heirs can afford, resulting in a forced sale of the business simply to pay estate taxes.)

The transfer of ownership to employees can take several forms. One involves giving shares of nonvoting stock (or rights to buy common stock) based on service. At the owner's death, this stock converts into voting common stock at some predetermined conversion ratio. In addition, employees may be required to put up cash at this time. Needless to say, the transfer mechanism is clearly less important than the underlying issue of whether the approach attracts and retains a solid staff.

Production   Establishing a production process involves decisions about how the company's products will be produced. Because of their size, small businesses are very often less efficient than their larger counterparts. The added cost of this inefficiency must be considered as the owner makes decisions about production. Since large amounts of money needed to purchase sophisticated, automated production equipment are generally not available to the small firm, the owner necessarily employs more labor in the production processes. Even though labor is the dominant input, decisions about the balance between labor and machinery still must be made by the owner.

Also, all phases of production are as important to the small firm as they are to the large one. This includes the purchase of raw materials, the process of converting raw materials to finished products, and the storage of finished products in inventory until they are sold. The local countertop manufacturer is just as concerned about turning formica into a finished counter as General Motors is in turning raw materials into Cadillacs.

Marketing Considerations

If a small business expects to be successful, it must get its products to the right place, at the right price, at the time when the customer's ready to buy. This process is the essence of the marketing problem that small businesses face. According to the Dun and Bradstreet *Business Failure Record,* 50 percent of failures come from inadequate sales, 25 percent from competitive weaknesses, and 3 percent from poor location. These facts indicate the necessity for sound marketing decisions.

Location   The purpose of a good location is to attract customers and generate sales. Choosing

TALKING BUSINESS

"Everyone gets into the business for the romance of it," says David Lett, owner and operator of a small winery, Eyrie Vineyards, in Dundee, Oregon. "I'm not in the wine business to make money. I'm in it to make wine." Lett's pride and joy is his pinot noir, made from the variety of grapes used for the great red wines of Burgundy. Not long ago, a 1975 Eyrie pinot noir was judged better than some of France's best vintages. But although Lett has made some fine wines, he has found it difficult indeed to make money.

Establishing a new vineyard requires a large investment in both money and labor, and nothing at all comes out until the fourth year. Even then, a small vineyard like Eyrie doesn't produce a large grape harvest, and Lett uses time-consuming old-world winemaking techniques; so he can't produce much wine in a year. Eyrie was started in 1965, and in 1981 Lett was just breaking even with $100,000 in sales.

Lett hopes to improve his cash flow by planting a variety of grapes from which he can produce a white wine that's ready to sell about six months after harvest, compared with two years for pinot noir. The year the newly planted vines will be ready to be harvested, 1986, Lett expects to produce about 5,400 gallons of the white wine—less than the Gallo winery bottles in an hour.

Source: Adapted from Sanford L. Jacobs, "Business Realities Can Ruin Romance of a Small Vineyard," *Wall Street Journal*, 21 September 1981, p. 27. Adapted by permission of The Wall Street Journal, ©Dow Jones & Company, Inc., 1981. All rights reserved.

the right location for a new business depends on the nature of the business itself. For example, a shop selling baby clothes and furniture would choose a location in a town where many young couples were living. A bait shop, on the other hand, would locate close to where its products were used without considering the age, income, or family distribution of residents in the area. The major requirement for the bait shop would be the presence of a nearby river, pond, or lake with good fishing.

A location scheme that's often followed is to consider the types of products the business is selling. For convenience goods, the location would need to be visible and easily accessible; and it would have to offer the customer a wide range of choices and substitutes. If the business sells shopping goods where customers compare prices, a location close to the competitor's should be chosen. The location is not as important to the customer as price, so comparing prices should be made simple and easy. Stores selling specialty goods have the least to consider about their location. Customers wishing to buy specialty goods will seek out the store as long as the location is not in a dangerous or blighted area.

Other factors that must be considered in locating a business are zoning, growth of the area, competition, real estate costs, taxes, traffic flow, and utilities' cost and availability. The owner can look to the local Chamber of Commerce and city and county offices for help in answering questions about these factors. The local SBA office and its management assistance programs also offer help with location studies.

Sales Channels   Sales channels decisions require that the owner plan a sales effort to move products from the company to its customers. The small manufacturing company can choose to market its goods directly to the consumer, or it can use the traditional middlemen channel, which includes the wholesaler and the retailer. In choosing the style of marketing to use, the company must consider the kinds of goods being sold, level of competition, promotion strategy, and the

Left, When selling goods where customers compare prices, retail businesses tend to cluster, as shown here in the lamp district in Manhattan. *Right,* Fotomats are located for convenience.

need for special expertise on the part of the sales staff.

Financial Considerations

Entrepreneurs generally do not have sufficient funds to establish a small business. Many of them find that they must obtain funds in addition to their own investment. Two types of financing are available: debt and equity. Debt (i.e. borrowed money) is the first source. Borrowed funds must be repaid with interest over a specified period of time. Equity funds are ownership funds that are raised through the sale of interests in the business.

Establishing Credit In order to borrow funds from lenders the business owner must show evidence of ability to repay the money along with interest. New businesses have problems in borrowing funds; generally, lenders make loans on the basis of the entrepreneur's credit reputation. The amount of borrowed funds available to a new business is limited. For example, banks generally limit loans to new firms; the amount is usually equal to about 25–35 percent of the funds required. In seeking to borrow, the new business faces stiff competition from established firms with favorable earnings histories. Lenders look for borrowers with established credit, experience in operations, and demonstrated repayment ability. Owners of new small businesses do not generally

possess these characteristics; so lenders must rely on the owner's abilities, the business plan, and a continuous business relationship with the borrower as guides for making loans to new small businesses.

Raising Capital Investors invest in the managerial ability of the owners of the firm. Lenders and equity investors alike will put their money only in those firms that they believe have strong potential for increased growth. The entrepreneur will typically need equity or ownership funds equal to about 65–75 percent of the total funds required to start the business. If the owner doesn't have the required equity, he or she must be prepared to give up some control and attract funds from investors in exchange for ownership interests. In addition to friends and relatives, the owner may look to a venture capitalist for financing. A **venture capitalist** is a professional investor who makes investments in risky small firms that are expected to achieve good fast growth and above-average returns.

The small-business owner may seek funds from a **Small Business Investment Company (SBIC).** SBICs are licensed by the Small Business Administration (discussed later in this chapter) and provide capital to small enterprises. The financing arrangement is negotiated between the SBIC and the business owner and may be equity investment, fully secured debt financing, or a combination of debt and equity financing. When the SBIC provides equity financing—that is, investment in the small business—it's prohibited from obtaining a controlling interest in the small business. The controlling ownership must be left in the hands of the owner. Some SBICs do more than finance their clients; they provide management assistance in the form of counseling on management and operational problems.

Accounting Considerations

A business owner must know where the business is going. Accounting records provide the information from which the owner monitors the progress of the business.

Setting up the Books   In setting up accounting records for a company, the books should be developed to provide the information needed by managers of the company. The accounting system should reflect the particular characteristics of the company for which they're designed. So a housing contractor's books would be quite different from a restaurant's. Effective recordkeeping should provide information about cash flow, sales, costs, inventory levels, and credits and collections. Good records provide a basis for:

1. verifying needs for credit and the sources of repayment;
2. comparison of results from period to period;
3. preparation of tax and regulatory reports;
4. verifying insurance claims in the event of a loss;
5. defining the value of the firm's equity, all or a portion of which may be sold to new investors or exchanged in a merger transaction; and
6. preparation of financial statements and special management reports.

If the owner is unsure what records are needed for the business and how to prepare them, a competent accountant should be hired to perform this function.

Tax Records   The business owner should be sure that the record system captures and maintains the data needed to properly and accurately report the company's tax liability. There are very few specific records that are required by law to be maintained for tax purposes. The IRS requires that records of payments to employees be maintained showing earnings, income tax withheld, and social security taxes withheld. Tax records should be designed and maintained so that tax returns can be easily prepared, and they should be retained at least three years in the event of an IRS audit.

MANAGING THE SMALL BUSINESS

Two stages of managerial expertise are required to bring the company through its life cycle from inception to maturity. In the first stage the firm is small and the owner maintains control over all aspects of its operation. The owner, who is also the manager, must run the company alone. But as the company grows, the role of the owner must change. This second stage requires the owner to place greater emphasis on the management function, since the company has grown to where one person can't do all the things needed to make the company function smoothly. Many of the decisions and day-to-day operations must be placed in the hands of others, freeing the owner to plan and direct (which are the important management tasks) the overall operation of the company.

Organization

Even though the organization of a small business may be very simple, it's still necessary to identify the areas of responsibility of the owner(s), managers, and each employee. The organization should be flexible yet at the same time provide for the specific assignment of duties. The **organization structure** is used to group together similar activities. There are several ways to do this, but the one most often used by small firms is the **functional organization**—the formal framework through which the practice of management is carried out. In this structure, work is grouped by business activity. Figure 4.1 depicts a functional organization along with a company profile for Barnes Custom Interiors, a small business in the Midwest.

This chart shows two broad functional areas: (1) production and installations—M. Barnes directs these activities; and (2) marketing and fi-

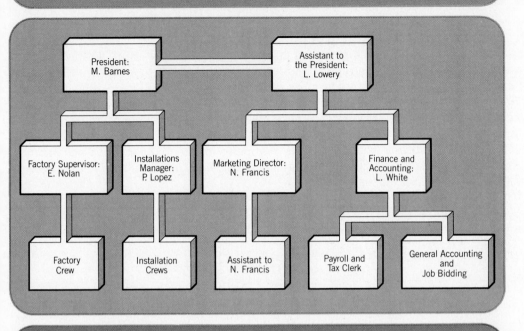

FUNCTIONAL ORGANIZATION FOR A SMALL BUSINESS: BARNES CUSTOM INTERIORS

President: M. Barnes

Assistant to the President: L. Lowery

Factory Supervisor: E. Nolan

Installations Manager: P. Lopez

Marketing Director: N. Francis

Finance and Accounting: L. White

Factory Crew

Installation Crews

Assistant to N. Francis

Payroll and Tax Clerk

General Accounting and Job Bidding

COMPANY PROFILE: *Barnes Custom Interiors*

Nature of business:	Designs and installs custom-made room interiors (specializing in kitchens). Also builds cabinets and other components.
Number of employees:	26
Number of supervisors:	6
Sales (1983):	$1,630,000
Profits after taxes (1983):	$66,400

FIGURE 4.1

nance—L. Lowery is in charge here. This company grew from a one-man operation, with sales of $26,000 in its first full year, to its present size. The organization chart suggests (and additional information would confirm) that M. Barnes is probably a production-oriented person who feels more comfortable in the factory than in the office. It appears that as his business grew and became more involved with marketing and financial problems, he hired an assistant with expertise in these areas. If we take the organization chart at face value, Lowery has as much authority as Barnes in managing the firm.

Informal Organization

The actual setting of authority and flow of decisions in a firm does not always correspond to what the owner thinks they are or to the way they're shown on the organization chart. While problems of this type are more typical of large organizations, they also affect small businesses. For example, it's highly unlikely that Barnes and Lowery share authority equally. If a dispute were to arise between production and marketing, it would need to be resolved by someone with authority

PERSPECTIVE ON SMALL BUSINESS

"Thoreau has a wonderful line about watching farmers walk down the Concord roads carrying their farms on their backs," says Jim Howard [a broker who arranges sales of small businesses]. "I see business owners carrying the same kind of burdens today when they've lost control.

"It's very common to find an owner who feels he's operating in a hostile environment. His employees are stealing from him, his suppliers are overcharging him, and he's working incredible hours just to survive," Howard adds. "If you look more closely at this kind of business, you'll find other signs of his loss of control, and the owner doesn't know it because he doesn't pay attention to financial matters. The premises will probably be a mess. The owner will often be cheating on his taxes and hostile about playing the game according to the same rules as everyone else."

An owner who's in control, says Howard, tends to operate in a very different way. Some of the techniques Howard recommends include the following:

1. *Be an Information Collector.* "The essence of any marketplace is that it's in a continual state of flux," Howard says. "You can either jump in and dominate it, or be a passive victim. In order to flow with the flux, you need information. You have to have the demographics of your market and be able to define your business concepts in terms of the need in the marketplace. You have to analyze the competition; define your share of the market today and in the future; position what you sell, either in terms of price, or quality, or service; and define the unique selling proposition of your business."

2. *Know Your Own Strengths and Weaknesses.* The owners of small companies, Howard points out, "tend to spend their time on the things they do well and get in trouble because they neglect the things they don't do well." When he was running a public relations firm, Howard created a self-evaluation checklist that he has since updated and offers to his broker-

age customers. On a scale of 1 to 10, this "Good Management Scorecard" touches on such skills as record keeping, planning, marketing, budgeting, company appearance, employee and business relationships, goal-setting, and problem-solving. An owner, says Howard, should track his own performance in these areas constantly and take steps to remedy his own shortcomings.

"But having a fixation on failure is itself a shortcoming," Howard adds. "It makes sense to build a business around something you do well."

3. *Build an Elite, Experienced Staff.* "I worked a long time on that word 'elite,'" says Howard. "I separate the world into true achievers and everyone else. The first bunch are the only kind I really feel comfortable about. And I realized, finally, that these people also need to *feel* elite."

Howard points out that in any reasonably large organization, the owner can exercise control only through the people who work for him. One of his own key qualifications for hiring employees for [his own firm]—which currently has 28 employees in five offices—is respect for the kind of management systems Howard advocates.

4. *Write Everything Down.* On a shelf behind Howard's desk is a row of notebooks he has filled with office procedures, business plans, manuals, and marketing ideas. His screening procedure for new business buyers is equally detailed: page after page of questions about goals, skills, financial resources, and even word associations. "We make people write down the silliest things," Howard concedes, "but it all helps define the business and the goals of the owner. When you write things down, you begin to see how everything connects."

SOURCE: Reprinted with permission of *Inc.* Magazine. Michael Rozek, "Take Charge, Says Jim Howard: Staying in Control," *Inc.*, January 1982, p. 56. Copyright © 1982 by INC. Publishing Company, 38 Commercial Wharf, Boston, MA 02110.

over both. Most likely Barnes would have to assume this higher role—at least temporarily—to resolve the conflict.

Also the chart suggests that interaction between various people—say, E. Nolan from the factory and L. White in accounting—does not take place, at least with respect to managing the business. But that may not be true. For example, because she controls the information flow in the company, White may actually exert some authority over Nolan.

By itself, informal organization isn't necessarily "bad." In fact, it may arise because the formal organizational structure isn't capable of getting the job done. Example: in addition to the information Nolan needs from White, he may also require her direction and guidance to do his job adequately. In this sense White's willingness to help actually benefits the company. Whatever the situation might be here, whether "good" or "bad," at the very least Barnes should be aware of it. He might also try to change the formal organization structure to bring it more in line with the way authority actually flows and decisions are actually made.

Human Relations

Management is the practice of getting things done through the efforts of others. In order to manage people effectively, the small-business owner must have the ability to inspire and motivate employees to perform as needed. Very often the owner must be willing to allow employees to participate in goal setting and decision making centered on their jobs. The **participative approach to managing people** helps in gaining an employee commitment and creating a sense of pride in working for the company. Even some large companies recognize this advantage and try to tailor their operations to gain a sense of "smallness." For example, 3M Company, with 87,000 employees, stresses worker individuality and flexibility. Gordon W. Engdahl, the company's vice-president for human resources, has commented:

We are keenly aware of the disadvantages of large size . . . we make a conscious effort to keep our units as small as possible because we think it makes them flexible and vital.[4]

Of course, these advantages accrue naturally to the small firm, and it makes sense for the owner-manager to use them as fully as possible.

Financing

Financing is an ongoing process that has both a long- and short-run dimension. In the long run, the owner will need permanent capital—either his/her own, or from additional owners, or borrowing long-term—to finance growth. The options here are many; you'll find them discussed at length in Chapter 18. One very important decision that usually needs to be addressed as the company grows is whether or not it should go public—that is, whether ownership should be shared with others. The successful business usually outgrows the availability of capital from the original owners or lenders, such as banks, credit companies, and insurance companies.

While there's often a certain glamour attached to going public, in some situations the original owners have regretted the decision and have tried to reverse the process by "going private." MAPI, Inc., a midwestern distributor of auto parts, is an example. Going public can raise more capital but can also bring additional headaches. MAPI's management estimated that it spent $75,000 in 1980 just to comply with additional record keeping related to being a public corporation.[5]

A short-run responsibility of financing is to maintain relationships with local bankers. Most firms try to establish and maintain a good working relationship with one or more banks that can provide several essential financial services such as checking accounts for both operations and payroll, financial advice, and—perhaps most important—short-term credit to finance seasonal needs. The entrepreneur should get to know several of the bank's officers and periodically talk with them about financial matters affecting the company. Bankers can also be very helpful in making contacts with other business people in the community. These contacts are often a fruitful source of new business.

OTHER ASPECTS OF SMALL BUSINESS

The growth of franchises and the development of more minority- and women-owned businesses have gained major attention in the 1980s. The federal government has focused more attention on small businesses as evidenced by the White House Conference on Small Business, which was held in January 1980. Also the Small Business Administration has attained a new visibility with the increased interest in small business by government leaders. These are a few of the changing elements of the small business environment.

Franchising

Franchising is a system of distribution in which a supplier, the **franchisor,** makes arrangements for a dealer, the **franchisee,** to handle the franchisor's product or service. The conditions of the arrangement are spelled out in a contract called the **franchise agreement.** Franchises may be developed for an entire business such as McDonald's, Dairy Queen, or Speed Queen Laundry. Other franchises are for exclusive distribution rights to a particular product. Examples of these are automobile agencies and Magnavox and Curtis Mathes television dealerships.

Contract Provisions The franchise agreement allows the entrepreneur to buy a "package" business consisting of a proven product, proven operating methods, and training in managing the business. The franchise agreement ordinarily requires the franchisee to accept certain obligations. The franchisee is generally required to:

1. make some minimum investment, usually in cash—though sometimes a deferred payment arrangement is made;
2. maintain a specified inventory;
3. purchase a standardized equipment package;
4. maintain a specific performance level in sales and/or service;
5. pay a royalty or franchise fee;
6. follow specified procedures;
7. participate in promotional efforts of the franchisor; and
8. maintain a continuing business relationship.

In return for these obligations, the franchisor generally guarantees some combination of the following rights:

1. use of a proven company name;
2. use of the company symbols and designs;
3. use of the proven operating facilities design;
4. guidance and training;
5. management assistance;
6. employee training;
7. wholesale prices on merchandise; and
8. financial assistance.

Advantages of the Franchise These are several advantages to buying a franchise, as opposed to starting a business of the same kind. First, the franchisee steps into a proven business with a minimum of personal experience. The franchisor's training program is designed to supplement

Three of the well-known franchise operations.

This ad, which appeared in the *Wall Street Journal*, emphasizes some of the advantages of franchising.

the franchisee's lack of experience and prepare the individual to learn quickly how to operate the business efficently. A franchise gives the business owner a recognized business in which customer acceptance, operating facilities, and management procedures have already been developed. The "package" aspects of the franchise combines proven methods with proven products. The franchisee generally lowers the risk of personal failure when investing in a franchise. The proven methods of the franchisor give the franchisee an income potential that develops more rapidly. The franchisor also stands ready to help the franchisee with management assistance and training that otherwise would not be available to a new business.

Disadvantages of the Franchise One major disadvantage of buying a franchise is the requirement of sharing the profits of the business. Most franchise agreements require payment of fees or royalties based on profits. Another disadvantage is the restriction of operating freedom of the franchisee. The franchise imposes standard operating

procedures, facilities, and inventory stock. This standardization reduces the control the franchisee has over the methods of business operation, and it can create problems. For example, when Mrs. Paul's Kitchens acquired the Arthur Treacher System, it insisted on an agreement with its franchisees whereby it would supply them with fish. But "the idea of serving precooked, reheated fish cakes on Mrs. Paul's orders didn't sit well with the franchisees."[6] Many franchisees defected from Mrs. Paul's and continued operations under different names.

The Small Business Administration (SBA)

The **Small Business Administration (SBA)** was created in 1953 by the Small Business Act. The agency was designed to provide broad assistance exclusively for small business. In establishing the SBA, Congress directed the agency to be the advocate for small business, support research into problems of small business, initiate ideas and innovations, and lead in identification of opportunities to aid the establishment of small business.

Objectives The SBA was mandated to develop programs and assist small business on three levels. The first level is the small business loan programs. These are designed to assist the financing of small business in expansion and modification of their operations. Loan programs for physical and economic disaster victims are administered by the SBA as well.

The second major program area where the SBA functions is in procurement assistance. The SBA seeks to ensure that small businesses receive a share of government contracts and purchases. Specialists with the various SBA offices are available to help small businesses bid for contracts and subcontracts.

The third objective of the SBA is to provide management training, counseling, and assistance. The SBA prepares and distributes many publications about various facets of managing small businesses, provides organized courses, and offers management counseling for small-business owners.

Loan Programs The small-business loan programs allow the small business to use the proceeds of SBA loans for working capital, equipment pur-

ON THE FIRING LINE

The SBA: An Agency We Can Do Without?

Recognizing the importance of small-business ventures, Congress created the US Small Business Administration (SBA) in 1953 to support and further small business. Some think, however, that the SBA is a failure, significant only as a burden on taxpayers.

Others dispute this claim, citing the agency's programs and accomplishments. First, they note, the SBA provides small businesses with needed assistance in management. This is important since 90 percent of all business failures result from poor management. In one SBA program, SCORE, approximately 8000 retired business executives across the country volunteer their time to provide one-on-one counseling to small-business owners. Another program (Small Business Institutes) links advanced students in university business administration programs with owners of small enterprises. Under the supervision of faculty advisers, these students provide on-site management counseling to those who wish assistance. Such programs are highly efficient; they provide considerable management help at a minimum cost.

Second, continue the agency's supporters, the SBA provides a wealth of business-related information through publications and workshops. These are usually designed to focus on specific problems that small-business owners face—accounting practices or tax regulations, for example.

A third function of the SBA, its supporters note, is to help small business owners obtain loans. Banks are often unwilling or unable to make such loans on their own due to regulatory limits, risks involved, or length of term requested.

Further, it's the SBA's responsiblity to see that small businesses receive a fair share of federal government contracts. The agency refers small firms for these contracts and helps them unravel the red tape involved in obtaining them. It can also award noncompetitive contracts to "socially and economically disadvantaged" business owners as a means of helping their businesses become self-sufficient.

SBA critics, by way of contrast, argue against the agency's continued existence. What successes it has had, they claim, have come at phenomenal expense. To illustrate, they note that as of 1979, 3400 enterprises had received assistance under the minority loan program but only 30 were still in operation. Part of the problem with the agency, they maintain, is its ill-defined purpose. Loans are made or guaranteed on a first-come, first-served basis. How specific types of businesses fit into the total economy is not considered. Yet this lack of long-range vision reduces chances that loan assistance will be productive.

Those who would like to abolish the SBA also note that the agency has failed miserably in aiding minority enterprise. All too often, they say, members of minority groups have been set up as fronts by well-to-do business people in order to obtain these government contracts.

Moreover, under the direct loan program, businesses in nonminority areas are given loans about 41 percent larger than those in minority areas. No wonder the default rate in minority areas is higher, they observe; minority borrowers don't receive enough to get their businesses on solid footing.

All SBA loans, complain the agency's foes, have been an enormous waste of taxpayer money. To justify its own existence—and appropriations—the SBA had to spend its loan funds. Caution was sacrificed in the interest of sustaining the bureaucracy; every office had to fill its quota of loans. The irony of this, according to these critics, is that the banks naturally went ahead and made loans to low-risk businesspersons, leaving the SBA to underwrite high-risk borrowers. In the case of many SBA loans, there was almost no hope of repayment. In fact, borrowers began to assume that loans would not have to be repaid. The inevitable result, of course, is that SBA losses have been high: for example, close to 40 percent of all direct loans were left unpaid over one recent nine-year period.

Those who support the SBA respond by asking two questions of the critics: If not the SBA, who then will provide the management counseling that small-business owners so desperately need? And who will act as their advocate and representative in the complex and threatening realms of big government and big business?

chase, and building construction. The SBA offers two types of loans for small business. The first type is the guaranteed loan. This loan is made by a commercial bank and guaranteed by the SBA. Currently the SBA can guarantee 90 percent of the face value of the loan up to a maximum amount of $500,000.

The other type of small business loan is the direct loan, which is made directly by the SBA. Direct loans come from funds appropriated by Congress and are intended for use specifically as direct loans. SBA direct loans are generally available only to businesses that are unable to get financing from any other source. The SBA also administers some other loan programs. Examples of these are economic opportunity loans made to economically disadvantaged persons, loans made to Small Business Investment Companies, disaster loans, and pollution control loans.

Management Assistance The SBA's management assistance program is designed to provide management and technical assistance to strengthen small-business management. The SBA provides these management assistance services in several ways:

- Management courses are offered dealing with operating businesses. These are often cosponsored with educational institutions and business associations.

- Management Assistance Officers who are employees of the SBA provide individual assistance and counseling to small-business owners.

- Publications, both free and for sale, are offered on management, marketing, and technical aspects of small business.

- Small Business Institute (SBI) programs in cooperation with colleges and universities offer free management counseling by assigning student teams to work on the problems that a small business may be having.

- The Service Corps of Retired Executives (SCORE) and Active Corps of Executives (ACE) programs also offer free counseling services for small business. These groups are made up of experienced volunteers who wish to assist small-business managers.

- The Small Business Development Centers (SBDC) program is a pilot program in which the SBDC brings together resources of the community, university, and state government for the benefit of the owner of a small business. The pilot program began with eight centers and has been expanded. However not all states have access to an SBDC.

Opportunities in Small Business

Small business is an important part of the economy of the United States. For this reason small business has been the focus of much attention. Two sectors of the small business arena have benefited substantially from this attention: minority-owned businesses and women-owned businesses.

Minority-Owned Businesses In 1977 there were 560,000 minority-owned businesses in the United States. This number has increased by 31 percent since 1972. By 1977 these firms were employing 424,000 people and produced 22.2 billion dollars in receipts. Today minorities own more than 5.5 percent of all U.S. businesses. Nearly all minority businesses are small businesses, and 80 percent of them have no employees. Minorities have traditionally entered the service and retail trade, where profit margins tend to be rather thin. The **Office of Minority Business Enterprise (OMBE)** was established by the Department of Commerce in 1969 to encourage and assist minority business to enter other industries. OMBE has been helpful in its efforts to secure entrepreneurial capital for minorities.

The SBA established the **Minority Enterprise Small Business Investment Company (MESBIC)** loan program in 1968. This program makes loans to companies that are organized to supply capital to minority-owned small businesses. In 1978 there were 86 MESBICs licensed by the SBA; they made 439 financings, totaling $22.6 million. Thirty-six percent of the firms financed in 1978 were new businesses. Through the efforts of both government and private enterprise, minority businesses have been able to make some progress in developing more profitable ventures. Business receipts have increased by 69 percent in the period 1972–1977, while the number of these firms increased by only 31 percent and employment by 21 percent.

A black owner of a printing business; a bank owned and run by women.

Women-Owned Businesses In 1977 there were 702,000 women-owned businesses in the United States. This number represents 7.1 percent of all firms and accounts for total revenues of $41.5 billion. The majority of women-owned businesses are in the wholesale and retail trade and services industries. Women, like the minorities, have faced discrimination; however some progress is being made by women with passage of equal-credit laws and establishment of several women-managers' assistance programs by the SBA and other agencies. Women have also faced the problem of tradition. Entrepreneurship was not a job for a woman. She had to be a nurse, a teacher, a secretary, a wife, a mother—but never a manager or business owner. These traditional conceptions are changing somewhat. More women are enrolling in business training programs and in business management programs in college.

The future opportunities for women in small business should increase. As more women see the fading of tradition and gain the confidence, training, and experience to exert their own independence and ingenuity, they should be able to establish and run a business just as well as their male counterparts do. Sandra Winston, author of *The Entrepreneurial Woman*, advises:

> *Women have special and unique circumstances that can either help or hinder them in their efforts to become entrepreneurs. The first step is to recognize these circumstances and turn them to your advantage.*

SUMMARY

Small businesses provide a variety of goods and services that give consumers wider choices in the marketplace, because small businesses function in areas where larger businesses could not afford to operate. The Small Business Administration (SBA) defines a small business as "one which is independently owned and operated, not dominant in its field of operation, and meets certain standards of size in terms of employees or annual receipts." By this definition, about 97 percent of all nonfarm businesses are small. These businesses are usually classified into four major categories—service, retail or wholesale, construction, and manufacturing.

The small business has several operating advantages: it's able to react quickly to changes in operations; it can give a "personal touch" to its handling of customers; and it may be able to survive on the receipts generated by a limited market. Disadvantages faced by the small business include limited managerial skill, inadequate capital-raising capacity, and excessive government regulation.

Fifty-five percent of new businesses fail within the first five years of operation. The most common reasons are lack of business experience, lack of financing, lack of sufficient sales, poor location, lack of business records, improper accounts receivable management, insufficient stock turnover, poor inventory control, and improper markups. Obviously, then, it's necessary to consider many factors in order to set up a small business successfully.

First, the entrepreneurial capability of the owner must be evaluated. Next, a detailed business plan must be developed. Legal considerations must be taken into account, including what form of organization the business will use. Managerial considerations include staffing and establishing a production process. Marketing considerations, such as choosing the proper location and sales channels, are especially important. Financial considerations include whether—and how—to use debt or equity financing. Accounting records must be set up to provide information needed by managers. Tax records must be kept as well.

Two stages of managerial expertise are required to bring the company through its life cycle from inception to maturity. First, the owner is a promoter, acting both as a manager and as a worker. As the business grows, the owner must delegate more work to others and concentrate on managing.

Organization of the enterprise is important; areas of responsibility of owner, managers, and employees must be identified. Small businesses most often achieve this end through use of the functional organization. Other ongoing management concerns include human relations and financing.

Important current trends in small business include the growth of franchises and the development of more minority- and women-owned businesses. The federal government has focused more attention on small business, and the Small Business Administration has gained new visibility with the increased interest in small business shown by government leaders.

KEY TERMS

commitment
construction
  businesses
experience
franchise agreement
franchisee
franchisor
functional
  organization
manufacturing
  businesses
Minority Enterprise
  Small Business
  Investment
  Company
  (MESBIC)
Office of Minority
  Business Enterprise
  (OMBE)

organization structure
participative
   approach to
   managing people
retail and wholesale
   businesses
sacrifice
service businesses
Small Business
   Administration
   (SBA)
Small Business
   Investment
   Company (SBIC)
venture capitalist

REVIEW QUESTIONS

1. What is the definition of *small business* as identified by the Small Business Administration (SBA)?
2. What are the types of the typical small business?
3. How many small businesses are started each year? How many fail—and for what reasons?
4. What are some important financial and accounting considerations in starting a new business? What marketing information would be helpful?
5. What does an organization chart show? How does informal organization differ from formal organization?
6. List typical contract provisions found in a franchising agreement.
7. What's the Small Business Administration (SBA) and what are its objectives?
8. What's a MESBIC?

DISCUSSION QUESTIONS

1. Explain three advantages and three disadvantages of small business.
2. Is it easy to identify the qualities that would ensure success for a man or woman who would like to start a new business? Explain.

3. What are the key considerations of a business plan?
4. Why is staffing important and what approaches might be used to build a qualified and capable staff?
5. Explain some advantages and disadvantages associated with franchising.
6. Describe the SBA's loan programs and it's management assistance program.

CASE: THE ADVENTURESOME LIBRARIAN

Chris Jordan was the head librarian at a midwestern university, but he was not really pleased with his job. Appropriately enough, he liked to work with books. However most of his time was *not* spent working with books and helping people find the resources they needed in the library. Instead he found himself having to appease faculty members who were not getting the service they needed from the reference room, or having to deal with students caught tearing pages out of encyclopedias. There was also a lot of thievery, which compounded the unpleasantness. Furthermore, there was the time spent with the university bureaucracy, concerned about the budget, never allowing him to purchase all the books needed to do a first-class job.

Chris was really at the end of his rope. It was a hassle to even think about changing careers at this stage of his life, but he was fed up with his job, and he had decided to try something else. He could probably go into teaching—perhaps Library Science at some small college. But another option, which came to him in a flash, was to go into business for himself.

A business for a librarian—what would that be? The answer, naturally enough, was a *book store*. The idea really appealed to Jordan. He could be his own boss and surround himself with people who liked to work with books—maybe housewives with degrees and talents, who could work well with customers. The prospect of a bookstore became more and more attractive, and finally he decided to make the break.

Jordan began to plan, putting his ideas down on paper. A notebook took shape—a real feasibility study of a business dream: costs for rent and furnishing the building with bookshelves and display cases, costs for advertising on radio, maybe television (and of course the newspapers), some wage figures for three helpers (for instance 20 hours a week for each at $3.35 an hour—minimum wage), and a few other miscellaneous figures. There really couldn't be much else needed to start a business, but Jordan trusted his instincts and vowed he would play it by ear as the thing developed.

1. Does it appear that Jordan has the qualities required for an entrepreneur?
2. Does Jordan have all the information he needs to start a new business? What details would you add?
3. What financial considerations will be important to Jordan as he starts his new business?

CASE: A NEW KICK—TENNIS AND SOCCER

Tennis had been Joni Lever's life for the past ten years. She was the owner-manager of an exclusive tennis club in a midwestern city with a population of around 200,000 people. Joni's dad financed the club, which cost about a million and a half dollars to build, and for the first two years he enjoyed a good return on his investment. Tennis was very popular and there was only one other competitor with an indoor club. So initiation fees were fairly high—$75.00 for a single membership, $150 for a family—and court costs for playing were $10.00 an hour.

Two hundred people comprised the original membership list, and court play was about 75 percent capacity for the first couple of years. Prospects were very encouraging and it looked as if the club was really going to generate substantial revenues and profits. But then business began to fall off in the third and fourth years as tennis seemed to lose its luster across the nation—at least as far as the high hourly court costs were concerned. Business took a beating. In spring and summer things got worse as play dropped off when other clubs entered competition, and the country clubs put on advertising campaigns to attract members back to their tennis courts and golf courses. So the club has been losing money for about five years, and Joni and her dad are getting kind of desperate. Court use has dropped to 50 percent and membership is below 120.

Joni's latest idea is to turn four of the courts into an indoor soccer field, since soccer has been getting more and more popular all the time both locally and nationally. Besides, she likes the game and has played it since high school. This makes quite a combination: soccer and tennis. Joni is very optimistic that soccer will come to the rescue of tennis and restore past profitability.

1. Do you think Joni and her dad gave up too soon on the tennis club? What could be done to revive interest in the club and possibly generate revenues for tennis?
2. What preliminary market study and financing plan do you think Joni should consider before leaping into soccer?

A CAREER IN BUSINESS

There are more opportunities for you in business than in any other career field. Unlike engineering, social work, or most other occupations, business can accommodate an infinite variety of interests, personality types, challenges, and compensation levels. Educational requirements vary from a two-year degree to a Ph.D.

A few generalities can be made about a business career. Verbal and written skills are important for almost any business position. Regardless of what you learn in school, if it cannot be communicated to others, your advancement will be limited. Moreover good communication skills will enable you to sell your ideas and proposals to others. Usually a business person must be able to pay attention to details when examining records and preparing reports. Some basic mathematical and accounting skills will help in analyzing and using budgetary and statistical data.

Many professional business positions require managing the work of others. Successful supervisors have good human relations skills. They understand how people interact in work groups, the importance of informal opinion leaders, motivation techniques, and how to maintain morale within the organization. A good manager can communicate effectively, develop plans, organize human and material resources, and create control systems to make certain that work activities conform to plans.

If you are contemplating a career in business, you should consider the following questions:

1. Are you willing to let people working for you make decisions?
2. Can you "make your point" in a group discussion?
3. Do you work calmly and efficiently under pressure?
4. Will you work more than eight hours a day and sometimes take work home?
5. Do you have the ability to separate and identify key points and opportunities from masses of information?
6. Do you have patience with other people?
7. Are you self-disciplined and do you have good self-control?
8. Can you generally see the broad perspective when planning?
9. Have you considered how a professional

business position might change your life-style?

10. Do you have good analytical skills?

The above list is not comprehensive nor is it intended to be. Our objective is simply to stimulate your thinking about the question, "Is a business career really for me?" A positive answer to the above ten questions is a step in the right direction. On the other hand, if your response is *no* to every one of them, you should probably look elsewhere for a career.

When planning to establish a small business, the owner-manager may do everything: financial planning, site selection, determining the building or space needed, layout, furniture and fixtures, and all the details required to open a business. Next is personnel selection, putting together a management team to perform other necessary functions: production, sales, credit, collections, etc.

Most small businesses can't afford the luxury of specialization; so the manager and perhaps a few assistants perform all these functions—regardless of qualifications and special training. Some professional assistance must be provided, such as *legal counsel* for licenses, filing government forms, drawing up contracts; *accountants* for systems and records; *advertising* experts; and perhaps *engineers* and *architects.* In most cases a lawyer and an accountant must be consulted to get a business started. These and other experts need not be permanent members of the staff but can be hired as consultants. Small-business owners/managers usually assume most of these functions, at least until they begin to generate revenues; then they add functional specialists as warranted.

Additional information on business opportunities is offered at the end of each major part of the text. The career sections begin with a general discussion of the field, educational requirements, trends, and potential pitfalls. Next, representative jobs are described in detail. Other information provided for each position includes: (1) most likely places of employment, (2) skills required, (3) employment outlook through 1990, and (4) salary ranges. By examining the variety of jobs, you will be able to develop a richer appreciation of the field.

PART 2

MANAGEMENT

CHAPTER   5

THE
MANAGERIAL
PROCESS

After studying this chapter you should be able to:

1 Describe the roles of a manager.
2 Enumerate the steps in the decision-making (problem-solving) process.
3 Describe the various management decision styles.
4 Explain the four functions of management.
5 Understand the importance of setting objectives to the success of a business.
6 Describe the channels of communication and explain their use for people in management.
7 Explain the managerial skills and their relationship to the functions of management.

97

True to form, Tom Coronado—manager of employee relations for Huse Manufacturing Company—pulled into his reserved company parking space early. It was 7:30 Monday morning—usually the most hectic day of the week, with more than its share of problems. But first the good news: Friday had been payday. Now the bad news: Monday of every week turned up Friday's payroll errors. With new hires, overtime work, and different wage rate categories, there always seemed to be mistakes in figuring wages and paychecks.

To make matters worse, in recent weeks these errors had been on the increase. Reason: a new computerized payroll system. Long live progress, Tom thought. He was also thinking—with concern—about a 10 o'clock meeting scheduled with the exec V-P on this very subject. Tom would have to report on how the new system was working out. Right now, though, he needed to find at least an hour of quiet to get his report together.

Fortunately his office was quiet and Tom was able to review a couple of computer printouts. But shortly after 8 o'clock the phone began to ring. His secretary wasn't in yet, so Tom had to personally take six calls in 20 minutes. The first five were about errors in the payroll checks: two calls were from shop supervisors, one was from a worker on the night shift, one from the production superintendent, and one from the local union president. This last was the most sweat; the union leader's parting shot was "When in blazes are you going to straighten out this payroll mess?" The sixth call was from Tom's secretary. She wouldn't be in today.

Over the next hour Tom was able to correct most of the payroll errors—with a little help from his friends. These included payroll clerks, the production superintendent, a junior systems analyst, and one hourly-paid worker. By 9:30 Tom thought he was ready to stick his phone in a filing cabinet and sit down with his materials for a last review before the 10 o'clock meeting. Five minutes later the phone started ringing. It was Ted Brokenshire, president of the Metropolitan Personnel Association. Would Tom be willing to give a talk at the association's next meeting?

By the time he hung up the phone, Tom realized he had talked away the rest of his prep time before the meeting. It was 9:57. Quickly he pulled together his notes and materials and walked the two corridors to the vice-president's office. The secretary waved him right in to a meeting that lasted two hours. But they were two hours well spent, Tom thought. The problems and the progress of putting in the new payroll system were taken apart, analyzed, gone over, and put together again. And despite the recent increase in mix-ups, implementation was actually two weeks ahead of schedule.

Tom came out of the meeting feeling good and ready to go ahead on the assignment. As he entered his office it also occurred to him that he had a few more ingredients for that talk he had to give to Metro Personnel. Then his eye caught the clock: 12:20. Now for some lunch, he thought. He remembered that he hadn't had breakfast, and now he felt like a big plate of shrimp Lo Mein. Then the phone rang.

Tom finally left for lunch at 2:30. As he pulled into the parking lot of the Shanghai Dynasty, he recalled that they were closed Mondays.

THE WORK OF A MANAGER

A manager's job, like Tom's, consists of many planned and unplanned activities filled with communications with many people. Often, too, these people are outside the organization. But in addition to this wealth of interaction with others, a manager also has to solve a variety of problems by making many decisions during the day. Often, these decisions must be made quickly by examining a situation and recognizing the possible outcomes of alternative solutions. Throughout a long and busy day a manager must fill several roles in order to manage successfully.

Managerial Roles

Management brings about improvement in organizations by setting goals and then integrating human, material, and information resources toward the accomplishment of those goals. The rather abstract term *management* really refers to flesh-and-blood managers of organizations. An **organization** is a group of people deliberately assembled to set, plan, and accomplish specific goals. A **goal** is some desired future condition or state of affairs,

such as a 15 percent rate of return on investment, toward which the organization is exerting itself. A manager, then, is that person who directs the organization in the pursuit of its goals. The goal of Edwin Land, founder of Polaroid Corporation, was to produce and successfully market a true push-button camera that would produce an instant color print. In 1972 he reached his goal with the creation of the Polaroid SX-70 camera. From the inception of his idea to its final execution, Land set goals, assembled people, integrated and directed their efforts, and measured performance against expected results.

A manager such as Land fills three sets of managerial roles (see Figure 5.1). One set consists of relationships with other people (interpersonal) as figurehead, leader, and "go-between." The role of figurehead is mostly ceremonial, as when Land presided over the press conference that introduced the SX-70. The figurehead role is less directly related to the job of managing company resources. Leader behavior has to do with taking charge of a department or other group and seeing to it that the necessary jobs are performed. Leadership moves the group toward the group goal.

The role of "go-between" finds a manager developing and maintaining contacts (linkages) outside his or her own department. Higher-level managers help link the entire organization to-

FIGURE 5.1

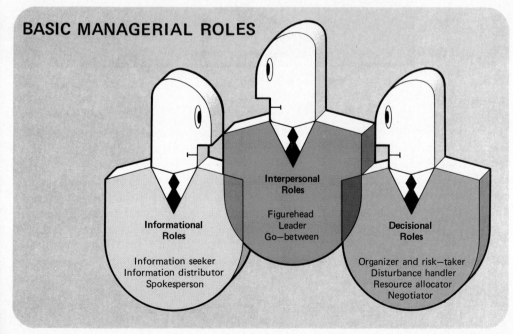

BASIC MANAGERIAL ROLES

Informational Roles

Information seeker
Information distributor
Spokesperson

Interpersonal Roles

Figurehead
Leader
Go—between

Decisional Roles

Organizer and risk—taker
Disturbance handler
Resource allocator
Negotiator

Managers engaged in problem solving.

gether. These contacts feed the manager information that proves helpful in managing the department or the firm. Throughout the lengthy developmental period of the SX-70, Edwin Land had to keep in constant contact with many Polaroid managers including the heads of research and development, marketing, and production. These discussions helped him in making many crucial decisions.

A manager's contacts with other managers and subordinates provide the basis for the second set of managerial roles: those of information seeker and information distributor. As information

seeker, the manager is always searching for information that will make it easier for the firm to achieve those goals for which he or she has a particular responsibility. An article in a trade magazine, for example, might furnish the manager of a J. C. Penney store with information on how to reduce shoplifting. In turn, as information distributor, the manager usually distributes important new information to subordinates. The Penney manager might communicate to the salesclerks advice on how to spot potential shoplifters.

Through the manager's role as spokesperson, other information is released to those outside the department (and possibly the firm) who can help the manager accomplish his or her goals. The J. C. Penney manager might inform the local police department of the store's new policies on shoplifting and ask for the department's help.

The third set of managerial roles involves decision making. When a new firm is created, the manager as organizer and risk taker must decide how to organize it and must be prepared to take the attendant risks. As a disturbance handler, a manager must make decisions that will put a stop to any disruption of work and restore order. Needless to say, this role demands sensitivity, tact, and the peacemaker's touch. Edwin Land, for example, had to intervene and settle disagreements and conflicts between departments during the production and marketing phases of the Polaroid SX-70 camera.

A manager, as resource allocator, must also decide how to organize resources. This involves approval of projects and the authorization of major budgets. And when lower-level managers disagree on a matter, the manager has to be a negotiator in the effort to reach a final decision. It's not too much to say that the skills of a diplomat are useful to a manager in this role.

Although the above roles might appear to be easily distinguishable from one another, in practice they often overlap. As we've seen, the story of Tom Coronado illustrates several managerial roles, including that of leader, disturbance-handler, and information-distributor. A manager must be adept at quickly and easily stepping into and out of various roles as situations demand and conditions change. If you were to accompany Edwin Land through a full workday, you'd see the interrelated and dynamic nature of these managerial roles. Land meets with top managers, prominent customers, labor representatives, supplier-company managers, and many other people in the course of a single day's activities.

Problem-Solving, Decision-Making, and Communication

A manager's typical workday involves solving problems, making decisions, and communicating those decisions to other people. Of course, many problems are routine or anticipated and can be dealt with according to established procedure.

For example, if an employee at Exxon is unhappy with his or her pay raise, the following procedures can be set in motion: first, a meeting is held between the supervisor and the employee. Then, if the problem is not resolved, the compensation administrator from the personnel department talks with the employee. So there's a series of procedures already established to handle exactly this type of routine problem.

Sometimes, however, problems are not foreseen. The situations that generate them are often unique and unplanned-for. To try to follow a routine procedure would most likely be impractical as well as inappropriate. By their very nature, such problem situations are hard to plan for in advance, as when the workers of an Exxon refinery engage in a wildcat (unexpected) strike.

A unique and unexpected problem requires that a manager search for a solution. Naturally, the manager must first be aware that an unusual problem exists. (As obvious as this sounds, it's really important.) Initially, the manager will try to clarify and define the problem. Once the problem is understood, the manager outlines alternative solutions. These must be weighed and evaluated carefully, after which the manager makes a decision selecting one or a combination of two or more alternatives. The next step is to put the solution/plan into action (implementation). The manager is still not finished, though, since it is necessary at this stage to follow through and see whether the course of action has succeeded in solving the problem. Figure 5.2 shows the problem-solving process.

But it's rare that a manager makes a decision and solves a problem without some interaction with other people. Good communication is required for gathering information to solve an important problem. In turn, the nature of managerial communication depends on the decision style of the manager. **Decision style** refers to how a manager interacts with employees to solve a problem. We can isolate three distinctive decision styles: the autocratic, the consultative, and the group-centered. Each style has its own different quantity and blend of employee involvement in decision making.

In **autocratic decision style,** the manager solves a problem and issues a related order to employees. (In some cases, the order is itself the solution.) There's only a minimum amount of employee involvement and communication. In-

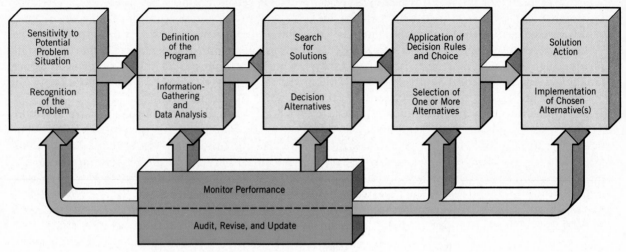

Sensitivity to Potential Problem Situation	Definition of the Program	Search for Solutions	Application of Decision Rules and Choice	Solution Action
Recognition of the Problem	Information-Gathering and Data Analysis	Decision Alternatives	Selection of One or More Alternatives	Implementation of Chosen Alternative(s)

Monitor Performance

Audit, Revise, and Update

FIGURE 5.2

formation flows in one direction: from manager to employee. Joe Lopez, as plant manager of Gaylord Container Corporation, uses the autocratic style when he decides to reduce production in order to keep finished-product inventories at minimal levels. He makes a decision and instructs the production superintendent to implement it.

In **consultative decision style,** the manager shares the problem with employees and asks for their suggestions. Still, it's the manager alone who in the end makes the decision. The communication pattern is as follows: (1) information is given to employees by the manager; (2) it is then exchanged among employees and fed back to the manager; and (3) finally, the decision is made by the manager and issued to employees. A bank vice-president recently met with three of her consumer-loan officers to discuss policies for making automobile loans. After hearing what the loan officers had to say, the vice-president established rules for making loans.

In **group-centered decision style,** manager and employees meet as a group to discuss the problem, to generate alternative solutions, and to come up with a solution by mutual agreement. The group-centered style can often be observed in the laboratories of the DuPont Company. There, problems encountered in research are often unprecedented, so that all those working on a project must participate in sharing information and making decisions.

"All in favor say 'Goody'!"

Drawing by Ed Arno; © 1975 by The New Yorker Magazine, Inc.

PERSPECTIVE ON SMALL BUSINESS

Until two years ago, production workers at the Chester Cable Corporation simply made wire. Day after day, they spun and spooled thousands of feet of plastic-coated copper filament in dozens of sizes, colors, and shapes.

A lot of that wire came back as fast as it went out. Truckload after truckload, an average of $70,000 worth of wire every month, landed back on the company's loading dock, rejected for poor workmanship.

Quality control supervisor Steve Rodvansky had wrestled with this frustrating and costly problem ever since he joined the $25-million company in 1977. He talked with customers, tightened up inspection procedures, and tried—without much luck—to get production workers to take quality seriously.

Rodvansky knew his problem had to be solved by the workers who actually produced the wire at the company's Chester, N.Y. plant. "You can't inspect quality into a product," Rodvansky says. "You've got to build it into the product in the first place."

But Rodvansky had trouble getting this point across to his production workers—until the day he walked into the plant with an electronic TV game that one of Chester Cable's customers made. On a whim, he'd picked up the game to show how wire eventually ended up in a consumer product.

"Suddenly," he recalls, "everyone got very excited. I was demonstrating the game plan to Pam Van Dunk, an extrusion operator who made the hair-thin wires that went into the game's connector cable. She showed it around the plant, and insisted I get samples of other products that use our wire.

"I know it sounds too simple to be true, but that demonstration turned out to be the beginning of an answer to our quality control problems," he says.

For the next nine months, Rodvansky rounded up examples of dozens of products that used Chester Cable's wire, and showed workers that the wire they cranked out made an important contribution to these products.

Slowly, Rodvansky's message took effect. Instead of just making anonymous lengths of wire, Chester Cable's workers began to feel they were helping to make important and interesting products. The new understanding almost eliminated the company's quality problems: For the last year, the amount of wire returned for defective workmanship has dropped from an average of $70,000 a month to a fairly stable $4000.

SOURCE: Reprinted with permission of *INC.* Magazine. Excerpted from Carol Rose, "You Can't Inspect Quality into Your Products," *INC.*, October 1980, pp. 123, 125. Copyright © 1980 by INC. Publishing Company, 38 Commercial Wharf, Boston, MA 02110.

THE MANAGERIAL PROCESS: PLANNING

Many of the day-to-day activities of a manager are composed of the managerial functions of planning, organizing, directing, and controlling (see Figure 5.3). Although these functions can be separated for purposes of analysis and discussion, in actual practice they form a tightly integrated process and cycle of behavior that consists of (1) thinking about a problem, (2) taking action, and (3) reviewing the decision and making any necessary adjustments.

Planning is a future oriented activity that requires setting objectives and designing the strategies, policies, and methods necessary for achieving them. Planning helps an organization progress from its current position to a more desirable position. For example, good planning might make the difference in helping the owner of a small gift shop raise profits from $50,000 to $100,000 a year. More specifically, planning is deciding in advance what needs to be done, how a job is to be performed, when an activity is to be undertaken, and who the participants in an activity are going to be. The objectives and strategies that flow from the planning process provide the foundation for the organizing, directing, and controlling functions of management.

DYNAMIC NATURE OF THE MANAGEMENT PROCESS

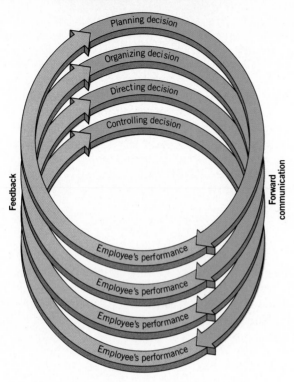

FIGURE 5.3

Importance and Purposes of Planning

The purposes of planning are (1) to provide a framework to help the firm reach its objectives and (2) to form a foundation for organizing, directing, and controlling decisions and activities. Planning is extremely important because of the concrete advantages it confers on a business. First, planning greatly increases an organization's chances of success. Second, planning provides direction for coordination of decisions and programs. When managers at all levels of the firm have knowledge of plans, they can better coordinate and direct their employees. Third, planning encourages the development of capable, forward-thinking managers.

A forward-thinking manager is one who can anticipate problems and opportunities and take appropriate action, rather than wait for problems to develop and suddenly present themselves. Robert Taylor, president of Minnetonka, Inc., recognized in the early 1970s that its Village Bath product line might reach its maximum potential in the mid-1970s. Village Bath toiletries include soap balls, bubble baths, bath oils, and shampoos sold primarily through gift shops and drugstores. Taylor realized that he needed a new product line to serve as a vehicle for growth. The result was Softsoap, a pump-dispensed liquid hand soap. By 1981 Softsoap was one of the best-selling hand soaps in the world.

In contrast to being forward-thinking, a reactive manager responds to a problem that has already done its harm. Although skill is needed here too (if only to remedy the matter in the most efficient way), a reactive manager is clearly less desirable than one who can think ahead.

Providing Direction through Objectives

An organization's general purpose or **mission** is its reason for existence. The mission of a hospital is to provide high-quality medical care for the community. Our military organizations and the Department of Defense exist to protect U.S. citizens, property, and interests from foreign encroachment and invasion. In the 1920s Henry Ford established the mission of the Ford Motor Company. This was the production and marketing of passenger cars at low cost, so that nearly every family could buy a car. The mission was accomplished by successfully assembling and marketing a highly standardized — and saleable — product.

From an organization's mission statement, objectives can be created and pursued. **Objectives** of the business firm are sometimes stated in broad terms when addressed to the general public as part of the company's public relations effort (see Figure 5.4). However objectives can be specific, hoped-for results that can be expressed in quantitative and measurable terms with timetables set for achievement. For example, Procter & Gamble may set as one of its objectives "to increase sales of Bounty paper towels by 5 percent within the next 6 months." From this objective, a sales representative may in turn formulate a derived objective. This might be "to increase the number of sales calls [customer contacts] by 10 percent over the next 90 days."

Carefully stated and explained objectives serve as guidelines and provide direction for managerial decisions and employee action. Additionally, objectives help bring about consistency in various programs and activities. Program consistency in

THE DOW CHEMICAL COMPANY OBJECTIVES

To seek maximum long-term profit growth as the primary means to ensure the prosperity and well-being of our employees, stockholders and our customers by making products that the people of the world need, and to do so better than anyone else

To attract and hire talented, competent people, and compensate them well for their performance

To provide our employees with opportunities for career growth and decision making

To protect our employees by continuing the development of safe work practices

To continue our commitment to individual freedom and equal opportunity

To practice stewardship in the manufacture, marketing, use and disposal of our products

To share in the world's obligation for the protection of the environment

To make wise and efficient use of the earth's energy and natural resources

To be scrupulously ethical in our daily conduct

To grow through continuous innovation of our products and processes

To be responsible citizens of the different societies in which we operate

To make this world a better place for our having been in business

April, 1979

FIGURE 5.4
Courtesy Dow Chemical.

turn means greater operations efficiency—the generation of more output (product or service) for a given amount of input. Thus when Georgia-Pacific Corporation eliminates almost all material waste in producing paper, it has achieved a high degree of efficiency. Finally, objectives serve as criteria for evaluating performance and determining organizational effectiveness. Effectiveness is the accomplishment of objectives.

Types of Plans

Plans vary along several lines, including (1) the time frame for accomplishment, (2) who does the planning and who initiates the plan, (3) coverage, (4) level of detail, (5) accuracy and predictability, and (6) the purpose of the firm. Table 5.1 shows several types of plans used by managers.

Strategic Planning   **Strategic planning** is long-range, comprehensive, and takes into account the firm's environment as well as the organization itself. Such plans are formulated by executives (top managers) and put into action by lower-level managers. A strategy helps answer questions about (1) the type of business a firm should offer its customers in terms of product, services, and location, (2) market opportunities, and (3) what resources are necessary in order to offer the right products and services to present and potential customers. Figure 5.5, taken from the Evans Products Company's 1980 annual report, shows what one company is doing in its strategic planning.

Almost every major company recognizes the importance of strategic planning. In 1981 Edgar Griffiths was fired as RCA Corporation's chairman because of a lack of strategic, long-range planning. One RCA executive noted, "While Griffiths was chairman, long-range planning meant, What are we going to do after lunch?"[1] Griffiths' emphasis had been strictly on short-term earnings.

Tactical Planning   **Tactical planning** is short-range (often less than one year) and more detailed, being based on central planning decisions. It focuses on current operations of the business. Some plans can be in the form of policies, procedures, or rules. A **policy** is a standing decision that serves as a guideline for making subsequent decisions in particular situations. A **procedure** is an ordered series of steps to be followed in accomplishing something. **Rules** tend to be very narrow and specific plans for carrying out a policy; they prescribe regularity in behavior. An example of a tactical plan is the Walden Book Company's "media-hot" plan. A media-hot book is one being currently promoted on TV talk shows or having some connection with a current movie or TV show. Each week, every manager of the 700 Walden Book Stores receives a list of media-hot books. The media-hot books are then grouped on "media tables" in high-traffic areas where the browsers are sure to see them. "Finger tags" say such things as "'Now a Movie" or "As Seen on the Merv Griffin Show." The "media-hot" tactical plan has re-

TABLE 5–1

Characteristics of Plans and Levels of Planning

Characteristic	Types of Plans	
	Strategic Planning (long-range)	Tactical and Operational Planning (short-range)
Time frame	One to five years	One week to one year
Level of management and who plans	Top or executive management (chief executive officer, vice-presidents, directors, and division heads)	Lower or supervisory management (unit supervisors, first-line supervisors, assistant foremen)
Coverage	External environment and entire organization	Smaller structural units and offices
Content	Broad and general (goal and policy statements)	Detailed (timetables, procedures and rules)
Accuracy and predictability	Uncertain (hoped-for accuracy + or − 10% to 25% of goal)	Reasonably certain (hoped-for accuracy + or − 2% to 7% of goal)
Purpose and use	Establish mission and long-term goals	Implementation and activation of plans

sulted in a sharp increase in sales. The plan was developed by top managers of Walden but is carried out by each bookstore manager.

All levels of management are involved in the planning process. Executive-level managers spend more time in planning activities than do middle- and lower-level managers. For the most part, lower-level managers, like the Walden Book Store managers, carry out the strategies and policies issued by top managers. Technical and operational knowledge is relatively more important for lower-level managers, while top managers must have more imaginative skills in creating long-range plans. For example, the local bookstore manager must know the details of how to step up a media display table; on the other hand, top management is concerned with how to make the 700-unit chain grow during the next five years.

Information for Effective Planning

To develop goals and successful plans, managers need an organized method of collecting, evaluating, condensing, arranging, and presenting reliable information. Organized in this way, information becomes an instrument of control for use by managers. Any plan of more than a one-year range is usually expected to be more uncertain than plans of shorter duration. This uncertainty arises because of the difficulty of predicting what will happen in the not-so-immediate future. However, sometimes uncertainty can be reduced by management's getting additional information.

Many progressive firms have developed a **management decision support system (MDSS)** to aid them in planning. This is a computer-based system that categorizes, stores, and analyzes information from many sources. An MDSS supports the planning, controlling, and operations functions of the firm by generating timely information for many routine decisions. It can also use mathematical models to solve unique, one-of-a-kind problems. The Equitable General Insurance Company has developed a very innovative decision-support system. The company's "paperless" policy-issuing facility, called the Serv-U-Center, uses a network of 140 computer terminals to process and provide immediate access to customers' policies, to generate reports, and to measure productivity.

THE MANAGERIAL PROCESS: ORGANIZING

Organizing is the process of creating structure, relationships, and other orderly arrangements in order to make the best use of a firm's assets. The result is (or should be) greatly increased chances

Strategic Plan 1981-1985

The primary objectives of Evans' long-term strategic planning are to (1) identify and anticipate trends in our major businesses, (2) explore opportunities within the expected market environment, and (3) evaluate alternative investments. Some of the key trends, strategies and operating plans developed in 1980 to achieve profitable and consistent growth over the plan period are summarized here.

Key Trends

More homes are being fixed up these days than are being built. There are several good reasons why this is happening. High new home prices and mortgage rates are making remodeling existing homes the more attractive financial alternative... Turnover in the nation's 87 million housing units is spurring improvements by new owners... Rising energy costs are continuing to prompt installation of energy conservation products... Old homes in inner cities are being restored at a record rate.

"Do-It-Yourselfers" spur growth in home improvement product sales

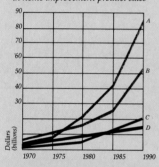

Home improvement product sales by types of retailers:

A *Home centers ("Do-It-Yourselfer" sales exceed 80% of total sales.)*

B *Contractor-oriented lumber & building materials (L&BM) dealers ("Do-It-Yourselfer" sales are less than 30% of total sales.)*

C *Consumer-oriented L&BM dealers ("Do-It-Yourselfer" sales are between 50% and 80% of total sales.)*

D *Hardware stores*

Source: National Home Center News and Frost & Sullivan

Basic Strategy

Emphasize marketing directly to the consumer through retail building materials stores and the sale of affordable, custom-built homes. Focus manufacturing activities on specialty products and products used by the growing remodeling market.

Operating Plans

Retail Stores:

By 1985 our *Retail Group* anticipates operating 450 stores and a near doubling of revenues.

The percentage of sales to the growing "Do-It-Yourself" market should increase due to:

1. The above-average growth rate inherent in the market.
2. Emphasizing cash-and-carry stores in the new store program.
3. Enlarging and remodeling dual yards, which serve both the consumer and contractor, to accommodate increased consumer sales. Dual yards will continue to be operated where substantial contractor business is available.

We plan to expand our market penetration in the 20 states we now serve, and to expand into additional states.

Existing stores will be continually evaluated in terms of the need to remodel, relocate or remerchandise. The primary goal is to improve our return on investment.

We will strive to maintain our strong consumer image as the "building materials specialist" by stocking ranges of merchandise which allow the customer to choose quality products at a variety of price levels. Equally important is customer assistance from free literature and knowledgeable sales personnel.

Personnel training programs will be intensified to enhance customer service, as well as to provide management for our increasing number of stores.

Custom-Built Homes:

Through increased penetration of existing markets and entering into new market areas, our *Homes Group's* output is expected to approach its current rated capacity by 1985.

Evans Financial Corp. will continue to develop innovative loan programs that are responsive to home loan market conditions and to maintain reliable external investment sources to fund such programs.

Manufacturing:

Our *Shelter Products Group* plans to increase the portion of its building product sales to the remodeling market. The Group plans to enter new market areas, as well as to serve existing sales areas more efficiently by opening additional plants for the manufacture of aluminum doors and windows and kitchen cabinets.

Our *Forest-Fiber Products Group* anticipates improved profitability from its wood products activities as higher operating rates and improved efficiencies are attained in more favorable markets. Additional offshore markets will be developed.

The Group's battery separator business is expected to strengthen its market position primarily by capitalizing on technological advances as its markets expand.

FIGURE 5.5

Reproduced from Evans Products Company's 1980 Annual Report.

of success. In 1980 Pan American and National airlines merged. As part of the merger they attempted to integrate their routes, maintenance facilities, and other resources. But when the reservations services of the two airlines were combined, service was so poor that about one third of the calls were never answered. This organization problem wasn't fully corrected until mid-1981. Meanwhile losses of potential sales were in the millions of dollars.

Importance and Purpose of Organizing

Pan American and National are large companies. But even many small business firms have relatively complex systems consisting of different tasks, several departments, numerous raw materials, and a number of people. The purpose of the organizing function is to bring about the coordinated and integrated effort of all parts to reach

TALKING BUSINESS

"Because a company has a long-range plan doesn't mean it knows where it is going," says Benjamin B. Tregoe, chairman of Kepner-Tregoe Strategy Group, Inc., a Princeton, N.J. consulting firm.

"A lot of companies in the US are deluding themselves."

He says many US companies get in trouble because they have not developed a vision of the future. He considers most long-range plans that now guide business "visionless"—actually one-year plans that measure performance against the previous year.

"I don't know of a single company that will say to a manager, 'You will not get a bonus this year because five years ago you said we would be here and we are not,' " Tregoe says. "Everybody who contributes to the plan knows that it can be revised after the next year's planning cycle, so it is basically a short-range plan."

American business should shift to strategic thinking, he says. Strategic thinking, which is just catching on here, has been thriving for years in Japan and West Germany. "Those countries have had to think in terms of world markets and where to put their resources in order to survive," Tregoe says.

Tregoe says US industry generally has been hurt by failing to think in terms of international markets.

"If you stop and think about it, there are very few examples of any products in the US that are really designed for world markets," he points out. "Our mentality has been to produce for our own markets and if we sell a product somewhere else, fine. The Japanese don't think that way."

Source: "The 'Visionless' Long-Range Company Plan," p. 37, reprinted by permission from *Nation's Business*, November 1980. Copyright 1980 by *Nation's Business*, Chamber of Commerce of the United States.

the company's goals. This is accomplished by designing a structure of tasks, positions, and work units—such as you can see in a McDonald's restaurant. There, the order-takers, food-preparers, and cleanup people work at different tasks in different locations with different equipment.

The importance of the organizing function is, of course, the contribution it makes to the accomplishment of plans. The structure of people, positions, departments, and activities forms the framework within which company goals are to be accomplished. Through organizing, the correct ordering of tasks can produce an efficient workflow. Proper relationships can be established between departments, and appropriate resource allocations can be made. Again, this can be seen even in a busy, crowded McDonald's when you place a special order.

Change and Reorganization Business firms, hospitals, government agencies, and other organizations are continually undergoing changes, growth, and advancement (or decline). Many changes are expected and result from carefully laid plans. Others are unforeseen and can create problems. The amount and impact of change are strongly influenced by the organization's environment. The business environment is basically made up of the social, political, economic, and technological factors that affect a firm's operations.

Some organizations are more likely than others

TALKING BUSINESS

Honeywell Inc., traditionally a people-oriented company, recently has been moving even closer to participative management. Viewing people positively is the basis of Honeywell's humanistic approach to management—or "humanagement." "Organizational objectives—such as increased productivity—are attainable only if they are consistent with individual objectives—such as self-esteem," says Dr. Jim Renier, head of Honeywell's Control Systems division and a leader of the humanagement movement.

Managers, according to this approach, shouldn't strive to change workers' attitudes to conform to organizational needs; rather, they should find out workers' views and structure jobs around them to achieve the most benefit for both the workers and the organization.

That isn't always easy. It places great demands on managers, who may never have had the chance to develop the human relations skills needed to manage effectively while sharing decision-making responsibility with workers. It also means managers must take a longer-term view than they are accustomed.

But the approach seems to be gaining ground at Honeywell. The success of the company's quality circles is a good example. These teams of workers, who gather to discuss work environment and productivity-related problems, have been responsible for improvements in many Honeywell plants. Ten such teams in one facility, for example, improved assembly productivity by 46 percent; at another facility, twenty-eight teams saved the company $625,724 in one year by reducing assembly hours.

Such results seem to support the humanagement philosophy—that people want to do a good job and that by helping them, management helps the company as well.

Source: Adapted from Perry Pascarella, "Humanagement at Honeywell," *Industry Week*, July 27, 1981, pp. 33–36. Used by permission.

to face rapid and often unplanned changes. For example, there is rapidly changing sales potential in the integrated circuit industry as new technology is continually brought to the marketplace. It therefore becomes essential for management to develop a flexible organization structure. Changes in structure can be made without great disruption when workers can be shifted from one department to another or when departments can be combined or new ones created.

In contrast to a rapidly changing environment, many firms operate within stable, slowly changing industries. For them, a somewhat rigid and formal organization structure may be more appropriate. For example, the container industry (bottles and cans) changes very slowly. The technology and raw materials used today are very similar to what they were 15 years ago. The American Can Company therefore has a great deal of permanency in its corporate structure.

DIRECTING

After an organization has been designed and its plans carefully developed, the next stage is the carrying out of those plans. Employees with the needed expertise and authority must set in motion those activities that are necessary for carrying out the plans and accomplishing overall objectives. **Directing** is guiding and motivating employees in order to help the firm move toward its goals. Leadership, communication, and motivation are key elements of directing.

The Nature of Directing and Supervising People

Managers are responsible for guiding the company in the right (or planned) direction. Primarily this means directing employees and controlling their work activities to see to it that the organization's goals will be met. For this, the skills of leadership, communication, and motivation are essential ingredients. In particular, the manager must understand what motivates a worker to do those things necessary to accomplish tasks and goals.

Appropriate incentives can help stimulate people to perform at their most capable levels. This high level of performance is more likely when the manager's leadership is encouraging and his or her communication is supportive and non-threatening. The manager's communication must include not only what is to be done, but also how well the employee has performed the task. Feedback, then, is an important element in the improvement of performance. Suppose you happen to take a job this summer at Disneyworld. As an employee, you'll have to follow a lengthy set of rules and regulations. Suppose, further, that somewhere along the way you make a mistake. If your supervisor brings this to your attention—in other words, gives you feedback—you can correct yourself.

Planning and organizing tend to be of greater concern to managers at the higher levels of organization, while directing and controlling activities are more important to managers in lower-level—that is, supervisory—positions. Supervisors have direct contacts with workers and frequently have wider spans of management than do executive-level managers. **Span of management** is the number of people directly reporting to a manager or supervisor. Some manufacturing supervisors have managerial spans as large as 60 to 80 employees. With this many direct employee contacts, a supervisor's skills of leadership and communication become crucial.

Leadership

Leadership is the exercise of influence of one person over another for the purpose of attaining some specified goal. Successful leadership is based on (1) the nature of the task and its accompanying goal, (2) the followers and their responsiveness to leader directives, and (3) the leader's ability to communicate and to influence behavior. In short, leadership is a function of the leader, the follower, and the situation.

Effective leadership depends on a leader's style and behavior. **Leadership style** is the way in which a leader succeeds in encouraging the follower(s) to accomplish a productive activity. Certainly, one kind is the **job-centered leader,** whose efforts are largely directed toward doing those things necessary for completing the task. Planning and organizing the workplace, assigning work duties, inspecting worker output, and closely following work rules and procedures—these are common traits of the job-centered leader.

Another kind of leader is more concerned about his/her followers and tends to be an **employee-centered leader.** Such a leader has (1) an understanding and appreciation of the personal needs of employees, (2) a desire to develop meaningful work-related relationships with employees and others, and (3) a concern for expanding the capabilities of employees as individuals and as a group.[2]

Job- or task-centered supervisors tend to be more autocratic (highly authoritarian) in their dealings with employees. In contrast, employee-centered supervisors display a democratic (or participative) approach. What this means is that job-centered leaders make decisions and issue orders with little or no input from subordinates. Employee-centered leaders, on the other hand, permit subordinates to participate in making work decisions and determining what is to be done. Both approaches can be very appropriate. In most cases, the effective supervisor is one who's capable of being concerned with both the task and the employee.

H. Ross Perot, as chief executive officer of Electronic Data Systems, Inc., is known as a very task-oriented leader. He has been very successful in developing and marketing computer software packages and integrated computer services. Another successful computer executive is a very employee-centered leader. Jim Treybig, President of Tandem Computers, a specialty computer manufacturer, leaves most of his calendar blank for employee drop-ins. Typical conversations discuss company strategy, tactics to help managers sell the company to a prospective customer or employee, and employees who have a problem their manager cannot solve.

ON THE FIRING LINE

American Business Leadership: A Lost Art?

According to Konosuke Matsushita, founder of Japan's huge Matsushita Electric Industrial Co., the twenty-first century belongs to Japan. Some observers of the American business scene are beginning to wonder if he may be right.

Some analysts ascribe the failures of US business to management, specifically its self-centered lack of interest in technology. For example, they say, tire manufacturers refused to sacrifice heavy investments in standard bias-belted tires to compete with the French firm Michelin when it introduced radials. As a result, Michelin is now manufacturing tires in the US.

American managers, these critics say, are not what they used to be. Back in the first half of this century, businesses were not so big and leaders came up through the ranks. Then in the 1950s and 60s corporations grew, merged, diversified, and became conglomerates. To manage these new, unwieldy organizations, profit centers were set up. Financial managers were hired to head them.

These new managers were usually outsiders, M.B.A.s and lawyers with no roots in the businesses they were to run. They evaluated the performance of the diverse divisions in their charge on the basis of quarterly reports—statements of short-term earnings. And so it was that top-level executives in the US became obsessed with short-term profits. They forgot that for a business to be a success, it must invest in the future, in new technology, in improved products and processes.

But other analysts suggest the picture is not as bleak as it seems. American business executives are now assessing their failures and the successes of Japan's leaders.

While some US firms need to ponder the Matsushita model, others seem to be models themselves. Delta Airlines, for instance, led the industry in service and profits in 1980. Its 1979 net income made up a fourth of the entire industry's earnings. Delta chairman W. Thomas Beebe's views on management are much like those of Matsushita. He does not like to bring outsiders into management: "Usually it turns out to be an ego trip, which is bad for the company. We want people who will enjoy and want to be working for the team."

At Delta and at other companies like it (such as IBM), there are no stars. In the example and success of these organizations, the American business community is rediscovering the value of selfless leadership. In fact, teachers at the top business schools in the country are preaching its virtue, the media are telling its stories, and nervous executives are touring Japan to study it. That is why many still maintain that the twenty-first century will not be Japan's after all.

Communication

Communication involves information-sharing between two or more people. Interpersonal communication occurs in face-to-face situations involving two people or a small group of persons, with each one having an opportunity to talk with the others. An organization communication system consists of various communication channels that gather and transmit information throughout the organization. Interpersonal and organization communications can be carried on formally or informally. A memorandum or report is a formal communication device, while casual talk between employees during break periods is an example of informal communication.

An organization's formal communication system normally has vertical and horizontal channels, with messages being sent through meetings, memos, posters, reports, and even closed-circuit TV. A vertical channel means that messages are passed up and down the management structure. A horizontal channel means passing a message from one person to the next on the same level within the organization. An informal system of

One of the most important management functions is good communications.

communication (known as the *grapevine*) may also exist and frequently parallels the formal system (see Figure 5.6). Face-to-face communication is the primary means of message transmission in the informal system: in just this way—through the grapevine—you may have heard about which teachers to study with and which ones to avoid.

The effectiveness of a supervisor depends heavily on his or her interpersonal communication skills. Most of a supervisor's daily activities require many interpersonal contacts with employees, superiors, and other supervisors. A supervisor's message must therefore be sent with words and cues that are readily understood by the message receiver. If a message fails to be understood, there must be adequate means of feedback for two-way communication, so that the failure can be reported. Also, the sender and receiver must work to avoid misunderstanding caused by noise. Noise is anything that prevents a message from being sent and clearly received, such as static in a telephone line, loud machinery in a manufacturing plant, or other people talking in a room (see Figure 5.7).

Motivation

Along with leadership and communication, a manager must be able to motivate his or her em-ployees to perform satisfactorily. **Motivation** is an internal state that causes us to behave in a particular way. Managers can to some extent stimulate and direct employee behaviors. Through encouragement, appropriate incentives, and then proper reinforcement, a supervisor can motivate a person to work and try harder. Jim Quick, supervisor at a Winn-Dixie Stores warehouse, praised Ed Gerloff for loading a truck in record time. This praise helped motivate Ed to continue working at a fast pace.

In business, a worker's motivation can be increased by (1) giving various rewards (promotion, wage increase, praise and recognition), (2) designing challenge and variety into jobs—for example, giving the worker more difficult and interesting (but achievable) tasks to perform, and (3) changing aspects of the immediate work environment, such as giving a skilled worker at the Drexel Heritage Furnishings manufacturing plant new and better tools with which to build and design bedroom furniture. These motivational techniques can be adjusted by a manager to make the employee's work and environment quite pleasant. Seeing an opportunity of satisfying personal needs through work, the employee may work harder. So when a Red Carpet realtor works longer hours and makes more sales calls, her sales commissions begin to rise, with the result that she may be motivated to work even harder.

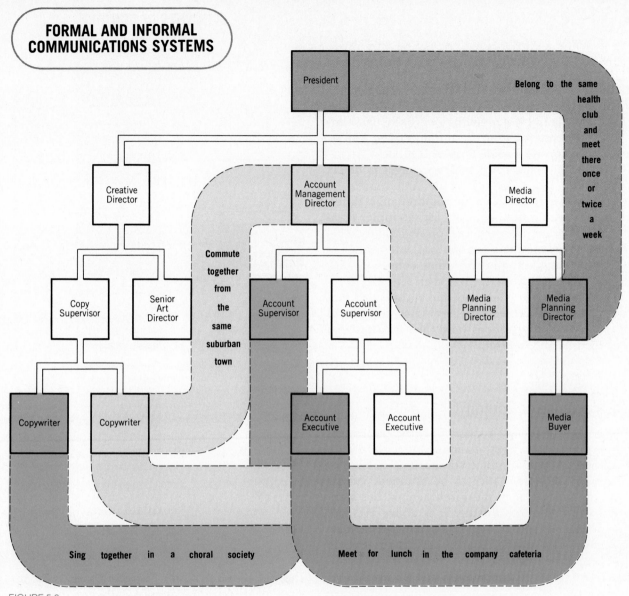

FORMAL AND INFORMAL COMMUNICATIONS SYSTEMS

President

Belong to the same health club and meet there once or twice a week

Creative Director

Account Management Director

Media Director

Commute together from the same suburban town

Copy Supervisor

Senior Art Director

Account Supervisor

Account Supervisor

Media Planning Director

Media Planning Director

Copywriter

Copywriter

Account Executive

Account Executive

Media Buyer

Sing together in a choral society

Meet for lunch in the company cafeteria

FIGURE 5.6

FIGURE 5.7

THE INTERPERSONAL COMMUNICATION PROCESS

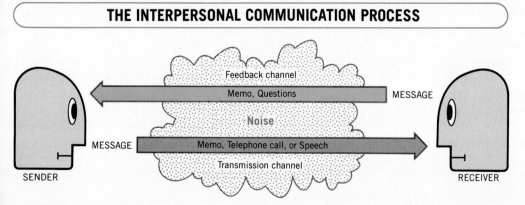

Feedback channel
Memo, Questions
MESSAGE

Noise

MESSAGE
Memo, Telephone call, or Speech
Transmission channel

SENDER

RECEIVER

CONTROLLING

Control is a process that ensures that what is being done agrees with the plans developed. The control process is based on (1) establishing standards of performance, (2) measuring employee and organizational performance, (3) correcting mistakes, and (4) containing or wholly eliminating deviations from the plan or objectives. The essence of control is some form of feedback. An active feedback system enables a manager to detect problems before they become unmanageable. This makes corrective action and change easier. In the writing of this book, for example, standards were established based on readability, coverage of topics, quality of analysis, interesting examples, and a number of other considerations. The original manuscript was then sent out to reviewers to measure how well the authors had met the publisher's objectives. Necessary corrections and reviewer suggestions were then incorporated in the final manuscript.

The Nature and Importance of Control

The control process consists of three basic steps (see Figure 5.8). First, standards of performance are set. A **performance standard** is a level or amount of performance to be attained. Actual performance is then measured against this standard to determine whether it is above average, good, merely acceptable, or less than satisfactory. Performance standards are usually expressed in concrete, quantitative terms. A firm might establish as a standard an annual return on investment of 18 percent. A customer service representative might be required to make call-back responses on almost all customer complaints within 75 minutes. A supervisor might have to respond to all worker grievances within 2 working days.

The second step of the control process is to measure actual performance and then compare this performance against the previously established standard. To measure its overall performance, a company might examine its actual rate of profit against its desired rate of profit.

The third step in the control process is taking corrective action when necessary. If results are below an acceptable level, some remedy is required to bring about acceptable performance. Assume

ELEMENTS OF CONTROL

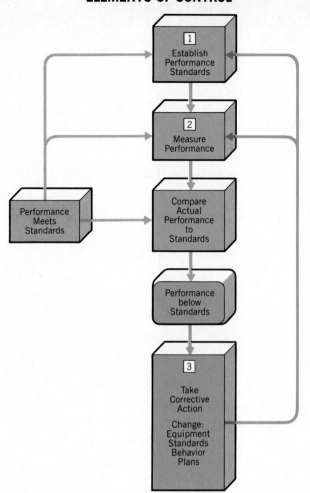

FIGURE 5.8

that the Bell Telephone Company has a standard that all directory-assistance calls are to be answered within an average of 5 rings. If a report reveals an average of 7 rings, management will have to put more information operators on duty. If the cost of hiring additional operators is too great, Bell will have to lower its service standards.

Why are management control and performance feedback systems important? First of all, they allow managers to determine the success of planning, organizing, and directing activities (see Figure 5.9). They also enable employee and workgroup behavior to be more easily directed toward organizational goals. Finally, a good control system means the firm's resources can be more systematically allocated and efficiently put to use.

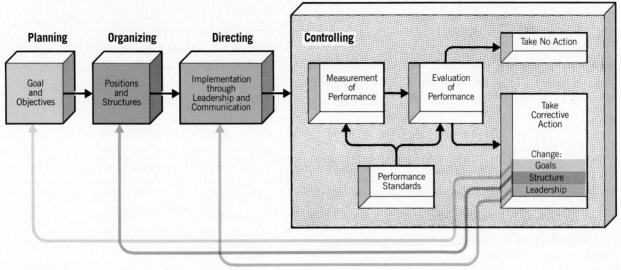

FIGURE 5.9

Types of Control

There are three basic types of control: (1) precontrol, (2) interactive control, and (3) postcontrol. All three types are used in most firms.

A **precontrol device** is one that is established before any work is performed. It is forward-looking and set in anticipation of various problems. A work rule or procedure, such as "always wear safety glasses when operating a wood lathe," is an example of a precontrol device. General Motors assembly-line workers who operate spray-paint machines are told that smoking on the job could subject the worker to a disciplinary layoff. This is a very important safety control device aimed at preventing a fire or explosion.

A control that operates while work is being performed is known as an **interactive control.** A lever, dial, or valve on a piece of equipment that can be adjusted while the equipment is in operation is an interactive control device. At GM, the automatic sprayers have a control valve that lets the operator vary the thickness of the paint.

Postcontrols are based on delayed feedback. Information is directed back to the manager after an operation has been completed. A final inspection on the GM assembly line can send a car back for missing parts or because of poor workmanship, among other reasons. Similarly, almost every company receives an end-of-the-month financial statement—a common form of postcontrol. In some cases, corrective action can be taken only in the future, such as faster collection of accounts receivable, which also becomes a measure of precontrol.

Control Techniques

Many control techniques can be developed and used in a variety of situations. A specific technique of financial control, for example, is the budget. This is a precontrol device, since it specifies in advance how much money can be spent on various items before work activity begins. The budget is also a form of interactive control because receipts and expenditures can be measured against the budget at any time during the budget period. Finally, the budget can serve as a postcontrol device by allowing total expenditures at the end of the budget period to be examined against the beginning budget.

Management and Organization Audits The **management and organization audit** is a periodic examination of the entire organization, including objectives, strategies, functions, and processes. It's a comprehensive control approach used to evaluate the quality of management. The audit examines managerial strengths and weaknesses and provides the foundation for developing better means of control (see Table 5.2).[3]

Normally a management and organization audit is conducted only once every two to five years. The process begins with the selection of the audit team or task force. Seven to eleven persons may serve as the auditors. After the design of audit procedures, the audit team gathers data for analysis. Information is assembled through use of questionnaires, interviews, evaluations, and examinations of various reports and documents. The data are then analyzed and an audit report is prepared, its findings presented in a report with charts, graphs, and tables. From start to finish, the audit of a large business firm like Xerox Corporation or Bankamerica Corporation may take as long as one year. It emphasizes improvements and typically recognizes noteworthy accomplishments besides giving company owners an idea of how well the managers and employees are performing.

PERFORMANCE AND MANAGERIAL EFFECTIVENESS

Every company hopes to get acceptable performance from its employees. **Performance** is the manner in which an action or task is carried out. Good performance depends on accountability and effectiveness. Accountability is the responsibility an employee owes an immediate superior for the resources assigned—e.g. information, personnel, raw materials, tools—and the performance or result expected from those resources. This might take the form of assembly of a product or the compilation of a report. Managers are held accountable by their immediate superiors for results. A production supervisor at a Georgia-Pacific Corporation sawmill is responsible for the board feet of lumber produced each day.

Effectiveness refers to the extent to which goals are achieved and tasks accomplished. Managers who produce expected results and continually strive to improve their performance will certainly be considered effective. If the Georgia-Pacific supervisor consistently meets the daily quota of board feet, his manager will consider him effective. Much of the improvement in managerial

TABLE 5–2
The Organizational Audit

- Should we be in this business?
- Are our objectives the right ones?
- Do we really know where we are headed?
- Is the business we think we're in really the one we are in?
- Do we have a good planning process?
  - Were there any external factors ignored?
  - Did we cover all alternatives in planning?
  - Did we get all of the available information?
  - Were our plans linked together?
    - Short-range to long-range?
    - Unit to department to division, etc.?
  - Was planning overly constricted by policy?
- Is our organization functioning well?
  - Do we need all of the units we have?
  - Are all units worth their cost?
  - Is the arrangement of units as efficient as possible?
  - Are any units understrength? Overstrength?
  - Do we need any new types of units?
  - Do we have a plan for managerial succession?
- What is the state of our policy manual?
  - Are policies up to date?
  - Do we need any new policies? In what area?
  - Are policies restricting initiative and creativity?
- What is the state of our management group?
  - Do managers operate effectively as a team?
  - Do they consult one another?
  - Where are information centers located, and are they effective?
  - Do strategic decision makers have access to the information needed?
  - Do personality clashes inhibit the functioning of the management team?
- Do managers pursue official objectives?
  - Do personal objectives clash with organizational objectives?
- Is the organization complying with the law?
- Do all managers comply with the law?
  - Equal employment opportunity?
  - Antitrust?
  - Payoffs and bribes?
  - Other laws and regulations?
- Are we in tune with social issues?
- Do we operate in accord with prevailing ethics?
- Do we accommodate interest groups?

SOURCE: Arthur Elkins, *Management, Structures, Functions and Practices,* © 1980. Addison-Wesley, Reading, MA. Page 452. Reprinted with permission.

TALKING BUSINESS

MBO programs have been implemented in many, perhaps most, large US businesses, often with great success. However, problems, usually caused by faulty implementation, have also been met with. John H. Jackson, management teacher, consultant, and author, gives the following example:

MBO came to Organization M with great fanfare from corporate headquarters. A series of seminars was conducted for operating managers explaining in great detail the process to be followed. Each manager was given target improvement areas for his or her unit. These then were to be "sold" to employees and subordinate managers.

The old performance appraisal system was replaced with a performance appraisal system replete with MBO jargon and required reports on initial meetings, goal setting meetings, follow-up meetings, appraisal meetings and performance levels relative to the objectives which had been set. Among the items on the new performance appraisal form was a rating of the subordinates' attitude toward MBO.

A consultant was called in after the first year's operation to audit the MBO system. Among the consultant's findings were the following major points:

An MBO system existed in form but not in spirit. Planning and goal setting were done in a manner consistent with MBO procedures *but* in important areas they were dictated by the superior.

MBO was used as a whip. Such great emphasis was placed on achieving goals subordinates would try to set absolute minimum objectives wherever they could to avoid failure. Further, adjustment of objective levels when a change in circumstances dictated a review of the original objectives hardly ever was done. It was made clear performance was critical and career continuation required a high level of goal attainment. Some upper level managers even calculated "percentage of total objectives achieved" on subordinates and compiled lists comparing individuals. Finally, the increase in paperwork was a major problem. . . .

Perhaps the most basic difficulty organization-wide was making a participative technique work properly in an essentially autocratic organization.

Source: Quoted material from "Using Management by Objectives: Case Studies of Four Attempts," by John H. Jackson, pp. 78–81 of the February 1981 issue of *Personnel Administrator*, copyright 1981, The American Society for Personnel Administration, 30 Park Drive, Berea, OH 44017.

performance can be generated through increased efficiency. Efficiency is the ratio of actual output to actual input. The Georgia-Pacific supervisor has increased efficiency by carefully scheduling the delivery of cut timber to the mill. This has resulted in less idle time for the saw operators.

Essential Managerial Skills

Managerial performance and effectiveness depend on taking skillful and timely actions. A skill is the ability, acquired through learning, to do something competently. Continued managerial success is determined by three kinds of managerial skills: technical, human, and conceptual.[4]

Technical Skills Technical skills are the specialized knowledge, procedures, processes, and methods that a person has at his or her command and brings to the job. For example, the Georgia-Pacific supervisor was a saw operator for 15 years before becoming a foreman. So the work and techniques that he supervises are well known to him from training and later experience. Engineers, plumbers, accountants, and architects all have technical skills acquired through experience and education. Knowledge of the managerial process and knowing how to plan, organize, direct, and control make up many of the technical skills of a manager.

Human Skills **Human skills** are primarily those that are used in working with people to accomplish organizational goals. A manager with good human skills is typically a leader who can also communicate with and motivate others. Ability to work with people, sensitivity to their needs, and a willingness to let subordinates make some decisions on their own are prime ingredients of human skills.

Conceptual Skills Creativity and the ability to think of the organization as a system are important **conceptual skills.** Possessing these, a manager can then view the business as whole, understand how its various parts fit together, and see how it relates to other organizations. For example, Tom Landry, coach of the Dallas Cowboys, must be able to foresee how well his men will play together as a team, as well as know the individual capabilities of each player.

Obviously, all three managerial skills are very important. However their usefulness will vary as your career progresses up the managerial ladder. Technical skills tend to be used more frequently at lower levels of the organization. It would be difficult for the Georgia-Pacific foreman to be effective without detailed knowledge of the sawmill and its equipment. Conceptual skills are called into play more often as a manager assumes positions of greater authority and responsiblity. Good human skills are necessary throughout one's career.

Management by Objectives and Results

Over the last 35 years, thousands of firms like Texas Instruments, General Dynamics Corporation, and the State Farm Insurance Company—as well as other types of organizations such as the U.S. Department of Health and Human Services—have tried to improve performance through a system called **management by objectives (MBO).** Introduced by Peter Drucker, a prominent management philosopher, MBO is an approach to management by which goals or objectives are set for managers. Next their performance is evaluated, based on whether they have reached their objectives. MBO, then, is an attempt to measure both manager effectiveness (by determining whether goals have been reached) and the individual's contribution to the overall success of the company.[5]

There are many variations in programs of management by objectives. Some of the more common characteristics are:

1. The superior and the employee strive to develop a clear, mutual understanding of the employee's job and its responsibilities, with special attention devoted to areas of potential performance improvement.
2. Mutual goal-setting sessions are held that involve
   (a) formulating specific job objectives,
   (b) setting time limits and target dates for accomplishment,
   (c) the superior and employee agreeing on and recording the objectives.
3. Action plans are specified that detail the "means" for accomplishing the objectives.
4. The action plans are carried out by giving the employee enough freedom to perform those activities necessary for goal attainment.
5. There is a periodic review of performance, including
   (a) an evaluation to determine whether the objectives have been accomplished and
   (b) a setting of new objectives or a modification of existing but unmet objectives.
6. Performance rewards are issued by the superior for successful employee behavior.

At first glance, MBO appears rather simple. However, it does not work out to be as easy as it looks. Management must specify realistic objectives and gain genuine superior/employee subordinate participation in the MBO program. Managers must also recognize that reaching goals is often the result of group efforts as well as of individual contributions. Aside from accomplishment of objectives, a number of benefits can be realized from an MBO program. These include (1) better superior/employee relationships, (2) improved planning and control systems, (3) more effective interpersonal communications, and (4) positive effects on employee motivation.

SUMMARY

Management brings about improvement in organizations by setting goals and then integrating human, material, and information resources toward the accomplishment of these goals. A manager (1) conducts relationships with other people as figurehead, leader, and go-between, (2) acts as information seeker and information distributor, and (3) makes decisions as organizer and risk taker, disturbance handler, resource allocator, and negotiator.

A manager's typical workday involves solving problems, making decisions, and communicating those decisions to other people. Some problems are routine and can be dealt with according to established procedures. Unforeseen problems require that the manager find a solution by being aware that an unusual problem exists, clarifying and defining the problem, conceiving alternative solutions, weighing and evaluating them, choosing a solution, implementing it, and following through to see if it succeeds. Good communication is required for gathering information to solve problems. The nature of the communication depends on the decision style of the manager—autocratic, consultative, or group-centered.

The managerial functions of planning, organizing, directing, and controlling form a tightly integrated process and cycle of behavior that consists of a manager's (1) thinking about a problem, (2) taking action, and (3) reviewing the decision and making any necessary adjustments.

Planning requires setting objectives and designing and coordinating the subgoals, policies, procedures, and methods for achieving them. Planning is based on the organization's mission and on its specific objectives. Strategic planning is long-range, comprehensive, and takes into account the business environment of the organization as well as the organization itself. Strategic plans are formulated by top managers and carried out by lower-level ones. Tactical planning is short-range and detailed, is based on central planning decisions, and

focuses on current operations. Tactical plans can take the form of policies, procedures, or rules.

In order to develop objectives and plans, managers need an organized method of collecting, evaluating, condensing, arranging, and presenting sound, reliable information. Computer-based management decision support systems are a new aid in information management.

Organizing creates structure, relationships, and other orderly arrangements to make the best use of an organization's assets and to bring about coordinated and integrated effort of all parts to reach the organization's goals. Organizations continually undergo change. Rapid change calls for flexible organization structure, while stable, slowly changing industries may have more rigid and formal structures.

Directing is guiding and motivating employees to help the firm move toward its goals. This activity calls for skills in leadership, communication, and motivation.

Controlling ensures that what is being done agrees with management's plans. The control process is based on establishing standards of performance, measuring performance and comparing it with the standards, and correcting mistakes when necessary. The essence of control is feedback. Three basic types of control are precontrol, interactive control, and postcontrol. The management and organization audit is a comprehensive control approach used to evaluate the quality of management.

Good employee performance depends on accountability and effectiveness. Successful managerial performance is determined by three kinds of skills—technical, human, and conceptual. Over the last 30 years, many firms have attempted to improve performance by using the management-by-objectives (MBO) system, by which goals are set and performance is evaluated based on whether the objectives have been met.

KEY TERMS

autocratic decision
 style
conceptual skills
consultative decision
 style
control

REVIEW QUESTIONS

1. What are the roles of a manager?
2. Describe the steps in the decision-making process. In what sequence do they occur?
3. What are the four functions of management? Briefly describe each.
4. Describe the three types of control. Why is each important?
5. What are the three management skills? Which is more important to upper management? To lower-level managers?
6. Describe the three elements in an organiza-

tion's communication system. How are they used?
7. What is the distinction between efficiency and effectiveness?
8. Explain why goals should be quantifiable and measurable.

DISCUSSION QUESTIONS

1. What are the three leadership styles? Which would be most appropriate for assembly-line workers? retail clerks in a medium-size department store? a door-to-door encyclopedia sales force? a group of college professors?
2. What effect have unions and government regulations had on managers' rights to manage? Give several examples.
3. Give examples of strategic and tactical planning for: a manufacturer of commercial airliners, a toy maker, a men's clothing store, Burger King.
4. Is your present work supervisor (or immediate past supervisor if you are not now employed) employee- or task-centered? Justify your opinion.
5. Is a budget a planning or control device, or both? How is it used by managers?
6. What is the effect of change (or lack of change) on the performance of organizational structure? Give several examples including a manufacturer of desk-top computers, a maker of railroad equipment, and a conglomerate.

CASE: THE STRONG MANAGER AND HIS BLOOMING BUSINESS

George Greene is president of the blooming and thriving Greene Thumb Company, a $6 million dollar family-owned nursery business. Instead of enjoying the excitement of a growing business, Greene found himself overwhelmed by management problems growing like weeds all around him. Advance purchasing decisions had been wrong; sales were lagging; new product shipments were late coming in, (so that deliveries would be late to customers); employees were demoralized; customers were grumbling; accounting records were in a mess; tax returns were due; and piles of paperwork on Greene's desk seemed to get higher every day.

Ordinarily this energetic, middle-aged executive would have mustered his courage and began tackling the problems. But now he stared at a piece of bad news that wouldn't go away. The medical report from his doctor showed high blood pressure and possible heart problems. His management roof was caving in, just at a time when the company should be gearing up for the annual frenzy of fresh spring business. *Now* what was he going to do? Nobody could run the company the way he did. And how *did* he run it? With a strong hand, as his father did—the *indispensable man.* Like father, like son.

But wait a minute: what about his top employees? These were five people who had been with the company anywhere from 6 to 20 years: Len Powers, the CPA; Don Dixon, who did the purchasing; Mary Ziegler, advertising and promotions; Sam Shore, the lead salesman; and son George Jr., who had just completed a degree in Business Administration, with a major in Personnel (he had worked on and off at the nursery since high school).

Well, maybe this would be a good time for a staff meeting—although George never really put much faith in meetings. There was usually too much work to be done to waste time in meetings!

1. How did George Greene get into this predicament anyway?
2. What should he do about it?
3. Is there much hope for the survival of the business—and George?

CASE: THE PRESIDENT LEFT NO FUTURE

Howard Anthony was a very creative president. Heath Company was born of his dreams and schemes. After World War II, he stumbled on a great idea that really made a fortune for him and for those who backed him to form a corporation and launch the Heathkit Company. He bought surplus parts from the government, mostly for aircraft, and sold them directly to people who needed parts for their airplanes. These parts included airspeed indicators, clocks, altimeters, and all kinds of other gauges and gadgets which could be sold for much more than he paid for them but still cheaper than new parts and gauges being manufactured for public purchase.

When these supplies were exhausted, Anthony had made enough money to continue adding new products for sale in the marketplace. He sensed that most people like to do things themselves, so he put together meters and gauges that were partially finished, providing essential components that could not be readily manufactured or fabricated in the garage. He made voltameters, ammeters, oscilloscopes, and many other gadgets that were fun for do-it-yourselfers to assemble. He included manuals, diagrams, and instructions to guide anyone who was motivated to complete the kit. His products sold like popcorn at the movies, and Anthony was well on his way to being a successful entrepreneur.

Howard Anthony was not the best administrator—his strengths lay in invention, innovation, and creativity. He loved to dream up new ideas, put them on the drawing board, make schematics and diagrams, then manufacture them, and put them up for sale. He was best on the earlier stages of this process and not the later. Yet he always managed to lure friends with administrative and managerial talents to help him run the company to get the job done. With such a genius creating new products as fast as they could be manufactured and sold, the future of Heathkit looked very bright and promising. And Howard Anthony had made his million, and in the process rewarded his managers very generously.

Then one bright sunny day Howard Anthony took off in his airplane to fly across Lake Michigan to Chicago or some other big town when his plane went down in the lake. All of his wonderful ideas for future products, innovations, and inventions seemed to drown in the lake with this brilliant man.

1. What were Howard Anthony's strengths, and were they enough to make the company successful?
2. What were Howard Anthony's weaknesses and how could they have been corrected?
3. What should his managers have done to guarantee the future of this creative organization?

CHAPTER 6

THE INTERNAL ORGANIZATION

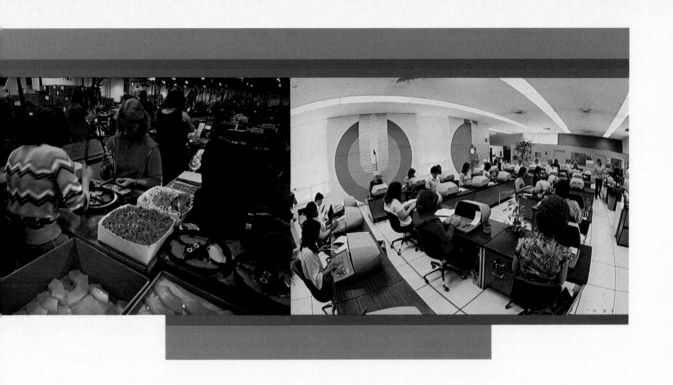

After studying this chapter you should be able to:

1 Describe the considerations in building a formal organization.
2 Understand how external environments influence organizational development.
3 Understand the impact of technology on organizational design.
4 Explain the difference between formal and informal organizations and how each functions.
5 Describe organizational authority and the sources of authority.
6 Explain the bases for organizing departments within an organization.
7 Understand the roles of line and staff members of an organization.

Twice Lars Nivelius and Bengt Ågren built up a successful construction business. The first time, it was for a large Swedish corporation. The corporation swallowed up their creation, making it part of a division with a hierarchical chart full of little square boxes defining limits of responsibility. In typical pyramid fashion, site supervisors report to project leaders who report to vice-presidents who report to the president.

Nivelius and Ågren were offered top jobs with the new division, but a huge corporate hierarchy held no appeal for them. Using their own savings, they set up offices in a small hotel and submitted their first construction bid. Three days later they got the job, and within two months the new enterprise—Bygg Gruppen—had won two more.

Here was the chance to organize the way they really wanted to. Looking at their organization chart, you see not a pyramid but a molecular (i.e. interconnected) structure with circles showing overlapping areas of responsibility. There are no vice-presidents or supervisors. Each of the firm's eight project leaders acts as a profit manager and reports directly to the co-owners.

BG's success is attributed to these project leaders, each of whom earns the same salary—and more than they'd get at bigger firms. They also share 20% of profits. Each has complete autonomy, performing all the tasks usually done by functional experts, such as quantity surveyors, estimators, and site managers. Project leaders must even find contracts. They draw up their own bids, specify materials, rent machinery, and hire subcontractors. They also deal with all the technical and labor problems on the site.

Every two weeks the eight project leaders meet as a group with the two co-owners. Says Nivelius, "At these meetings, everyone gets to know what everyone else is doing, and what problems they have. . . . We also review the status of each project and discuss such things as the quality of a new subcontractor's work and new business." Adds Ågren: "If a project leader with a lot of work knows of new business that he can't handle, he will pass that on to other project leaders. We try to share out the workload."

Central control and monitoring originate from the co-owners. The firm minimizes costs by having a central buying function, operating without a storage yard, renting almost all machinery and equipment—and relying wholly on the subcontractors for skilled workers, such as plumbers, roofers, and electricians. BG's masons know how to wield hammers, and their carpenters know how to work with trowels. "We have no demarcation problems," says one project leader, "simply because the workers want and are encouraged to learn new skills, and the unions accept this."

Dick Söderholm, a project leader, sings the praises of molecular organizational structure this way: "In a larger firm I carried out one function. . . . Here I am everything. I am the guy who turns a piece of paper into a finished product. It's an exciting task. But there is great satisfaction in being your own boss and making your own decisions without having to go through layers and layers of bureaucracy."

Adapted by permission from Jules Arbose, "A Construction Company That Really Works," *International Management* 37 (January 1982): 36–38. Reprinted by special permission from International Management. Copyright © McGraw-Hill Publications Company. All rights reserved.

THE NATURE OF AN ORGANIZATION

An organization—molecular, pyramid, or other—is a group of individuals acting in different but interrelated roles designed to achieve a goal. The formal organization, with its channels of authority and accountability, reveals the interrelations of these roles and suggests something of the inner workings of a firm. Figure 6.1 shows a typical organization chart. Its structure lays out a framework for accomplishing activities and tasks. The information provided by an organization chart can be useful to managers and employees. However, there is much important information *not* found in the formal chart, as you will see later in the chapter.

Organization Structure

Structure implies order, design, and interrelation. **Organization structure,** then, is the order and design of relationships among employees, jobs, and departments within the firm. These relationships consist of human, material, financial, and information resources. For example, each Sears store has a customer service desk and a customer services manager who communicates with employees of the accounting department about returned merchandise.

The management hierarchy generally develops in a pyramid fashion (see Figure 6.2). The pyramid can be roughly divided into three categories: top management, middle management, and supervisory management. Top managers are responsible for broad, sweeping decisions that determine the nature and scope of the company. They must decide where to build new plants, what new products to offer, and what goals the company should pursue. Middle managers are more involved with planning for a shorter time span and often take part in solving day-to-day problems. Middle managers include department heads, plant managers, deans at universities, and office managers in various branches of government.

Supervisory managers are responsible for the activities of nonmanagement workers such as production-line employees, clerks, salespersons, and maintenance workers. Supervisory managers are less involved in future planning and must monitor and evaluate worker progress weekly, daily, or sometimes continuously.

The organization chart reveals a certain amount of stability in the relationships among people, jobs, and departments. However, formal relationships can change quickly when management decides to redesign the structure. Moreover the informal interpersonal relationships that exist among managers and employees can be very different from those formally displayed on the chart. The informal social structure may at times be

FIGURE 6.1

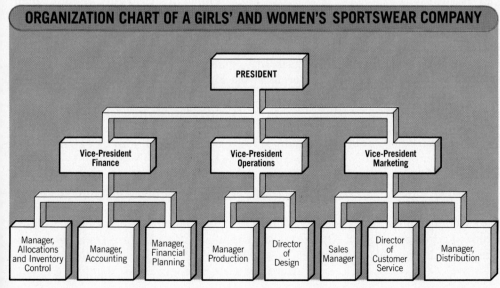

ORGANIZATION CHART OF A GIRLS' AND WOMEN'S SPORTSWEAR COMPANY

PRESIDENT

Vice-President Finance · Vice-President Operations · Vice-President Marketing

Manager, Allocations and Inventory Control · Manager, Accounting · Manager, Financial Planning · Manager Production · Director of Design · Sales Manager · Director of Customer Service · Manager, Distribution

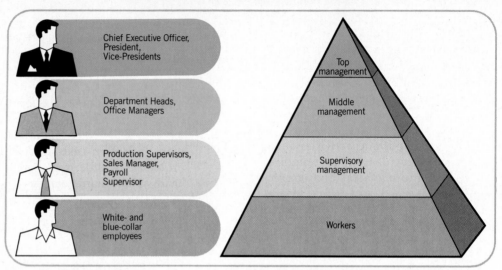

FIGURE 6.2

even more efficient in accomplishing various tasks. For example, at a Levi Strauss plant in California, the manager's secretary was friendly with one of the supervisors. Through this informal relationship, the supervisor learned of coming changes in the plant's production schedule before news of the changes reached others via the formal channels. This enabled the supervisor to get a head start on planning manpower requirements in scheduling vacations and time off.

Structural Building Blocks, Formal Considerations

The basic building block for creating an organization's structure is the organization's primary task. The primary task is the activity or set of activities that forms the basis for an organization's existence. The primary task of Findlay Enterprises, a residential subdivision developer, is to create real estate value through installing streets, sidewalks, water pipes, and other services necessary for homebuilders to construct and sell houses. The primary task of General Motors is to design, assemble, sell, and deliver safe, fuel-efficient cars.

There are several important considerations in designing a structure to accomplish the firm's primary task. These include (1) division of labor, (2) span of control, (3) the hierarchy, and (4) departmentation.

Division of Labor and Specialization The primary task can be broken down into smaller tasks, with a separate worker or group of workers assigned to perform each of these subtasks. This process of dividing the work and assigning tasks to workers is commonly labeled *division of labor*. At Findlay Enterprises only one of five supervisors is responsible for the installation of water and sewer pipes. Many examples of labor division can be found in the activities of a large manufacturing firm. These range from the assembly line to the office to the shipping dock, where distribution takes place. In some areas of the business, division of labor may be more extensive than it is in other areas. For example, in a Ford auto assembly plant some workers install only front-door-window glass—a very specific task.

When a company further divides its primary task into smaller work units, *specialization* increases (see Figure 6.3). As a worker becomes a specialist and performs one or a small number of tasks, he or she develops greater skill—and presumably greater efficiency—in doing the assigned job. However under conditions of extreme, routinized division of labor, the job may become too simple and repetitive. This may lead to reduced motivation, boredom, and therefore decreased production. A good example of this can be seen in an auto assembly plant where a worker may install only rearview mirrors. In recent years many firms (e.g. SAAB, Texas Instruments, General Motors) have experienced these conditions of rou-

DIVISION OF LABOR AND WORKER SPECIALIZATION IN DEVELOPING A NEW PRODUCT

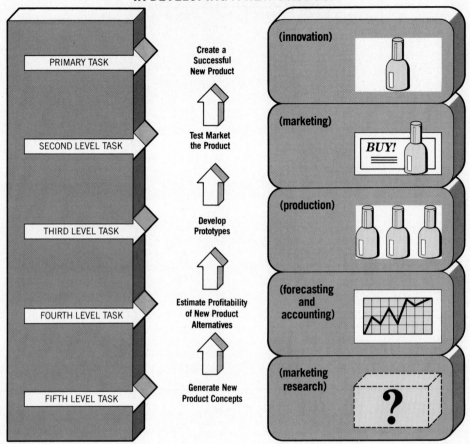

FIGURE 6.3

tinization. They have begun to reverse the trend by expanding an employee's job to increase job challenge and worker motivation.

Span of Control   The number of employees reporting directly to a manager determines the manager's **span of control**. A manager's span of control could be as narrow as 2 or 3 employees or as wide as 50 to 80. If hundreds perform basically the same job, a single supervisor may be able to manage as many as 60 of them effectively.

Such might be the case at a Levi's plant, where hundreds of sewing machine operators are working from identical patterns. On the other hand, a manager can probably effectively supervise only a small number of employees (8 or fewer) if they perform complex and different tasks. This would probably be the case with 8 research chemists at G. D. Searle, a large manufacturer of pharmaceuticals. In addition to being affected by the

nature of the task, span of control is also affected by whether (1) employees are located together or not, (2) the manager can effectively delegate task responsbilities, and (3) employees are skillful and highly motivated.

The Managerial Hierarchy   An aspect of organizations that is closely related to management span is the managerial hierarchy. **Hierarchy** refers to the number of levels of management within the business, arranged by degree of authority. A wide span of control usually implies few managerial levels. Narrow span produces more levels of management (see Figure 6.4). Wide span of control creates what is called a **flat structure** while a more narrow span results in a **tall structure** (and more managers). Tall structures sometimes become bureaucracies, with more managers than are actually required to accomplish the organization's goals. This can be very expen-

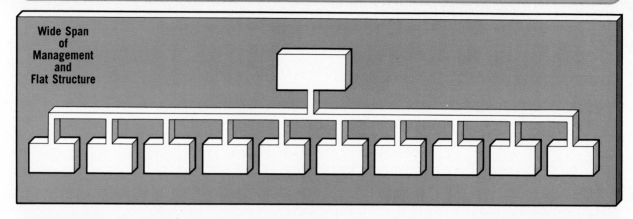

FLAT AND TALL STRUCTURES WITH SAME NUMBER OF POSITIONS

Wide Span
of
Management
and
Flat Structure

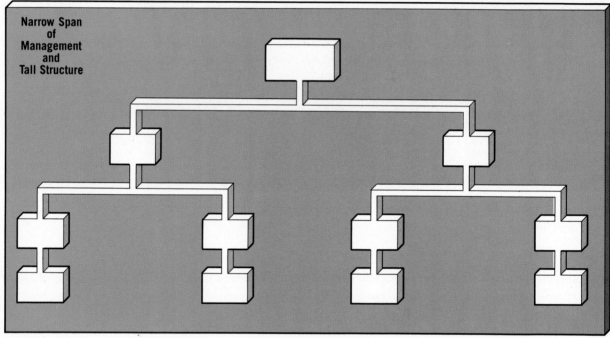

Narrow Span
of
Management
and
Tall Structure

FIGURE 6.4

sive and can also slow down the decision-making process.

With the organization changes taking place in Sears, Roebuck, its relatively flat structure is giving way to a taller organization structure. You perhaps already know that colleges and universities tend to have relatively flat structures. There are only two or three levels of administration between the faculty member and the president. Military organizations, however, usually have many levels (or ranks) of management and are considered relatively tall organizations.

Departmentation   Over the years an organization like General Motors expands from a few people and one product to hundreds (or thousands) of employees and many products. As growth occurs, it becomes necessary to group people, products, and various resources into departments, and divisions. The process of establishing departments is called **departmentation.** Several departments may be organized into a division. The basis on which an organization is divided includes such elements as major business function, product produced or sold, production process, type of cus-

TALKING BUSINESS

To draw workers into the process of improving quality, corporations are turning their backs on the old style of "scientific management" that grew out of Frederick Taylor's theories early in the century. It's now recognized that quality suffers when employees are assigned to isolated, limited tasks and don't understand what they are doing. Unfeeling managers and uncaring workers often become adversaries despite mutual interests. Today workers are being asked to think about what they are doing and how it can be done better. The quality circle is a popular vehicle for involving blue-collar employees in quality and other improvements. In Japan, about 5 million workers belong to circles of about ten people each. The circles made their mark in the US early in the 1970s when GM used them to help turn around a badly demoralized plant at Tarrytown, New York. Quality improved markedly, while absenteeism and grievance claims dropped. About 85 GM plants are now experimenting with circles. Ford and Chrysler are working on similar ideas, with the enthusiastic cooperation of the United Auto Workers.

Some 200 US companies are trying circles, though not always successfully. Unless the workers get some training and help from a quality specialist, circles can become aimless kaffeeklatsches. [But many companies agree that quality circles can work. Says the president of one manufacturing firm,] "We are seeing enormous results in better quality and better processes."

Source: Excerpted from Jeremy Main, "The Battle for Quality Begins," *Fortune*, December 29, 1980, pp. 28–33. ©1980 Time Inc. Courtesy of Fortune Magazine.

tomer, and territory or geographic area. General Motors is primarily organized along product lines (e.g. its Chevrolet, Pontiac, Oldsmobile, Buick, and Cadillac cars). However geographic areas are the basic lines along which GM arranges its sales forces, customer services, and dealer relations.

Product and functional forms of departmentation are the most common (see Figure 6.5), although in many large manufacturing firms departments of all types will be found. Products are sometimes grouped into divisions. For example, Procter & Gamble has 12 divisions: (1) packaged soap and detergent, (2) bar soap and household cleaning products, (3) industrial chemicals, (4) food products, (5) toilet goods, (6) paper products, (7) cellulose and specialties, (8) crushing, (9) coffee, (10) industrial cleaning products, (11) industrial food, and (12) international. (The twelfth is the exception to organization by product; here the basis is geographic.)

Within each product division there may be several functional departments to carry out various

activities (e.g. finance, personnel, manufacturing, marketing and sales, distribution and transportation). Sales territories may be defined by geographic areas; or sales representatives may be grouped by type of customer. IBM sales representatives are divided by size (large v. small) of computer purchased.

Many commercial banks, for example, group people, jobs, and activities in three different ways and so have three basic forms of departmentation (see Figure 6.6). One departmental form is to group together those people and jobs concerned with loans. This is product departmentation. Each loan officer is responsible for review and approval of loan applications, distribution of loan proceeds, and collection of the borrowed money. This permits the loan officer to develop a more thorough knowledge of loan and investment documents and customers' financial needs.

Another form of bank departmentation is grouping persons and jobs concerned with banking services and operations. These include check-

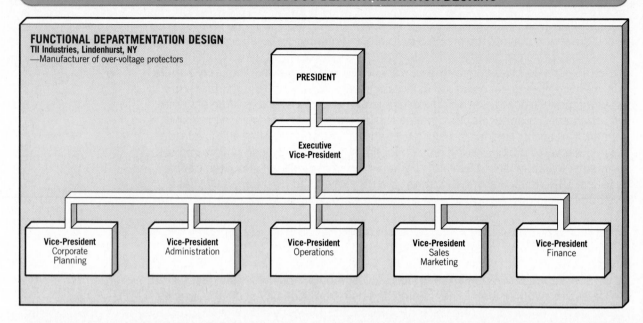

FUNCTIONAL DEPARTMENTATION DESIGN
TII Industries, Lindenhurst, NY
—Manufacturer of over-voltage protectors

PRESIDENT

Executive Vice-President

| Vice-President Corporate Planning | Vice-President Administration | Vice-President Operations | Vice-President Sales Marketing | Vice-President Finance |

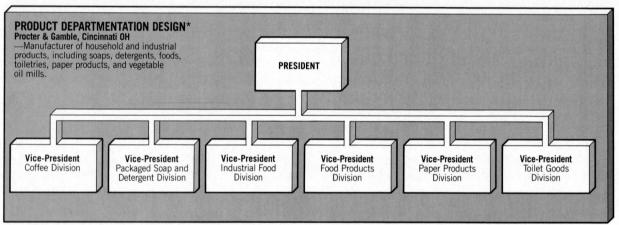

PRODUCT DEPARTMENTATION DESIGN*
Procter & Gamble, Cincinnati OH
—Manufacturer of household and industrial products, including soaps, detergents, foods, toiletries, paper products, and vegetable oil mills.

PRESIDENT

| Vice-President Coffee Division | Vice-President Packaged Soap and Detergent Division | Vice-President Industrial Food Division | Vice-President Food Products Division | Vice-President Paper Products Division | Vice-President Toilet Goods Division |

*Excerpted from the P&G organization chart

FIGURE 6.5

ing and savings accounts, deposits and withdrawals, currency exchange, and related tasks. This is functional departmentation. While the loan departments may not require very many officers and employees, several of these standard banking services may require relatively large numbers of employees (e.g. tellers, check processors). Each service is a different basic process or sequence of banking operations.

A third form of bank departmentation would be based on location (or geographic area), since a bank may have several—or even, like Citicorp, many—branches located throughout city, county, and state. Each branch offers various standard services and lends money to customers. The branch manager would be most knowledgeable about any unique and different conditions of the area. He or she could make adjustments in banking hours, changes in certain service procedures, and modifications of the criteria used in making loan decisions.

Regardless of which specific departmental form(s) an organization has, people, machines, and other resources are grouped to make for greater unity of direction to accomplish the firm's goals.

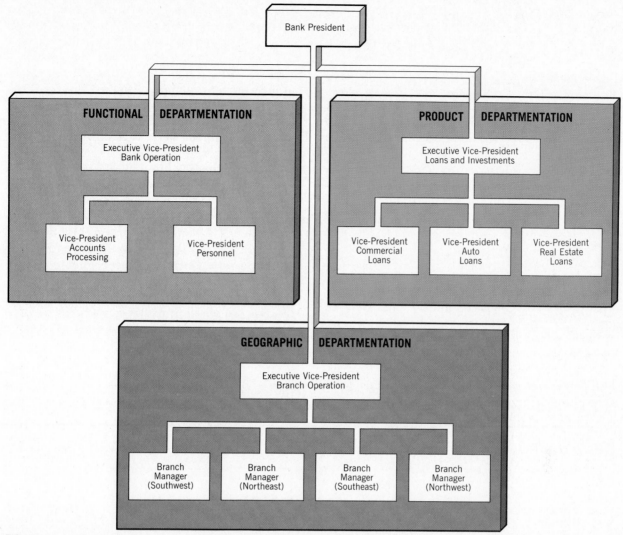

FIGURE 6.6

The Informal Organization

The formal aspects of the business such as are shown by the organization chart are of great importance. But the informal characteristics can also play a major role in developing an effective organization. These aspects of the firm are referred to as its **informal structure or organization.**

The organization chart shows the formal authority relationships as they exist between superiors and employees throughout the organization.

There are many other relationships (some work-related and others not) between people at the same organizational level and between persons at different levels in different departments that are not shown on the chart. Many of these unrecorded relationships are based on friendship.

Over time these informal relationships may develop into an informal network of communication channels. For example, Pat Gray is sales manager for the Peabody Coal Company and frequently has lunch with Ed Selchert, the mining supervisor. Pat and Ed have no formal link in the organization structure—they are in different areas of the company—yet they communicate almost daily. If Pat is having difficulty meeting a shipping date, Ed will usually use his influence to help Pat meet the deadline.

Sometimes such informal channels are referred to as the *grapevine* or *rumor mill* or the *intelligence network*. The informal network can at times work very efficiently in transmitting various messages. However, information conveyed in this way is not necessarily accurate. Consider the student intelligence network at a school, with its "inside info" about instructors and their course requirements, especially term papers and examinations. How accurate is this kind of information? You might not like to have your grades depend on it.

HOW THE ENVIRONMENT AFFECTS ORGANIZATION DESIGN

A business firm is created to fulfill some product or service need as determined by the marketplace. Avis Inc. was founded to give business travelers automobile transportation. However some years later Budget Rent-A-Car was established to give the traveler more economical automobile transportation. For a company to produce and sell its services, it therefore has to interact continuously

with others in the external environment. As we have already seen in Chapter 5, the business environment is a complex of social, political, economic, and technological factors that affect a firm's operations. The "others" in a firm's external environment include business firms, government agencies, suppliers of materials, consumers, labor unions, and financial institutions—to name several (see Figure 6.7).

The characteristics of these other organizations and the unique relationships that develop between them and the firm influence the organizational design of the firm. For example, employment requirements as specified by the federal government's Equal Employment Opportunity Commission (EEOC) have caused firms like Motorola and State Farm Insurance to create affirmative action offices within their personnel departments. Competition by Budget and other economy car rental firms has caused Avis to open up more offices serving smaller markets (local airports) than it probably would otherwise do.

Relationship of the Firm to Its Environment

Once a business has been formed and begins to operate, its basic concerns revolve around survival

Information often travels through the grapevine.

THE RELATIONSHIP OF A BUSINESS FIRM TO ITS EXTERNAL ENVIRONMENT

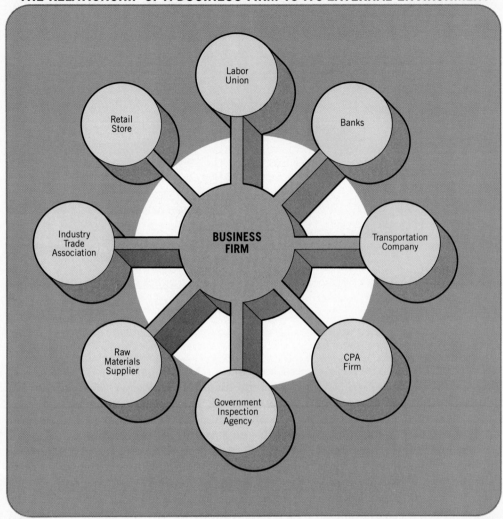

Labor
Union

Retail
Store

Banks

Industry
Trade
Association

**BUSINESS
FIRM**

Transportation
Company

Raw
Materials
Supplier

CPA
Firm

Government
Inspection
Agency

FIGURE 6.7

and growth. To survive, a business firm must develop and maintain beneficial exchange relationships with various organizations in the business environment. An exchange occurs when a company or person obtains a desired object from another company or person by offering something in return. Two very important exchange relationships are (1) buying supplies and raw materials for cash or credit and (2) making sales to customers for cash or credit. Many exchange relationships are built on mutual dependence—that is, the relationship by which certain organizations are *interdependent*. Whirlpool Corporation has for years greatly depended on Sears Roebuck as the primary buyer of its major home appliance products. For its part, Sears has depended on

Whirlpool production and quality. General Motors depends on Borg-Warner Corporation for its car transmissions. In turn, Borg-Warner depends on GM for a major share of its sales revenues.

Organizational interdependencies mean that business firms operate as open systems. An **open system** is a firm that continuously engages in exchange transactions with the external environment. As such, it gets various resources (capital, raw materials, etc.) from the environment, transforms them into a product, and then delivers the product to the environment by selling it (see Figure 6.8). For example, Borg-Warner supplies transmissions that ultimately become part of Chevrolet, Buick, and other GM cars, which are then delivered to dealers that sell them to buyers.

THE BUSINESS FIRM IS AN OPEN SYSTEM

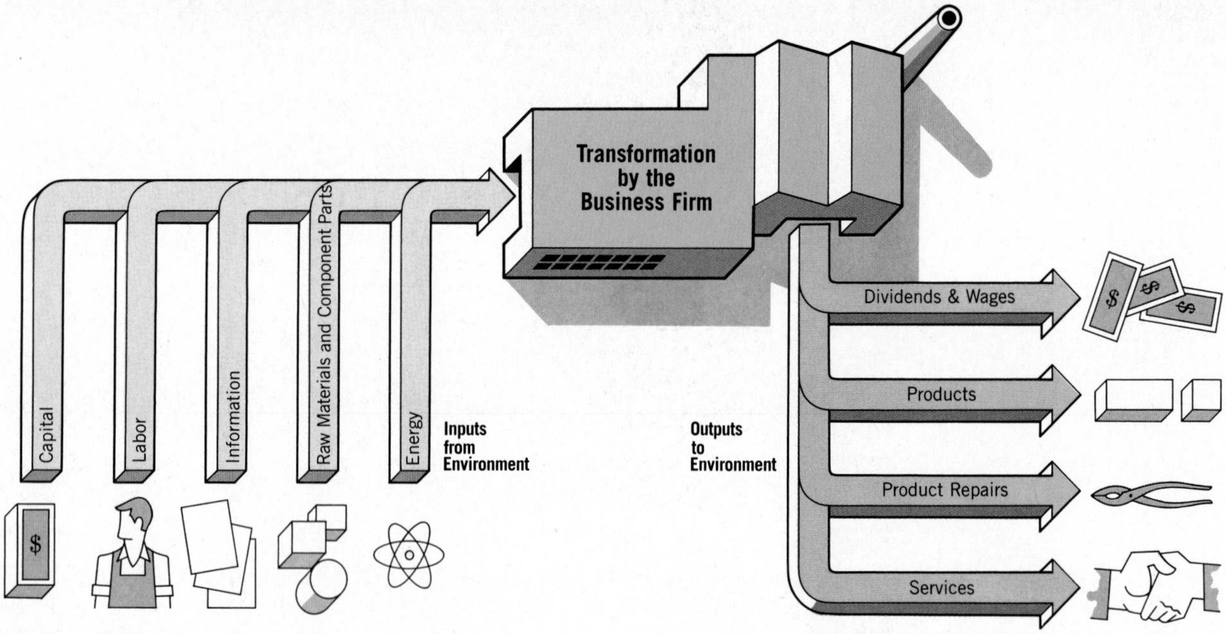

Transformation by the Business Firm

Inputs from Environment

Capital | Labor | Information | Raw Materials and Component Parts | Energy

Outputs to Environment

Dividends & Wages

Products

Product Repairs

Services

FIGURE 6.8

(Some of these buyers may be Borg-Warner employees!)

To keep the business system flowing, favorable relationships with organizations and various groups in the environment must be maintained. For Borg-Warner to continue selling transmissions to GM, it must produce a high-quality product that meets GM's standards. Also, the business must be able to anticipate—and adjust to—changes that may occur within the environment. For example, in recent years the public's concern for automobile safety has necessitated the addition of many safety features to our cars.

Environmental Change and Uncertainty

For some firms, environments are relatively stable with changes taking place very slowly, as in the steel and iron industries. Other firms operate within rapidly changing environments that have high degrees of uncertainty. The clothing and fashion industry experiences swift—almost sudden—change, with its attendant risk. In fact fashion designers must constantly anticipate changes in apparel trends and the shifting tastes of the consumer. Once the cloth has been cut, the designer and clothing manufacturer have committed large resources to a particular clothing style. If their prediction of consumer acceptance turns out to be wrong, financial losses may be large.

To prevent such loss and minimize threats to its growth and survival, a firm may have to adopt a set of flexible structural arrangements. The Minnesota Mining & Manufacturing Company (3M) reorganized its ten business groups into four product-service sections as a response to changes in the firm's environment. Top management believed that the old organizational structure was too fragmented to allow the firm to develop an integrated line of office products, a necessity in today's market.

Environmental Changes Environmental change (and disturbance) can come from a variety of sources and affect businesses in different ways. Some changes can be predicted while others cannot. More than anything else, general economic conditions and the federal government probably influence the firm most directly. For example, Congress may enact an increase in the minimum wage. This type of change is usually announced sufficiently in advance so that business firms and other organizations can make the necessary adjustments in personnel staffing and work scheduling. Some firms will be greatly affected, requiring major adjustments. Other firms

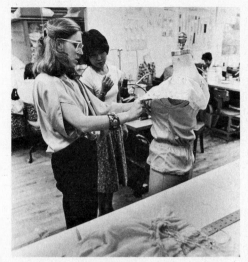

In the fashion industry, styles can be changed almost overnight. But in some of the metals industries, change occurs very slowly.

will be minimally affected, if at all. An increase in the minimum wage means major changes for firms like Wendy's and Jack-in-the-Box in the fast-food industry. On the other hand, steel manufacturers like Bethlehem and U.S. Steel are rarely affected by such a change because of the high wage they pay their employees.

Responding to Environmental Changes Environmental changes may require organization adjustments, some more substantial than others. If a change outside the firm is likely to recur, but only infrequently, then changing some procedure may be all that is needed. However a major disturbance in the environment that occurs frequently enough could lead to an important change within the organization. Suppose that the quality of the Borg-Warner supplies and materials used by General Motors began to decline; suppose too that there were not any available substitutes. This would be immediately signaled by GM's quality control department, which would then more carefully inspect incoming parts. The head of this department thus serves as an important link in GM's ties to Borg-Warner and other suppliers.

The Importance of People Who Meet the Public

The new quality control department head may operate outside the immediate boundaries of the firm as much as within them. What are these boundaries? They can be defined in terms of the firm's physical plant, product market, labor market, and other contacts with the environment by management personnel and other employees. In short, the firm has multiple **boundaries** (points of contact) with other organizations and interested groups. Several persons (such as the chief executive officer, the marketing researcher, the personnel director, a sales representative, and a labor negotiator) work at or near these various boundaries. Each **boundary spanner** (person who comes into contact with others outside the firm) links the firm with the environment. The success of the firm greatly depends on the effectiveness of these boundary spanners.[1]

At General Motors, boundary spanners include the corporation's purchasing agents and its sales representatives. Purchasing agents acquire raw materials and other goods and services for the organization. Salespersons hope to sell GM cars to retail dealers. Besides performing the routine tasks of purchasing raw materials and closing sales, these people gather information to help the company better foresee problems and exploit opportunities.

Information Gathering One of the important duties of a boundary spanner involves data gathering. Sales representatives, for example, are continually seeking information about competitors' products. A GM salesperson is always interested in how consumers are reacting to new Ford prod-

PERSPECTIVE ON SMALL BUSINESS

Perhaps as much as any other company, Celestial Seasonings Inc. was a product of the 1970s: a free-spirited outfit born of flower children picking herbs in the mountains and mixing them for "tea," which they began selling to natural-food stores.

With characteristic fancy, the company took its name from a founder's brother's girlfriend whose nickname was, really, Celestial Seasonings. Then it went on to give the world Red Zinger, Morning Thunder and other brews, and to help launch the market for herb teas. All the while, its energetic young managers combined some very hard work with a happy sort of love-and-peace approach that some observers dubbed "cosmic capitalism."

But now it is the 1980s, and the cosmic capitalists have grown up. Herb tea is big business, with industry sales of perhaps $70 million a year; the closely held Celestial Seasonings, with annual revenues of around $16 million, is the leader of the industry. As might befit its position, it is behaving a little differently than it used to.

It is becoming mainstream.

[The company, founded in Boulder, Colorado, in 1971 by Morris J. (Mo) Siegel and John Hay, who were "looking for something to do one summer," now makes 40 kinds of herbal tea. During the years 1976–1981, its sales increased fivefold, attracting the attention of such industry giants as Thomas J. Lipton, Inc., which is now entering the herb-tea business.]

But Celestial Seasonings' success has come at the expense of its old image. Once a shining light of the counterculture, the company now has found such middle-American acceptance that its products are to be found on many neighborhood grocery shelves. It advertises in such magazines as McCall's and Redbook.

And it has been hiring managers away from such establishment enclaves as PepsiCo Inc., Coca-Cola Co., J. M. Smucker Co.

Celestial Seasonings still isn't Procter & Gamble by a long shot. But it also isn't that charmed cottage industry—men gathering herbs and blending them for tea, their wives sewing muslin bags to hold it—that many of the company's early supporters hoped might bring a fresh spirit to the corporate world.

"Somewhere along the line, Mo and the others had to make a decision whether they were going to run this like a real live American business, or were they going to continue to hold eight-hour staff meetings every Wednesday and dwell on philosophical attributes of tea bags," [says a former associate, Jeff Morgan].

"From a business aspect," he adds, "the right decision was probably made: to treat it like a business."

SOURCE: Excerpted from Eric Morgenthaler, "Herb Tea's Pioneer: From Hippie Origins to $16 Million a Year," *Wall Street Journal*, May 6, 1981, pp. 1, 17. Reprinted by permission of The Wall Street Journal, © Dow Jones & Company, Inc., 1981. All rights reserved.

ucts. Much of this information is obtained through routine contacts with established customers (GM dealers). Some information also comes through talking with competing sales representatives at industry trade fairs and conventions—such as the U.S. auto show held annually in New York.

Problems and Opportunities Potential problems and opportunities must be quickly acted on by the firm that operates within frequently changing environments. Once again, the data-gathering activities of people working at or near organizational boundaries can be helpful to management. Problems can be more easily identified,

Sales reps act as boundary spanners.

ished products and services (outputs). Technology is therefore essential for effective performance of the firm's primary task. Some technologies are highly sophisticated and computer controlled, such as spot-welding robots on the General Motors auto assembly line. Other technologies are handicraft in nature and depend on the manual skills of the worker, as in the manufacture of finely tooled cowboy boots using exotic leathers.

Technology and organization structure are closely interrelated. For example, there are few departments at the Tony Lama Company because western boots are made there by handicraft methods (that is, a bootmaker performs all the tasks necessary to produce a pair of boots). In contrast to this, there are many departments and subassembly workflows in a Ford Motor Company plant, where technology is very sophisticated and machine-paced.

opportunities more readily seized. Specialists in market research and systems engineering for Continental Telephone Corporation helped that firm change from a rural telephone company to a sophisticated supplier of data and voice-communication services.

THE IMPACT OF TECHNOLOGY ON ORGANIZATION DESIGN

The **technology** of an organization includes the equipment, methods, and knowledge necessary for transforming raw materials (inputs) into fin-

Job Design and Workflow

The relationship between technology and organization structure can be further illustrated by looking at the design of jobs and the flow of work and materials into, through, and out of the organization and its various departments. Actually, there are several workflows in business organizations. These include raw materials, assembly, information and paperwork, orders and instructions, and financial resources. People are stationed in work positions along these flows (see Figure 6.9). By

FIGURE 6.9
Alberni Pulp and Paper flow chart.

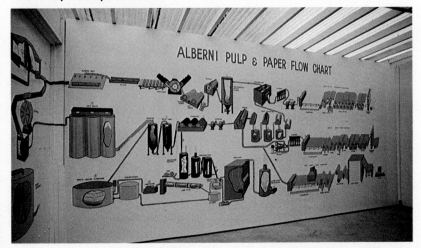

following patterns of work and identifying critical jobs along these flows, it's possible to design an organization from the bottom to the top. Knowledge of the sequence of each activity and its subtasks provides the basis for designing workers' jobs.

Making Jobs More Pleasant   An important development of the Industrial Revolution in the United States had to do with making jobs simpler and more highly specialized. Division of labor and creation of the assembly line greatly increased work productivity. However, as we've already seen, extreme task specialization has also resulted in boredom and dissatisfaction, as with the worker at GM who bolts wheels on new cars all day long. Consequently jobs and work patterns at many progressive companies have been reanalyzed to make them more satisfying. Two approaches to overcoming worker dissatisfaction are job enlargement and job enrichment.

   Job enlargement means expansion of the scope and responsibilities of a job so that a worker experiences greater satisfaction and interest, hopefully resulting in increased productivity. This may mean performance of a greater number of tasks. So a windshield assembler at GM, instead of installing only windshields, installs *all* auto glass for *both* doors and car body as an enlargement of the job. **Job enrichment** means boosting productivity and interest by providing greater authority, new responsibilities, more challenge, and the opportunity of increased personal achievement and recognition. The windshield assembler's job might be enriched by being assigned the responsibility of inspecting work performed by other auto glass installers.[2]

Putting Jobs in a Logical Order   In many businesses, such as the Equitable General Insurance and Levi Strauss, the order or sequence of performing various tasks is critical. A pair of Levis must be cut from a bolt of cloth before zipper and pockets can be sewn in. An Equitable adjuster must know the limits of a policy and the amount of damage — as well as the validity of the claim — before the claims department can issue a check. This sequencing of tasks is called **task interdependency.** In some situations two or more tasks may need to be performed simultaneously, such as the installation of windows while the walls of a new house are being framed.

Types of Technology

Every firm uses technologies that have unique features. However, among technologies there are at least three general types: (1) job-shop and small-batch, (2) continuous-process and mass-production, and (3) interactive and information-based.

Job-Shop and Small-Batch Jobs   Job-shop and small-batch technology can range from a small handicraft operation — as when an artist hand-paints fine china — to a large, highly automated manufacturing plant. The distinguishing feature of both a **job-shop operation** and a **small-batch operation** is that each finished product is unique and requires different skills, materials, and equipment. Job-shops also very often fill specific orders. A specially designed pair of western boots from Tony Lama and a specially equipped jet produced by Cessna Aircraft for GM executives are examples of products produced on a small, or single-batch, basis.

Continuous-Process and Mass-Production Jobs   There are many standardized products that are manufactured in large quantities using the technology of **continuous process** and mass production. Generally, raw materials are continuously fed into the manufacturing process, often on a 7-day-week, 24-hour-day basis. This in turn yields lower costs and larger (mass) volume. Many foods, cars, chemicals, and appliances are produced in plants with sophisticated equipment using standardized techniques. Some machinery is even computer controlled. Such production plants are usually machine intensive rather than labor intensive. For example, Exxon's oil refineries call for very few workers and much expensive *equipment* to produce gasoline. The refineries are therefore machine intensive. Those workers who are required tend to be highly skilled with broad training. Most manufacturers of high-quality furniture, such as Henderdon and Baker, are still labor-intensive. That is, *workers* predominate — in this case, skilled craftsmen using hand-operated tools to produce fine furniture.

Interactive Based Jobs   Some products and services are individually provided to meet the client's or customer's needs. Common examples are

Three types of technology: small-batch stained glass window shop; continuous process oil refinery; interactive-based legal services.

ON THE FIRING LINE

Job Enrichment—More Profits or More Problems?

For the last several years, companies have sought to enrich jobs. They have hoped thus to increase worker interest and reduce absenteeism and turnover. They have used various strategies. Work settings have been cleaned up, lighted better, decorated. Plants have been located in industrial parks, where they are surrounded by woods and green belts. Cafeterias have been subsidized, and hours made more flexible. Recreation programs and physical fitness centers have been introduced. Employers are experimenting with 35-hour workweeks, work-at-home arrangements and job sharing programs. A few companies have also introduced sabbatical programs. By offering 12-week vacations every seven years (in addition to regular time off), they hope to lure employees into staying.

Yet another tack is to involve workers in decision making. This, some believe, can relieve the monotony of menial and clerical work. Perhaps even more important, it is intended to help workers identify with organization goals.

Is this massive effort to please employees worth it in dollars and cents? Does it have any effect on productivity?

Many argue that there are no returns on such investments in the quality of work life. Workers, they claim, view these programs with suspicion; "you don't get something for nothing." Steel companies and the United Steel Workers Union agreed to set up "productivity committees" in the early 1970s. The committees were intended to involve workers in decision making. But the workers saw them as attempts to speed up

work. The problem was made worse when managers ignored workers' suggestions for improving production processes. Similarly, a pet food plant in Kansas failed in its effort to redesign its production process. It has returned to its original assembly-line approach.

Some workers, it has been found, take the monotony of an assembly line in their stride. They even take advantage of it. The mechanical nature of their jobs allows them to pass the time chatting with coworkers while they work. In one GE plant where such workers were given "enriched" assembly jobs, they filed a grievance.

On a more basic level, altering the production plan to create identity groups and offer workers more responsibility may, after all, be the answer. Despite the failures noted earlier, European and Japanese industries have had marked success in this. So, too, have some American companies—Delta Airlines, for example. (See On the Firing Line: American Business Leadership, in Chapter 5.)

Perhaps, then (job enrichment advocates suggest), the failures—in the pet food plant, the steel companies, and GE—are not because the concept is bad. They may be failures of management to find the right way to upgrade jobs. Perhaps management just gave up too quickly. Or perhaps managers lacked the skills required to put the program into effect. They may need to learn to listen to workers. Indeed, Øglaend's production manager has a telling comment: "It is necessary for managers to accept that the problem is never what we think it is. The problem is what the workers think it is."

the services of doctors, lawyers, and hairstylists. This **interactive-based technology** is one in which information feedback is frequently a critical element. An example of interactive technology is the automated teller machine ("cash machine") used by some banks. The customer punches a personal number on a keyboard and can then deposit

money, receive cash, transfer funds from savings to checking, or even pay a third party to a transaction. The consumer interacts with an automated teller machine in order to receive a banking service.

The sophistication of the technology determines the amount of control necessary to ensure that a firm offers products or services of consistently high quality. In the manufacture of fuels even a very minor error could make a batch of gasoline—thousands of gallons—unusable without complete reprocessing. The producer of Häagen-Dazs ice cream has been known to throw out over 30,000 gallons because "it didn't taste quite right."

Controls, which furnish regulation and also act as safeguards, are necessary to prevent mistakes. Controls may be very elaborate; they may require a complex organizational structure with many levels of authority and highly specialized units or departments. The U.S. Strategic Air Command is such an organization. Accidental nuclear war must of course be prevented.

In many large-scale organizations all three types of technology (small-batch, continuous-process, and interactive) can be found. This is the case at the General Dynamics plant where the F-16 fighter jet is manufactured. Some parts of the F-16 must be individually made by highly skilled machinists. This is a small-batch operation. Other assembly operations (wing and tail) use an interactive technology because the various part connections must be frequently tested for stress as assembly proceeds. And many of the plastic and chemically coated electronic parts and connecting wires for the F-16 are manufactured by continuous-process operations.

BRINGING AN ORGANIZATION TO LIFE: AUTHORITY AND RESPONSIBILITY

It should be clear by now that technology and the environment have a substantial impact on the development of the formal organization. Once established, the structure comes to life through the authority exercised and the responsibilities discharged by managers and workers. The authority and responsibility relationship between a superior and employee rests on the concept of **unity of command.** This means that each employee reports to only one superior. The series of unbroken one-to-one authority and reporting relationships that begins with the lowest level of the organization and progresses to the top level is called the **chain of command.** Bausch and Lomb, the world's largest manufacturer of contact lenses, provides an example. There Anthony LaPaglia,

president of the Analytical Systems Division, reports to James Edwards, president of the Instrument Group, who in turn reports to Daniel Gill, corporate president and chief executive officer.

When a Manager Has Authority and Influence

Unity of command is closely related to the concepts of power, authority, and influence. **Power** is the ability to exercise control over others. **Authority** exists by formal arrangement and approval. Here an individual possesses the power to make decisions and give orders. Thus it is customary for a superior in an organization to control the behavior of his or her employees.

Influence is a form of power that gets things done by persuasion rather than by command. Stated another way, it's the ability of one person to get someone else to perform some mutually beneficial task. For example, if Anthony LaPaglia can convince James Edwards to alter some aspect of Instruments Group policy, he has exercised influence. Influence is an important ingredient of supervisory leadership.

Sources of Authority

There are at least three important sources of authority within the business firm. One is based on *position*. Regardless of *who* occupies a position, a certain amount of authority is vested in it by the owners of the organization. However employees answer to a *person* as well as to a position. A superior may have a certain amount of personal authority in addition to the authority vested in his or her position. This personal authority stems from the individual's *expertise*, or technical knowledge and skill. For example, Anthony LaPaglia's special knowledge of analytical instruments provides him with authority based on expertise.

A third source of authority is based on the employee's *acceptance* of the superior's authority and ability to command. If employees do not accept and act on a manager's order, the manager has no authority. If Peabody Coal Company miners refuse to go into a mine because of some safety hazard, the supervisor has little if any authority to force them to mine coal under unsafe conditions.

Delegation and Accountability

In an organization of any size it's impossible for the top manager to keep all the authority and make all decisions. Authority and responsibility, then, are delegated throughout the organization to lower-level managers. **Delegation** is the downward distribution of job duties and corresponding authority to people in the organization. The acceptance of these job tasks and this authority creates a set of responsibilities for the employee. In accepting **responsibility** an employee becomes accountable for the job duties and authority assigned. When a Radio Shack store manager instructs a salesclerk to change prices of various items, the clerk is obliged to use the new prices in making sales. Overall responsibility for performance of delegated tasks is kept by the superior, who's responsible for checking on, and guaranteeing, the performance of his or her subordinates.

Although delegation may seem a relatively simple matter, many managers are reluctant to delegate sufficient authority. This reluctance can be overcome if the manager develops greater confidence in his or her employees.

CHOICES FOR DESIGNING ORGANIZATIONS

The amount of delegation of authority is closely related to the design of a company. Most organizations, regardless of size, will use several structure and design approaches, since there's no single best way to design a company's organization.

Line and Staff Arrangements

A **line organization** is one in which there are direct, clearly understood lines of authority and communication flowing from the top of the firm downward, with employees reporting to only one supervisor. As long as store managers for Sears, Roebuck have good technical skills and knowledge to solve merchandising problems, the line organization may be the only type of structure needed. But in large stores with thousands of products, managers need help in managing the operation. This assistance is usually in the form of a staff organization. A **staff organization** is those persons, working by themselves or in small groups, who provide advice, recommendations, and specialized support services to line managers. Members of the line organization (store manager and department heads in Sears) in the day-to-day management of operations make decisions and take actions directly connected with the firm's primary task of selling merchandise. Staff specialists (Sears' credit analyst, inventory control specialist and cost accountant) help the line managers accomplish the firm's objectives.

Production, marketing, and financial functions of the business firm are the chief elements of the line organization. Public relations, personnel, legal, consulting, and other support functions are examples of staff organization (see Figure 6.10). Staff units are shown as dashed or broken lines on the organization chart.

Position and Authority Line and staff managers may not always be easily distinguishable. The major differences between line and staff personnel are based on authority and the use of specialized knowledge.

Line authority is the right to issue decisions and orders concerning production, marketing, finance and other line functions. Much of this authority is based on the individual manager's position in the organization. **Staff authority,** based primarily on specialized and expert knowledge, is the right to advise, assist, or support line man-

"And this, gentlemen, is Mr. Quodley, my immediate inferior."

Drawing by Stan Hunt; © 1972 by The New Yorker Magazine, Inc.

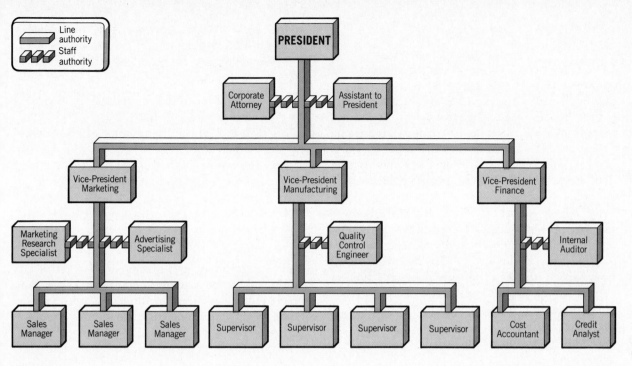

Line authority
Staff authority

PRESIDENT

Corporate Attorney

Assistant to President

Vice-President Marketing

Vice-President Manufacturing

Vice-President Finance

Marketing Research Specialist

Advertising Specialist

Quality Control Engineer

Internal Auditor

Sales Manager

Sales Manager

Sales Manager

Supervisor

Supervisor

Supervisor

Supervisor

Cost Accountant

Credit Analyst

FIGURE 6.10

agers and other staff personnel. As chief legal counsel for Tyson Foods, a major poultry processor, Larry French regularly attends company board meetings; and he advises the firm's president on legal matters almost daily.

People in the line organization need general managerial skills and must be able to make full use of the specialized knowledge of a staff member. In many situations, however, the line manager may not be willing to use the advice or service of the staff specialist. At American Can Company's Dixie Cup Division, the parent company supplied staff scientists to research plastic products for the division. Dixie's line managers were experts on wood fiber products and refused to yield to the plastics experts in the container lab. In the end, a number of disgruntled staff scientists were transferred elsewhere or left the company. Such a situation is an example of **line-staff conflict.** Lacking direct authority, the staff person pushes for acceptance from line managers. The line manager may strongly resist the new ideas of the staff specialist or fail to keep staff personnel adequately informed about line problems.

To overcome these potential conflict situations, line managers and staff specialists need continually to recognize each other's value in making the organization successful. One approach to

making the line-staff relationship work more smoothly is the development of functional authority.

Functional Authority **Functional authority** is a combination of line and staff authority in which a specialist is delegated direct authority for supervising some specialized area of activity. Functional authority is often found in labor and industrial relations. In a unionized company like Whirlpool Corporation, one or more specialists may be given the job of dealing directly with the union on a continuing basis. The plant manager at Whirlpool's Evansville, Indiana plant delegates to the director of labor relations the responsibility of negotiating, administering, and interpreting the labor agreement. During contract negotiations, labor relations specialists may ask for information from line managers and other staff specialists. While the contract is in effect (which could be for a period of three years), line managers depend on the labor relations specialist when the firm needs to make labor relations decisions. Should it become necessary to add a second shift to increase production of washing machines, the Whirlpool plant manager will rely on the labor relations director to work out any special problems with the union.

Centralization and Decentralization

Delegation rarely means assigning absolute authority to lower-level managers. Usually, varying degrees of authority and responsibility are delegated. Under **centralization,** only a limited amount of authority in an organization is assigned downward. **Decentralization** is a situation where considerable authority and decision-making freedom are delegated to lower-level managers.

How Much Should a Firm Decentralize? A number of things need to be considered when determining how much authority to delegate. Some of these are (1) the size of the organization, (2) how rapidly the external environment changes, (3) the willingness of employees to accept greater authority, and (4) the geographic dispersion of the organization.

Decentralization is usually the best policy when:

1. the organization is very large, such as Exxon, McDonald's, McDonnell Douglas, Ford, and IBM;
2. the firm is in an industry that's both mature and slow to change (examples include textiles, bulk chemicals, and rail transportation);
3. employees are willing and able to accept greater responsibility; some companies are known for having progressive, young management teams that are eager to "try their wings" (examples include Apple Computer, Federal Express, Texas International Airlines, E. F. Hutton, and Digital Equipment);
4. the company is geographically widespread, such as J. C. Penney, Mobil, Pan American World Airways, and Du Pont.

Companies such as IT&T, CBS, and Polaroid have remained relatively centralized. Some managers prefer centralization because it leads to (1) the development of top managers with a broader view of things and (2) tighter financial and other controls. On the other hand, centralization may mean that lower-level managers don't have sufficient opportunities to develop their skills. And problems may not be solved speedily enough. Top management may be too busy to worry about a productivity slowdown at the Newton, Iowa

plant—and the local manager lacks the authority to unsnarl the problem.

When management decides to decentralize it expects the following benefits.

1. Quicker decisions in solving problems at lower levels.
2. More rapid development of lower-level managers.
3. Reduction in the day-to-day involvement by top management in minor details of running the organization.
4. More highly motivated lower-level managers because of their greater freedom to make decisions.

If, however, lower-level managers do not have adequate skills or training, costly mistakes may result. This is one reason why companies such as Sears have begun to *re*centralize instead of *de*centralize.

In practice, the amount of authority delegated to lower levels of management varies not only from organization to organization but also from function to function within the organization. It's fairly common for a manufacturer to decentralize its production operations while greatly centralizing financial decision making. For many years this has been the managerial strategy of General Motors, Motorola, General Electric, and Firestone.

Project Management and Matrix Organization

Project and matrix organization arrangements are relatively new and have been developed by firms in high-technology industries, including aerospace, electronics, and electrical equipment. Citibank, Dow Corning, Shell Oil, Texas Instruments, Bechtel, and TRW Systems are a few of the business firms that are project-oriented and that have successfully developed matrix designs to meet project-development needs.

When Bell Helicopter decides to bid on a major government helicopter contract, it pulls together people from several departments to work on this special project. A senior engineer may be assigned to head it up with a special task force. The project director is given enough authority to gather and manage the resources needed to accomplish the project's goals. This is referred to as **project man-**

TALKING BUSINESS

For a company with some 87,000 employees and annual sales in excess of $6 billion, Minnesota Mining & Manufacturing Co. spends a lot of time "thinking small."

"We are keenly aware of the disadvantages of large size," says Gordon W. Engdahl, the company's vice president for human resources and its top personnel officer. "We make a conscious effort to keep our units as small as possible because we think it helps keep them flexible and vital," he says. "When one gets too large, we break it apart. We like to say that our success in recent years amounts to multiplication by division." . . .

3M has manufacturing plants in 91 communities around the US, and only five of them employ 1000 persons or more. Although the average company installation employs 270, the median number is 115. Most of the plants produce many different products, and that variety helps cushion downturns in any one product line. It also allows workers to change assignments from time to time.

The same principles are applied to the company's managerial and technical employees. Work is thought of in terms of the "project," which can be a product or a market segment. Projects rarely involve more than a dozen managers and professionals.

"One consistent request we get from our people is that they be allowed to run a business of their own," says Robert M. Adams, 3M's vice president for research and development. "Our project system gives a lot of them the chance to do just that."

Source: Excerpted from Frederick C. Klein, "Manageable Size: Some Firms Fight Ills of Bigness by Keeping Employee Units Small," *Wall Street Journal*, February 5, 1982, pp. 1, 25. Reprinted by permission of The Wall Street Journal, © Dow Jones & Company, Inc., 1982. All rights reserved.

agement. If Bell wins the contract, the team will be joined by others to supervise production of the aircraft. When the contract expires, the managers and workers return to their regular departments. The project director may then be given some other special project to manage.

Project management is usually temporary. However the management of several projects over a period of time may lead to the development of a **matrix organization**—one with vertical and horizontal authority relationships (see Figure 6.11). Matrix structure helps an organization meet the special needs that a variety of projects present. This means, for example, that the vice-president for production is in charge of production schedules for each project under him or her (vertical authority). But at the same time, the director of a single project is in charge of that entire project, including research, design, production, sales, accounting, etc. (horizontal authority). Naturally this arrangement leads to overlapping authority. A production scheduler on project assignment, for example, would report directly to the project director and indirectly (or secondarily) to the vice-president for production. In matrix organizations, project team members have a dual allegiance—to the project and to their respective departments.

Why Do Firms Use Project and Matrix Organizational Arrangements

A primary advantage of project and matrix design is the teamwork approach. This draws on the unique talents of such groups as engineers, accountants, salespersons, and production special-

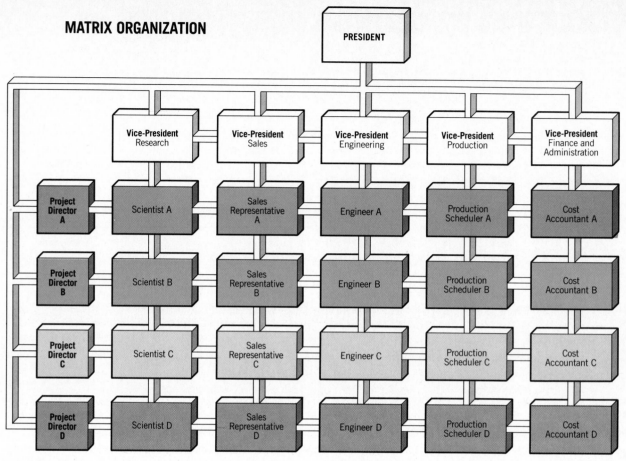

MATRIX ORGANIZATION

FIGURE 6.11

ists, making it easier to tackle complex and unique tasks. This teamwork approach also gives top management greater flexibility in the distribution and redistribution of resources. And because there is one team (and team leader) for a specific project, more effective control can be exercised. This means reduced project development time and lower costs. In short, the project director can more easily coordinate all project resources and activities.

Some Drawbacks of Project and Matrix Organizations Despite the important advantages that we've noted, project and matrix arrangements do pose some problems. The functional specialist— say in production, engineering, or marketing— assigned to a particular project has a dual allegiance and must report to two superiors. So a project director (*horizontal authority*) could tell a marketing specialist to promote a product one way while a marketing manager (*vertical author-*

ity) might recommend a completely different approach. The two-way reporting relationship could also lead to conflict between the project director and the functional manager—in this case, the marketing manager.

There's another disadvantage of project and matrix arrangements: a functional specialist may be assigned and reassigned to several projects within a short period of time, without working on any one project long enough to become fully effective. Also, there's little time to develop worker loyalty and good teamwork.

SUMMARY

An organization is a group of individuals acting in different but interrelated roles to achieve a goal. Organization structure is the order and design of relationships among employees, jobs, and departments within the firm. These relationships consist of human, material, financial, and information resources. The basic building block of an organization's structure is its primary task—the activity that forms the basis for its existence. Considerations important in designing a structure to carry out this task include (1) division of labor, (2) span of control, (3) management hierarchy, and (4) departmentation.

Organizations must continuously interact with other organizations in the external environment, and this interaction can influence the structure of the firm. The firm must develop and maintain beneficial exchange relationships. Two important such relationships arise from buying supplies and raw materials and from selling to customers.

Some firms operate in relatively stable environments, while the environments of some others are rapidly changing. Organizations may have to adopt flexible structures to cope with change. General economic conditions and the federal government are probably the external agents of change that affect firms most directly.

The firm has multiple points of contact, or boundaries, with its environment. Boundary spanners link the firm with the environment and thus greatly affect the firm's success. One of the most important duties of a boundary spanner involves data gathering, which can help management identify potential problems and opportunities.

Technology also affects organization structure. Departmentation may be based on level of technology. Analyzing workflow through the departments provides a basis for organization and job design. Three general types of technology are (1) job shop and small batch, (2) continuous process and mass production, and (3) interactive and information-based.

An organization's structure comes to life through the authority exercised and the responsibilities performed by managers and workers. The authority and responsibility relationship between a superior and a subordinate rests on the concept of unity of command. The series of unbroken authority relationships from bottom to top of the organization is the chain of command.

Unity of command is closely related to the concepts of power, authority, and influence. Three sources of authority within the firm are position, personal authority based on expertise, and the subordinate's acceptance of the superior's authority. Delegation is the downward distribution of job duties and corresponding authority to people within the organization. The amount of delegation of authority is closely related to the company's design.

A line organization contains direct, clearly understood lines of authority and communication that flow from the top of the organization downward. A staff organization consists of persons who provide service and specialized support services to the line managers. The main differences between line and staff personnel are based on authority and the use of specialized knowledge. The possibility of line-staff conflict is sometimes avoided through the development of functional authority—a combination of line and staff authority that involves delegation to a specialist of direct authority for supervising some specialized area of activity.

The degree of authority and responsibility delegated to lower-level managers depends in part on the degree of centralization of the organization. Whether the organization should be centralized or decentralized depends on (1) its size, (2) how rapidly its external environment is changing, (3) the willingness of subordinates to accept greater responsibility, and (4) its geographic dispersion. Often the degree of centralization varies from function to function within an organization. Project and matrix organizational structures are relatively new, project oriented arrangements developed by high-technology industries.

KEY TERMS

authority
boundaries
boundary spanner
centralization
chain of command
continuous process
decentralization
delegation
departmentation
flat structure
functional authority
hierarchy
informal structure or
   organization

interactive-based
 technology
job enlargement
job enrichment
job-shop operation
line authority
line organization
line-staff conflict
matrix organization
open system
organization structure
power
project management
responsibility
small-batch operation
span of control
staff authority
staff organization
tall structure
task interdependency
technology
unity of command

REVIEW QUESTIONS

1. What are the four major considerations in designing an organization to accomplish its primary task?
2. Name at least three major sources of authority in an organization. Briefly describe each.
3. Explain how the formal and informal organizations are structured within the same business firm.
4. Describe the three types of technology that affect organizational design.
5. What are the basic forms of organizing departments? Give an example of each.
6. Explain the basic functions of line and staff members within an organization.
7. Describe the conditions under which a company should decentralize.

DISCUSSION QUESTIONS

1. Draw an organization chart for your college and the firm for which you work. What is the chain of command? Are they tall or flat structures?
2. Which of the following would be line, staff, or functional members of an organization: production supervisor, executive secretary, auto design engineer, personnel manager, labor relations vice-president. Which might be more than one?
3. Why is unity of command an important aspect of every organization? What could happen if there were no unity of command?
4. What is the distinction between job enlargement and job enrichment? How would the application of each have changed a job you have held?
5. Under what conditions is a project form of management appropriate? Give at least two examples.
6. What effect would the installation of a headquarters computer or the beginning of a recession have on a company that was decentralized? Why?
7. How and why would the span of management differ for: workers on an automobile assembly line, workers building a Boeing 747, salespersons selling copying machines in a major city, copywriters in an advertising agency.

CASE: PYRAMIDS AND PLATFORMS

The story of Sears, Roebuck and Co. has been a dramatic one, especially under the leadership of the dynamic and imaginative General Robert Wood, who headed the company from 1928 to 1954. Through the ups and downs of the economic cycle Wood led Sears to the point where it dominated retail merchandising and set a model for companies large and small to follow. In the 1920s the company was strictly a mail order house serving rural America, with centralized leadership and organization. Under General Wood's direction, it became the nation's largest retail chain, with hundreds of full-service stores scattered across the US. When Wood took over and the organization grew in leaps and bounds, he vowed to decentralize operations to give local managers more authority to make decisions affecting their local markets.

To assist managers, Sears hired thousands of specialized staff in advertising, marketing research, promotion, pricing, purchasing, store engineering, computer science, and other technical areas. This was to give managers all the help they needed in making informed and strategic decisions in the battle for customer loyalty, sales, and profits.

The organizational structure was still recognized by Sears as a flat projection of authority and responsibility—as against the traditional big-company approach of building pyramids, with hierarchies of management reaching the tallest proportion. These pyramids of management represented the principles that were commonly recognized for efficient operations: unity of command, chain of command, span of control, division of labor, and specializations that were bound to result in greater efficiency plus savings and maximization of profits.

General Wood delighted in exploding this myth of management principles (and their execution) with a flourishing business following World War II and continuing through the 1960s and most of the 1970s. By 1978, however, problem signs began to appear: profit margins declined, and after more than two years of sluggish performance, Sears was forced to make some organizational changes. Many of these changes meant taking authority away from local managers and returning it to higher-level management in central positions: purchasing, standardization, advertising, promotion, computerization and financial control.

Thus the pyramids began to form and local platforms to diminish. Local retail store managers found their authority disappearing, and they had to check all decisions with higher headquarters—all the characteristics of the large corporate enterprises that had survived through the Depression years.

The story of Sears, Roebuck—even with the brilliant leadership that it has enjoyed over the years—seems to display a pattern of operation, and a design for organizational structures, almost "predestined."

1. What are the advantages of a centralized organizational structure?
2. What are the advantages of a decentralized organizational structure?
3. Why did Sears find it necessary to change its organizational structure?

CASE: PAR FOR THE SMALL BUSINESS: 100

Jack Murphy, an ambitious entrepreneur, spoke of "100" as if it were par on a golf course. Speaking at the annual meeting of the South Bend Chamber of Commerce, Murphy contended that the optimum size for a small business organization should not exceed 100 employees, including management. He claimed that when the number got over 100, it was very difficult for people to communicate face-to-face in the conduct of daily business—to maintain the kind of relationships necessary to make a business operate efficiently. Murphy was indeed talking about "Span of Control," "Channels of Communication," "Performance Reviews," and other functions of management. He himself had organized three such businesses and handed them over to his sons-in-law (he had four daughters).

Jack Murphy had come out of big business—he had been Director of Training in a huge corporation. Having risen from the ranks, he knew what skills were needed throughout the plant. Showing his disdain for bureaucracies, he said that as long as big business was as inefficient as it is, there'd always be a place in the economy for the small, enterprising businessman. His success in his own three businesses, each numbering close to 100 employees, was built on his creative imagination and the ability to figure out products that were needed in the marketplace, but which could not be manufactured efficiently by big corporations. His first business was manufacturing parts for nuclear submarines. The second specialized in designing small auxiliary motors for activating various space-vehicle systems. His latest venture was the production of heat pumps for hot tubs, sauna baths, and swimming pools.

Jack Murphy ended his talk with a description of the tall pyramids that seem to burgeon in the large corporation, so far separating top management from the workers that most managers don't know what's going on in the plant. He contended that efficiency was best promoted in flat-type organizations, where management could work directly with labor to accomplish objectives.

1. How practical is Jack Murphy's approach to business organizations?
2. What would be the advantages of maintaining a flat organization of 100 employees or less?

CHAPTER 7

HUMAN RELATIONS
IN BUSINESS

After studying this chapter you should be able to:

1   Understand the nature of human relations in business.
2   Explain the difference between Theory X, Theory Y, and Theory Z.
3   Understand the importance of the psychological contract between employer and employee.
4   Describe the hierarchy of worker needs.
5   Describe job motivators and job maintenance factors.
6   Explain the nature and structure of work groups and how they affect productivity.
7   Describe the importance of role and status in work groups.
8   Understand the process of effective leadership.
9   Understand group decision-making and problem solving.

Send a labor-management delegation to Japan and the two parties may end up looking at the same thing from different perspectives. Management admires the productivity. Labor likes the worker consultation and "family" atmosphere surrounding employee security. Both are really looking at human relations as they affect both production and worker satisfaction.

Yes, East is East and West is—*what*? Members of the Ford-UAW delegation that sojourned those ten eye-opening days in the land of the rising yen wondered just that. What are *they* doing that we might be doing, maybe even better—?

One thing Peter J. Pestillo, Ford vice-president for labor relations, noticed was that the Japanese were more concerned with human relations than with labor relations. Not that they were trying to stifle labor disputes; just that they seemed to be supplying the kind of plant atmosphere that made people want to work productively.

Donald F. Ephlin, UAW vice-president and director of the Ford Department, agreed. Naturally enough, he felt that Ford ought to increase its worker consultation and discuss business matters on the shop floor. He also wanted to see U.S. auto makers give their workers more security. That would make workers much more receptive to ideas involving improved productivity. At present, he said, workers feel that improving productivity might land them out of a job. In Japan this couldn't happen, since the big companies have a lifetime employment policy. Yet Ephlin was no more demanding this concession than Pestillo was about to offer it.

But none of this tells the whole human relations story. Ephlin conceded that the UAW puts more emphasis on individuals, while the Japanese put the group first. That just may be the way the American worker wants it. And if in some respects the American record on human relations may be more glowing than its oriental counterpart.

"I saw one man doing five operations, whereas in the U.S. he might do two—he was literally running." This was management talking (Ford's assistant director of manufacturing engineering & systems, also on the Japan trip); the individual Japanese worker just seems to have more individual tasks. According to Ford's man, the Japanese system allows managers to make employees work harder.

The delegation also observed that relief time is shorter in Japan; that the workplace lacks the elaborate heating and air conditioning systems that are typical in the U.S.; that Japan employs more than twice as many robots as the U.S.; that the Japanese union is a company unit, unlike its independent American counterpart.

Adding the pluses and minuses, the pros and cons, both sides could see their visit as a sort of object lesson in—human relations. Consensus: that this was an area ripe for improvement by both the company and the union. The twain were meeting.

Based on John Hartley, "Looking for Better 'Human Relations,' " *Automotive News*, 20 July 1981, p. 34. Used by permission.

HOW PEOPLE BEHAVE IN ORGANIZATIONS

Not just in Japan or only recently, but over the last 50 years management practitioners, teachers, and researchers have continually argued that *people* are the business firm's most important resource. As such, managers and workers can be employed effectively or wasted. Even the most highly qualified group of police officers available may become unhappy, lose interest, and eventually leave the force. The officers must be given interesting jobs, made to feel that they are part of an effective crime-fighting team, and be personally recognized for their contributions.

An effective manager can organize and stimulate employees to reach company goals. To be that effective, a manager must possess a variety of human relations skills. These include the ability to understand employee habits and attitudes and to make decisions that will increase worker motivation. In short, an effective manager needs to understand the nature of human relations in a business, nonprofit organization, institution, or government agency.

Human Relations

Human relations is the study of the importance of individuals as they interact on the job. The result is a body of theory, knowledge, and practice devoted to explaining both group and individual behavior. Behavior that takes place within a business is, of course, restricted in a number of ways and at times even closely controlled. This is also true of the college classroom. If you think about your own behavior in this course, you'll see elements of restriction and control. But even though behavior is controlled by the teacher, it's nevertheless appropriate for the situation. For example, you refrain from talking in order to hear the lecture—and out of courtesy to the other students.

It doesn't take much imagination to realize that certain behaviors are undesirable in an organization, such as an employee fighting with a supervisor. As a future manager, you must be concerned with making the organization function smoothly and minimizing undesirable behavior.

Much behavior can be understood by observing the actions of people as they work. For instance, Frank Parsons, a foreman in the kitchen at a large food processing plant, watches the catsup preparation crew seasoning ingredients to add to 200 gallons of tomato pulp. He's making sure the crew performs this task properly. We can't completely understand Parsons' behavior just by watching him. His thoughts, motives, and attitudes cannot be directly observed; they can only be assumed. For example, Parsons told the preparation crew that there would be no more smoking on the job. He probably issued this new rule because he felt that smoking might contaminate a large batch of catsup. On the other hand, maybe Parsons simply doesn't like to be around people smoking cigarettes.

The mere fact that certain behavior is required or suggested by various rules and regulations doesn't necessarily mean that employees will do as they're told. And the results of their failure to do so aren't always undesirable, either. For example, at a major plywood manufacturer's Shreveport mill the plant manager, concerned about having to lay off loyal employees, instructed the plant accountant to inflate sales and production figures. The accountant refused and reported the incident to the home office. As a result, the plant manager was terminated. Change and progress might be held back if managers and workers always "went by the book." An Army supply officer can often get the materials a unit needs much faster by avoiding "official supply channels."

Work Motives, Values, and Attitudes

Arnie Davis, a steelworker at U.S. Steel, goes to work five days a week and hasn't missed a day of work in 10 years. Brad Shelton, a young corporate attorney for Bell Telephone, takes affidavits, rate cases, and other legal documents home with him each night for additional study and review. Why do Brad and Arnie act the way they do? Most adults have a positive feeling toward being productive. And many Americans have an ethic (a principle of moral conduct) that work is good and essential for one's physical, social, and economic well-being. This so-called **work ethic** means that people place a high value on working—and that they do enjoy working. Because people recognize the importance of working, they (1) get to work on time, (2) try to do a good job, (3) offer suggestions for work improvement, and (4) respond to supervision.

"The other employes hate your guts, Mervin.
Keep it up."

Good work attitudes and job performance usually bring about **job satisfaction.** This is the pleasure experienced when you have done a good job, whether you're a carpenter's helper, grocery store clerk, amusement park ride operator, or president of a major corporation. When workers experience job satisfaction, employee morale is high. *Morale* measures the degree to which employees see their needs being satisfied by the job, expressed in satisfaction. Much of this positive feeling may flow from the work itself. For many people, work is a way to achieve various ends. Money from your paycheck can be used to make car or tuition payments, buy clothes, and go to sporting events, movies, concerts, and the theatre.

If workers aren't happy, the result can be numerous problems for the company. In fact worker discontent can mean lost sales, poor profits, bad publicity for the firm, and even bankruptcy. These are several "signs" that should tell management that it has a problem. High absenteeism is a key indication of worker dissatisfaction. Instead of striking, police and firemen in Cleveland, Chicago, Philadelphia, and other cities and towns have staged "sick-ins," calling in to report nonexistent illness. High absenteeism on assembly lines often yields major production cutbacks and quality control problems.

High absenteeism may ultimately result in high turnover among workers. One of America's largest manufacturers of consumer packaged goods is reputed to have a sales-force turnover of over 30 percent a year. A marketing research firm in Dallas loses over 80 percent of its new interviewers each year. The workers dislike the low pay, rude customers who slam the phone or door in their face, and the pressure to complete more interviews with more detailed answers.

Another sign of worker unhappiness is poor-quality service and deliberate damage to products. When employee time-off provisions at one of the country's largest airlines were conservatively rewritten, the result was a big increase in lost and incorrectly shipped baggage. Worker sabotage at the Lordsburg, Ohio plant of General Motors resulted in thousands of vehicles with windshields broken, upholstery slashed, ignition keys broken, and carburetors clogged with washers. A subsequent management crackdown produced mounting worker resentment. Three months later, the workers went on strike, costing GM an estimated $45 million. Strikes—the ultimate form of worker discontent—will be discussed in Chapter 9.

Work and the Nature of Man: Theories X and Y
In a large Chicago company, there was an office manager who rigidly enforced a "no beverages" rule from 9:00 A.M. to 4:00 P.M. This was the period when clients were likely to visit the office. Any secretary caught during those hours with a soft drink or coffee was vigorously scolded by the manager in front of other employees. This tale illustrates Douglas McGregor's **Theory X** approach to managing people, which assumes that:

1. the average person has an inherent dislike for work and will avoid it if he/she can;
2. because people don't like to work, most workers must be controlled, directed, or threatened with punishment to get them to put out enough effort to achieve organization objectives;
3. the average person prefers to be directed, wishes to avoid responsibility, has relatively little ambition, and wants security above all. [1]

This view of people suggests that managers must constantly prod workers to perform and must closely control their on-the-job behavior. In contrast to the authoritarian Theory X managers, we have those who follow **Theory Y,** which assumes that:

1. work is as natural as play or rest;

TALKING BUSINESS

In the early 1970s the success of the Japanese approach to management in a number of industries attracted admiring attention far and wide. American research into the Japanese model yielded a so-called **Theory Z**, explained at length in William Ouchi's celebrated book, *Theory Z: How American Business Can Meet the Japanese Challenge.* The Theory Z approach to management has many Japanese elements, but they are more or less westernized, reflecting US cultural values. The significance of Theory Z emerges from a contrast of traditional American management with its Japanese counterpart. Differences are most apparent in seven important areas:

Length of Employment	Relatively short-term; worker is subject to layoffs if business is bad.	Lifetime; layoffs never used to reduce costs.	Long-term but not necessarily lifetime; layoffs "inappropriate"; stable, loyal work force; improved business conditions don't require new hiring & training.
Rate of Evaluation & Promotion	Relatively rapid.	Relatively slow.	Slow by design; manager is thoroughly trained & evaluated.
Functional Specialization	Considerable; worker acquires expertise in a single functional area.	Minimal; worker acquires expertise in the organization instead of a functional area.	Moderate; all experience the various functions of the organization & have a better sense of what's good for the firm rather than for a single area.
Decision Making	Done on an individual basis.	Much more consensual, allowing input from all parties concerned.	Emphasizes consensus; higher quality, easier implementation.
Responsibility for Success or Failure	Assigned to the individual.	Shared by a group collectively.	Assigned to the individual.
Control	Very explicit & formal.	More implicit & informal.	Relatively informal but with explicit performance measures.
Concern for Workers	Focuses on work-related aspects of worker's life.	Extends to whole life of the worker.	Relatively concerned with worker's whole life, including the family.

The Theory Z approach to management, in contrast to the traditional American model, depends on trust, subtlety, and intimacy. There is already some evidence that Theory Z management contributes both to organizational performance and to individual emotional well-being. Firms that exemplify the Theory Z approach include IBM, Eastman Kodak, and Hewlett-Packard.

Based on Jerry D. Johnson, "Theory Z."

2. the threat of punishment isn't the only means of getting people to work—people will exercise self-direction and self-control and try to achieve organization goals if they believe in them;

3. workers can be positively motivated and will try to accomplish an organization's goals if they believe that they'll receive future rewards;

4. the average person learns, under proper conditions, not only to accept but also to seek responsibility;

5. most workers have a relatively high degree of imagination, ingenuity, and creativity and are willing to help solve problems.

Should you as a manager follow Theory Y, you'll recognize individual worker differences and continually encourage worker learning and self-devlopment. In short, a Theory Y approach to managing people builds on the idea that worker and organization interests are the same. For example, Mark Athon, a sales representative for NCH Corporation (an industrial chemical manufacturer), surpassed his monthly sales quota with a big order of janitorial cleaner. Athon received a bonus in addition to his regular sales commission.

Obviously he benefits from the added reward, and the firm gains from the increase in sales.

Putting Theories X and Y Together Upon first encountering Theories X and Y, you could easily draw the conclusion that a Theory Y managerial philosophy is always more appropriate. This is because today's business is relatively sophisticated and has a more educated work force. Many firms, including Dresser Industries, TRW Systems, Procter & Gamble, and Texas Instruments, have adopted variations of a Theory Y approach and have used Theory Y in their training programs for managers.

Despite the general appeal of Theory Y and the rejection of Theory X by many, under certain circumstances the more controlled and authoritarian approach of Theory X can be as effective as Theory Y. Upon graduating from college and/or business school and beginning your career, you'll probably face an X-Y "fork" in the managerial road. You may even find that something of a combined approach—say Theory Y coupled with strong elements of control and authority—is useful, allowing also for change in emphasis as work circumstances themselves change.

TALKING BUSINESS

American corporate executives have been bowing deep to Japanese-style management lately.

They have bought William G. Ouchi's book in sufficient droves to put it on the best seller list. Management and business magazines are full of articles about the wonders of Japanese business.

It has become a "fascination," says James W. Begun, a young assistant professor at Cornell University's Graduate School of Business and Public Administration. But, he maintains, the value of Japanese-style management has been oversold. . . .

Mr. Begun finds most of the goals of Japanese-style management unobjectionable, however, and in fact, often desirable. It is better to have happy workers than sad workers, for managers to be sensitive rather than insensitive to the problems of their employees.

He's afraid, though, that should the fascination of American executives with Japanese-style management not boost productivity as desired, they will reject the many positive elements of a more humane management style. Thus Begun wants managers of US corporations to have a more balanced view of Japanese-style management.

"Japanese organization is romanticized in the literature," he says. Yet it includes elements of racism, sexism, paternalism, resistance to change, innovation, or deviation, the crushing of individual expression, and an inability to make quick decisions.

Japanese employees, he noted, are expected to put company before family. They have a derogatory term for those who act contrariwise—"wife-lover."

Oddly, younger Japanese are now insisting on the greater individuality that is normal in the US. "Things should be less Z-like in the future in Japan." says Begun. "Young people are demanding a full life outside of work." Management styles are already changing in fast-moving high-technology firms.

So, US management may become more Japanese-like, and Japanese management more American-like. It is hoped the cross will be as healthy as hybrid corn.

Excerpted by permission from David R. Francis, "Is the Japanese 'Theory Z' Really a Management Acme?" *Christian Science Monitor*, 1 April 1982, p. 10. Reprinted by permission, *The Christian Science Monitor*, © 1982; The Christian Science Publishing Society. All rights reserved.

ATTACHMENT TO THE ORGANIZATION— THE PSYCHOLOGICAL CONTRACT

When Frank Parsons went to work for the food-processing firm, he had various expectations about the company and its benefits for himself and his family. Similarly, management expects Parsons to work hard in return for a given amount of reward (money, nonwage compensation, benefits, recognition, and so forth). Companies like this usually try to convey work expectations through training, job descriptions, and production standards. Frank Parsons and other workers develop reward expectations through information covering wage rates, other compensation, benefits, job transfer opportunities, and job promotions.

Many company and worker expectations are conveyed by means of various forms and documents, such as union contracts and written job descriptions. But there are also many *un*written expectations between the worker and the company. These unrecorded expectations are called the **psychological contract.** For example, Parsons may expect to use the company car for personal use, such as taking his son's Little League baseball team to out-of-town games. When both Parsons and the company consistently meet each other's unwritten expectations, this psychological contract strengthens Parson's attachment to the firm. On the other hand, if Parsons and the firm fail to meet each other's expectations, the psychological contract is broken. Frank Parsons may lower his performance and be fired, or he may simply quit.

Let's take a closer look at the actual relationship between workers and managers and among the workers themselves. After reading the rest of this chapter, you'll be able to (1) better understand your own motivation to work and (2) identify the human relations skills you'll need when you graduate.

MOTIVATION FOR EFFECTIVE PERFORMANCE

One reason why some people work very hard and others don't is because of differences in employee motivation. We can begin to explore worker motivation by examining employee needs.

Nearly 100 years ago Frederick Taylor, in his studies of scientific management, advanced the idea that motivation was influenced chiefly through monetary rewards and assurances of job security.[2] Many years later researchers under the direction of Elton May at the Hawthorne Works of the Western Electric Company in Chicago noted that elements of the social system of work had an impact on employee motivation and, consequently, on levels of production. These views of management and the worker were drawn on by psychologist Abraham Maslow in the development of his needs hierarchy theory of human motivation.

Employee Needs

The **needs theory** of motivation proposes that people act in order to satisfy or fulfill various needs. A **need** is a want of something requisite, desirable, or useful. A person who feels a need is moved to correct the situation. When you're hungry, you look for and eat food to eliminate the feeling of hunger. The process by which need is satisfied is shown in Figure 7.1.

Five categories of human needs that we all experience are shown in Figure 7.2. This theoretical model, pioneered by Maslow, is known as the **hierarchy of motivations.** According to Maslow's theory, one tends to satisfy lower-level (physiological) needs, such as hunger and thirst, before being concerned with needs of a higher order, such

FIGURE 7.1

NEEDS-BEHAVIOR DIAGRAM

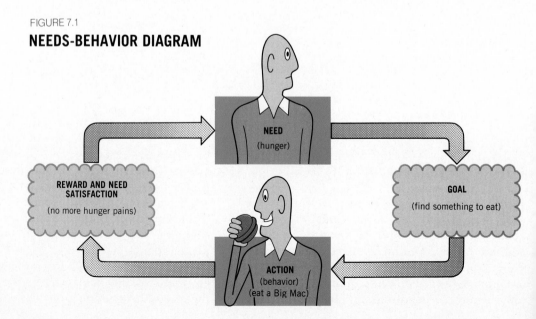

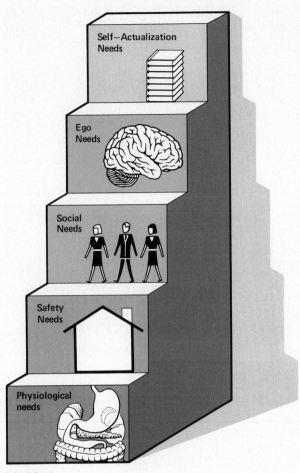

Self—Actualization
Needs

Ego
Needs

Social
Needs

Safety
Needs

Physiological
needs

FIGURE 7.2

ence on employee motivation in American society.

Safety and Security Needs Protection from work hazards and from loss of job are important concerns at the second level (**safety needs**) of the so-called hierarchy of needs. Occupational health and safety legislation, seniority provisions in labor agreements, and various forms of insurance are ways in which the attempt is made to satisfy these needs. The physical safety of workers is not a problem in most job situations. However there is increasing concern that many employees are suffering from lack of psychological safety. This is due to increasingly stressful work situations. Suppose that you were a stockbroker with a seat on the New York Stock Exchange. You'd be under continuous pressure to buy and sell millions of dollars' worth of stock at the right times and in the right amounts for clients. Over a period of weeks and months, such daily work pressure could affect your physical and mental health.

Social and Affiliation Needs The need to interact with others and affiliate with (belong to) work groups is the third category in the hierarchy of human needs. **Social needs** include those for belonging, for acceptance by others, and for giving and receiving friendship and love. Informal social groups, both on and off the job, provide avenues for the satisfaction of these needs. For example, your friends at school help satisfy your need for belonging.

Formal work groups, like the "quality circles" used by Japanese industrial firms and by many American firms (e.g. Nashua, Xerox) can also help meet workers' social needs. A **quality circle** is a small group of workers who meet periodically to find solutions to production problems. A typical quality circle might be a small group of machine maintenance mechanics in an International Harvester plant who meet on a regular basis. Discussion might focus on preventive maintenance schedules for materials-handling equipment.

Ego and Self-Concept The fourth category of human needs takes in what are called **esteem needs.** These are needs that are reflected in a person's self-worth (ego) and reputation. When one's ego (or self-evaluation) and reputation are about equivalent, one experiences relative satisfaction. Suppose that your college professors have evaluated you as an outstanding student with consider-

as social needs. You may not care about "meaningful dialogue" if you haven't eaten in five days.

Only unsatisfied needs, says the theory, can strongly influence behavior. A satisfied need is not likely to be a motivator. You'll not pull into a McDonald's if you just had a big turkey dinner. In short, once a need becomes relatively satisfied, its importance diminishes and another need emerges to stimulate other behaviors.[3]

Physiological Needs The most basic human needs are **physiological needs** (i.e. bodily in nature). The needs for food and clothing emerge and reemerge continually. A person lacking food, love, and esteem would more likely try to satisfy hunger first. Because of social security, compensation, and other employment laws, most of us are assured of enough money to satisfy physiological needs. Higher-order needs are therefore enabled to assume greater significance. They are likely to have a more direct and stronger influ-

Some companies have elaborate safety procedures and equipment to safeguard employees.

able leadership potential. Suppose too that you not only achieve superior grades but enjoy the achievement. Finally, you look forward to translating all this into professional leadership. If this describes you, you're already experiencing ego satisfaction. For an employee, praise and recognition from managers and others in the firm can contribute to the development of a healthy ego.

Achievement and Fulfillment The highest level of needs is called **self-actualization** — living up to one's potential and capabilities. Presumably if you're becoming everything that you're capable of becoming, self-actualization is taking place. Realization of your own potential is the pinnacle of the need hierarchy. John Y. Brown's building of the Kentucky Fried Chicken empire from $2 million to $288 million probably resulted in a high level of self-actualization.

Self-actualization is closely linked to the need to achieve. The **achievement motive** is the desire to accomplish or reach personal goals.[4] It strongly relates to person's **level of aspiration,** or the standard of performance by which one measures whether goals have been reached or not. There's no doubt that a person like John Y. Brown has a high level of aspiration.

Motivational and Maintenance Factors

When you go to work for a company, there are several factors that may affect your work motivation and degree of job satisfaction. Those factors listed in Table 7.1 as **job satisfiers** according to Frederick Herzberg will satisfy and motivate workers.[5] They are — or should be — all part of a workers' actual job. They correspond more or less to the ego and self-actualization needs discussed above. In contrast, the potentially dissatisfying elements tend to lie outside the actual job itself but are considered important aspects of the work environment. They're called factors of job maintenance for the employee.

TABLE 7–1

Factors That Affect Worker Motivation

Job Satisfiers and Motivators	Job Maintenance Factors (Potential Job Dissatisfiers)
Achievement	Company policy
Recognition	Supervision
Work itself	Work conditions
Responsibility	Interpersonal relations
Advancement	Salary and benefits
Growth	Security

TALKING BUSINESS

A new breed of manager is bringing subtle but important changes in the ways that corporations deal with their rising young executives.

Loyalty to the corporation, deference to superiors and other tried-and-true ways of getting ahead are low priorities of these young men and women managers.

For them, leisure time is more coveted than overtime, and self-satisfaction is as important as making the boss happy or collecting ever larger salaries. Above all else, they want their work to be "meaningful.". . .

The research firm of Yankelovich, Skelly & White, which monitors workers' attitudes and values for corporations, finds these traits typical of the new breed:

- They focus primarily on themselves rather than on a larger group.
- They expect to be paid well—and the less they like their work, the better they expect to be paid for doing it.
- They are relatively unfazed by the threat of being fired.
- They want "feedback" from their superiors.
- They are unwilling to put up with boredom and want their work to be stimulating.

Source: Excerpted from Alvin P. Sanoff, "The 'Me Generation' in the Executive Suite," Reprinted from *U.S. News & World Report*, March 9, 1981, pp. 71–72. Copyright 1981, U.S. News & World Report, Inc.

Job maintenance factors are those things that are required to keep a worker on the job, such as good working conditions. Yet maintenance factors rarely motivate workers. Good working conditions won't cause an employee to work harder. On the other hand, poor working conditions may cause a worker to quit. To motivate, management must offer recognition and advancement opportunities. Still, maintenance factors can help to satisfy a worker's physiological, safety, and social needs. Salary and benefits can be seen as helping to maintain health. Protective clothing can help reduce safety hazards on the job. Rest breaks can provide time for chatting with coworker friends.

Task Design and Job Enrichment If you accept a job that has many motivational factors, you should experience job satisfaction, increased motivation, and effective performance. A lack of job motivators, however, doesn't necessarily lead to dissatisfaction and poor performance. It simply means that you may not be motivated to do more.

To make a job more exciting and rewarding (as well as to increase productivity), a manager can enrich the job. Job enrichment is done by making a job more challenging and responsible, leading more readily to recognition and advancement. Job responsibilities are often expanded to include planning as well as self-evaluation of job performance and results. Job enrichment has been employed at AT&T, and the result has been improved work performance. Telephone switching system installers have participated with management in defining the nature of the installer's job. Workers have also helped decide what constitutes good and acceptable (as well as unacceptable) performance. It should be noted that not all workers want increased responsibility or greater challenges. These workers would not be candidates for job enrichment.

Expectations and Job Outcomes

Theories X and Y and the hierarchy of needs are two explanations of employee motivation. Another theory, offered by Victor Vroom, is that employees are motivated to exert effort and pro-

PERSPECTIVE ON SMALL BUSINESS

Ottis Stull, the top manager of a $2.4-million electrical contracting business, was normally a pleasant-natured man with an easy smile. He had a strong marriage and two healthy children. But after carrying out a subcontract on a large industrial rebuilding project, Ottis Stull changed. At the age of 35, he had burned himself out.

"I didn't crash until the job was finished," he recalls. "I'd thought all along that when it was over, I'd sit down and relax. But I couldn't."

Stull's condition had developed slowly, and he had not realized that anything was wrong. But in the wake of his biggest job to date he experienced a letdown, and his psychological burnout began to manifest itself clearly. He became continually exhausted and frustrated. He couldn't relax. He was edgy and too quick to judge, frequently reacting to the slightest provocation with anger. Stull's wife Sally insisted that he get help.

Like most victims of burnout, Stull had worked too hard too long, had tried to endure too much stress over too short a time. Burnout does not strike suddenly, leaving its victims "sick" where they were "well" the day before. Instead it develops gradually. It knows no threshold, just as the line between social drinking and alcoholism is obscure. Even persons not suffering from burnout can on occasion exhibit one or more of its symptoms. But although the condition can make a shambles of a life, a victim can recover, just as Ottis Stull recovered thanks to a program of psychological counseling and changes in his work style.

Stull's case is not unusual, either in its cause or its solution. According to Dr. Edward Stambaugh, the clinical psychologist who worked with Stull, an estimated 10% of Americans succumb to burnout every year. And it isn't unusual for burnout to strike the CEOs and top managers of smaller companies.

Compared with their counterparts in larger corporations, smaller company managers have to do more of everything themselves, because they don't have large staffs to rely on. And even entrepreneurs who have support staffs observes Stambaugh, don't always use them properly.

"All the entrepreneur possesses is locked up in his one little company," notes Stambaugh. "It is his dream, his vision, and there's precious little to fall back on if it goes bust. The very single-mindedness of purpose that makes the entrepreneur ideal for starting a company can easily become a threat as the company grows and there are more and more stimuli and demands on the owner's attention. All these can combine for a solid case of burnout."

SOURCE: Reprinted with permission of *INC.* Magazine. Excerpted from Donna L. Sammons, "Burn Out!" *INC.*, December 1980, pp. 57–58, 62. Copyright © 1980 by INC. Publishing Company, 38 Commercial Wharf, Boston, MA 02110.

---

duce because of their expectations about various job rewards and outcomes.[6] Stated differently, **expectancy** is the employee's estimate of his or her chances of accomplishing some goal (outcome) and receiving a reward. If an employee believes that by working hard the chances of receiving a bonus or promotion are reasonably high (80 percent, for example), he or she will exert substantial effort.

On the other hand, when someone believes that hard work isn't likely (say 20 percent or less) to lead to valued rewards, effort may only be minimal and job performance low. Motivation and job performance, according to this theory, therefore depend on how the employee views his or her chances of success. Assume that you walked into a class at the beginning of a new term and the instructor told the class that an *A* grade was almost never given but everyone would likely receive a *B*. Your motivation to study might very well decline.

Productivity is often enhanced when working conditions are improved.

Motivation, Performance, and Job Satisfaction

Employees work to receive rewards that they can use to satisfy their needs, just as you may work during the summer to pay tuition for the fall. The extent to which needs can be satisfied by working influences a person's motivation. You may lose your motivation if you begin spending all that you earn. Since you then cannot save enough to pay your tuition, you may become unhappy with the job. You may also lose your motivation if for some reason you cease to need the money gained through work. Managers need to understand this important relationship of factors. In it, motivation, performance, and job satisfaction are all linked to one another and money may play an especially important role.

The Role of Compensation in Motivation

Of the various job rewards (such as promotions, increased job security, transfer, bonus, recognition, and others), the pay raise is one of the most clear-cut, well understood, and highly valued. Few would argue against the idea that business firms should pay for performance. It follows that the worker receiving the highest performance evaluation should be given the largest raise.

A pay raise tied to performance (and not to promotion, seniority, etc.) is called a *merit increase*. Suppose Judy Lane feels that her improved performance will result in a bigger pay raise. If money is very important to Judy, her increased motivation should result in more effort. Or suppose that you were a bank loan officer and that the bank had a bonus program that rewarded officers for reaching loan goals. The expectation of getting a large bonus would strongly encourage you to work harder.

Money can be a powerful motivator when it is closely tied to performance with frequent and large pay increases.[7] In other words, if accomplishing a major work goal today doesn't result in a pay increase for approximately a year, money isn't considered a strong motivator. Why? In the worker's thinking, the goal achievement is not tied to the financial reward. Unfortunately, there are several reasons why management cannot always follow this policy. Four of these are (1) wage provisions of union contracts may specify that workers receive the same pay rate regardless of effort and merit, (2) the money with which to pay substantial and frequent raises may be lacking, (3) inflation and cost-of-living factors may disrupt compensation structures, and (4) there may be problems in effectively measuring employee performance.[8]

INTERPERSONAL RELATIONS AND GROUP BEHAVIOR

At Drexel Heritage Furnishings, manufacturers of quality household furniture, many managerial decisions are made by individual supervisors and then communicated to individual workers. This one-on-one leadership is undoubtedly most appropriate for Drexel and a good number of other companies. (Many Drexel workers are skilled artisans who individually fashion pieces of furniture.)

There are times, however, when a company manager needs to deal with subordinates on a group basis. Also, there are many businesses whose workers perform tasks together, as when the waitress, busboy, and cook in Denny's Restaurant work together to prepare and serve meals. Interpersonal relations (relations between people) is therefore an important concept for managers to understand.

Development of the Work Group

Every organization contains groups. Some groups are deliberately set up, while others are formed naturally and informally by people who work together. A **group** is a social unit consisting of two or more people who share the same goal and who cooperate to achieve it. A **work group** is a group that has been created to accomplish a specific task. The terms *committee*, *task force*, *team*, *crew*, and *work gang* are frequently used to describe work groups. As a future manager, you should know that (1) nearly every business has one or more work groups, (2) employees may belong to several different groups, and (3) work groups can both advance and frustrate the goals of the business.

Norms and Standards of Behavior   Remember from Chapter 6 that employees can be placed in departments in order to create an efficient organization. For example, a marketing research department may be created and filled with people who have the skills necessary for test-marketing new products or surveying consumer needs. Over time, the workers in this new department will establish work norms. One of these work norms may be that if a researcher tests a new product idea, he or she should issue a final report to management within 12 weeks.

A **norm** is a standard of behavior or performance used for determining if the actions of a member of a specified group are acceptable or unacceptable. A researcher who took six months to write a final report would be going beyond the work norm. And a worker who conforms to group norms will be more highly accepted than one who does not conform. Many of the accountants in the St. Louis office of a New York accounting firm usually take an extended lunch hour (nearly two hours) on Fridays. A young, energetic accountant decided that to get ahead more rapidly, he was going to work during the lunch hour on Fridays. He found that after a few weeks many of the other accountants were a little more distant in their dealings with him. Why? He didn't conform to their social and work norms.

In one famous study, a work group—14 employees at the Western Electric Company—was observed for several months.[9] The social scientists watching these workers found that they established their own norm about what they considered a fair day's work. Employees who performed at or near the output norm were highly regarded by most members of the group. However those who performed either considerably above or considerably below the norm were avoided and called either "rate-busters" or "chiselers." It so happened that the amount of work considered normative—that is, acceptable by the group—was less than what the company considered acceptable. In short, output at Western Electric was restricted by the group.

Role and Status   Each of the members of a work group has a role to play. The term **role** has two features. First, a role is a set of expectations about what an individual can and cannot do when holding a particular work position. For example, Lisa Kirkland, an insurance claims supervisor in a regional office of State Farm Insurance, expects claims processors to be at work on time. Similarly, the officeworkers expect Kirkland to be available for help when an unusual claim is received.

A role is also the actual behavior displayed by the occupant of the role. Lisa is usually available for assistance throughout the workday. There may be times however when she must be away from the office—such as for special meetings. So her basic role and actual behavior may be somewhat different.

The job a person holds, and the nature of that job—in other words his/her power and social position—help to determine that person's **status** within a group. Lisa, the claims supervisor, may have a special nameplate, the largest desk, and the newest typewriter as status symbols. At Bell Telephone corner offices, a carpet on the floor and more buttons on your telephone are considered status symbols. At a highway sign shop in which one of your authors once had a summer job, a tape measure functioned as a status symbol. Possession meant that its owner, who wore it on his belt like a badge of honor, was a painter

rather than a helper. Status symbols help identify the role a worker plays.

Within the work group a person may occupy several roles, either on a formal basis or informally. Most roles can be grouped into either task roles or group maintenance roles. **Task roles** are the activities aimed at getting the job done. At the sign shop, lettering the signs, spraying a sealer coat, and packing the finished sign were task roles.

Maintenance roles help to develop and sustain good relationships within the group. When issuing a work order to make a dozen stop signs, the shop supervisor is using task role behavior. If the supervisor resolves a disagreement between a shipping clerk and a sign painter, he or she is playing a maintenance role. We'll see more of these roles in the following examination of effective leadership.

Effective Leadership for Group Performance

Pierre Du Pont was 20 years old when he first reported for duty at the family's powder works in 1890. In a dingy shed that passed for a lab, Du Pont could find little modern equipment and less management responsibility. After eight frustrating years, he teamed up with two cousins to buy the family business for $12 million. Over the next 17 years—first as treasurer, then president—he led Du Pont to its place as a vast modern corporation. But he could not have acomplished this task alone. On the contrary, he was aided by a troop of brilliant lieutenants. The point is that Pierre Du Pont was a great leader. Leadership is found in most businesses—whether huge corporations like Du Pont or a small highway sign shop.

Leadership is the exercise of command, direction, or influence in a skillful and responsible manner in order to achieve specific goals. Effective leadership takes place when followers (such as Pierre Du Pont's lieutenants) do the things necessary for attainment of goals. The process of leadership involves two things: (1) setting goals and defining what activities need to be accomplished, and (2) strengthening the ties among group members and keeping the group together.

Setting Goals and Activities for the Group   As a leader, Pierre Du Pont had to plan and control work activities while at the same time motivating subordinates. A leader must initiate activity, seek information, give job instructions, take corrective action to solve work problems, and give rewards for a job well done.

Strengthening and Maintaining the Group

In trying to accomplish a goal—whether it be assembling an automobile, selling an insurance policy, or making gunpowder—the leader must guard against doing anything that could destroy the group. Showing favoritism, for example, could be destructive. Instead a leader must provide encouragement, be friendly and responsive to others, and try to reduce tensions should disagreements arise. In these ways a leader builds group cohesiveness and helps to preserve it. When a Ford production supervisor offered a compromise that helped solve a problem in the engine assembly area, the assembly group was kept working smoothly and hurt feelings were soothed.

Group Cohesiveness and Performance

In many businesses—such as most major airlines, Bell Telephone, and the U.S. Army—employees are assigned and reassigned to work groups or departments without being much, if at all, consulted. This makes it necessary for employees to adapt themselves to a new work environment rather quickly. Orientation programs are one of several ways a supervisor can make entrance or transition into a new assignment easier for new employees. Another would be to introduce new employees to their coworkers. The more quickly people get to know one another, the more quickly the department can function effectively.

A department's performance may strongly depend on group cohesiveness. The **cohesiveness** of a group consists in its members' sense of solidarity and their desire to remain in the group, as well as a tendency to resist outside influences. Cohesive-

Teamwork helps to get the job done more quickly and efficiently.

ness can help departmental performance—or it can reduce productivity (recall the restriction of output at Western Electric). At SAAB, the Swedish automotive manufacturer, group togetherness of the four-person engine assembly teams actually increased productivity.

Determinants of Group Cohesiveness A number of factors tend to increase work-group cohesiveness. These include:

1. similarity of group-member interests—e.g. belonging to the same engine assembly team;
2. the degree to which members depend on one another in the performance of their jobs—e.g. the sales staff at Xerox depending on quality maintenance by the service group in order to keep customers happy;
3. existence of a common threat to the group—e.g. American Airlines announcing to its employees that it was closing its New York headquarters and moving to the Southwest;
4. exercise of leadership within the group—e.g. William Paley assembling the great managerial team that created and built the CBS network;
5. the degree to which members participate in decisions affecting the group—e.g. university department faculties participating with the department chairperson in decision making.

The manager can also influence performance by developing a closely knit group. This tends to be much easier when the work group is relatively small (15 or fewer employees).

Consequences of Group Cohesiveness The development of group cohesiveness may take several weeks or months. The audit teams of Peat, Marwick, Mitchell & Company, one of the "big eight" accounting firms, have typically enjoyed much group cohesiveness. This has yielded major advantages for the company, some of which are (1) increased output, (2) greater company loyalty, (3) less employee turnover, and (4) reduced absenteeism.

On the other hand, group cohesiveness can also lead to some undesirable outcomes, such as (1) restriction of output, (2) resistance to change, and (3) conflict with other work groups. Employees can be united *against* the firm as well as united in support of it. A strike or work slowdown, for example, is a united effort against the company. Recall the GM Lordsburg plant example mentioned earlier in the chapter.

Group Problem Solving and Decision Making

Another aspect of group dynamics rests with the group's ability and willingness to contribute to the solving of business problems and the making of business decisions. Of course, many decisions of consequence to the firm are made by managers as individual contributors to organizational success. However, in many problem situations subordinate employees can on a group or team basis greatly contribute to problem solving and decision making. For example, the introduction in the 1980s of General Motors' subcompact J-car was based on a series of product decisions made by an executive committee. The amount of this group involvement is often a function of the decision style of the manager.

Decision Style of the Manager Decision style is the degree to which a supervisor involves other people in solving problems and making business decisions. A leadership and decision style that relies on employee input is basically a democratic process. For example, when John De Lorean, president of De Lorean Motor Company, asked his employees for advice about marketing the DMC sports car, he was using a democratic decision style. An autocratic style, on the other hand, would permit very little employee involvement in decision making.

Approaches for Group Decision Making Groups function in businesses as committees, task forces, and study teams. The most commonly found permanent group in a business is the *board of directors*. This group of top managers, elected by the corporation's stockholders, charts corporate strategy and adopts major policies for the firm. The board of directors, like most other formal groups, functions as a unit of interacting people. Decisions of the group may be made by majority vote or through reaching a consensus.

The type of problem it tackles will help determine how a group makes a decision. For example, if a problem is very unstructured (not easily specified), a **brainstorm** approach may be used.

Group members first discuss the problem and then offer all ideas and solutions that they can possibly think up. No idea is criticized or discarded during the first phase of brainstorming, no matter how unusual it may sound at the time. After members have exhausted their search for ideas, they begin to sift and evaluate the alternatives and try to arrive at a decision. A brainstorming session must be chaired by a strong moderator to keep it on course, and it's usually kept reasonably short. The Hoover Company used brainstorming to think of ways that vacuum cleaner sales could be improved. The result was the first such appliance to be offered in a variety of colors.

Although group decision making has many benefits, it also has its drawbacks. Some of these are (1) the difficulty in pinpointing who is actually responsible if something goes wrong, (2) the greater length of time it takes to make a decision (3) the possibility that one person will dominate and influence other group members, and (4) the group pressure to force acceptance of a decision that some group members may not agree with.

Despite the disadvantages of group decision making, there are also some advantages. The knowledge of the group is usually greater than that of any one person. This may lead to a larger number of ways to solve a problem. When more people participate in finding a solution to a problem, there tends to be greater acceptance of the decision. Finally, there's the likelihood of better understanding of the decision and less opportunity of a breakdown in communications.

When you become a manager, you'll often have to choose between individual and group decision making. Some things to consider are (1) the amount of time available for reaching a decision, (2) the importance of making the "right" decision, (3) the need for employee acceptance of the decision, and (4) the amount of information available for making a decision.

RELATIONS BETWEEN GROUPS AND THE ORGANIZATION

Work-group performance depends on individual efforts within the group. It also depends on a supervisor's relationships with other supervisors. Supervisors have a dual role. On the one hand, they function as managers. On the other, they themselves are subordinate to higher-level managers.

Linking Pins for Between-Group Development

A lower-level manager can be thought of as a **linking pin.** The supervisor links the work group he or she manages with the employee group immediately above it. As regional sales manager for

FIGURE 7.3

THE LINKING PIN CONCEPT

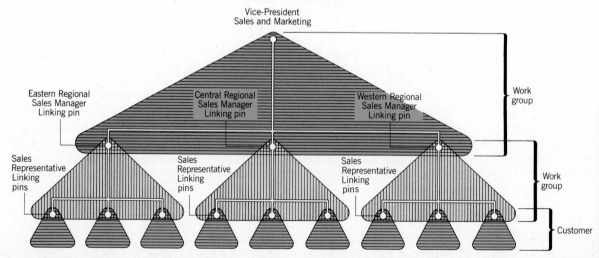

Source: From *New Patterns of Management,* by Rensislikert, p. 105. Copyright 1961 by McGraw-Hill. Used by permission of McGraw-Hill Book Company.

ON THE FIRING LINE

**Corporate Boards—
Democracy or Tyranny?**

As Americans, we like to affirm the principles of democracy. We say we believe that people have the right to be represented. When institutions make policies that affect their lives, people should take part in the policy-making, we insist. Yet there is one large sector of the American scene where democracy does not exist. Business and industry are the mainstays of our economy and our way of life. Business and industry, however, do not cherish the notion of corporate democracy. US corporations do not want to give employees any role in their policy-making processes. They do not want employees elected by their peers to sit on their boards of directors.

Curiously, in this democratic society objections to such a scheme come from all sides. Top management in business and industry has several objections to any such plan. Corporate boards, it says, function to make policy and to execute it. Worker directors might well provide important insights in the policy-making process. But their own self-interest would interfere with any executive function. Their concern with salaries, benefits, and job security would conflict with corporate goals. Management's ability to make speedy and effective decisions would to this extent be limited. The result would be inefficiency and lower productivity.

Moreover, corporate executives maintain, workers should not be involved in carrying out management policy. They are not trained managers; they are therefore not qualified. And they would, practically speaking, be bossing themselves. Furthermore, says management, a corporate board with workers seated on it would lose the unity necessary to conduct business.

As representatives of all employees, employee board members have to take whatever position employees adopted. They would not be free to consider issues as individuals. This would turn the board into a forum for labor negotiations. It would give unions more power than they already had. A development of this sort, executives are convinced, would hurt productivity. Finally, corporate officials note, there is the matter of the law. Currently, corporate directors are required to concern themselves only with what is best for the shareholders. For employee directors, the interests of employees would clearly be of prime concern. Thus to seat them on a board would be illegal as well as unwise. Corporate democracy, executives insist, is a political ideal—a form of socialism that we should avoid at all costs.

Oddly enough, a recent national survey showed that Americans believe that if "the people who worked in the companies selected the managers, set policies, and shared in the profits," the country would be in better economic shape. In fact, proposals for seating workers on boards of directors have been heard more frequently in the last decade. The advantages, say some, could be great. And they reject the fears and arguments of those against worker directors.

These advocates note that workers actually do own huge quantities of corporate stock—in their pension funds. Though the billions of dollars in these funds are controlled and invested by banks and insurance companies, they belong to workers. Thus workers should have a say in corporate policy.

Nashua Corporation, a paper products and office equipment manufacturer, Randy Beckham links his group of sales representatives to the national vice-president of sales and marketing (see Figure 7.3).

As a linking pin, the supervisor can hinder as well as help other work groups and departments to reach their goals. If Beckham failed to tell his supervisor about an important new piece of office equipment that a competitor was going to introduce in six months, Nashua's new product development group would be at a disadvantage.

Conflict and Cooperation Between Groups

Relationships between work groups usually exist because of various tasks that are of common concern to them. The production scheduling and logistics departments of a GM assembly plant must work together to make sure that Olds Cutlass and Pontiac Trans Am cars arrive at dealers on time.

When two groups face a common problem or share joint responsibility, they must work together. In some situations, however, scarce resources or unsatisfactory relations between group supervisors may result in conflict between the groups. Let's assume that a sales representative for Cessna Aircraft in closing a sale promises a customer that the Cessna Citation jet just ordered will arrive within 90 days. By the time the sales order is transmitted to the Cessna manufacturing department, 5 days have passed. Meanwhile, the production department already has 12 back orders for the Citation and will require 150 days for manufacture and shipment. Here, then, is potential for conflict between the sales and manufacturing departments. But conflict may be resolved—through negotiations between the two departments, through mediation efforts by a higher-level manager, or by the customer's agreeing to a longer delivery schedule.

Information Flows and Communication

As we have just seen, one approach to resolving disagreements between groups is for the immediate supervisor of the two conflicting groups to step in. For a situation demanding immediate action, this will surely be the most appropriate and (hopefully) effective approach. A senior vice-president of Cessna could, for example, dictate that Citation orders be moved ahead of other aircraft orders. However when time is less critical, a better approach would be to let the departments "talk it out."

Timely and accurate information can be transmitted quickly through the use of a computer information system. Suppose that the Cessna representative had been able to telephone his or her department and tie into a computer system that contained the Citation production schedules. Right then and there the sales representative would have known that the 90 day delivery time was not possible. Information provided by the computer would have prevented interdepartmental conflict and meant greater cooperation between sales and production.

SUMMARY

It is often argued that people are the business firm's most important resource. To use this resource effectively, managers must understand human relations.

Most adults have a positive feeling toward being productive, and many Americans subscribe to a work ethic. Good work attitudes and job performance usually lead to job satisfaction, which in turn creates high morale.

To manage workers, some managers follow the authoritarian Theory X approach, while others follow the more worker-centered Theory Y. Although Theory Y may be more appealing, Theory X can still be effective, as can a combination of the two.

Workers and organizations expect certain things of each other. Some expectations are formally set out; other, unwritten, expectations are called the *psychological contract.* When worker and organization consistently meet this contract, their attachment is strengthened.

Performance is based in part on motivation. Frederick Taylor advanced the idea that motivation was mainly affected by such external factors as monetary rewards and job security. Later, researchers observed that elements of the social system of work affected employee motivation. Maslow drew on both these views when he developed his hierarchy of needs theory of human motivation, which proposes that people act in order to satisfy needs and that, once lower-level needs are satisfied, a higher-level need emerges to stimulate other behavior. This hierarchy includes physiological needs, safety and security needs, social and affiliation needs, needs related to ego and self-concept, and needs related to achievement and fulfillment.

Several factors can affect work motivation and job satisfaction. Job satisfiers are factors that motivate workers; they relate to the job itself and correspond to needs related to ego. Maintenance factors tend to lie outside the job but can be necessary to keep the worker on the job; they generally relate to physiological, safety, and social needs.

Workers may also be motivated to produce because of expectations about various job rewards and outcomes. Managers must understand the relationship of motivation, performance, and job satisfaction. Money can be a particularly important motivator.

Understanding interpersonal relations can help managers deal with workers in groups. Every organization contains groups; some are deliberately set up, while others are informal. Workers in groups set work norms and value group members who conform to them, while rejecting members who do not. Each member has a role consisting of the expectations relating to the position as well as to actual behavior in the position. The position of the role relative to the rest of the group determines the holder's status. A person can occupy several roles, either formally or informally. Most roles are either task or maintenance oriented.

Effective leadership of groups involves (1) setting goals and defining what activities are to be accomplished and (2) strengthening ties among group members to keep the group together. The true test of effective leadership is when followers do the things necessary for attainment of goals. A department's performance may depend on group cohesiveness, which is affected by many factors and takes time to develop. Cohesiveness yields major advantages but may also lead to disadvantages, depending on whether the group is united in the organization's interests or against it.

Another aspect of group dynamics involves the group's ability and willingness to help solve problems and make decisions. A supervisor who uses a democratic decision style involves group members in these tasks, while an autocratic manager tends to permit little such involvement. Approaches to group decision making vary with the type of group and the type of problem. Group decision making involves both benefits and drawbacks.

Work-group performance depends not only on efforts of workers within the group but also on the supervisor's relationships with other supervisors. As linking pin, the supervisor can hinder or help other work groups. Groups must also sometimes work together to solve problems. When groups are in conflict, supervisors can step in or the groups can work out the conflict themselves.

KEY TERMS

achievement motive
brainstorming
cohesiveness
esteem needs
expectancy
group
hierarchy of
    motivation
human relations
job maintenance
    factors
job satisfaction
job satisfiers
level of aspiration
linking pin
maintenance roles
need
needs theory
norm
physiological needs
psychological contract
quality circle
role
safety needs
self-actualization
social needs
status
task roles
Theory X
Theory Y
Theory Z
work ethic
work group

REVIEW QUESTIONS

1. What is meant by the term "work ethic"?
2. Explain the distinction between job satisfaction and employee morale.
3. What are the basic assumptions of Theory X and Theory Y?

4. What are the five levels (hierarchy) of needs according to Maslow? Briefly describe each.
5. Enumerate the motivational and maintenance factors.
6. How does expectancy affect employee motivation?
7. What are the two important elements of effective leadership?
8. Explain the five determinants of group togetherness.

DISCUSSION QUESTIONS

1. Describe how affiliation with a work group might change individual behavior. Give an example, preferably from your own experience.
2. Why does a worker who tries to set a good example by outproducing coworkers sometimes end up rejected by the group?
3. Explain why an increase in pay may not act as a motivator for every employee.
4. Review Maslow's hierarchy of needs. Which needs does your present (or past) place of employment satisfy? Which needs were not satisfied? Why?
5. How might the psychological contract between employer and employee differ for the following persons: production worker, office clerk, cab driver, store manager.
6. Would you consider your present (or past) employer a believer in Theory X or Theory Y? Give examples of his/her actions to support your belief.

CASE: HAWTHORNE REVISITED

Tom Witty, a recently promoted supervisor, had just learned about a survey by the University of Michigan showing that American workers of all types believed they didn't receive enough information to do their jobs well. Tom was determined to give his workers all the information they needed, and he wanted to try out some of the programmed learning techniques he had just acquired from his recent seminar conducted by the American Management Association. He also wanted to be sure he gave the workers a chance to express themselves about their jobs.

So Tom set about to do a worker survey throughout the plant as an input to his new training program. He used tape recorders to get information, and at first the workers were a little leery about having their voices recorded in these interviews. But Tom assured them that this information would be used to improve their jobs, and who could be against that?

Tom was going to revolutionize the on-the-job training program with a brilliant idea: he would take all his information about jobs and the correct ways of performing tasks on the assembly line and then put it on computer videotapes to be made available on TV monitors placed strategically throughout the plant. The monitors would display job instructions at each step in the assembly line, so that workers would be reminded of the most efficient procedures to be followed in performing their jobs and improving production.

This new approach would take the place of on-the-job training sessions that had previously been offered by lead supervisors and instructors. Money would be saved by using TV monitors instead of people. Tom had worked out all the cost details. In terms of hourly wages and supervisors' salaries, Tom could really save money for the company. He was sure he'd ultimately be rewarded for this breakthrough in training.

1. How do you think the workers will receive this innovation in training?
2. Was Tom right in his assessment of workers and their desire to learn to improve their jobs?
3. Is there anything wrong with this approach, and will the workers receive this innovation with open arms and receptive minds?

CASE: ANY SUGGESTIONS ON SUGGESTIONS?

The managers of the Golden Music Company prided themselves on their outstanding employee relations programs—especially their Suggestion System. John Daly, the personnel manager, played a very active role in screening suggestions, since he's the one who introduced the system and set up the ground rules. As Daly was sifting through the newest load of suggestions, he came across one that really caught his attention. A young lady on the production line, Mary Weather, suggested that by altering the head of a screw on the arm of the record changer, the operation would be improved considerably. As a matter of fact, many changers had been returned by customers who claimed that the arm was hanging up from time to time, interfering with the smooth operation of the machine.

This was a real breakthrough for Mary Weather, and of course she would be rewarded handsomely for such an imaginative and technically sound suggestion. Not only did the suggestion improve the operation of the record changer, it saved the company money, yielded more satisfied customers, and resulted in improved profits. Sure enough, Mary was the star of the show at the annual banquet, receiving the congratulations of the president and an attractive prize of $2500.

John Daly was very happy at this high point in his personnel career. But his pleasure was short-lived. To everyone's surprise, Mary Weather was no longer greeted warmly in the engineering department. Research and development was not exactly sending her flowers. And certain levels of management were turning a cold shoulder to the recently crowned star of the Suggestion System.

1. What happened to cause Mary Weather's star to dim?
2. Why was the engineering department and R and D unhappy with Mary?
3. What could be wrong with such a remarkable suggestion system?

CHAPTER 8

HUMAN RESOURCES MANAGEMENT

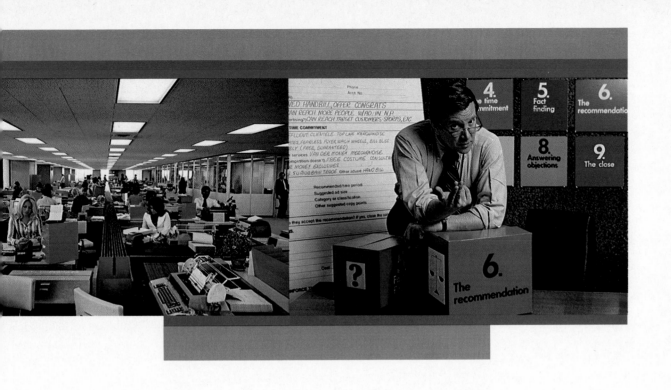

After studying this chapter you should be able to:

1 Describe the nature and activities of the personnel function.
2 Understand how human resources managers perform their functions.
3 Describe the importance of the personnel function to employees and to management.
4 Explain how employees are recruited and selected.
5 Describe the methods by which employees are trained and developed.
6 Understand the importance of the performance appraisal in human resources management.
7 Explain the different forms of compensation and their importance to employees.
8 Describe the role of the federal government in preventing employment discrimination.

Bill Danner *assumed* his managers were satisfied with their jobs—that is, until the day he found out that his sales manager was leaving the company to start a business of his own. Danner, the 40-year-old president of Trak Inc., had always figured that if he hired bright, hard-working people and gave them something constructive to do, they'd keep themselves interested in helping his company succeed. And Trak's performance seemed to prove him right. In 10 years, the Massachusetts-based marketer and manufacturer of cross-country skis, boots, and poles, had grown to $36 million worldwide in revenues, to 10 percent pretax profits, and to a 25 percent share of the U.S. market.

But Danner's sales manager, Eric Eidsmo, said Danner was wrong. Eidsmo told his boss that he knew meeting Danner's sales quotas and keeping the sales force happy was good for Trak—but it wasn't enough for him. As Danner and Eidsmo talked, Danner discovered that his bright, ambitious sales manager wanted more than just sales managerial experience—and he wasn't getting it.

So Danner had a problem. He hadn't really given much thought to whether he could fit the ambitions of a highly motivated manager like Eidsmo into the framework of Trak. One thing he *did* know, though: he couldn't afford to lose a good manager and the kind of idea person who could help Trak grow. Plus he didn't want Trak's sales and marketing or product plans walking out the door. And he didn't want to write off the time he had invested in training and learning to work with Eidsmo.

Source: Adapted with permission of *INC.* Magazine. Susan Benner, "He Gave Key People a Reason to Stay with the Company," *INC.*, September 1980, p. 42. Copyright © 1980 by INC. Publishing Co.

NATURE AND OBJECTIVES OF THE PERSONNEL FUNCTION

Trak's a relatively small company compared to the giants of the ski industry. But hiring and keeping good people is just as important for the small firm as for the large one. In fact the loss of key personnel may severely dampen a small company's serviceability and growth prospects. Intel, the high-technology semiconductor manufacturer, and Marathon Oil Corporation both faced lower growth prospects in the mid-1980s due to the loss of several key employees.

For this reason and others that we shall see, the personnel function has become increasingly important within the organization. There's now greater top management involvement with the personnel function. Top managers are participating in personnel planning and policy making. Why have top executives become more involved? Their expanded role is due primarily to the realization that the personnel function can have an important impact on the firm's profitability.

Many out-of-court settlements have resulted in large cash awards to current and former employees of firms found guilty of employment discrimination. The American Telephone and Telegraph Company settled two employment discrimination suits for a total of $63 million in backpay awards.

The increased involvement by top management is also indicated by the rotation of upper-level managers through the personnel department as part of their training for top executive positions. Many chief executive officers have spent from one to three years as the top personnel official in their organizations.[1] Richard D. Wood, before being named chairman of the board, president, and chief executive officer of Eli Lilly & Company, occupied the top job in personnel for more than two years. W. T. Beebe, chief executive officer of Delta Airlines, was once the firm's senior vice-president for personnel.

Also—and perhaps due to upper management's interaction with the personnel function—the status of the chief personnel officer has been elevated. This is evidenced by the change in job title from *manager* or *director* to *vice-president*. Frequently the vice-president reports directly to the president.

Still another development of importance to the personnel function is the use of the computer to improve record keeping and reports. Even relatively small firms like Menasco Manufacturing, a helicopter parts subcontractor, use the computer for personnel activities, especially payroll and compensation matters.

Personnel Activities

Raw materials, capital items, human resources, and information are essential ingredients for building a good organization. Effective management of human resources is the primary concern of the personnel function.

Historically, personnel management has been concerned with the recruitment, hiring, training, testing, evaluation, and promotion of employees (with all of the planning these imply). The personnel function has also involved employee benefit programs, management-union relations, and organizational compliance with laws and regulations.

Over time, human resources management developed out of the personnel function, until—especially in larger firms—it has become a separate function in its own right. **Human resources management** is concerned with maximizing worker satisfaction, improving worker efficiency and ensuring a sufficient number of quality employees to meet the organization's objectives. This often takes the form of programs to develop employees' interests and talents through training and retraining, based on insightful evaluation of performance and abilities.

We shall examine human resources management in the overall context of the personnel function. The personnel function begins with the job interview (or other hiring arrangement) and ends with disengagement from *all* connection with the firm. Even retirement doesn't end the relationship, since retirement benefits are an ongoing connection between the firm and the former employee.

In summary, important activities within the personnel function are:

1. personnel planning and forecasting,
2. employee recruitment and selection,
3. employee training and development,
4. performance evaluation and career development,
5. compensation and employee benefits,
6. labor relations.

The last of these activities will be covered in Chapter 9. The first five are conducted in logical order, with personnel planning beginning the chain of events.

Personnel activities are linked in such a way that a change in one may eventually lead to an adjustment in all others (see Figure 8.1). For example, American Airlines finds that the vice-president for airport operations will be retiring in six months. Personnel records reveal that three people are good candidates for the airport-operations position vacancy, all three of them division managers. Besides the internal search for a replacement, A. V. Casey, American's president, decides that an external search should also be conducted.

After four weeks of recruiting, five people (including the three inside managers) are identified as candidates. A week later, the job is offered to one of the division managers, Aileen Loredan. After two salary negotiation meetings, Aileen accepts a specially designed compensation package. During the next four months she's sent to Stanford Business School to participate in a four-week executive training and development program. Finally, two weeks before becoming airport operations manager, she has a complete physical examination. The doctor recommends that Aileen get more exercise. She then receives a physical fitness prescription from Quick and Associates, an executive health-fitness consultant.

Even by omitting all the decisions that preceded Aileen's promotion—beginning with her hiring by American—this story shows that one personnel decision leads to others. Also, a number of personnel specialists and managers may be involved. In fact it's common to find three levels of management making most personnel decisions: (1) top management, (2) lower-level operating (line) managers, and (3) staff specialists and managers within the personnel department. The focus of this chapter is on the third group. Figure 8.2 illustrates the personnel department of one major (and huge) corporation—Dresser Industries. Dresser is a diversified multinational supplier of equipment and technical services to energy and natural resource industries.

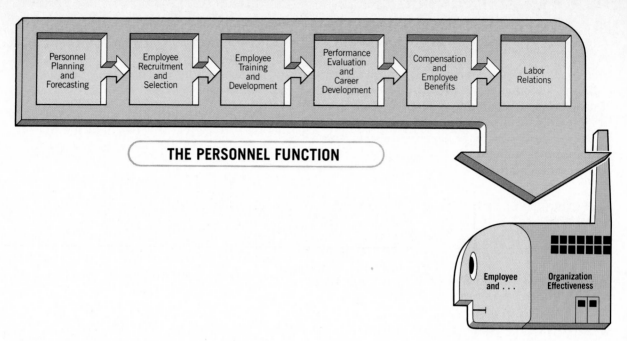

FIGURE 8.1

FIGURE 8.2

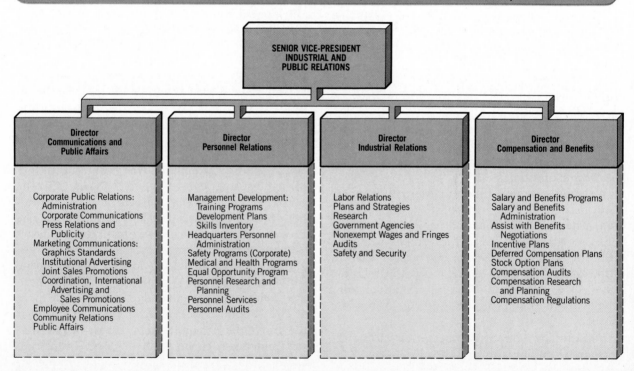

Source: Allen R. Janger, *The Personnel Function: Changing Objectives and Organization* (New York: Conference Board, 1977), p. 24. Reprinted by permission.

TALKING BUSINESS

Just as women have gained a footing in nearly every occupation once reserved for men, men can be found today working routinely in a wide variety of jobs once held nearly exclusively by women. The men are working as receptionists and flight attendants, servants and even "Kelly girls."

The Urban Institute, a research group in Washington, recently estimated that the number of male secretaries rose 24% to 31,000 in 1978 from 25,000 in 1972, while the number of male telephone operators over the same span rose 38%, and the number of male nurses, 94%. Labor experts expect the trend to continue.

Source: Excerpted from Carol Hymowitz, "More Men Infiltrating Professions Historically Dominated by Women," *Wall Street Journal*, February 25, 1981, p. 25. Reprinted by permission of The Wall Street Journal, © Dow Jones & Company, Inc., 1981. All rights reserved.

Objectives of the Personnel Department

The overall objectives of the personnel function are (1) to maximize the effectiveness of human resources, (2) to satisfy employee needs in helping the employee achieve a successful career, and (3) to provide a source of competent, well-trained employees for the various departments in the company. For the personnel department to accomplish its goals, personnel managers must have a clear understanding of the objectives of the entire organization.

Relationships Between the Personnel Specialist and the Operating Manager

The personnel department typically supports the line (or operating) segment of the business. Personnel specialists perform many jobs that are of help to line managers in making personnel decisions. Basic personnel policies come from top managers and executives. These policies are essential contributions to the personnel function, and without them personnel has no mission. Given this overall direction by top managers, specialists then design the company's personnel programs. The primary responsibility for using these programs lies with lower-level operating managers in manufacturing, marketing, and other functional areas (see Figure 8.3).

Suppose that an office manager in the claims department of Metro Insurance needs an additional clerk typist. To fill this need, the manager sends an employee requisition form to the personnel department. There a specialist in the employment office places an ad in the "help wanted" section of the *New York Times* or other suitable media. Applicants for the job are interviewed and tested by the personnel specialist. Those applicants meeting the minimum hiring requirements are taken to the office manager for further, in-

FIGURE 8.3

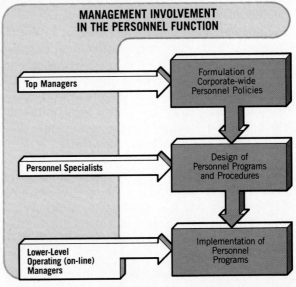

MANAGEMENT INVOLVEMENT IN THE PERSONNEL FUNCTION

Top Managers → Formulation of Corporate-wide Personnel Policies

Personnel Specialists → Design of Personnel Programs and Procedures

Lower-Level Operating (on-line) Managers → Implementation of Personnel Programs

depth interviewing. Of the six applicants who are interviewed, one is offered a job by the office manager.

After accepting the offer, the new employee is sent back to the personnel department to be added to the payroll and to establish a permanent personnel record. Throughout this process, the office manager and the personnel specialist must keep in mind two very important personnel policies. One policy affirms that the company is an "equal opportunity employer." The other specifies that the company "attempts to hire the most qualified person available for every vacant position."

Three distinct roles of the personnel department can be seen in the Metro example. The first is to help design personnel policy. The employment specialists design recruitment and employee selection programs based on the employment philosophy and policies of top management. Secondly, many of the routine tasks of recruiting and employee record keeping are provided by the personnel department. Service, then, is a distinct role of the personnel function. In its third role, the personnel department acts as a control unit for the rest of the organization. It makes sure that employment discrimination doesn't take place and that highly qualified job applicants are hired.

HUMAN RESOURCES PLANNING

Personnel and human resources planning involves (1) defining future human resources needs or requirements, (2) examining the current inventory of human resources (number and qualifications of existing employees), and (3) determining the strategy for moving from the firm's current work force to the desired size and quality of work force. **Personnel planning** helps a firm to have the correct number of people with the appropriate skills at the right places and at the right times.

Personnel planning begins with a review of strategic corporate plans. By understanding the mission of the organization, personnel planners can better forecast human resource needs. When American Airlines moved its headquarters from New York City to Fort Worth, much personnel planning was necessary to carry out this important decision. Planning involved whom to trans-

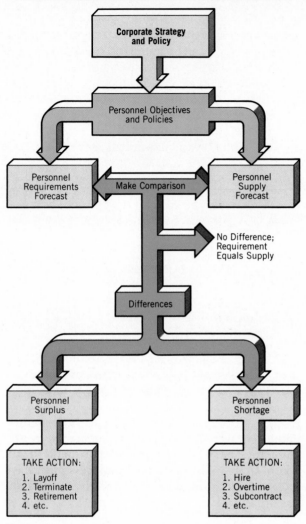

PERSONNEL PLANNING PROCESS

FIGURE 8.4

fer, when to move them, and how to orient those employees to their new job surroundings.

Usually two forecasts are generated: (1) a human resources demand forecast to estimate employment needs, and (2) a supply of labor estimate to find the number of people within the organization who will be available to fill jobs in the future. Next specific personnel objectives are made in the areas of recruitment (e.g. number of persons to hire), employee training, compensation, and other personnel programs. Action plans are then constructed from the program objectives. An action plan is a detailed statement setting forth just how the personnel objectives can be accomplished. Finally, reports are used to provide feedback. If the feedback reveals some problem areas, the planning system and other personnel programs may need to be redesigned (see Figure 8.4). A well-designed personnel information system can furnish much of the information for effective planning.

Role of Human Resources Information Systems

All personnel activities need information about employees. This information can be entered into an information system that permits systematic data input, storage, and retrieval for the personnel function (see Figure 8.5). During the last 20 years many business firms, including PepsiCo, Monsanto, and Owens-Corning, have created computerized personnel information systems.

A major function of the computerized personnel information system is to identify and describe characteristics of employees. Also, many information systems contain data about job characteristics, labor market conditions, payroll budgets, fringe benefit eligibility, and job openings in the organization. General Motors has hundreds of bits of information about its managers coded for information storage and processing. When a managerial position opens at GM, a list of employees with the necessary qualifications is automatically generated from the personnel information system. From this list a person may be selected and promoted to fill the vacancy.

Job Analysis and Design

Characteristics of jobs are very important data for successful personnel planning. A **job** is a collection of tasks and responsibilities, making up a unit of work, that may be performed by one or more people. Information about a specific job is put together through a program of **job analysis.** This is the systematic study of a unit of work, or job, in terms of its tasks and processes. A job analyst collects information about a job by identifying the tasks and employee skills needed for effective job performance. For example, when General Dynamics was awarded the F-16 fighter plane contract, several new industrial engineering jobs were created. Job analysts from the personnel department gathered task and job information from department heads and supervisors to assist re-

cruiters in hiring college-graduate engineers to fill these jobs.

The tasks and responsibilities of a job—including the authorizations, limits, conditions, and other elements built into it—are usually listed in the **job description.** The skills, knowledge, and abilities necessary for the job are recorded in another document called the **job specification.** These forms help the personnel planner to decide whether existing jobs are adequate for carrying out a new program. At General Dynamics it was necessary to create several new mechanical engineering jobs to be filled by persons with knowledge and work experience in nonmetal aircraft parts.

Work Scheduling and the Altered Workweek

Another important consideration in planning for human resources is the scheduling of work. Common work schedules consist of 8-hour work shifts—either one, two, or three of them in a 24-hour period. A one-shift business presents fewer planning problems than does a multishift operation with overlapping work crews. Even the standard 8-hour workday of 8:00 A.M. to 5:00 P.M. (with a one-hour lunch period) can be troublesome. It may be hard to fix the minimum number of employees required if the amount of work fluctuates from one hour to the next, as it does in a supermarket. The seasonality of various products (e.g. fruitcakes, swimsuits, snowmobiles) and services (e.g. ski lodges, swimming pool cleaners, and professional sports) can also create problems in personnel planning. During the harvest season for many vegetables, the H. J. Heinz Company has to increase its plant work force by three or four times to help process the vegetables.

Many retail and industrial firms, such as General Tire and Smith Kline Corporation, have in recent years experimented with **altered workweek** schedules. These work plans are major departures from the standard 8-hour day, 5-day week schedule. Two variations of the altered workweek are the compressed schedule and flexitime. The **compressed workweek** involves scheduling 40 hours of normal work into less than 5 days or working less than 40 hours a week but receiving 40 hours of pay. Three examples of this arrangement are (1) 4-day week, 10-hour day—a schedule used successfully by Kraftco's Sealtest

A PERSONNEL INFORMATION SYSTEM

DATA INPUT

DATA OUTPUT

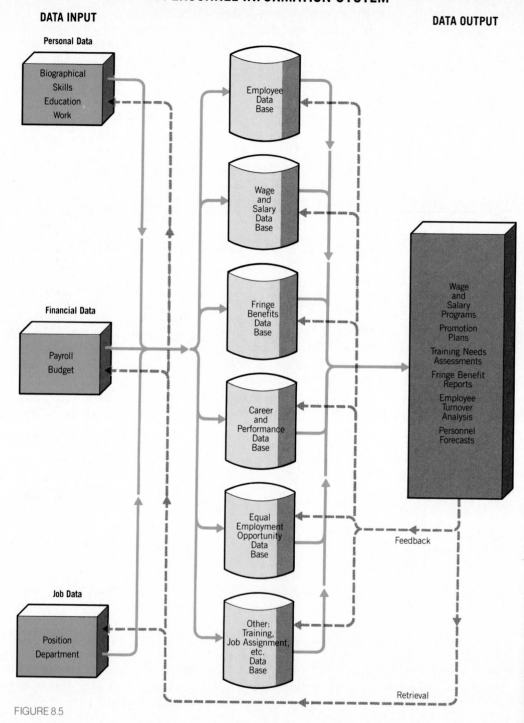

Personal Data

Biographical
Skills
Education
Work

Financial Data

Payroll
Budget

Job Data

Position
Department

Employee
Data
Base

Wage
and
Salary
Data
Base

Fringe
Benefits
Data
Base

Career
and
Performance
Data
Base

Equal
Employment
Opportunity
Data
Base

Other:
Training,
Job Assignment,
etc.
Data
Base

Wage
and
Salary
Programs

Promotion
Plans

Training Needs
Assessments

Fringe Benefit
Reports

Employee
Turnover
Analysis

Personnel
Forecasts

Feedback

Retrieval

FIGURE 8.5

Foods; (2) 3-day week, 12-hour day—used by Lipton Tea; and (3) 4-day week, 9-hour day—a variation at Scoville Manufacturing.

Flexitime means that all employees must be present and working during a core (high-volume) work period of the day (say from 9:30 A.M. to 2:00 P.M.). The remaining hours are completed whenever the employee wants. Under this type of arrangement 40 hours of flexitime has been successfully applied to operations at the Social Security Administration in Baltimore.

EMPLOYEE RECRUITMENT AND SELECTION

Internal and External Labor Markets

When a firm creates a new position or an existing job becomes vacant, a personnel search begins to identify people with the right qualifications. There are two job-applicant pools where qualified persons can be found. These are the internal and external labor markets. The **internal labor market** is within the organization, while the **external labor market** lies outside it.

Many businesses such as Sears, Pepperidge Farms, and State Farm Insurance attempt to fill non-entry-level positions from within the company. If there are no qualified internal candidates, the organization may search the external market. Entry-level jobs (or trainee positions) are typically filled with people from the external labor market.

The internal search for applicants usually results in some reassignment of human resources through either promotion (upward movement), transfers (movement at the same level), or demotions (downward movement). Externally, the employee search process involves (1) developing sources of applicants, (2) issuing information about job openings, and (3) trying to attract qualified prospects to the firm.

Methods of Recruitment and Job Information

Recruiting attempts to find and attract qualified and compatible applicants from the external labor market. For this purpose the organization may advertise, solicit on college campuses, use employment agencies, or hire the services of outside recruiting firms. In most situations, the nature of the job opening determines the recruiting method. There are major differences between recruiting assembly-line workers and trying to attract professional/managerial employees. Boeing Aircraft would not recruit an experienced engineer the same way it would recruit a janitor. Nor would it be likely to recruit a top-level manager in exactly the same way it recruited an engineer.

Attracting Nonmanagement Personnel Unskilled workers are usually attracted to a company through radio and newspaper advertising, employee referrals, and the job placement services of the joint federal-state U.S. Training and Employment Service (USTES). The Texas Employment Commission and Iowa State Employment Service are examples of state agencies of USTES. Radio ads for jobs have been used successfully by Texas Instruments, Wang Laboratories, and many other companies. With the information received

Most companies post job openings for their employees.

from USTES or a "help wanted" ad, prospective employees usually apply directly to the employer at the job site. Regardless of the method, applicants are ordinarily given limited but specific job information. Topics covered include time and place of work, wage rate, name of immediate supervisor, times of rest breaks, and equipment used. The labor market for nonmanagement workers is usually no more than 30 miles from the job site.

College and Professional Employee Recruiting Positions requiring highly specialized skills and knowledge call for a different recruiting strategy. For entry-level managerial and professional positions, many firms look to the college campus. Recruiters are sent by IBM, Xerox, Exxon, Shell Oil, J. C. Penney, and many others to colleges and universities across the country to conduct preliminary interviews with thousands of students who are nearing graduation. Students get information from specially prepared company brochures, annual reports, and position descriptions (see Figure 8.6).

Employment Agencies and Executive Search Firms For professional and managerial positions above the entry level, many firms rely on private employment agencies and executive search firms. An **employment agency,** such as Snelling and Snelling (which has offices in many large U.S. cities), helps job applicants and employers by coming up with an acceptable employment match. Employers list job openings with such an agency, on whose door applicants knock seeking professional jobs. When an employer hires an applicant, a fee is paid to the agency by the employer or the individual. This fee could be as much as one month's salary.

An **executive search firm,** such as Paul Ray and Associates, operates much like a private employment agency. However it rarely assists job applicants. Rather, the search firm works almost exclusively with employers to recruit people for middle management or executive-level positions. Often the executives reached by a search firm on behalf of an employer are already employed and may not be seeking new positions. The employer attempts to lure away a qualified person from another company by going through the search firm. This technique is sometimes called "pirating of employees," the search firms being dubbed *headhunters* and *people pluckers*. There are approxi-

"...AND THE RECRUITER FROM IBM — DID YOU ALSO TELL HIM THAT AT COLLEGE YOU MOSTLY SAT ON A ROCK BY THE SEA, TRYING TO FIND YOURSELF?"

mately 300 prominent and specialized recruiting firms scattered worldwide.

The Employee Selection Process

After people have been attracted to the firm and applications have been received, employment specialists begin the screening and reviewing process, with perhaps some applicants eventually being offered jobs. This employee selection process consists of several steps, of which each is a progressively more difficult hurdle for the applicant to leap over. A diagram of the selection process is shown in Figure 8.7.

Initial Screening The first two steps in the selection process together make up the initial screening; these two can occur in either order. They are the preliminary interview and the employment application form—the two most commonly used selection tools. The preliminary interview tends to be rather short, often lasting less than 15 minutes. This interview is part of a rough screening process. It is usually structured, and the questions asked are very specific.

We believe our first responsibility is to the doctors, nurses and patients, to mothers and all others who use our products and services ■ In meeting their needs everything we do must be of high quality ■ We must constantly strive to reduce our costs in order to maintain reasonable prices ■ Customers' orders must be serviced promptly and accurately ■ Our suppliers and distributors must have an opportunity to make a fair profit ■

We are responsible to our employees, the men and women who work with us throughout the world ■ Everyone must be considered as an individual ■ We must respect their dignity and recognize their merit ■ They must have a sense of security in their jobs ■ Compensation must be fair and adequate, and working conditions clean, orderly and safe ■ Employees must feel free to make suggestions and complaints ■ There must be equal opportunity for employment, development and advancement for those qualified ■ We must provide competent management, and their actions must be just and ethical ■

We are responsible to the communities in which we live and work and to the world community as well ■ We must be good citizens—support good works and charities and bear our fair share of taxes ■ We must encourage civic improvements and better health and education ■ We must maintain in good order the property we are privileged to use, protecting the environment and natural resources ■

Our final responsibility is to our stockholders ■ Business must make a sound profit ■ We must experiment with new ideas ■ Research must be carried on, innovative programs developed and mistakes paid for ■ New equipment must be purchased, new facilities provided and new products launched ■ Reserves must be created to provide for adverse times ■ When we operate according to these principles, the stockholders should realize a fair return ■

△ Early responsibility, diversity, and growth characterize the array of functional career opportunities at Johnson & Johnson. Some of our professionals, shown here, discuss their careers later in this brochure.

Johnson & Johnson is the largest and most diversified health care products company in the world. We rank among the top 100 of the Fortune 500 U.S. industrial corporations, with sales of about $5 billion. Our products range from the well-known BAND-AID Brand Adhesive Bandage to the most advanced medical diagnostic imaging equipment.

We are a highly decentralized family of 150 companies—each with responsibility for charting its own course for the future. When you work for a Johnson & Johnson

company—whether in marketing, sales, engineering, finance, research, or another function—you're part of a relatively small, highly autonomous organization, rich with the vast resources of Johnson & Johnson. That makes you a vital contributor from the beginning. And that's the Johnson & Johnson difference.

We can offer you a unique opportunity to play an important part in an important company—and in an atmosphere in which bright, talented people can make a difference wherever they start.

FIGURE 8.6

An excerpt from a Johnson & Johnson recruiting brochure.

FIGURE 8.7

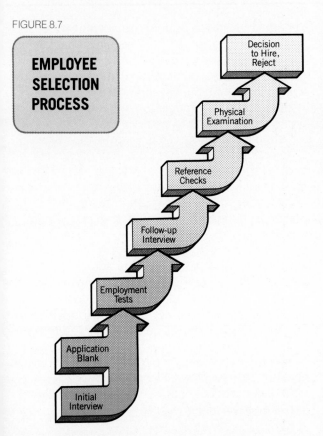

EMPLOYEE SELECTION PROCESS

Decision to Hire, Reject

Physical Examination

Reference Checks

Follow-up Interview

Employment Tests

Application Blank

Initial Interview

Employment application forms tend to be relatively short, contain specific questions, and can be coded for computer processing and storage (see Figure 8.8). Some firms attach numerical weights to various items, creating a weighted application blank. Those items that are considered more accurate predictors of successful job performance, such as previous work experience, are weighted more heavily. These weights can be converted to a scoring system to determine the total score of the application. The higher the score, the better qualified the candidate is supposed to be.

Employment Testing After initial screening, the applicant may be asked to take one or more employment tests (see Table 8.1). These tests attempt to measure the person's general intelligence and knowledge, aptitude, skills, work interests, and personality (see Figure 8.9). Some may test performance on samples of work or artificial job tasks. A typing test, for example, attempts to measure an applicant's ability to type efficiently and accurately. A work sample requires that the applicant perform a "mock" job task. Thus Roadway Express might ask a prospective driver to take a road test in an eighteen-wheeler.

ON THE FIRING LINE

Should Education Get Down to Business?

What is the purpose of education? Is it to improve the mind? Is it to humanize the spirit? Is it to prepare for a job? Who should decide?

In the last few decades, the demand has increased for career, and particularly business, education. Knowledge in many fields has burst out of the grasp of any one individual. Science and technology have become unbelievably complex. Many believe that the person who does not prepare for a specific career in college will be unable to compete in the job market upon graduating. They go on to say that today's students are wise to foresake the liberal arts education highly prized in times past for courses in business.

The ability to function in business, these critics stress, is a key to power as well as money. Power, in our country, is vested primarily in big business and in government. These two domains of our economy are tightly interwoven, and the principles of business are basic to both. Even minority and antiestablishment students are turning to business education. They feel that to make headway in society, they must learn the skills required to run a business.

Colleges and educators who promote liberal arts education are elitist, say those in favor of business education. They would have American education designed for the masses. In their view, a liberal arts education—foreign languages, literature, philosophy, political theory, for example—has little value for the masses. What everybody needs most is a means of support. The fact that those who do still opt for a liberal arts education are largely the well-to-do is evidence, they say, that such schooling is indeed a luxury. And the number of liberally educated Ph.D.s who drive taxis, do construction work, wait tables, or have low-paying clerical jobs underscores the uselessness of such training.

Teachers in the liberal arts know that the number of college-age students will dwindle in years to come. They are also aware that students are more interested in preparing for jobs than in taking their classes. Thus their efforts to compel, or at least induce, students to take their courses is self-serving. Without students they will have no jobs. In a free society, however, students must be allowed to choose what type of education they receive. The numbers speak for themselves. As many as one out of every four entering freshmen is choosing to study business.

Despite these strong arguments, others take an opposing view. They believe a liberal education is important for everyone. Their position is supported by recent studies, employers' reports, and the admissions policies of some of the most prestigious graduate schools of business. Take Stanford University, for instance. Its business school prefers to admit well-rounded students. Fifty-five percent of the class of 1980 had undergraduate majors in the social sciences or humanities, 30 percent in science and engineering—and only 13 percent in business.

Emphasis in business curricula is on numbers—profits and losses. Yet business success is heavily dependent on more human factors. The ability to relate and talk to people—to colleagues, employees, clients—requires an understanding of human nature. And that understanding—not to mention the writing skills and vocabulary often found wanting in employees—is best nurtured through a more liberal education.

To think logically, to analyze diverse issues, to question that which is commonly accepted, and to communicate—these skills are of supreme importance. They are the skills of dynamic leadership, insist those in favor of a liberal arts education. Without the leadership qualities and diversity liberal education encourages, business would suffer. A senior executive at American Can talked not long ago about the success of his company's recruiting policy. American Can hires high-achiever liberal arts graduates as well as MBAs and accountants. The liberal arts recruits, he noted, were highly effective in unstructured projects—projects where the business school graduate's "numbers-first" approach was not suitable.

And so the debate goes on. Should education get down to business or not?

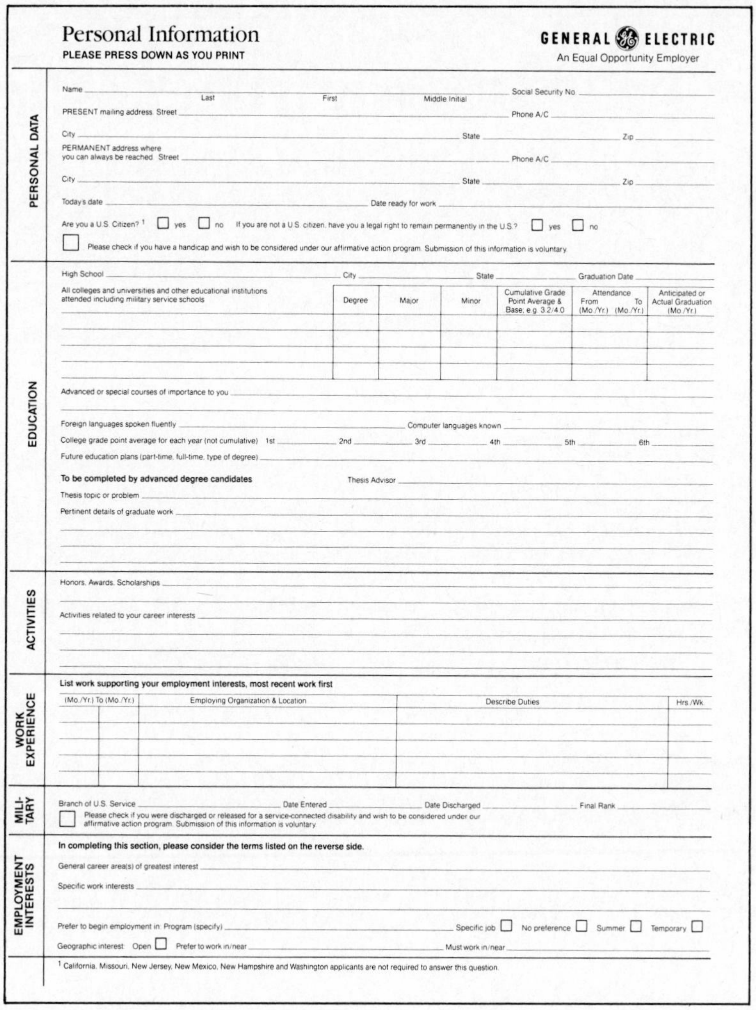

FIGURE 8.8
A job application blank from General Electric.

Personal Information
PLEASE PRESS DOWN AS YOU PRINT

GENERAL ⊛ ELECTRIC
An Equal Opportunity Employer

PERSONAL DATA

Name ____
Last ____ First ____ Middle Initial ____ Social Security No ____
PRESENT mailing address Street ____ Phone A/C ____
City ____ State ____ Zip ____
PERMANENT address where you can always be reached Street ____ Phone A/C ____
City ____ State ____ Zip ____
Today's date ____ Date ready for work ____
Are you a U.S. Citizen? ▢ yes ▢ no   If you are not a U.S. citizen, have you a legal right to remain permanently in the U.S.? ▢ yes ▢ no
▢ Please check if you have a handicap and wish to be considered under our affirmative action program. Submission of this information is voluntary.

EDUCATION

High School ____ City ____ State ____ Graduation Date ____
All colleges and universities and other educational institutions attended including military service schools | Degree | Major | Minor | Cumulative Grade Point Average & Base; e.g. 3.2/4.0 | Attendance From (Mo./Yr.) To (Mo./Yr.) | Anticipated or Actual Graduation (Mo./Yr.)

Advanced or special courses of importance to you ____
Foreign languages spoken fluently ____ Computer languages known ____
College grade point average for each year (not cumulative) 1st ____ 2nd ____ 3rd ____ 4th ____ 5th ____ 6th ____
Future education plans (part-time, full-time, type of degree) ____

To be completed by advanced degree candidates   Thesis Advisor ____
Thesis topic or problem ____
Pertinent details of graduate work ____

ACTIVITIES

Honors, Awards, Scholarships ____
Activities related to your career interests ____

WORK EXPERIENCE

List work supporting your employment interests, most recent work first
(Mo./Yr.) To (Mo./Yr.) | Employing Organization & Location | Describe Duties | Hrs./Wk.

MILITARY

Branch of U.S. Service ____ Date Entered ____ Date Discharged ____ Final Rank ____
▢ Please check if you were discharged or released for a service-connected disability and wish to be considered under our affirmative action program. Submission of this information is voluntary.

EMPLOYMENT INTERESTS

In completing this section, please consider the terms listed on the reverse side.
General career area(s) of greatest interest ____
Specific work interests ____
Prefer to begin employment in: Program (specify) ____ Specific job ▢ No preference ▢ Summer ▢ Temporary ▢
Geographic interest: Open ▢ Prefer to work in/near ____ Must work in/near ____

[1] California, Missouri, New Jersey, New Mexico, New Hampshire and Washington applicants are not required to answer this question.

TABLE 8-1

Common Employment Tests

Type of Test	Example	Test Measures
Intelligence or mental ability	General Aptitude Test and Employee Aptitude Survey	Verbal and numerical ability, word fluency, reasoning ability, and other areas
Job skills and knowledge	Work sample and achievement tests (typing, shorthand, office machine test)	Finger and manual dexterity, speed and accuracy, reaction time, and precision control
Personality test or inventory	California Psychological Inventory and Edwards Personal Preference Schedule	Aggressiveness or passivity, cooperativeness, introversion or extroversion, and dominance or submissiveness
Vocational interest test	Strong vocational interest blank and Kuder Preference Record	Individual interest in relation to vocational categories, including scientific, literary, social service, and other broad fields

FIGURE 8.9
Sample questions from the instruction section of the Wonderlic Personnel Test

WONDERLIC

PERSONNEL TEST

FORM I

NAME..Date...............
(Please Print)

READ THIS PAGE CAREFULLY. DO EXACTLY AS YOU ARE TOLD.
DO NOT TURN OVER THIS PAGE UNTIL YOU ARE
INSTRUCTED TO DO SO.

This is a test of problem solving ability. It contains various types of questions. Below is a sample question correctly filled in:

REAP is the opposite of

    1 obtain,   2 cheer,   3 continue,   4 exist,   5 sow ....[5]

The correct answer is "sow." (It is helpful to underline the correct word.) The correct word is numbered 5. Then write the figure 5 in the brackets at the end of the line.

Answer the next sample question yourself.

Paper sells for 23 cents per pad. What will 4 pads cost? ....[...]

The correct answer is 92¢. There is nothing to underline so just place "92¢" in the brackets.

Here is another example:

MINER   MINOR — Do these words have

    1 similar meaning,   2 contradictory,   3 mean neither same nor opposite? ....[...]

The correct answer is "mean neither same nor opposite" which is number 3 so all you have to do is place a figure "3" in the brackets at the end of the line.

When the answer to a question is a letter or a number, put the letter or number in the brackets. All letters should be printed.

This test contains 50 questions. It is unlikely that you will finish all of them, but do your best. After the examiner tells you to begin, you will be given exactly 12 minutes to work as many as you can. Do not go so fast that you make mistakes since you must try to get as many right as possible. The questions become increasingly difficult, so do not skip about. Do not spend too much time on any one problem. The examiner will not answer any questions after the test begins.

Now, lay down your pencil and wait for the examiner to tell you to begin!

Do not turn the page until you are told to do so.

Interviewing the Applicant The **selection interview** is the most widely used tool for making the actual hiring decision. It can be used to gather in-depth information about the applicant's work experiences and training, his/her skills and abilities, how well he or she communicates, and his or her personal mannerisms. For a managerial or professional position, such as that of internal auditor, the applicant might be screened for more than an hour by several interviewers using open-ended (nonspecific) questions. Example: "Why do you think you would enjoy working for our company?" Obviously, this question can not be answered with a simple "yes" or "no."

Selection Criteria and the Hiring Decision A criterion is a guide or standard used to help reach a decision—in this case, to hire or not to hire.

Several criteria are often used to decide whether to offer someone a job, and they are almost always based on the job requirements. For example, a theoretical minimum test score could be set to measure an applicant's skill in mathematics or English. Applicants scoring above the minimum level would be given further consideration for the job.

Other, more general, criteria are also used to help find the "right person." One survey has shown that *nonmanagement* employees rated as tops by their bosses have a number of work attitudes in common. These attitudes are often used as criteria for hiring new employees. What is the profile that emerges from these attitudes? The top-ranked worker tends to:

- Put family or love first in order of what's important.

- Take great pride in his/her work.
- Work long weeks.
- Have no college degree (surprise!).
- Think money is important, but not nearly as necessary as the satisfaction of doing a job well.
- Think accuracy is the most important element of a job well done.[2]

Affirmative Action and Equal Employment Opportunity

As a result of federal and state legislation it is illegal for employers to discriminate against job applicants and employees or otherwise to treat them unfairly. Hiring, training, and job promotion decisions must be unbiased and based on qualifications, credentials, and performance. Discriminatory or unfair employment practices by the firm may result in a wide range of penalties, including loss of government contracts.

Legal Environment and Requirements Key federal laws governing the relationship between the employee and the employer include Title VII of the Civil Rights Act (1964), the Equal Pay Act (1963), the Age Discrimination in Employment Act (1967), and the Equal Employment Opportunity Act (1972). These acts forbid an employer to discriminate on the basis of age, race, sex, color, national origin, religion, or handicapped status. For example, it's unlawful to discriminate against people who are between the ages of 40 and 70 years. An employer also cannot legally pay different salaries to males and females doing equal and the same work.

Role of Government Agencies The two most prominent federal agencies that enforce employment discrimination laws are the **Equal Employment Opportunity Commission (EEOC)** and the **Office of Federal Contract Compliance Programs (OFCCP).** The EEOC was created by the 1964 Civil Rights Act, which authorizes it to investigate and resolve charges of employment discrimination. The Act also empowers this agency to file lawsuits on its own against employers. Court action against employer violators may require that companies promote, pay back-wages, or provide additional training to employees who suffered discrimination. In 1980 the Motorola Company had to make large back-pay awards

and offer special training to minorities that had been discriminated against.

The OFCCP (created by Executive Order 11246) polices firms under government contract to make sure that applicants and employees get fair treatment. A major part of its enforcement activity involves review of the contractor's affirmative action plans and programs. If there is a major violation of this executive order, the OFCCP can recommend cancellation of a firm's government contract. **Affirmative action** involves a major effort by employers to significantly expand the number of minority applicants.

EMPLOYEE TRAINING AND MANAGER DEVELOPMENT

The personnel department tries to bring about a suitable match between the new employee and the job; but rarely is the match perfect. The firm must therefore train the employee to perform the job efficiently and effectively.

Training Needs and Development Objectives

A **training and development program** attempts to increase the knowledge and skills of the employee, making him or her more productive and efficent for the firm. In general, training and development programs are concerned with (1) orientation of new employees, (2) improving performance of employees in their present jobs, and (3) preparing people for more job responsibilities and promotions.

Designing Training and Development Programs

A common view of learning is that it's a "relatively permanent change in behavior that occurs as a result of practice or experience."[3] After a newly hired supermarket clerk has received job instructions and been given time to practice on the cash register, the clerk will perform more efficiently. Thus training objectives are often stated in behavioral terms as well as in knowledge and skill levels. Behavioral objectives state what the desired behavior of an employee should be after training. So the supermarket clerk, following training, would be expected to look for mismarked prices on items and to ring up a shopper's

TALKING BUSINESS

Even the appearance of discrimination in job interviews can lead to lawsuits, says Edward R. Koller Jr., executive vice-president of Howard-Sloan Associates, a New York–based executive search firm. In a pamphlet called *Careful Questions*, the firm offers interviewers the following suggestions:

- Write your questions ahead of time. Remove references to age, sex, color, creed, religion and national origin.
- Don't imply that the job is available only to members of one sex by saying "she must show initiative" or "he has to be a hard worker."
- Don't ask—
  How old are you?
  What is your date of birth?
  Do you have children?
  What is your race?
  What church do you attend?
  Are you married, divorced, widowed, single?
  Were you ever arrested?
  What type of military discharge do you have?
  What clubs or organizations do you belong to?
  What is your political affiliation?
  Do you rent or own your home?
  What does your spouse do?
  Who lives in your house?
  Have your wages ever been attached or garnisheed?
  What is your maiden name?

Source: Adapted from "Conducting a Safe Job Interview," pp. 21–22, reprinted by permission from *Nation's Business*, November, 1981, Copyright 1981 by *Nation's Business*, Chamber of Commerce of the United States.

purchases accurately. If employees come up with the desired behavior, the training can be considered successful. The grocery clerk who always calls out prices to the customer should be successful at identifying errors in pricing.

Training materials may be in print form, but films and video and audio tapes are finding increasing use. Techniques and methods of training can be broadly classified as either on-the-job- or off-the-job. Off-the-job methods tend to involve more expensive and formal settings, such as the classroom. An example of formal training is a three-day conference on employee selection conducted by Harvard Business School. On-the-job training is usually done by supervisors and coworkers. Supervisors, for example, train new employees through orientation and specific job instructions. Various on- and off-the-job methods are presented in Table 8.2.

TABLE 8–2

Methods of Employee Training and Development

On the Job	Off the Job
Job instruction	Lecture
Apprenticeship	Role playing
Coaching	Films and video tapes
Internship	Simulation
Special projects	Vestibule training
Job rotation	Programmed instruction
Assistantship	Case study
	Conference or workshop
	Sensitivity training
	Apprenticeship classes

Training of a railroad engineer.

Employees learn and acquire skill and knowledge in several ways. Some of these are (1) experimentation, (2) discussion and exchange of information with others, (3) reading, and (4) questioning of concepts and ideas. Each person has a unique style of learning. However there are sufficient similarities in the way individuals learn so that specific training materials and techniques can be used with relatively large groups of workers.

On-the-job methods tend to be very direct and quickly applicable to the employee's job. Some of these involve (1) job rotation, (2) coaching, (3) special assignments on projects, (4) specific job instructions, and (5) frequent performance appraisals. Regardless of the method, the employee is usually given very quick and concrete feedback about results. Corrective action can be taken by the employee shortly after learning of a mistake.

Off-the-job training may take the form of special classes, workshops, and conferences. These may involve lectures, films, computer-assisted instruction, questionnaires, and the discussion/solution of case problems. Usually methods and materials are used that are interactive, problem centered, and experience based. Learning and feedback take place on an individual basis or through small-group activities. The participation of trainees in discussing and analyzing study materials aids the transference of knowledge and experience from the classroom to actual job situations.

PERFORMANCE APPRAISAL AND CAREER DEVELOPMENT

Another important personnel function besides training is performance appraisal and career development. Knowledge of results from a performance evaluation can stimulate an employee to work harder. In the early 1970s Emery Air Freight saved millions of dollars and greatly improved workforce performance through frequent performance feedback from supervisors to freight packers and handlers. **Performance appraisal** means comparing actual performance with expected employee performance. Expected performance is set by establishing performance standards.

Let's take the case of Fred Bartin, sales representative for Black & Decker, the general machinery and tool producer. B & D established sales objectives of (1) a 20 percent increase in total sales-dollar volume and (2) a 10 percent increase (in sales-dollars) in average sales per customer for Fred. The first objective will have to be met within six months; but Fred is given only three months to reach the second. To accomplish these objectives, Fred must find more customers while at the same time selling more products to those who are already customers.

To reach the first goal, Fred plans to contact five potential customers in each of the first three months of the sales performance plan. During the last three months, follow-up contacts will be made to complete the sale. Fred also plans to make more use of the telephone with existing Black & Decker customers. This will give him more time for face-to-face meetings with potential customers.

Career Planning and Development

If Fred remains with Black & Decker, he'll receive career planning help from the personnel department. Career planning and development has become quite popular, especially for managerial and professional employees. A **career** is a series of

TALKING BUSINESS

Working from the premise that an employee's problems can mean management headaches, Control Data Corp. is now selling a dial-for-help program it has been using in-house for seven years. The plan (which costs some $15 per employee per year) involves a 24-hour "800" telephone hot line that allows workers to call for aid with any personal or family problem, work-related or not, ranging from morale to mortgage payments, from alcohol to alimony. Administered through Control Data's health-care arm, the Life Extension Institute, the scheme provides confidential counseling or referrals and, if need be, private face-to-face meetings with professionals. One manager of the program, Dr. Stephen Duvall (his doctorate is in counseling), says the plan aims for maximum usage, noting that during the seven years it has been available to Control Data's 48,000 employees, 30,000 have used it. Humanitarianism aside, Duvall says, the economics of the plan are plain. Any corporation, he says, knows how much it spends—and loses—handling employees in the "disciplinary process" (counselor talk for firing), which can take up to 90 days from the time a worker begins to be a problem. So far, Control Data has netted 37 outside customers, including the National Basketball Association, which has a $100,000-a-year deal for its players.

Source: "Trends: Dial 800 for Help." Reprinted by permission of *Forbes* Magazine from the June 22, 1981, issue, p. 10.

jobs, roles, and statuses through which a person progresses until retirement (see Figure 8.10).

Careers are typically viewed as having four stages: (1) organizational entry and apprenticeship, followed by (2) several years of skill and technical development with supervisory responsibility, leading to (3) the midcareer years of successful and improving performance, and ending in (4) late career with stable performance and general management responsibilities (see Figure 8.11).

You'll have a big stake in planning your career. You'll have to (1) appraise your strengths and weaknesses, (2) explore job opportunities, and (3) establish career goals. To help employees map out a career plan, many firms (e.g. NCR Corporation, General Motors, and AT&T) provide career counseling services. The job and career progression program at Sears, Roebuck, for example, helps to identify the most likely series of jobs through which managers can advance. A person may begin as an assistant department manager.

The next step is to department manager. From this point a successful career might lead to group manager, store manager, vice-president of regions, and so on.

The Assessment Center and Measuring Employee Potential

A new method for identifying employees with managerial potential is known as the assessment center, pioneered in 1959 by American Telephone and Telegraph. The **assessment center** involves an intensive one day to a week in which a group of candidates is rated by a team of personnel assessors. The candidates are put through interviews, case problem discussions, job simulations, and decision exercises. After lengthy evaluation of each participant by the observers, recommendations are made for further training, promotion, or job performance counseling. Assessment centers have also been effectively used by American Airlines, Boise Cascade, and Exxon Corporation.

POSSIBLE CAREER PATHS IN A LARGE PHARMACEUTICAL CORPORATION

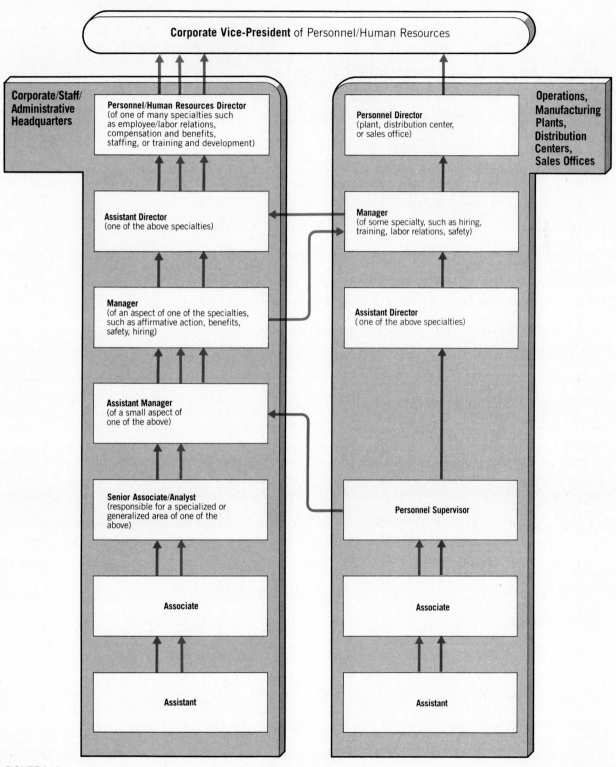

FIGURE 8.10

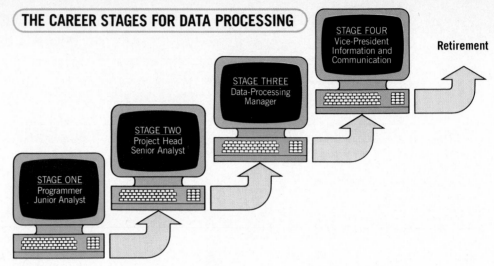

THE CAREER STAGES FOR DATA PROCESSING

STAGE FOUR
Vice-President
Information and
Communication

Retirement

STAGE THREE
Data-Processing
Manager

STAGE TWO
Project Head
Senior Analyst

STAGE ONE
Programmer
Junior Analyst

FIGURE 8.11

COMPENSATION AND EMPLOYEE REWARDS

The compensation and reward system of all organizations is closely linked to the performance appraisal process. People with higher performance levels receive larger pay increases and other rewards. A good salary and benefits program can greatly increase employee motivation.

Wage and salary structures reflect the importance of an organization's jobs. Jobs of greater importance to the firm are compensated at higher wage and salary rates. Jobs of equal importance are paid at the same rate. The hourly wage or weekly/biweekly/monthly salary a person receives is also based on his or her performance level. If the job performance of one assistant manager for a Skaggs Alpha Beta supermarket is better than another assistant manager's, he/she will probably receive a large salary increase or be paid at a higher level.

External Influences: Competitive Compensation

The firm must also be concerned with the wages and salaries paid by competitors. Many large companies like AT&T, Burlington Northern Industries, Baxter Travenol Laboratories, and Westinghouse conduct wage and salary surveys to see what other firms are paying. From this information the employer can decide to pay above, at, or below current salary ranges for its various jobs. In general, most firms try to pay competitive salaries on an industrywide basis.

Equity and Pay Satisfaction

Satisfaction is a positive feeling about some event, accomplishment, person, or activity. Pay satisfaction is important because if employees are not satisfied with pay, absenteeism and employee turnover may increase. Performance on the job may also suffer. When employees are satisfied with their compensation, they also tend to be satisfied with their jobs and their employers.

Pay satisfaction is also more likely when an employee's job inputs (contributions of hard work, experience, training, and education) and job rewards (job transfer or promotion, pay increases, and benefit improvements) are the same (or nearly so) as those of other employees in the same job. If the input/output ratios aren't commensurate, the employee will probably be unhappy.

Methods of Payment

Employees are usually paid by the amount of time worked, the amount of goods produced, or some combination of time and output. Hourly wages are usually paid lower-level workers (such as machinists and assembly-line employees), while managerial and professional employees are paid weekly, biweekly, or monthly salaries. Rates for specific jobs are fixed by job evaluation procedures, using the company's pay ranges for those jobs and making adjustments for external factors (rates paid by competitors and general economic

PERSPECTIVE ON SMALL BUSINESS

Walter Lesniowski, president of Thermo-Kold Equipment company of Oaklyn, N.J., knows from experience what a well-explained benefits program can mean. In 20 years his company has grown from a two-man operation to service commercial refrigeration equipment into a major distributorship for five lines of ice makers, refrigerated cabinets, and commercial scales. The company now has 3 corporate officers and 15 other full-time employees and does $2.5 million in annual sales.

Lesniowski credits a clear explanation of benefits with an improved team spirit that has reduced employee turnover. "Our employees now have the same loyalty and dedication to the company that the owners have," he says. "That's important in an industry in which summertime emergency repair calls can often mean inconvenient overtime duty."

Each November, Thermo-Kold invites employees and spouses to a benefits meeting. There the company's independent insurance agent, Earl Seely, clearly explains the company's benefits program. He usually speaks for about an hour, then spends another hour or so meeting with employees for discussions over coffee.

In the presentation itself, Seely relies on flipcharts, summarizing the items that make up the company's benefits package, including government-required benefits and items such as paid vacations. "This is a good opportunity to remind employees about benefits they might otherwise take for granted," he says.

Seely clearly explains each benefit, using examples and case histories—preferably of Thermo-Kold employees—whenever possible. "A benefit always seems more immediate if the person you work next to is the person involved in the example," Seely says.

Seely also attempts to anticipate potential dissatisfaction with the value of company contributions. He shows that to receive comparable coverage an employee working for himself would have to *subtract* the same amount or more from his earnings that the company has *added*. If a company contributes $3500 in benefits payments for an employee earning $14,000, the total effective compensation is $17,500. That same employee, working for himself and earning $14,000, would have a net spendable income of $10,500 or less if he had to purchase the same benefits out of his own pocket.

SOURCE: Reprinted with permission of *INC.* Magazine. Excerpted from Ernest H. Schell, "Take the Wraps Off Your Benefits Package," *INC.*, August 1980, pp. 72–73. Copyright © 1980 by INC. Publishing Co.

---

conditions). A person's salary or wage may also be determined by merit and performance evaluations. If you as a production foreman received the highest performance rating in the plant, you'd be given the largest salary increase.

Although it is less common, some employees are paid by the number of units of product produced. These payment plans usually have an incentive feature so that pay increases when performance increases. For example, a tiremaker at Goodyear might be paid $3 for each tire up to 18 tires a day. For any tires over 18, the worker would receive $4 a tire. Completion of 23 tires during a workshift would result in pay of $74.

Benefits and Services

Fringe benefits and employee services are forms of nonwage compensation. A **fringe benefit** is a form of pay in addition to the wage or salary. **Employee services** are activities and services offered to employees to improve morale and working conditions. For example, the Zale Corporation operates a day-care center for its employees. A few benefit items are required by federal and/or state legislation, but most are voluntarily provided by the employer. Three benefits employers *must* provide are (1) unemployment compensation, (2) worker's compensation, and (3) social security (Old Age, Survivors, and Disability Insurance). Under the first two, employees receive benefits during periods of unemployment or for lost worktime due to a work-related injury. For the third benefit a number of services are available from the social security program. However the benefit that one is most likely to receive is a social security payment. Employers partially pay for all three of these benefits.

A number of voluntary benefits come in the form of paid nonwork time (holidays, sick days, and vacations). Other employer-paid benefits include insurance programs (life, health and hospitalization, and disability), profit-sharing plans, pension and retirement programs, stock purchase options (to buy company stock), and special bonuses for outstanding performance.

In addition to these, many firms—such as Bell Helicopter and J. C. Penney—provide other services including social and recreational programs, free parking, merchandise discounts, tuition reimbursement for college and other study, and a company newsletter.

Retirement Pension

One of the most important and expensive benefits is the retirement pension, fast becoming even more important as people live to an older age. Most employees participate in the social security program through the so-called payroll tax. Retirement benefits are financed by equal employer and employee contributions. These have increased substantially in recent years (at the same time as the social security system itself has been threatened with economic failure). In addition to social security, many employers provide pension benefits through voluntary (private) programs.

What You Can Expect

Along with the increased importance of pension and retirement programs, there are several other important trends in employee compensation. One factor is the continually increasing cost of living. With more firms giving cost-of-living wage increases, less money becomes available for merit raises. Many firms, such as International Har-

"Retirement plan? I wouldn't worry about that. You'd be out of your mind to work here that long."

From *The Wall Street Journal*, by permission of Cartoon Features Syndicate.

vester, have signed union-negotiated agreements calling for the payment of automatic wage increases one or more times a year to offset increases in the cost of living. These payments are called *cost-of-living adjustments* (COLA); they first came into existence through collective bargaining contract negotiations between the United Auto Workers Union and General Motors.

Also, the costs of most benefits and services have increased faster than wage and salary increases have. This is particularly true of health and hospitalization insurance premiums. For employers like Ford and U.S. Steel, costs now equal more than 40 percent of the total compensation dollar.

Finally, problems have risen concerning the number and variety of fringe benefits. Labor unions continue to push for expansion of paid nonwork time. At the managerial level, tax considerations and the increased competition for high-talent managers have stimulated the development of individualized compensation packages. These allow upper-level managers flexibility in designing compensation items to meet their personal needs. Tax, insurance, and investment consultants frequently have to be brought in to create these unique compensation packages, sometimes referred to as *compensation cafeteria.* The menu includes such payment devices as salary increases, bonus awards, deferred bonus, fringe benefits and prerequisites, additional life insurance, qualified and nonqualified stock options, deferred retirement compensation, and phantom stock plans — rather a rich diet.[4]

SUMMARY

For a number of reasons, the personnel function has assumed increasing importance within the organization. The primary concern of the personnel function is the effective management of human resources. Human resource management, which is concerned with maximizing workers' satisfaction improving worker efficiency, and ensuring a sufficient number of quality employees to meet the organization's objectives developed over time out of the personnel function and has become a separate function in many firms.

Important activities within the personnel function are: (1) personnel planning and forecasting, (2) employee recruitment and selection, (3) employee training and development, (4) performance evaluation and career development, (5) compensation and employee benefits, and (6) labor relations. The overall objectives of the personnel function are (1) to maximize the effectiveness of human resources, (2) to satisfy employee needs by helping the employee to achieve a successful career, and (3) to provide competent, well-trained employees to the various departments within the company. To accomplish these goals, personnel managers must have a clear understanding of the objectives of the organization, since these objectives form the basis of personnel policies.

The personnel and human resources planning activity involves (1) defining future human resource needs and requirements, (2) examining the current inventory of human resources, and (3) determining the strategy for moving from the firm's current work force to the one desired. Job analysis and design are important components of successful personnel planning. The tasks and responsibilities of a job are usually listed in the job description. The skills, knowledge, and abilities necessary for the job are given in the job specification. Another important consideration in planning for human resources is the scheduling of work. Factors that complicate scheduling include multishift operations, fluctuations in workflow, and such altered workweek plans as compressed schedules and flexitime.

The personnel function of employee recruitment and selection takes place when a new position is created or an existing job becomes vacant. Qualified indviduals can be found in either the internal labor market or the external labor market. Recruiting attempts to find and attract qualified applicants from the external market. After people have been attracted to the firm and applications have been received, employment specialists begin the screening and reviewing process. First comes the initial screening, which includes a preliminary interview and the completion of an employment application form. Then the applicant may be asked to take one or more employment tests. The selection interview is the most widely used tool for making the actual hiring decision. Several federal laws involving discrimination must be considered in the hiring decision.

Training and development programs attempt to increase the knowledge and skills of the employee. Such programs generally are concerned with (1) orienting new employees to the firm, (2) improving the performance of employees in their current jobs, and (3) preparing people for more job responsibilities and promotions. Techniques and methods of training can be broadly classified as either on-the-job or off-the-job.

Another important personnel function is performance appraisal and career development. The compensation and reward system of the organization is closely linked to the performance appraisal process. Firms must also be concerned that their compensation systems be competitive with those of other firms in their industry. Employees are usually paid by the amount of time worked, the amount of goods produced, or some combination of the two. Fringe benefits and employee services are forms of nonwage compensation. Some benefit items are required by law, but most are voluntarily provided by the employer. One of the most important and expensive benefits is the retirement pension. Other important trends in employee compensation are cost-of-living adjustments, the increasing costs of benefits and services, and the increasing complexity in the number and variety of fringe benefits offered.

KEY TERMS

affirmative action
altered workweek
assessment center
career
compressed workweek
employee services
employment agency
Equal Employment
   Opportunity
   Commission
   (EEOC)
executive search firm
external labor market
flexitime
fringe benefit
human resources
   management
internal labor market
job
job analysis
job description
job specification
Office of Federal
   Contract
   Compliance
   Programs (OFCCP)
performance
   appraisal
personnel planning
recruiting
selection interview
training and
   development
   program

REVIEW QUESTIONS

1. For what three reasons has the personnel function assumed increased importance within business organizations?
2. What are the six important activities of the personnel department?
3. Describe the relationship between the personnel specialist and the operating manager.
4. What are the differences between job analysis, job specification, and job description?
5. Name the three objectives of the personnel department.

6. What is the sequence of steps in the recruitment and selection process?
7. Describe the methods of employee training and development.
8. What are the purposes of performance appraisal?

DISCUSSION QUESTIONS

1. How would the employee selection process differ between an entry-level job and a middle-management position?
2. When would a business firm attempt to promote from within the company, and when would it go to the external labor market for non-entry-level jobs?
3. What effect, if any, have government-directed affirmative action programs and the EEOC had on the ability of a business to hire the most qualified applicant?
4. Under what conditions are employment tests appropriate? When might they be illegal?
5. What kind of training program would be most appropriate for: an electrician, a telephone operator, a college-graduate management trainee, an assembly-line worker.
6. What is the effect of the personal income tax structure in determining whether an employee prefers an increase in direct pay or fringe benefits?
7. Describe the fringe benefits that might be offered to employees of an airline, a bank, a supermarket, and a computer manufacturer. How might these fringe benefits change the level of direct pay?

CASE: MBO—WITHOUT A FULL DECK

A management consultant was called in from Northeast State University to consult with a large insurance company about some of its morale problems. A few months before, another visiting consultant had completed an attitude survey and found that morale was at a very low level, while turnover was very high, especially among middle managers. Unfortunately, the managers who left were the most talented ones who had completed university degrees that the company had paid for, and who had also completed the management development seminars offered by the company.

At the suggestion of the first consultant, the executive committee had decided to initiate a Management by Objectives program—along with a possible profit-sharing plan—*if warranted.*

The new consultant from the university had just begun to conduct seminars to acquaint the various department heads with the principles and practices of MBO, and with the various steps in implementing the program. He had completed discussions of tying performance reviews to MBO by establishing "quantifiable and measurable objectives" for individuals and relating these to department objectives linked with production and profitability, suggesting that each department should ideally be treated as a "profit center," accountable for costs and revenues—virtually developing "income statements" for each department.

To the department heads in the seminar, this seemed like a great idea—very practical, too; but there was one hitch: the vice-president for finance would never accept any such scheme, especially if it meant sharing company profit figures with department people. As a matter of fact, when the vice-president learned of this whole approach (he had been out of town when the executive committee had discussed the launching of an MBO program in the company), he hit the ceiling, claiming that "sharing profit figures with the employees will be the downfall of the company; after all, what do they know about financial matters—return on investment, owner's equity, responsibilities to the stockholders, and all the other intricate details of running a profitable company?"

There went the MBO program, the management seminars, the employee attitude survey—and immediate prospects of reversing the high turnover and the low employee morale: the consultant was sent back to his university.

1. What do you think of the position taken by the vice-president for finance? Is his reaction justified?
2. What are some other ways to interpret peformance reviews and rate people for promotions and raises besides profits and losses?

CASE: THE RIGHT CHOICE?

Bob Payne, newly appointed assistant personnel manager, has a choice to make between three applicants for the position of clerk typist. *Qualifications*: typing skill, 60 words per minute; type letters and reports from rough draft; part-time receptionist; light bookkeeping and filing; some college desired but not required. Salary: minimum wage.

Three finalists were screened from 28 who applied. Number one, a very attractive blonde with typing speed of 80 words per minute, 2 errors; bachelor's degree in psychology; previous experience in part-time office jobs while attending college. Bob told her she was "a cinch for the job."

Number two, black woman, well groomed and poised; 65 words per minute, 1 error; associate degree in secretarial science from a community college, plus one and a half year's experience as clerk typist.

Number three, older woman—45 to 50 years of age—wife of attorney; recently returned to job market after two children grew up, married, and left home; typing speed 65 words per minute, 1 error; currently working toward business degree; worked for husband for year when he opened his office.

1. Which candidate should get the job? Justify selection.
2. Did Bob commit any errors in his interviewing?

CHAPTER 9

MANAGEMENT AND LABOR

After studying this chapter you should be able to:

1 Understand the historical development of the trade union movement in the United States.
2 Explain how employees benefit by becoming union members.
3 Understand the role of federal legislation in the growth of unionism.
4 Describe the structure and objectives of labor organizations.
5 Describe the collective bargaining process.
6 Explain the levels of union security.
7 Describe the trends of the union movement in the 1980s.

- Prior to the 1979 convention of the American Federation of Labor–Congress of Industrial Organizations (AFL-CIO), a women's group within the organization forced the labor organization to move its convention site from the traditional location—Miami—to Washington, D.C. Reason: Florida had failed to ratify the Equal Rights Amendment.

- At its November 1979 convention, the ailing 84-year-old George Meany officially resigned as president of the AFL-CIO. Meany had been the organization's unchallenged leader for 24 years. Lane Kirkland, who had been secretary-treasurer of the AFL-CIO since 1969, became Meany's successor and only the second president of the organization.

- Toward the end of contract renewal talks between the Chrysler Corporation and the United Auto Workers (UAW), Chrysler agreed to nominate Douglas Fraser, UAW president, for its board of directors. In 1980 Fraser became an official member of the 18-person Chrysler board.

- During 1980, as a reaction to the slump in auto sales, the continuing increase of auto imports, and the mass layoffs of U.S. auto workers, the United Auto Workers tried to secure federal legislation requiring that Japanese firms build autos in America. Earlier in the year, Honda Motor Company had announced plans to construct a $200 million auto assembly plant in Ohio.

- Hundreds of New York City firms, anticipating a major transit strike, spent thousands of dollars to arrange temporary housing and transportation for their employees. Much of the money was for nonrefundable deposits on hotel rooms, rental cars, buses—and bicycles. Even a brief shutdown of the New York City transit system can increase business costs by billions of dollars. Fortunately, the strike did not take place.

You may consider these events mild in comparison with the union organizing struggles and labor strikes of the 1930s. Yet they do illustrate the nature of recent labor-management relationships. Some of the more important trends are:

1. the changing age, sex, and racial mix of the labor force—with white males no longer a majority in the employed labor force;
2. a new generation of labor union leaders at all levels of the labor movement—more specifically, changes in high-level positions in the AFL-CIO, United Auto Workers, and United Mine Workers;
3. the rapid push for greater union involvement in the affairs of business—much of this connected with union drives to improve the quality of worklife;
4. the major employment declines (and union membership losses) in several basic industries (auto, steel, and coal)—advances in technology and import increases being two important reasons for these changes;
5. the continuing increase in unionization of public and professional employees—with the federal government more unionized than the private employment sector.

THE LABOR FORCE, LABOR UNIONS, AND UNION MEMBERSHIP

People who have chosen to work are defined as the **labor force**. This includes those looking for work and those temporarily absent from work. In the early 1980s the United States civilian labor force held over 105 million people. Labor unions represented over 20 million of these. Although American unions do not cover the world, many of them do represent workers in Canada and Puerto Rico. Approximately 1.4 million union members are located outside the United States.

A **labor union** is an organization of workers formed to deal with the employer on a group basis in order to pursue common goals. These include higher wages, shorter work hours, and better working conditions. Labor unions also include public (teachers and police officers) and profes-sional (medical doctors and athletes) employee as-sociations. Many of these have come into exis-tence only during the last quarter century. The American Nurses Association, the National Foot-ball League Players Association, and the Idaho Employee Association are examples of employee associations.

The American labor movement has generally grown over the years. Union membership grew very rapidly between 1932 and 1946, then de-clined slightly and leveled off before resuming growth between 1949 and 1953 and again be-tween 1962 and 1973 (see Figure 9.1).

FIGURE 9.1

MEMBERSHIP IN NATIONAL UNIONS, 1930-1978; COMBINED WITH MEMBERSHIP IN EMPLOYEE ASSOCIATIONS, 1970-1980

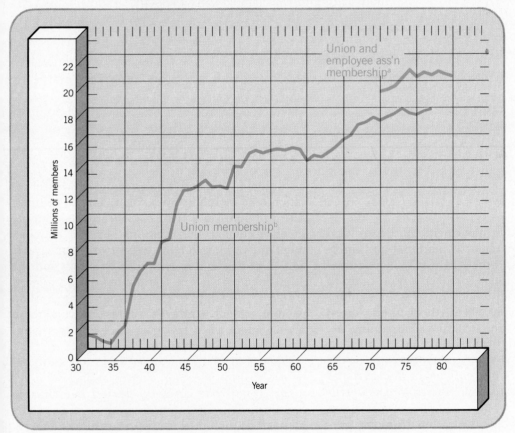

Source: *Directory of National Unions and Employee Associations, 1979,* Bulletin 2079, Bureau of Labor Statis-tics, p. 58; "Corrected Data on Labor Organization Membership—1980" (USDL-81-446), 18 Sept. 1981, Bureau of Labor Statistics, p. 3.

Note: Excludes Canadian membership but includes members in other areas outside the U.S. Members of AFL-CIO directly affiliated local unions are also included. Members of single-firm and local unaffiliated unions are excluded. For the years 1948–52, midpoints of membership estimates, which were expressed as ranges, were used.

[a] Statistics for employee associations date from 1970, given by Bureau of Labor Statistics only as consolidated with statistics for unions.

[b] Separate union statistics discontinued by Bureau of Labor Statistics after 1978 and consolidated with statistics for employee associations.

TALKING BUSINESS

"Bust the Union Busters!" is organized labor's slogan in its fight against consultants and law firms that help employers avoid or end unionization. Keeping unions out is a growing business, a business union leaders allege often wins by using unethical or illegal techniques—for example, teaching managers to harass, intimidate, and threaten workers. The "union busters," of course, deny the accusation. Says one consultant, "our purpose in every campaign is to give employees the right to make an informed choice."

The unions' counterattack includes publishing a monthly newsletter (Report on Union Busters, or the RUB sheet); picketing and otherwise disrupting management seminars on union busting; pressing for federal government action against consultants; and holding advanced training courses for union organizers.

Some union officials would like to get tougher on union busters. One union organizer predicts "more confrontations in the street against these consultants. I'm talking about strikes to the bitter end. Either we go down or the employers go under."

Source: Adapted from Joann S. Lublin, "Labor Strikes Back at Consultants That Help Firms Keep Unions Out," *Wall Street Journal*, April 2, 1981, p. 25. Adapted by permission of The Wall Street Journal, © Dow Jones & Company, Inc., 1981. All rights reserved.

Labor Union Organizations

The American Labor movement consists of local unions, joint union councils, national and international unions, and the AFL-CIO labor federation. The average union member is most familiar with his or her local union. Local unions (numbering more than 60,000 in the United States) vary in terms of size, structure, bargaining arrangements, and officer election procedures. In most cases, the local union (or simply *local*) is the basic building block of a national or international union. As an affiliate of the International Brotherhood of Teamsters, for example, a local union would generally follow the national union's constitution, bylaws, and regulations. The constitution and operating manual of the national union usually determine the number of local officers, their election procedures, the frequency of local meetings, the financial arrangements with the national organization, and the local's participation in negotiating labor agreements.

Many activities take place at the local union level. There are three primary functions of the local union: (1) collective bargaining, (2) worker relations and membership services, and (3) community and political activities. Collective bargaining involves contract negotiations between management and organized labor every two or three years as well as day-to-day grievance handling and the adjustment of worker complaints due to alleged employer violations of the labor agreement. Shop or department **stewards** represent workers to management when trying to resolve worker complaints.

Discussion of union issues takes place at the monthly union meeting. Financial and other reports are given, officers elected, committee appointments announced, and special events planned at the meetings. Also, members may receive copies of the local's newsletter and information from the national union.

American unions have never shown much interest in forming a labor political party. But they do often become involved in political affairs. Usually workers are politically active at the local level. They participate in voter registration drives and they campaign for local candidates who support labor union interests. Some members also join lobbying efforts at the state, county, and city levels of government. Often, too, a union member may be running for municipal office or some higher political position. You may recall that Ronald Reagan, early in his career, was president of the Screen Actors Guild.

National Unions   A **national union** consists of a group of many local unions in a particular industry, skilled trade, or geographic area. The scope of a national union and its affiliated local units is called its **jurisdiction.** A union's jurisdiction is measured by geographic area, number of firms or employers, type of work, or industry or occupation where the union has a special interest. Unions have usually organized themselves around either of two jurisdictions: craft (or skilled trade) and industry. A **craft union** (carpenters, plumbers, bricklayers) is one that organizes and represents workers in a single craft or occupation. An **industrial union** (e.g. auto workers, steelworkers, and food and commercial workers) serves a single industry, regardless of occupation and level of skill. Recent years have seen the development of the **mixed union,** which tries to organize and bargain for a wide variety of workers. For example, the Teamsters Union not only represents truck drivers, but it also negotiates for nurses, schoolteachers, police officers, sanitation engineers, fire fighters, and secretaries.

As an umbrella organization for most of the American labor movement, the AFL-CIO represents the memberships of 112 labor unions, or about 54 percent of the unions and employee associations. These organizations in turn represent nearly 70 percent of all union members. The three largest labor organizations (Teamsters, National Education Association, and Auto Workers) do not belong to the AFL-CIO (see Table 9.1).

The AFL-CIO passes new rules and regulations at its convention, held every two years, in which delegates from the member unions participate. Between conventions, the president and secretary-treasurer, with the assistance of the executive council and general board, run the AFL-CIO. (See Figure 9.2 for a chart of the organizational arrangements within the AFL-CIO.) The AFL-CIO avoids interfering with the affairs of member unions, and it particularly avoids collective bargaining activities. It does, however, provide help to member unions in the areas of lobbying and legislative activities, labor education programs, union organizing drives, and political activities.

Why Employees Join Unions

During the early developmental years of the union movement, workers joined because they felt that unions were the answer to overcoming poor working conditions, cruel supervisors, poverty-level wages, and long working hours. Undoubtedly, many workers in today's labor force join unions hoping for greater security of job and income. Unions also offer employees the opportunity of meeting other workers, making new friendships, and developing leadership skills through election to a union position. Sometimes workers join unions for the opportunity of acquiring some control over their work environment. Workers are frequently genuine believers in the goals of the labor movement and look up to labor leaders as heroes.

DEVELOPMENT OF AMERICAN LABOR UNIONS

American labor unions have a history that closely follows the economic development of the United States. Toward the end of the eighteenth century, groups of skilled craftsmen formed guilds or societies to ensure that only quality products were produced and to resist employers' attempts to lower their wages. Some of these people were self-employed. Others belonged to small craft organizations of carpenters, shoemakers, and printers that were to be found in New York, Boston, and Philadelphia. Collective bargaining, as practiced today, had its beginnings in some of these early labor organizations. Organizations of shoemakers or printers often protested an employer's effort to hire "two-thirders" or "half-way" journeymen. These were workers who had not completed an apprenticeship (training) program and who were willing to work for less than the skilled workers.

Many of these early unions also pushed for higher wages and shorter working hours by threatening to strike. But employer opposition was often successful, and workers were hard hit by the depression after the panic of 1837. Some of the employer success was due to the courts. Employers fought craft unions by hiring nonunion workers and by filing claims in court to have labor organizations declared illegal. The courts found that a group of workers trying to raise wages was a conspiracy and therefore a crime against the pub-

TABLE 9-1

Labor Organizations Reporting 100,000 Members or More, 1980[a]

Labor Organization	Members (× 1000)	Labor Organization	Members (× 1000)
Teamsters (Ind.)	1891	Retail, Wholesale	215
National Education Association (Ind.)	1684	Government (NAGE) (Ind.)	200
Automobile Workers (Ind.)	1357	Transportation Union	190
Food and Commercial	1300	Iron Workers	184
Steelworkers	1238	Nurses Association (Ind.)	180
State, County	1098	Railway Clerks	180
Electrical (IBEW)	1041	Fire Fighters	178
Carpenters	784	Painters	164
Machinists	754	Transit Union	162
Service Employees	650	Electrical (UE) (Ind.)	162
Laborers	608	Sheet Metal	161
Communications Workers	551	Bakery, Confectionery, Tobacco	160
Teachers	551	Oil, Chemical	154
Clothing and Textile Workers	455	Rubber	151
Operating Engineers	423	Police (Ind.)	150
Hotel	400	Boilermakers	145
Plumbers	352	Bricklayers	135
Ladies' Garment	323	Transport Workers	130
Musicians	299	Postal and Federal Employees	125
Paperworkers	275	Printing and Graphic	122
Government (AFGE)	255	Woodworkers	112
Postal Workers	251	Office	107
Mine Workers (Ind.)	245	California	105
Electrical (IUE)	233	Maintenance of Way	102
Letter Carriers	230		

SOURCE: Bureau of Labor Statistics.

NOTE: All organizations not identified as (Ind.) are affiliated with the AFL-CIO.

[a]Based on reports to the Bureau of Labor Statistics.

lic.[1] The criminal conspiracy argument was upheld by state courts until 1842.

The Knights of Labor

In 1869 a small group of clothing workers secretly founded the Noble Order of the Knights of Labor. For the next decade the Knights grew at a slow but steady pace. By 1879 total membership had reached 10,000, and at this point the Knights came out into the open. Membership quickly increased to almost 1 million by 1886. Almost as rapidly, membership dropped to below 100,000 by 1893 and gradually declined until the organization disappeared in 1917.[2]

The **Knights of Labor** was one of the first major national labor organizations. However it was never very effective in improving the life of the working person.

The Knights were concerned with broad social issues and ambitious economic programs and reforms. More than that, they wanted to move from a strongly competitive society to a cooperative one, in which workers and employers would mutually benefit. The Knights also felt that workers' interests would be better served by public ownership of utilities, abolition of child and convict labor, and greater social and legislative emphasis on those who worked in mass-production jobs.

Leaders of the Knights did not like to use strikes in order to effect change. But many local and district units did become involved in strikes, a good number of which were successful, especially those against the Wabash and other railroads. However later strikes in the railroad and meat

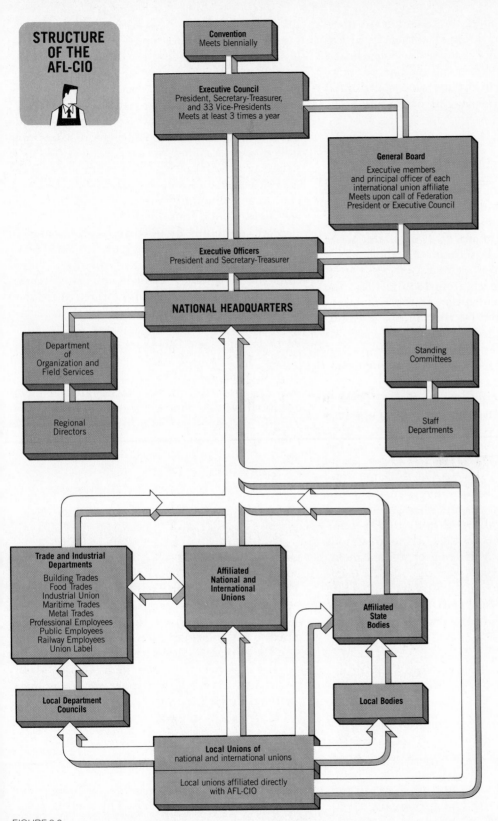

STRUCTURE OF THE AFL-CIO

Convention
Meets biennially

Executive Council
President, Secretary-Treasurer, and 33 Vice-Presidents
Meets at least 3 times a year

General Board
Executive members and principal officer of each international union affiliate
Meets upon call of Federation President or Executive Council

Executive Officers
President and Secretary-Treasurer

NATIONAL HEADQUARTERS

Department of Organization and Field Services

Regional Directors

Standing Committees

Staff Departments

Trade and Industrial Departments
Building Trades
Food Trades
Industrial Union
Maritime Trades
Metal Trades
Professional Employees
Public Employees
Railway Employees
Union Label

Affiliated National and International Unions

Affiliated State Bodies

Local Department Councils

Local Bodies

Local Unions of
national and international unions

Local unions affiliated directly with AFL-CIO

FIGURE 9.2

Source: *Directory of National Unions and Employee Associations, 1977*, Bulletin 2044, Bureau of Labor Statistics, p. 2.

packing industries failed. In 1886 a bomb incident during a mass meeting of workers in Chicago's Haymarket Square resulted in violence and death. These strike defeats and the bad publicity generated by the Haymarket riot contributed greatly to the end of the Knights' organization.

Emergence of National Unions and the American Federation of Labor

Many of the craft groups within the Knights were unhappy with its philosophy and activities. In 1881 they formed the Federation of Organized Trades and Labor Unions, five years later to be called the American Federation of Labor (AFL). Under the leadership of Samuel Gompers, president almost continuously from 1886 to 1924, the AFL dropped the philosophy of the Knights of Labor and emphasized (1) the concept of exclusive jurisdiction for member unions, (2) local union authority, and (3) collective bargaining and strikes to improve wages, hours, and working conditions.

Exclusive jurisdiction means that a member union of the AFL was given free rein to organize all workers within a skilled trade or craft. Other unions were then prohibited from organizing the same craft. Each union was also free to develop its own constitution and program of collective bargaining. Such relationships among member unions—and between them and the AFL—helped the AFL grow and prosper despite a good many jurisdictional disputes. By 1904, 120 craft unions had joined with the AFL for a combined membership of over 2 million workers. The AFL encouraged its member unions to try for immediate wage gains and improved working conditions, set down in a written labor agreement.

Rapid Union Growth and Development of the Congress of Industrial Organizations

The AFL was the major force on the labor scene for nearly 50 years. However with the Great Depression in 1930 came a severe reduction of workers in the building trades. Just when the Wagner Act revived the AFL's fortunes by guaranteeing labor's right to organize and to bargain collectively, a crisis developed within the AFL, posed by the efforts of mass-production workers to estab-

lish industrial unions. The AFL persisted in refusing to allow union organization on an industrial basis. Under the leadership of John L. Lewis, president of the United Mine Workers of America, the AFL's position was successfully challenged. The UMW had for several decades been a member of the AFL. However it had grown and developed as an industrywide union, containing skilled and unskilled workers, rather than as a strictly craft union. This was a compromise of the AFL's doctrine of exclusive jurisdiction. Lewis argued that a union organized along industry lines was better than a craft union.

After continuing disagreements with leaders of some of the larger AFL unions, in 1935 Lewis took his union and a handful of others and bolted from the AFL. They formed the Committee for Industrial Organization (CIO), three years later to be called the Congress of Industrial Organizations. With the financial backing of the Mine Workers union, the CIO launched union organizing drives in several mass-production industries, including the auto and steel industries. The CIO was very successful thanks to its aggressive membership drives. After a brief period of having been caught by surprise, AFL unions aggressively counterattacked and recruited to its ranks thousands of industrial workers. The stage was set for a major contest.

The AFL and CIO: Rivalry and Merger

Until the early 1950s, AFL and CIO unions competed against one another for new members. They also tried to raid each other's existing membership, but this effort produced few gains and cost much money. Soon the AFL and CIO decided to end their own hostilities and call a truce. On December 5, 1955 the two organizations merged into one labor movement. George Meany became its president and spoke for a combined membership of over 16 million workers.

The Labor Movement of the 1980s

After the AFL-CIO merger in 1955 the labor movement experienced a lull. This was due to the growth of the economy coupled with increasingly complex economic conditions, and to greater re-

TALKING BUSINESS

The rise of specialized education for business managers, with masses of students chasing M.B.A.s and companies chasing the best of the students, is having a parallel on the other side of the bargaining table.

Not only are labor leaders in general better educated today than their predecessors—the late George Meany never finished high school; his successor as AFL-CIO president, Lane Kirkland, has a bachelor's degree in foreign service—but more and more people with labor studies degrees are coming to the fore in the union movement.

Joel S. Denker, associate professor in labor studies at the University of the District of Columbia, reports in [his] book, *Unions and Universities: The Rise of the New Labor Leader*, that at least 20 community colleges are awarding an associate degree in labor studies and an equal number of four-year colleges and universities are offering undergraduate studies in labor history, labor and politics, collective bargaining and labor law.

Three universities—Rutgers, the University of Massachusetts at Amherst and the University of the District of Columbia—are now awarding master's degrees in labor studies. As recently as 1964, no degree programs in labor education existed. Universities were offering mostly noncredit courses on techniques of union leadership.

Source: "Trends: Labor Leaders Now Rise by Degrees," p. 24, reprinted by permission from *Nation's Business*, March 1981, Copyright 1981 by Nation's Business, Chamber of Commerce of the United States.

sistance by unorganized employees to union membership. But in the mid-1980s the American labor movement is again coming to life. This is illustrated by (1) an increasing number of national and international union mergers, (2) intensified organizing drives of the AFL-CIO to unionize clerical, technical, and professional employees, (3) attempts by many unions to strongly influence the management of pension funds, and (4) sophisticated contract and legislative proposals for increasing union-member income and job security. Also, in 1981 the United Auto Workers rejoined the AFL-CIO to swell the ranks to approximately 18.3 million workers.

THE LEGAL ENVIRONMENT OF UNIONISM

The Norris–La Guardia Act (1932)

The role of the courts in the settlement of labor disputes has grown over the years. Prior to 1932, when a company was faced with a strike or picket line, it could get a court order, called an injunction, requiring that laborers go back to work. If

"There was a time when blue collar looked blue collar."

Drawing by W. B. Park: © 1982 The New Yorker Magazine, Inc.

union members failed to obey the injunction, the court could impose prison sentences or fines.

Along with labor injunction, employers were successful in using the courts to enforce yellow dog contracts. A **yellow dog contract** was an agreement by an employee that, as a condition of being hired, he or she would not join a labor union. If the employee broke the contract, he or she could be fired and blacklisted. The **blacklist** contained names of workers who were involved with the unions. Circulated among employers, it kept many workers from being hired.

The **Norris-LaGuardia Act** (also known as the Anti-Injunction Act) largely ended the use of injunctions by employers and prohibited its use among other things to avoid strikes. It also made yellow dog contracts unenforceable.

The National Labor Relations Act of 1935 (Wagner Act)

The Norris-LaGuardia Act resulted in an increase in union organizing activities, especially in the mass-production industries. But employers had no legal obligation to recognize unions as bargaining agents for employees. Unions tried to change this by urging Congress to pass a law that would require employers to deal with labor organizations. In 1935 Congress responded by passing the National Labor Relations Act, commonly known as the Wagner Act, which, in the words of political scientist Richard Watson, "ushered in the 'Golden Age' of organized labor in the United States."

The basic purpose of the **Wagner Act** was to encourage the creation of unions and more collective bargaining. The law also provided a means for peacefully resolving disputes over union representation. Congress included a set of provisions in the Wagner Act to help protect an employee's rights; these provisions are called **employer unfair labor practices.** For example, it is unlawful for an employer to discriminate against an employee because the employee is involved in union activities. Also, an employer cannot sponsor a labor organization or fire an employee for joining a union (see Table 9.2). To enforce the law, the Wagner Act set up the National Labor Relations Board (NLRB), which was empowered to hear appeals from unions and to issue orders to employers.

TABLE 9–2

Employer Unfair Labor Practices Under the Wagner Act

The employer shall not:

- Interfere with, restrain, or coerce employees in the exercise of their rights to organize, bargain collectively, and engage in other concerted activities for their mutual aid or protection.
- Dominate or interfere with the formation or administration of any labor organization or contribute financial or other support to it.
- Encourage or discourage membership in any labor organization by discrimination with regard to hiring or tenure or conditions of employment, subject to an exception for valid union-security agreements.
- Discharge or otherwise discriminate against employees who have filed charges or given testimony before the NLRB.
- Refuse to bargain collectively with an authorized representative of a majority of employees in an appropriate bargaining unit, or refuse to discuss wages, hours, and working conditions.
- Enter with the union into a "hot cargo" agreement, by which the employer agrees not to do business with another company that the union has targeted in some way.

The Taft-Hartley Act of 1947

Until the Supreme Court upheld it (1937), the Wagner Act met with strong resistance from employers—and even with noncompliance. Subsequently, in the light of increasing union strength, the act was viewed by many as pro-labor. It was finally amended in 1947 by the Labor-Management Relations Act, known as the **Taft-Hartley Act,** passed by Congress over a presidential veto.

Most importantly, Congress (1) created a set of union unfair labor practices; (2) outlawed jurisdictional strikes (disputes between two unions over claims to the same work), secondary boycotts or strikes (a boycott or strike against an employer because it is doing business with another employer whose workers are on strike), and the closed shop (the requirement that one be a union member before being hired); (3) outlined procedures for dealing with strikes of major economic consequence, including federal injunction against strikes of 80 days' duration when these threaten the national health or security; (4) broadened the range of things an employer could do in dealing

ON THE FIRING LINE

Right-To-Work Laws: An Anti-Union Strategy?

According to national labor law, workers in business and industry may by majority vote elect a union to represent them. It then becomes the union's responsibility to negotiate their contracts and file grievances in their behalf. In more than half of the states, once a union is voted in, one of two possible arrangements may exist. The unit of workers represented may become either a union or an agency shop. In the *union shop*, all employees are required to join the union. In the *agency shop*, employees may choose not to join. Nonetheless they must pay all the fees to the union that union members pay. In theory, the fees are payment for union representation. They do not, however, differ from the cost of membership. Thus there is little real difference between agency and union shops.

In states with right-to-work laws, still another arrangement is possible. In an *open shop* workers are not required to join the union elected to represent them—*nor do they have to pay the union any fees*. A move is currently under way to pass right-to-work laws in all states presently without them. Those in favor of such laws advance arguments focusing on individual freedom and the need to make union leadership more responsive to the membership.

A right-to-work law does not threaten the existence of unions, say many right-to-work campaigners. It simply forces unions to work effectively for their members. Unions must offer real benefits for the money they receive from workers. If they do not, workers will not support them with membership and money. No longer will union leaders be able to spend millions of dollars on political causes in which their membership has little interest. Right-to-work laws will force unions to concentrate, and properly so, on representing the interests of members to management. Individual workers will have a new measure of freedom under such laws. In fact, say those in favor of right-to-work laws, workers should be permitted to decide to whom they will be responsible—union or management. Similarly, workers should not have to pay the sizable union membership fees against their will.

Those who oppose right-to-work laws believe their purpose is to sap unions of their power. The laws, they insist, merely encourage "free riders"—workers who contribute nothing to the cost of collective bargaining and representation yet gladly accept the improved wages and fringe benefits these gain them. The financial burden on union members grows as the number of free riders increases. Worker morale is bound to suffer in an open shop situation.

Opponents of right-to-work laws are also concerned with the balance of power. Reduced union funding, they point out, will mean cutbacks in the labor lobby at all levels of government. Passage of laws to protect working people will then be harder to achieve. Big business lobbies will be able to steamroll legislation right over labor. A system of checks and balances on power is crucial to the survival of the US as a free nation, say those opposed to right-to-work laws. Organized labor has served as an effective counterbalance to the powers of corporate giants. The labor movement must be strong to fight for and preserve workers' rights. Business is always ready, they insist, to exploit workers. They note, for instance, that some of the best contributors to a right-to-work campaign in Missouri were business owners fined for violating federal occupational health and safety standards.

While both advocates and opponents frequently assume that so-called right-to-work laws weaken unions, there is little hard evidence to this effect. Two recent studies, in fact, indicate workers are no less likely to join unions in right-to-work states than in other states.

with unions; and (5) further defined the rights of employees.

Like employers, unions were prohibited from doing certain things, called **union unfair labor practices.** For example, it became unlawful for unions to charge excessive dues. Monthly dues of $100 would be considered too much when the employee (union member) earned only $1000 in the same period. Also, unions were restrained from having so many members picketing a business that nonstriking employees were prevented from entering or leaving the plant (see Table 9.3).

Immediately following World War II union strike activity dramatically increased. Lengthy strikes disrupted the economy, and many businesses and people suffered. To deal with strikes Congress passed the **national emergency strike procedures** as part of the Taft-Hartley Act. These procedures give the president of the United States the right to declare a national emergency if a strike creates major health or safety problems and to bring a halt to the strike through legal action. A court order forces the strikers to go back to work for up to 80 days (known as the *cooling-off period)* while the employer and labor negotiators attempt to resolve their differences. The national emergency strike provisions have been used approximately 35 times between 1947 and the early 1980s.

The National Labor Relations Board

Enforcing the Wagner and Taft-Hartley acts is the job of the **National Labor Relations Board (NLRB).** The board has five members, each serving a five-year term of office, and about 50 regional and field offices scattered throughout the United States. Enforcement means (1) the investigation of charges of employer or union unfair labor practices, and (2) the supervision of union representation elections to determine whether employees want to be represented by a union. If the NLRB finds an employer or union guilty of an unfair labor practice, a remedy is issued by the board. For example, if an employer fires a worker for union involvement, the NLRB will issue an order (**remedy**) against the employer, requiring that the employer rehire the employee with back-pay for wages lost. Remedies can also be issued against unions when they violate the law. If union negotiators refuse to meet with employer repre-

TABLE 9–3
Union Unfair Labor Practices Under the Taft-Hartley Act
The union shall not:

- Restrain or coerce employees in the exercise of their rights under the act.
- Restrain or coerce an employer in the selection of his bargaining or grievance representative.
- Cause or attempt to cause an employer to discriminate against an employee on account of his membership or nonmembership in a labor organization, subject to an exception for valid union-shop agreements.
- Refuse to bargain collectively (in good faith) with an employer if the union has been designated as bargaining agent by a majority of the employees.
- Induce or encourage employees to stop work with the object of forcing an employer or self-employed person to join a union or of forcing an employer or other person to stop doing business with any other person or firm (secondary boycott).
- Induce or encourage employees to stop work with the object of forcing an employer to recognize and bargain with the union when another union has been certified as bargaining agent (strike against a certification).
- Induce or encourage employees to stop work with the object of forcing an employer to assign particular work to members of the union instead of to members of another union (jurisdictional strike).
- Charge an excessive or discriminatory fee as a condition of becoming a member of the union.
- Cause or attempt to cause an employer to pay for services that are not performed or not to be performed (featherbedding).
- Require membership prior to employment.

sentatives to negotiate a contract, the NLRB can issue an order to force the union to bargain in good faith.

The Labor-Management Reporting and Disclosure Act of 1959 (Landrum-Griffin Act)

Shortly after the AFL-CIO merger in 1955, some national unions—among them the Teamsters and the Bakery Workers—were accused of poor financial management, labor racketeering, rigged elections for officers, bribery of union officials, and other illegal activities. The scandal caused Congress to set up an investigation, resulting in passage of the Labor–Management Reporting and Disclosure Act, often called the Landrum-Griffin Act.

Unlike the Wagner and Taft-Hartley acts, this law dealt primarily with the internal affairs of labor unions. The **Landrum-Griffin Act** contained (1) a union-member "bill of rights," (2) requirements for the annual filing of detailed union-related reports and documents with the secretary of labor, (3) a set of rules for conducting elections for union officers, and (4) various safeguards to ensure that the unions didn't go bankrupt.

COLLECTIVE BARGAINING: NEGOTIATION OF A LABOR AGREEMENT

Collective bargaining is the process of negotiating, administering, and interpreting the labor agreement. This process involves both management and labor. However when management and labor do not agree on an issue, a third party may become involved.

Collective bargaining is overseen by the National Labor Relations Board. It focuses on anything to do with work including wages, hours, working conditions, and pensions. The object of collective bargaining may be either a contract, an agreement over a grievance, or an adjustment of worker complaints.

Much of the bargaining process takes place through face-to-face meetings. Demands, proposals, and counterproposals are exchanged during several rounds of bargaining. The end result is (hopefully) compromise and agreement. The starting positions of labor and management establish the **zone of bargaining,** in which the initial difference may be too wide to produce worthwhile discussions. The union's range of acceptance must overlap management's own range of acceptance before agreement can be reached. For example, assume that the Carpenters Union demands a $0.90 per hour wage increase but is willing to accept $0.60. U.S. Homes, a major homebuilder, initially offers a $0.20 per hour increase but is willing to settle for $0.40. In this case no zone of realistic bargaining exists. Both parties are outside each other's range of acceptance. When this happens, labor may strike (see Figure 9.3).

The Substance of Bargaining

The results of collective bargaining are written into the labor agreement, some provisions of

FIGURE 9.3

THE BARGAINING ZONE

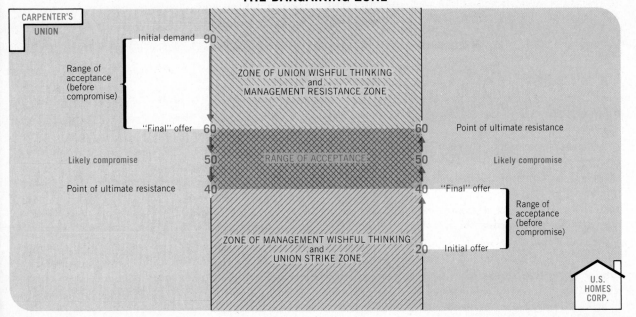

Contract negotiations between Buick and final assembly workers union, Flint, Michigan.

which are mandatory and others voluntary. A mandatory item is one that relates to wages, hours, and working conditions. An employer must be willing to discuss and respond to a *mandatory* issue. But there's no obligation to respond to *voluntary* items. A union's "demand" that the employer announce the date and time of union membership meetings over the plant's intercom system would be a voluntary item.

Labor agreements can range in length from a few pages to as many as 350 — as in the agreement between General Motors and the United Auto Workers. Of course, provisions in these agreements vary greatly from one company and union to the next.

Union Security   One of the most important issues for a union is union security. This is an agreement that imposes some form of union membership on employees. The most restrictive form of union security is called a **closed shop.** Under this arrangement a person must be a union member in good standing before being hired as an employee. The Taft-Hartley Act made the closed shop illegal. The most common union security clause today is the **union shop.**

Closely related to union security is the **dues checkoff.** Under this clause union members annually authorize the employer to automatically deduct the amount of union dues and assessments from their paychecks. These funds are then given

to the union in a lump sum at the end of the pay period. The checkoff helps the union remain in good financial condition.

Management Rights   When a firm becomes unionized, gone are the days of running its business any way it wants. Unionization obviously poses a challenge to management's authority and decision making, and management may resist any weakening of its power. Fortunately for itself, management has certain rights in collective bargaining. One way of exercising these rights and resisting union interference with its authority is to put a management rights clause in the labor agreement.

Approximately 70 percent of all labor contracts have some form of management rights provision.[3] A typical clause gives the employer all rights to manage the operation except as these rights are modified through specific terms of the labor agreement. For instance, the contract might modify the employer's promotion policy by specifying that seniority be considered in making promotion decisions. When the United Auto Workers union gave up more than $1 billion in pay concessions to help rescue Chrysler Corporation, it demanded a revision of Chrysler's management rights clause. This clause had given the company "exclusive rights to manage its plants and offices and direct its affairs and working forces." The modified agreement required that

TALKING BUSINESS

In 1980, Chrysler Corporation agreed to put Douglas Fraser, president of the United Auto Workers union, on its board of directors. Such an unusual interaction between business and labor might have been expected to provoke problems; but both Chrysler officials and union members have praised Fraser's performance.

"He acts just like a normal board member. He doesn't give the sense of being just a labor advocate," says Robert B. Semple, a Chrysler director. At the same time, however, Fraser was instrumental in the board's decision to set up a committee to study the personal and social impacts of plant closings, a move Fraser credits with keeping several plants from being closed. And while some Chrysler directors think Fraser's position helped make bargaining with the union easier, union officials are confident his presence on the board hasn't compromised his effectiveness in contract bargaining. "He didn't give anything away," says a member of the Chrysler rank-and-file negotiating committee.

In spite of Fraser's success, it remains to be seen whether the experiment will be extended to other major auto manufacturers, as the UAW hopes.

Source: Adapted from Robert L. Simison, "Chrysler Lauds Strong Performance of UAW's Fraser as Board Member," *Wall Street Journal*, March 12, 1981, pp. 27, 33. Adapted by permission of The Wall Street Journal, © Dow Jones & Company, Inc., 1981. All rights reserved.

management consult with UAW local committees on all decisions that "might adversely affect" job security, such as layoffs and plant shutdowns.

Another common management rights provision is a lengthy list of specific areas that are not subject to the contract's grievance procedure and collective bargaining. A long-form management rights clause might contain the right to (1) schedule working hours, (2) hire and fire workers, (3) set production standards, (4) promote, demote, and transfer workers, and (5) determine the number of supervisors in each department. These "rights," also known as *management prerogatives*, are matters of potential disagreement between labor and management. There are no hard and fast rules governing them.

Wages and Benefits Much time and effort are devoted to provisions for wage increases and fringe benefit improvements for the life of the contract. Wage increases can be (1) an immediate across-the-board percentage or cents-per-hour increase, (2) a deferred wage increase based on an annual improvement factor (productivity increase), and (3) a cost-of-living adjustment. A **deferred pay increase** is one that becomes effective later during the contract period. For example, at the beginning of the second and third years of a three-year contract, employees could receive across-the-board wage increases of 5 percent and 3 percent. Management meanwhile hopes that productivity will increase enough to offset these wage increases.

Many contracts contain **cost-of-living adjustment (COLA)** clauses that mean automatic wage increases as the cost of living advances. Typically, an adjustment provision calls for an hourly wage increase of $0.01 cent per hour for a specified rise in the consumer price index (CPI). The index is a measure by which the Bureau of Labor Statistics determines changes in living costs.

Besides wage increases, unions demand improvements in various fringe benefits. In some industries, such as steel and auto manufacturing, fringe benefits make up 40 percent of the total compensation bill. These benefits include (1) higher wage rates for overtime work, holiday work, and less desirable workshifts, (2) insurance programs (life, health and hospitalization, dental care), (3) payments for nonwork time (rest periods, vacations, holidays, and sick leave), (4) pensions, and (5) income maintenance plans. A fairly common income maintenance plan, such as that offered by General Motors, involves **supplementary unemployment benefits.** These benefits are paid from a fund, established by the employer, to workers on temporary layoff and are in addition to state unemployment compensation benefits.

Seniority and Job Security Cost-of-living adjustments, supplementary unemployment benefits, and still other benefits give an employee a certain amount of financial security. But financial security in turn is often directly related to job security. This is the assurance in some degree that workers will keep their jobs, regardless of economic conditions. Seniority, discussed in about 90 percent of all labor contracts, is the main way that job security is determined in collective bargaining agreements.[4] **Seniority** is the length of continuous service with the firm and is used for several purposes in collective bargaining. One of these is to determine an employee's eligibility for benefits, such as vacations, severance pay (additional pay given to employees who leave the company), and pension benefits. Seniority is also used to determine job assignments. These job rights can be used in bidding for higher-paying jobs, shift preferences, overtime work, and job transfers.

Other Major Issues Two other important bargaining issues are the duration of the contract and the no-strike and no-lockout clauses. The length of the contract period has tended to increase over the years. It is now most commonly three years. What has permitted this longer interval between contract renewals is, among other things, the wage protection now built into many agreements through cost-of-living adjustment clauses.

Strike and lockout provisions can be found in nearly all contracts. Under the no-strike clause the union agrees not to strike during the term of the contract. In turn, the employer gives a no-lockout pledge: the firm agrees not to shut the business down and force workers off their jobs. When a company uses a lockout, it hopes to get the union to change its position on some crucial issue. For example, trucking companies in Chicago have locked out drivers to force the union to accept their wage offers.

COLLECTIVE BARGAINING: CONTRACT ADMINISTRATION AND INTERPRETATION

The Grievance Procedure

The principal means at the union's disposal for policing the labor contract is the grievance procedure. A typical first step, under a United Auto Workers contract at the International Harvester Company, is taken when the aggrieved employee (employee with a problem) presents a grievance either in person or in writing to the supervisor. A union steward may be at the meeting to hear the grievance. In most cases, a **grievance** occurs because the worker feels that management has violated some provision of the collective bargaining agreement. (Often this involves interpretation of the contract.)

At step two, after the grievance has been put in writing, discussions take place between the employee and one or more union officials (such as a chief steward), and the supervisor and other managerial employees. Usually the other managerial employees include a labor relations specialist and the plant manager.

If the problem is not solved at step two, it goes to the next level. At this stage the local union president and a representative from the national union get involved along with the plant manager or a top executive of the division or company. If there's still no agreement, the union may request arbitration.

Labor Arbitration

The final step in the grievance procedure involves arbitration. **Grievance arbitration**—usually voluntary but sometimes compulsory—is a way to settle disputes using an impartial third party. This may be either a single arbitrator or a panel. The arbitrator reviews the grievance at a hearing and makes a decision (known as the *award*). This decision is binding on both labor and management and must be carried out. Only occasionally can it be appealed through the courts. If an arbitrator finds that Roadway Transport has wrongly discharged a truck driver, the company may be required to rehire the driver and pay him for wages lost.

PERSPECTIVE ON SMALL BUSINESS

What happens when an employee's grievance reaches arbitration?

Most grievances don't go that far. For Labconco, a small Kansas City, Missouri manufacturer of laboratory equipment, less than 5 percent of the grievances filed in 1981 ended in arbitration, according to Joan Park, Labconco personnel manager.

But some problems can't be settled by the company and the union. For Labconco, one such problem involved a worker's attendance record. Discipline for workers with attendance problems involves four progressive steps—a verbal warning, a written warning, a three-day suspension, and finally firing. Before a worker is given a warning, though, the company offers counseling; and after the disciplinary process has begun, it can be canceled if the worker's attendance improves.

Jack Pritchard, an assembler, had received a great deal of both counseling and discipline. Finally, when he left work early one day to appear as a defendant in court, he was fired. Pritchard filed a grievance the next day. Supporting the grievance, the union claimed he had been fired unjustly, because his absence was unavoidable, and asked that he be reinstated.

Three months later, having passed unresolved through the three stages of the grievance procedure, the case was presented before a professional arbitrator, a college dean paid by the company and the union and chosen by them from a list supplied by the Federal Mediation and Conciliation Service. The arbitrator, whose decision is binding, must determine whether the contract between the company and the union has been violated. At issue in this case was the discharge clause, which says "no employee shall be discharged, suspended or disciplined without just cause."

The hearing began with opening statements by the company and the union. Then the company called its witnesses—its director of administrative services, Mel Wise; its production manager, Dick Rosewicz; and the manager of Pritchard's department, John Jud. Through testimony and exhibits, the company's lawyer, John Bestor, presented his case: Labconco's attendance rules had been formulated with the union's cooperation and implemented with the union's approval. In accordance with the rules, Pritchard had been counseled often, had received many verbal and written warnings, and had even twice been suspended for three days before he'd finally been fired.

But why fire him for an absence he really couldn't avoid? That absence was part of a pattern Pritchard apparently was unable to change, the company said. So many allowances had been made for him already, explained the production manager, that "we were on the cliff-edge of discriminating against other employees." Further, Pritchard hadn't tried to change the court date or inform the company of it until the day before it was scheduled to take place.

The union's witnesses—Pritchard himself and the union steward for his department—didn't refute the company's testimony but focused on the personal problems—an invalid wife, a large family, seemingly unending health and financial problems—that made it hard for him to meet the demands of his job. "With all the problems that this brother has had . . .," asked the union representative, "why did the company have to take the day to terminate the man when they knew full well he had to be in court?"

More than a month after the hearing, the arbitrator's decision was released. In essence, it said that the company's attendance rules were reasonable and that the company had the right to enforce them reasonably, even when absences might seem beyond the employee's control. The union had produced no evidence to show the company had enforced the rules in a "capricious or discriminatory manner." Though Pritchard's problems invited sympathy, "leniency or clemency is the prerogative of the employer rather than of the arbitrator." The company's action was upheld.

SOURCE: Information courtesy of Labconco Corporation, Kansas City, Mo. The grievant's real name was not used.

The arbitration hearing is usually an informal proceeding with witnesses being called for testimony and cross-examination. Before the hearing, the union and employer submit a joint statement to the arbitrator that spells out the grievance situation. This helps the arbitrator understand the issues and make a decision.

Industrial Conflict, Strikes, and Other Labor Activities

The major recourse that a union has for putting pressure on an employer is to strike—but this is also usually the action of last resort taken by the union (see Figure 9.4). Although the strike may work an economic hardship on the employer, it also means loss of pay to the employees. On the average, fewer than 3 percent of American workers are involved in strikes each year. And—with few exceptions—strikes tend to be relatively short. A strike lasting longer than one month is considered unusual. The 110-day strike of the United Mine Workers union in 1978 was one of the longest strikes in the history of the union.

The most common type of strike is the eco- nomic strike over issues such as improvement in wages, pensions, vacations, and other benefits. This action usually results from a strike vote of the union membership. The strike normally begins immediately after the old labor agreement has expired and management and labor have failed to agree on new contract terms. Occasionally a group of union employees or the entire local union will strike while the contract is in effect, thereby violating it. This action is often illegal and is called a **wildcat strike.** Although organized and nonspontaneous, it is without the approval of the national union. A **sympathy strike** is mounted by workers not directly involved in a collective bargaining dispute to support the strikers directly involved.

A **labor boycott** occurs when union members and others are urged by the union to stop doing business with an employer with whom the union has a dispute. For example, if the Food and Commercial Workers Union has a dispute with Shop Rite supermarkets, it might instruct its members not to buy groceries from the Shop Rite stores. This is an example of a *primary* boycott. It differs from a *secondary* boycott, which is aimed at those dealing with the employer that's having a dispute

FIGURE 9.4

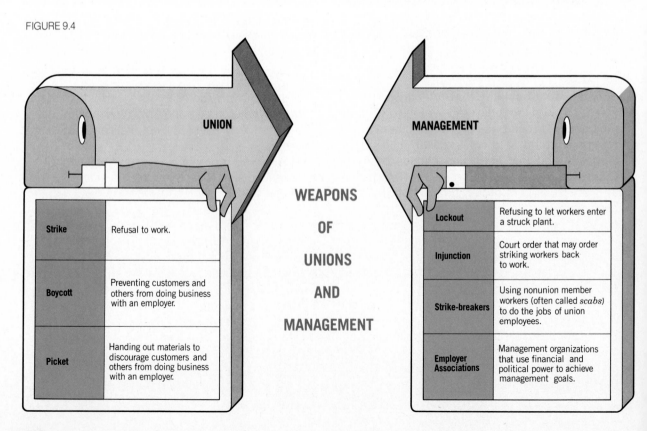

WEAPONS OF UNIONS AND MANAGEMENT

UNION

Strike	Refusal to work.
Boycott	Preventing customers and others from doing business with an employer.
Picket	Handing out materials to discourage customers and others from doing business with an employer.

MANAGEMENT

Lockout	Refusing to let workers enter a struck plant.
Injunction	Court order that may order striking workers back to work.
Strike-breakers	Using nonunion member workers (often called *scabs*) to do the jobs of union employees.
Employer Associations	Management organizations that use financial and political power to achieve management goals.

One of the most dramatic strikes in the early 1980s involved Air Traffic Controllers, inconveniencing many air passengers.

established a picket line, locking the gate simply makes picketing easier.

Strikebreakers — new employees hired to replace striking union workers — can also be a powerful weapon of management. The *Washington Post* replaced workers in order to break a strike by the typesetters union. The problem often faced by management is finding qualified personnel to take the place of union workers. Typically, workers that possess such skills belong to a national union.

Management has sometimes relied on an injunction to keep workers on the job. An **injunction** is a court order that restricts the union from interfering with a plant's production. In the past, management faced very few difficulties in obtaining an injunction. Today injunctions are invoked only when there are acts of violence or damage to the employer's property.

On a national level, management's counterpart to the AFL-CIO is the National Association of Manufacturers (NAM). The NAM maintains a vigorous and massive lobbying effort aimed at influencing Congress and the executive branches of government. It conducts extensive public relations work and does research in the area of labor relations. The NAM structure is not as highly organized as the unions but the power and financial resources of its employer members enable it to have a significant impact on labor legislation.

with a union. If a union were to call for the boycott of a trucking firm used by the employer, this would be an example of a secondary boycott, which is illegal under the Taft-Hartley Act.

Management's Options

Management is not without weapons of its own in disputes with labor. One of the more effective is the lockout. A **lockout** is the refusal to let workers enter a plant or building in order to work. In one recent case, 15,000 employees of job contractors to dressmakers in New York City were locked out in a disagreement over contract terms. Sometimes a lockout can play into union hands if the gate is closed indefinitely. Overhead costs continue whether the gate is open or closed. If a union has

Mediation and Conciliation

Management and labor can avoid using their entire arsenal of weapons in a labor dispute through mediation and conciliation. Both approaches involve third-party neutrals. In **conciliation** the third-party neutral tries to keep the parties to a dispute focused on the issues of disagreement. He or she acts as a channel of information to be exchanged between the parties. **Mediation** is a stronger form of intervention. Here the neutral engages in substantive discussions with union and management negotiators in separate meetings and in joint sessions. Additionally, the mediator makes suggestions to the parties in the hope that concession and compromise will result. In contrast to arbitration, the mediator has no authority to issue binding decisions on the disputing organizations. Effective communication and persuasion are the primary tools of the mediator.

Strikes often have repercussions beyond the organization itself. The New York City transit strike resulted in a long hike to work over the Brooklyn Bridge for many commuters.

SUMMARY

The labor movement in the United States has generally grown over the years. The US labor movement consists of local unions, joint union councils, national and international unions, and the AFL-CIO labor federation. The three primary functions of local unions are (1) collective bargaining, (2) worker relations and membership services, and (3) community and political activities. A national union consists of many local unions in a particular industry, skilled trade, or geographic area. An umbrella organization, the AFL-CIO represents about 54 percent of US unions and employee organizations.

Forerunners of US labor unions were the late-eighteenth-century guilds formed to further workers' interests. Partly because of the courts, employers' opposition to these groups was frequently successful. The Knights of Labor (1869–1917) was one of the first major national labor organizations; however it was not very effective in improving the life of the working person. In 1881 many of the craft groups within the Knights left it to form the Federation of Organized Trades and Labor Unions, later called the American Federation of Labor (AFL). Under Samuel Gompers, the AFL rejected the broad social and economic goals of the Knights of Labor to concentrate on such practical matters as (1) the concept of exclusive jurisdiction for member unions, (2) local union authority, and (3) collective bargaining and strikes to improve wages, hours, and working conditions. In 1935, after a conflict within the AFL, John L. Lewis, president of the United Mine Workers of America, left the AFL to form the Committee for Industrial Organization (CIO), later called the Congress of Industrial Organizations. Until the early 1950s, AFL and CIO unions competed for membership. Various problems caused the two groups to merge in 1955 into one, with George Meany as president.

The role of the courts in the settlement of labor disputes has increased over the years. The Norris-LaGuardia Act included several provisions favorable to unions, such as those prohibiting employers' use of injunctions and yellow dog contracts. In 1935 Congress passed the National Labor Relations Act (Wagner Act), which encouraged the creation of unions, set out employer unfair labor practices, and established the National Labor Relations Board (NLRB). This act was amended in 1947 by the Labor-Management Relations Act (Taft-Hartley Act), which placed a number of restraints on union activities. Enforcing the Wagner and Taft-Hartley Acts is the job of the NLRB. In 1959 Congress passed the Labor-Management Reporting and Disclosure Act (Landrum-Griffin Act), which dealt primarily with the internal affairs of unions.

Collective bargaining is the process of negotiating, administering, and interpreting the labor agreement. One of the most important issues for the union in negotiating this agreement is union security. Closely related is the provision for a dues checkoff. To protect its rights against union encroachment, management often includes a management rights clause in the labor agreement. Much time and effort in negotiations are devoted to provisions for wage increases and fringe benefit improvements. Job security, another union concern, is assured mainly through seniority provisions.

The main way in which the union polices the labor contract is through the grievance procedure. Typically, the first step involves the employee's presenting the grievance to the supervisor, perhaps in the presence of the shop steward. Subsequent steps involve progressively higher levels of union and company officials. Finally, the grievance may be submitted to binding arbitration.

The union's major recourse for putting pressure on the employer is the strike. Mediation and conciliation are two of the most common approaches for resolving labor disputes stemming from contract negotiation differences.

conciliation
cost-of-living
    adjustment (COLA)
craft union
deferred pay increase
dues checkoff
employer unfair labor
    practices
exclusive jurisdiction
grievance
grievance arbitration
industrial union
injunction
jurisdiction
Knights of Labor
labor boycott
labor force
Landrum-Griffin Act
lockout
mediation
mixed union
national emergency
    strike procedures
National Labor
    Relations Board
    (NLRB)
national union
Norris-LaGuardia Act
picket
remedy
seniority
stewards
strikebreakers
supplementary
    unemployment
    benefits
sympathy strike
Taft-Hartley Act
union shop
union unfair labor practices
Wagner Act
wildcat strike
yellow dog contract
zone of bargaining

KEY TERMS

blacklist
closed shop
collective bargaining

REVIEW QUESTIONS

1. What are the objectives of a labor union?
2. Describe the important pieces of federal legislation that have benefited the labor movement.

3. What is the difference between a craft union and an industrial union?
4. Name the three mandatory items of collective bargaining.
5. What are the weapons or tools of management and labor in a dispute?
6. Describe the three levels of union security.
7. What are the six trends affecting current labor-management relations?

DISCUSSION QUESTIONS

1. Which of the following persons are likely to become members of a union: airline pilot, janitor, college professor, author, dentist. Why?
   What roles do unions take in political campaigns? Give several examples.
2. Are there advantages to management in having its work force unionized? If any, what are they?
3. Can unions be considered a monopoly? If so, how?
4. In today's economy are unions as necessary as they formerly were to protect the rights of workers? Explain.
5. In recent years large numbers of women have entered the work force. What has been the effect on union membership? What effect will it
6. fect on union membership? What effect will it have in the future?
7. Many recent union contracts have included a cost-of-living adjustment. If this adds to inflation, does it benefit the workers or not?

CASE: FORD'S NEW MODEL MANAGEMENT/LABOR CONTRACT

Headlines in newspapers across the country announced the member ratification of the historic contract with UAW. According to these reports, "The pact guarantees union members more job security while promising Ford savings of up to $1 billion." The result of the voting from 56 Ford Locals was 3-1 in favor, as related by Douglas Fraser, UAW president, who expressed pleasure with the member endorsement.

Ford chairman Philip Caldwell said: "March 1 [1982] is a date we shall long remember as an important milestone on our road ahead." He added:

"There is, I am convinced, a clear understanding in our plants and at all levels throughout the company of what we all have to do to regain our national competitiveness."

Ford had 54,261 workers on indefinite layoff; car sales were sluggish, and the company recorded over $1 billion losses in 1980 and 1981—not a very healthy environment for workers or management or the country.

The new contract, with an expiration date of September 1984, required Ford's autoworkers to give up all eight paid personal holidays per year, accept a wage freeze for the contract's duration, and defer cost-of-living allowance payments for nine months.

Ford's chief negotiator, Peter J. Pestillo said: "This may be the most critical point in time in our history and we get to put labor relations behind us."

1. Why did these management and union leaders putting so much emphasis on the historical significance of this contract?
2. Did the contract settlement favor management or labor?

CASE: THE MIFFED MEN IN BLUE

The police department for this midwestern city of approximately 300,000 people had been operating for the past two months with an acting chief of police. The previous chief had suffered a heart attack, and had been out of service for that period of time.

The acting police chief had for two years been the deputy chief, so he was a likely candidate for the vacant position. Of course, in compliance with Equal Opportunity guidelines, many candidates had to be interviewed before the final selection was made.

One factor that had to be considered by the mayor and the council was renewal of the police union's labor contract, due to expire in three months. The new chief therefore had to have experience in union relations and negotiations as well as a good track record demonstrating an ability to run the police department in a city of this size.

The mayor, after duly considering all the candidates—with extensive interviews for inside as well as outside candidates—decided to offer the position to an outsider. His decision was approved by the city council, and the new man, Tim Mahan, was invited to take over the job.

On the appointed day, Mahan met with the mayor, the city council, and the press to accept his new position and to hold a brief press conference. All went well until a union spokesperson rose to challenge Mahan's appointment.

Through its attorney the union had asked for an injunction to delay the official assumption of his responsibilities by the new chief, on the grounds that he had failed to qualify for the position. The union alleged that he had insufficient experience as chief in a city of comparable size—one of the criteria for eligibility.

The press had a field day describing both sides of the argument. One editorial comment was that the "inside" candidates were miffed because they felt that they had not been given due consideration for the position. Others criticized the mayor and the city council for not doing their homework and checking out the precise qualifications of the candidate.

The case hung in the balance for a few days while a court considered the arguments. Finally, the challenge was thrown out. The new police chief was found qualified in accordance with eligibility rules, and he was duly reinstated in the position by the mayor (with the applause of the city council).

1. How would you evaluate the merits of this case and the differing points of view that came out of the challenge of the new appointment?
2. Are there likely to be some repercussions when the union contract is renegotiated?
3. What chances do you think the new police chief has for successful managerial control over the police department?

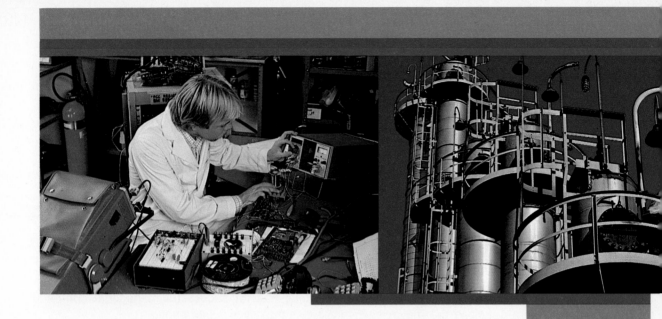

C H A P T E R   10

PRODUCTION AND
OPERATIONS
MANAGEMENT

After studying this chapter you should be able to:

1 Understand how the production function converts factors of production into outputs.
2 Explain the basic production processes.
3 Understand the important steps in production planning.
4 Describe the quanitative and qualitative factors in determining plant location.
5 Explain the process of inventory control.
6 Describe the steps of production control.

"Let your imagination fly." Advancements in technology may well create the basis for new business opportunities, but Bell Helicopter Textron's credo for the eighties seems to suggest that it's really the *imaginative application* of those advancements that makes the opportunities pay off.

Imaginative applications have certainly paid off for Bell, helping to make the Fort Worth company—which is also Textron's Inc.'s biggest operating division—the world leader in the helicopter industry. Bell has built and delivered over 25,000 helicopters to the commercial and military markets. Not bad, especially when they're selling a product that Wilbur Wright dismissed because ". . .we soon saw it had no future."

There's no doubt today that the helicopter has a bright future. And to ensure its place in that future, Bell is moving aggressively ahead, not only with technological improvements to the product itself, but also with technological reindustrialization of the manufacturing processes used to build it. And the most pervasive influence is that of the computer.

Manufacturing processes and computer systems go hand-in-hand at Bell. Today, stand-alone computer systems are at work in functions like shop floor control and inspection. But tomorrow, all these systems and more will be tied together into a single computer-integrated manufacturing network extending from sales orders all the way through manufacturing.

"Our computer integrated manufacturing network will link all the functions essential to building helicopters," explains R.K. (Dick) May, senior vice president of operations. "And we think it will be one of the biggest productivity improvers our industry has seen."

Donald E. Hegland, "Bell Helicopter—Flying on the Leading Edge," *Production Engineering*, January 1981, pp. 59–61. Reprinted with permission .

The ability to achieve productivity gains as demonstrated by Bell Helicopter is important to the long-run success of the business firm. It's been said that if most manufacturing businesses were stripped down to their bare essentials, there'd be only two: the need for people to make the product (production), and the need for people to sell the product (marketing). Of course, this statement is an oversimplification of the business enterprise. Still, we'd have to agree that the production function plays a major role in any business organization—regardless of whether it sells a product or a service.

The production process has long been a subject of study. Back in the eighteenth century, Adam Smith recognized that **specialization of labor** in manufacturing—that is, having a worker perform one or several tasks in the manufacture of an item rather than performing all the tasks—could be economically beneficial. Other contributors to the study of production include Frederick W. Taylor, who outlined the concepts of scientific management and who pioneered time study and work study; Frank B. Gilbreth, who developed motion study of jobs; and Henry L. Gantt, who developed a means of comparing the relationship between planned and actual production performance. All three flourished around the beginning of this century. There have been numerous other contributors and studies since that time. There will be renewed emphasis on the production process in the United States now that many companies such as Bell Helicopter have made the improvement of productivity a major goal. In this chapter we will focus on the production process and how it is managed.

THE PRODUCTION PROCESS

The purpose of the **production function** in the business enterprise is the conversion of inputs, sometimes referred to as **factors of production,** into outputs—the finished product. Figure 10.1 diagrams this process.

We see from the diagram that the final output from a production process doesn't have to be a tangible product. It's usual to think of a company like General Electric combining steel, rubber, copper, and many other inputs to produce something as concrete as a dishwashing machine; but it's necessary to expand our thinking to include organizations whose function it is to provide a service. For example, the Humana Corporation is in the health care business, which centers on the operation of hospitals. Humana provides the service of combining medical personnel, equipment, supplies and related components, and sick patients to produce the desired output—healthy individuals.

Classifying Production Processes

Production can be classified in three different ways. First, we can look at how inputs are converted into final outputs. This is called the **conversion process,** and two forms are identified: analytic and synthetic. Second, we can see if the conversion process runs continuously or intermittently, which is referred to as the **conversion system.** Third, we can classify production by the nature of demand for the product—whether production is for specific orders or for inventory. We'll now take a look at these classification schemes.

Analytic vs. Synthetic In an **analytic process,** the basic input is broken down into component parts. For example, when the Aluminum Company of America (ALCOA) manufactures aluminum, the raw material—bauxite, which is mined—is processed to extract the aluminum. Petroleum products are similarly the result of an analytic process. At Exxon, crude petroleum (the input) is refined into a whole host of products, such as home heating oil, gasoline, jet fuel, and petrochemicals, to name a few.

On the other hand, a **synthetic process** is one in which the basic inputs are combined to produce the final product. An automobile is the result of the combination of thousands of component parts. Electronic equipment—such as television sets, stereo receivers, and hand-held calculators—results from a synthetic process.

FIGURE 10.1

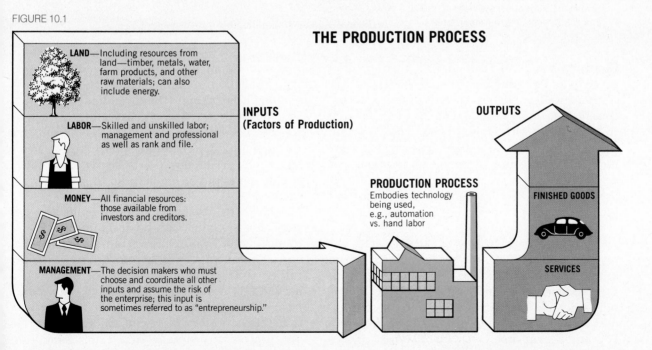

THE PRODUCTION PROCESS

LAND—Including resources from land—timber, metals, water, farm products, and other raw materials; can also include energy.

LABOR—Skilled and unskilled labor; management and professional as well as rank and file.

MONEY—All financial resources: those available from investors and creditors.

MANAGEMENT—The decision makers who must choose and coordinate all other inputs and assume the risk of the enterprise; this input is sometimes referred to as "entrepreneurship."

INPUTS
(Factors of Production)

PRODUCTION PROCESS
Embodies technology being used, e.g., automation vs. hand labor

OUTPUTS

FINISHED GOODS

SERVICES

(Top) An analytic production process: phosphate plant. (Bottom) A synthetic production process: Advent Stero assembly line.

Continuous vs. Intermittent In a **continuous process,** long production runs are made, and the equipment is rarely shut down. Raw materials are continuously fed into production. Usually unit costs are lower with such a system, since specialization of labor and special-purpose machines are used. The production of petroleum products and many chemicals is accomplished by a continuous production system. Mass-production industries, such as the automobile industry, fall into this category.

An **intermittent process** is one in which the product is usually in process of completion over an extended period of time—the time it takes for the product to be "put together." General-purpose machines are usually used, but not continuously. They are set up to produce different products at different times. Custom orders are usually produced by an intermittent process. Intermittent production is characteristic of many job-order machine shops (the so-called job-shop), custom furniture, and almost all construction projects.

Figure 10.2 depicts an intermittent flow and a continuous production flow. Clearly, continuous production would be much easier to schedule.

To Order vs. To Inventory Meeting the demand for a product can be accomplished (1) by producing (or by purchasing from an outside vendor, if the company is a retailer or wholesaler rather than a manufacturer) the item when needed (**"to order"**) or (2) by taking the product from storage into which it was placed at an earlier time (**"to inventory"**). The product of a continuous process is generally stored for some time between production and sales. Thus Exxon's gasoline production continues at varying levels throughout the year. However the heavy demand period occurs during the summer driving months. The industry hasn't been capable of meeting summer gasoline demands from production and has had to draw on inventory during those months.

Determining the Input Mix

An **input mix** refers to a specific combination of inputs used in production. Of course, in actual practice a plan for the mix must be very detailed, spelling out specifically what kind of inputs to use and in what quantities. However in general dis-

cussion the mix is viewed often as the combination of only two inputs—capital and labor. (*Labor* is a fairly straightforward term, but *capital* can be confusing. It often refers to money—that is, financial capital—but it can also mean real things such as machinery and buildings. For the sake of simplicity, let's think of capital as all inputs other than labor and management.)

It's important to understand that technology is often embodied in the capital a business buys. If you want the latest technology in data processing, you need to buy a computer and not an adding machine. So, in making capital expenditure decisions, management "locks in" a specific technology for as long as the capital lasts. To illustrate, the claim has been made that U.S. steelmakers were reluctant to incorporate new technologies in

FIGURE 10.2

EQUIPMENT AND PRODUCTION FLOW

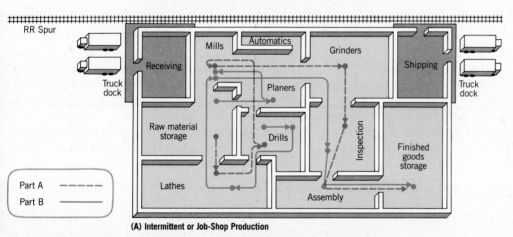

(A) Intermittent or Job-Shop Production

(B) Continuous Production

SOURCE: Elwood S. Buffa, *Modern Production/Operations Management,* 6th ed. (New York: John Wiley & Sons, 1980), p. 467. Reprinted by permission.

steelmaking at the end of World War II because they still had plant and equipment capable of producing steel with the older methods. Not burdened with existing plants—they were bombed to oblivion—the Germans and Japanese rebuilt their steel industries to incorporate the very latest technologies in steelmaking. Their enormous competitive edge in world markets, and even in the U.S., during the 1950s and 60s is, unfortunately, documented history.

The Role of Automation We generally think of **automation** as the replacement of human effort by automatic machines used to control production processes. There's no question that automation has played a significant role in the development of American and world industry. It's no less certain to play a larger role in the future. General Electric, for example, not long ago invested many millions of dollars in its dishwasher manufacturing plant in Louisville, Kentucky to make it the most modern facility of its type in the world. Renovation called for replacing over half the existing equipment with more sophisticated machines and automated assembly equipment.

In many situations, the production process is completely carried out and monitored by mechanical and electronic devices: that is, machines are controlling machines. Chrysler Corporation provides an example: in its state-of-the-art Jeffer-

son Assembly Plant, where the fuel-efficient K-cars are built, "steel-collar workers" (robots) are used to make nearly 3000 welds on each K-car body. One stage of this process is shown in Figure 10.3. Here the Robogate fixture automatically welds together the two sides and underbody panel of each car.

PRODUCTION PLANNING

A major input to the production process is management expertise. It wouldn't be possible for industry to produce the many different products that it does—and in such large quantities—without very careful planning.

Analyzing the Product

For the production manager to begin planning for production, he or she must completely analyze the product. Levi Strauss might begin with the general concept of a "fashion jean," but eventually this must be made concrete and specific. The exact specification of the product then leads to a whole host of decisions ranging from raw materials through machinery and manpower scheduling. The form that *physical specifications* take varies depending on the product. In a machine

FIGURE 10.3
Robogate robots help bring Chrysler K-cars to life.

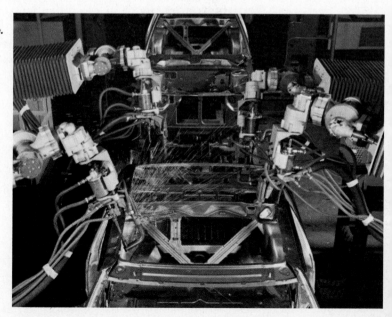

ON THE FIRING LINE

The Robot Revolution—Are We Ready for It?

Growth in productivity is a telling measure of the health of a nation's economy. For years, the US passed this test with ease. Until 1965, US productivity increased each year by an average of 3.4 percent. But then the productivity growth rate began to drop. Meanwhile, productivity in Japan has grown by leaps and bounds. Indeed, some believe Japan may soon assume the role of world economic leader—a role we like to believe is ours. How can this be?

There are many possible answers. Robots, for example. Robots are one very important reason for Japan's production gains. Robots, almost everyone agrees, are the troops of the second industrial revolution. In Japan both industry and labor are embracing these hardened soldiers with open arms. By some estimates, Japan had nearly 14,000 robots in use in 1981. Japan's robot population is far greater than that of any other country. In the US, for instance, there were only about 4000 robots in use in 1981.

The robot revolution, like the first industrial revolution, will make production much more efficient. Robots don't require coffee breaks, weekends and nights off, or vacations. They can work three shifts, round the clock. They can do work people cannot do—dangerous or very heavy work. They do not require retirement pensions or other benefits, and they don't go on strike. What's more, robots have been getting cheaper, while the cost of labor has gone up. Robots used in the auto industry, for example, cost about $4.50 an hour. The average auto industry blue-collar worker, however, earns around $14 an hour in wages and fringe benefits.

Japan already has an indisputable edge on the market with its large robot work force. Japanese industry has had an easy time introducing robots. One reason for this is that the Japanese government encourages their use. In fact, it supports a program to lease robots to small and medium-sized companies, which might otherwise not be able to afford them. Another reason is a singular tradition of Japanese business and industry: Japanese companies generally guarantee their employees jobs for life. Their workers have no fear of losing jobs to robots.

Unless US firms quickly build their force of robots, say many, they'll never regain their lead in the world market. The onslaught of the Japanese mechanical army threatens the very life of the ailing auto industry. In the 1970s, 450,000 Japanese workers were producing 2.5 to 3 million cars a year. In the 1980s, it was predicted, the same work force—with the help of robots—would be able to produce *four times* that many cars.

In the last couple of years, too, the Japanese have developed totally automated factories. There is Yamazaki Machinery Works, for instance. Its robots do almost all the work. Only twelve people operate three shifts—six on the first, six on the second, and none at night. An equivalent system without robots would require 220 workers. And in a Japanese vacuum cleaner plant, robots reduced the needed work force from several hundred to eight people.

Offices are being taken over by robots. The second-largest bank in the country, Citibank, has opted for automation. In the first stages of the process alone, automation reduced the staff by 40 percent. What this means, we're told, is that soon after the advent of robots there will be only two basic types of jobs. First, some unskilled labor will still be important to keep the robots going. Workers will wait on robots, feeding them parts or changing their tools. Such jobs will be as dull as—or duller and more tedious than—assembly-line jobs. Second, a high level of technical education will be needed for any other robot-related jobs—robot maintenance or programming.

shop, specifications are usually available in the form of an engineering drawing. In an industry manufacturing food products, we would expect the product specification to be provided in the form of a recipe. These specifications should tell the manager all that he or she needs to know to be able to make the product.

The *raw materials specifications* tells the production manager which raw materials — and of what quality — should be used in the manufacture of the product. Should Levi's new jeans be made with a 10- or 12- ounce denim? It should also indicate if material substitutions are permissible. For example, the specification of galvanized nails for use in exterior construction might indicate that aluminum nails are an acceptable substitute.

Value Analysis **Value analysis** is the process by which a product is completely analyzed in terms of its cost and intended use in order to determine the least costly (but still satisfactory) specification for the product. The purpose, of course, is to minimize the cost of production. A value analysis should reveal such information as alternative but less expensive materials, product simplification for economy, and alternative but cheaper manufacturing methods.

In one instance, as a result of value analysis, a company was able to substitute molded nylon for low-carbon steel in the manufacture of a carburetor component. The result was a 50 percent savings. The change in materials made possible the elimination of several manufacturing operations.

Minimizing Cost

The performance of most production managers is evaluated on the basis of cost of production rather than on the more usual factors of profit or return on investment, which are applicable elsewhere in the company. RCA must produce its television sets to have comparable quality with Zenith's and to be price competitive. To do this, it must produce at the lowest possible cost. The production of a product involves several cost areas, which we'll now look at.

Raw Material Costs Raw material costs for a manufactured product can range from a very

small amount to a substantial portion of the final cost. Small savings in unit material cost can often result in large dollar savings when production costs are totaled.

Labor Costs Labor costs are a major component for many industries, especially those that are considered service industries, such as health care, education, and food service. A major determinant of labor cost is the skill level required to produce the output. In general, the higher the skill level required, the higher the cost. A Brooks Brothers' hand-tailored suit will cost about five times as much as one from Richman Brothers.

Equipment Costs **Equipment Costs** are major cost items for mass-production industries, such as automobiles. Each time a new model is introduced, much of the tooling must be replaced at considerable cost. In 1980 Chrysler spent more than $100 million in the 20-week conversion of its Jefferson Assembly Plant to produce K-cars.[1] The design of the product from the production standpoint must therefore take into account design standards and their related impact on equipment costs.

Energy Costs Until fairly recently, energy costs were considered a minor component of total production cost for most industries. With the rising cost of oil, natural gas, and electricity, energy costs must now be examined as critically as other production costs. As a result, some industries — such as the aluminum industry, which consumes large amounts of energy in the conversion process — have been able to make notable progress in reducing energy requirements over recent years in an attempt to reduce overall production costs.

All of the above costs must be considered as related when making production decisions. A company may save money in the initial outlay by purchasing low-efficiency electrical equipment — and then spend many times the initial savings in future energy costs. The key to minimizing costs is to minimize the sum of all cost categories together, not each cost considered separately. This concept is demonstrated for a hypothetical example in Table 10.1 where three different production methods are evaluated on a least-cost basis. It's assumed that each method produces the same quantity and quality of output.

Costs of Alternative Production Methods[a]

Input Component	Production Method		
	A	B	C
Raw material	$ 50	$ 45	$ 35
Labor	150	100	80
Equipment	40	75	150
Energy	10	20	30
Total	$250	$240[b]	$295

[a]Costs in thousands.
[b]Least cost method.

CHOOSING A PLANT LOCATION

A major strategic decision that must be made in the earliest stages of planning for production is the location of the plant. A mistake made at this stage can be very costly since it's usually far from easy to relocate a plant once production begins. There are many factors to consider prior to locating a plant. Among these are the market, the sources of materials, transportation facilities, and the potential for future expansion. These factors are related to the geographical region of location. Once the region is pinpointed, a specific location is determined by study of the communities within that region and the availability of plant sites within each community.

Quantitative Factors

Many of the factors determining plant location can be readily investigated and reduced to costs. Because of the huge importance of raw materials to the production process, many companies make the availability of raw materials the major consideration in their decision where to locate. Companies in the extractive industries, such as mining, would be concerned to attempt to locate near the source of supply. A company producing processed food would also consider the availability of raw material to be a prime consideration. Dole, pineapple packers, located their processing and packing plant in Hawaii, close to the pineapple fields.

There are several labor-related issues to consider in deciding on a plant location. Regional labor patterns such as labor-pool size, labor-pool skill levels, and productivity history are all important. Wage rates and the extent of unionization are important determinants of the ultimate cost of production.

The availability of transportation to bring in raw material as well as to transport the final product to market is important to many companies. Take, for example, a milling company (such as Ethan Allen, mentioned earlier) which produces manufactured goods using wood as the raw material. This company would usually find it necessary to select a plant site located along a railroad sid-

The relatively low wage-rate structure attracts labor intensive industry, like furniture production, to the south, while favorable climatic conditions limit production of pineapples to places such as Hawaii.

ing so that raw materials could be moved in to the plant and the final products moved out to market.

During the last decade, energy costs and availability have assumed a prominent role in the cost structure of American industry. There are major regional differences in the cost of electrical power, ranging from the Northwest, where energy costs are relatively low (a major portion of the electricity is generated by hydroelectric plants), to the Northeast, where heavy reliance is placed on electricity generated by expensive imported oil.

Regional taxes at the time the location decision is made (and afterward) play an important role. State corporate income taxes, property taxes, sales taxes, payroll taxes, and others increase the cost of doing business. Taxes can vary tremendously from location to location throughout the country. Along with its higher energy and labor costs, the Northeast has a history of higher taxes—whereas the southern states (the so-called Sun Belt) have a history of lower taxes, and many companies have chosen to locate in, or relocate to, this area. Numerous localities offer tax incentives to get companies to locate within their borders.

Qualitative Factors

There are many important location considerations that are not easily reduced to figures and statistics but that are nevertheless important. The quality of local government, the attitude of the

FIGURE 10.4

An ad attempting to attract new industry to the state of Arkansas.

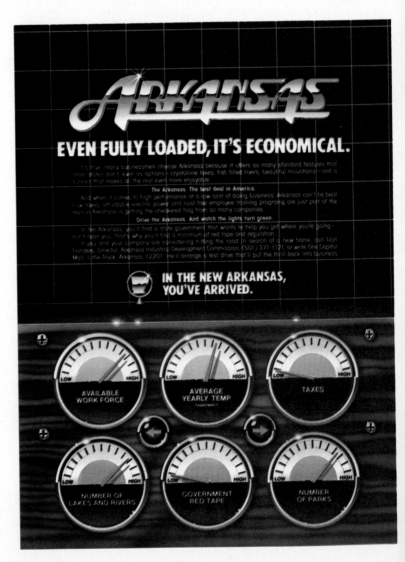

community toward business, and general living conditions are among these considerations.

Moreover community attitudes toward business, as well as the quality of government, are often reflected in the regulations and ordinances that govern the local site and conduct of business. Zoning regulations, which are locally imposed, can be especially revealing. We'd all agree that many existing ordinances are appropriate, but there are some that can severely limit the economic operation of a production facility. For this reason, locating a plant calls for a close look at such matters as local waste-disposal and pollution regulations.

Site Selection

Once the region of the country and a particular community within that region are selected, it's necessary to select a specific site for the plant. Site considerations include the availability of existing structures, construction needs, land size and cost, utilities, and proximity to transportation—to name several. All of the information necessary to make the site selection must be carefully researched. Many communities that are trying to attract industry have formed development agencies whose function it is to provide just such information. Many areas actively advertise in order to attract new business. One such ad run by the State of Arkansas is shown in Figure 10.4.

As with most other production-related decisions, the appropriate objective for the plant location decision is the minimization of cost. This means that all of the factors we've considered have to be taken into account so that the final choice is the lowest cost alternative consistent with qualitative considerations and the firm's achievement of its production goals.

PURCHASING RAW MATERIALS

The purchasing department has traditionally been viewed as a necessary but not particularly exciting part of the business. Its function is to arrange for all purchases of materials and supplies necessary to run the business. Like most production-related functions, purchasing is a cost center where money is spent. However, it's important to recognize the opportunity to increase profit through cost reduction in the purchasing process.

As with most decisions related to production, the **minimization of cost** is the primary objective of the purchasing department. Additionally, though, the purchasing department must be concerned with the availability and quality of materials purchased. If materials aren't available when needed, the cost of lost production and lost sales can be significant when compared to the material cost. If quality is lacking, waste and scrap may be excessive, and the final product may fall below standard.

Shopping for Supplies

A major responsibility of the purchasing department is to shop for and buy needed materials, supplies, or other ingredients. Procter & Gamble, Beatrice Foods, and other food processors have been able to use a variety of oils—soybean, cottonseed, safflower, and others—to produce margarine. This adds considerable flexibility when their production departments submit purchase requisitions. After a requisition is submitted, the purchasing department must determine sources, prices, quality, and availability of items to be purchased.

Price Price is always an important consideration in making any purchase. In some cases a supplier will be able to charge a fixed price for its product. However when orders are placed frequently and in large quantities, the purchasing agent is often able to negotiate the price.

In more usual situations, bids are frequently requested from several suppliers able to meet the requirements. The contract, however, won't necessarily be awarded to the lowest bidder, since price isn't the only consideration.

Delivery Costs An additional cost adding to the total cost of supplies is that of transportation from the supplier to the purchaser. This cost depends on the distance and speed of delivery as well as the physical characteristics of the material.

Quality Purchasing materials from the lowest price source may in fact turn out to be expensive if the quality of the material is inadequate for its intended function. A major responsibility of the

PERSPECTIVE ON SMALL BUSINESS

For sizable multinational companies, selecting expansion and relocation sites is easy. Their top managements, often aided by in-house facilities planners and outside consultants, continually review the relative cost-effectiveness of various production and distrubution units around the country and the world and regularly examine alternative locales. Despite difficulties and frustrations, large corporations usually have both the experience and the personnel for a wide variety of site selection activities.

Not so for the smaller, more entrepreneurial organization. Deciding whether to move or expand is usually a one-time decision that no one in the company is equipped to handle. As a consequence, management may repeatedly postpone the move or expansion possibility from month to month and then from year to year. Or else someone within the company, usually the production manager, is designated to explore a new location on a special-assignment, "when you get time" basis. Often this person interprets the assignment (usually correctly) as being a matter of second-guessing the chief executive's preferences rather than coming up with an original and sensible recommendation. Not surprisingly, such assignments are frequently delayed indefinitely.

An Alternative Approach

Small companies can obtain outside assistance in site selection decisions that is not only competent but also free. Approximately 7,500 professional area development groups now operating in the United States, usually under the control or direction of a state development agency, are willing and able "to serve as the smaller company's whole site team." . . .

A situation recalled by John Foltz, executive director of the Louisiana Office of Commerce & Industry, illustrates the range and sophistication of aids that may be available to alert small business owners:

"When Olympic Fastening Systems of California decided to expand, one phone call they placed was to our office. We learned from them that Vice President of Manufacturing H. L. Williamson and President Frank Nance would be in Little Rock, Arkansas on another matter; we arranged to pick them up in a state airplane, fly them to Louisiana, and show them the type of site they were seeking in two towns, both of which provided a program of speculative industrial building.

"They ultimately selected the town of Vivian. In addition to briefing the company, we also advised the two towns as to what the company was seeking, assisted town leaders in presenting their advantages and, perhaps most important, helped town leaders construct their already planned speculative buildings to Olympic's specifications.

"Overall, we were able to arrange it so that Olympic received not only a tailor-made speculative building program but also a free start-up training program and a full 10-year tax exemption in a town that was able to prove without any doubt that the company was wanted there."

SOURCE: Reprinted by permission of the Harvard Business Review. Excerpt from "Outsiders Can Ease the Site Selection Process," by Ted M. Levine, Harvard Business Review, May–June 1981, pp. 12, 14. Copyright © 1981 by the President and Fellows of Harvard College; all rights reserved.

purchasing department is to monitor the quality of its purchases. In this way it assures the production departments that they won't have defective materials that could increase their costs because of poor performance.

Purchase Planning

Purchase Planning is the efficient planning of material purchases to ensure, on the one hand,

Buy-or-Make Considerations: Auto manufacturers routinely buy tires from manufacturers such as Goodyear (right), rather than producing them themselves.

that there's sufficient materials inventory when it's needed and, on the other hand, that there's not so much inventory that it will hurt the financial position of the company. For example, a six-week supply of coal in its yard might be considered satisfactory by a public utility.

The main determinant of when purchases are made is the time that's expected to elapse between the placement of the order and the receipt of the materials—the so-called **lead time.** This lead time varies depending on the supplier, the material being ordered, and the distance it must travel from its origin. Specialty metals or custom-made ball bearings, for example, could take several months from the time an order is placed until they arrive at the plant for use in production.

While firms such as Toyota, the Japanese automobile manufacturer, will maintain raw material and component inventories, ranging from a few minutes to a few hours of production, other companies will buy materials to meet their production needs for an extended period of time. They're then following what's called a policy of **forward buying.** Even though the inventory investment cost will generally be higher with forward buying, there are reasons why it may be desirable. Appliance manufacturers, such as Frigidaire, Whirlpool, and Westinghouse, have historically purchased and inventoried larger amounts of steel than usual when there was a threat of a steelworkers' strike. If these companies didn't have enough steel to last the duration of a strike, they'd have to shut production down. Another reason for inventorying larger amounts of material is the prospect of a price increase—a common enough occurrence over the past decade.

INVENTORY, PRODUCTION, AND QUALITY CONTROL

A major function of production management is the control of inventory, production, and quality. This generally involves the measurement of results against plans and subsequent adjustments of inputs as necessary.

Controlling Inventory

The control of inventories is a major responsibility of the production manager. Inventory is used to serve several purposes. Its obvious use is to meet demand for the product. Just as important is the use of inventory to smooth production; that is, machines generally operate at different rates, and in many cases inventory at various stages of manufacture is necessary to keep all workers busy. The last use of inventory is speculation: many companies keep larger inventories than usual in anticipation of a strike or price increase.

Types of Inventory There are three basic types of inventory distinguished by their place in the production cycle. **Raw materials inventory,** used to start production; intermediate inventory, known as **work in process,** which includes products at any of the various stages of production prior to completion; and **finished goods inventory,** which is stored to meet customer demand.

Level of Inventory The appropriate level of inventory is of great concern to the management of any company. There are several cost categories that must be considered in determining the best level of inventory. The **cost of holding** the inventory consists of investment, storage, handling, insurance, and shrinkage (goods not available for sale for one reason or another). Since this cost increases as the level of inventory increases, there's an incentive to keep inventories low. However the lower the level of inventory, the more frequently orders will have to be placed, thereby increasing the **order cost.** A final cost to consider is the cost of maintaining an inadequate level of inventory — the so-called **shortage cost.** The lower the level of inventory, the more likely shortage cost will be incurred. In determining the best level of inventory, the inventory manager must assess each of the three costs and minimize their total.

Monitoring Inventory In order to manage inventory levels properly, management must be able to keep track of the movement, or lack of movement, of the various items in inventory. Most companies maintain what's referred to as a **perpetual inventory.** This is simply a system that keeps continuous track of all major inventory items and identifies orders, sales, and receipts as they occur. The task of monitoring inventory has been aided by the use of computer programs. Most computer manufacturers, such as IBM and Control Data, have software packages that not only track inventory levels but actually calculate order quantities and print the purchase order at the appropriate time. A recent study by Booz-Allen & Hamilton, a leading management consultant, has found that those American manufacturers which were most successful during the 1970s utilized some sort of computerized inventory management technique.[2]

Routing and Scheduling Production

The routing and scheduling of production are additional tasks that are an integral part of the job of a production manager. **Routing** is the process by which the manager specifies the machines — and the sequence of operation of those ma-

Computerized parts storage at Midland-Ross Corporation.

TALKING BUSINESS

Toyota's famous "just in time" materials movement system isn't unusual in Japanese factories. Raw materials inventory is not stockpiled on the plant floor, as it is in many U.S. manufacturing facilities; rather, materials are doled out in small batches as needed. Vendors often make three or four deliveries a day so that manufacturers can avoid keeping excess stock in the plant.

Even work-in-process inventory is minimal. The movement of inventory through the assembly process is steady, because the incidence of rejects and of machine failure is very low. Thus, stockpiles of extra parts are seldom needed.

As one senior manager in a Japanese plant said, "We feel that inventory is the root of all evil. You would be surprised how much you simplify problems and reduce costs when there are no inventories. For example, you don't need any inventory managers or sophisticated inventory control systems. Nor do you need expediters, because you can't expedite. And, finally, when something goes wrong, the system stops. Immediately the whole organization becomes aware of the problem and works quickly to resolve it. If you have buffer inventories, these potential problems stay hidden and may never get corrected."

Source: Adapted by permission of The Harvard Business Review. Adapted from "Why Japanese Factories Work," by Robert H. Hayes, *Harvard Business Review,* July–August 1981, p. 59. Copyright © 1981 by the President and Fellows of Harvard College; all rights reserved.

chines—as an order progresses from start to finish. Closely related to routing is **scheduling,** which specifies and controls the time it takes for each task to begin and end.

Sequencing Production   There are many quantitative tools that have been developed to aid in deciding on the most efficient **sequencing of production** (sequencing of machines) necessary to manufacture a product. Once the sequence is determined, the routing of jobs as they move through the production facility is usually accomplished with the aid of a route sheet. The route sheet generally contains all the information related to a specific sequence of machine operations for a particular job. Additionally, the document may contain information related to the operation and setup times, materials, and other details as necessary.

Using Gantt Charts   Gantt Charts, named after Henry Gantt, who originated the chart, are used in the scheduling of production. They graphically measure the relationship between scheduling and actual performance. Figure 10.5

shows an example of a Gantt Chart. The left-hand column lists those activities that are required to complete a particular job. The bars are used for the time scale, which is used to schedule the activities as well as measure the progress of each activity against the schedule.

In the example that Figure 10.5 presents, the activities of scheduling, designing, and ordering are complete; however, the latter two were completed after the date planned. Note, too, that design started ahead of schedule. Materials delivery has begun, but behind schedule. As of the review date (October 8), the machine components activity has not begun and is already behind schedule.

There are many mechanical and magnetic board-type devices that are available to facilitate the use of Gantt charts. A Gantt chart is most useful in situations where there aren't many tasks, where task times are relatively long (days or weeks rather than hours), and where the job routings are short and relatively simple.

PERT-CPM Methods   One of the major shortcomings of Gantt charts is that they are static devices, as are other graphic-type models. Also, for

A GANTT CHART

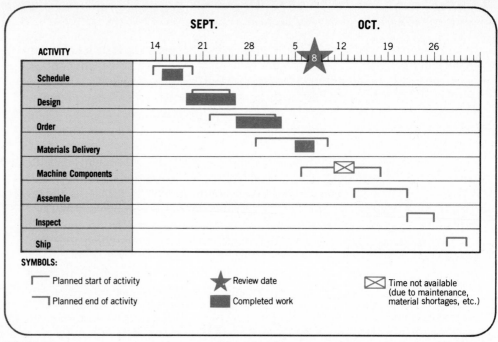

SYMBOLS:

⌐ Planned start of activity

⌐ Planned end of activity

★ Review date

▮ Completed work

⊠ Time not available (due to maintenance, material shortages, etc.)

FIGURE 10.5

complete jobs with many separate but connected tasks, these charts don't have the capability of indicating the inter-relationships between tasks. This deficiency is overcome by so-called **network models,** such as PERT (Program Evaluation and Review Technique) and CPM (Critical Path Method). McDonnell Douglas, Boeing, General Electric, and other companies connected with the space program were pioneers in the development of these approaches. In many instances, the government contract specified that PERT-CPM techniques be used to monitor progress on the contract.

In these techniques a network chart is developed by breaking the project into a sequence of events and the activities leading to those events. A network is drawn showing the order of priorities of the various events. This makes it possible to plan for effective completion of the project. Figure 10.6 is an example of a CPM network.

In the case of **CPM (Critical Path Method)** a single time-estimate is developed for each activity. For **PERT (Program Evaluation and Review Technique)** three time-estimates are developed for each activity in order to take into account time variability. The time required to traverse

each path is computed by adding up all required activity times along the path. The path having the longest time is designated the critical path and represents the shortest possible period of time in which the entire project can be completed. For the sample network of Figure 10.6, the critical path consists of events 1-4-7-9-10, requiring a total time of 37 days $(15 + 10 + 12 + 0)$.

Network models are best suited to situations in which the precedence relationships and reasonable time estimates can be established. One important feature of these models is that they permit the manager to determine the overall effect of a delay in the completion of a particular task. It also makes it possible to figure the effect on the schedule of a reallocation of resources from one task to another. In addition, computer programs are available to help with PERT-CPM schedules.

Controlling Quality

In recent years the quality of goods manufactured in the United States has come under discussion, taking on the proportions of a major business issue. The quality of a product is measured by com-

CPM NETWORK

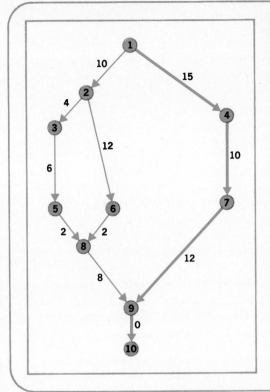

SYMBOLS:

①　Events

$\xrightarrow{\quad 9 \quad}$　Activities (days)

EVENTS:

1. Start
2. Materials for components *A* & *B* Received
3. Machining of *A* Complete
4. Polishing of *A* Complete
5. Machining of *B* Complete
6. Materials Received for Component *C*
7. Component *C* Formed
8. Assembly of *A* and *B* Complete
9. Mounting of *C* on Assembly Complete
10. End

FIGURE 10.6

paring the finished product to some preselected standard. It's the job of the **quality control** manager to regulate the inputs to a production process to ensure that the output—the final product—conforms to this standard. The quality control department is therefore important for several reasons. Its objectives include reducing returns, reducing scrap, increasing output through fewer rejects, and reducing raw material defects through careful monitoring of vendor quality. These objectives must balance quality against the cost of maintaining that quality.

A relatively recent innovation in American industry is the **Quality Control (QC) Circle,** which has been used in Japan. This concept, discussed in Chapter 7, recognizes that the quality of a product is determined not only by machinery but also by the motivation of the workers involved in the production. A QC Circle is basically a group of workers and managers who periodically meet to study methods for improving quality. Most firms using this technique have found it beneficial. One

"LET'S FACE IT — WE HAVE NO QUALITY AND WE HAVE NO CONTROL."

TALKING BUSINESS

"Hey, take a look at this window," complains John Latini as he rolls up the hard-to-crank rear window of a Lynx station wagon. "If you can't roll the window up easily with two fingers it's no good," he says.

Latini, manager of Ford's huge Wayne, Michigan, plant, is responsible for seeing that Ford Escorts and Mercury Lynxes are built as defect free as possible. To do that, he spends as much time as he can on the plant floor, inspecting cars rolling off the assembly line, talking with workers, listening to their complaints and ideas.

It wasn't long ago, Latini recalls, that top management cared only about how fast and how cheaply cars could be made, "no matter if there was a glaring defect here or there." Ford still wants high production and low costs, but foreign competition and changing consumer preferences have given quality control top priority.

Ford installed $40 million worth of new equipment in Latini's Wayne plant in 1979 as an investment in the quality of Escorts and Lynxes—new models to be introduced as Ford's answer to high-quality foreign subcompacts. The two models will have to be especially good to overcome Detroit's image of poor quality. So far, owners of the cars have reported 30 percent fewer problems than owners of other Ford models.

Source: Adapted from John Koten, "Quality Controller: A Ford Plant Manager Tries to Limit Defects in Escort, Lynx Models," *Wall Street Journal,* 15 May 1981, pp. 1, 17. Adapted by permission of The Wall Street Journal, © Dow Jones & Company, Inc., 1981. All rights reserved.

such plant—the GM plant in Tarrytown, New York—has seen a major improvement in the quality of output due to the use of just such a technique.

SUMMARY

The purpose of the production function is the conversion of inputs, sometimes referred to as factors of production, into outputs—finished products or services. Production can be classified according to the conversion process the inputs undergo, the conversion system used, or the nature of demand for the product.

An input mix is the important first decision confronting production managers, and closely related to this is the question of how much capital and labor to employ in the production operation.

The production process involves much careful planning. The production manager must first completely analyze the product, a process that in-

cludes value analysis. Since the performance of most production managers is evaluated on the basis of cost of production, they must pay particular attention to minimizing costs. Cost areas include raw materials costs, labor costs, equipment costs, and energy costs. The sum of all these costs, rather than each separate cost, must be minimized.

A major strategic decision to be made in the earliest stages of planning for production is the location of the plant. First a geographic region must be chosen, then a particular community, then a specific site. The appropriate objective for the plant location decision is minimization of cost.

The purchasing department arranges for all purchases of materials and supplies needed to run the business. Here again, minimizing cost is the primary objective, but additional considerations include availability and quality of materials. The department must shop for supplies, considering sources, prices, quality, and availability. Delivery costs must also be considered. A manufacturer may sometimes have to decide whether it would be more cost-effective to make or to buy a certain product.

Purchasing raw materials efficiently must be done to ensure that the production process is not interrupted. Purchase planning assists in maintaining an optimal inventory level.

Not only raw materials inventory but other inventories as well must be controlled. Inventory serves several purposes: meeting demand for the product, smoothing production, and speculation. The three basic types of inventory are raw materials inventory, work in process inventory, and finished goods inventory. The costs of having too much or too little inventory must be assessed and minimized to determine the best inventory level. To monitor the movement of items in inventory, many companies maintain a perpetual inventory system.

Routing and scheduling of production are additional tasks of the production manager. Gantt Charts, PERT, and CPM are scheduling aids. The manager must also send out the instruction to begin work and must completely specify what work is to be done.

Finally, controlling quality of the finished product is a consideration of growing importance. The quality control manager compares finished products to a preselected standard to ensure quality. At the same time, the cost of maintaining that quality must be considered. To meet these objectives, managers are using a new technique called Quality Control Circle.

KEY TERMS

analytic process
assembly line
automation
continuous process
conversion system
cost of holding
Critical Path Method (CPM)
equipment costs
factors of production
finished goods inventory
forward buying

Gantt Charts
input mix
intermittent process
lead time
minimization of cost
network models
order cost
perpetual inventory
production function
Program Evaluation and Review Technique (PERT)
purchase planning
quality control
Quality Control (QC) Circle
raw materials inventory
routing
scheduling
sequencing of production
shortage cost
specialization of labor
synthetic process
"to inventory"
"to order"
value analysis
work in process inventory

REVIEW QUESTIONS

1. Name and describe the four factors of production.
2. What is meant by the term *production function*?
3. What is the difference between analytic and synthetic production processes? How do continuous and intermittent production processes differ?
4. Describe what is meant by the input mix.
5. What are the major considerations in determining plant location?
6. Name and describe the four important considerations in purchasing materials and supplies.
7. What kinds of inventories are there? What costs should a manager assess in determining the best inventory level?
8. Describe routing and scheduling.

DISCUSSION QUESTIONS

1. How might the production process differ in a brewery, a printing plant, a refrigerator assembly factory, a television repair shop?
2. Has automation increased or reduced production costs? In what way?
3. Explain how a manufacturer can use value analysis to cut cost without sacrificing product quality.
4. Why are most of the older industrial plants of the US located in the northeastern part of the country? What factors explain why business have migrated from the "snow belt" to the "sun belt"?
5. Can the Critical Path Method be used to plan the construction of a new building? In what ways would CPM be helpful to the builder?
6. Explain how a quality circle could be helpful in both controlling quality and reducing costs.

CASE: OUTBIDDING THE BIDDERS

Bud Robertson was a private contractor who always prided himself on his ability to keep track of costs so that he could make intelligent bids for contracting jobs. Through the years he had progressed from building one residential dwelling to six large houses, which he constructed simultaneously for speculation in a booming real estate market.

During the last few years Robertson concentrated on large luxury-type homes—four and five bedrooms with family rooms, game rooms, large dining rooms, living rooms, and often with two fireplaces and triple garages. His last contracts were for $150,000–$200,000 homes, on which he netted around $20,000–$35,000 per house.

Robertson operated out of his own place—a big luxury home he'd built some ten years before. With three acres of grounds, home also meant ample space for keeping his trucks and equipment without violating building codes. His wife and four sons (ranging from 14 to 19 years) all helped in the business, which really kept overhead down. His competitors were a little bitter about Bud's successful operation, but he earned their respect. He always knew the costs of the equipment and sup-

plies he was using—and of course in his situation labor was always kept under control.

But when the housing market became somewhat depressed, Bud Robertson decided that he'd go into the motel and apartment building market. He was confident that he could handle this situation despite the more complex nature of controlling costs—as well as bidding against competitors who had many years of experience in this bigger league.

Even if Robertson was very efficient in dealing with costs for $100,000 homes with 8 to 12 rooms—how was he going to handle a motel with 120 units and a cost of $1 million to $1.5 million? How was he going to keep track of all the components: plumbing equipment, electrical circuits, cement blocks, roofing, water pipes, bathroom fixtures, lighting fixtures, windows, etc.?

His sons were very excited about the big business they were about to launch. They felt that they were ready; two of the boys had attended electrical school and plumbing school, and each had his license. Meanwhile the younger boys were learning the trades in high school. All were ready to meet their competition in making bids, constructing motels—and then on to bigger buildings and newer worlds to conquer.

1. What chance do Bud Robertson and his sons have of meeting their competition in this big-construction league?
2. What knowledge and skills should they have to compete intelligently?
3. What new technology might they add to assist them in competing in this new market?

CASE: BEWARE— UNFRIENDLY ROBOT

A class from the College of Engineering was visiting the Sperry-Vickers plant in hopes of being introduced to the company robot. This turned out to be a friendly enough monster, placing parts into a machine-tooling mechanism, withdrawing them after they had been finished, and then placing them on a conveyor belt.

It was easy to see that the robot had taken the places of several workers and the tour guide explained that the robot was capable of working 24 hours a day, 7 days a week; it never got sick, never took a coffee break; it always did its job as programmed.

However that statement's not altogether accurate—the robot did get sick once in a while when one of its circuits shorted out. And of course it had to be reprogrammed to perform slightly altered functions. The company was rather "humane" in its dealings with the robot, even going so far as to purchase a second robot—so that robot number 1 wouldn't be all alone. So here were two robots really performing efficiently—a source of improved productivity, and a major threat to human workers who could be replaced by these friendly monsters.

The tour guide went on to tell a story that was none too pleasant. It seems that one of these robots was involved in an accident in Japan and actually killed a worker. The worker had gotten in the way of the robot, was knocked down, then was crushed against other machinery—a totally unforeseen accident. From that time on, some protection was built in to protect workers from robots who went about their work without paying attention to nearby humans.

A fence had been constructed around the robot here in the plant to prevent any such accident from occurring. Meanwhile the robot went on about its work, performing its functions perfectly. But one could not help avoid speculating about the future, with these mechanized creatures multiplying as they proved to be greater aids in industrial production.

1. Since the advent of *Star Wars* people have been intrigued by robots. What do you think about the use of robots in American factories?
2. Is the robot the answer to increased productivity and efficiency in the manufacturing plant?
3. What about the fear of robots competing with humans?
4. Shouldn't humans be given priority over these monsters?

A CAREER IN MANAGEMENT

Many students in Colleges of Business elect a "management major." Management principles and practices apply in any kind of organization, regardless of the nature of the product, process, or service involved. A person concentrating in management will have a strong background in psychology, sociology, group dynamics, social psychology, all supported by research in human relations, that will be an appropriate background for a manager in any kind of enterprise, whether a profit-oriented firm, government, or not-for-profit organization.

The mid-1980s and beyond will be very bright for college graduates seeking a career in management. You should realize, however, that you don't graduate from college one day and become a manager the next. A path often followed is to first become a management trainee. This will entail learning company policy, the nature of the industry, operating procedures, and organizational structure. It may require a stint on the production line, working in a warehouse, or other "blue-collar" job. Upon satisfactory completion of the training program, which may last from several weeks to several years, you'll enter a field of specialization as a manager. These include opportunities in sales, production, accounting, personnel, industrial relations, credit, finance, and research and development. Middle and higher level managers are selected from the ranks of sales managers, production managers, controllers, human resource managers, and so forth.

Where the Opportunities Are

1 ■ MANAGER OF HUMAN RESOURCES

This is the new name for a more comprehensive position, formerly titled the personnel manager. The manager or director of human resources has responsibility for personnel matters throughout the organization. This staff position provides service to all the line operations in a business, be it manufacturing, retailing, accounting, or others. The manager of human resources has overall responsibility for all the personnel functions—recruitment, interviewing, screening, hiring, training, wage and salary administration, health, safety, and all the fringe benefits that may be in effect in any organization. In large corporations, this job may carry the title of vice-president of personnel, or vice-president for human resources, or it may be titled director or manager or supervisor of that department.

Places of Employment   Throughout the country in profit and not-for-profit organizations.

Skills Required   A few jobs for persons with a two-year degree. Most employers prefer four-year programs.

Employment Outlook thru 1990   Private sector: excellent; public sector: good.

Salaries   Personnel management trainee:

$12,000; manager of human resources: $22,000–$50,000 + .

2 ◼ BANK OFFICER AND MANAGER

Approximately 25 percent of all employees working in the banking industry are in positions of management, or are officers—including president, vice-presidents, treasurer, comptroller, branch manager, loan officers, personnel officers, and other officials. These people oversee all operations of service provided by banks from individual checking accounts to letters of credit for financing world trade. As banks continually adapt their services to meet their customers' needs, so does the function of bank management positions change and grow to accommodate these additional services. Examples include such new offerings as revolving credit plans, charge cards, accounting and billing services, and money management counseling.

Places of Employment Almost every community of 1000+ population. Primary opportunities lie in the financial centers, such as New York, Chicago, St. Louis, and San Francisco.

Skills Required Four-year program or M.B.A. Many trainees and managers continue their education through programs provided by the American Bankers Association.

Employment Outlook thru 1990 Excellent.
Salaries $11,500–$20,000 for trainee position; $25,000 + for vice-president.

3 ◼ RESTAURANT MANAGER

From the roadside diner to a large nationwide chain to fast-food restaurants and cafeterias—and even to the exclusive evening gown and tuxedo dining atmosphere—managers and proprietors include a large share of the work force. They may perform such duties as bookkeeping, menu planning, budgeting, food preparation and sanitation, or earn a salary functioning as managers for others. In any case, their duties encompass all aspects of the operation to ensure proper service .

Places of Employment Every city and town in the country. Most positions are in the larger metropolitan areas. Opportunities are increasing fastest in the Sun Belt.

Skills Required Two- or four-year program depending on employer. A few hotel chains and restaurants insist on a hotel/restaurant management degree.

Employment Outlook thru 1990 Good.
Salaries Vary significantly from company to company. Trainee: $10,000 + ; owner/manager of successful metropolitan area restaurant: $100,000 + .

4 ■ CITY MANAGER

With the increase in urban problems—growth versus decay of the inner cities, industrial expansion—there's increasing need for people with managerial skills. City managers are usually appointed by elected officials, such as city councils, and the managers are responsible to that governing body. The duties of the city manager include tax collections and disbursements, law enforcement, public-works projects, hiring department heads and supporting staffs, and preparation of annual budgets (to be approved by the city officials). Other duties may include collecting rents, designing traffic control, crime prevention, urban planning, etc.

Places of Employment Generally, cities with populations over 50,000. A few smaller affluent communities have moved to the city manager concept.

Skills Required Master's degree in public administration. Some cities will accept a person with a four-year degree and several years' experience as an assistant city manager.

Employment Outlook thru 1990 Very good as cities seek out professionally qualified managers—not politicians—to handle complex city affairs.

Salaries Assistant city managers: $15,000–$25,000; city managers: small city, $26,000; medium-to-large cities, $50,000 + .

5 ■ CREDIT MANAGER

Credit managers have responsibility for assessing credit applications and accepting or rejecting applicants. Their regular duties call for analyzing financial conditions of individuals, checking credentials, and working with other department managers—especially sales—to establish credit policies and implement some credit practices.

Places of Employment Most openings are in medium-to-large cities.

Skills Required Four-year program.

Employment Outlook thru 1990 Average.

Salaries Trainees: $13,000; assistant credit managers: $14,500–$18,000; credit managers: $25,000–$40,000.

6 ■ RETAIL STORE MANAGER

There are some 2,700,000 retail trade workers, and of those some 10 percent may be considered managerial or supervisory. The job of the retail store manager is to coordinate all store operations, plan work schedules, and control advertising, ordering merchandise, pricing, displaying, and selling. The manager is always concerned with employee and customer relations in addition to store security, personnel services, expense control, and planning all phases of the merchandising and selling procedures. Managers work longer hours than do salespeople and clerks, planning merchandising strategy, taking inventory, and completing reports.

Places of Employment Throughout the country. As chains continue to discover opportunities in smaller communities, positions will be available in communities of under 15,000 population. Careers with traditional department stores are primarily limited to the medium-to-large cities.

Skills Required Two- or four-year program. National chains require a four-year degree. Positions as department heads, division managers, and corporate executives may be available for those who survive the rigors of first-line management to take on added responsibilities at higher levels.

Employment Outlook thru 1990 Average.

Salaries $12,000–$17,000 for assistant managers; $17,000–$50,000 + for managers, plus commissions and/or bonuses for sales volume and profits generated.

7 ■ RETAIL FOODSTORE MANAGER

In the various types of foodstore—supermarket, small grocery store, convenience store, and specialty foodstore—the manager coordinates all store operations. These duties often include planning work schedules and controlling advertising, ordering, pricing, hiring, and especially customer relations. Managers may assist clerks and stockboys in their day-to-day functions or may supervise and assist in the delicatessen sections, film processing, check cashing, and catering. Other responsibilities include store security, personnel matters, expense control, and planning possible competitive strategy.

Places of Employment Throughout the country. Most growth is in the Sun Belt region.

Skills Required Four-year program. In the smaller owner/operator grocery store a manager may have learned the business from stockboy on up or may have learned the trade in a family-owned store. More and more formal education is becoming essential in the growing retail foodstore business, with the ever-expanding offerings of product, services, and nonfood items.

Employment Outlook thru 1990 Average.

Salaries Trainees: $14,000–$18,000.

8 ■ PURCHASING MANAGER

If materials, supplies, or equipment are not on hand when they're needed, the entire production process or workflow in an organization could be interrupted or halted. Maintaining an adequate supply of necessary items is the purchasing manager's responsibility. This includes more than just buying goods and services, however. Market forecasting, production planning, and inventory control are all part of the job. Purchasing managers supervise purchasing agents or industrial buyers, who carry out the actual purchase process.

Places of Employment Over half of all purchasing managers work for moderate-to-large manufacturers. The remainder are employed by government agencies, construction companies, hospitals, and schools. These opportunities exist everywhere yet are concentrated in large industrial and governmental centers such as Washington, D.C., Chicago, Pittsburgh, and Los Angeles.

Skills Required Two- or four-year program. More employers are requiring an M.B.A.

Employment Outlook thru 1990 Good; excellent with an M.B.A.

Salaries Junior purchasing agent: $18,500; purchasing managers: $27,000–$60,000. The federal government pays entry-level purchasing agents $12,000–$14,000.

9 ■ STATION MANAGER (RADIO/TV)

The station manager of a small television or radio station may also be the owner and may play an active role in various functions of the four major departments: programming, engineering, sales, and general administration. In large stations of metropolitan cities, the station manager may be titled Director of Directors, since he's in communication with directors of programming, continuity, radio and television, public service, etc. In either case, his function is to control all aspects of production—from budgeting to presentation of programming—to inform, educate, and entertain the viewing and listening audience.

Places of Employment New York, Chicago, and Los Angeles offer the most opportunities. However positions can be found in medium-to-large cities throughout the country.

Skills Required A four-year program with a specialization in broadcasting, mass communications, telecommunications, speech, or journalism provides an excellent background for the station manager. However emphasis in programming, management, and marketing may be sufficient education for efficiently operating a television or radio station.

Employment Outlook thru 1990 Good, especially in cablevision. Competition for higher-management positions is vigorous; the ratings game can be ruthless and take its toll at all levels.

Salaries Managers in small communities: $15,000–$25,000; managers in larger cities: $30,000–$65,000.

Management Careers—A Final Note

This by no means exhausts the position descriptions for managers, as there are multitudes of managers in every conceivable business function. There are traffic managers, public relations managers, office managers, building managers, department managers, manufacturing managers, and administrators at all levels. The opportunities for advancement from line operations, sales positions, or general administrative work are numerous for those who have ambitions to move upward and assume more responsibility. Higher-level management positions entail many more administrative skills, and most companies provide supervisory and managerial training for those who are willing to accept more responsibility. Many companies also encourage their potential managers to continue their education in colleges and universities. Some companies even pay tuition to assist in management development. The future looks promising for those willing to put out the effort.

PART 3

MARKETING MANAGEMENT

CHAPTER 11

THE
MARKETING
PROCESS

After studying this chapter you should be able to:

1 Explain the marketing concept.
2 Describe how the four elements of the marketing mix relate to one another.
3 Discuss the use of the marketing concept for the marketing of services and intangible products.
4 Explain various approaches to market segmentation and why a marketer would want to consider this.
5 Clarify the use of product differentiation by marketers.
6 Evaluate how a product has been positioned in the market.
7 Understand how market research is used to minimize marketing risk.
8 Explain the importance to the marketer of understanding consumer behavior.

A. C. Gilbert & Company: never a very large firm—but it did hold its own rather handsomely among the top ten toy manufacturers. Time: the 1950s, when Gilbert's sales were reaching over $17 million. For many years, Gilbert had been the household name in science toys—chemistry sets, microscopes, the famous Erector "engineering" sets—known to generations of boys and their fathers. Now, in an era of cold war, sputniks, and technology, science was pulling out in front as a national priority. What could be better for Gilbert?

As events later showed, *lots* could have been better for Gilbert. By the end of the 1950s, the toy market was changing. Although the new decade brought with it prosperity and, in particular, a booming toy market, it was not a market that Gilbert was familiar with. For one thing, a new nationwide promotional medium—television—had taken a front-row place in toy marketing. TV was fast eclipsing Gilbert's old standbys, the toy catalog and the handsome window display.

There was still another way that the toy market was changing. Customers were bypassing the "traditional" toy stores, hobby shops, and department stores in favor of self-service, high-volume supermarkets and discount stores. And what were *these* dealers pushing? Mainly low-priced, heavily advertised toys in attractive packages that functioned as selling tools.

As for Gilbert, it didn't recognize that the toy environment was changing, bringing with it an ever worsening problem for the venerable firm. Finally, when the rude awakening did dawn on the company, it was met with frantic activity in the product line—a line that had gone relatively unchanged for decades. Now, in one year's time, that line was greatly expanded to include 50 new toys. These were directed not only to the traditional target market of 6-to-14-year-old boys but for the first time to girls and preschoolers.

Having strayed from its time-honored base, Gilbert found itself in the business of toys it was not used to making. Low in price, low in quality, and geared to large-volume sales, the new product line strained the company's engineering and production capabilities. The result could have been predicted: poorly designed toys of not very good quality, with disappointing customer appeal.

Nothing Gilbert later did served to restore the image of the reputable toymaker. A company/brand image is a precious thing. Long in building, it can't for long take punishment and abuse. In 1967, a bankrupt A. C. Gilbert threw in the towel.

Source: Adapted by permission from Robert F. Hartley, "A. C. Gilbert Company—Complacency, Then Desperate Reactions—Result: Failure," in *Marketing Mistakes*, 2d ed., ed. Robert F. Hartley (Columbus, Ohio: Grid Publishing, Inc.), pp. 181-192.

The A. C. Gilbert story shows that poor marketing can be fatal (or very costly) to any organization. Marketing can be thought of as getting the *right goods or services* to the *right people* at the *right place* at the *right time* at the *right price* using the *right promotion techniques*. This is referred to as the "right principle." As you can see, marketing managers control many factors that ultimately determine marketing success. Gilbert's management didn't have the right products available in the right place, nor did they use the right promotional strategies.

In a broader sense we can define **marketing** as the performance of those business activities directed at satisfying needs and wants through the exchange process. What is exchanged? Typically, consumers exchange money for goods and services. In order to help the exchange process, market-managers follow the "right principle." If Hometown Ford dealer doesn't have the "right" car for you, there will be no sale (no exchange of money or credit for a new automobile).

THE MARKETING CONCEPT

In order to stimulate sales, many firms have adopted the marketing concept. Briefly, the marketing concept sees the customer's needs and wants as primary. It therefore takes the satisfaction of those needs and wants as the principal function of the business. The foundations of the **marketing concept** are (1) consumer orientation and (2) goal orientation.

Consumer orientation means that marketing managers identify the groups of those people who are most likely to buy their products. This is done by assembling data about potential customers or by analyzing the existing market, both of which yield a market profile. Next the company tries to determine how it can best meet the needs of these groups. Being consumer oriented often means that managers must do research to explore consumer desires or to get reactions to new product ideas and concepts. You'll probably not be surprised to learn that Procter & Gamble spends over $220 million each year trying to find the "right" products for the marketplace.[1]

Although consumer orientation is necessary for success, it can be carried too far. After all, a profit oriented firm is first of all in business to earn a reasonable return on investment. The consumer, of course, is out to get the "best buy" — the highest quality for the lowest possible price. A firm can't try so hard to satisfy the consumer that it strives to supply the "best buy" when this represents the "worst sale" — that is, threatens the firm's return on investment objectives. You might very well want to buy a new Cadillac for $5000. You wouldn't be alone. However the Cadillac Division of General Motors would be foolish to sell the car at that price because it would lose money and not meet its profit goals. (At GM the cost of employee benefits alone amounted to $900 per vehicle in 1980.) Therefore **goal orientation** must be part of the firm's marketing concept. That is, the firm

must have its own goals clearly before it. These will be of both a financial and a nonfinancial kind. In summary, the marketing concept is finding out what the consumer wants and then producing it at a reasonable profit.

Implementing the Marketing Concept

The marketing concept may strike you as very logical, yet modern marketing didn't evolve until fairly recent decades. Before that, most firms were production oriented. **Production orientation** sees buyers as wanting to obtain goods at the lowest possible cost. To meet this desire, the firm concentrates on having an efficient and economical production system. A production orientation is internal in nature. Management talks with itself and asks, What can we do best? What is the easiest thing for us to produce? What are the least costly items to manufacture? Production orientation reasons that if a company's product is economical and the best that it knows how to manufacture, someone will want to buy it. In the long run many companies, like Studebaker Automotive and A. C. Gilbert, failed because they produced *what they could manufacture best* (that is, most easily) rather than *what consumers really wanted to buy.* To avoid becoming another A. C. Gilbert, many companies — such as General Foods, Pillsbury, General Electric, and General Mills — began using the marketing concept in the early 1960s. Their almost immediate success soon found other firms accepting the marketing concept.

The Marketing Mix

When General Electric and others began to establish the marketing concept, they also created a marketing mix. A **marketing mix** is a unique blend of (1) product and service offerings, (2) a distribution system created to reach a specific group of consumers called the *target market*, (3) pricing, and (4) promotion. These activities are the means by which a marketing manager plans to satisfy target consumers. Each element of the mix has a critical role to play in the process. For example, the very best product of its kind may fail if it is not properly promoted. Yet by the same token even a mediocre product may have some short-term success with very extensive advertising. Coldsnap, a make-at-home ice cream product, was introduced in 1978 by General Foods with heavy advertising. The initial public response was pleasing because many people's curiosity was aroused by the advertising. But there were very few repeat buyers, and the product was withdrawn from the market-place the very next year. As a company spokesperson noted, "Coldsnap was doomed from day one. Who wants to go through that complicated process to make ice cream?" Yet without the promotional blitz, Coldsnap wouldn't have enjoyed even a modest initial success.

As it did with Coldsnap, the marketing mix usually begins with the development of the product and/or service offerings. Some companies primarily market *products*, such as Anheuser-Busch — beer; Milton Bradley — toys and games; Gillette — personal grooming products; Joe's Nursery, which grows and guarantees its flowers and shrubs. Other firms offer *services*, such as Delta Airlines — air travel; Merrill Lynch — financial services; Warner Communications — entertainment; and Comet Cleaners, which offers one-hour dry cleaning at no extra charge. *Product* in a marketing context refers not only to the physical unit but also to the package, the warranty, the service after the product has been sold, the brand and company image, and a host of other things. Thus *product* is an all-encompassing term, meaning the total of benefits offered, and relating to every element of the product.

After a product or service has been created for a target market, it must be effectively distributed to the "right" people. Distribution is basically how a product flows from the producer to the consumer. The institutions that help move the product from the manufacturer to the ultimate buyer are called **middlemen.** Two of the most common categories of middlemen are wholesalers (who primarily sell to retailers) and retailers (who sell to ultimate consumers).

The third element of the marketing mix is pricing. Even if a good product is available when and where consumers want to buy it, it must be sold at a fair price. In other words, the consumers must believe that they are getting good value for their money or they will not buy the product. Sometimes a special introductory price will be used to try to get people to buy a new product. In other cases, price reductions are used to sell goods that would perhaps have gone unsold.

Coupons help businesses sell products.

PERSPECTIVE ON SMALL BUSINESS

Anyone who still believes you have to have money to make money has never met Larry Ross and Martin Blinder. These two young men transformed their avocation into their vocation—and developed a thriving art-publishing business, making a million bucks in the process.

When the bearded team founded Martin Lawrence Limited Editions in 1975, they had little more to go on than determination and a keen appreciation for fine art. Both were art collectors and in their mid-20s. Their initial investment of only $500 went toward subleasing an office, buying a desk and obtaining a telephone.

Today their business, based in Van Nuys, Calif., a Los Angeles suburb, grosses more than $20 million annually. They own four galleries in Hawaii and two in Southern California and distribute limited editions of fine-art prints to some 1200 other galleries throughout the world. Among the prominent artists they distribute are Salvador Dali and Victor Vasarely.

Ross and Blinder attribute the success of their company—it is now among the top four or five art publishers worldwide—to creative marketing in an otherwise staid industry. "We take a Madison Avenue approach to fine art," says Blinder.

For example, in 1977, they offered *Lincoln in Dalivision* in an edition of 1190 hand-signed lithographs, heavily advertised and imaginatively packaged in portfolios that included special viewing monocles and framable certificates of authenticity. When seen through the monocle from the proper perspective, *Lincoln in Dalivision*, otherwise an abstract, is a portrait of the American President....

The $500 Martin Lawrence investment is still multiplying, with a gallery just opened in Sherman Oaks, Calif. Eventually they want to own a string of galleries around the world. They are also branching out into music publishing.

Financial success aside, Ross and Blinder derive personal fulfillment from what they do. "Many people think of art as being too expensive to own," says Blinder, "but we help make it possible for many individuals of modest means to enjoy both the esthetic and investment value of fine art."

SOURCE: Excerpted from "The Entrepreneurs: The Art of Making a Million," p. 18, reprinted by permission from *Nation's Business*, April 1981. Copyright 1981 by Nation's Business, Chamber of Commerce of the United States.

The final element of the marketing mix is promotion. **Promotion** is made up of personal selling, advertising, sales promotion, and publicity. Together these have been referred to as the *promotional mix*. A good promotion campaign can sometimes do much to increase a company's sales. Dr Pepper went from an obscure, regional bottler to America's third best-selling soft drink by first promoting "America's Most Misunderstood Soft Drink Ever" and later "I'm a Pepper, he's a Pepper, she's a Pepper, we're a Pepper, wouldn't you like to be a Pepper too?" On the other hand a poor campaign can spell disaster for a good product. Alka-Seltzer's advertising agency created a very amusing promotional campaign during the mid-1970s. Perhaps you remember the theme—"I can't believe I ate the whole thing!" Although very catchy, it wasn't effective in increasing sales against the competition. A new campaign and advertising agency were then chosen.

Advertising may be defined as any paid form of nonpersonal presentation of goods and services (or ideas) by an identified sponsor. This may be through such media as newspapers, broadcasts, mail, and films—making use of print, radio and television, and direct mail. Personal selling involves direct personal communication between individuals, often verbal and face-to-face. Personal selling is *always* done on a one-to-one basis.

Sales promotion is a catchall that includes

trade shows, catalogues, premiums, coupons, contests, and games—to name a few. Sales promotion is exclusive of advertising and largely comprises marketing "events."

Publicity also plays a special role in the promotional blend. Good publicity, such as American Airlines being ranked number one among frequent flyers year after year, helps stimulate sales. On the other hand, bad publicity can hurt or even bankrupt a company. A newspaper story of the kind that talks about the financial problems of Braniff Airways or the poor on-time service record of Eastern Airlines creates bad publicity and can be very damaging.

Publicity, then, is any news item or story about a company or organization and can be either good or bad. A public relations department in a company releases favorable stories to the news media in the hope that they will be printed or reported. Good public relations help create goodwill and prestige for a company.

The public relations department also prepares speeches for company executives, takes photographs and distributes them to the media, prepares internal newsletters, and may communicate with stockholders and customers. The unique blend of sales promotion, advertising, publicity, and personal selling is called the *promotional blend.* The promotional blend skillfully combines these variables in an effort to stimulate sales.

Marketing's Work Functions

The marketing mix determines the ultimate success of a product or service, and even of a company. So far we have discussed major areas of marketing responsibility—pricing, distribution, promotion, and the product. Let's take a closer look at the specific functions of the marketing department. Figure 11.1 shows the functions for which marketing is normally responsible.

The various work functions have been subdivided into two areas—those concerned with generating demand or sales, and those concerned with servicing the demand after it has been created. Several tasks, such as general marketing administration, financing, and marketing research, support all the other activities necessary to generate and service demand.

The nature of the market (e.g. dispersed vs.

concentrated, large customers vs. small customers, sophisticated buyers vs. uninformed purchasers), the availability of qualified personnel, the firm's management philosophy, and tradition can all influence how the marketing concept is applied and the specific functions carried out by a marketing department.

The Broadened Concept of Marketing

The marketing mix can be applied to nonbusiness situations as well. In the 1970s it was recognized that the marketing concept was just as valuable for nonprofit organizations as for those seeking a profit. Charities, hospitals, universities, museums, and many other organizations are becoming marketing oriented. Hospitals, for example, identify their "target market." This would include patients most likely to want certain medical services, such as pain clinics and cancer research centers. Hospital administrators then determine how they can most effectively serve the patients' needs.

A hospital advertisement that "headaches can be the early sign of brain tumor, but a CAT scan can reassure you that everything is normal" would be a highly unethical form of marketing. On the other hand, public service announcements of a new visiting policy that allowed children to see their mothers and the newborn would cost nothing. At the same time, it would inform the public of a new service that didn't increase health care costs.

University Hospital, connected with Boston University, uses preprinted newspaper inserts to reach about 500,000 homes. The message is designed to make the public aware of the hospital's "product offerings." University Hospital selected six services for which it was well known and promoted them as "Centers of Excellence."

Fine-arts groups are using new pricing and promotion strategies to maximize the number of people attending their performances (see Figure 11.2). Many nonprofit groups are using publicity and advertising to establish a positive image of their organizations. Perhaps one of the most successful public relations programs for almost a generation has been Jerry Lewis' annual Muscular Dystrophy Telethon—successful too as a fund raiser. How about your school? Does it effectively use the broadened marketing concept?

MARKETING'S FUNCTIONS

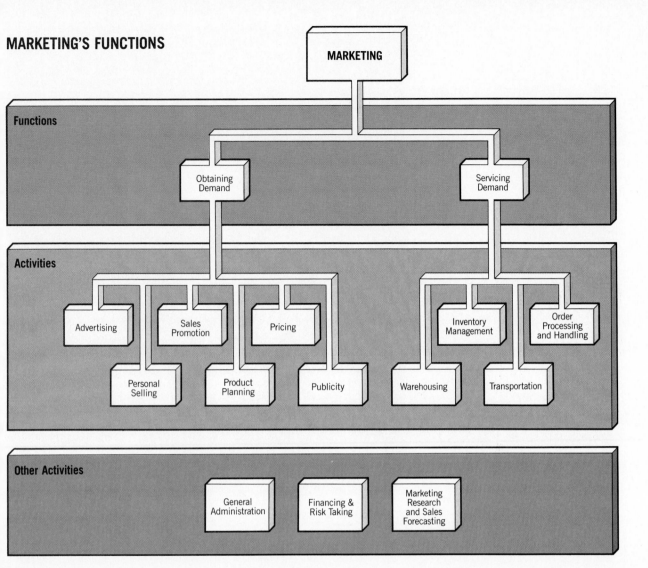

FIGURE 11.1

THE TARGET MARKET
Segmenting the Market

For a nonprofit organization, like the New York Philharmonic Orchestra—or a profit oriented firm, such as General Motors—to use the marketing concept successfully, there must be a thorough understanding of the target market. One technique that is often used to aid in developing a clear picture of the target market is called *segmentation*. **Market segmentation** is a process of separating, identifying, and evaluating various strata or layers of a market. Thus a market might be stratified (broken into groups) on the basis of (1) families with children and (2) families without children. There are some people who are more likely to buy a certain product than others. Families with young children are very likely, for example, to buy hot cereals. You can be sure that the Quaker Oats Company knows this and plans its marketing mix accordingly. Thus market segmentation is the process of dividing a total market into segments that are related and identifiable for the purpose of designing a marketing mix.

Ten small reasons to support the arts.

Take a look at a child's face the first time he creates his own painting. Or the first time she discovers the piccolo.

You'll see what we mean when we say the arts are for kids, too.

Unfortunately, many schools don't have the resources to bring the arts to their students. But your business does.

For example, one small company donated musical instruments to its local elementary school. Another helped underwrite scholarships for talented young students. We even know of one medium-sized company that brought an entire symphony orchestra to its local schools.

In fact, there are scores of ways your business can help open young minds. You'll not only bring the arts to kids, but in a way you'll be investing in the future of America.

For more information, write to: Business Committee for the Arts, Inc., 1501 Broadway, Suite 2600, New York, New York 10036 or call 212-921-0700.

Support the arts for America's sake.

Photography by Steve Steigman

FIGURE 11.2
Marketing the fine arts.

How Markets Are Segmented There are five basic forms of market segmentation:

1. demographic: by age, sex, income (because this is the most common form of segmentation, we shall examine it separately in the next section);
2. geographic: by region, urban or rural;
3. psychographic: by lifestyle, personality, values, or attitudes;
4. by benefit: e.g. tastes good, feels good;
5. by volume: light user versus heavy user

Geographic is a very common form of market segmentation. For example, ice skates and snow skis are sold in the northern states, while swimsuits and suntan lotion are sold primarily in the "Sun Belt" states and only seasonally elsewhere. People's buying habits for many types of products vary by regions of the country (see Table 11.1).

Psychographics refers to the development of psychological profiles of consumers and their lifestyles. A **lifestyle** is a distinctive mode of living, analyzed by looking at a person's typical activities, interests, and opinions. Marketing managers can

ON THE FIRING LINE

Paid Political TV Ads—Bane or Blessing?

Has the time come to call a halt to use of paid political TV ads? Should we prohibit selling candidates on TV like soap, dog food, or razor blades? Some believe that paid political TV commercials should be banned. Such ads have done and will do untold harm to our government and political system, they say. To back up their claim, they offer the following evidence:

First, there is the matter of cost. TV time is expensive. Packaged TV ads came into wide use in campaigns some 20 years ago. Since that time, the costs of campaigns involving TV have *quadrupled.* Recently, one senator spent $7 million to gain reelection.

Second, say critics, paid political ads dangerously distort the public's view of candidates. Like product ads, they are designed to create an image that will appeal to everyone. To do this, they play to viewers' emotions and avoid serious content or issues.

Third, TV campaigns have to a large degree destroyed party politics. According to these same critics, candidates do not need party endorsement and party support so much any more. They rely instead on two people: the campaign consultant and the campaign pollster. The pollster finds out what the people want to hear. The campaign consultant's job is to create ads that give the candidate a winning image. It is to tell the candidate how to look and sometimes how to say what the people want to hear.

Fourth, the critics continue, candidates these days are highly dependent on their consultants. Consultants are thus gaining considerable power, before *and after* elections. Often they have a say in political decisions, including appointments. Yet their expertise is in advertising, not government.

On the other hand, many believe paid political advertisements are a vital part of the political process. They too have arguments to support their stand. First and most important, they say, TV is the only way to reach all the voting public.

Second, with packaged TV, candidates are more fully in control of their campaigns, say proponents. Before TV became the vital core of most campaigns, candidates had to rely on volunteers. Volunteer efforts could easily get out of control. With TV campaigning, however, massive forces of volunteers and the countless headaches they bring are not needed to reach the people.

Third, proponents continue, it is not possible to pull the wool over the public's eyes with political TV ads. The viewing public is growing ever more sophisticated. Viewers now see through the superficial ads. Disenchantment, and sometimes disgust, is the response obtained time and again in studies of public attitudes toward politics and politicians. In fact, some analysts believe TV exposure may reduce politicians' chances of staying in office. This, they say, is precisely because they cannot sustain the campaign image created for them. The public is getting wise—and so are the politicos. Thus the trend in TV ads will soon be away from image and back to content.

The main reason for allowing political ads on TV, say those in favor of them, is that they are one aspect of free speech. To ban them would be to limit the right to free speech. It would be political censorship. We cannot deny candidates for public office access to the people. To do so would be to jeopardize our democratic system and basic liberties. Candidates must not be restricted, on TV or anywhere else, as to what they say or how they say it.

As all these arguments suggest, the paid political ad on TV has both advantages and disadvantages. Some European countries, plagued by the same issue, have chosen an interesting solution. They allow candidates to purchase TV time for campaigning. They do not, however, permit *packaged* commercials. Thus they avoid to a large degree the visual appeals to conscious and subconscious emotions that give TV ads a bad name.

Roy MacGregor, "The Selling of the Candidates," *Maclean's*, 7 May 1979, p. 50.

TABLE 11-1

Heavy and Light Users for Twenty Major Markets

Product	The Best	The Worst
Beer & ale (% of drinkers who consume)	Milwaukee (67.9)	Dallas/Fort Worth (44.2)
Bicycles (% adults who ever bought)	Minneapolis/St. Paul (30)	Atlanta (18.5)
Brief cases (% adults who ever bought)	Los Angeles (12.9)	Cincinnati (6.2)
Canned chili (% of homemakers who use)	Dallas/Fort Worth (72.7)	Boston (6)
Deodorants & antiperspirants (% adults who use once a day)	Baltimore (88.1)	Minneapolis/St. Paul (78.3)
Foreign travel (% adults who traveled in past three years)	Seattle/Tacoma (38)	Cincinnati (10.8)
Fur coats (% adults who ever bought)	Detroit (11)	Cincinnati (6.4)
Insecticides (% of homemakers who use at least once a month)	Houston (61.9)	New York (26.4)
Life insurance (% adults who currently have)	Pittsburgh (80.3)	Miami (53.4)
Lipstick (% of women using at least twice a day)	Seattle/Tacoma (58.2)	Cincinnati (35.6)
Men's neckties (% men who bought one within 12 months)	Cleveland (18)	Pittsburgh (10.2)
Motor oil (% adults who buy)	Dallas/Fort Worth (64.8)	New York (40.8)
Panty hose (% women who bought in past month)	Houston (61.1)	Miami (39.7)
Paperback books (% adults who bought in last 30 days)	Seattle/Tacoma (53.2)	Dallas/Fort Worth (31.3)
Popcorn (% adults who buy for home use)	Minneapolis/St. Paul (54.3)	Miami (26.5)
Restaurants (% adults who visited in past month)	Seattle/Tacoma (72.6)	Washington D.C. (54.9)
Scotch whisky (% of drinkers who consume)	New York (35.9)	Cincinnati (9.6)

SOURCE: Reprinted from p. 107 of "More Bang for the Dollar" with the special permission of *Dun's Review,* October 1978. © 1978, Dun & Bradstreet Publications Corporation.

learn much about consumer needs and wants by examining lifestyles. Winchester Arms found that purchasers of shotgun ammunition are likely also to enjoy fishing, are "do-it-yourselfers," and tend not to oppose violence on television. Thus a more complete picture of the target consumer begins to emerge than simply knowing that the "average" shotgun ammunition purchaser is between 21 and 35 years of age.

There are lifestyles associated with the chic suburbanite, the devoted family man, and numerous others (see Figure 11.3). Miller Beer, for example, dramatically increased its sales by appealing to a glamorous blue-collar lifestyle. Advertisements showed railroad engineers, tugboat captains, and lumberjacks happily drinking Miller Beer after a hard day's work. Since most heavy drinkers of beer are in blue-collar occupa-

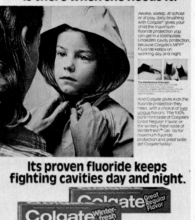

FIGURE 11.3
Ads appealing to different lifestyles.

tions, they could readily identify with the advertisements.

Another form of segmentation develops markets based on what a product will do rather than on consumer characteristics. A good example of this "benefit" segmentation is the toothpaste market. Some toothpastes are segmented by the claim made for them that they'll get teeth extra white (e.g. Pepsodent), others by the claim that they'll prevent cavities (e.g. Crest). One toothpaste (Ultra-Brite) even promises to provide the user with sex appeal!

For almost every product, there are heavy, moderate, and light users, as well as nonusers. These categories form the basis of segmentation by volume. It's not unusual or surprising to find that heavy users account for a large portion of the total sales of a product or service. Many firms often target their marketing mix to a heavy-user segment. McDonald's, for example, targets a large portion of its promotion to young children, since they're heavy users of fast-food hamburgers. The heavy users of industrial helicopters are petroleum and pipeline companies. Thus the Bell Helicopter salesperson's time is heavily weighted in favor of the petroleum industry.

The American Demographic Market

The most common form of segmentation is demographic, which develops markets based on age,

TALKING BUSINESS

Ford Motor Co. experimented with psychographics in 1971 after it had brought out the Pinto. The first television commercials presented the Pinto as a frisky, carefree little car. The car was identified with the pinto pony. When a Pinto car was seen whisking down a country road on your television screen, there, superimposed over it, was a galloping pony. But initial sales were disappointing, and Ford decided to change the commercials.

The new commercials were based in part on a psychographic study done by Grey Advertising. The study, which examined the attitudes of people identified as potential Pinto buyers, made it clear that they were not looking for friskiness; they wanted a practical and dependable little car. Grey came up with an ad campaign that portrayed Pinto as just that. Instead of comparing its performance to that of a pony, Grey chose to show Pinto on a split screen with the old Ford Model A, a car of legendary reliability and value. Shirley Young, Grey's executive vice-president and research director, notes pointedly that Pinto went on to become the largest-selling subcompact in the U.S.

Excerpted from Peter W. Bernstein, "Psychographics Is Still an Issue on Madison Avenue," *Fortune*, 16 January 1978, pp. 78–80, 84. © 1978 Time Inc. Courtesy of Fortune Magazine.

---

sex, and race. The American market has a wealth of interesting population characteristics. A first examination shows us that the percentage increase in population has been falling since 1950. We are fast moving toward zero population growth. This means that the average woman of childbearing age will not produce the two children required to replace herself and her husband (given the fact that some children die before reaching their teens).

As people born during the post-World-War-II baby boom get older, the largest single market will shift from teenagers to people in their late 20s. The average age in 1985 will be 32. Since there are going to be fewer teenagers and more people entering middle age, Levi Strauss and other bluejean manufacturers are beginning to emphasize jeans cut for the more mature figure. Revlon is pitching its formerly teenage oriented Natural Wonder cosmetic line to a broader, 13-to-40-year audience and using older models to promote it.

Another major population segment that continues to grow very rapidly is people over age 55. This group will probably continue to grow into the twenty-first century (see Figure 11.4). As medical care improves, the life-span of the aver-

As Levi's major market grew older, it altered its product line.

age American rises. A survey by the Bureau of Statistics of the Department of Labor reveals that of those products sold in America each year, households headed by a person 55 or older (36 percent of all households) account for:

- 42 percent of smoking supplies other than cigarettes,
- 41 percent of coffee,
- 37 percent of all over-the-counter drugs,
- over 30 percent of lawn and garden products,
- nearly 32 percent of paper towels, napkins, and tissues.[2]

Helena Rubinstein has already introduced a new line of skin care projects for women over 50 called Madame Rubinstein. The Leeming/Pacquin Division of Pfizer has developed New Season, a shampoo-conditioner for people over 50. And Noxell's Cover Girl, a leading makeup for young women, has introduced its Moisture Wear makeup line for older women, which includes a moisturizing wrinkle stick. Gerber Products, which for years had announced that "Babies are our business, our only business," dropped that slogan when it began selling life insurance to the older generations. Wrigley's chewing gum has also found an older market segment. It has been turning out Freedent, a product for denture wearers that's stickproof.

In addition to age, populations can be segmented by income. The upper middle group ($25,000–$50,000) will grow faster than any other during the 1980s. Why? A primary reason is that the number of families with more than one wage earner is increasing. By 1990 this segment will account for roughly one third of all U.S. households. Rising incomes mean larger markets for luxury items as interest and buying power tend to be dispersed. More and more marketing managers are targeting goods and services to families that can afford the "good life" as the percentage of lower-income families in America declines.

Sometimes, as incomes rise and family situations are altered, changes in demand for products can be rather subtle. The Consumer Power Company, a Michigan gas and electric utility, forecasts that two-income families will reduce the need to build new generating plants. When both family members work, their gas and electricity needs tend to decline.

Minority markets are also growing during the 1980s and becoming more diverse (see Figure 11.5). The continued increase in size of the Hispanic community (about 20 million consumers) is now rivaling the total number of persons in the black market. As a result, Spanish-language media and Hispanic oriented products and services will continue to grow.

Blacks now constitute more than half of the population of five major cities and between 40 and 50 percent in eight other cities. This concentration creates a market that's physically accessible. There are some obvious advantages in marketing to a concentrated consumer group rather than to one that's physically dispersed. Fewer stores are needed to reach the consumer. Also, specialized media, such as black oriented radio stations, can be used to present a selling message.

Product Differentiation and Market Segmentation

Segmentation is dividing a market using one or several criteria—such as race, benefit, income—and then deciding on a marketing mix to reach the market segments with the greatest profit potential (see Figure 11.6). Segmentation is there-

FIGURE 11.4

AGE-GROUP SHIFTS, 1980–1990

Projected change in population segments
Based on population projection of 243,513,000 in 1990

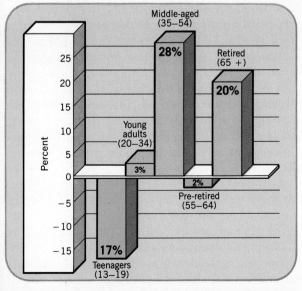

Source: U.S. Department of Commerce, Bureau of the Census, "Projections of the Population of the U.S.: 1977 to 2050," Series P-25, no. 704, and Series P-20, no. 800.

FIGURE 11.5

Minority advertising reflects the growth and diversity of minority markets.

FIGURE 11.6

AUTOMOBILE MARKET SEGMENTED BY INCOME

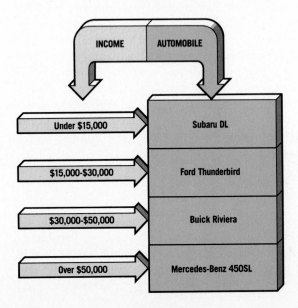

INCOME	AUTOMOBILE
Under $15,000	Subaru DL
$15,000-$30,000	Ford Thunderbird
$30,000-$50,000	Buick Riviera
Over $50,000	Mercedes-Benz 450SL

fore a market oriented strategy. **Product differentiation,** on the other hand, has a different goal: distinguishing one firm's goods or services from another's. The difference can be either real or superficial. When Boeing introduced the 747 Superliner, it offered an airplane that had some very real advantages over other models. It would fly longer distances on less fuel and carry more passengers (up to 500) than other airplanes. What Boeing had done was examine the need of a market segment and then design an airplane to meet that need.

At the other extreme are such products as regular gasoline, aspirin, and some soaps and toothpastes. These are differentiated mostly by packaging, brand names, color, and/or smell. The marketer is introducing a product similar to existing products and attempting to convince the target market that it's different from all the rest. If the marketer can succeed in this, the firm will reap greater demand for its product and may be able to sell it at a higher price. For example, St.

Joseph's aspirin costs much more than store-brand aspirin, yet they're all acetylsalicylic acid. Calvin Klein jeans is another example of product differentiation at its best. By putting the famous designer's name on the back pocket, Klein has been able to jack up prices over what the same jeans would have sold for without the Calvin Klein name. Pantyhose was a fairly colorless product until L'Eggs came along with its name and an egg-shaped package and sales rack. Promotion was effectively used both to inform the consumer and to persuade her to purchase L'Eggs.

In short, product differentiation begins with *a product* and then asks, "How can we make it different from all the rest?" Market segmentation begins with *the total market* and asks, "What are the characteristics of the overall market and how can important segments be served?"

Marketing Positioning

The marketing mix that's created for a product or service depends on whether a firm is following a market segmentation or product differentiation strategy. But it also depends on the firm's positioning strategy. **Positioning** is the strategic placement of a product in the market. Every effort is made to convey the desired image and to make the product attractive, thereby maximizing the chances of sales and minimizing the element of risk. However, a product's place finally depends on how the consumer perceives the product. So positioning is essentially how the target market views the product relative to all possible substitutes. Perhaps the best example is in the cigarette industry. Marlboros are positioned as a very "masculine" cigarette. Camels are positioned in a similar place but in a nonfilter market rather than a filter one. At the other extreme Virginia Slims and Eve are positioned as very "feminine" cigarettes. Virginia Slims is a more "active" feminine cigarette than Eve. Others, like Kools, aren't positioned in a masculine/feminine sense (see Figure 11.7). Dr Pepper is positioned as an unusual soft drink—"not a Cola, but so much more." And 7-Up has similarly placed itself as an "Un-" (uncola). Meanwhile Pepsi attempts to position itself as a cola drink that most people prefer over Coke in taste tests. Pepsi also projects itself as preferred by those with a youthful outlook on life (the "Pepsi generation").

MARKETING RESEARCH

What Is Marketing Research?

The Pepsi taste test is a form of **marketing research.** This may be defined as the planning for, collection, recording, and analysis of data relative to the marketing of goods and services, and the communication of those results to management.

FIGURE 11.7
Masculine, "neutral," and feminine positioning of cigarette ads.

TALKING BUSINESS

Old products need not die—they can be revitalized through repositioning. According to Franchellie Cadwell, an advertising executive, products can be repositioned in two ways: the brand character can be changed to broaden the product's appeal; or new uses for the product can be found.

The repositioning of Ivory Bar Soap offers an example of the first method. By the late 1960s, Ivory's market share had been eroded by deodorant, perfumed, and other specialty soaps. But the growing popular movement toward "natural" products offered a perfect means for Ivory to be repositioned as a pure, "natural" soap.

Arm & Hammer Baking Soda, taking advantage of the same consumer movement, chose to find new uses for its product. All-purpose Arm & Hammer had been all but forgotten among the convenience products and cleansers, deodorants, antacids, and personal care products that proliferated in the 1950s and 1960s. With the emphasis on additive-free products, however, Arm & Hammer could be positioned as a safe, natural product for multiple uses, including new ones—deodorizing the refrigerator and treating swimming-pool water, for example.

These repositioning strategies turned old, faltering products into vital new ones.

Adapted from "Repositioning Can Do Wonders for Golden Oldies," *Advertising Age*, 25 August 1980, p. 12. Reprinted with permission from the August 25, 1980, issue of Advertising Age. Copyright 1980 by Crain Communications Inc.

Market research helps to determine which products and services consumers want—which colors, tastes, package sizes, and so forth they prefer—and what types of promotional themes will most likely appeal to target customers. Marketing research is a separate business function of fairly early origin. An 1879 mail survey of state agricultural officials by the N. W. Ayer & Sons advertising agency has been identified as the earliest marketing research study.

Who Does Research?

Three types of organizations actually design and conduct the bulk of the marketing research studies: (1) corporate marketing research departments, (2) advertising agencies, and (3) independent marketing research firms. Corporate marketing research departments can be found in the structure of such manufacturers as Carnation, General Electric, and Pepperidge Farm; retailers, such as J. C. Penney, Montgomery Ward, and Southland "7-11" stores; and service corporations, such as Braniff Airways, Avis, and Merrill Lynch.

Large advertising agencies also conduct many research studies. These studies are directed toward a client's needs and are often launched by the client. For example, Procter & Gamble may be concerned about how it should position a new toothpaste flavor relative to other toothpastes. The company will likely have its advertising agency do a study. For its part, the agency may try to pick the "right child" to show just how good the toothpaste tastes. Next it will film the same commercial using perhaps three different children. Consumers would then be shown the three commercials and asked such questions as which one was the most believable and which one they liked best. Such studies are routinely conducted to make advertising more effective.

An independent marketing research firm is a company whose primary business is selling marketing research services, both custom (one-of-a-kind studies) and syndicated. A **syndicated research service** compiles a standard set of specialized data on a continuing basis (every week, month, or year) and distributes it to subscribers. The famous Nielsen television ratings are an example of a syndicated service. Other syndicated services measure magazine readership, warehouse movement of products, and retail shelf audits.

Custom research firms set up one-of-a-kind research projects. Frequently these are studies in the new-product area. The researchers will test ideas for new products, alternative flavors, package designs, colors, and other variables.

The "production line" of market research is the **field service company**, hired by custom research firms and corporate market research departments to conduct the actual interviewing. The more than 300 field service organizations are found in major cities throughout the United States. For reasons of the cost, almost all market research firms use field services rather than their own interviewing staffs.

Gathering Data

The information gathered by field services from potential buyers is known as *primary data*. **Primary data** are data that are collected for the first time directly from the original source for the purpose of solving a problem under investigation. In contrast, **secondary data** can be obtained from a number of "middle" sources—such as government agencies, trade associations, research bureaus, universities, commercial publications (such as *Advertising Age, Sales Management,* and *Product Management*)—or else through internal records. Examples of internal records are sales invoices, accounting records, data from previous research studies, and historical sales data.

The advantages of secondary data are the savings in time and money over the expenses and effort involved in gathering primary data. The trick is making sure that secondary data will adequately meet the researcher's need. Since they were gathered to solve a previous problem, secondary data often won't answer a current situation. The manufacturer of Seven Seas salad dressings wanted to know whether consumers would buy a new Caesar's salad dressing flavor. There were plenty of *secondary* data about consumption of Caesar's salad dressing and consumers' preferences for other flavors. However these secondary data couldn't answer the one question that mattered: what the response would be to *Seven Seas'* particular blend of Caesar's salad dressing. The only way to solve the problem was to obtain primary data. Consumers were first asked to taste the new blend and then asked how it compared to others that they had tried.

Primary Data Primary data are usually gathered by some form of survey research in which questions are put to one or another kind of group in order to draw out the group's attitudes or behavior. There are three kinds of personal interview situations in survey research: door-to-door, mall intercept, and focus group interviews. The door-to-door interview is conducted in the respondent's home. This method can be very costly, both in the interviewer's travel time and in gasoline expense. Instead, more researchers are turning to mall intercept interviews. Field services using this technique intercept shoppers as they browse in shopping malls and interview them in the mall area or at a nearby research facility.

Mall interviewing is much more economical than door-to-door interviews, but the survey may not be adequate. The people who shop at the mall may not be typical of the community's population. A study conducted in the beautiful Waterworks in downtown Chicago would include few if any interviews with lower-middle-class (and below) Chicagoans. These people simply can't afford to shop there.

A **focus group** is another form of personal interview. Individuals are recruited, either at malls or by telephone, for participation in a group discussion called a *focus group*. The discussion is usually held in a conference-room setting with audio taping equipment. The room is also usually equipped with a one-way mirror for the benefit of client observers. During the group session a moderator will focus discussion on a series of prearranged topics. In a study of breakfast cereals, for example, the moderator might lead a group of product users into a discussion of such matters as their awareness of brands and their own rates of consumption. She might try to draw out the users' own words to describe their favorite cereals.

TALKING BUSINESS

Market researchers are experimenting with the capability to tailor television commercials to individual households. In tests being carried out in a number of medium-sized cities across the United States, market-research firms monitor and catalog the grocery-store purchases of thousands of volunteer families and transmit custom-tailored commercials to those families via cable TV. By continually monitoring these consumers' purchases, the researchers can tell how effective various commercials are in causing them to change brands.

Although this new technology presents exciting prospects for marketers, most do not believe its extension to everyday use will come soon. The logistics and costs of expanding the system across the country or even to large cities are prohibitive. Other objections are taking shape as well.

"I find it shocking," says Norma Rollins, director of the privacy project at the American Civil Liberties Union in New York City. "Trying to beam commercials specifically (into individual homes)—I see that as a very large invasion of privacy."

Adapted from Jeffrey H. Birnbaum, "Admen Excited over New Marketing Tool, but Critics Contend It Smacks of '1984,' " *Wall Street Journal*, 25 September 1981, p. 35. Adapted by permission of The Wall Street Journal, © Dow Jones & Company, Inc., 1981. All rights reserved.

CONSUMER BEHAVIOR

Attempts to study people's feelings toward cereals and other products reflect management's desire to understand and respond to consumer behavior and attitudes. **Consumer behavior** is the total of the decision processes and acts of people who are involved in buying and using products. When you decide to buy (or not to buy) a product or service, you're involved in a problem-solving task. By purchasing an item, you have hopefully acquired something that will satisfy some need. For example, you decide that you are hungry so you drive to McDonald's and order a Big Mac. The hamburger should for the time being solve your hunger pangs.

Problem Solving

Problem solving can occur on several levels: (1) routinized response behavior, (2) limited problem solving, and (3) extensive problem solving. Much of our consumer behavior, like the example of the Big Mac, is routinized response behavior. You're familiar with McDonald's and other available brands of hamburgers. You've probably tried all the other major fast-food hamburgers and know how they taste. And you've also eaten a Big Mac often enough to recognize that it can satisfy your hunger. The problem-solving task isn't difficult. You need little new information, and therefore the decision is routine in nature. In fact, routinized behavior is often habitual. If you have used Right Guard antiperspirant for many years and begin to run low, you may out of habit reach for the Right Guard package at the drug store.

Habitual purchase behavior marks a person as **brand loyal.** But even brand-loyal consumers will sometimes switch brands. Assume that Bristol Meyers comes out with a new antiperspirant that will keep a person completely dry for two days and that comes in your favorite fragrance. Or assume that another antiperspirant, such as Dial, is offering a special price discount. In either case you might be led to put Right Guard aside and try the other product—out of curiosity in the one case and a desire to save money in the other.

Limited Problem Solving Limited problem solving involves much more decision making than does routinized or habitual behavior. It usually occurs when a person is trying to choose between two or more brands in a familiar product class. A college student moving into an empty dorm room may decide to "liven the place up" with some music. From this comes the decision to buy a stereo system. The student has, then, selected the product class *stereos* instead of several others, such as televisions and radios. The student is generally aware of the benefits of each product class and has decided that a stereo would best suit his or her needs. The primary decision now is to select a brand—perhaps Pioneer, Sony, or Realistic. This decision-making process is referred to as **limited**

Informative advertising is used to aid the consumer in extensive problem-solving.

DON'T BUY A MAGNAVISION JUST BECAUSE IT PLAYS MOVIES.

Watch your favorite movie on Magnavision* and you'll hardly recognize it.

Because Magnavision gives you a sharp, astonishingly clear picture—better than any VCR can deliver. And most discs are recorded in brilliant stereo sound as well, so you can hear your movie sound track the way it was *meant* to be heard...a whole new dimension in video/audio entertainment systems.

But we didn't develop Magnavision just for movies.

Magnavision is a LaserVision player.

And you'll be able to do things with the LaserVision system that are impossible with other systems.

It all starts with a laser beam: the heart of Magnavision.

The laser beam picks up a picture from a special video disc (it's about the same size as a long-playing record, but it's made of tough aluminum plated acrylic).

Nothing touches the disc except a tightly focused beam of light which reads the 0.4 micrometer pit on the disc. So *there's nothing to wear out*, and you can expect to see the same sharp, clear picture time after time.

Variable speed slow motion, jitter-free freeze-frame on any of the standard disc's 54,000 individual frames, and a "Rapid Search" button let you find just the place you want, when you want it—in seconds.

This advanced technology also gives you *room-filling stereo sound* (you can play it

through your own stereo system—frequency response is 40 to 20,000 HZ ± 3db).

You can enjoy movies, shows and concerts (wait till you hear Olivia Newton-John's* new video *Physical* disc in stereo!).

And the list grows longer every day.

There are also more and more "interactive" laser discs available—that's where the fun begins.

These are *discs that let you participate*, using the Magnavision wireless Infrared Remote Control.

You can learn *How to Watch Pro Football* (and be quizzed afterwards); or try all the games and puzzles on the Grammy nominated *The First National Kidisc*.

You can go on art gallery tours and attend classical, pop or rock concerts.

Don't know how to filet a flounder? Take the *Master Cooking Course* from Craig Claiborne and Pierre Franey. Just put your Magnavision into "Slow Motion" and they'll show you exactly how it's done.

You can see it all on Magnavision right now.

Just stop in at your nearest Magnavision Dealer, push the "PLAY" button, and step into the future. *To find your nearest dealer, call toll-free 800-447-4700.*

© 1981 N.A.P. CONSUMER ELECTRONICS CORP. A NORTH AMERICAN PHILIPS COMPANY *Olivia Newton-John ®, MCA, ©Original Programming Associates Inc.

MAGNAVISION

MAGNAVOX
The brightest ideas in the world are here today.

problem solving. A person engaged in limited problem solving will often try to get further information from advertising or perhaps by visiting with friends before making the purchase selection. For example, the student might speak with the dormmate down the hall to get her opinion as well as to ask about her Superscope stereo system.

Extensive Problem Solving Extensive problem solving is the most complex form of purchase decision making. The consumer is not familiar with the product class or the brands available. This means that it will be necessary to search extensively for information before making a purchase decision. The product may involve social risk: Will my friends approve? It can also have considerable economic impact on the buyer: Is this the best use of my money? For many people, home video recorders present a broad problem-solving situation. Because they have never owned or used a home video recorder, they must first familiarize themselves with it and then decide whether it's suitable for their needs. Once this decision is made, the various brands—such as Sony-Betamax, Panasonic, Quasar, and RCA—must be weighed.

Many high school students also face extensive problem solving when trying to decide whether to go to college (college being the product/service class). Once the decision is made to go to college rather than get a job, a brand (specific university or college) must be chosen.

When consumers are faced with broad problem-solving situations, marketing managers often use highly informative promotion. For example, an advertisement for a Magnavox LaserVision player doesn't stop with promoting the quality image of Magnavox products. It must also stress the benefits of owning any video player while emphasizing the unique advantages of Magnavox.

Consumer problem solving isn't always based on the deliberation of a single person. Actually, a number of people can be involved. These are the influencer, the purchaser, the decision maker, and the user. To illustrate, consider the Jones family in Toledo, Ohio. Frank Jones has just reached 18 and is entering his freshman year in college. He has saved some money, and with the help of Carl Jones, his father, he hopes to buy his first automobile. Susan, Frank's mother, has always been quite conservative and worried about young Frank's finances at college. She suggests that Frank consider only economy cars that get at least 30 miles to the gallon. Her role in the purchase decision is that of influencer. An influencer is someone whose opinion is valued in the purchase decision-making process.

Frank, of course, wants a car that has plenty of power and that also fits his image of a sharp, "with-it" college freshman. The person that will actually make the decision (and most of the payments) is Carl Jones. He decides on an economical Ford Escort, which both has enough class for Frank's image and is economical enough to suit Susan Jones.

The decision maker is the one who chooses both the product class and the brand. In this case, the product class is an automobile rather than other forms of transportation, such as a motorcycle or a bus. But although Mr. Jones has made the decision to buy a Ford Escort, he relies on his brother Fred to make the actual purchase. Fred happens to work at a Toledo Ford dealership and can save a large amount on the purchase price. Fred, then, is the actual buyer who completes the process. Thus four persons were involved in the purchase decision: an influencer—Susan; the decision maker—Carl; a purchaser—Fred; and the user—Frank Jones.

SUMMARY

Marketing is the performance of those business activities directed at satisfying needs and wants through the exchange process. In order to facilitate exchange, marketing managers use the "right principle"—getting the right goods or services to the right people at the right place at the right time at the right price using the right promotional techniques.

Until fairly recently, most firms were production oriented. Today, however, many firms have adopted the marketing concept, which identifies the satisfaction of the consumer's needs and wants as a principal function of the business enterprise. The foundations of the marketing concept are consumer orientation and goal orientation.

Implementing the marketing concept involves establishing a marketing mix—a unique blend of (1) product and service offerings, which include the total of benefits offered, (2) a distribution system created to reach a specific group of consumers, called the *target market*, (3) pricing, and (4) a promotional mix, or blend, which includes personal selling, advertising, sales promotion, and publicity. These activities are the means by which a marketing manager plans to satisfy target consumers. The marketing mix can be applied to nonbusiness as well as business situations.

Success in implementing the marketing concept depends on a thorough understanding of the target market. One technique often used to this end is market segmentation. The five basic forms of segmentation are: demographic, geographic, psychographic, benefit, and volume.

The marketing mix for a product depends on whether the firm creates it by using market segmentation (a market oriented strategy) or product differentiation—a product oriented strategy that emphasizes differentiating the firm's product from others. The marketing mix also depends on the firm's positioning strategy—the strategic placement of the product in the market.

Much can be learned about consumers through marketing research, which involves planning, collecting, recording, and analyzing data related to the marketing of goods and services and communicating the results to management. Marketing research is carried out by (1) corporate marketing research departments, (2) advertising agencies, and (3) independent marketing research firms, which offer both custom and syndicated services. Field service companies are often hired by custom research firms and corporate research departments to conduct the actual interviewing. Marketing researchers can use primary data, gathered through door-to-door, mall intercept, and focus group interviews, or secondary data, obtained from a number of "middle" sources. Using secondary data saves time and money, but the data may not adequately meet the researchers' needs.

Emphasis on marketing research reflects management's desire to understand consumer behavior—the decision processes and acts of people involved in buying and using products. Consumer behavior involves decision making, which can take place on several levels: (1) routinized response behavior, which is often habitual and can involve brand loyalty, (2) limited problem solving, which usually involves choosing between two or more brands in a familiar product class, and (3) extensive problem solving, which involves searching extensively for information about both product class and brands. A particular consumer decision may involve a number of people, including the influencer, the purchaser, the decision maker, and the user.

KEY TERMS

advertising
brand loyal
consumer behavior
consumer orientation
field service company
focus group
goal orientation
lifestyle
limited problem
   solving
market segmentation
marketing
marketing concept
marketing mix
marketing research
middlemen
positioning
primary data
product
   differentiation
production
   orientation
promotion
psychographics
publicity
sales promotion
secondary data
syndicated research
   service

REVIEW QUESTIONS

1. In what way will the attitude of a business that is marketing oriented differ from one that is production oriented?
2. What are the basic elements of the marketing mix? Is one more important than the other?
3. List five ways of segmenting a market.
4. Explain how product differentiation differs from market segmentation.
5. What is the basic principle behind product positioning?
6. What are the basic types of market research?
7. Describe three types of problem solving that influence consumer behavior.

DISCUSSION QUESTIONS

1. Can the marketing concept be applied effectively by a small, sole-proprietor form of business or is it best for larger businesses with more management? Explain.
2. How would the marketing mix differ for each of the following firms or organizations: United Airlines; Henrietta's Hair Style Salon; Caterpillar Tractor Co.; Revlon cosmetics; Evanston, Ill. (pop. 80,000) chapter of the American Cancer Society; Burger King; George and Harry's machine tool rebuilding shop.
3. a. List at least three ways in which a manufacturer of jeans might segment the market by demographic characteristics.

   b. Describe at least three ways in which the same manufacturer of jeans might consider segmenting the market by attitudes or lifestyle.
4. Explain under what circumstances a marketer would feel that product differentiation would be more important than market segmentation.
5. Look for the following products and their advertising and describe how you believe each is positioned: Mercedes-Benz automobiles, Seven-Up, K mart stores, Apple Computer, Head and Shoulders Shampoo.
6. When would a marketer want to consider using primary research? Secondary research?
7. Describe the kind of problem solving that might be involved in purchasing the following consumer products: a low-cost calculator for use in an introductory math course, unleaded gasoline, a new pair of dress shoes, whether to buy a foreign or American compact car, a six-pack of beer.

CASE: TO MARKET, TO MARKET. . . OR NOT TO MARKET?

Karen and Ben Tate live in a suburb of a major metropolitan area. For the last ten years both have been working for the same major hotel chain, where they've risen to middle management positions in the restaurant and catering departments. Now, in their early 30s, they'd like to fulfill a dream of having their own restaurant. Karen's a gourmet cook with experience in kitchen operation and food buying. While she prefers the preparation, flair, and presentation of continental gourmet cooking, she's equally adept at provincial European foods and all kinds of fish and sea food. Ben's expertise, on the other hand, is in overall management and small group catering.

They recently learned of space that will become available in two months. They estimate that after remodeling, they could have an ideal kitchen and room for 40 customers. They have the necessary capital to start and have to make a firm decision in two months.

1. What marketing decisions do Karen and Ben have to make?
2. What questions would you want answered if you were in their position?
3. What recommendations would you have for getting the questions answered?

CASE: IN & OUT OF POSITION

In the late 1950s, Helene Curtis was one the country's largest marketers of shampoos, hair preparations and other toiletry items. Distribution was broad, and their products could be found in almost all food, drug, department, variety, and general stores. In 1957 the researchers in their shampoo laboratory made a technical breakthrough and for the first time were able to blend into a shampoo sulfur, a medication frequently used by dermatologists in the treatment of dandruff. Millions of people with simple dandruff could now treat the problem by shampooing three to four times a week instead of massaging the scalp with a sulfur-based ointment.

Yellow in color and packed in a blue jar that was enclosed in an attractive red, black, and white box, *Enden* (a jargonal combination of the words *end dandruff*) was almost an overnight success. Sales skyrocketed, and within two years Enden was among the country's leading shampoos. However, follow-up research among users revealed that while they were quite satisfied with the product, most would go back to their regular shampoo once the dandruff symptoms went away and would come back to Enden only when the symptoms returned.

Two years later, Procter & Gamble developed Head and Shoulders, a lotion-type dandruff treatment shampoo packed in a bottle. Advertising as well as the package showed a woman with long beautiful blond hair. P & G advertised heavily and within a few years the new product became the top-selling shampoo in the country. Enden sales fell drastically. Research with Head and Shoulders users indicated that most used the shampoo regularly and had switched from other shampoos to this.

1. Comment on the differences in target markets and the positioning of the two products.
2. Do you think Helene Curtis should have been able to predict the consumer's attitudes and acted differently?

CHAPTER 12

PRODUCT AND SERVICE OFFERINGS

After studying this chapter you should be able to:

1 Define the meaning of a product from the marketing manager's point of view.
2 Describe a product classification system for consumer and industrial goods.
3 Explain the procedure of good product development.
4 Evaluate the different stages of the product life cycle.
5 Explain the advantage of branding and packaging to the producer and the consumer.
6 Discuss the importance of product safety.

Perhaps you've had—and enjoyed—a Chipwich. Or maybe you've only heard of the Chipwich—or worse yet, maybe you're wondering "What's a *Chipwich*??"

That must have been the question on the minds of thousands of New Yorkers on May I, 1981 as they passed any of 60 carts set up on strategic corners of midtown Manhattan. Beside each was a vendor outfitted in a safari-like uniform, keeping up a patter of street talk with passersby, urging them to try a Chipwich.

Passersby got the point and put their money where they wanted their mouths to be: digging into a Chipwich. After only four hours, vendors had sold out their $25,000 stock on their first day of busiwich—er, business.

Now what's a Chipwich? you ask, if you don't already know. A Chipwich consists of vanilla ice cream sandwiched between two chocolate chip cookies and studded with chips along the edge. It's the sweet brainchild of New Yorkers Richard LaMotta and Bruce Nevins. LaMotta created the novelty while operating a shop called The Sweet Tooth in Englewood, N.J. Nevins provides the marketing acumen that's propelling remarkable sales of the snack food.

The Burry Division of Quaker Oats was interested in licensing the production rights to Chipwich and test marketed the product in Minneapolis and Philadelphia. But LaMotta declined the deal, preferring to maintain quality control himself. Instead, he pieced together $500,000 from friends to capitalize production.

New York streets are flowing with food vendors, but the clean appearance of the Chipwich carts and vendors gives the product a sharper profile than most. Unlike Good Humor and other ice-cream vendors, Chipwich is a 12-month-a-year operation. Plans called for moving the carts indoors during the winter and expanding the program to the Sun Belt states.

But cart sales are just an introductory phase for Chipwich. Nevins, chairman of Premium Products Sales, is lining up distribution through supermarkets, the main delivery mechanism for ice-cream products. "The carts provide a great sampling program while yielding profits," he says. "They give the product a personality, and they're building a consumer base. When people see the product in their supermarket freezers, they'll be much more likely to buy it."

"Eventually we plan a national rollout," Nevins continues; once that's complete, he expects sales in the $50-$100 million range. "The novelty business is relatively unsophisticated. Products are not marketed aggressively. We intend to change that."

Word of mouth has been the primary promotion to date, but with very satisfactory results. Nevins contrasted Chipwich's popularity with that of Perrier mineral water, which he helped introduce to America. "After two months, product awareness was 65 percent in New York. That's 10 points higher than Perrier after five months."

Adapted by permission from Kevin Higgins, "Chipwich Cools off New York; National Distribution Planned," *Marketing News*, 4 September 1981, p. 5, published by the American Marketing Association.

WHAT IS A PRODUCT?

Before a manager ever selects a channel of distribution or sets a price or develops a promotional strategy, he or she must first know what type of product or service will be sold. As the Chipwich story illustrates, the product is primary. The manager's art and skills revolve around the product: what it is and what it does, what it means to the business and what it can do for the business. But how is the very idea of *product* to be understood?

Marketing uses a broad definition of **product**— any want-satisfying good or service as well as its perceived tangible and intangible attributes and benefits that people attribute to it. A product isn't simply a physical object but many other things which are symbolic in nature. People often consume things not simply for what they are but for what they mean. Why would a man in the heat of summer wear a tie consisting of several layers of cloth wrapped tightly around his neck, except for some symbolic value that it may possess for him: it may be a badge of taste or convention; or it may advertise that its wearer is a white-collar worker; or it may denote a certain rank within society.

Service after the sale, the image of the brand, the image of the retail store, packaging, warranty, attachments, instructions, color—all are part of a product's attributes (see Figure 12.1). So

FIGURE 12.1

THE TOTAL PRODUCT CONCEPT

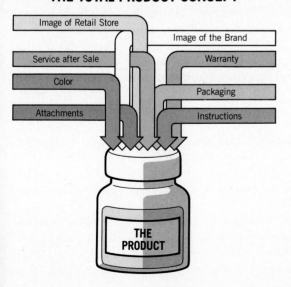

if a manufacturer produces two identical men's suits, one with a Saks Fifth Avenue label sewn in it and the other with none, we consider these two different products. The Saks Fifth Avenue suit has much more prestige than one without any label, even though the quality of the material and the cut are the same. For this reason, marketing managers would consider these same *suits* two different *products*. And the prices of these two garments would be significantly different. Why? Because there are people who are willing to pay for status symbols—in this case a label. Symbolism plays a role in their thinking and in their consumer behavior.

New Products

When a product or service is brought to the marketplace, it must have the "right product attributes" in order to be successful. It must also possess satisfactory elements of the marketing mix — price, promotion, and distribution. General Electric may come up with another attachment for a food processor, and S. C. Johnson & Son may change the color of Agree shampoo. But these actions alone may not cause people to see the items as new products. General Foods offers many "new" cold cereals, hot cereals, powdered drink mixes, and even coffees to the market every few years. But these cannot be considered major product developments.

Marketers must be careful in deciding whether to position their product as new or simply as an improvement over an existing one. Should Procter & Gamble have promoted Pringles as an improvement over exisiting potato chips or rather as a new kind of snack food? In 1968 Pringles was placed in limited (test) markets. The product offered consumers a convenient canister pack and guaranteed unbroken, uniform-size chips. National distribution of Pringles began in 1975 with P & G spending about $45 million on promotion. For a while, consumers responded. But as early as 1974 sales had already begun to falter in the test markets. When the novelty of the package wore off, it was found that Pringles was at a taste disadvantage.

Procter & Gamble also found that the packaging of Pringles was appealing to someone who wanted a can of chips that would last a month without going stale. That fact alone, however, did

TALKING BUSINESS

not make for large volume in repeat customers. In early 1981 the brand's market share sank to about 3 percent of the $2.3 billion potato chip market. Advertising and research were slashed, and one of the two Pringles production plants were converted to a plant for making paper products. By late 1981 P & G was testing a corn chip product that might gain a foothold in the multibillion-dollar snack food market. And with this latest development came an old question: whether to position it as a new product or an an improvement of an existing one.

PRODUCT CLASSIFICATION

Consumer Goods

Products such as Pringles fall into the broad general category of **consumer goods**. These are goods and services purchased and used by the ultimate buyer. Electric razors, sandwiches, cars, stereos, magazines, and houses are all consumer goods. To understand the nature of consumer goods better, we shall examine them under three major groupings: convenience goods, shopping goods, and specialty goods (see Figure 12.2). The classification system is based on the amount of effort consumers are willing to make to acquire the product.

Convenience Goods   **Convenience goods** are relatively inexpensive items that require little shopping effort. Soft drinks, candy bars, milk, bread, and small hardware items are typical convenience goods. We buy these routinely day in and day out without much if any preplanning. This does not mean that consumer goods are unimportant, obscure items. Some, such as Pepsi-Cola, Pepperidge Farm, Jeno's Pizza, and Sure Deodorant, are very well known. Since convenience goods are inexpensive, they need wide distribution in order to sell in sufficient quantities to meet their manufacturers' profit goals. Therefore they are sold in all kinds of outlets from gas stations to department stores. People expect convenience goods to be easy to buy.

Shopping Goods   **Shopping goods** are usually more expensive than convenience goods and are found in fewer stores. These items are often bought only after a brand-to-brand and store-to-store comparison of price, lifestyle compatibility, suitability, and style. (Stores are also compared for such things as service and credit policies.)

Shopping goods include such items as furniture, automobiles, and some clothing. While convenience goods are bought with little preplanning, a shopping good may have been decided upon some months or even years before the actual purchase. You may decide that you're going to buy a new car when you get out of college. You

TYPES OF CONSUMER GOODS AND THE SEARCH EFFORT FOR THEM

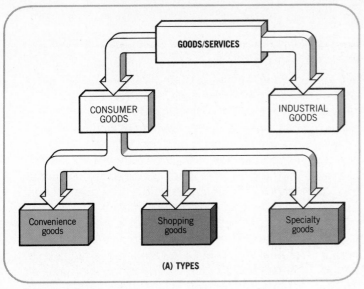

(A) TYPES

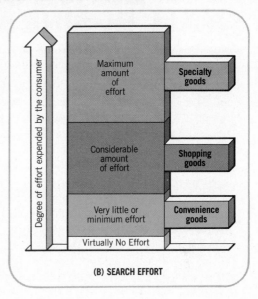

(B) SEARCH EFFORT

FIGURE 12.2

may already be comparing models, styles, and other details. More importantly, you're beginning to set some money aside each month.

Some shopping goods, such as appliances, generally have the same features and perform the same functions. Brand names can then be quite important, since consumers often view them as indicators of product quality. Heavy advertising by firms such as RCA, Sony, and General Electric contribute to higher levels of brand awareness

Three types of consumer goods: convenience, shopping, and specialty.

PERSPECTIVE ON SMALL BUSINESS

[In 1977] the micro-softwear industry didn't exist. The first "personal computers" were introduced in 1975, but they were sold as kits and had no keyboards or video monitors: you used them by flicking on-off toggle switches and watching flashing red lights.

Now the installed base of personal computers has passed the 1 million mark and is forecast to grow as much as 50% a year for the next decade. The demand for programs, or software, to run these machines has mushroomed. In 1981, sales of micro software totaled about $500 million. By 1985, forecasts suggest that sales will range between $1 billion and $5 billion.

The beginnings of this now-hot industry were inauspicious. Late one night in January 1975, Bill Gates was playing poker in his Harvard dorm. He was losing heavily, when a friend showed him that month's issue of *Popular Electronics*. The cover featured the first personal computer, called an Altair. "I decided that I better buy one," says Gates, who had been planning to go into law despite an extensive back-

ground in programming. "I thought it was a better use of my money than losing at poker."

Gates did buy an Altair. With his good friend Paul Allen, who was working at Honeywell Inc.'s Boston facilities, he began writing a programming language. The two of them had decided that these little machines needed a simple, "high-level" language with which users could write programs. (High-level means that it's easy for people rather than machines to understand.)

Gate's dorm room at Harvard became the site of weeks of what Gates fondly calls "working in the hard-core mode." They named their finished language Microsoft BASIC and started Microsoft Inc. to market it. They've since sold more than 600,000 copies of Microsoft BASIC, and the company, which they moved first to Albuquerque, N. Mex., and then to Seattle, had revenues of $15.8 million last year [1981].

SOURCE: Reprinted with permission of *INC.* Magazine. Excerpted from Steve Ditlea and Joanne Tangorra, "The Birth of an Industry," *INC.*, January 1982, pp. 64–70. Copyright © 1982 by INC. Publishing Company, 38 Commercial Wharf, Boston, MA 02110.

and consumer preference. As a result, the prices for widely advertised shopping goods may be higher than for less well knows manufacturers' brands. Also, some shopping goods are highly nonstandardized, such as furniture and better clothing. The consumer in this case is searching for suitability, image, and lifestyle compatibility rather than just the lowest price.

Specialty Goods   When consumers search long and hard for specific goods or services and refuse to accept substitutes, the objects of their search are referred to as **specialty goods.** Expensive jewelry, designer clothing, expensive stereo equipment, limited-production automobiles, and gourmet food products fall into the specialty good category. Since consumers are willing to spend much time and effort to find specialty goods, distribution is often limited to one store (or at the most two) in a given region. The product may be found only at Neiman-Marcus, Gucci, Gump's, or some other exclusive store.

For one person a product may be a convenience good; for another, a shopping good; and for yet another, a specialty good. A child with some change to spend may search long and hard before deciding which candy bar to buy. On the other hand, some adults seem to be hooked on Milky Way candy bars. That is the only candy bar they will eat, and if it's not available, they'll forgo the extra calories. For *them* a Milky Way is a specialty good. But for most of the target market a Milky Way is simply a convenience good. So the marketing manager must know how at least a majority of the consumers view the product. The marketing mix is then designed to appeal to the perceptions of the target market. If most people view an item as a convenience good, then it should be promoted, priced, and distributed as a convenience good.

Industrial Goods

Just as consumer goods are bought by the ultimate user, **industrial goods** are bought by businesses or institutions for use in making other goods or for rendering a service. Industrial goods can be broken down into six major categories: installations, accessory items, raw materials, component parts and materials, services, and supplies (see Figure 12.3).

Installations   **Installations** are large, expensive capital items—goods that have a long life-span and that get special tax treatment. As such, they help determine the scope and profitability of a company. Large production equipment, buildings, and other major capital items such as airplanes are considered installations. If General Motors shuts down an outdated assembly plant and builds a new installation using assembly-line robots, the results will greatly boost the profitability of producing cars by slashing costs. One major reason why American automakers fell behind the Japanese during the 1970s is that they were stuck with a large number of outdated and inefficient installations. It will probably be the mid-1980s or

after before investment in new plants and equipment cuts costs enough to compete effectively with foreign car manufacturers.

Accessories   **Accessories** do not have the same long-run impact on the firm as installations. Still, they're considered capital goods. Accessory items are usually less expensive and more standardized than installations. Examples include word processing equipment, small machine tools, and forklift trucks. If GM should buy one more word processing machine than it really needs, the effect on long-run profitability won't be noticeable. However to build a new automotive assembly plant (an installation) with the wrong specifications or outdated technology could pose a serious setback to the firm. Because accessories are less expensive and usually have no important long-run consequences for the firm, they may be acquired by a purchasing agent rather than by top management.

Raw Materials   **Raw materials** are classified as expense items—costs incurred in the operation of a business that are charged against income for a specific period. Raw materials are those resources from which finished goods are made. They are items that undergo no more processing than is required for economy or protection before being incorporated into the final product. Raw materials can be further classified as "natural" products—

FIGURE 12.3

TYPES OF INDUSTRIAL GOODS

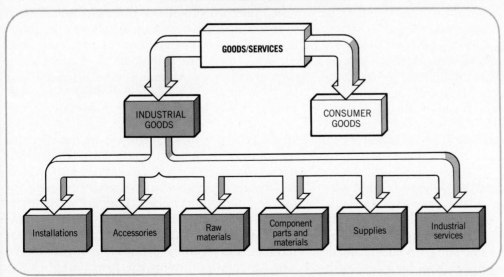

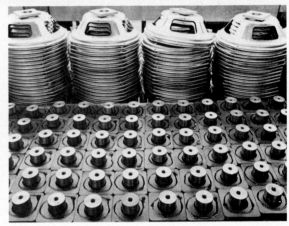

Three types of industrial goods: installations, raw materials, and component parts and materials.

for example, minerals, forest products, and farm products. Because the total supply of raw materials is limited, they're subject to broad regulation both in the United States and in foreign countries.

Farm products—a category of raw materials—are grown seasonally, with the result that storage and shipment play a large part in total price. In addition, most crops lend themselves to more efficient growth in certain regions; examples are citrus fruits in California and Florida, cotton in the South, and potatoes in Idaho and the West. This regional specialization requires extensive transportation to get farm products to the ultimate consumers. The long distances involved mean higher shipping costs.

Component Parts and Materials Component parts and materials—which, like raw materials, are also incorporated into the end product—do not occur naturally. They're humanly pùt together. Some component parts are custom-made items such as a set of brake shoes for a new auto-

mobile, a keyboard for a minicomputer, or a special pigment for a paint. In other situations component parts may be standardized for sales to many industrial users. Integrated circuits for minicomputers, cement for the construction trade, and steel for various applications are standardized components and materials. Buyers of component parts and materials look for product consistency. The component part must continuously meet the demands of the industrial user. A Chrysler Motors engine assembly line would come to a screeching halt if the pistons began varying by one-sixteenth inch or more.

Supplies The fifth category of industrial goods is **supplies.** These are items that are bought routinely and often in large quantities by the purchasing agent. Supplies are set aside, available for use, and dispensed at need. They are useful to the firm in the conduct of its business, but they're expense items and don't become part of the final product. They also have minimum impact on the long-run profitability of the firm. Supply items include pencils, pens, paper, paper clips, typewriter ribbons, stationery, and the like. Distribution of supply items is wide since most buyers will rarely search for them. In essence, supply items are the convenience goods of the industrial market.

Services   **Services** is the final category of industrial goods. Service organizations are used to plan, facilitate, or support company operations. They can vary from highly sophisticated consulting firms to janitorial businesses. Service purchasers must be convinced of the need to hire special skills outside the firm, having first determined if the need can be better met internally. Management must also be persuaded of the cost effectiveness of going to a service organization.

NEW-PRODUCT DEVELOPMENT

The Importance of New Products

Whether industrial goods or consumer goods, new products form the lifeblood of many companies. Without new products, most firms would cease to grow. A recent study shows that firms get an average of 15 percent of their current sales volume from products introduced within the past five years.[1] If firms don't change their product mix to meet the changing needs of the target market, in the long run they'll fail. Most successful products eventually decline in sales and profits and are phased out. So new products are needed to fill the gap.

Risks and Rewards of Development   Despite its importance, the development of new products usually proves risky. About 40 to 50 percent of new products introduced during the 1970s and early 1980s turned out to be failures.[2] In fact the list of all new-product failures seems almost endless. The Ford Motor Company lost over $50 million on its Edsel model. Listoral (produced by the manufacturer of Listerine) failed because consumers could not associate the Listerine brand name with a product that was a household disinfectant.

Interestingly, product failure doesn't mean that the product fails entirely to sell. It simply means that the product hasn't met management's expectations. Post breakfast cereals with freeze-dried fruit, Frost 8/80 Whiskey, and Campbell's Red Kettle Soups were all withdrawn because sales didn't meet expectations.

The New-Product Development Process

To increase a new product's chances of success, a manufacturer uses the new-product development process. Steps in the process (see Figure 12.4) are:

1. opportunity exploration,
2. screening,
3. developing a preliminary profit plan,
4. creating a marketing mix,
5. test marketing, and
6. market introduction.

Opportunity Exploration   The first step in new-product development is **opportunity exploration**—searching for and getting new ideas or concepts for products. Ideas can come from almost anywhere. Customers, investors, retailers, employees, market research, and even competitors can be sources for new-product ideas.

Sometimes companies will set up brainstorming sessions to try and hatch ideas for new products or services. Brainstorming has for its goal getting a group of people to think of all the possible ways of varying a product/service or of solving a problem.

FIGURE 12.4

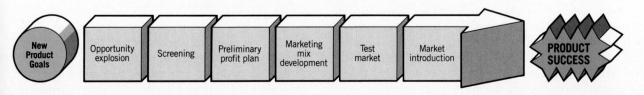

THE NEW-PRODUCT DEVELOPMENT PROCESS

New Product Goals · Opportunity explosion · Screening · Preliminary profit plan · Marketing mix development · Test market · Market introduction · PRODUCT SUCCESS

Criticism isn't allowed, no matter how silly the idea may seem at the time. Emphasis is on the sheer quantity of ideas, with assessment put off until later. General Foods' development of Cycle dog foods began in a brainstorming session.

Screening   Once the ideas are gathered, the second step is to screen them and reject obvious misfits. A product might be a misfit simply because of development costs or because of unavailable technology or low sales potential. Or it just might not fit in with existing products. It would be very difficult for the Bic Company, the manufacturer of disposable pens and lighters, to manufacture and market motorcycles. The company simply doesn't have the expertise, the sales and distribution, or the know-how to produce and market such products effectively. For the same reason, it would be hard for Yamaha to manufacture and market disposable pens and lighters.

A Preliminary Profit Plan   The screening step eliminates those product ideas that are obviously poor fits. The next hurdle is called a **preliminary profit plan.** At this point management begins to take a serious look at the product concept (the idea for a new product). Financial statements are developed that project potential profits over a period of time (usually five years). This means that sales, production costs, financing charges, and development expenses must all be estimated.

The Marketing Mix   If a product shows a reasonable profit potential, the firm begins to develop a prototype (an original model) and a marketing mix (discussed in Ch. 11). After prototype models of the product are created and laboratory tested, small pilot production plants may be set up. Next the name is conceived, promotion strategies are developed, and positioning and channel-of-distribution strategies are created.

Test Marketing   The next hurdle for a new product is **test marketing.** This is the "acid test" for the product concept and its positioning. Anywhere from one to several cities are chosen that are considered typical of the market for the product. The product is then placed in stores and advertised in the local media. Finally, sales results are measured. Test marketing evaluates the product concept under "battle conditions." If the product is successful there, it is assumed that it will be successful in the market as a whole.

Hanes rolled into an Orlando, Florida test market positioning Underalls as "panties and panty hose all-in-one that will eliminate panty lines." After five months of test marketing, Underalls achieved a 24 percent share of the department store market.

Market Introduction   Only about 50 percent of all products survive test marketing. Those that make it past the last hurdle are then introduced to the entire marketplace, or "rolled out nationally." New-product development is a long and costly process. Only about one idea in 58 finally reaches the marketplace as a new product. Despite all the work and expense of preparing the product for the marketplace, there's no guarantee of survival. About two out of three products that make the national scene will be successful. Underalls became very successful and was followed by a host of imitators. Panty hose "all-in-one" is now the fastest-growing segment of the hosiery market.

THE PRODUCT LIFE CYCLE
Characteristics of the Life Cycle

After a product reaches the marketplace it enters the product life cycle. The **product life cycle** is total sales from a product over a period of time (see Figure 12.5). As a product goes through the life cycle, the marketing manager must revise the marketing mix as the product matures and finally dies. A product life cycle typically has four stages:

1. introduction,
2. growth,
3. maturity, and
4. decline and death.

These four stages can be roughly characterized by the kinds of consumers identified with them by some marketers:

1. innovators,
2. early majority,
3. late majority, and
4. "laggards."

Before we examine the stages of the life cycle a few further points should be made.

Actual product life cycles are often not the smooth curves that Figure 12.5 shows. Instead,

STAGES

IN

THE

PRODUCT

LIFE

CYCLE

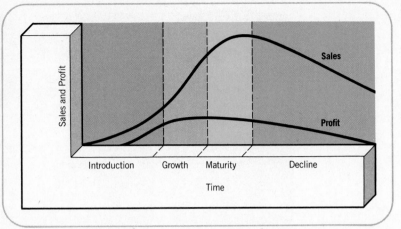

FIGURE 12.5

there will be bumps, hills, and valleys due to a number of factors that can affect sales. And not all products go through every stage in the life cycle. In fact many will not even make it out of the introductory stage. Also, the length of time products stay in any one stage can vary greatly. Some fad items, like "pet rocks," move through the entire life cycle in a matter of weeks. Others, such as filter cigarettes, stay in the maturity stage of the life cycle for decades.

A product does not necessarily go from maturity into decline. The death of a product isn't always certain. An item can sometimes be *repositioned* so that there's a new growth phase in the cycle. **Repositioning** has to do with changing the image or perceived uses of the product. A classic example of repositioning is Johnson & Johnson's Baby Shampoo. When the U.S. birthrate fell, Johnson & Johnson's shampoo, which was already a dull sales performer, became even more sluggish. However, through advertising, the product was repositioned as a shampoo gentle enough for everyday use—by *every* member of the family. To further this idea, macho men such as Fran Tarkington were shown using Johnson & Johnson's Baby Shampoo. Sales skyrocketed, and the product became the best-selling shampoo in the world.

Stages of the Life Cycle

Introduction   When a product enters the life cycle it faces many obstacles on the path to success. The **introductory stage** is characterized by little competition, frequent product modifi-

cation, limited distribution—and a high failure rate. Sales in the introductory stage come from consumers whose perceived needs best fit the product's characteristics. This is referred to as the *core market*. Production costs and marketing costs are high because of the absence of sales volume. And then there are often "freebies"—giveaways distributed free in order to acquaint and attract customers. So profits are usually small, if any, in the introductory stage. Promotion is based on developing product awareness: "how the product meets your needs."

Growth   After the product successfully moves through the introductory phase it enters the growth stage. The **growth stage** is the period when sales are mounting at an ever increasing rate. In April 1980 Minnetonka Inc. introduced Softsoap. By early 1981 Softsoap had entered the growth stage of the cycle and had already captured 7 percent of the $1 billion U.S. soap market.

Large companies begin to acquire small pioneering firms that don't have adequate funds for market expansion. Many competitors enter the market as firms jump on the bandwagon. Profits increase greatly during the growth phase due to strong demand. Promotion emphasis begins to evolve—from informing the consumer about the new product to aggressively promoting the brand name and the differences between product alternatives. For example, in 1981 Minnetonka spent $15 million on TV commercials to tell consumers why the "me-too" products weren't as good as

ANNCR: (OVER) Johnson's Baby
Shampoo presents Bucky Dent - and
Bill Russell.

BUCKY: My hair's a mess after every
game.

BUCKY: So I hafta shampoo every day.

BILL: Yeah - - but shampooing that
much worries me.

BUCKY: Then don't use anything harsh;
use Johnson's. It's gentle enough to use
everyday - -

BUCKY: Johnson's doesn't dry out
your hair. Leaves it clean, thick and
healthy looking.

BILL: Would Johnson's do that for me?
BUCKY: No tears, no runs, no errors.

BILL: (TAKE) Johnson's Baby Shampoo.
BUCKY: It's gentle enough to use every-
day.

BILL: From Johnson & Johnson.

**Repositioning has made Johnson's
Baby Shampoo one of the largest-selling
in the world.**

Softsoap. Minnetonka also gave out 200 million coupons and placed a variety of ads in women's magazines.

Distribution becomes important in the success of a product in the growth stage. If the item isn't available when the consumer wants it, sales will be lost. Minnetonka succeeded in getting 99 of the top 100 grocery chains to carry Softsoap.

Toward the end of the growth phase, profits reach their highest point. As firms develop economies of mass production, prices begin to fall, and increased competition serves to drive prices down even further.

Maturity   When sales continue to mount, but at a decreasing rate, the product has moved into the **maturity stage** of the life cycle. Most products that have been on the market for a lengthy period of time are in the maturity stage. So a majority of marketing strategies are designed for mature products. For example, it's common for a company to bring out several variations of a basic product during its maturity phase. Koolaid was originally offered in three basic flavors. Today there are over ten flavors of Koolaid plus sweetened and nonsweetened varieties. Passenger cars are in the maturity phase; even though the num-

ber of models has been declining, there's still something for everyone.

Competition continues to be very stiff at the maturity stage of the life cycle. Here manufacturers use price, service, and repairs as means of distinguishing their products from others. Product design tends to focus on product differentiation (how to distinguish this product from other similar products?) rather than on improving the *function* of the product (how can it be made better?). Promotion is often intense during the early phases of the maturity stage as manufacturers compete for market shares. The result can be the creation of strong brand loyalties. Pepsi-Cola, Marlboro Cigarettes, and Tide laundry detergent have millions of loyal customers.

In the latter phases of the maturity stage, sales, prices, and profits begin to fall and marginal competitors drop out. As a retailer's profit margins decline, the incentive to carry the product lessens. Inventory is reduced and less shelf space is devoted to the merchandise. This usually results in a further decline in sales.

Decline   When sales begin permanently to fall, the **decline stage** has set in. The rate of decline is governed by how rapidly consumer taste is changing and new substitute products are being placed on the market. Many convenience goods go into rapid decline as new and better products are offered to consumers. Others are phased out over many years, such as nonelectric watches, black-and-white TV sets, and convertible automobiles. As demand falls, major competitors leave the marketplace. By an interesting sequence of events, small specialty firms reenter the market and buy manufacturing rights to the "abandoned" product. They then sell to the original core market—the very segment (though not necessarily the same individuals) who first gave the product its success. Producers of rocking chairs, horse carriages, and pure maple syrup have gone through this process.

BRANDING AND PACKAGING

When a product becomes part of a line, it must be given a brand name. **Brand** is a very broad term. It identifies a product or service by word, name, symbol, design—or a combination of these things. Organizations use brands to identify their product and service offerings and to distinguish them from all others. A **trademark** is the legally protected design, name, or other identifying mark associated with a company or its product.

A world without brands would be very hard to imagine. Estimates are that the average consumer sees about 1500 of these every day.[3] If everything came in a plain brown wrapper, life would be less colorful and competition would soften. There'd be no incentive to put out a better product, since the consumer could not readily tell one merchant's goods and services from another's. There'd perhaps be little pride in one's work and no credit for good quality or responsibility for bad work.

Advantages of Branding

Advantages to the firm Registration of a trademark provides legal protection to a firm. But ownership of a trademark has no value in itself unless the brand has a positive image among target customers and is well known. Names like RCA, Kleenex, Pepsi-Cola, and Xerox are worth hundreds of millions of dollars to their firms. Marketing managers strive to build brand identi-

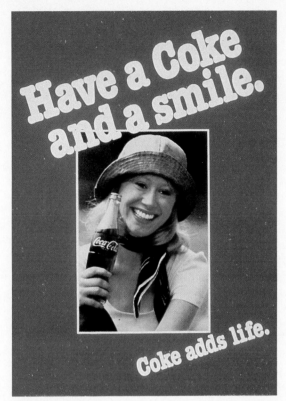

FIGURE 12.6
A Coke reminder ad.

fication and then brand loyalty for a product or service. And brand loyalty often means that firms can charge higher prices than they could if their offerings were seen as almost identical with competing goods and services. Once a satisfactory brand image is developed, it must be kept up. Coca-Cola spends millions of dollars a year reminding people of the Coca-Cola name and product (see Figure 12.6).

Advantages to the Consumer The business firm is not the only one to benefit from branding. Consumers, too, benefit importantly. Branding simplifies shopping decisions by aiding in product identification. If you go to a Kroger or Safeway store and buy a frozen Totino's Pepperoni Pizza, take it home, and find it thoroughly enjoyable, then the product has a positive image in your mind. You will likely make a note of the brand name. Then, the next time you go to the store, you can run your eye over the brands in the frozen pizza section. Finding the Totino's Pepperoni, you can expect to have about the same eating experience. This would be totally impossible if there were no brand names. Instead, just as in the central markets of developing nations, you would have to inspect each item and try to determine which one (in this case, which pizza) looked best for your needs.

Types of Brands

Family Branding Another way branding can help simplify is by helping us identify new products that we may want to buy or avoid. Perhaps you enjoy Green Giant frozen vegetables such as peas and carrots, corn in butter sauce, or broccoli with cheddar cheese. If you feel that these are quality products, a new Green Giant frozen vegetable would probably be of interest to you. Using the Green Giant name on a number of different products is referred to as **family branding.**

The question arises just how far a family brand can be stretched. In other words, when are products perceived as no longer being "in the family"? Would it be going too far to put the Green Giant label on frozen pastries? What about frozen meat entrees? You'd probably agree that putting the Green Giant label on dog food would be stretching the family brand. However, Ralston Purina puts its distinctive (and registered) "checkerboard square" on a number of breakfast cereals, dog foods, cat foods, and food products for a variety of barnyard animals. But as we noted earlier, Listerol failed because consumers didn't stretch the family brand from Listerine mouthwash to a household disinfectant.

Manufacturers' and Dealer Brands You probably recognize such names as Polaroid, Drexel, Bobby Brooks, and Suzuki. These are referred to as **manufacturers' brands** or **national brands.** The term *national brand* may not always be accurate, since many manufacturers serve only regional markets. Brands of wholesalers and retailers are referred to as **dealer brands** or **private brands.** The word *private* implies that the product is distributed only in the retailer's or wholesaler's own distribution channels. Sears Roebuck has several well-known dealer brand names including Craftsman and Diehard. J. C. Penney often uses the name Penncrest, and Montgomery Ward has many products with the Airline brand name. The Independent Grocers Association, a large wholesale grocery organization, uses the dealer brand name Shurfine. In major retail chains, the sale of dealer-branded merchandise exceeds that of manufacturers' brands. Sears' own brands now account for over 90 percent of the company's volume.

Dealer brand names tie the consumer to the retailer or wholesaler. If you want to get a Kenmore washing machine, you must go to Sears. Also, profit margins are usually higher on dealer-branded merchandise than on manufacturers' brands. However, dealers must stimulate the demand for their product. Promotion costs have made Sears one of America's largest advertisers. This can cut heavily into the higher profit margin. And if a dealer brand name is of poor quality, the dealer can't blame the manufacturer but must assume the responsibility. So an unsatisfactory experience with a dealer brand name may mean the loss of a customer to the retailer or wholesaler. But if, for example, a customer has a problem with a manufacturer's brand bought at J. C. Penney, he/she may simply exchange it for a different manufacturer's brand (or even a Penney brand) and so remain loyal to the store.

For a small retailer, a manufacturer's brand can help bring in new customers and enhance the retailer's prestige. For example, a small bicycle repair shop in a midwestern college town acquired a franchise to repair and sell Schwinn bicycles. Sales grew rapidly. The shop was remodeled and became one of the most successful university-community retailers. Extensive promotion of their products by large national manufacturers encourages rapid sales turnover. Moreover most manufacturers offer frequent deliveries to their retailers. This allows the retailers to carry less inventory, which in turn means that they need less working capital.

Manufacturers' brands carry with them two potential drawbacks for wholesalers and retailers. First, the manufacturer's brand will usually carry a smaller profit margin than a dealer can earn on his or her own brand. Second, a manufacturer keeps control over the distribution of its brand. For example, it can decide to offer the product to a different dealer and drop the original wholesaler or retailer. It can be too bad for the small retailer who spends years developing a franchise if suddenly the brand is taken away and given to another retailer, or if a company store is opened nearby. In one southwestern city a couple worked for many years developing a U-Haul trailer busi-

TALKING BUSINESS

Air France, Owens-Corning Fiberglas and the Safeco Insurance Company use him in their advertising. The Brabo Corporation sells him as a bendable doll, Stromberg-Carlson will introduce a $99.95 telephone shaped like him and D. Gottlieb & Company is planning to use him on a pinball machine.

The Pink Panther has joined Mickey Mouse, Snoopy and Al Capp's Schmoo in the zoo of cartoon animals that return millions of dollars in licensing revenues to their owners—United Artists in the case of the panther.

"It's an explosion," said William Dennis, general manager of merchandising and licensing at the film company. "The increased revenues are coming from two sources—new licensees plus accelerated efforts and introduction of new products by existing ones."

The panther's success as a merchandising symbol came slowly. He first appeared in the United Artists film "The Pink Panther" in 1964. Today about 60 domestic companies and 175 overseas own licenses to exploit the panther and his sidekick, Inspector Clouseau. They pay anywhere from $5,000 to $50,000 for the license itself, plus at least 6 percent of the revenues they derive from sales of Panther products.

"What's happening is that the Pink Panther is taking on a life of its own," said Mr. Dennis. "He's growing faster than Mickey Mouse or Snoopy, but no doubt they still have higher incomes."

"The Pink Panther has an image associated with affluence," said Donald Van Polt, an owner of Saddleman Inc., a sportswear specialty house. "His image portrays the Rolls-Royce of characters." Saddleman will soon introduce pink-and-white orlon sweaters embroidered with foot-tall panthers. They will sell for $30 in resort boutiques and sporting goods stores.

Next? United Artists and a group of businessmen are discussing a fast-food chain using the panther symbol. It would be called Le Pink Panther Croissanteries.

"Heir to Mickey Mouse?" *New York Times*, 1 March 1981, p. F-19. © 1981 by the New York Times Company. Reprinted by permission.

ness. U-Haul later opened a gleaming company-owned facility with new equipment a few blocks away from the original dealer. This competition put the independently owned firm out of business.

Generic Products

As retail prices continue to rise, consumers look for new ways to save money. One such avenue that became popular in the late 1970s and early 1980s was the sale of generic products. Starting from nearly zero in 1977, generics grabbed 5 percent of the $200 billion grocery market by 1981.[4] A **generic product** does not carry a brand name. Instead it is a no-frill, low-cost product that simply has the name of the type of merchandise on the box: Laundry Soap, Paper Napkins, Corn Flakes, and so on.

Despite their popularity, there are still fewer than 500 generic items available in the consumer markets. However, about one third of the nation's grocery stores now stock generics. The quality of generic products varies from manufacturer to

Natural, expensive and juvenile packaging.

manufacturer. Generally it's somewhat lower than the quality of well-known dealer and manufacturers' brands. Consumers seem to be willing to sacrifice some quality in order to obtain the appreciably lower price of the generics. That generic products are cheaper is mostly due to the absence of advertising and other promotional costs.

Packaging

Often the promotional claims or positioning concepts of well-known brands are reinforced by themes and claims printed on the package itself. Packaging is a big business in the United States, with sales of approximately $50 billion a year. Packaging consumes over half of all U.S. paperboard and glass production.[5] The package and the product are usually viewed as one and the same by customers. Often, seemingly minor changes in packages can make a large difference in sales. The use of silver or gold foil, for example, creates an air of heightened value about a product. The green paper wrapper used by Listerine antiseptic—suggestive of army medic supplies?—identifies and distinguishes it from all other mouthwash products.

Good packaging as a means of promoting sales is not limited to consumer goods. A plant that assembles refrigerators had a policy of buying gasket materials from two suppliers. The purchasing policy was to have equal quantities of the two brands in stock. However the easy-to-dispense features of one gasket package more than doubled its use in the plant. In another case, a manufacturer of metal springs uses cartons with compartments for each spring—a feature that adds as

much as 25 percent to the cost of the product. But industrial buyers are willing to pay the extra cost since the packaging saves labor time otherwise spent in untangling boxes of springs. The springs are also less easily damaged when kept separate than when they're dumped together into a box.

Packaging can also be used as a basis for market segmentation. Different size packages, for example, can appeal variously to heavy users and light users. Today many supermarkets are devoting more shelf space to products for the single-adult family. Cereals come in small, medium, large—and in some cases giant—sizes depending on the number of children within the family. Beer can be bought in small banquet-size containers, half pints, pints, quarts, and even kegs. It's important to remember that in this self-service world the package is the last chance to make a sale at the point of purchase. A well-designed package may complete the sale if the consumer is wavering between two brands. By the same token, an unattractive package may lose a sale that

From *The Wall Street Journal*, by permission of Cartoon Features Syndicate.

TALKING BUSINESS

The toothpaste cap that drops on the bathroom floor or, worse, down the sink. The little aspirin tin that refuses to open when, as instructed, you "press red dots with both thumbs." The breakfast cereal that goes stale because the inner bag tears or won't reseal securely. The last bit of skin lotion or shampoo that's retrievable only by balancing the plastic bottle upside-down for a while.

These are only a few examples of packages that don't always do what you want them to do. They're annoying, result in costly waste and often lead shoppers to switch to another brand. A familiar packaging problem even inspired light verse writer Richard Armour to this lament: "Shake and shake the ketchup bottle, none'll come and then a lot'll."

Companies routinely redesign package graphics, change ad agencies and distribute millions of coupons to sell their products, but changes in "physical packaging" come much slower. As a result, marketers may be overlooking ways to satisfy customers and stay ahead of competitors.

"When you have products that are almost identical, physical packaging could make the difference," says Roy Parcels of Dixon & Parcels, a New York designer. "You don't have to be a major company to get a marketing edge by changing your packaging."

was stimulated through advertising. A study has shown that one third of the consumers presold by advertising switched products when confronted with more attractive packages.[6]

PRODUCT SAFETY

Packaging plays a role in the promotion of product safety. First, warning labels help consumers avoid products that may be potentially hazardous to their health. (Consider the warning found on all packages of cigarettes.) Second, packages that are potentially dangerous are now required by law to be made "childproof." (You've perhaps wrestled with a childproof medicine container in an effort to open it.) Bathroom disinfectants, insecticides, antifreeze, and a variety of other products now have childproof lids. Despite these improvements, over 30,000 Americans are killed every year in accidents involving products, 110,000 are permanently disabled and 20,000 are injured.[7]

Product Liability

The growing public awareness of product safety problems has resulted in a huge increase in the number of product liability lawsuits. For example, the Lubbock Manufacturing Company, which makes tanks for hauling hazardous materials, until 1975 had had only a small number of minor claims, which never exceeded a few thousand dollars. In late 1975 the driver of one of Lubbock's tank trucks, filled with 9000 gallons of liquid propane swerved to avoid hitting the car immediately ahead as he rounded a curve. The tank broke loose, overturned, and slammed into a concrete abutment. The propane gushed out in a fireball that killed 16 people, including the driver, and injured 44 more. A jury ultimately assessed a $50 million judgment against Lubbock.

Manufacturer Defenses A manufacturer or retailer faced with a product liability suit has three basic defenses. First, if a consumer finds

ON THE FIRING LINE

The Consumer Product Safety Commission: A Right to Life?

The birth of the Consumer Product Safety Commission (CPSC), an independent regulatory agency established by Congress in 1973, was greeted with acclaim. It was considered a triumph in the battle to balance consumer rights with the special interests of business and industry. The new arrival on the regulatory scene was assigned four major missions: (1) to protect consumers against "unreasonably" risky products, (2) to help shoppers evaluate product risk, (3) to develop uniform product safety standards, and (4) to investigate causes and means of preventing product-related sickness, injury, and death. Almost from the start, however, the commission's right to life was in question.

Critics view the CPSC's power to ban products from the market and set safety standards as a threat to an already troubled business community. For example, they cite the dire economic effects on 125 small producers when TRIS, a flame-retardant chemical found to cause cancer, was banned. Ironically, TRIS had been developed at the agency's own recommendation, in order to make children's sleepwear safer. "The costs of being completely safe are horrendous," says John A. Howard, a professor at the Columbia Graduate School of Business. In fact, many believe the costs of meeting safer standards and doing the increased paperwork necessary to comply with commission regulations may not only bankrupt numbers of small businesses but may also add considerably to product prices and thus fan inflation. They point out, too, that the bureaucrats on the CPSC payroll are living out of the taxpayer's pocket.

According to its critics, the CPSC's massive task of overseeing approximately 10,000 different kinds of products and about 2.5 million

firms is beyond the capacity of the small underfunded agency. The format prescribed by Congress for the agency's functioning has not only slowed the development of standards to a snaillike pace but has also allowed industry excessive influence in the process. Given the fact that nearly two thirds of all product-related injuries are due to misuse, poor maintenance, or other human errors and thus cannot be prevented by regulation, who needs the CPSC? A free market situation in which business and industry are legally liable for harmful products is the answer, they maintain.

Proponents of the commission disagree. Concerning the problem of cost, they cite a 1968 study indicating that injuries related to consumer products amounted nationwide to $5.5 billion in medical expenses, lost income, and death and disability payments. In contrast, they note, the per item cost of making products reasonably safe is not necessarily excessive—for instance, $3 to $4 for a mattress that a burning cigarette cannot ignite. Furthermore, they argue, the free market does not provide consumers with protection from unreasonable product risk. As one former member of the Federal Trade Commission observed, competition "may sometimes lead to 'shaving' of costs of manufacture involving some sacrifice of safety." Legal liability for dangerous products and the consumer's right to sue are no sure guarantees that products will be made safe. Individuals may eventually manage to force corporations to make monetary compensation for product-related harm and to redesign dangerous products, but actual losses can never be recouped—losses of limbs or even lives.

that a product is defective and continues to use it, the manufacturer is relieved of responsibility. If you buy a new car and several months later receive a letter saying that the car is being recalled, this is considered adequate notification of a product defect. A few years ago Subaru sent out a letter recalling models of its station wagon for repair of a seatbelt mechanism. If, after receiving the letter, you had been injured because of a faulty seatbelt, Subaru wouldn't have been held liable.

A second defense is misuse of the product. A man used a hairdryer in his garage to dry paint on a toy wagon that he had just sprayed. A spark from the dryer ignited the volatile paint fumes that had collected in the closed garage, causing an explosion. The hairdryer manufacturer was sued, but the courts rejected the suit on the grounds that the hairdryer was being misused.

Yet another defense is if the product isn't defective in the first place. Nevertheless, lawsuits may arise in such instances. A Michigan woman tried to reach into her locked car through a side-vent window to get her ignition key. She struck her eye on the sharp point of the vent window, putting it out. A jury held the window wasn't defective and that its design was adequate for normal use.

SUMMARY

A broad definition of product includes any want-satisfying good or service as well as its perceived tangible and intangible attributes and benefits. A new product can be defined as a good or service that provides a significant increase in consumer satisfaction and that has no direct substitute. Marketers must be careful in deciding whether to position their product as a new one or simply as an improvement over an existing one.

The two broad general categories of products are consumer goods and industrial goods. Consumer goods—goods and services bought and used by the ultimate buyer—can be classed as convenience goods, shopping goods, or specialty goods, depending on how much effort consumers are willing to exert to get them. Industrial goods are bought by organizations for use in making other goods or for rendering a service in the operation of a business or institution. These goods include six major categories: (1) installations, (2) accessory items, (3) raw materials, (4) component parts and materials, (5) services, and (6) supplies.

To succeed, most firms must continue to put out new products. But new-product development can be risky; many new products fail: they don't meet management's expectations. Steps in the new-product development process are (1) opportunity exploration, (2) screening, (3) developing a preliminary profit plan, (4) creating a marketing mix, (5) test marketing, and (6) market introduction.

After a product reaches the marketplace, it enters the product life cycle. This cycle typically has four stages: (1) introduction, (2) growth, (3) maturity, and (4) decline and death. Not all products go through every stage, and the length of time products stay in a stage can vary dramatically. Products do not necessarily go from maturity to decline; repositioning can create a new growth phase. Profits usually are small in the introductory phase, reach a peak at the end of the growth phase, and then decline.

Products usually are given brand names. *Brand* is a broad term identifying a product or service by word, name, symbol, design, or a combination of these things. Organizations use brands to identify their products and services and to distinguish them from all others. Brand identification can lead to brand loyalty, which often allows the firm to charge higher prices and maintain market share. Branding helps consumers to simplify shopping decisions by enabling them to identify products so that they can continue to buy the ones they like while avoiding those they do not like. Brand identification can be extended to include new products through the use of family branding. Some brands are manufacturers', or national brands; others are dealer, or private, brands. Generic products carry no brand at all.

Often the promotional claims or positioning concepts of well-known brands are reinforced by themes and claims on the package itself. Packaging can promote sales and serve as a basis for market segmentation. It also plays a role in the promotion of product safety through inclusion of warning labels and "childproofing."

Growing public awareness of safety problems has resulted in a huge increase in product liability suits. Manufacturers' defenses against such suits are (1) the consumer's knowing a product is defective and continuing to use it anyway, (2) the consumer's misusing the product, and (3) the product's not being defective in the first place.

KEY TERMS

accessories
brand
component parts and
  materials
consumer goods
convenience goods

dealer brands
decline stage
family branding
generic product
growth stage
industrial goods
installations
introductory stage
manufacturers'
   brands
maturity stage
national brands
opportunity
   exploration
preliminary profit
   plan
private brands
product
product life cycle
raw materials
repositioning
services
shopping goods
specialty goods
supplies
test marketing
trademark

REVIEW QUESTIONS

1. What are the principal attributes that are used in defining a "product"?
2. What are the three basic classifications of consumer goods, and how do they differ from each other?
3. Describe the five forms of industrial goods.
4. What are the main elements of the new product development process?
5. Describe the key characteristics of each of the four elements of the product life cycle.
6. Explain how packaging can help define a target market.
7. What are the manufacturer's defenses in a product liability suit?

DISCUSSION QUESTIONS

1. Explain why the concept of "product" cannot be discussed or defined in purely physical terms.

2. What would you consider to be the product attributes for: a McDonald's hamburger, your income tax return prepared by H & R Block, a set of Craftsman screwdrivers from Sears, a box of cornflakes.
3. Name at least one new product in each of the following areas that in the last ten years has reached importance: automobile tires, food preparation, medical diagnosis, banking.
4. Under what circumstances would a manufacturer of jeans market the product as: a convenience good, a shopping good, a specialty good.
5. Dick Storinger, the owner of Oakton Pharmacy, needed a new typewriter in order to type prescription labels. He went to Harvey's Office Supplies and after trying out a few decided on a new Smith-Corona electric portable, the same model his daughter bought for her school work. Did Dick buy a consumer good or industrial good? Explain.
6. Is it necessary that all new products go through all phases of the new product development process? Explain.
7. Why is it impossible to describe the product life cycle in exact time periods?
8. Name three types of product for which the brand is very important. Also name three kinds of product for which you would never consider investing money to develop brand identity.
9. Which of the following items do you feel could have good consumer acceptance as a generic product: automobile tires, ice cream, staples, scientific calculator, running shoes, panty hose, gasoline, men's briefs. Explain.
10. Consider the case of Lubbock Manufacturing Co. (p. 293). Do you feel the firm should engineer its tank to prevent a recurrence of the accident?

CASE: FROM LEVI'S TO THE CLASSIC LOOK

Everybody knows of Levi's, a household word in the clothing industry for many years, actually dating back to 1853, when Levi Strauss set up a dry goods store in San Francisco and sold pants to minors. Levi's have been synonymous with bluejeans over the decades. As for jeans, their fortunes took a big upsurge in the 1970s, when it seemed that almost everyone was wearing them.

Realizing that not only do jeans sometimes fade but that the basic bluejean market was likely to fade, the aggressive marketeers at Levi Strauss expanded its line to include many new products—shoes, shirts, corduroy pants, athletic gear, and "action suits." The action suit was a polyester stretch suit that neatly filled the gap between the informal jean and the informal suit. It was quite popular and succeeded in capturing another segment of the market.

Then the daring young men at Levi Strauss decided to launch out into another market clientele—the young sophisticated executive who dressed a little more formally but with a touch of informality, all in good taste. This new look was identified as the "Levi Tailored Classics"—a line of suits, sport coats, and slacks that would add a touch of distinction to the young executive. This Levi Tailored Classic was not made of cotton or polyester but *wool* with fine tailoring.

As the date for launching the new look approached, the company began to run into problems. With its quality and tailoring, the Tailored Classic cost more than the competition. Retailers resisted it, feeling that even the prosperous young executive would not pay the higher price for this new look. Even the salesmen balked at the prices of the new line, and sales lagged in the test markets being probed. However the company pushed ahead with advertising and promotion, trying desperately to change the image of Levi Strauss in an entirely new market.

Finally, this most daring attempt to open a new market foundered. Levi Strauss retreated to analyze its failure and to determine upon a new strategy for this bold venture.

1. Why do you think this new venture for Levi Strauss Company was unsuccessful?
2. What kinds of stores should be selected to carry this new Tailored Classic Line?
3. In light of the high risk in this venture what action would you take in trying to ensure the success of this product?

CASE: CLEANING UP—AN EASY PROFIT

"Starting up a cleaning business would be a cinch!" At least that's what a resourceful college student said as he told a friend how tired he was of working for other people. So he was going to try his hand as an *entrepreneur* with a cleaning and maintenance business.

"All you have to do is hire a night crew—go out and solicit some clients—and you're in business." That's how he explained it to another friend who happened to be a marketing major. The friend hit him with: "Have you decided what your target market will be, your marketing mix, your media selection—?" More questions were forthcoming from his commercial law professor, who asked him about licenses, personal liability, and bonding of employees. This was to say nothing of all the questions thrown at him by his accounting buddies, who carried on about start-up costs, cash flow, income tax returns, etc.

Anyway, this brave young man started the business and hired some people to work nights (this was an all-night business). When last observed, he was heading for the bank—but whether to make a deposit, float a loan, or declare bankruptcy, remained to be seen.

1. What do you think the chances of success are for this daring entrepreneur?
2. What problems is he likely to encounter when launching his business?
3. What marketing questions should he ask himself, and what information does he really need in order to launch and maintain a successful cleaning business?

CHAPTER 13

PROMOTION STRATEGIES

After studying this chapter you should be able to:

1 Explain how promotion strategy is used in the marketing mix.
2 Describe the elements of the promotion mix.
3 Relate the use of promotion to the product life cycle.
4 Evaluate the extent of effectiveness as well as the limitations of advertising.
5 Define different types of advertising.
6 Classify the specific uses of different advertising media.
7 Explain the role of selling in promotional strategy.
8 Discuss the various applications of sales promotion.

Charmin's Mr. Whipple; Palmolive's Madge the Manicurist; Folger's Mrs. Olson; the Pillsbury Dough Boy; Kellogg's Tony the Tiger; and Old Lonely, the Maytag repairman—they all have something in common besides their talent for interrupting your favorite programs—a talent developed over many years. But that's precisely it: they've been around so long, they've far exceeded the life expectancy of characters in TV commercials. They've buried many of their lesser-known cousins and have even outlived many of the shows on whose backs they rode over the years.

Take Old Lonely, for example. The melancholy repairman will soon have been around for 20 years—and with nothing to do: all those Maytag washers out there, and not a one to fix! They're too dependable! Oh, well. . . . But before Old Lonely came slouching across the screen and into our consciousness, Maytag's ad campaign was using forgettable testimonials: real customers raving about the product, not surprisingly—and not too interestingly.

In advertising, the big thing is to stand out from the crowd. Old Lonely is a brand identifier: he may not stand up straight, but he stands out. Maytag estimates that more than $20 million has gone into the Old Lonely ads. It's paid off: Old Lonely scores twice as high as other commercials in consumer awareness surveys, according to Maytag.

Although Mr. Lonely is viewed as a nice guy, a character doesn't have to be liked to be long-lived. Mr. Whipple, the supermarket owner, has been hassling shoppers about squeezing the Charmin since 1964 and is sometimes regarded negatively by TV viewers. But, Mr. Whipple still lives . . . somewhere . . . because he has made Procter & Gamble's Charmin the top-selling toilet paper by giving it an identity as a soft tissue. Other brands touted by less irksome commercials have little or no image.

In the world of TV commercials, "It's better to be noticed and disliked," says an ad executive who can't stand Mr. Whipple, "than not to be noticed at all."

THE COMMUNICATIONS PROCESS

Although Mr. Whipple isn't always much liked, he *does* communicate to the target market the idea that Charmin is a quality, soft bathroom tissue. The essence of promotion of any kind is **communication**. Communication is the process by which messages—such as attitudes, emotions, and feelings—are exchanged between people through a common system of symbols.

Communication basically takes two forms: explicit and implicit. **Explicit communication** is the use of language as a symbol to establish common understandings between people. **Implicit communication** involves "intuitive interpretation" of symbols or gestures. A friend may look at you and say, "Really nice job!" This is explicit communication. But nonverbal actions can vary the meaning. If your friend is smiling when those words are spoken, you should be pleased by what you hear. On the other hand, if your friend is frowning, your reaction will be something else. Nonverbal communication—such as a frown, a gesture with the body or hand, shuffling one's feet, or looking down at the ground—often tells more about the true meaning of what's being said than the words themselves.

Promotion

The broad goals of promotion are either to reinforce existing behavior or to modify it. In either case, this is done by stimulating the demand for goods or services. Much of Coca-Cola's advertising is designed to reinforce existing behavior — that is, to keep millions of people drinking Coca-Cola. When you see an advertisement for Orville Reddenbacher's Gourmet Popcorn, the goal is usually behavior modification. The advertiser is trying to get you to purchase Orville Reddenbacher rather than the most popular brand, Jolly Time. For years, Schlitz beer has been faced with a steady decline in market share. Expensive promotional time was bought for use during the 1981 Super Bowl showing a taste test between Schlitz and Miller beer drinkers. The goal, of course, was to achieve behavior modification — getting Miller drinkers to try Schlitz beer.

Promotional Tasks

All promotions are designed either to inform, to persuade, or to remind target audiences about the firm's goods and services (see Figure 13.1). A product that's in an early stage of its life cycle, such as Warner Two-Way Cable Television, gets heavy **informative advertising** to explain its merits to potential buyers. People won't buy something until they know why and how it's going to benefit them. Can you imagine what the advertising was like for the original microwave ovens? The manufacturer had to explain that this was a new product that cooked without direct heat. Social critics are usually agreed that truly informative advertising is useful to the consumer: it helps him or her to make better, more informed choices.

Consumer activists often decry the second task of promotion, which is persuasion. They assert that **persuasive advertising** causes us to buy many things that we don't really need and thus stimulates demand artificially. Yet persuasion is the most common form of promotion and is a valid means of accomplishing promotional goals. Think, for example, of the clothing and stereo sales ads in your local college newspaper. Persuasive advertising is the primary promotional task when the product enters the growth stage of the product life cycle. This is because other similar products have entered the market and there's increased competition.

When a good or service enters the maturity phase of the life cycle — such as Hertz Rent-a-Car, Salem Cigarettes, and Bell Telephone — the firm uses large amounts of **reminder advertising.** The purpose of reminder advertising is to maintain

FIGURE 13.1
The promotional tasks: informative, persuasive, and reminder ads.

"top-of-the-mind" awareness. Bell Telephone, for example, reminds you to use long distance. Hertz reminds you that you don't have to run through airports—Hertz will have a car already reserved and waiting for you.

The Promotional Mix

Several forms of promotion can be used to achieve behavior modification or reinforcement of existing behavior. The unique combination of advertising, personal selling, sales promotion, and public relations (publicity) is called the **promotional mix.** How much advertising rather than personal selling, for example, a firm uses in its promotional mix depends on several factors (see Figure 13.2). Usually, advertising and personal selling are the primary components of a promotional mix. These are supplemented by sales promotion and public relations. The final blend and its proportions are all related to:

1. the nature of the product,
2. market characteristics, and
3. available funds.

The Nature of the Product Many industrial goods, such as large machines, buildings, and custom-made items, require personal interaction between the seller and the prospective buyer. Plans must be drawn and details worked out. Personal selling, then, usually plays a large role in the promotional mix of industrial goods. Advertising is used to create a positive image for the industrial product and to locate potential buyers. The Cessna Citation Aircraft, designed to serve as a company plane, is advertised is *Business Week,* the *Wall Street Journal*, and other business publications. Every ad contains either a coupon or a phone number for a prospective buyer to use in finding out more about the Citation. This form of advertising, besides projecting a favorable image, helps locate potential buyers. When a prospect has been located, personal selling takes over. Each Citation, for example, has a custom-fitted interior to meet the unique needs of its corporate owner. In addition, a number of accessories can be added to vary the plane's capabilities.

In contrast to industrial products, consumer goods are usually made for the mass market. It would be silly for a salesperson to travel from the home office to a mountain cabin to discuss and

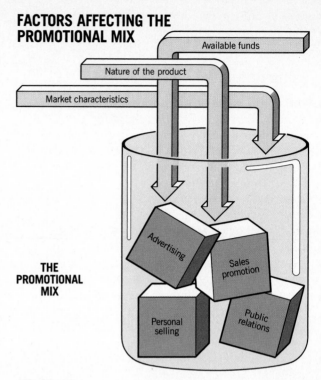

FACTORS AFFECTING THE PROMOTIONAL MIX

FIGURE 13.2

explain various alternatives and then go back and have a deodorant custom-blended for one person. Most consumer goods are rather inexpensive and could not support the cost of salespeople's time and effort. So advertising is the major element in the promotional blend for most consumer goods. Advertising is used to create brand awareness and to persuade the consumer to buy one product rather than another. Personal selling is used for some specialty goods such as jewelry, television sets, furniture, and appliances. Salespersons are rarely used in retail stores to sell such convenience goods as combs, cereals, pencils, and paint. However, they're used in the channel of distribution by manufacturers to sell large quantities of goods to wholesalers and retailers.

Market Characteristics A promotional blend of more advertising and sales promotion, and less personal selling, will be used when there are (1) widely scattered potential customers with (2) good product knowledge, and (3) a large target audience of brand-loyal customers. But with custom-made industrial goods, personal selling is required regardless of market characteristics.

If merchandise must be stocked on shelves—as are bread, milk, and other convenience goods—

then personal selling and delivery to the retailer are necessary. Retailers often depend on the company salesperson to stock the shelves. And many manufacturers prefer to deliver and stock their own merchandise to ensure an attractive display and adequate shelf space for their wares. At the same time, many of these convenience goods will be backed with large advertising campaigns aimed directly at the consumer.

Available Funds   The amount of available promotional funds is often the most important factor determining the nature of the promotional blend. A manufacturer without sufficient capital may have to rely heavily on free publicity to develop awareness among potential buyers. Although a company recognizes the need to hire a sales force, it may not be able to justify the expense. Even smaller, well-capitalized manufacturers and retailers may not be able to afford the advertising rates of such major publications as *Business*

Week, *Time*, and *McCall's*. Sometimes the small organization can effectively reach its target audience through direct mail when other alternatives are not economically feasible. The success of direct mail depends on whether target consumers are easily identifiable and if mailing lists are available.

THE IMPORTANCE OF ADVERTISING

The dollars spent on advertising by major corporations can be mind-boggling, as shown in Table 13.1. Procter & Gamble, for example, spent over $615 million in 1979 on advertising. That is an average of over $1.6 million a day, seven days a week. Of the top ten advertisers, all are consumer goods organizations; two are retailers (Sears and K mart); one is a regulated monopoly (AT&T); and the rest are manufacturers. This outlay by Procter & Gamble is even more amazing since it

TABLE 13–1

America's Top 50 Advertisers, 1980

1	Procter & Gamble Co.	$649.6[a]	26	Heublein Inc.	$170.0
2	Sears, Roebuck & Co.	599.6	27	RCA Corp.	164.3
3	General Foods Corp.	410.0	28	Unilever U.S. Inc.	158.3
4	Philip Morris Inc.	364.6	29	General Electric Co.	156.2
5	K mart Corp.	319.3	30	Seagram Co. Ltd.	152.0
6	General Motors Corp.	316.0	31	Gillette Co.	151.0
7	R. J. Reynolds Industries	298.5	32	Chrysler Corp.	150.3
8	Ford Motor Co.	280.0	33	Nabisco Inc.	150.0
9	American Telephone & Telegraph	259.2	34	Consolidated Foods Corp.	149.2
10	Warner-Lambert Co.	235.2	35	Norton Simon Inc.	149.0
11	Gulf & Western Industries	233.8	36	International Telephone & Telegraph Corp.	143.0
12	PepsiCo Inc.	233.4	37	Time Inc.	141.9
13	Colgate-Palmolive Co.	225.0	38	Richardson-Vicks	134.0
14	McDonald's Corp.	207.0	39	Loews Corp.	132.8
15	Ralston Purina Co.	206.8	40	CBS Inc.	132.4
16	American Home Products	197.0	41	Chesebrough-Pond's	128.3
17	Bristol-Myers Co.	196.3	42	Dart & Kraft	128.3
18	Mobil Corp.	194.8	43	American Cyanamid Co.	125.0
19	Esmark Inc.	189.9	44	Pillsbury Co.	124.0
20	Coca-Cola Co.	184.2	45	J. C. Penney Co.	108.0
21	Anheuser-Busch	181.3	46	Revlon Inc.	105.4
22	Johnson & Johnson	177.0	47	Schering-Plough Corp.	100.0
23	Beatrice Foods Co.	175.0	48	Quaker Oats Co.	99.7
24	U.S. Government	173.0	49	DuPont	98.3
25	General Mills	171.1	50	B.A.T. Industries Ltd.	95.8

SOURCE: "Fast Facts," *Advertising Age*, 10 September 1981, Vol. 52, No. 38, p. 1. Reprinted with permission from the 10 September 1981 issue of Advertising Age. Copyright 1981 by Crain Communications Inc.
[a]Total ad dollars in millions.

doesn't include the costs of personal selling, sales promotions, and public relations. The figure is larger than the budgets of all but a handful of U.S. cities and exceeds the budget revenues of many of the world's nations.

What Can Advertising Do?

Why do firms like Procter & Gamble and General Foods spend so much money on advertising? What can advertising really do? With something like 1700 newspapers, 6000 AM-FM radio stations, 3000 magazines, 600 TV stations, thousands of billboards, and billions of pieces of direct mail, advertising must have some impact on us.

Advertising can be influential where people don't hold strong attitudes or opinions. It can't, however, change strongly held values. Advertising will never convince men and women to shave their heads or most Americans to eat dog meat. These things would be contrary to strongly held cultural values. For advertising to be effective, it must reflect and reinforce *existing values*. An effective ad might convince a man to buy Haggar slacks rather than Levi's dress pants. However a Haggar ad for a man's kilt would be ineffective. Why? Kilts are not worn by men in our society. Many, in fact, would associate them with dresses, and for a male to wear a dress in our society is taboo.

There's no doubt that good advertising can *alter* demand for a product or service. But it's highly unlikely that advertising can *manage* demand. Economist John Kenneth Galbraith has claimed that big advertisers can manage demand. In other words, a firm could increase demand for its offerings by spending large sums of money for advertising. If this were wholly true, though, the huge sales slump experienced by General Motors, Ford, and Chrysler during the early 1980s would never have occurred.

FIGURE 13.3
Institutional ad.

Types of Advertising

If a company is trying to improve its image, it engages in what's called **institutional advertising.** This is the attempt to create a favorable picture of the company, its ideals, services, role in community affairs, and the like. While some institutional advertising is aimed at the company's target audience, other institutional advertising may be directed to stockholders or simply the public at large. Institutional advertising usually does not seek action on the part of the audience. Instead, it tries to create a more favorable image for the company in the minds of consumers (see Figure 13.3).

One aspect of institutional advertising that has become heated in recent years is known as **advocacy advertising.** The idea is to take a stand on certain issues and proposals of a controversial social or economic nature. Advocacy advertising has sometimes been called *grass roots lobbying.* Many energy companies, for example, have used advocacy advertising to try and influence public opinion concerning government regulation of the petroleum industry. An example of an advocacy ad is shown in Figure 13.4. Estimates are that in 1979 Mobil Corporation spent over $4 million on advocacy advertising. One result was that 90 percent of government, congressional, and other prominent leaders read a Mobil advocacy ad.[1]

A good image often strengthens the effectiveness of product advertising. When Phillips Petroleum runs an institutional ad that discusses the funding of the U.S. Olympics swimming team by Phillips, the company hopes this positive image will carry over to ads for Phillips Trop-Arctic motor oil. Product advertising is the advertising of a specific good or service. When used to stimulate demand for a new good or service, it's referred to as **pioneering advertising.** In 1980 when Clairol brought out Sonic Scrub, a sonic denture cleaner, and promoted the product through mass advertising, the company was engaging in pioneer advertising.

Another type of product advertising, which became popular during the 1970s, is called **comparative advertising.** In comparative advertising two or more specific products, mentioned by name, are compared in terms of product/service features. A commercial that compares Dial deodorant with Sure deodorant is a comparative ad. Many American automobile ads now compare features of domestic cars with those of the im-

FIGURE 13.4
Advocacy ad.

U.S. STEEL TAKES A STAND ON CLEAN AIR.

"An updated Clean Air Act can mean healthy air, healthy industry and more jobs."

The Clean Air Act urgently needs revision. The Act should be updated to encourage rather than inhibit industrial growth without impairing continued environmental progress. No one can deny it takes a healthy, productive economy to assure the success of any program concerned with the quality of American life.

The enactment of legislation currently before the Congress, the Luken Amendments, will revise the Clean Air Act in a manner which recognizes both the need to protect public health and the need for economic recovery. This bill, introduced by Congressman Luken (D-Ohio) and co-sponsored on introduction by Congressmen Madigan (R-Ill.), Traxler (D-Mich.), Hillis (R-Ind.), Dingell (D-Mich.) and Broyhill (R-NC), has strong bipartisan support because of its balanced approach to this complex problem.

The steel industry is proud of its own record on clean air. At United States Steel, nearly $1 billion worth of air pollution control facilities have resulted in the control of over 95% of our air emissions. There has been substantial improvement of air quality in areas where our plants are located.

But studies show that some aspects of the Clean Air Act are delaying industrial development and the construction of badly needed energy facilities without significant air quality benefits. The stifling of industrial growth cannot provide a stable basis for a healthy economy or a healthy environment. Many jobs—both present and future—are at stake. That's why we believe a properly updated Clean Air Act is in the best interest of all Americans.

We join many concerned Americans in urging Congress to enact the Luken Amendments which update and streamline the Clean Air Act to help create a healthy balance between economic and environmental goals.

That's what we think. What do you think?

United States Steel
600 Grant Street, Pittsburgh, PA. 15230

USS

For a cold with these multiple symptoms: nasal and sinus congestion, runny nose, aches, pains, fever and coughs, COMTREX gives you more kinds of relief than Contac, Dristan, Bayer, Anacin, Extra-Strength Tylenol or Dristan Nasal Spray.
And COMTREX has a non-aspirin formula for gentle, effective pain and fever relief. COMTREX Multi-Symptom Cold Reliever, available in tablets, liquid and capsules.

COMTREX®
Multi-Symptom Cold Reliever

Comparative advertising has grown in popularity. (Reproduced by permission of Bristol-Myers Company © 1981)

ports. Typically, the American cars are promoted as cheaper yet with equivalent features. Coca-Cola and Pepsi-Cola continue to be one of the most vivid examples of comparative advertising during the 1980s.

Is comparative advertising the most effective way to advertise a product? Again, the answer depends on the quality of the advertising. The chairman of Kenyon and Eckard Advertising, one of America's largest agencies, puts it this way: "We employ the comparison advertising technique only in significant product attribute areas where we have a demonstrable superiority and where the major competitive brand is perceived more positively than our brand."[2]

Advertising Media

Both product and institutional ads are found in all the major media. But which of the media is/are "just right" for a given advertiser? Cost is an obvious consideration. And just as important as cost is the audience reached by the media. When examined across media, costs are usually placed on a "CPM" basis—the *cost per thousand* members of an audience. Assume that Hewlett-Pack-

ard wanted to advertise its scientific handheld calculators and had decided that the best approach was through a magazine that would reach the target audience. In 1981 the CPMs for one black-and-white page in major science magazines were as follows:

Magazine	CPM
Science '81	$11.67
Discover	17.48
Science Digest	18.00
Scientific American	18.21

Source credibility—the trust that the consumer places in the media—is also important in media selection. Radio, for example, tends to have lower credibility than major retail catalogs. Independent TV stations often have lower credibility than major network stations.

The reproduction capability of a given medium is also important. Some print media, such as newspapers, don't produce four-color pictures as well as high-quality, slick-paper magazines do. In addition, the advertiser must be aware of lead times required. Magazines often need final advertising copy and layout several months before go-

TALKING BUSINESS

According to conventional wisdom, advertisers should avoid humor in their commercial messages. However, the success of many TV commercials that depend on humor to get their messages across seems to refute this advice.

Harry Wayne McMahan, a commercial consultant, lists some examples of advertising campaigns that are both humorous and successful; here are a few of them:

Chiffon margarine. The "mother nature" spoof was credited with making Chiffon No. 1.

Culligan water conditioners. A series of 10-second and 20-second cartoons and the line, "Hey, Culligan Man," made this service nationally known. . . .

Dr Pepper. Its humor-coated "spectaculars," geared to a younger generation, have upped sales 15% a year for the last six years.

Hawaiian Punch. A mad little 20-second spot won out over a pool of five (the others were shelved!), and ran for three years. Whereupon RJR Foods bought it and took the little West Coast product national (with the same little "Punchy" character that still runs today, 15 years later!).

Jell-O. Here is a parity product that was second to Royal gelatin. When Jell-O decided to stage itself as a "fun product" the success began.

The list, according to McMahan, goes on and on: Miller Lite; 9-Lives, featuring Morris the cat; Polaroid; Vlasic pickles; Xerox; and many more.

Quote from Harry Wayne McMahan, "No Joking; Humor Sells!" *Advertising Age*, 29 December 1980, p. 19. Reprinted with permission from the December 29, 1980, issue of Advertising Age. Copyright 1980 by Crain Communications Inc.

ing to press. So the advertiser loses a certain amount of freedom and may be unable to alter the message to meet changing marketing conditions. Local radio ads, however, offer almost unlimited **timing flexibility.** New copy can be written in the morning and heard on the radio within the hour. This is also true of local TV ads.

Still another consideration in selecting media is the **"noise" level.** Noise has a special sense here: it is anything that makes comprehension of the message more difficult. Television almost always requires both audio and visual attention for a promotional message to be fully understood. This dual requirement increases the potential for "noise"—for example, through unequal attention paid to both the audio and the video. Special magazines such as *Flying* and *Plant Engineer* appeal to readers highly interested in the articles.

The advertiser in these magazines is competing with a "high noise level" due to interesting and informative articles. Direct mail usually has the lowest noise level of all media. There is no other advertising, neither is there any element of news or entertainment to compete for readers' attention. (The problem, of course, is to get the recipient to open and read the direct mail piece!)

Finally, some media have very long life-spans, while others are short. Printed media, such as specialty magazines, usually have a long life-span. Many people keep *National Geographic* for a number of years. Newspapers, in contrast, have a very short life-span—typically, one day. And radio and TV commercials have a very short life-span—perhaps the shortest. Once the commercial is seen or heard, its life-span has been completed. Many magazines further their life-span because of a high pass-along rate. This means that more than one person will read the publication. *Time*, *Newsweek*, and *Reader's Digest* have pass-along rates of three or better.

Newspapers Newspapers are America's most popular advertising medium. About half of all American adults read a newspaper every day. One problem with newspaper advertising is, again, the high "noise" level. An ad not only competes with other ads but also with news and entertainment stories as well. But newspapers are an excellent medium when a company is trying to sell a product within a local market. In fact, local advertising makes up the great bulk of newspaper promotions.

Automobiles, transportation, tobacco, and food are the most popular newspaper advertising categories. Also, business reply cards and four-color advertising inserts are becoming common forms of newspaper advertising. About 15 billion advertising pieces are inserted in the newspapers each year. And most newspaper ads can be prepared quickly, at a reasonable cost, with a short lead time.

Magazines Magazines exist for almost every interest group and market segment imaginable. There are magazines for railroad hobbyists, golfing, surfing, skateboarding, roller-skating, archery, bird dogs, sewing, home decorating, firefighting equipment, and hundreds of other subjects. Magazines have a higher cost per thousand readers than do newspapers. But they'll often have a lower cost per potential customer because magazines appeal to special audiences. A manufacturer of a home composter will find most newspapers have lower cost per thousand than does the magazine *Organic Gardening*. Yet almost every reader of *Organic Gardening* will have some interest in a composter, whereas only four or five out of a thousand newspaper readers could be expected to share this interest.

Some magazines help create a positive image for the products advertised in them. When a relatively unknown manufacturer of a food processor advertises in *Gourmet* magazine, the image of the processor may be enhanced in the minds of the readers because of the positive image of *Gourmet*. *Parents* and *Good Housekeeping* magazines help their advertisers project a quality image by letting them use the *Good Housekeeping* and *Parents* "Seal of Approval."

Our readers track celestial bodies.

Our readers love imported cars. They have a passion for performance and an eye for the engineering that produces it. 49% of them own at least one imported car. 57% of their car purchases are new-car buys. With an average household income of $37,500 they can buy just about any one they want.

All reasons why SCIENTIFIC AMERICAN carried more imported-car ad pages last year than any other consumer monthly.

Our readers do their thinking at the very highest levels and they do their living there as well.

Media must also advertise to attract advertisers.

Radio There are more than 7000 radio stations in the United States, ranging from all news to hard rock, and everything in between. Every corner of the country can be reached by at least some radio station. There are four major radio networks—CBS, NBC, Mutual, and ABC—that offer both news and entertainment programs. Radio stations can reach select geographic audiences (Asbury Park's WJLK reaches people living in Asbury Park and the north Jersey shore). Every station positions itself in the marketplace, and this enables advertisers to reach specific target markets. Such products as Clearasil are advertised on hard rock stations. Mercedes-Benz and Cadillac automobiles are usually promoted on "beautiful music" FM stations. Some stations depend on DJs and other radio personalities to build a loyal audience. Popular radio personalities can be effective in selling to local consumers.

Television Television offers advertisers huge audiences, low cost-per-contact, and an absence of simultaneous competition from other stories and ads. Television also has many of the advantages of personal selling. For example, a product such as a G.E. dishwasher can be demonstrated on TV. People spend more time with TV than any other medium. Of the total population aged 18+, people watch television an average of 3 hours and 57 minutes a day, listen to radio 3 hours and 27 minutes a day, and spend an average of 27 minutes a day with a magazine.[3] It's estimated that upon completion of high school, a student will have spent 11,500 hours watching TV. Adding time spent at the movies and in listening to records, tapes, and radio, 20,000 hours will have been spent with the media—nearly twice the time spent in class.

The growth market for television during the 1980s is pay-TV, cable, and over-the-air (satellite) transmission. In addition to carrying major network programs, cable operators are originating a number of programs of their own. These include local sports, news, cultural, and even educational programming. Many cable operators also feature services such as Home Box Office, which offers first-run movies and other special entertainment features.

Although many TV program markets can be segmented demographically by lifestyle, the products advertised must usually be of broad appeal, such as food, cars, and appliances.

Direct Mail   As an alternative to network TV and other media, many advertisers are relying more heavily on direct mail. Of course the efficiency of direct mail depends primarily on the quality of the mailing list. If the list does not represent users of the product, the best promotional message in the world can be a dismal failure. Mailing lists are available from brokers for about $50 for 1000 names. Moreover these lists can be broken down in hundreds of different ways. For example, if you want to reach veterinarians in New York City with earnings over $75,000 a year, such a list is available. An effective direct mail piece usually brings a response rate of about 1 or 2 percent. Anything lower than 1 percent is considered a failure.

Outdoor Advertising   Outdoor advertising is an inexpensive medium that offers a large amount of flexibility. A billboard will reach a fairly specific geographic market, but there is little or no audience selectivity. In addition, billboards obviously cannot have a long-selling message. They contain few words, and they are often just barely glimpsed.

Each billboard is seen by a wide variety of income and age groups as well as lifestyles. Advertisers usually base their billboard locations on census tract data. (A census tract is a small, permanent, relatively homogeneous area used in collecting census data.) They assume that people who are most likely to see a certain billboard will have demographic characteristics similar to those of the tract in which the billboard is located. In some cases, billboards are an effective means to reach ethnic and minority groups (see Figure 13.5).

Advertising Agencies

Many companies rely on advertising agencies to create and monitor their campaigns. A full-service agency furnishes five services: creative services, media services, research, merchandising advice, and campaign design and planning (see Figure 13.6). The creative department develops promotional themes and messages, writes copy, designs layouts, takes pictures, and draws illustrations. Media service groups select the media mix and scheduling.

Many advertising agencies also perform market research studies for their clients. Depending on the agency-client relationship, the agency may be involved in new-product development, image

"The program, 'Alternative Energy Sources' will not be shown tonight, thanks to a grant from a major oil company."

From *The Wall Street Journal,* by permission of Cartoon Features Syndicate.

FIGURE 13.5

Billboard ad aimed at a minority market.

measurement, package studies, and positioning research. In addition, agencies conduct research on advertising themes, copy, desirability of specific models, and media effectiveness. Some agencies go beyond the advertising function and provide merchandising advice. They will develop contests, point-of-sale displays, premium offers, and brochures for a client's sales force.

Almost every advertising agency works with its clients in campaign design and planning. In some cases campaign planning is placed completely in the hands of the agency. Other firms prefer to do much of the work in-house and rely on the agency for media scheduling and postcampaign evaluation (usually, however, left to marketing research).

Agency Switching As we noted, measuring the effectiveness of advertising is difficult at best. Also, the advertiser continually demands creative freshness and originality. Advertisers can be rather fickle in their relationship with agencies. In the early 1980s more than 500 large accounts (each over $500,000) changed agencies per year. In 1981 a record $1.4 billion in advertising billings changed hands. Airlines led the seeming stampede, the reason given being deregulation of the industry, bringing with it new competition and a number of changes in management. As one agency chairman put it, "When there are management changes, there are agency changes." Airlines switching included Pan Am, American, Continental, Braniff, Southwest, Northwest, Re-

FIGURE 13.6

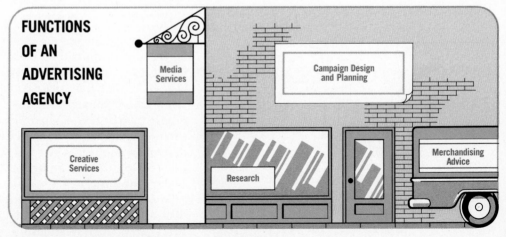

Source: Reprinted by permission of Television Bureau of Advertising.

PERSPECTIVE ON SMALL BUSINESS

When David Featherly took over as president of Sport Shacks Inc. last year, he knew the company needed to reach a wider variety of advertising prospects. Sport Shacks, a White Bear Lake, Minn., franchiser of sporting goods stores, had relied on newspaper advertising to generate prospective franchisees since it was founded in 1974. The strategy worked well, particularly when the ad campaign focused on business publications and the financial sections of newspapers in major markets. But the law of diminishing returns had set in. That's when Featherly decided to explore the possibility of advertising on cable television.

"We were looking for 1 person in 10,000," says Paul Zak, the media specialist who worked with Martin Lambert Advertising in Chicago to put together a cable advertising program for Featherly. "We were looking for people who watch sports—not just the passive sports observer but the hard-core sports junkie. We also needed someone who could afford a $35,000 to $50,000 investment."

Sport Shacks invested $8,000 in a 10-day test on the Entertainment and Sports Programming Network (ESPN), a 24-hour sports cable network which now has over 8.5 million subscribers. A commercial featuring Bobby Douglass, former football and baseball star, was produced at a cost of $2,700. It was aired 14 times, and a toll-free number was used to record responses, as well as the date and time of the call.

Featherly set a goal of 100 responses for the first week of the test. He got 165 the first night. By the end of the 10-day test, there had been 593 calls, of which 86 were judged to be "very qualified" leads. In contrast, newspaper advertising had produced an average of 100 qualified prospects every six months.

The most telling argument for cable, however, came when it was pitted directly against network television. In a Salt Lake City test, Martin Lambert aired the same Sport Shacks commercial on both the sports cable channel and ABC's "Wide World of Sports." The cable commercial pulled more responses.

More and more small businesses like Featherly's are exploring the potential of advertising on cable TV and reaping its benefits. Like a rack of specialty magazines, cable TV's many channels give the advertiser a wide choice of narrowly focused programming at a cost roughly comparable to spot radio announcements.

SOURCE: Reprinted with permission of *INC.* Magazine. Excerpted from Joanne Kelleher, "Cable Goes to Work," *INC.*, May 1981, pp. 168, 171. Copyright © 1981 by INC. Publishing Company, 38 Commercial Wharf, Boston, MA 02110.

public, Scandinavian, French, U.T.A., Jet America, Golden Gate, Pacific Southwest, and Midway. Leading the pack was Eastern Airlines, with its prize $54,000,000 account—a sizable portion of the $268,200,000 that was switched in the transportation industry alone in 1981.[4]

In fact every year there are several accounts worth over $25 million apiece that change hands. This can be disastrous to the earnings and profitability of the agencies, which usually receive a 15 percent commission of total billing. Sometimes, however, a change of agencies is justified because promotional goals haven't been achieved. In other cases advertisers change for emotional rather than rational reasons. Also, it must be pointed out that thousands of accounts, both large and small, remain with a single agency for many years.

When a major advertiser is thinking about a change of advertising agencies, it will invite a number of agencies to make sales presentations. These presentations must be carefully thought out and well designed because millions of dollars are resting on the outcome. The persons who make agency presentations are professional salespeople.

PERSONAL SELLING AND SALES MANAGEMENT

In a sense, every person in the business organization performs a selling role. Managers must continually sell their ideas to other managers and their subordinates. The president must sell his or her strategy for running the company to the board of directors.

The Professional Salesperson

Not everyone who is engaged in the selling profession is a professional salesperson. Nor is a professional salesperson simply someone who makes a lot of money. Instead a **professional salesperson** has three primary characteristics: (1) complete product knowledge, (2) creativity, and (3) knowledge of the customer's needs. The professional salesperson understands every aspect of the product line. And he or she knows how to fit the product or service creatively to meet the needs of the potential buyer. For example, an Alcoa salesperson was able to illustrate to General Motors executives how the substitution of aluminum for steel in many automobile parts could greatly improve miles-per-gallon performance.

In addition to creativity and product knowledge, a professional salesperson thoroughly understands the needs of the potential buyer. He or she also has a pleasant personality, is familiar with a wide variety of subjects and issues, and manages his or her time well. The professional salesperson is enthusiastic about his or her job, and the sales presentation is based on benefits of the product rather than on the hardware itself. Potential buyers are more interested in what a machine will do for a company than in its appearance.

The Selling Process

Another characteristic of the professional salesperson is a thorough knowledge of the selling process (see Figure 13.7). The selling process consists of the approach, presentation and demonstration, handling objections, closing the sale, and follow-up. Although selling styles vary from company to company, the basic selling process always remains the same.

Prospecting   Before a salesperson approaches a potential buyer, he or she should first engage in prospecting. **Prospecting** is the process of identifying those firms and persons most likely to buy the seller's offerings. Not everyone is equally likely to be a prospect—that is, to buy. A salesperson for Bell Telephone who is seeking to sell the Dimension Three business communication switchboard first examines the number of existing business lines and other telephone equipment. If there are too few lines, the prospect is not likely to trade up to Dimension Three. On the other hand, if there are too many lines, a larger telephone switching system would be necessary.

The Approach   After the persons or businesses most likely to purchase have been identified, the approach is made. An important element of the approach is making certain that the decision maker is identified. When a presentation is made to the wrong person—that is, one without authority to buy—considerable time and energy may be wasted.

A good approach includes the salesperson's telling the prospect why he or she wants an appointment and setting a specific date and time. Most importantly, the approach should attempt to generate excitement and enthusiasm in anticipation

FIGURE 13.7

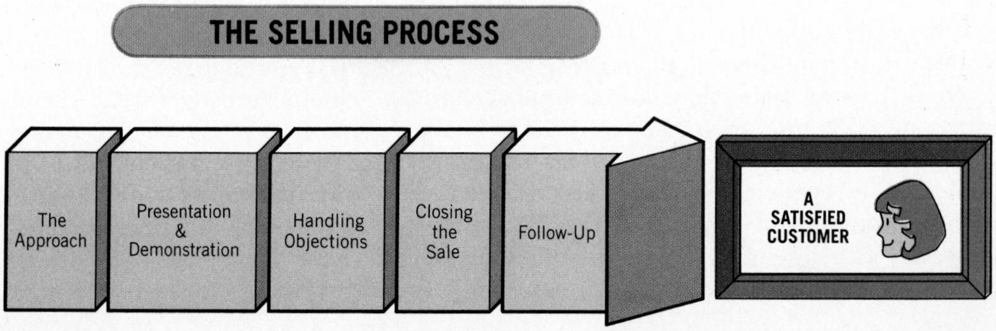

THE SELLING PROCESS

The Approach — Presentation & Demonstration — Handling Objections — Closing the Sale — Follow-Up — A SATISFIED CUSTOMER

of the salesperson's visit. For example, the salesperson might say, "I think I can cut your shipping and delivery time by an average of two days."

Presentation and Demonstration   After the approach is made, the salesperson then makes his or her presentation. This can run the gamut from *fully automated* to completely unstructured. A fully automated presentation usually involves movies, slides, or a filmstrip. The salesperson sets up the equipment and waits until the presentation is over to answer questions and take the order. At the other extreme is the completely unstructured presentation with no format whatever.

A memorized or **"canned" presentation** is sometimes used to sell products to final consumers, but rarely is it used in industrial sales. Instead, the industrial salesperson often employs an organized presentation. Xerox salespersons calling on a prospective business client use an outline or checklist for the presentation, but they have complete authority to alter the presentation as needed. This approach gives a personal touch to the presentation yet ensures that all important points are covered.

Handling Objections   Almost every sales presentation, whether highly structured or completely unstructured, will be met with some objection. Rarely does the customer simply say, "I'll buy it," without asking any question or voicing any concern. The professional salesperson's preferred way of handling objections is first to try to *anticipate* objections. A Xerox salesperson, selling the 9500 Duplicator, might well run into concern over price. In response to this, he or she might say: "Yes, it *is* more expensive than some other copier/duplicators; but with the 9500 you get offset-quality copies at far below what offset printing equipment would cost. It also turns out 120 copies a minute, and it can give two-sided copies—which reduces paper cost! Moreover the 9500 can automatically sort copies into almost limitless numbers of sets."

Closing the Sale   After the salesperson has satisfied the prospect's objections, it is time to close the sale. Even old pros sometimes have difficulty in closing a sale because this is the moment of truth. Perhaps the easiest way to close a sale would be simply to ask for it: "Mr. Jones, would you like to purchase this equipment?" Another technique is to proceed as though the deal were

concluded: "Mr. Jones, we'll have this equipment in and working for you in two weeks!" (If Mr. Jones doesn't object, you can assume that the sale has been made.)

Follow-up   The salesperson's job isn't completed when a sale is made. In effect, it's really just beginning. The salesperson must turn in the order properly and promptly. While this may sound relatively easy, an order for a complicated piece of industrial equipment can involve several hundred pages of detail. These must be carefully checked to ensure that what's custom manufactured is what was actually ordered. After the product has been delivered to the customer, the salesperson must follow up with a routine visit to make sure that the customer is satisfied. A follow-up call may also present the opportunity of making an additional sale. At the least, it will build goodwill for the salesperson's company and perhaps provide an opportunity for future business. One sale is often not worth the time and expense involved. Repeat sales over many years is the usual goal.

SALES PROMOTION AND PUBLIC RELATIONS

The effectiveness of personal selling can be increased through sales promotion and public relations. Sales promotion attempts to stimulate immediate purchase action or modify a person's attitude about a company or product or service.

Samples, Premiums, and Coupons

The major forms that sales promotion takes are premiums, samples, and coupons. We receive over 1200 coupons per household per year and redeem only about 4 percent of them.[5] Sixty three percent of all adult females redeem coupons, whereas only 35 percent of men do.[6] A coupon is really a controlled price reduction designed to stimulate immediate sales. In contrast, a premium tries to add value to a good or service by offering a gift or prize at minimal or no cost in order to get a customer to buy an item. When Hills Bros. brought out a line of flavored coffees, it offered buyers of the new coffee a half gallon of free ice cream. The consumer had only to buy the ice cream and send a refund slip to Hills Bros. The goal was to get people to try the flavored coffees

FIGURE 13.8
Hubert Clock.

such as Bavarian Mint, Toffee, Mocha, Almond Mocha, and Cafe Mocha. The promotion also advised that by mixing ice cream in the flavored coffees, the consumer could create an exotic beverage or dessert.

Chicago's Harris Bank has been highly successful in using Hubert, the stuffed lion, to pull in new savings accounts. Hubert, according to an advertising executive, is an excellent vehicle for Harris Bank because ". . . it is soft-selling, warm, institutional love that reaches right into your kids."[7] The success of Hubert led to a Hubert wake-up alarm clock (see Figure 13.8). The alarm clock was credited with making many new customers for Harris Bank and with projecting a warm, friendly image to existing account customers.

Sampling isn't as popular in America as it once was, because of its high cost. Although food processors may offer free samples from time to time in grocery stores, the day of free door-to-door sampling has almost passed. Instead manufacturers are using **co-op sampling,** in which several different products are delivered in the same container at the same time. Another trend is offering a "trial size" container as a **salable sample.** Retail-

Trade shows are an important way to make sales.

ON THE FIRING LINE

Public Utilities—What Right to Advertise?

In the interests of efficiency, state governments grant monopoly status to the corporations that supply electricity and gas. To safeguard consumers, however, regulatory agencies oversee these monopolies. One major responsibility of these regulatory agencies is to set the rates consumers pay for service by the public utilities. They examine the utilities' operating expenses and financial status to determine when it is necessary to raise rates. Federal law directs these agencies to examine advertising expenses and, if appropriate, to prohibit utilities from charging ratepayers (consumers) for the cost of promotional or political advertising.

Promotional advertising, as defined by the Public Utilities Regulatory Policies Act of 1978 (PURPA), encourages the use of service provided (gas or electricity). The promotional effort may be direct in its approach or indirect. An example of indirect promotion is urging consumers to install equipment and/or appliances that increase use. The purpose of *political advertising*, as defined by PURPA, is to influence public opinion regarding legislation, public administration, elections, or controversial issues of public importance.

Recently the extent to which state regulatory agencies may restrict these two types of advertising has become a source of controversy. At issue are two central problems: (1) the right of "commercial" free speech and (2) the monopoly status of the utilities.

Commercial Free Speech

Commercial free speech is a relatively young concept embracing the right of business and industry to speak out. It includes both political and promotional speech. Some would deny corporations the right to publicize their political views. These people fear that big business is too well moneyed and too powerful. They believe that through massive advertising campaigns it can adversely affect the course of the country's future. They point, for example, to the promotion of nuclear power plants. The Three

Mile Island accident, they say, clearly demonstrated the danger of such plants. The serious structural defects discovered in the Diablo Canyon plant in California in 1981 served only to underscore the ominous message of Three Mile Island. The problem of safe, long-term storage of the radioactive waste these plants produce has not been resolved either. Yet electric utilities are pushing hard for more and more nuclear plants. Consumer protection groups that are aware of the danger cannot possibly hope to raise funds enough to counter the massive and convincing ad campaigns of these huge corporations, according to this view.

Monopoly Status

Utilities are monopolies. And with monopolies, there is always a danger that prices charged will be higher than necessary—higher than a normal competitive market would permit. Whether political or promotional advertising by utilities is appropriate should hinge in part on how it is financed. When ratepayers do not benefit directly from utilities' advertising, they should not have to pay for it. Advertising that provides consumers with information on how to reduce utility bills offers a direct benefit, for example. Advertising encouraging consumers to buy electric appliances does not. Ads that offer no direct benefit, many feel, should be paid for entirely out of shareholders' profits. The cost, they say, should not be considered part of the essential operating expenses used as a basis for setting rates.

Public utilities' advertising will no doubt remain a matter of controversy for some time. For the present, though, some state regulatory commissions have found a way to sidestep the issue. They do not analyze each utility's every ad for its effect on ratepayers. Instead, they simply set a percentage limit on the amount of operating funds to be used each year for goodwill, informational, and institutional advertising—usually a small fraction of 1 percent.

L'eggs, one of the most successful point-of-purchase displays in recent years.

ers like salable samples because they earn a small profit. They also give the manufacturer a return on its costs. However in order to charge even a nominal price (such as 25¢) for a two-ounce sample-size container of Jergens hand lotion, there must be at least some interest in the product.

Trade Shows and Conventions

Trade shows and conventions are an important part of sales promotion. There are approximately 6000 such meetings held each year in the United States covering almost every type of product. These meetings give manufacturers and wholesalers the chance to display their wares to a large audience of potential buyers at relatively low cost. About 80 million people attend trade shows and conventions each year.

Point-of-Purchase Advertising

Point-of-purchase advertising (POP) is promotional material (displays, printed material, etc.) placed inside retail stores (or windows), usually

TALKING BUSINESS

To increase sales of the Ottawa Citizen, promotion manager Ben Babelowsky organized a gold rush contest. Before it was over, the newspaper was selling 1,500 more copies a day, and thousands of treasure hunters had picked over practically every corner of the Canadian capital.

Eight one-ounce gold wafers with a retail value of more than $4,000 were hidden in one spot. Each day the Citizen published a drawing with clues, false leads and instructions that "the gold is in a public place and it isn't necessary to dig or damage anything to find it."

The treasure hunters looked just about everywhere. Even the window sills of Prime Minister Pierre Trudeau's office building weren't immune. A hunter who was convinced the gold was in a bird's nest checked every tree along the city's seven-mile canal.

Jailkeepers had to call police to clear the district jail of treasure hunters after a newspaper drawing indicated the prison might be a hiding place. Police headquarters also was a target. Before searchers were cleared from there, they had pulled insulation from the crevices of the building's exterior walls.

No one was seriously hurt in the hunt, but there were some close calls. A gold hunter forced his way into the car of a young woman shouting "you've got the gold and I want it." He was detained for a psychiatric examination. Police arrested another hunter for drunkenness after he threatened anyone approaching a section of the park that he had staked out.

The police worried that the whole thing might get out of hand, but they tried to be cooperative. After all, some of them were looking for the gold, too.

Promotion manager Babelowsky says gold hunters tried calling him late at night to wheedle further clues. "I've found the gold," said an early-morning caller. "Guess where I am?"

Unlike a treasure hunt in Britain, set off by the best-selling book Masquerade, the Citizen contest already has a winner. In fact, it has two. An engineering student found one cache of wafers in a canal wall pipe after only four clues. So the Citizen ran the contest again. An employee at the government mint found the second set of wafers three weeks later, tied to a tree near a cross-country snow trail.

Now Mr. Babelowsky is working on a new campaign for the Citizen, which regularly sells 180,000 papers on weekdays and 225,000 on Saturdays. He thinks the gold hunt is one of his best promotions ever, but he wouldn't recommend it in a big city like New York. "There'd be blood in the streets," he says.

next to the advertiser's goods—that is, where they are bought by consumers. It's an attempt to stimulate purchase at the point of sale. Point-of-purchase displays can be very effective, sometimes doubling or tripling a company's sales. The biggest task is getting retailers to use the manufacturer's POP material. Retailers have only a limited amount of space. The POP materials they receive are often bulky and unassembled, so there may be little incentive to erect the display. A large

FIGURE 13.9

The press kit introducing Kodak's new disc camera and photography system contains photos, descriptive literature and diagrams in a large binder.

retailer receives hundreds of POP displays a year, from which it must choose those that will most increase profits.

Public Relations

Public relations, like sales promotion, can be a vital link in the promotional mix. **Public relations** is any communication or activity that tries to increase the prestige or create a favorable public image of a product, an individual, or an organization. It's largely concerned with **publicity**—information about a product, person, or company—and is featured by the media. Publicity is free, since the media are not paid. An organization may, however, bear the expense of paying a public relations firm to generate publicity.

Publicity can be good or bad. Naturally a firm's public relations department tries to create as much good publicity as possible. For this reason one of its main tools is the press release—a formal announcement of some "newsworthy" occasion or event. It may be the start of a new program, the introduction of a new product, or the opening of a new plant (see Figure 13.9).

Public relations complements the role of advertising by building product or service credibility. Since publicity isn't paid for directly by a company, it doesn't carry sponsor bias. A news story about the reliability of a Chevrolet pickup in the automobile section of the *New York Times* would probably be more believable to a potential buyer

than would an ordinary ad that stressed the same reliability. A third party (in this case the *New York Times*) has the effect of validating the story and removes the sponsor identification. This despite the probability that the automobile editor of the *Times* got his information from a press release put out by Chevrolet.

SUMMARY

The essence of promotion is communication. Communication takes two forms: *explicit*, which involves the use of language, and *implicit*, which involves intuitive interpretation of symbols or gestures.

The broad goals of promotion are to reinforce existing behavior or to modify it in order to stimulate the demand for the promoter's goods or services. All promotions are designed to inform, to persuade, or to remind target audiences about the firm's goods and services. Which of these functions is chosen depends in part on the product's stage in the product life cycle.

The unique combination of advertising, personal selling, sales promotion, and public relations (publicity) used to reinforce or modify behavior is called the promotional mix. Usually, advertising and personal selling are its primary components. The final blend and its proportions are related to (1) the nature of the product, (2) market characteristics, and (3) available funds.

Advertising can be influential where people do not hold strong attitudes or opinions. It cannot change strongly held values; rather, it must reflect and reinforce existing values. Good advertising can alter demand for a product or service, but it is unlikely that it can manage demand.

Institutional advertising attempts not to sell specific products but to promote a favorable image of the company, its ideals, services, role in community affairs, and the like. Advocacy advertising is a controversial type of institutional advertising in which the firm takes a public stand on issues of a social or economic nature.

Product advertising is the advertising of a specific good or service. When it is used to stimulate demand for a new product, it is called pioneering advertising. Another type, comparative advertising, compares two or more specific products by name in terms of their attributes.

Both product and institutional advertisements are found in all the major media. Which medium is chosen by a particular advertiser depends on cost, market selectivity, source credibility, reproduction capability, timing flexibility, noise level, and life-span. Types of media include newspapers (the most popular US advertising medium), magazines, radio, television (the medium with which people spend the most time), direct mail, and outdoor advertising.

Many companies rely on advertising agencies to create and monitor their campaigns. A full-service advertising agency furnishes five services: creative services, media services, research, merchandising advice, and advertising planning. It is not uncommon for advertisers to change agencies, sometimes for emotional rather than rational reasons.

Personal selling is another major component of the promotional mix. An effective professional salesperson has three primary characteristics—complete product knowledge, creativity, and knowledge of the customer's needs. To make a sale, the salesperson follows the selling process, which consists of the approach, the presentation and demonstration, the handling of objections, the closing of the sale, and the follow-up.

Sales promotion attempts to stimulate immediate purchase action or to modify a person's attitude about a company or product. A major form of sales promotion is the distribution of premiums, samples, and coupons. Trade shows and conventions are an important aspect of sales promotion, as is point-of-purchase advertising.

Public relations involves any communication or activity that attempts to enhance the prestige, or create a favorable public image, of a product, individual, or organization. It is largely concerned with publicity featured by the media.

KEY TERMS

advocacy advertising
"canned" presentation
communication
comparative
　advertising
co-op sampling
explicit
　communication
implicit
　communication
informative
　advertising
institutional advertising
"noise" level
persuasive advertising
pioneering
　advertising
point-of-purchase
　advertising (POP)
professional
　salesperson
promotional mix
prospecting
public relations
publicity
reminder advertising
salable sample
source credibility
timing flexibility

REVIEW QUESTIONS

1. Explain the two basic forms of communication.
2. What are the three primary tasks of promotion strategy? Can they all be applied at the same time?
3. Find two advertisements for consumer advertising that you would consider to be informative advertising, persuasive advertising, and reminder advertising.
4. How do the different elements of the promotion mix relate to one another?
5. Can advertising be used effectively to get people to switch brands of toothpaste? How about hospitals? Explain.
6. Every year during the Christmas–New Year season Seagrams, a major manufacturer and importer of whiskey, gin, vodka, wine, and other alcoholic beverages, runs an ad with the major line, "When you're having one more for the road, make it coffee." How would you describe this form of advertising?
7. If you were a marketer and wanted the flexibility to change your ads quickly, which media would you consider?
8. What are the major advertising advantages

and disadvantages of: radio, newspaper, TV, consumer magazine, billboards.

9. Explain the difference between professional and nonprofessional salespersons.

DISCUSSION QUESTIONS

1. Explain how different factors in the marketing situation affect the promotional blend.
2. If you were a medium-sized manufacturer of specialized machinery, what are some of the important issues you would have to consider in developing a promotion strategy? Where would you probably place the most emphasis?
3. For each of the stages of the product life cycle describe how the promotional blend would change for a new consumer product for which you expected wide use.
4. Should public utilities, such as electric companies, use advertising to influence people's thinking about nuclear energy? Explain.
5. Do you think it is unfair for a marketer to run ads naming competitors' products and suggesting that they are inferior? Explain.
6. Direct mail is considered the most expensive advertising medium. Why would a marketer want to use it?
7. "Advertising sells!" Do you agree? Explain.
8. In recent years there has been a marked increase in the use of premiums by banks. Since all banks generally offer identical services, what do you feel they hope to gain by the premium offer?
9. Review the expenditures of the top 50 advertisers as reported by *Advertising Age.* Do you think some companies spend too much on advertising? Why?

CASE: WOULD YOU BELIEVE FISH FARMS?

Ask any farmer across the country, the early 1980s have been a disaster. But something is happening in the Mississippi Delta. Suddenly a new product is born, and with it farmer entrepreneurs are giving birth to a new industry—catfish farming! For miles one can see symmetrical ponds, twenty acres each, filled with catfish. In one recent year alone, the number of catfish acreage jumped more than 50% and the number of catfish farmers doubled. To make some comparisons, catfish yield about $400 profit an acre as opposed to $80 an acre for cotton; but expenses are high. Still, the industry is booming, and so far the market has been able to absorb most of the catfish produced. The question is: can the market be expanded to absorb the potential productivity of this burgeoning industry? The market so far has been confined to the South, where people have eaten catfish for years; but it still has a rather unglamorous image in the West, the Midwest, and the Northeast. Will the Yankees bite on the bait of this new industry? Or does the lowly catfish carry a stigma that cannot be changed with advertising and promotional appeal?

Changes in the eating habits of Americans have been taking place with astounding results. In the 1960s Americans were eating almost 150 pounds of red meat annually. By the late 1970s this amount had diminished somewhat; meanwhile the market for poultry and fish was increasing in leaps and bounds, with people eating fish by as much as 11 to 13 pounds annually—a 17% hike over the 1960s. And that increase was mainly in fresh and frozen fish, not a canned or cured fish like tuna.

This new crop of catfish has raised great hopes for people of the Mississippi Delta. Is it possible that the people of America could catch "Catfish Fever"?

1. What kind of marketing strategy could be employed to make catfish a popular food for the American dinner table?
2. How could the media be used to improve the image of the catfish, turning this typical southern fish food into a popular treat along with the hotdog, hamburger, and country fried chicken?

CASE: APPLES— NOT FOR EATING

The very mention of the name Apple Computer brings a gleam to the eyes of most beholders. Two young dropouts from college started a little business in a garage and parlayed it to a booming financial venture soon to join the ranks of the Fortune "500." They pooled their talents and produced the attractive plastic box with a keyboard that became the prototype for the personal computer, which they vowed to put into every home in America. From the outset this team of geniuses, later joined by a venture capitalist who put in $250,000 of his own money to become an equal partner, launched a successful enterprise that seemed to do everything right through the stages of Apple I, II, and III—sales surging from $2.7 million in 1977 to $200 million in 1980, capturing 23% of the $2.2 billion worldwide market in personal computers.

The big Apple has now come to a critical juncture in its short history. It has a substantial share (23%) of the market in personal computers, but it must fight off an army of aggressive competitors—Radio Shack, Xerox, IBM, and all the rest.

Apple can hold its own by maintaining the innovative edge with research and development, but it will need more than that to meet such giants as Xerox, whose competing personal computer has been jokingly named by its engineers "the worm"—because they would like to see it eat up the Apple.

1. How successful do you think the promotional strategy for this new personal computer has been?
2. What marketing strategy do you think would be suitable in helping the Apple maintain its market share and go on to compete successfully in the market?

CHAPTER 14

DISTRIBUTION
MANAGEMENT

After studying this chapter you should be able to:

1 Explain the importance of distribution management to a marketer.
2 Describe how different channels are used for consumer goods and industrial goods and services.
3 Justify the cost of distribution for long channels.
4 Decide when a marketer would use intensive, selective or exclusive distribution.
5 Discuss the functions of wholesalers and their relationships to marketers and other middlemen.
6 Distinguish between wholesalers, manufacturer's agents and brokers.
7 Contrast different kinds of retail operations.
8 Explain the goals of physical distribution.
9 Discuss the advantages and disadvantages of different forms of transportation in the movement of goods.

No-frill, cash-and-carry retail outlets are no longer news; today one hasn't far to go for the savings they offer. But until lately, the retailer hasn't had any such place to turn to. Now all that is changing, as cash-and-carry wholesale centers crop up throughout the U.S. Among them, few are going as all-out as Makro Self-Service Wholesale Corp.

Enter any of Makro's burgeoning centers—200,000 sq. ft. of shelves and aisles on a 16-acre site where 35,000 stock items in 45 major product categories beckon. Setting Makro further apart is its combination of food and nonfood offerings. Fully 75% of a retailer's needs in nonfood items can be found, and when it comes to foods, "We have everything," says general manager Mark Van Stekelenberg.

Not surprisingly, then, customers come in the thousands from grocery stores, restaurants, catering firms, convenience shops, associations, clubs, and independent retail stores. The concentration of numerous supply lines reduces their shopping trips to less than a fourth of the time it used to take them—and reduces cost too. But those in the nonfood sector—general merchandisers, fashion retailers, specialty and small store owners—also flock to Makro; perhaps not for their main products, but for additional supplies, such as cleaning materials and stationery. Says Van Stekelenberg, "Most small offices without a contract cleaner go to the store around the corner and pay the full price for cleaning materials. If you compare apples with apples, we are cheaper for the small business."

Suppliers—and these include most national brands—are kept happy too. They like this efficient way of approaching a market with 35,000 to 40,000 wholesale customers per distribution center without having to service it with a sales force and distribution system. That alone means a 20%-25% savings for them.

And of course Makro's happy seeing customers keep coming back, making up the $100 million annual sales volume that each center averages. Self-service greatly cuts down on manpower and reduces overhead; self-transportation eliminates the need for delivery personnel; and Makro's cash-only rule means no need for a credit department. A largely computerized billing and inventory control system further reduces staffing requirements and stores a giant information base on customers. "We ask them what they like and what they dislike," says Van Stekelenberg. "That's a strong weapon, and it's one of the reasons we've been so successful."

Based on "Dutch Firm Expands No-Frills Idea to U.S. Self-Service Wholesale Centers," *Marketing News*, 2 October 1981, pp. 1, 11, published by the American Marketing Association.

DISTRIBUTION CHANNELS

The Makro story illustrates the several dimensions of distribution. To focus on just one: manufacturers liked the "efficient way of approaching a market with 35,000 to 40,000 wholesale customers per distribution center. . . ." Distribution can limit, or sometimes enhance, the sales of a quality product. For example, as distribution costs increase, the retail price of the product must also increase. Remember that a quality product must be available at the right place and at the right time and must be sold at the right price.

Channels Defined

A **channel of distribution** is the sequence of marketing institutions (such as wholesalers and retailers) through which a product passes on its way from the producer to the final user. The distribution system focuses on the process of physical transfer of goods and services and on their ownership in each stage of the marketing sequence. Since channel institutions — such as manufacturers, wholesalers, and retailers — tend to form buying and selling relations among themselves, they can be viewed as a system. Some of the common channels of distribution are shown in Figure 14.1. The members of those channels are described in Table 14.1.

Basic Channel Systems

There are some institutions that help move products from the producer to the consumer, or ultimate user, but that aren't actual channel members. A channel member performs the **negotiating function.** This is the buying and selling of the merchandise and the transference of title of ownership from one institution to another. Organizations that don't perform negotiating functions aren't true members of the channel. A bank, for example, extends credit to members of channels of distribution. However, it's not directly involved in the buying, selling, negotiating, and ownership of the merchandise as it moves from one institution to another. So a bank isn't a mem-

FIGURE 14.1

BASIC DISTRIBUTION CHANNELS

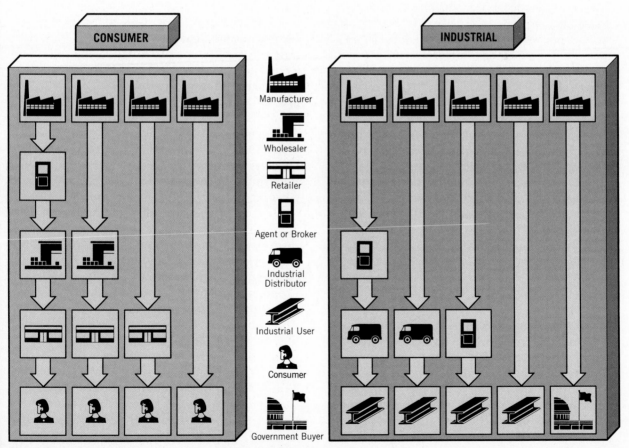

Source: Carl McDaniel, *Marketing*, rev. ed. (New York: Harper & Row, 1982), p. 369. Copyright © 1982 by Carl McDaniel. Reprinted by permission.

TABLE 14–1
Common Channel Members

Manufacturers Manufacturers convert raw materials to finished products.

Agents and Brokers Agents and brokers do not take title to the merchandise and rarely handle the merchandise itself. A broker brings the buyer and seller together. Brokers are common in markets where it is hard to find potential buyers and sellers. An agent is a representative of a manufacturer or wholesaler. Agents do not take title and have little, if any, authority over the terms of a sale.

Industrial Distributors These are independent wholesaler organizations that purchase related product lines from many manufacturers and sell to industrial users. An industrial distributor often maintains a sales force to call on account executives, make deliveries, extend credit, and provide information.

Industrial Users Industrial users buy products for internal use or for further processing as part of the production process. They include manufacturers, utilities, airlines, railroads, and service institutions such as hotels, hospitals, and schools.

Government Buyers State, local, and federal government purchasing agents buy virtually every good and service imaginable. Because of the quantities and specifications involved, these transactions are usually between the government and the manufacturer. Manufacturers are invited to submit proposals and prices for specific goods and services.

Wholesalers Wholesalers sell finished goods to institutions, e.g. schools and hospitals. They also sell products to retailers and manufacturers. The historical function of a wholesaler has been to purchase from the manufacturer and sell to the retailer.

Retailers Retailers sell to the ultimate consumer and industrial end users.

Consumers Consumers are the end users of consumer goods.

SOURCE: Carl McDaniel, *Marketing*, rev. ed. (New York: Harper & Row, 1982), p. 368. Copyright © 1982 by Carl McDaniel. Reprinted by permission.

ber of the channel. A market research company will help determine which retail stores are most likely to sell the highest volume of the product. However it too isn't a member of the channel of distribution. It's simply a helping agent. Banks and market research companies aid in creating an efficient flow of merchandise from the producer to the consumer.

Consumer Channels Figure 14.1 shows there are two basic types of channels of distribution: one for consumer goods and the other for industrial products. The "long" channels of distribution such as manufacturer → agent/broker → industrial distributor → industrial user are most likely to be used for less expensive products. Why? Take a pocket comb, for example. It might sell for 30¢, and one fast-food store might order 50 pocket combs a month. Let us assume that the Ace Comb Company has a manufacturing plant in New York City. If it shipped boxes of 50 combs to each of 2000 fast-food stores in California, the cost would be huge. This would be a very uneconomical way of getting the combs to the final consumer.

Instead Ace Comb might sell 50,000 combs in one economical shipment to a wholesaler in Los Angeles. The wholesaler would then distribute the combs to fast-food stores all over California. The long channel of distribution here is a much more economical way to get the products to the retailer than shipping in small lots directly from the manufacturer. Adding a middleman does not always increase costs. The cost of shipping a box of 50 combs from New York to a single Seven-Eleven in San Diego would probably be greater than the cost of manufacturing.

Industrial Channels Industrial-good channels are usually much shorter than consumer-good channels. This is because the price of most industrial goods is much greater than consumer-good prices. A can of corn sold at a Safeway supermarket costs much less than a new Clark forklift truck sold through the manufacturer. As we saw in Chapter 12, many industrial items are custom-made for the end user. The manufacturer must have direct contact with the buyer in order to meet special requests and needs. For example, Dana Corporation's subsidiary Wichita Clutch Company sells huge clutches for Marion Machine Company stripping shovels, used for coal and other forms of strip-mining. Wichita's engineers work with Marion designers to produce clutches to exact specifications.

In addition to large custom-made clutches, Wichita makes a variety of standardized clutches and parts sold through industrial distributors. An **industrial distributor** is somewhat like an industrial department store that serves a particular industry. There are industrial distributors in petroleum, mining, aircraft, and many other industries.

Intensity of Market Coverage

The type of product sold partly determines the intensity of market coverage. Distribution can be thought of in three basic degrees: intensive, selective, and exclusive (see Figure 14.2). Wichita's large custom-made clutches are sold *exclusively* from the factory, while its standardized clutches are widely (*intensively*) distributed and are available "off-the-shelf."

Intensive When a firm strives for **intensive distribution,** it is looking for maximum market coverage. It wants to sell the product in every outlet where there are potential customers. Consumer goods such as ice cream, bread, candy, soft drinks, hardware items, and light bulbs are often distributed intensively. Usually the product is of low cost and is bought frequently by the consumer. This means that a lengthy channel of distribution is necessary. Coca-Cola, for example, is sold in just about every retail store and business imaginable. It can be vended from a machine in the corner of almost any establishment. Can you imagine the cost of one can of Coca-Cola if it were all bottled in Atlanta and then shipped to every single outlet?

Selective **Selective distribution** means that dealers are screened to exclude all but a few out-

Some products are available only in very few locations.

FIGURE 14.2

DEGREES OF MARKET COVERAGE

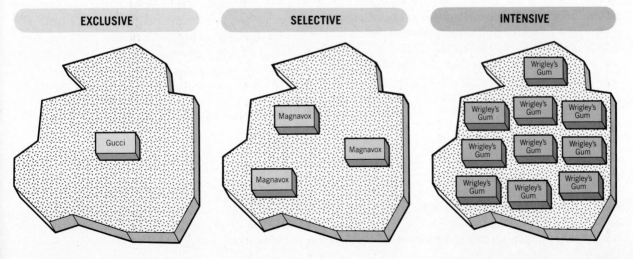

lets in one area (such as a city). Since the number of retailers handling the product is limited, the consumer must be willing to seek out the product and drive (or otherwise travel) to the store to get it. Hunter ceiling fans are distributed selectively. Television sets, stereo components, cars, and well-known brands of clothing like Levi's, Bobbie Brooks, and Wranglers are distributed selectively. Manufacturers use a variety of considerations when choosing dealers for each area. Levi's, for example, might search for retailers that offer high-traffic locations in regional shopping malls. Magnavox would perhaps screen for TV retailers that could offer high-quality customer service. All manufacturers tend to exclude retailers who are poor credit risks or who have a weak or negative image.

Exclusive   When a manufacturer selects one or, at the most, two dealers per area, it's using **exclusive distribution.** Because there's only one retailer, consumers often must drive far to get the product. Therefore only items that are in strong demand by the target audience can be distributed exclusively. If Wrigley's chewing gum were sold in only one drugstore per city, Wrigley would soon be out of business. The same would probably be true if Magnavox had only one retailer per city. However Gucci clothes and accessories, Estée Lauder cosmetics, Rolls-Royce cars, Corum watches, and Bill Blass clothing are distributed exclusively with great success.

WHOLESALING
What Do Wholesalers Do?

Manufacturers who use selective or exclusive distribution normally don't go through wholesalers but instead sell directly to the retailer. On the other hand, firms using intensive distribution often rely on wholesalers. A **wholesaler** is a "middleman" positioned between the manufacturer and the retailer. Wholesalers typically sell finished products to retailers who in turn sell to the final consumer.

Wholesalers also sell to other institutions like manufacturers, schools, and hospitals, who use the product to perform their basic mission. A manufacturer, for example, might buy typewriting paper from Nationwide Papers, a paper wholesaler. A hospital might buy its cleaning sup-

plies from Lagasse Brothers, one of the nation's largest janitorial supplies wholesalers. Sometimes wholesalers sell to manufacturers, who then use the product in the manufacturing process. A small manufacturer of custom boats, for example, may buy batteries from a battery wholesaler. For gauges, switches, and the like it will turn to an electrical wholesaler. And some wholesalers sell to other wholesalers in what then becomes a further step in the distribution process.

About one half of all wholesalers offer financing for their clients. This means that they sell to the retailers on credit and usually expect to be paid within a 60 day period. In contrast, cash-and-carry wholesalers operate just like a retail store. The retailer goes to the wholesaler, selects the merchandise, pays cash, and then transports it to the retail outlet.

Many wholesalers, like the cash-and-carry wholesaler, perform the storage function. That is, they stock merchandise and provide it for the retailer on an as-needed basis. Part of the storage function usually involves **"breaking bulk."** This means that when the wholesaler receives a boxcarload or truckload shipment, it's broken down into smaller, more usable quantities and sold that way to the retailer. If a boxcarload of Chiquita bananas is shipped to St. Louis, there is probably no one grocery store that could sell all of the bananas before some of them spoiled. Instead the bananas are shipped to a produce wholesaler who breaks them down into smaller lots and so can sell them to many grocery stores. It's usually more economical to ship in bulk to a wholesaler, who in turn sells smaller quantities to local merchants.

Because wholesalers usually serve a limited area, they're often located closer to the retailer than is a manufacturer. The retailer can thus get faster delivery and lower costs of goods from the wholesaler than from the manufacturer. A retailer can reduce its inventory if it knows that the wholesaler stands ready to restock the retailer's shelves within a day or less. A lower inventory means that the retailer has less money tied up in inventory. It also means that the risk of loss due to fire and theft is reduced.

Merchant Wholesalers

There are three major categories of wholesalers: merchant wholesalers, manufacturers' sales

Wholesalers often take carload quantities and break the bulk into smaller more usable quantities for shipping to retailers.

branches, and agents and brokers (see Figure 14.3). A **merchant wholesaler** has two major characteristics: (1) it buys manufacturers' products for its own account and resells them to other businesses, and (2) it operates one or more warehouses where it receives merchandise, takes title to it, stores it, and later ships it to the buyer. In contrast to an agent or broker, the merchant wholesaler buys goods for itself rather than for someone else. By taking title to the merchandise, a wholesaler owns it and can dispose of it and set policies for it in any manner the wholesaler sees fit. An agent or broker works for either the manufacturer or for the retailer and has almost no say

FIGURE 14.3

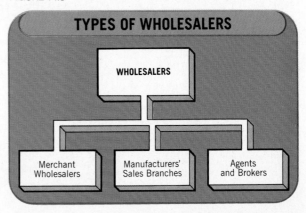

TYPES OF WHOLESALERS

WHOLESALERS

Merchant Wholesalers

Manufacturers' Sales Branches

Agents and Brokers

about delivery dates, price of the product, and the like.

Many merchant wholesalers are also full-service wholesalers. This means that they not only carry stock but they also usually have a sales force to call on customers. In addition they offer credit, make deliveries, advise clients, and service the products they sell. So a full-service wholesaler means just that: it offers a complete line of services to the retail customer.

Manufacturers' Sales Branches

A second major category of wholesalers is manufacturers' sales branches. A **manufacturer's sales branch** is similar to a full-service merchant wholesaler, because it performs many of the same functions. But a manufacturer's sales branch is managed, owned, and completely controlled by a manufacturer. Merchant wholesalers account for about half of all wholesale sales, while manufacturers' sales branches make up an additional 40 percent.

Manufacturers' sales branches are the most rapidly growing form of wholesaling. One of the main reasons for their popularity is that they enable the manufacturer to maintain very close control over its inventory. This has been particularly true in the automotive, transportation equipment, and forest products industries. Some manufacturers have set up sales branches because of dissatisfaction with merchant wholesalers. The wholesalers may have been unwilling to adequately promote the manufacturer's products to retail customers, or they may have carried inadequate inventories. As a result, many manufacturers in the hardware, drug, and clothing industries have created their own sales branches.

Agents and Brokers

Manufacturers' sales branches have also replaced some agents and brokers whose work is to represent manufacturers, wholesalers, and retailers. Because brokers and agents do not take title to goods, they have very little control over the sales policies of the merchandise. Agents and brokers receive a commission based on sales volume. Usually they perform very few functions, and so their rate of commission is quite low. They account for slightly less than 10 percent of all wholesale sales.

Manufacturers' Representatives   A **manufacturer's representative,** also called *manufacturer's agent*, represents one or more noncompeting manufacturers of goods bought by one type of trade. A manufacturer's representative is a salesperson who functions as an independent agent rather than as a salaried employee of the company. He or she takes neither title nor possession of the merchandise. If a manufacturer's representative makes a sale, he or she receives a commission. If the agent doesn't make a sale, there's no payment made by the manufacturer. Manufacturers' representatives are found in a variety of industries, including electronics, packaging machinery, clothing, food service equipment, hardware, automotive hand tools, furniture, building products, toys, and housewares.

Brokers   Like the manufacturer's representative, the **broker** doesn't take title to the merchandise. Instead he or she brings a buyer and seller together. Brokers are found in markets where there isn't adequate market information for a buyer and seller to find one another easily. Usually a broker will locate a potential buyer or seller for the other party and then let the two work out a sales contract. The broker doesn't get involved in setting the price, quantity, quality, or any other aspect of the sale. Brokers are common in real estate, agriculture, insurance, stocks, commodities, and mortgages.

RETAILING

Wholesalers serve many of the 28 million Americans who are engaged in some type of retail business. Of these, almost 16 million work in service retail concerns such as barber shops, lawyers' offices, and amusement parks. Most retailers are in small business. But less than 10 percent of all retail businesses account for over half of all retail sales and employ about 40 percent of all retail workers. Obviously, then, retailing is an industry dominated by the giant organizations such as Sears Roebuck, J. C. Penney, Safeway, K mart, and Montgomery Ward. Sears is America's largest retail organization and employs almost 400,000 people in the United States.

Choosing a Store

There are usually many retail outlets to choose from. So it's important that the retailer understand why a consumer will pick one store over another. One of the most important factors in governing retail shopping is the store's image—how a consumer views the given retailer relative to other retailers. Image has many sides to it such as friendliness of personnel, quality of merchandise, level of service, convenience, and ease of access. Store images also tend to have a "halo effect": the general image of the store tends to dominate other considerations. For instance, someone holding a very positive image of the Target stores might perceive the quality of merchandise to be higher than that of similar goods in other discount stores. Retailers are continually striving to improve their image. They often conduct semiannual studies of customers and potential customers to measure their image strengths and weaknesses. If a store doesn't do as well as a major competitor in personnel friendliness, it may begin a retraining program for its salesclerks. The store will conduct another image study later to see if the training has paid off.

Advertising can also make an important contribution to a retailer's image. High-fashion advertising, for example, can give a retailer a "with-it" type of image. Bloomingdale's, the New York department store, uses this type of advertising very effectively to portray a fashion image. On the other hand K mart uses full-page ads that promote inexpensive merchandise at reduced prices to convey a discounter's image.

Risk In addition to image, perceived risk helps determine where a person shops. There are two types of risk that are of concern to consumers: social and economic. **Social risk** means that what a person buys—or where he or she buys it—is seen as affecting how other people view that person. For example, buying the "wrong" suit might give a businessperson a poor image. A banker might not buy a suit at K mart or Target because of concern for social risk.

Retailers use advertising to aid in creating their image.

CALVIN KLEIN: Pure, Sure SweatShirting

PERSPECTIVE ON SMALL BUSINESS

Bill Rodgers just wanted to run. A world-class marathon runner, Rodgers had no particular desire to own three jogging-equipment stores and a rapidly expanding wholesale running-gear firm or, for that matter, to endorse Golden Butterscotch Life Savers.

But Rodgers also had to earn a living—a practice that often clashed with his demanding training regimen. In 1977, two years after he won his first Boston Marathon, Rodgers was a special-education teacher in Everett, Mass. "They started putting pressure on me to quit running during my lunch hour," Rodgers says, "so my wife and I decided to go into business."

Bill Rodgers the runner became Bill Rodgers the reluctant businessman. He didn't know the first thing about operating a retail store, but at least he could continue running. . . .

With the aid of his brother Charlie Rodgers, accountant Russell McCarter, and runners who were literally hired off the street to sell shoes, the first Bill Rodgers Running Center opened at the basement site of an old neighborhood dry cleaners in Boston, in October 1977.

Business didn't exactly boom on the first day. Despite a steady stream of family, friends, and curiosity seekers, the store grossed only $14. Customers were satisfied merely to hobnob with Rodgers and partake of the opening day festivities. Some people, in fact, were just looking for the dry cleaners.

"We were all crazy to do it," laughs Charlie Rodgers, "because we didn't know what we were doing." No one, he adds, had the foggiest notion how to cash out at the end of the day or keep a proper set of books.

Despite the opening day folly, Rodgers was confident. He knew there was a large, affluent body of casual and serious runners who would have no qualms about spending $40 on a pair of running shoes. He also suspected he could market his name: he was constantly in the public eye thanks to his victories at the Boston and New York marathons (he's won four of each), less well-known races, and various media appearances.

His confidence was justified: the store's sales climbed steadily, and brother Charlie settled in as the manager. They opened two more retail outlets—another in Boston and a smaller store in Worcester, Mass. In 1978 he took the next step—a wholesale clothing line, a logical extension of his running-gear stores. [To start the clothing line, Rodgers collaborated with Rob Yahn, a former employee of runner-entrepreneur Frank Shorter.]

SOURCE: Reprinted with permission of *INC.* Magazine. Excerpted from Hank Gilman, "Rodgers & Company Runs on a Fast Track," *INC.*, May 1981, pp. 142–148. Copyright © 1981 by INC. Publishing Company, 38 Commercial Wharf, Boston, MA 02110.

A second form of risk is economic. **Economic risk** is the possibility that a purchase decision will greatly reduce the consumer's budget and not yield substantial satisfaction. Studies have shown that vacuum cleaners, automobile tires, typewriters, draperies, china, stereo systems, and some clothing tend to have high economic risk. When consumers perceive a product as having low social risk, they may be willing to buy it at a department or discount store. On the other hand products with high social risk often occasion negative attitudes toward some department and discount stores. The upper-income consumer would probably prefer to buy an item with high social risk (such as expensive clothing) at a specialty shop. If an item has high economic risk (such as a new stereo system), the buyer will want to make sure that the dealer is reputable and can be trusted.

Methods of Retail Operation

Department Stores When you go shopping, you have a wide variety of stores from which to choose. One that all are familiar with is the **department store.** This has many different departments located in one building to achieve more effective promotion, buying, service to the customer, and control. Each department is usually managed by a buyer. This person selects the merchandise for the department, displays it within the department, and may manage department personnel. Higher management sets broad policies concerning types of merchandise to buy and their price ranges in order to create a certain store image. For example, K mart merchandise is usually much more economical and sometimes of lower quality than what one finds at Marshall Field in Chicago or the Broadway stores in California.

Today there are almost no large independent department stores. Most are owned by national chains. The three largest chains—Federated Department Stores, Dayton-Hudson, and May Department Stores—have combined sales of over $11 billion a year. Federated is huge, operating about 275 stores throughout the United States. Two of its better-known stores are Abraham & Straus in the northeast and Bloomingdale's in New York. Federated also has I. Magnin and Bullocks on the West Coast, Burdine's in Florida, Foley's and Sanger-Harris in Texas, and Goldsmith's in Tennessee.

Mass-Merchandising Shopping Chains The **mass-merchandising shopping chain,** such as Montgomery Ward, Sears, and J. C. Penney, is like a department store in many ways. But it's different because of its huge sales volume, promotional budgets, store brands, and number of stores. Sears, for example, is a giant organization. Its annual sales of over $17 billion are greater than those of the three largest department store chains combined. Sears operates 854 stores across the nation. Perhaps due to its size, Sears had difficulty in developing a strategic plan during the late 1970s and early 1980s. It used an approach that by and large failed, trying to attract the more affluent customer by stocking expensive, high-fashion merchandise, ignoring its image as "the provider of goods for America's heartland."

Both J. C. Penney and Montgomery Ward have also experienced problems during the past fifteen years. For example, the mass-merchandising shopping chains usually buy directly from manufacturers rather than going through wholesalers. All three chains (Sears, Penney, Ward) have had trouble from time to time with supplier relations.

Because of their many stores throughout the nation, Sears, Penney, and Ward engage in heavy TV advertising. National network advertising helps them build their image and create brand loyalty for such products as the Diehard battery and Signature refrigerators and freezers.

Specialty Stores Both mass-merchandising shopping chains and department stores have experienced difficulty in coping with specialty stores. As the name implies, the **specialty store** sells a single line of merchandise, such as women's clothing, sporting goods, bedroom furniture, and gifts. Specialty stores usually carry a greater variety of merchandise in their area of specialization than would a mass-merchandising shopping chain or a department store. And some specialty stores have evolved into rapidly growing chains, such as The Gap (a store that caters to the "jeans generation"), Hickory Farms (a specialty food store), and Margo's LaMode (a women's clothing chain). As with other retailers, the image, quality of merchandise, and friendliness of personnel are important in determining who will shop at a specialty store.

Discount Stores A **discount store** carries lines of merchandise that enable it to sell high volume at a low price. Discounters usually handle well-known branded merchandise, such as Zenith and General Electric, as well as their own store brands. Most discount chains also carry a full line of inexpensive clothing, sheets and towels, and other soft goods. Large discount chains like Wal-Mart, K mart, and Target typically offer well-lit parking lots, convenient shopping hours, and easy-to-see (and locate) merchandise groupings. In contrast to the other retailers we have examined, discount stores have little clerical help within the departments and no extra services such as delivery.

K mart, the nation's second-largest nonfood retailer, has long relied on centralized advertising and the promotion of discount prices. More than 4000 newspaper-ad pages are produced each week, appearing in more than 1000 papers reaching 55 million readers.[1] The first K mart opened in 1962; by 1981 it had penetrated 270 of the

ON THE FIRING LINE

Subsidized Supermarkets: Can They Hush the Cities' Growling Bellies?

The big supermarket chains are suffering, and for several reasons. The grocery business has always operated on a financial tightrope. The markup on food items is typically no more than 1 percent. To make a profit, grocers have to do a high-volume business. In the last five years, however, the real annual growth rate of the grocery market fell to 0.3 percent. Consumers are buying less; their real income has been eaten away by inflation.

In city centers, supermarkets are particularly hard pressed to make ends meet. The cost of land in most cities prohibits construction of new stores. Consequently, inner-city supermarkets are small—squeezed into old buildings—and cannot stock a large mix of products.

Inner-city residents typically have relatively low incomes. They tend not to buy the luxury products, such as prime beef, on which grocery stores make their best profits. Stocking perishables becomes a problem, as does cash flow. Crime and vandalism take a bite out of inner-city supermarket profits too.

As a result, supermarket chains are pulling out of inner cities. In some sections of many large cities the number of supermarkets has declined from 30 to 60 percent in the last five to ten years. If this continues, food distribution may become a problem of crisis proportions.

More and more people believe that the answer lies in subsidizing the development of supermarkets in inner cities. This could take many forms. To stimulate development, some local governments have exempted businesses in certain areas from property taxes for 5, 10, or 15 years. Taxes on income could also be made favorable for inner-city enterprises. Government can also underwrite or provide low-interest loans to encourage development. Cities have sometimes lowered the price of land they own when selling to suitable developers. Subsidies can also take the form of coordinated municipal services—well-designed bus routes, for instance.

Some insist that subsidizing inner-city supermarkets is a moral imperative. Inner-city ghetto dwellers are typically members of ethnic minorities. Of all people, they can least afford to travel miles or pay outrageous prices for their food. Yet for years they have been the victims of discrimination by business and government.

Subsidies are economically sound in the long run, claim those who favor them. As business has left the urban areas for the suburbs, the tax base that supports the cities' essential public services has declined. Inner-city residents, with their low incomes, cannot pay taxes adequate to keep the cities functioning. Yet they, more than anyone, need the public services. Encouraging inner-city business will lead eventually to a larger tax base. Furthermore business is what stabilizes a community, say those who favor subsidies. Stability should be a preeminent concern, given present conditions in urban ghettos.

Subsidies are not the answer, insist others. No one is starving because a supermarket is not just a few blocks away. Government give-away programs, once enacted, are hard to reverse. Subsidies are paid for with taxes. Government at all levels is having difficulty meeting the demands on its tax revenues. And no one wants a long-term tax increase.

Taxes aside, these same people say, subsidies have adverse effects on a business. Once subsidies begin, management no longer has to worry about pleasing the customer. The big concern becomes keeping on the good side of the government officials in charge of doling out aid.

Besides, the time for subsidies is past, the argument continues. We can expect to see inner cities and inner-city supermarkets revive in the near future. Suburban development is no longer as appealing as it once was. Land costs are higher, environmental standards are frequently very severe, and customers are less willing to spend money on gas to shop at great distances from home. More and more, developers are interested in renovating existing structures in city centers. This and the new no-frills warehouse supermarket, where services and product brands are reduced to a minimum, may be just what is needed to turn city supermarkets into high-volume, profit-making operations.

country's largest metropolitan areas. All major policy decisions are made at K mart's Troy, Michigan headquarters.

Direct Retailing   **Direct retailing** means selling to the consumer in his or her home, using a catalog, telephone, or direct-mail piece. The convenience of ordering from home amidst rising gasoline prices, while at the same time avoiding crowds of shoppers, all works to the advantage of direct retailing. Sales amount to over $100 billion a year. The largest direct retailer is Sears, with catalog and telephone sales of over $2.5 billion. Every three months Sears distributes about 16 million of its famous catalogs.

Direct-mail retailers send approximately 30 billion pieces each year to prospective buyers. Direct mail is no longer an inexpensive form of promotion due to the rising cost of postage, mailing lists, paper, and envelopes. However its virtue is that it can reach a very specific target audience. For example, if an organization wanted to reach those plastic surgeons living in Florida who had bought a new home within the past two years, a mailing list for this target market could be purchased. The cost, however, would be about $100 per 1000 names. Mail-order retailers operate out of warehouse-type facilities in order to maintain a low overhead. Given the wide array of merchandise that can be found in catalogs, mail-order retailers

Specialty stores in shopping malls and mass-merchandise shopping chains are two forms of retail operation.

TALKING BUSINESS

Many shoppers can testify that finding a competent sales clerk—or any sales clerk—is often next to impossible. Partly because of the decreasing supply of well-trained salespeople and the increasing cost of paying them, U.S. retailers have moved from an emphasis on customer service to an emphasis on price and value promotion.

Stores that cater to the upper crust—for example, Neiman-Marcus or Gucci shops—still maintain a high level of service. "We'll do anything" for a customer, says a Neiman-Marcus vice-president. "We can't afford to lower our level of service. If we start to slip there, we become more ordinary."

More typical, though, are stores such as Sears, J. C. Penney, and Montgomery Ward, which have cut back on sales help and replaced it in many cases with such expedients as more informative packaging and signs to direct customers to merchandise.

That customers accept, and sometimes even prefer, such indirect help is partly the result of the influence of discount stores, which taught customers the advantages of trading off better service for lower cost. The Target discount chain, for example, offers almost no service at all; but it does offer Calvin Klein jeans for $25 a pair, $17 less than at more service-oriented stores, and Seiko gold quartz watches that normally sell for $295 for $200.

"If a customer has to make the choice between waiting an extra five minutes in line and saving money," says Target's president, "he'll put more value in prices."

Adapted from Steve Weiner, "Find It Yourself: Many Stores Abandon 'Service with a Smile,' Rely on Signs, Displays," *Wall Street Journal*, 16 March 1981, pp. 1, 20. Adapted by permission of The Wall Street Journal, © Dow Jones & Company, Inc., 1981. All rights reserved.

---

offer many products that cannot be found in smaller communities.

Door-to-door retailing has declined in use during the past 25 years. Rising crime rates and gasoline costs are two major factors accounting for this trend. Companies such as Amway, Fuller Brush, Avon, and Tupperware have created variations on the door-to-door selling operation. They ask individuals to host "parties" where prospective buyers are brought together for a demonstration of products. The companies, of course, hope that those attending will feel motivated to buy something.

Another type of direct marketing is telephone selling. It's estimated that the average American household receives about 19 calls a year from businesses selling products and services.[2] You're not even safe from telephone sales calls if you have an unlisted telephone number. Firms use "random digit dialing" machines to reach those families without listed telephone numbers. Telephone selling is certainly not restricted to shady land-developers or aluminum siding contractors. Sears, J. C. Penney, and many major department stores regularly use telephone selling.

Factory Outlets The **factory outlet** is closely related to direct selling, since it offers merchandise directly to the final consumer from the factory. Factory outlets are popular for a wide variety of products such as furniture, food products, clothing, and housewares. Usually factory outlets sell goods far below the average retail price because both the wholesaler and the retailer are bypassed. The merchandise offered is often slow-moving returned goods or factory seconds, which also helps contribute to the lower sales price. The location of a factory outlet and the character of its physical layout often closely resemble those of a warehouse rather than of a modern retail store. In fact most factory outlets originally were located adjacent to the factory itself. However the popularity and profitability of these stores have prompted manufacturers to branch out, with more locations serving higher-traffic areas. Today there are at least 8000 outlets across the United States compared with fewer than 1000· about a decade ago. Many are owned by large clothing manufacturers such as London Town Corporation (London Fog coats) and V. F. Corporation (Vanity Fair and Lee jeans).

Catalog Showrooms   The growth of the **catalog showroom** has been just as dynamic as that of the factory outlet. This is not surprising since catalog showrooms have many cost advantages over other retailers selling similar kinds of merchandise. Sales cost, display cost, and service cost are usually substantially below those of traditional stores. One of the most important features favoring showrooms is competitive pricing. On key lines of products in which catalog showrooms specialize, such as jewelry and housewares, the price difference is quite large.

PHYSICAL DISTRIBUTION

Physical distribution is important to retailers, wholesalers, manufacturers, and consumers because it is concerned with getting the finished product through the channel of distribution. A simple example of physical distribution is getting a G.E. blender from the G.E. manufacturing facility to a Sears store in Moscow Mills, Missouri. The importance of distribution is obvious enough. If the product is not available to sell, consumers will often go somewhere else to find it. Even when items must be ordered — as from a catalog — if it takes too long to get the goods, consumers will try to get them elsewhere.

Goals of Physical Distribution

Physical distribution has two major goals: to offer quality service and to minimize cost. Sometimes these two goals can be conflicting. Good service increases the chances of repeat sales and the possibility that the firm will get new customers. Distribution service is measured by **order cycle time.**

This is the elapsed time between placing an order and the customer's receipt of the merchandise in good condition. The order cycle time for getting a Chevrolet built to your specifications might be 90 days, while the order cycle time at a McDonald's drive-in-window might average 4 minutes. Generally speaking, the shorter the order cycle time, the better the service and the happier the customer is going to be.

It is important to maintain quality service in order not to lose customers. But by the same token, if service is "too good," the cost may be huge. General Motors can't have every possible color, model, and style of car available in every dealership across the country. The inventory cost would be out of sight. Therefore most manufacturers try to provide a reasonable amount of inventory at crucially located warehouses. When a dealer runs out of a special product or has a special request, it can be quickly obtained from a warehouse.

Cutting distribution costs isn't especially difficult. The Levi Strauss Company, for example, could eliminate all of its warehouses and all of the inventory of blue jeans within its warehouses. If a retailer such as The County Seat wanted to stock Levi's, Levi would receive the order, manufacture the product, and ship it by either rail or barge — the two least expensive forms of transportation. By eliminating all of the finished-good inventory of Levi's — operating directly from orders received, using slow modes of transportation, and selling their warehouses — Levi Strauss could greatly reduce the cost of distribution. But this way it might take The County Seat six months to get the order of blue jeans. With that order cycle time, you can be sure that The County Seat would start selling Wranglers, Lee, or some other brand of jeans, and dump Levi's.

Physical distribution objectives therefore become a balancing act between the service and cost. The manufacturer must find a happy balance. Service must be reasonably good to avoid losing customers, but the manufacturer must not make service so fast and efficient that it loses money.

Modes of Transportation

One function of physical distribution is to determine how merchandise will be shipped. A physical distribution manager can choose from air, highway, rail, water, and occasionally pipelines. Each of these offers certain unique advantages and disadvantages (see Figure 14.4).

Air Normally, the fastest way to move goods between two points is by air. On the other hand, air is the most expensive means of shipment. Expense, however, refers strictly to the cost of airfreight. When other things are taken into consideration—such as the ability to eliminate a warehouse because of the speed of air delivery, or the reduced necessity for packing—the total cost of distribution may be less when using airfreight.

Ordinarily, merchandise shipped by airfreight is of high unit value, such as computers, medical diagnostic equipment, and critical replacement parts. Some perishable items are also shipped by airfreight (e.g. flowers and pineapples from Hawaii, bread from Paris, and lobsters from Maine).

The use of huge 747 Superjet airfreighters, roll-on containers, and swing-tail cargo planes has helped reduce the cost of airfreight. However the skyrocketing cost of jet fuel and the limited capacity of a single airplane as compared with trains and ships still limit the growth of this carrier.

FIGURE 14.4

RELATIVE ADVANTAGES OF THE BASIC MODES OF TRANSPORTATION

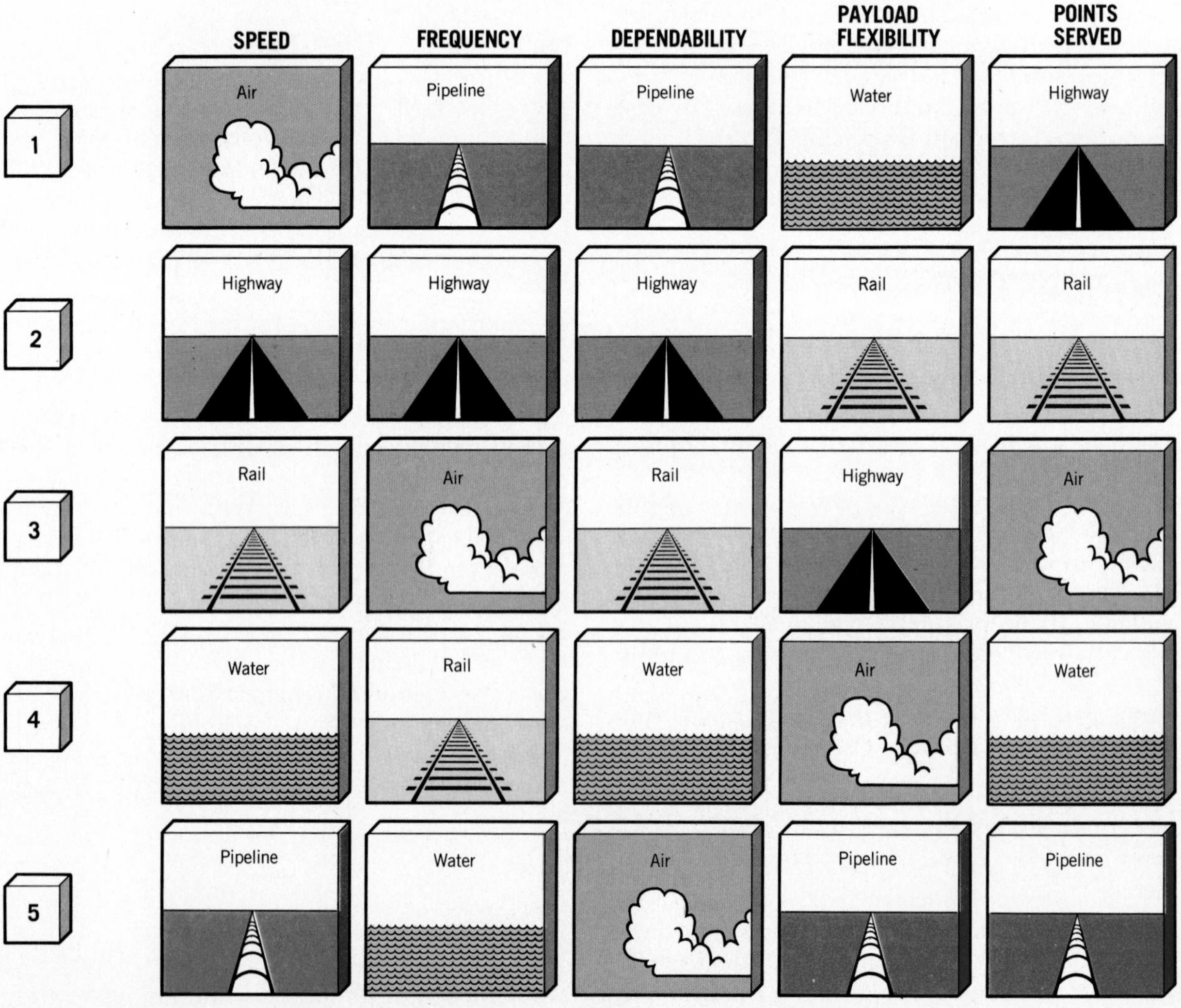

	SPEED	FREQUENCY	DEPENDABILITY	PAYLOAD FLEXIBILITY	POINTS SERVED
1	Air	Pipeline	Pipeline	Water	Highway
2	Highway	Highway	Highway	Rail	Rail
3	Rail	Air	Rail	Highway	Air
4	Water	Rail	Water	Air	Water
5	Pipeline	Water	Air	Pipeline	Pipeline

Source: Adapted from J. L. Heskett, Robert M. Ivie, and Nicholas A. Glaskowsky, Jr., *Business Logistics* (New York: Ronald Press, 1964), p. 71. Adapted by permission.

TALKING BUSINESS

Within the next few years, shopping at home by cable television or video cassette may become commonplace. Already, several marketers and cable TV companies are exploring the possibilities of video shopping.

One way to shop at home involves cable TV programs that allow manufacturers to demonstrate products and offer general buying advice. "We call the show an 'infomercial'" a cable TV executive says of one such program. "It isn't pure generic information and it isn't a commercial."

At present, such programs mostly act as an aid to the sellers' other marketing activities while providing information for the consumer. Conceivably, though, viewers might someday be able to ask questions or place orders directly through their television sets.

Adapted from Theodore J. Gage, "Video Shops Around for a Future," *Advertising Age*, 2 November 1981, p. S-8. Adapted with permission from the November 2, 1981, issue of Advertising Age. Copyright 1981 by Crain Communications Inc.

Highway   Although airfreight is limited by the availability of airports, trucklines provide the most flexible form of hauling freight. Many of them provide door-to-door service in almost every community in the United States. Door-to-door service can also help reduce packing costs. And truck rates are usually lower than airfreight. In fact trucks sometimes provide faster door-to-door delivery than airfreight within distances under 250 miles. This is because the goods don't have to go from airport to airport, as well as to and from the airport.

Trucks are quite dependable unless they are hampered by severe weather conditions. However trucks are limited by the volume that they can carry with any single load. Because trucks offer a fairly smooth ride as compared with railroads, they are best suited for handling finished goods and fragile items.

Rail   For almost a century, railroads have been the backbone of America's freight transportation system. The growth of trucklines almost eliminated rail service to smaller markets. Railroad service goes from terminal to terminal and is relatively slow. To offset the lack of speed, railroads offer low rates on carload lots of merchandise.

Rough handling, coupled with a lack of speed, make rail transportation ideally suited for raw materials.

Railroads also offer piggyback service and **containerization.** A manufacturer using **piggy-back service,** such as S. C. Johnson (Johnson's Wax), drives a special truck to a piggyback freight yard. There a huge crane picks up the trailer portion of the truck (the container) and places it on a railroad flatcar. It is then shipped to a distant city to another piggyback freight yard where, again, a Johnson's representative has a tractor waiting. The trailer is then off-loaded, attached to the tractor, and driven away.

Another unique rail service is known as the unit train, which goes between two points only and carries a single bulk commodity such as coal. Burlington-Northern runs a coal unit train with almost 100 cars daily from the coal fields of Wyoming to an electric power generator that supplies electricity for the city of San Antonio.

Water   Still another major carrier of bulk commodities is America's inland waterways. New large tugboats have greatly increased the capacity of many barge lines. Also, special barges can now

Some of the common modes of transportation: barges, air cargo jets, and containerized shipping.

handle such items as asphalt, corrosive chemicals, and even refrigerated commodities. The major limitation of the waterways lies with the number and length of their routes. Service is usually slow, and some northern rivers cannot be used at certain times of the year. Water is usually the cheapest means of moving raw materials and semifinished goods over long distances.

Pipelines   Pipelines are also slow but maintain a continuous flow of product. There's no route flexibility, and capacity is limited by the diameter of the pipe. Weather is almost never a consideration with pipelines. Gases, liquids, and some insoluble solids such as coal (movable in a watery mixture or suspension called a *slurry*) are the primary products moved through pipelines. Pipeline routes move in only one direction, with storage terminals at the receiving end. Pipelines require the least amount of energy of all carriers to move an item from one point to another.

SUMMARY

A channel of distribution is the sequence of marketing institutions through which a product passes on its way from the producer to the final user. The distribution system focuses on the process of physical transfer of goods and services and on their ownership in each stage of the marketing sequence. Channel members engage in the negotiating function—that is, the buying and selling of the merchandise and the transference of title of ownership. Organizations that do not perform negotiating functions are not true members of the channel.

There are two basic types of channels of distribution—one for consumer goods and the other for industrial products. Long channels of distribution are most likely to be used for less expensive products. Industrial-good channels are usually much shorter than consumer-good channels, because most industrial goods are more expensive than most consumer goods. Many industrial goods are custom-made for the end user. Industrial goods are also sold through industrial distributors. Distribution can be intensive, selective, or exclusive. The degree of intensity of market coverage depends in part on the type of product involved.

Firms that use intensive distribution often rely on wholesalers. Wholesalers typically sell finished products to retailers. They also sell to other institutions, such as manufacturers, schools, and hospitals, who use the product to perform their basic missions. Some wholesalers sell to other wholesalers. Wholesalers provide a wide variety of functions for the manufacturer and retailer, including selling, financing, and storing merchandise.

The three major categories of wholesalers are (1) merchant wholesalers, (2) manufacturers' sales branches, and (3) agents and brokers. Merchant wholesalers buy manufacturers' products and resell them to other businesses. They operate one or more warehouses, where they receive the merchandise, take title to it, store it, and later ship it to the buyer. Full-service merchant wholesalers offer a complete array of services to the retail customer. Manufacturers' sales branches perform many of the same functions as full-service merchant wholesalers, but they are managed, owned, and completely controlled by the manufacturer. Agents and brokers do not take title to goods; they are paid by commission according to sales and perform few functions.

Some 28 million people in the US are engaged in some type of retail business. It is important that the retailer understand why a consumer picks one store over another. One of the most important factors in this choice is the store's image. Perceived risk—both social and economic—also helps determine where a person shops. Types of retail operations include department stores, mass-merchandising chains, specialty stores, discount stores, direct retailing methods (catalogs, direct mailings, door-to-door sales, and telephone sales), factory outlets, and catalog showrooms.

Physical distribution is important to retailers, wholesalers, manufacturers, and consumers. Its two major goals are to offer quality service and to minimize cost to the company. Sometimes these two goals conflict, and the company must find the balance that offers service good enough to prevent loss of customers but not so good that the manufacturer loses money. One function of physical distribution is to determine how merchandise will be shipped. Goods can be moved by air, highway, rail, water, and occasionally pipeline. Each offers unique advantages and disadvantages.

KEY TERMS

"breaking bulk"
broker
catalog showroom
channel of
    distribution
containerization
department store
direct retailing
discount store
economic risk
exclusive distribution
factory outlet
industrial distributor
intensive distribution
manufacturer's
    representative
manufacturer's sales
    branch
mass-merchandising
    shopping chain
merchant wholesaler
negotiating functions
order cycle time
physical distribution
piggy-back service
selective distribution
social risk
specialty store
wholesaler

REVIEW QUESTIONS

1. What are the basic functions of members of a channel of distribution?
2. Why are distribution channels for many consumer goods long channels?
3. Cite at least three reasons why channels for industrial goods are usually shorter than those for consumer goods.
4. What are the principal functions of a wholesaler from the manufacturer's point of view? From the retailer's point of view?
5. What are the major characteristics of a merchant wholesaler?
6. What are the distinguishing differences between a manufacturer's agent and a broker?
7. What advantages do shopping centers and malls offer the retailer? What are some of the disadvantages?
8. What kinds of goods are best suited for rail shipments?
9. What advantages do trucks have over most other forms of physical distribution?

DISCUSSION QUESTIONS

1. Why are there differences between consumer and industrial channels?
2. In what way are intensity of market coverage and length of distribution channel related?
3. Explain why the same brand and model of some popular stereo equipment can be found in audio equipment stores, discount stores, and catalog showrooms?
4. In what way can store image affect the sale of designer jeans?
5. In the previous chapter on product strategy you learned how to categorize three classes of consumer goods—convenience, shopping, and specialty. What relationships do you see between these and types of retail stores?
6. What in the operations of mass merchandisers enables them to often sell the same item for less than a department store or specialty store?

CASE: IBM SWIMS A NEW CHANNEL—TO SEARS

With Apple II making such a splash in the personal computer market, distributing its fast-selling Apples through various outlets, (including franchised stores and other companies willing to carry this lively new product), IBM gave up its exclusive marketing (direct from manufacturer to consumer) and made an agreement with Sears to market its small computers along with its competitors—Hewlett-Packard, Exxon, and others. Test stores for this new marketing plan opened their doors for business in Dallas, Chicago, and Boston, and sales exceeded the expectations of market managers.

This new marketing approach is distinctly separate from regular Sears stores. What we have here are specialty stores that stock personal computers, copiers, word processors, calculators, and other products made by the manufacturer. Some other large manufacturers, including IBM, Digital Equipment Corporation, and Xerox Corporation, have opened their own stores and plan to open more. So business is booming through new channels of distribution for the once exclusive companies that used only their direct channels from manufacturer to commercial consumer.

Of course, Sears is to be congratulated on its role in this marketing strategy. Its new stores will include a "Learning Center Room" in which salespersons will demonstrate the equipment and provide information on operating all these business products and solving business problems.

Time will tell how this new strategy works. Meanwhile, IBM and its collaborating competitors are waiting with fingers crossed for the latest sales figures on what's happening in the new specialty stores in the marketplace.

1. What chance do you think IBM has of competing in the personal computer market, since its reputation has been built on huge computers in the high-cost range, traded exclusively through IBM sales representatives?
2. Do you think the Sears image is compatible with the IBM image, and what will be the result in the marketplace?
3. What are the chances for a successful introduction of computers into the home? Is this new approach in distribution the best way to get personal computers into the middle-class American household?

CASE: A FACTORY SUITS YOU CHEAPER

The Kuppenheimer Factory Outlet opened its doors about four years ago and is now a thriving business. It boasts a quality line of suits, coats, slacks, shirts, belts, ties—direct from the factory to you for less money.

Kuppenheimer is a well-known name in men's suits, dating back many years along with Hickey Freeman, Palm Beach, Hart, Schaffner & Marx, and other quality lines of men's wear. A few years ago Hercules Pant Company bought out Kuppenheimer and decided to set up factory outlet stores across the country. Competition could be met head-on by lower prices resulting from the elimination of middlemen. Walton Clothes were also involved in the transaction.

Now these merged companies are involved in the mix and match game as they manufacture pants in Columbus (O.) and coats and vests in Hialeah (Fla.) and Loganville (Ga.), which end up on the racks in the outlet store.

The factory outlet store is a model of efficiency, with suits neatly arranged by sizes in long rows from the front to the back of the store—on both walls. Shorter racks in the middle carry sport coats flanked by tables of multicolored slacks stacked neatly in rows according to size. Interspersed are cases of shirts arranged for quick selection to go with the suits and sport outfits. Tie racks are found at the front of the store with easy access for completing outfits near the checkout counter. There are belts near the slacks counters too.

All this efficiency is reflected in lower prices. A quick check of price tags up and down the rows reveals a price range in suits from $69.95 to $149.95; sport coats from $49.95 to $99.50; and shirts, belts, and ties reasonably priced to match any combination. Top coats and raincoats are also available.

The business seems to be holding its own, given economic conditions. In fact, the future looks bright as long as disposable personal income is available. With the competition in quality men's suits priced from $200 to $400, the Kuppenheimer line stands a good chance of making it.

1. How convincing is the appeal of the shortened channel of distribution, with suits furnished directly from the factory to the consumer?
2. How do you compare the image of Kuppenheimer with Hart, Schaffner & Marx and Hickey Freeman labels? Are they all high-quality men's clothes?

CHAPTER 15

PRICING STRATEGIES

After studying this chapter you should be able to:

1 Describe the role and importance of pricing to the marketer.
2 Discuss alternative pricing objectives.
3 Explain the use of skimming and penetration policies in pricing new products.
4 Understand different pricing tactics used by marketers to maintain competitive positions.
5 Explain how pricing can be used psychologically.

K. Douglas Martin came to Scripto, Inc. in 1978 to put the company back on the road to financial health. Writing instruments were Scripto's main product, but the firm was strong only in mechanical pencils, a small segment of the market. Martin knew that the right product was needed—a ball-point with appeal to a young audience. This was the audience Scripto had when it headed the market in the 1950s, but which it lost when that generation moved on. The right product would also have to quickly pay back investment and return a profit. But what *was* the right product?

At just this point, Gillette announced its Eraser Mate, an erasable ink pen. The new product soon began to rise in consumer interest and trade reaction. But Scripto had been researching the same idea since 1964 and had already filed for patents. Just such a product seemed to satisfy Martin's objectives: it was a ball-point, it appealed to a young audience, and it satisfied high margin requirements.

After quickly overcoming technical obstacles to developing the pen, Scripto sped up market research plans. By auditing warehouse withdrawals at two drug chains, Martin could compare the unit movement of Gillette's Eraser Mate with two high-volume pens—Flair markers and Paper Mate 98¢ ball pens.

Eraser Mate's $1.69 price was high compared with the two other products. Despite that, it captured 40% of the unit movement of all three products. Unit movement even exceeded that for Flair, which weighed in at only one third the retail price of Gillette's pen.

At this point Martin paused. Scripto's strategy was to reach the young adult audience, including teenagers. But a $1.69 tag would normally mean a product was an adult purchase item. So it became important to research the actual demographics of Eraser Mate.

The results were a big surprise: 65% of users were under 18, and a full 42% fell in the 11-14 age bracket. Says Martin, "For a product retailing at almost $2, that was astounding." The fit with Scripto objectives was getting closer. Everything looked Go. And since "stick" pens are the largest segment of the writing-instrument market (1 billion + units a year), Scripto decided to go even further and produce the world's first *disposable*, erasable pen.

From then on it was a matter of putting together the details: product configuration, consumer positioning, packaging, promotion, communication, and pricing. Students were interviewed and researchers learned they felt that 98¢ would be a reasonable price for an erasable, disposable pen. "This price point was verified in subsequent placement tests using our actual product and, importantly, it gave us the margin we were looking for, Martin says. "So 98¢ became our price point."

At 98¢, the Scripto Erasable Pen is being snatched up; and it's putting Scripto back on the road to financial good health. "Erases the ink, not the paper," says the ad copy. It might have gone on to say, "Erases red ink best."

Adapted by permission from "Success of Scripto Erasable Pen Due to Marketing Research: CEO," *Marketing News*, 23 January 1981, p. 8, published by the American Marketing Association.

THE NATURE OF PRICING

Why Pricing is Important

The Scripto story shows that price can be an important tool both to stimulate sales and to restore a company's fortunes. Most specifically, though, pricing is important to the marketing manager because the manager must charge the right price to enable the company to earn a fair return on its investment. A price that's too high or too low won't achieve that objective. If the price is too high, customers will not buy the product or service, and the firm will go out of business. If the price is too low, sales may be extremely good — but the firm may be incurring a loss. This actually happened with the A & P food chain during the late 1970s. Its program, WEO ("Where Economy Originates"), was very successful in stimulating sales. However A & P experienced a huge financial loss for the duration of the program.

There are many factors that impact on why managers are concerned about pricing. Inflation, recessions, government regulations, rising consumerism, skyrocketing energy costs, and shortages of raw materials all bring home the importance of pricing to the marketing managers. Each of these factors makes it more of a challenge for the company to establish the "right price."

Price as an Allocator

Price plays a very important role in our American free-enterprise economy. It's a basis for allocating goods and services among consumers, businesses, and units of government. **Free enterprise** means that you have the right to engage in any economic endeavor that you wish. Taken to its limits, free enterprise implies the ability to compete freely, unhampered by (excessive) government restrictions. You may open a barber shop or you may become a lawyer; you can drive a bulldozer or be a salesperson. The American government plays a smaller role in guiding business conduct than do the governments of many other nations.

Our government also plays a relatively minor role in allocating resources compared with many countries. For example, it does not tell U.S. Steel *how much* iron ore it will receive from *which* mines. Nor does it tell U.S.S. who will receive the output from its mills. Similarly, government doesn't tell you how much milk, bread, clothes, and other consumer goods you can buy.

However, perfectly free enterprise is as common as the unicorn. Thornton Bradshaw, then president of Atlantic Richfield, put it this way some years ago:

"the myth of American free enterprise persists. . . I think it is time to look at our economic system realistically. My own premise is that business does not now operate in a free-enterprise system, but rather as part of a unique mix of private and government forces."[1]

But yet somehow the huge outpouring of goods and services of American business must be allocated. There must be *some* orderly and rational distribution. This is the role of the price mechanism. In effect, income can be viewed as **"dollar votes."** If people believe that a retailer or other merchant has established a fair price for a good or service, they "vote" for (purchase) that product. So if you think that McDonald's makes a good hamburger and that it has established a fair price for its Big Mac, you'll vote for (purchase) that hamburger. When you buy a Big Mac, you're in effect saying. "Keep producing the Big Mac hamburger, McDonald's! It meets my needs and is a reasonable value for the money." And Ronald M. hears you.

Business firms that do a good job of satisfying the needs of the consumer receive more dollar votes (sales). The sales revenue may then be used by firms like McDonald's to buy additional resources. These include hamburger buns, pickles, ketchup, and labor to cook the hamburgers to produce more output, such as Big Macs. Companies that don't satisfy the consumer lack the dollar votes and can't effectively compete for resources because of lack of funds. They'll eventually switch production to another product or go out of business. Minnie Pearl's Fried Chicken, for example, could not attract enough dollar votes (sell enough chicken) to keep the franchise solvent. It finally went out of business.

Pricing Objectives

Establishing the "right price" means reaching the company's objectives. It's important for a company to set pricing objectives that are realistic and

TALKING BUSINESS

measurable. They should be attainable with the resources that are realistically available to the company. And they should also be measurable in order to determine if pricing goals are being met.

Profit Maximization   A goal often mentioned by companies is **profit maximization.** That is, the firm should continue to produce units of output as long as the revenue is greater than cost. This will yield the largest possible profit on a product or service.

Bill Boswell is a residential housebuilder in Portland, Oregon. Bill's houses are conventionally designed and sell for $100,000 each. His costs and revenue projections are shown in Table 15.1. Bill feels that he can sell as many as 15 houses a year at the price he's established. Notice in column 3 that the cost per house drops for each of the first four units. By having several houses under construction at the same time, Bill can afford to hire a full-time crew. This is a much more economical measure than subcontracting each task to an independent contractor. Another reason that costs are falling is that Bill can order materi-

als in greater quantities and receive quantity discounts.

But Bill decides to have six houses under construction at the same time. Bill feels that six is the most that he can personally supervise at one time.

TABLE 15–1

Boswell Builders' Projected Cost and Revenues for Building Homes

(1) Output (House)	(2) Sales Price	(3) Cost of the Current House Built	(4) Profit on the Current House Built	(5) Total Profit
1st	$100,000	$ 80,000	$ 20,000	$ 20,000
2nd	100,000	75,000	25,000	45,000
3rd	100,000	73,000	27,000	72,000
4th	100,000	70,000	30,000	102,000
5th	100,000	70,000	30,000	132,000
6th	100,000	77,000	23,000	155,000
7th	100,000	90,000	10,000	165,000
8th	100,000	115,000	(15,000)	150,000

Even with six homes, there's more work than can be handled by his crew, so additional help must be hired. By producing additional houses, Bill would need a full second crew and would have to hire a supervisor.

To maximize profits, Bill should construct seven houses a year. Even though the profit *per house* is falling for the sixth and seventh house (column 4), *total* profits are still rising (column 5). If Bill produces the eighth house, he'll have gone beyond profit maximization. That is, the cost of the eighth unit will be greater than the selling price, resulting in a $15,000 loss. Total profits would fall to $150,000.

Many companies don't have sophisticated enough accounting systems to give management adequate notice that its profit maximizing point is being reached. Because of this difficulty, many companies have turned to other, easier-to-measure pricing goals.

Target Return on the Investment   Companies like Johns-Manville, International Harvester, General Electric, and DuPont use **target return on investment** as their primary pricing goal. The company tries to determine the price that will give it a desired profitability in terms of either a return on investment or on sales. Return on investment is the net profit received from an investment after taxes.

Assume that a marketing manager estimates it's going to cost $2 million for Quaker Oats to develop, launch, and market a new hot cereal. If the net profit is forecast to be $200,000 the first year, the return on investment for the first year would be 10 percent ($200,000/$2,000,000 = 10%). Quaker Oats' top management might set a 15 percent return on investment as a satisfactory return for the company. The marketing executive can then use this standard to decide whether a given price and marketing mix combination is feasible. That is, will it yield the desired target return? Either (1) the new hot cereal would not be produced, or (2) the price and marketing mix would have to be altered so that it would yield at least a 15 percent return on investment. (The average target return on investment in large corporations is currently about 14 percent.)

Along with the projected target return on investment, management must evaluate the risk. A marketing mix that has the potential of earning a 25 percent return on investment might also be so risky that the firm *could* lose many millions of dollars. Usually high risk and profit potential go hand in hand. The higher the potential return, the higher the risk to the company, and vice versa. If Westinghouse could bring out an electric car, the potential return might be hundreds of millions of dollars. The risk, however, of competing with General Motors, Ford, and the imports in a market unfamiliar to Westinghouse could cost the company a fortune.

Market Share   Many companies feel that maintaining or increasing their **market share** (their percentage of the industry's total sales) is the key to their success. In other words, a reasonable market share will yield a reasonable return on investment. Research companies like A. C. Nielsen provide detailed market share reports for many different products and in a variety of industries. By purchasing this information, a firm can tell what portion of the market it has captured relative to its competitors. A Nielsen report is shown in Figure 15.1.

In many respects, market share and target return on investment are closely related. On an average, if a company can increase its market share by 10 percentage points, its return on investment tends to increase by about 5 percent.[2] A larger market share may increase profitability, to a

FIGURE 15.1
A Neilsen auditor gathering market-share information.

ON THE FIRING LINE

Windfall Profits: To Tax Or Not To Tax?

Profit is the American way. As a principle of business, it has helped make our country what it is. Profit is the essence of capitalism. It is the just reward for creativity and efficiency in business. Take away the opportunity to profit and there will be no incentive to produce more and better products. Productivity and progress will decline.

Still, can a profit be too big? Suppose by some lucky chance some few businesses suddenly come into billions of dollars of extra earnings. Oil companies, for example, prospered mightily when oil prices were decontrolled. Their added income was the result of neither efficiency nor inventiveness. Do such companies have a right to all that unearned income? Or should government use some of that money for the greater, common good? In other words, *should there be a substantial tax on windfall profits?*

Some take a stand in favor of taxing such profits heavily and cite a number of good reasons. Inflation has drained dollars of value. The actual buying power of people's income is now less than it was a few years ago. Given this state of affairs, why should some businesses be allowed excessive profits? Shouldn't they be required to return some of those profits to the people?

The government should put the revenue gained from windfall profits to work for everybody, say those in favor of a windfall profits tax. That may mean helping people out with their utility bills. Or perhaps developing needed work projects that can employ people who do not have jobs. It would seem appropriate, too, to use oil industry windfall profits to fund mass transit systems around the country. That might save millions of commuters the fortune they spend on gas. Using revenues from a windfall profits tax for research and development (R&D) of new energy sources would be still another sound approach.

Others, however, oppose the windfall profits tax. They maintain that business needs all the profits it gets—windfall and otherwise—since taxes still eat up almost half of corporate earnings. Then, too, the accounting systems used to calculate many firms' profits do not project a true picture. They overstate earnings for two reasons. First, inflation may cause inventory items to sell for more than was originally expected. This makes stated profits higher. But inflation also causes the cost of replacing the products—of production—to go up. The higher profits are rapidly eaten up by production costs. Second, inflation makes replacing old equipment and plants much more costly. This, too, is ignored when profit reports are written. Thus people mistakenly think businesses are better off than they really are.

Businesses have less to invest in making better, cheaper, or new products than they did five years ago. Good profits are a must for high productivity. And the argument goes, our nation's productivity must keep growing at a good rate for the standard of living to improve. People would not be so eager to tax windfall profits if they realized that U.S. productivity was dropping.

Business is not the main cause of inflation, insists the antitax group. High labor costs, the increase in the minimum wage, higher Social Security taxes, and higher prices on imported items are more to blame. In fact, with greater profits, businesses could better fight inflation. They would have more to invest in new products and markets.

In the end, it is the age-old dilemma of government: to tax or not to tax.

point, because of increased economies of mass production and greater control over pricing strategies. A firm with a large market share often becomes a price leader rather than a price follower.

Meeting Competition   The least aggressive pricing objective that a firm can pursue is **meeting competition.** The firm determines what competitors are charging and then prices at approximately the same level. For years many large retail department stores have followed this strategy. A store employs "shoppers" who go out and buy merchandise at competing stores. The merchandise is then analyzed to determine the price and quality of the product relative to the department store's own product mix. In addition to department stores, firms such as National Steel, Gulf Oil, Goodyear, and Continental Airlines have followed a strategy of meeting price competition. American Motors has striven to meet competitive prices for over 40 years.

Industries such as gypsum board, lumber, steel manufacturers and other highly concentrated industries have large firms that are price leaders. The remainder of each industry follows the leader. As a result, these industries have fewer price wars than those industries that are characterized by more active competition.

HOW TO PRICE A NEW PRODUCT

Pricing goals serve as guidelines in establishing a price for a new product. The goals provide direction for choosing either skimming or penetration price strategy. The price strategy enables a manager to develop a base price. The price is then "fine-tuned" with pricing tactics. We will first examine the two price strategies and then the pricing tactics (see Figure 15.2).

Price Skimming

A firm that charges a high introductory price is probably using a **price skimming** strategy. This means that as a product moves through its life cycle, the price is successively lowered to get all the sales the market will bear at each price level. Price skimming thus means "skimming off" the top or cream of the market. Price skimming also

TO SET A PRICE FOR A NEW PRODUCT

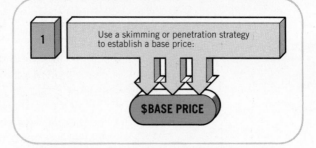

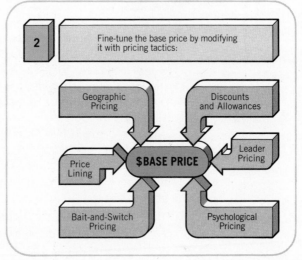

FIGURE 15.2

progressively brings the product within range of the more price-conscious consumer, enabling it to reach mass markets. Sometimes price skimming is called "sliding down the demand curve." Examples of products introduced by this strategy include minicomputers, home videotape equipment, and word processing equipment.

Skimming can be used when a product is well protected legally by a patent or copyright. This will aid in keeping competitors from entering the market and offering a cheaper version of the product. Skimming is often used when there is a major technological breakthrough that prevents competitors from quickly bringing out a "me-too" product. Skimming is also used when production can't be quickly expanded due to technological difficulties, raw materials shortages, or the inability of skilled craftspersons to turn out more than limited quantities. Hummel figurines, for example, are brought out each Christmas and sold at skimming prices. There are only so many Hummel artists that can produce these high-quality

TALKING BUSINESS

In the 23-year battle for market share between Bic and Gillette, pricing strategies have been an important weapon. In the early sixties, Bic introduced the 19-cent throwaway pen, which rapidly replaced Gillette's 98-cent Paper Mate as best seller. Results were similar in the disposable cigarette lighter market.

Then, late in the seventies, Bic threatened the "very core of Gillette's business"—the razor-and-blade market. Bic took advantage of Gillette's weakness at the low-priced end of the market by offering a disposable razor for "19¾ cents."

Gillette countered by trying to "out-Bic Bic. Even before the French company was ready to launch its razor in the U.S., Gillette brought out its own disposable razor, called Good News, and rushed it to supermarkets and drugstore counters, where it sells for 25 cents. Gillette justifies the premium by pointing out that, like the Trac II and Atra (Gillette's popular and profitable expensive brands), the new disposable features a twin blade, while Bic's razor employs the more traditional single blade." The distinction is important, since it undermines one of Bic's most successful marketing ploys—the claim that its disposables are just as good as the higher-priced competition.

By 1980, the firms had achieved virtually equal market shares; but these positions were not gained cheaply. Low profit margins caused Bic to lose $25 million on its razor over a three-year period. While the Good News produced a profit during this period, gains for the disposable mean losses for Gillette's more expensive products in the long run. Indeed, "Gillette's margins have already begun to slim down, as millions of shavers have forsaken the higher-priced blades."

Quotes from Linda Snyder Hays, "Gillette Takes the Wraps Off," *Fortune*, 25 February 1980, pp. 148–50. © 1980 Time Inc. Courtesy of Fortune Magazine.

---

items. If competitors should enter the market, the skimming price is usually forced down.

Advantages   Price skimming has several advantages for the marketing manager. If an introductory price is seen by consumers as being too high, the marketing manager can simply lower it. Skimming prices can be a way to test the market to find what buyers are willing to pay. An initial high price may create an image of quality and prestige for a new product or service. Consumers may therefore feel that they are getting a bargain when the price is ultimately lowered. This was true when microwave ovens went through a long period of "sliding down the demand curve."

Disadvantages   Price skimming is not without its problems. For one thing, it invites competition because of attractive profits. When Wella Balsam hair conditioner was introduced, it was priced at $1.98 a bottle. The average market price for creme rinses was $1.19. Alberto-Culver countered by introducing Alberto Balsam creme rinse, priced at $1.49, and spent much more on advertising than did Wella. Alberto Balsam soon claimed 60 percent of the hair conditioner market.

Some firms follow the price skimming strategy and tend to lower prices automatically as production costs decrease. Naturally, as prices are lowered, profits per unit decline, but total profits will increase if a sufficient number of additional units are sold at the lower price. Texas Instruments has for years followed the strategy of lowering prices as unit production costs decrease due to an increase in sales volume. The company could probably have maintained the higher price on many of its semiconductor products and received a higher profit, per unit, since its products represented state-of-the-art technology. However the company's ultimate goal seemed to be to maximize market share by lowering price even at the expense of profits.

For most products, skimming should be a short-range rather than a long-range strategy. If a firm is going to sell to a mass market, sooner or later it must reduce the price. There would never have been a mass market for digital watches, CB radios, or pocket calculators without "sliding down the demand curve." The mass market couldn't be tapped while the pocket calculator was selling for $150. (Epilogue: the same calculator ultimately sold for under $10.)

Penetration Pricing

If a company doesn't elect to use price skimming, it will probably follow a **penetration pricing** policy. Penetration pricing is philosophically at the other end of the scale from price skimming. The idea is to initially sell a good or service at a low, mass-market price and hope for a large sales volume.

Penetration pricing requires more accurate planning and forecasting than does skimming because the firm must gear up for mass production and marketing. When Texas Instruments entered the digital watch battle, its Lubbock, Texas production facilities could produce 6 million watches a year. At that time, this was the entire world demand for low-priced watches. If Texas Instruments had been wrong about the demand for its watches, the losses would have been staggering. (In 1982, TI got out of the digital watch business.)

Penetration pricing has several advantages. The relatively low price may induce consumers to switch brands. Texas Instruments convinced many people to switch from low-priced Timex watches to the new TI digitals. The strategy hopes to persuade consumers that the new product is a good substitute for the established one and that the new product has lower, more reasonable prices.

Another important advantage of penetration pricing is that it may discourage competitors from entering the market. Production of large quantities of a single product often lead to **economies of scale.** This means that as production is increased,

the average cost per unit tends to decline. For example, average cost of a new Ford or Chevrolet would be many times higher if it weren't for assembly-line, mass-production techniques. A Rolls-Royce costs over $100,000 as compared to $10,000 for a Ford Granada. This is in part due to the huge differences in output. The yearly production of Rolls-Royce is approximately 150 units — hardly a half day's production for the Ford Granada.

If Texas Instruments had produced only a few hundred watches a year, the cost would be over $100,000 per unit — due to the lack of economies of scale. Yet during the first year that Texas Instruments produced the digital, it shipped 4 million units. This enabled the company to *profitably* charge about $20 per watch. The only way a competitor could have entered the market with a similar product would be to charge about the same price. To meet that price, the competitor would also have had to achieve the same economies of scale that Texas Instruments did. All this would have represented a huge gamble for another electronics manufacturer. It would have had to sell about 4 million watches to get its cost down to that of TI. The market was not large enough for Texas Instruments *and* a competitor to sell 8 million digital watches. So the penetration pricing policy succeeded in discouraging potential competitors and eliminating most existing ones.

SPECIAL PRICING TACTICS

A skimming price or a penetration base price can be modified by using special pricing tactics. Among these are discounts and allowances, geographic pricing, price lining, leader pricing, bait-and-switch pricing, and psychological pricing.

Discounts and Allowances

Quantity Discounts A common way to change a base price is to offer a quantity discount. A **quantity discount** means that the price per unit is based on the number of units bought. The more units bought, the lower the price per unit. The quantity discount schedule shown here indicates that the purchaser who buys over 1500 units can save up to $6 per unit.

Quantity	Price per Unit
Fewer than 500 units	$10
500 to 1000 units	8
1000 to 1500 units	6
1500 units or more	4

A quantity discount:

- gives a consumer incentive to buy from one source rather than from a variety of dealers;
- reduces the selling cost and may shift some of the storage, finance, and risk-taking to the buyer;
- may increase the sales potential of a slow-moving item;
- is sometimes offered to increase sales during slack periods.

A quantity discount can be cumulative or non-cumulative. **A cumulative discount** is added up over a period of time. Referring back to the quantity discount schedule: let us assume that the buyer has three months in which to receive a quantity discount. Assume, too, that the first order is for 300 units, and the second for 400. If the second order is within the three-month cumulative discount period, the buyer will receive the $8 discount price on the 400-unit order only. This is because the 400-unit order marks the first time that the buyer is in the 500-to-1000 unit bracket. (The first order — 300 — plus 400 = 700.) A **non-cumulative discount** is a once-only reduction in price. It is based exclusively on the number of units bought at a single time. This number isn't applicable to a subsequent purchase.

Cash Discounts   A **cash discount** is a price reduction given to a buyer for paying a bill within a specified period of time — or for an immediate cash payment. Take, for example, an invoice with terms of *2/10 net 30*. This means that the customer will receive a 2 percent discount if the bill is paid within 10 days. It also says that the customer has a maximum of 30 days in which to pay the full amount. Suppose, then, that an office supply store orders a dozen electric pencil sharpeners and receives a bill for $250 with terms of 2/10 net 30. The bookkeeper will write a check for $245 (reflecting the 2 percent discount) if the bill is paid within 10 days. If the bill is not paid within the discount period, the full $250 will be due at the end of the 30 day period. Cash discounts are given because accounts receivable (money owed the company by those who charged their purchases) are expensive to finance. Also, with accounts receivable the company loses the benefit of putting the unpaid cash to work. Finally, accounts receivable can sometimes result in a collection problem. The cash discount encourages prompt payment.

Seasonal Discounts   A **seasonal discount** is offered to a retailer or wholesaler when goods or services are bought out of season. Seasonal discounts enable a manufacturer to maintain a steady level of production throughout the year. Toro, a manufacturer of lawn mowers, offers seasonal discounts to retailers in the fall and winter. This is to encourage them to buy earlier. That way, Toro's production keeps flowing smoothly.

Cash rebates are a form of price cutting.

Airlines, resorts, and hotels offer seasonal discounts during their slow periods or off-seasons to help offset fixed costs.

Functional Discounts   A **functional discount,** also called a *trade discount*, is a payment to members of a channel of distribution for performing their functions. Wholesalers and retailers, for example, are supposed to locate retail buyers, provide a proper assortment of merchandise, and carry a reasonable level of inventory. For performing these services, the manufacturer offers the wholesaler and retailer a discount. Assume that a manufacturer quotes a retail list price of $500 and functional discounts of 40 and 10 percent. The retailer's cost will be $300 ($500 minus 40%), and the wholesaler will pay $270 ($300 minus 10%). Manufacturers may give different functional discounts to different channel members because the services they perform will vary.

Allowances   Allowances are similar to discounts. If a retailer sets up a point-of-purchase display provided by the manufacturer, the manufacturer may include a quantity of "free goods" in the retailer's next order. This is a promotional allowance. A **promotional allowance** is either a cash or a merchandise payment to a retailer for performing a promotional task for the manufacturer.

Another form of allowance is a trade-in allowance. Perhaps you've received this if you've ever traded in a used car for a new one. Because of the large markups in full-size automobiles (around 18%) it is often difficult for the consumer to determine the real value of a trade-in allowance.

Geographic Pricing

In addition to discounts and allowances, base prices may be varied by using geographic pricing. Geographic pricing can be categorized as FOB, uniform delivered pricing (and zone pricing), and freight absorption pricing.

FOB Pricing   The term **FOB** means "free on board." This implies that the seller will place the merchandise free on board the truck or other carrier. If a price is quoted "FOB factory," the merchandise is placed on board the carrier at the factory. When goods are purchased "FOB shipping

point," the merchandise will be placed on the carrier at a warehouse or other location. The sales price excludes transportation charges. The buyer pays the shipping charges from the point where the merchandise is loaded on board the carrier. Any damage claim beyond the point of origin must be filed by the buyer against the freight carrier rather than against the seller. The total cost will generally be higher for purchasers the farther they are from the shipping point. This is because the total expense to them is the selling price *plus* the freight charges.

Uniform Delivered Pricing   If a manufacturer prefers that all customers who buy identical quantities of a product pay the same total cost, it can implement uniform delivered pricing. **Uniform delivered pricing** is sometimes referred to as "postage stamp pricing." The manufacturer computes the average cost of transportation and charges this fee to every buyer. That way the total cost for each buyer is the same regardless of where the buyer is located. In effect, this policy discriminates against buyers located close to the shipping point. Some companies use postage stamp pricing when they are trying to maintain a nationally advertised price. They don't want distant buyers to inflate the retail price by the extra cost of long-distance shipping. Postage stamp pricing is often found in the office equipment and paper products industries.

Zone Pricing   A variation of uniform delivered pricing is zone pricing (see Figure 15.3). A marketing manager using **zone pricing** computes the

FIGURE 15.3

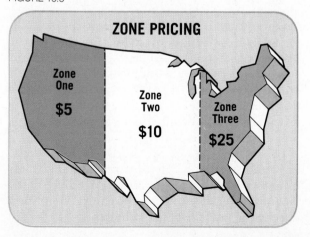

average freight charges within a given zone. Every buyer within the zone is then charged the average rate. If the Blue Diamond Almond growers used zone pricing, they might charge $5 a case in Zone 1, $10 in Zone 2, and $25 in Zone 3. Obviously the policy discriminates against buyers that are located closest to the seller within a zone. A buyer in Lawrence, Kansas should pay a lower freight rate for Blue Diamond Almonds (shipped from Sacramento) than a retailer in Chicago. Yet they'd both pay $10 a case, since each is in Zone 2. So zone pricing does work to the advantage of those farthest from the seller within a given zone.

Freight Absorption Pricing   As its name implies, **freight absorption pricing** means that the seller absorbs all or part of the freight charges. This policy is used to (1) break into new markets, (2) meet competition, or (3) increase sales, thus achieving greater economies of mass production. If the savings in production costs (due to economies of mass production) are greater than the cost of absorbing freight, the total profits of the firm will rise. Suppose that production costs drop $2 per unit and the company absorbs $1 in freight charges per unit. Using freight absorption pricing, the company still earns an additional dollar profit on each unit sold.

Price Lining

Managers can also use price lines to modify base prices. When a retailer or manufacturer sets a limited number of prices for a line of merchandise, this is called **price lining.** Sears might offer women's blouses at $15, $20, and $30. There would be no blouses available at prices in between these figures.

Price lines help simplify consumer decision making because there is a single price—say $20 for a wide selection of styles and brands of blouses. The retailer assumes that if the prices are viewed as reasonable, customers will concentrate on their purchases instead of responding to slight differences in price. Sears' management feels that it would not significantly increase sales by dropping the $15 line to $13.

By setting prices at two, three, or four levels, the retailer may be able to carry a smaller total inventory than it could without price lines. This means a lower investment in inventory, simplified purchasing, and fewer markdowns.

Price leader ads attract customers to the grocery store.

However price lines aren't without disadvantages. As costs continue to rise, the marketing manager is faced with either changing price lines or accepting a lower profit. Assume that Sears had been paying $10 for blouses that it was selling for $15. If Sears receives notice from the manufacturer that the $10 blouses are going to be raised to $12, Sears can either raise the price line to $17 or take a smaller profit per unit ($3 instead of $5). Frequent changes in the price line can result in consumer confusion and may create ill will for the merchant. An alternative is not to

Higher prices seem to suggest higher quality. The relation is dubious. The price on a higher quality product may be considerably higher than the product's extra quality. In 1979, University of Iowa professor Peter C. Reisz tried to relate the prices of 679 brands of packaged foods with their quality ratings as determined over 15 years by Consumers Union. His conclusion: "The correlation between quality and price for packaged food products is near zero."

Marketing men, however, sense that consumers are buying more than a mere commodity when they buy some goods. A $100 bottle of perfume may contain $4 to $16 worth of scent. The rest of the price goes for advertising, packaging and profit. Such perfume sells. . . .

Marketers say that consumer preference for higher prices extends especially to "ego-sensitive" merchandise such as perfume and other personal care products and goods that one way or another are kept on display. That suits the marketing men fine. "Almost invariably, there's more profit in premium products," says John Keon, a New York University marketing professor. "That's why so many companies want to go to the premium end."

change the price line, but rather to stock lower-quality merchandise as costs increase. However this strategy may prove damaging to the image of the firm and result in a loss of customers.

Leader Pricing

Leader pricing means that merchandise is priced below the normal markup or even below cost. Management hopes that leader prices will increase sales volume and profits. Leader prices may attract customers to a store where they wouldn't otherwise have shopped. Every Thursday you can pick up the grocery section of any major newspaper and see examples of leader pricing. Department stores and specialty stores also rely heavily on leader pricing.

Leader prices are usually set on items for which buyers are price sensitive. Supermarkets often feature coffee and bacon as leader prices. A good leader price is (1) well known, (2) priced low enough so that it is attractive to the marketplace, and (3) not already so low in price that a further reduction won't generate additional sales.

Bait-and-Switch Pricing

Leader pricing is a legitimate attempt by a manufacturer or retailer to attract customers by offering a bargain. **Bait-and-switch pricing** has a different motive—and is unethical. This strategy is used at the retail level to attract customers to the store by advertising an item for an unusually low price (the bait). Next, very aggressive personal selling is applied to trade the customers up. The retailer has no intention of selling the low-priced merchandise. An ad for a stereo specialty shop might say, "Sony Stereo System Only $12 a Month at XYZ Audio Center!" If you went to buy that stereo system, you'd probably find that it had "just been sold" or was "at our other store." Or they might have the stereo, but it would be so beaten and damaged that no one would want it. Next, the salesperson would say, "I realize that this is not much of a stereo. Now, over here I have a *really* fine unit that is only $399." This is the *switch* that may cause a susceptible customer to make a very expensive (and perhaps unaffordable) purchase. Bait-and-switch advertising is illegal under the Wheeler-Lea Amendment (1938) to the Trade Commission Act of 1914. From time to time some of America's largest retailers have been charged with bait-and-switch advertising, including Sears and Levitz Furniture Stores.[3]

Psychological Pricing

Odd-Even Pricing   Another special pricing tactic is psychological pricing. One form this takes is **odd-even pricing.** Dealers believe that consumers favor odd prices over even prices for most products. Instead of pricing a stereo system at $500, the seller will price it at $499.95 or $495. Presumably the customer views this as $400+ rather than $500, and so may feel less resistant. The odd-even pricing issue may seem trivial, but it isn't. If a retailer could sell just as many units at the higher (whole-dollar, or even) price, he/she would be foolish not to. After all, even pricing could add $100,000 to the profit of a retailer grossing $30 million.

While odd prices are used to imply a bargain, even prices are intended to denote quality. One would never find, for example, a hand-tooled pair of anteater cowboy boots priced at $799.95.

Instead, they'd be priced at $800. Fine jewelry, watches, and clothing are priced at $500, $1000, and $2000, but rarely at an odd price. The higher price is often associated with higher quality or status, the domain of prestige pricing.

Prestige Pricing   A second form of psychological pricing is called prestige pricing. **Prestige pricing** sometimes means that the product will be perceived as having greater value or higher quality simply by raising its price. A consumer who has a hard time determining the value of a product, such as an automobile tire, may assume that the highest-priced item possesses the greatest quality. But prestige pricing can in fact be associated with products of genuinely high value and quality, which could not be maintained if the price were cut by much.

High prices can indicate high status, especially in clothing. Rodeo Drive's specialty shops in Beverly Hills cater to the super-rich Hollywood crowd. By the same token, Cutter Bill's western wear serves the oil-rich urban cowboy. Exemplifying a common form of prestige pricing, a shirt that would sell elsewhere for $10.95 might sell for $50 at one of these specialty shops.

Examples of psychological pricing.

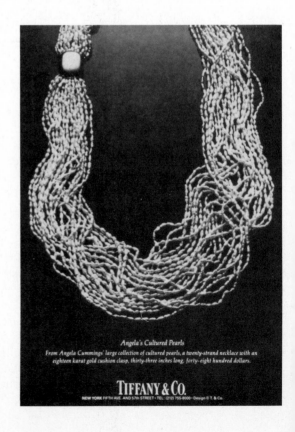

Angela's Cultured Pearls
From Angela Cummings' large collection of cultured pearls, a twenty-strand necklace with an eighteen karat gold cushion clasp, thirty-three inches long, forty-eight hundred dollars.

PERSPECTIVE ON SMALL BUSINESS

High-volume sales and mass marketing may be the goal of some small businessmen, but Edward and Thomas O'Gara are happy if they ring up three or four sales a week.

The O'Garas sell exotic cars, customized limousines, armorplated vehicles, and jet planes. Their showroom floor features merchandise like a 1964 Phantom V Rolls Royce for $125,000, a Clenet II limited edition convertible for $83,500, and a Stutz Blackhawk Coupe for $91,500.

While bottom line figures aren't disclosed, Ed, a 38-year-old ex-Navy fighter pilot with a master's in business administration, smiles and says, "The markups are profitable."

The two men started their exotic automobile sales operation, known as the O'Gara Coach Co., [in 1978] with an initial investment of $30,000. As it turned out, the customers who came by the Beverly Hills showroom had more than transportation on their minds. They also wanted security. The result was O'Gara International Ltd., a spinoff that markets armored vehicles—standard luxury cars with extras such as bulletproof tires and windows, armorplated sides, and plating under the floor to resist mine blasts. Tom O'Gara, 31, spends half of his time on the road, visiting clients in Saudi Arabia, Manila, London, Oman, and Rome. A company office in Washington, D.C., takes care of sales to foreign diplomats.

From conversations with exotic car shoppers, the O'Garas identified yet another market—people who aren't satisfied with conventional limousines. The two set up a plant at Canoga Park, Calif., where Lincoln Continentals or Cadillac Fleetwoods are cut in half and extended 42 or 48 inches. Plastic fittings are replaced with walnut, and accessories like a color TV set, videotape recorder, and bar complete with crystal glassware are installed. The price for such a town car is around $67,000, FOB Los Angeles.

"We're in the transportation business," Ed O'Gara says simply, then adds, "in the high end of it."

SOURCE: Norman Sklarewitz, "Need a Bulletproof Rolls with Full Bar?" *INC.*, December 1981, p. 19. Copyright © 1981 by INC. Publishing Company, 38 Commercial Wharf, Boston, MA 02110.

SUMMARY

In a free-enterprise economy, price is the basis for allocation of goods and services among customers, businesses, and units of government. If people believe a good or service is fairly priced, they will buy the product and so encourage its producer to keep supplying it.

The firm must charge the right price to earn a fair return on its investment. If the price is too high, customers will not buy the product, and the firm will go out of business; if the price is too low, sales may be good, but the firm may incur a loss. Prices are set according to the firm's pricing objectives, which should be realistic and measurable. Pricing objectives include profit maximization, target return on investment, maintaining or increasing market share, and meeting competition.

Pricing objectives serve as guidelines for choosing either a skimming or a penetration pricing strategy for a new product. The price strategy enables a manager to develop a base price, which is fine-tuned with various pricing tactics. The price skimming strategy involves charging a high introductory price; as the product moves through its life cycle, its price is successively lowered. A penetration pricing policy, on the other hand, involves initially selling a good or service at a low, mass-market price and hoping for a large sales volume. Since this strategy involves mass production and marketing, it requires more accurate planning and forecasting than does skimming.

Pricing tactics used to fine-tune the base price include discounts and allowances, geographic pricing, price lining, leader pricing, bait-and-switch pricing, and psychological pricing. Sellers can offer quantity discounts, cash discounts, seasonal discounts, and functional, or trade, discounts;

types of allowances include promotional and trade-in allowances. Geographic pricing relates to shipping costs; types include FOB pricing, uniform delivered pricing, zone pricing, and freight absorption pricing. Price lining involves setting a limited number of prices to cover a line of merchandise. Leader pricing is pricing merchandise below the normal markup or even below cost to increase sales volume and attract customers to the store. In bait-and-switch pricing, as in leader pricing, a low price is advertised. However, once in the store, the customer is urged to buy a higher-priced item. Bait-and-switch pricing is illegal. Psychological pricing includes odd-even pricing, which seems to make the customer perceive the price as lower than it is, and prestige pricing, which makes the customer perceive the product to have higher quality because its price is high.

KEY TERMS

bait-and-switch
   pricing
cash discount
cumulative discount
dollar votes
economies of scale
FOB
free enterprise
freight absorption
   pricing
functional discount
leader pricing
market share
meeting competition
noncumulative
   discount
odd-even pricing
penetration pricing
prestige pricing
price lining
price skimming
profit maximization
promotional
   allowance
quantity discount
seasonal discount
target return on
   investment
uniform delivered
   pricing
zone pricing

REVIEW QUESTIONS

1. How does "price" allocate goods and services?
2. What techniques can retailers employ to induce prompt payment?
3. When would a firm most likely use price skimming?
4. Who pays the freight on a shipment priced "F.O.B. Destination"?
5. What is meant by price lining?
6. Are bait-and-switch pricing and leader pricing essentially the same thing? Give examples.

DISCUSSION QUESTIONS

1. Since profit is a realistic goal for a business, why is it that all businesses do not set pricing objectives for profit maximization?
2. What pricing strategy would you most likely consider if you were going to market a new product and knew that your competition couldn't start producing for a year? Explain.
3. What kind of pricing objectives do you think would be best for a store featuring high-fashion designer clothes? Explain at least two approaches.
4. How can something as obvious as a retail price have a psychological dimension?
5. Bait-and-switch pricing is illegal in interstate commerce. Should the federal government also outlaw price skimming?
6. If price lining offers so many advantages to both the retailer and the consumer, why don't all retailers use this tactic?

CASE: TRYING NOT TO PASS THE BUCK

Panko's Paint Stores, a midwestern chain of discount paint and hardware stores, has been marketing paint under its own brand for some time. Part of Panko's success has been the ability to maintain a retail price much lower than national or regional brands. To do this, Panko's often finds it necessary to absorb increased costs in materials or production from its supplier.

One of Panko's best-selling items was a 16-oz. can of spray paint, held down to 99¢ for over four years. Not long ago Panko's was notified by the supplier that costs would increase again. The buyer at Panko's calculated that to maintain the same minimum profit, the price would have to be increased to $1.19. While this would still be lower than other brands, a good part of the price differential would be lost—and so might Panko's competitive edge. Panko's buyer also calculated that by coming out with a more slender can, which would be as tall as the old 16-oz. item but would hold only 14 oz., Panko's could hold the price at 99¢ for at least another nine months to a year.

1. If you were Panko's buyer, what would you want to consider before making the decision?
2. What other ways would you consider for dealing with the price increase?

CASE: HOW ARE THINGS IN GUACAMOLE?

A sad song's being sung in California these days. The sadness is the lament of an industry that's really "gone to the dogs." For several years an overabundant crop of avocados has resulted in a market at once glutted and depressed. And, with another record crop being anticipated, the future offers no relief.

With pricing of the product generally determined by supply and demand, this industry is in real trouble. Furthermore, not everybody likes avocados. The market seems to be confined primarily to California and adjacent states and to Southern states, which have been supplied by Mexico. The midwestern states and the East Coast sustain only a modest demand for the product.

Avocados are selling in stores from 20¢ in supermarkets to $1.50 in specialty stores, but profit has really gone downhill everywhere—despite a very low cost due to the oversupply. Some creative marketeers have tried to find other uses for the product. Well known, of course, is "Guacamole Dip," which has become quite popular in some circles. The latest brainstorm is to make pet food out of avocados. But, say some, "the dogs won't eat the stuff."

For years this unusual "fruit" has been a favorite of the well-to-do, who have cultivated a taste for unusual dishes. The avocado salad enjoyed a good market in these social circles—but now what's to become of the avalanche of ever-ripening avocados that are causing a glut in a depressed market?

1. What pricing strategies could be used by the creative marketer?
2. How can "prestige pricing" be applied to the product under these conditions?
3. What do you think the growers should do about this catastrophe in their industry?

Epilogue: Technical Pricing Information

DEMAND AND SUPPLY

The Nature of Demand

A pricing goal of meeting the competition ignores both supply and demand. However market share and profit maximization both rely on demand estimates. Demand is the quantity of a product or service that will be sold in the market at various prices for a specified period of time.

The quantity of a product that people will buy depends on its price. The higher the price, the lower the number of products or services that will be demanded. The lower the price, the more products or services will be demanded. This concept is illustrated in Figure 15.A1 which examines the demand per week for pretzels at a local bakery at various prices and plots it in graphic form. This is called a demand curve. The vertical scale of the graph shows different prices of pretzels measured in dollars per package. The horizontal scale measures the quantity of pretzels that will be demanded per week. For example, at a price of $1.50, 85 packages will be sold per week.

The demand curve slopes downward and to the right. This indicates that as the price of pretzels is lowered, more is demanded. Stated another way, if a greater quantity is put on the market, then hopes of selling all of it will be realized only by selling it at a lower price.

One reason why more is sold at lower prices than at higher prices is that lower prices bring in new buyers. While this might not be so obvious with pretzels, consider the example of steak. As the price of steak gets lower and lower, some people who are not eating steak will probably start

DEMAND SCHEDULE AND CURVE FOR PRETZELS

Price per Package	Packages Demanded per Week
$3.00	35
2.50	50
2.00	65
1.50	85
1.00	120

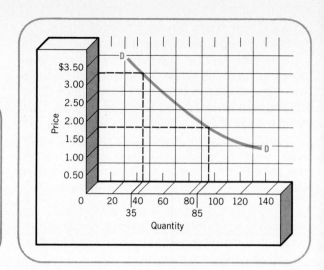

FIGURE 15.A1

buying it rather than hamburger. And, with each reduction in price, existing customers may buy extra amounts. If the price of pretzels gets low enough, some people will buy more than they have bought in the past.

The Concept of Supply

The demand schedule relates prices to the amount that customers wish to buy. The supply schedule is a relationship between prices and the amount of a product that producers are willing and able to supply. Figure 15.A2 illustrates the supply schedule for pretzels and the resulting supply curve. Unlike the falling demand curve, the supply curve for pretzels rises upward and to the right. This means that at higher prices, pretzel manufacturers will obtain more resources (flour, yeast, salt) and produce more pretzels. If the price consumers are willing to pay for pretzels rises, producers can afford to buy more pretzel ingredients. Therefore, output tends to increase at higher prices because more packages of pretzels can be sold and greater profits earned.

FIGURE 15.A2

SUPPLY SCHEDULE AND CURVE FOR PRETZELS

Price per Package	Packages Supplied per Week
$3.00	140
2.50	130
2.00	110
1.50	85
1.00	25

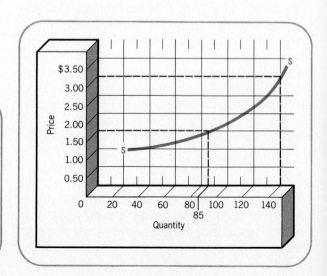

How Demand and Supply Establish Prices

At this point, let's combine the concepts of demand and supply to see how competitive market prices are determined. Up to now we have been saying that if price is x amount, then consumers will purchase y amount of pretzels. But how high or low will prices actually go? Related questions are: how many packages of pretzels will be produced? how many consumed? We cannot predict consumption by looking only at demand curves. Nor can the supply curve alone forecast production. Instead, Figure 15.A3 answers these questions by revealing what happens when supply and demand interact.

At a price of $3, the public would demand only 35 packages of pretzels. But suppliers stand ready to place 140 packages on the market (data from the demand and supply schedules). This would create a surplus of 105 packages of pretzels. How does a merchant get rid of a surplus? By lowering the price.

If the price were $1, then 120 packages would be demanded, but only 25 would be placed on the market. A shortage of 95 units would be created. If a product were in short supply and you wanted it, how would you entice the dealer to part with one unit? The answer is to offer more money (pay a higher price).

Now, let us examine a price of $1.50. At this price 85 packages are demanded and 85 are supplied. When demand and supply are equal, a state called *equilibrium* is achieved. A temporary price above equilibrium—say $3—creates a surplus. This is because suppliers stand ready to place more packages of pretzels on the market than consumers are willing to buy. A surplus therefore places a downward pressure on prices. A temporary price below equilibrium—say $1—results in a shortage, because demand for pretzels is greater than the available supply. Shortages force an upward pressure on price. As long as demand and supply remain the same, temporary price increases or decreases will tend to return to equilibrium. At equilibrium there's no inclination for prices to rise or fall. But an equilibrium price may not be reached all at once. There may be periods of trial and error as the market for a product or service moves toward equilibrium. Yet sooner or later demand and supply will settle down in proper balance.

PRICING TECHNIQUES

Sometimes retailers and manufacturers will ignore or minimize the importance of demand and price their products on the basis of cost. Pricing strictly on the basis of cost creates two problems. First, the price may be too high, reducing or eliminating sales. Second, the price may be too low, with additional profits simply thrown away. For example, when Texas Instruments first brought out its Speak and Spell electronic toy, it was operating at plant capacity and still could have sold thousands more. This was true even though many retailers were adding a generous markup to the wholesale price. If Texas Instruments had first established demand and then established a price, it could have reaped greater profits and still sold all that it was capable of producing.

Markup Pricing

The most common form of cost-oriented pricing is markup pricing. Markup pricing means that a retailer adds a certain percentage to a product's wholesale cost to arrive at a retail price. So retail selling price = *cost plus markup*. The cost is the expense of acquiring the goods for resale. The markup is the amount added to the cost in order to cover expenses and earn a profit. These rela-

FIGURE 15.A3

THE EQUILIBRIUM PRICE FOR PRETZELS

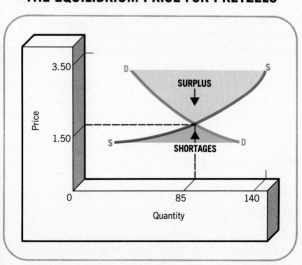

TABLE 15-A1

Markup Pricing

Cost to the retailer	$5	(71%)
Markup	+ 2	(29%)
Retail price	$7	(100%)

$$\text{Markup percentage} = \frac{\text{AMOUNT ADDED TO COST (MARKUP)}}{\text{PRICE}}$$

$$\text{Markup percentage} = \frac{\$2}{\$7} = 29\%$$

tionships are shown in Table 15.A1. An item that costs $5 and is sold for $7 carries a markup of 29 percent. If the firm had operating expenses (such as wages and utilities) averaging $1.50 per unit, the average net profit would be 50¢ per unit, or about 7 percent.

A question that management must resolve when using markup pricing is whether to charge the same percentage markup for all the merchandise in the store. For example, it was long a common practice in department stores to have a gross margin (what remains after subtracting cost of goods sold from sales revenue) of 40 percent. Furniture and jewelry stores have often charged a 100 percent markup. Many present-day retailers, however, are abandoning the uniform markup because of a better understanding of the nature of demand—and also because of competition. When department stores added a 40 percent markup to appliances, they became extremely vulnerable to discounters such as K mart and Target.

If merchandise doesn't sell, it usually is marked down. The *initial markup* and the markup for which the product sells aren't always the same thing. The initial markup is called the *markon*. Suppose, for example, that a retailer selling stationery has ultimately to cut the price from $7 a box to $6 in order to sell it. If the cost to the retailer was $5, the actual markup would only be $1 or 17 percent ($1 divided by $6). This figure is called the gross margin or the *maintained markup*.

A number of elements can influence markups. As we have already noted, there are traditional markups in some industries. Other elements include markups used by competitors and the image a store is trying to build. If a retailer is trying to create a prestige image, the average markup will be much higher than that of a merchant trying to develop a discounter image. From time to time, prices are lowered (the markup is reduced) for a sale. One objective of a sale is to bring people into the store who may not come otherwise. The merchant hopes that these customers will buy not only the sale items but also regular-price goods. Many retailers also try to trade the customer up from lower-priced to higher-priced goods. An exception is clearance sales, which are usually run at the end of the season to get rid of out-of-season stocks. In early spring, for example, Oshman's—a large sporting goods retailer—runs a clearance sale on ski equipment and accessories. This is to avoid having to carry the inventory over for another year.

Stock Turnover and Profits   Another element that influences the markup a manager places on goods is stock turnover. This is the number of times during a given period (usually a year) that the average amount of goods on hand (inventory) is sold and replaced. The formula is:

$$\frac{\text{Stock}}{\text{turnover}} = \frac{\text{net retail sales}}{\substack{\text{average retail value} \\ \text{of the inventory}}}$$

If a store had sales of $400,000 during the year and the average inventory at retail value was $45,000, turnover is:

$$\frac{\$400,000}{\$\ 45,000} = 8.8 \text{ times}$$

Stock turnover is a measure of the efficiency of a business. A lower rate of turnover may be a danger signal that something needs to be corrected. Inventory levels may be too high or there may be stock shortages and outages due to either shoplifting or poor recordkeeping. Rapid stock turnover often results in limited investment in inventory, less need for storage space, fresher goods, and fewer markdowns. Usually, higher stock turnover results in higher profits. A higher turnover means that there's less money tied up in inventory and that markdowns are minimized. Big markdowns are common with large, aged stocks of merchandise. If markdowns are too large, there may be no profits at all. At the same time, sales volume must reach a certain—usually quite high—level before all costs are covered.

The Break-even Concept

Manufacturers, wholesalers, and retailers are always interested to know how much volume must

Reduced prices often help stimulate inventory turnover.

be sold at a certain price before a profit is earned. This level of volume is called the break-even point. A manager must understand cost and revenue concepts to figure break-even points.

Total cost consists of total variable cost plus total fixed cost. Variable costs are those costs that change with levels of output. Wages paid to production-line employees and expenditures for raw materials are considered variable costs. For example, the total cost of raw materials depends on the level of production. Fixed costs are costs that don't vary with the level of output. A 25-year lease on a manufacturing facility is a fixed cost. The $4166-per-month rent must be paid whether production is one unit or a million units.

Total revenue, on the other hand, is a simpler matter. It's determined by multiplying the selling price by the number of units sold.

Grey Manufacturing has fixed costs of $50,000 and variable costs of $3 per unit (comprised of labor and raw materials). A research report provided to Grey management shows that it can sell up to 100,000 bottles of Grey after-shave lotion at $5 a bottle without having to lower its price. The formula for the break-even point in units is:

$$\text{Break-even point in units} = \frac{\text{total fixed cost}}{\text{fixed cost contribution}}$$

The fixed cost contribution is the selling price minus the variable cost—in this case, $5 − $3 (= $2). So $2 per bottle is the revenue that can be contributed to covering fixed cost. And after the break-even point is reached, this same $2 be-

comes *profit*. But when is the break-even point reached? We apply the formula and get:

$$\frac{\$50,000}{\$2} = \frac{25,000 \text{ units}}{\text{(bottles)}} = \frac{\text{break-even}}{\text{point}}$$

Grey Manufacturing will break even when it sells 25,000 units of after-shave lotion. At that point, total revenue will be $125,000 (25,000 units × $5 = $125,000). Total cost will be $125,000 ($50,000 fixed cost + $75,000 variable cost). Now, if Grey's forecasts are correct and it can sell 100,000 units, its total profits will be $150,000; that is, 75,000 units × $2. (Remember that for the first 25,000 bottles the $2 is applied to covering fixed costs.) Total revenue at 100,000 units would be $500,000 ($5 × 100,000), and total cost would be $350,000 ($50,000 fixed cost + $300,000 variable cost). Therefore total revenue ($500,000) minus total cost ($350,000) equals total profit ($150,000). So by using the break-even formula, Grey Manufacturing can quickly find out (1) how much it has to sell to break even, and then (2) how much profit can be earned if higher sales volumes are obtained (see Figure 15.A4). When a firm is operating close to the break-even point, management may want to take action to reduce costs or see if there's any reasonable way to boost sales.

FIGURE 15.A4

THE BREAK EVEN POINT FOR GREY AFTERSHAVE AT $5.00 A BOTTLE

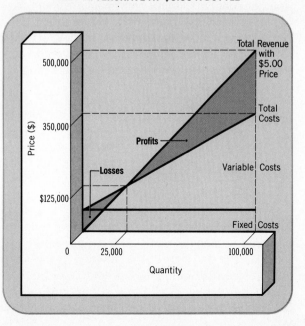

A CAREER IN MARKETING

The importance of marketing and marketing-related activities continues to mount in the United States. Top management realizes that in order to grow and effectively compete, a company must understand the marketplace and consumers' needs and wants. Marketing offers a rich variety of career opportunities, from highly technical marketing research analysis to very creative work in advertising.

Some positions—such as traffic manager, market research analyst, and product manager—are office oriented desk-type jobs. Others—particularly in sales, public relations, and advertising account executives—require wide contact with the public and outside corporations. For the past several decades, marketing has been a primary employer of business graduates. The greatest number of opportunities have been in the field of sales. The outlook for the remainder of the decade continues to be very bright for careers in marketing.

Where the Opportunities Are

1  RETAIL BUYER

All merchandise sold in a retail store, be it automobile tires or high-fashion clothing, appears in that store on the decision of the buyer. A buyer for a small store may purchase its complete stock of merchandise. Buyers who work for large stores often handle one or two related lines such as home furnishings, and decorative accessories. Buyers work within a limited budget and attempt to select the merchandise that will sell most quickly. They must understand their customer likes and dislikes and foresee fashion and manufacturing trends.

Places of Employment   Throughout the country. Most jobs are in major metropolitan areas.

Skills Required   Some jobs for persons with a two-year degree. Most employers prefer a four-year program.

Employment Outlook thru 1990   Good.

Salaries $15,000–$40,000 + bonus (mass merchandising buyer).

2 ■ MARKET RESEARCHER

A market researcher provides decision-making information for the marketing manager. Statisticians determine sample sizes, decide who is to be interviewed, and use quantitiative tools to analyze data. Research firm account executives sell research projects to advertising agencies, manufacturers, and retailers. They also act as "go betweens" with the research firm and the client to plan studies, give progress reports, and present results. Field supervisors hire research field services to do the interviewing. They are in charge of gathering the data quickly, economically, and accurately.

Places of Employment   New York, Chicago, and California are the homes of most large research firms. Other opportunities are with manufacturers and large retailers throughout the country.

Skills Required Research statistician: M.B.A.; account executive: four-year degree; field supervisor: for the most part a four-year program, some two-year.

Employment Outlook thru 1990 Fair to good in the places listed above. Fair elsewhere.

Salaries Research statistician: $18,000–$35,000: account executive: $16,000–$40,000 + ; field supervisor: $11,000–$20,000.

3 ■ MANUFACTURER'S SALESPERSON

Manufacturers salespersons sell mainly to other businesses—factories, railroads, banks, wholesalers, and retailers. They also sell to hospitals, schools, libraries, and other institutions. Most manufacturer's salespersons sell nontechnical products. Sales workers who deal in highly technical products, such as electronic equipment, are often called sales engineers or industrial sales workers. Some manufacturer's sales positions require extensive traveling.

Places of Employment Throughout the country.

Skills Required Nontechnical products: usually a four-year program; technical products: technical undergraduate degree plus an M.B.A.

Employment Outlook thru 1990 Very good to excellent.

Salaries Nontechnical: $15,000–$42,500; technical: $22,000–$60,000 + . Many positions also pay a commission or bonus for both technical and nontechnical sales.

4 ■ TRAVEL AGENT

Many travelers seek the assistance of travel agents—specialists who have the information and ability to make the best possible travel arrangements, considering the tastes, budgets, and demands of the customer. When travel agents make arrangements for their clients, they consult fare schedules and ticket prices often via computer terminals. Other guides and fact sheets often are used by agents to get information on hotel ratings, accommodations, and other tourist information.

Places of Employment Every part of the country, but concentrated in major population centers. Only 20 percent of all agencies are located in small towns and rural areas.

Skills Required Two year program.

Employment Outlook thru 1990 Excellent.

Salaries $10,800–$19,200.

5 ■ WHOLESALE TRADE SALESPERSON

Wholesale salespersons regularly visit buyers for retail, industrial, and commercial firms, as well as buyers for institutions such as schools and hospitals. They show samples, pictures, or catalogs that list the items their company stocks. Some wholesale salespersons check stocks for retailers to determine what should be ordered. Some workers help store personnel improve and update systems for ordering and inventory. A salesperson handling technical equipment, such as air-conditioning equipment, may give technical assistance on installation and maintenance.

Places of Employment Wholesale firms are often located in large cities but sales workers may be assigned territories in any part of the country.

Skills Required Depends mainly on the product line and market: either two-year or four-year program.

Employment Outlook thru 1990 Very good.

Salaries $12,000–$63,000 (experience in growth industries).

6 ■ PUBLIC RELATIONS WORKER

Public relations workers help businesses, government, universities, and other organizations build and maintain a positive public image. Public relations workers may handle press, community, or consumer relations; interest-group representation; fund-raising; speech-writing; and plant tours. They often represent employers at community projects.

Places of Employment Manufacturing firms, public utilities, transportation companies, insurance companies, and trade and professional associations employ many public relations workers. Also, a sizable number work for government agencies. Public relations workers are concentrated in large cities. More than half of the approximately 2000 public relations firms are in New York, Chicago, Los Angeles, and Washington D.C.

Skills Required Four-year program.

Employment Outlook thru 1990 Excellent.

Salaries $11,400–$37,200 (public relations director).

7 ■ PRODUCT MANAGER

In large manufacturing corporations, one key product may account for millions of dollars in sales. It is too important to leave the success of such products to chance. The product manager oversees the marketing of a product or products and is responsible for meeting profit objectives. Product managers must coordinate the activities of distribution departments, market research, advertising, and others to assure that the product has the "right" marketing mix. Working with many departments, yet lacking direct authority over any requires good human relations and planning skills.

Places of Employment Major population and industrial centers.

Skills Required Four-year program; some employers require an M.B.A.

Employment Outlook thru 1990 Very good.

Salaries $15,000–$58,000 (group product manager).

8 ■ ADVERTISING ACCOUNT EXECUTIVE

The advertising account executive is responsible for making sales to client firms. It is this person's responsibility to keep the client organization satisfied so that it remains with the agency. This involves understanding the client's needs and helping develop a package or campaign that will enable the firm to reach its promotional goals. A director of accounts (one step above account executive) assigns accounts to account executives whose interest and skills match clients' needs.

Places of Employment The greatest concentrations of large advertising agencies are New York and Chicago. Moderate-sized and smaller agencies are found in every metropolitan area.

Skills Required Four-year program.

Employment Outlook thru 1990 Good.

Salaries $15,000–$56,000 (major New York agency).

9 ■ ADVERTISING MEDIA PLANNERS

Media planners supervise all media purchases and plan when commercials will be shown and the media that will be used. Media planners are responsible for achieving the right media exposure for a campaign. This does not always mean getting maximum number of viewers, listeners, or readers per dollar. The image of media and its advantages and disadvantages must also be considered. A high-quality product would not be advertised in a sensational, newspaper-format magazine.

Places of Employment Same as advertising account executive.

Skills Required Four-year program or M.B.A.

Employment Outlook thru 1990 Good.

Salaries $13,000–$50,000 (major New York agency).

10 ■ DISTRIBUTION TRAFFIC MANAGER

A traffic manager is responsible for inbound raw materials and products and outbound finished goods. Handling methods, time in transit, packaging costs, warehouse costs, costs of intraplant movement, and the avoidance of waste and damage are part of the traffic management task. Most importantly, perhaps, traffic managers must understand the costs and services of alternative carriers in order to minimize expenses and maximize services.

Places of Employment   Throughout the country, particularly major industrial centers.

Skills Required   M.B.A.

Employment Outlook thru 1990   Very good.

Salaries $16,500–$38,000 (senior traffic manager).

PART 4

FINANCE

CHAPTER 16

MONEY AND THE FINANCIAL SYSTEM

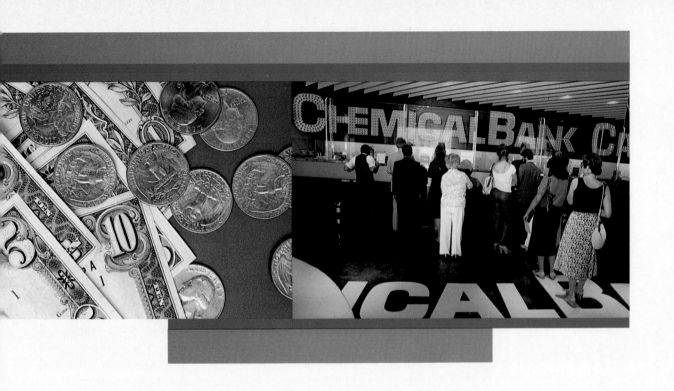

After studying this chapter you should be able to:

1 Define money and understand its three principal functions.
2 Discuss the importance of the physical characteristics of money.
3 Identify the key participants and various institutions in the U.S. financial system and understand the role of financial markets.
4 Recognize the structure, functions, and characteristics of commercial banks in the U.S. financial system.
5 Describe the role of the Federal Reserve System—its functions, how it sets monetary policies, and the techniques used to control the money supply.
6 Describe some new directions in banking—electronic funds transfer systems, plastic money, interest checking, etc.

Dyann Sherman of Los Angeles had her first inkling of trouble when she deposited a $3,000 check in her bank account via an automated teller machine and got a receipt with printing so faint it was barely legible. Worried that her only proof of the deposit was an all-but-blank slip of paper, Sherman called her bank after a couple of days to ask whether the money had been credited to her account. It hadn't.

Six days after she had deposited the money, Sherman's bank finally tracked it down. For reasons unexplained to her, bank employees servicing the teller machine had not used her encoded deposit ticket but had filled out a new one, accidentally transposing two digits in the process and directing the money to someone else's account.

The experience jolted her. "Normally I wouldn't have called to check the balance in my account," Sherman explains. "But if I hadn't, I might have bounced a check."

Automated teller machines (ATMs) and other means of electronic fund transfer (EFT) are the newest opponents in man's perennial battle with machines, and so far man has been stubbornly reluctant to yield. In most places the checkless society isn't much nearer than when it was first heralded a decade ago. [To reassure consumers who take a chance on EFT, Congress passed the Electronic Fund Transfer Act, which contains numerous consumer protection provisions for users of the systems. However, the law doesn't cover everything.]

To protect yourself, an official of the American Bankers Association offers this advice: Make deposits at electronic terminals by check rather than cash; checks may be outmoded, but they still can be traced.

Source: Excerpted from "Automatic Banking Can Cause You Trouble," *Changing Times*, June 1981, pp. 26–28. Reprinted with permission from Changing Times Magazine, © Kiplinger Washington Editors, Inc., 1981.

MONEY

Money—getting it, spending it, investing it—is a topic of prime interest to everyone, a basic part of life. For just that reason, it's important to understand what money is; it's important, too, to know what its characteristics are.

What is Money?

Without money, goods and services must be exchanged directly. This is called a **pure barter system.** Its inconveniences are staggering: someone who has fish and wants bread must search out and find someone who has bread but wants fish. Not only must their wants be complementary, but the quantities to be exchanged must be satisfactory too.

These inconveniences led even very primitive societies to a money system. Usually a commodity that had value in its own right (referred to as *intrinsic* value) was singled out as the medium of exchange. Money of this type is called **full-bodied money,** and the most familiar example is gold.

However other commodities—some of them very strange to us—have also been used. The American Plains Indians, for example, used horses as a means of exchanging goods. So one horse might have been worth three steers or 500 arrows or seven buffalo robes. Usually only one item was generally accepted as the unit in which the value of other goods was stated.

Basically, **money**—in whatever form—is anything that is generally accepted as a means to pay for goods and services.

In specific economic terms, money must be generally acceptable in payment for transactions, and it must easily measure value. That is, it should be easy to determine the relative value of goods and services in terms of units of money. Today money is the lubricant for the machinery of our economic system, but, like any lubricant, too much or too little can hurt the system it is supposed to protect.

The Principal Functions of Money

For money to be generally acceptable as a medium of payment for goods and services, it must serve three basic economic functions: (1) act as a medium of exchange, (2) serve as a standard of value, and (3) constitute a store of value. General acceptance requires these qualities.

As a **medium of exchange,** money can be used instead of goods to help make transactions. Having one common means of exchange—money—is much less complicated than a barter system. Money allows the exchange of goods and services to be an easy, simple process.

As a **standard of value,** money serves as a yardstick. It provides a means by which it's easy to measure the relative value of goods and services. With money whose value is accepted by all, goods and services can be priced in monetary units. A standardized pricing system helps in the exchange of goods and services. And as a unit of account, money is used to express and record transactions.

As a **store of value,** money can be used to hold wealth; that is, someone owning money can choose to hold it in preference to exchanging it for other assets that could also serve as a store of value. Because its value is easily eroded, during inflationary periods, money is a poor store of value when compared to, say, residential housing or gold. Of course, the reverse is true during deflationary periods as in the 1930s. Then, it made some sense to hold wealth in the form of money.

The Desirable Physical Characteristics of Money

Many early kinds of money would be unsuitable for widespread use today. Thus a horse isn't divisible into smaller units of exchange, and it could be

"Money may not be worth as much these days but I still love it."

From the *Wall Street Journal*, by permission of Cartoon Features Syndicate.

difficult to transport the horse over long distances. For money to be a suitable medium of exchange, it must have the physical characteristics of durability, portability, and divisibility.

If horses were used as money, there's the risk that the unit of exchange—the animal—would weaken or die. A truly useful form of money must therefore possess **durability**. Today currency meets that requirement. And, when it wears out, it can be replaced with new coins and bills.

Again, if horses were used as money, they'd be a difficult item to transport—and every other building would have to be a bank! **Portability** means simply that a good form of money must be easily carried and conveyed. Again, paper money meets the requirement; and checks can be as simply handled—and even mailed. Portable and mailable paper money helps in making transactions, whether they be local or distant.

Finally, how could you purchase a package of gum if the unit of exchange were horses? It wouldn't be easy; barring inflation, you'd probably have to trade your horse for a *lifetime* supply of gum! **Divisibility** refers to the fact that a good form of money must be easy to divide into smaller parts. All moneys today are very divisible. One dollar can be split into 100 cents, one Japanese yen into 100 sen, and one Saudi riyal into 100 ha-

TALKING BUSINESS

Moreton Binn has an affinity to Peter Stuyvesant. "He was the father of bartering," says Mr. Binn. "He traded $24 worth of beads for Manhattan Island. Not a bad deal."

Mr. Binn is owner and president of Atwood Richards, Inc., a New York City-based bartering firm that takes whatever a company can't sell, gives the company something it needs in return, then trades the acquisition to another company that can use it.

"In today's economy, money is depreciating so quickly that it makes sense to trade products, not dollars," says Mr. Binn. "Barter is a more creative way of completing traditional transactions."

Atwood Richards regularly deals with more than 100 companies. Its inventory contains everything from airplanes to pocket electronic calculators. The company, which began in 1957 as a subsidiary of a larger corporation, was acquired by Mr. Binn in 1974. Since then, trading has been spurred by a problem generic to business—excess inventory.

"Companies have invested money to produce a product, and if the product sits in a warehouse, the company is losing money every day," he says. "Instead of letting the inventory vegetate, the company can trade for something it really needs without spending a dime."

In the case of BSR, a British electronics firm, Atwood Richards acquired phonograph turntables. In return, BSR received plush hotel accommodations that Mr. Binn had acquired in another deal.

Source: Excerpted from "If You Can't Sell It, Trade It," *Nation's Business*, December 1979, pp. 81–82. Reprinted by permission of the Chamber of Commerce of the United States.

---

lala. Divisible forms of money help in making transactions of all sizes and amounts.

THE U.S. FINANCIAL SYSTEM

An important factor in the high standard of living that we enjoy in the United States is our well-developed financial system. The system efficiently serves its purpose: it allows those who need money to borrow it relatively easily (regardless of their geographical location); and it provides savers with a variety of investment opportunities.

Consider: a neighborhood of new homes constructed in Oregon is financed partially by savings of families in Virginia. The Virginians deposited their money in a local financial institution. That institution in turn looked for the most profitable way to use the money—in this case, as a mortgage instrument issued by another financial institution in Oregon. The process is complex, but it works remarkably well.

Households, Businesses, and Governments: Key Participants

As it happens, almost all Americans are participants in their financial system. Families saving for a rainy day or borrowing for a new roof, businesses borrowing to finance a new factory, state and local governments borrowing to build new schools—all are part of the system. It sometimes seems amazing how the system can so efficiently serve the needs of over 220 million people, millions of businesses, and thousands of government organizations. Yet it does.

Households are important participants in our financial system. Statistics bear out that American households in the U.S. are net savers: overall, they save more than they borrow. Obviously, many households borrow to finance various purchases. But on balance, households are net *suppliers* of funds to the financial system.

Most businesses depend on our financial system as a source of capital. Businesses constantly need financing for inventories, new factories, research, advertising, and many other productive activities. The financial system makes the transfer of household savings to businesses that need capital.

Governments also depend on the financial system. City, county, and state governments, school boards, special government agencies (such as electric power authorities), and the federal government are frequent borrowers of funds to finance various programs. State and local agencies, such as the Indiana Turnpike or the New York Port Authority, often finance large projects such as bridges, roads, office buildings, and parking structures with borrowed funds. And the federal government borrows constantly to finance its budget deficit.

How Financial Intermediation Works

Occasionally, capital suppliers deal directly with those who need it. For example, a wealthy realtor in Chicago lends money to a friend who intends to speculate in the commodity markets. But more frequently financial institutions become involved, acting as intermediaries between demanders and suppliers of funds.

Financial institutions take the money that savers entrust to them and invest it in the securities (e.g., IOUs, mortgages, bonds, stocks) that capital demanders issue to them. This process is called **financial intermediation,** and it's illustrated in Figure 16.1. The figure shows households as *net suppliers* of funds and businesses and government as *net demanders*. Of course, any individual household, business, or government may be a supplier or a demander, depending on its particular situation.

Financial Institutions

The heart of the financial system is its financial institutions — the go-betweens linking borrowers

FIGURE 16.1

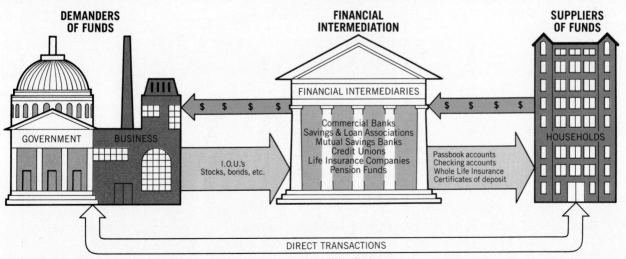

THE FLOW OF FUNDS IN THE ECONOMY

DEMANDERS OF FUNDS

FINANCIAL INTERMEDIATION

SUPPLIERS OF FUNDS

FINANCIAL INTERMEDIARIES

GOVERNMENT   BUSINESS

Commercial Banks
Savings & Loan Associations
Mutual Savings Banks
Credit Unions
Life Insurance Companies
Pension Funds

HOUSEHOLDS

I.O.U.'s
Stocks, bonds, etc.

Passbook accounts
Checking accounts
Whole Life Insurance
Certificates of deposit

DIRECT TRANSACTIONS
No Intermediation Necessary

and savers. Financial institutions include commercial banks, savings and loan associations, mutual savings banks, credit unions, life insurance companies, and pension funds. We'll briefly examine each of these institutions.

Commercial Banks There are some 15,000 commercial banks in the United States. A **commercial bank** offers the widest range of financial services, including checking and savings accounts, credit cards, consumer loans to finance cars and boats, etc., business loans, and home mortgages. Basically, the commercial bank is the "department store" of the financial institution industry. The other institutions are more specialized, although they are beginning to become more competitive with commercial banks by offering more services. Commercial banks are examined more closely later in this chapter.

Savings and Loan Associations There are about 5000 savings and loan associations in the United States. The **savings and loan association** used to offer only savings accounts; now it offers checking accounts as well. Savings and loans are very important sources of home mortgage loans; over one half of all U.S. home purchases are financed by savings and loans. This heavy dependence on real estate loans has hurt savings and loan associations during periods of high interest rates, such as the early 1980s. Many savings and loans will probably try to depend less on real estate loans as their source of income.

Mutual Savings Banks A **mutual savings bank** is a savings oriented institution that operates very similarly to a savings and loan association. One significant difference, however, is that a mutual savings bank distributes its profits to depositors. Of the approximately 500 mutual savings banks in the United States, most are located in the Northeast. Mutual savings are important financiers of homes in the areas where they're located.

Credit Unions A **credit union** is basically a savings cooperative. Its members usually have something in common; they may have the same employer or belong to the same church. There are approximately 23,000 credit unions, and to become a member of one you've got to deposit some minimal amount in a savings account with it. Members can borrow at the credit union, usually at favorable interest rates. Traditionally, credit unions made only short-term consumer financing loans; now some credit unions make long-term mortgage loans as well. Today credit unions offer customers checking accounts similar to those provided by savings and loan associations.

Life Insurance Companies There are approximately 1800 life insurance companies in the United States. A **life insurance company** is a significant participant in the financial markets. It can be very large—as many are—with substantial investments in stocks, bonds, real estate, and real estate loans. Prudential Insurance, for example,

Financial institutions offer and widely promote many services.

invested approximately $1.4 billion in real estate and $600 million in stocks during 1981 alone. Prudential's total investments in those areas are many times the amount for that year.

Pension Funds   **A pension fund** is a large pool of money that a company or government (state, local) sets aside for paying pension benefits to its employees. Pension funds are managed by the employers themselves as well as by life insurance companies, commercial banks, and private investment advisers. The total worth of pension funds today is several hundred billion dollars. Most are growing in size; to spur growth, they invest in stocks, bonds, and real estate. Very often they invest in the employees' company. To name just one, the Sears, Roebuck pension fund has a large investment in Sears' common stock.

Financial Markets

Transactions between demanders and suppliers of funds take place in what is known as the **primary market;** this is where *new* funds flow to demanders. The securities (stocks, bonds, etc.) given in exchange for funds in a primary market transaction can be resold in a secondary market. The **secondary market,** similar to a used-car market, is where securities that have already been issued are bought and sold. These securities and markets will be more thoroughly discussed in Chapter 17. The primary market can be subdivided into the money market and the long-term securities market. The **money market** consists of activities in short-term (maturity of less than one year) securities, while the **long-term securities market,** or **capital market,** is where long-term bonds, mortgages, and stocks are sold.

   Venture capital is basically long-term investment in high-risk, high-growth potential enterprises. Many new businesses are financed by venture capitalists, such as life insurance companies, pension funds, and wealthy individuals. Digital Equipment, the large computer manufacturer, was originally financed by venture capital investors. Government policies tend to encourage venture capital investments since new companies often develop new products and services, promoting economic growth.

THE UNITED STATES BANKING SYSTEM

The cornerstone of the United States financial system is its commercial banks. The size and scope of activities of each of these 15,000 institutions vary widely. However their function is basically one: to use the customer's deposits for the purpose of making loans and investing in securities. In this section we'll examine the structure of the American banking system and see how it works.

Structure

Banks are chartered by either state or federal government. A **bank charter** is basically a license to operate the bank. Because both the state and federal governments can issue bank charters, our banking system is different from that found in most other parts of the world. In most countries banks are chartered only by the national government. And most countries have far fewer banks than we do. Canada, for example, has several large nationwide banks plus several smaller provincial banks. The larger banks have branches in every Canadian province. In contrast, the United States has about 15,000 banks, many of which have no branches. Only one commercial bank has branch offices in more than one state. This is the Bank of California, headquartered in San Francisco and with branch offices in California, Oregon, and Washington. (The bank has multistate branches because it had them before federal legislation outlawed the practice.) Overall, the American banking system is much more fragmented than that of many other countries.

State Banks   State banks are chartered by state government agencies. In California, for example, the state banking commissioner issues bank charters. State banking laws differ from federal law, so many banks select a state charter if it's to their economic advantage. About two thirds of all U.S. banks are state chartered. However they tend to be smaller than federally chartered banks. State banks hold about 40 percent of the country's total banking deposits.

National Banks   National banks are chartered by the comptroller of the currency, an officer of the U.S. Treasury Department. All national banks must belong to the Federal Reserve System and must carry **Federal Deposit Insurance Corporation (FDIC)** insurance on their deposits. (We shall examine the Federal Reserve System and the FDIC more fully below). About one third of all U.S. banks are national banks, and they collectively hold about 60 percent of all banking deposits. Most of the very large commercial banks are national banks.

How can you tell if a bank has a federal or a state charter? It's simple: all national banks must incorporate the word *national* in their name. Wells Fargo Bank, N.A., for example, is a national bank: the letters *N.A.* stand for *National Association.* Bank of America, N.T. and S.A. (the largest U.S. bank) is also a national bank. *N.T.* and *S.A.* are abbreviations for *National Trust* and *Savings Association.* On the other hand, Morgan Guaranty Trust Company (the fifth largest U.S. commercial bank) is state chartered.

Functions

Commercial banks provide many necessary financial services, including accepting deposits and making loans. To explain more thoroughly how banks operate, let's examine a single bank—the Bank of Hawaii. This bank was originally chartered by the Republic of Hawaii (i.e. before U.S. annexation) in 1897; it's now chartered by the State of Hawaii. Bank of Hawaii is the largest commercial bank in the Aloha State, with 60 branch offices in Hawaii and 10 more on various Pacific islands including American Samoa, Guam, and the Marshall Islands. Despite its "exotic" locales, the bank's basic function is the same as that of State Bank, Main Street, Toulon, Illinois, and any other bank. That is, it accepts deposits from its customers and invests them, as well as its own capital, in loans to its customers, in bonds, and in other vehicles.

Table 16.1 presents the Consolidated Statements of Condition for the Bank of Hawaii as of December 31, 1980. These statements help us understand a bank's operations as well as its financial condition. The bank's *assets* are what it owns; the bank's *liabilities* are what it owes. Its *shareholders' equity* is that portion of the bank's assets that its shareholders own. (The following discussion of deposits, loans, and investments will be keyed to Bank of Hawaii's consolidated statements.)

Deposits Banks accept deposits from their customers. These can be **demand deposits,** which are checking accounts; **savings deposits**; or **time deposits,** which are **certificates of deposit (CDs)**[1]. These are IOUs issued by the bank, paying interest at a stated rate, and having a specific maturity. Bank deposits are owed to customers and can be withdrawn by them under the terms of the account. The Bank of Hawaii had approximately $2 billion in deposits (noted (*a*) in Table 16.1) as of December 1980. These deposits made up about 88 percent of the bank's $2.3 billion of funds (noted (*b*) in the table). This was a typical situation, since most banks acquire a large proportion of their funds through customer deposits.

Loans and Investments Banks use their customers' deposits to make loans and to invest in securities and other assets. The profit earned on these loans and investments is used to pay interest to depositors, to cover operating expenses, to pay taxes, and to pay dividends to shareholders. The Bank of Hawaii had about $1.4 billion in loans (noted (*c*) in Table 16.1) outstanding as of December 1980. This is what borrowers owed the bank. It also had approximately $416 million invested in various securities (noted (*d*) in the table). The bank had other assets, too, including $190 million of cash and non-interest-bearing accounts at other banks (noted (*e*) in the table). Banks keep cash on hand to cash customers' checks and to meet legal requirements.

So we can see the essence of financial intermediation: the bank uses its customers' deposits to finance loans and investments.

Types of Deposits

In general, there are three types of bank deposits: demand deposits (or checking accounts), savings deposits, and time deposits (certificates of deposit).

Demand Deposits These are deposits that can be drawn on without notice by means of checks—

TABLE 16–1

Bank of Hawaii Consolidated Statements of Condition

December 31 (in thousands of dollars)		1980	1979	1978
ASSETS				
Interest Bearing Deposits		$ 135,340	$ 57,000	$ 30,284
Investment Securities	(d)	415,548	387,367	334,569
Funds Sold		10,000	—	50,000
Loans		1,420,137	1,207,243	1,020,632
Unearned Income		(5,680)	(10,285)	(18,158)
Reserve for Possible Loan Losses		(14,605)	(11,472)	(7,685)
Net Loans	(c)	1,399,852	1,185,486	994,789
Net Lease Financing		22,977	21,439	10,698
TOTAL EARNING ASSETS		1,983,717	1,651,292	1,420,340
Cash and Non-Interest-Bearing Deposits	(e)	190,033	200,242	157,348
Premises and Equipment		55,064	43,403	43,083
Customers' Acceptance Liability		1,508	491	26,451
Other Assets		46,043	37,247	27,129
TOTAL ASSETS	(b)	$2,276,365	$1,932,675	$1,674,351
LIABILITIES				
Domestic Deposits				
Demand Deposits		$ 578,374	$ 601,555	$ 539,701
Savings Deposits		459,902	460,038	462,646
Time Deposits		691,697	566,434	352,488
Foreign Deposits		270,838	128,817	103,535
TOTAL DEPOSITS	(a)	2,000,811	1,756,844	1,458,370
Funds Purchased		48,785	9,550	21,670
Other Short-Term Borrowings		22,671	4,181	27,351
Bank's Acceptances Outstanding		1,508	491	26,451
Other Liabilities		42,840	29,084	21,672
Long-Term Debt		20,135	24,830	25,715
TOTAL LIABILITIES		2,136,750	1,824,980	1,581,229
SHAREHOLDERS' EQUITY				
Common Stock		14,908	13,267	13,267
Surplus		49,669	37,000	30,000
Undivided Profits		75,038	57,428	49,855
TOTAL SHAREHOLDERS' EQUITY		139,615	107,695	93,122
TOTAL LIABILITIES AND SHAREHOLDERS' EQUITY	(b)	$2,276,365	$1,932,675	$1,674,351

SOURCE: *Bancorp Hawaii, Inc., Annual Report 1980* (Honolulu: Bancorp Hawaii, Inc., 1981), p. 38.

NOTE: See text discussion under *Deposits* and *Loans and Investments* for the significance of (a)–(e) in the table.

or by withdrawal of funds. Until recently, interest wasn't paid on demand deposits. However beginning January 1, 1981 the **1980 Depository Institutions Deregulation and Monetary Control Act** went into effect, allowing most financial institutions to pay interest on certain types of checking accounts. These are commonly called **NOW (negotiable order of withdrawal) accounts.** Al-

TALKING BUSINESS

though Congress authorized their use in 1981, some institutions had been using them before then.

Savings Deposits These are passbook savings accounts. Ordinarily, withdrawals can be made at any time without penalty. Passbook savings accounts usually pay lower interest rates than time deposits. In the early 1980s the highest allowable interest rate on commercial bank passbook savings accounts was 5.25 percent annually.

Time Deposits These are funds kept on deposit for a minimum of 30 days and with a fixed maturity date. Normally, heavy interest penalties are charged to depositors who wish to withdraw time deposits prior to maturity. The receipt for a time deposit is a certificate of deposit (CD). Certificates have borne the highest rate of interest on deposits, amounting to more than 16 percent (for certain kinds).

Other Services/Conveniences

In addition to providing checking and savings accounts, commercial banks offer many other financial services. These include money-wiring facilities, safe deposit boxes, financial advice, and automated teller machines. As we saw earlier, because of the wide variety of services that commercial banks offer, they can rightly be regarded as the "department stores" of financial services.

Wiring Money Sally D'Angelo owns a bicycle store in Omaha. A friend of hers has just called from New York saying that some new French bikes are available at a 30 percent discount—if Sally can get the cash to New York by tomorrow. It sounds like a good deal, but how can the money be moved cross-country so fast? Very simply: Sally's bank can wire funds to the supplier's New York bank. This transfer of funds takes only a few minutes, even cross-country; and it usually costs under $10. By **wiring funds,** the transaction can be quickly consummated.

Safe Deposit Boxes   The risk of valuables like stocks, bonds, and jewelry is that they could become lost or stolen. And whereas a home safe could provide some protection, it's an expensive item — and a burglar could crack it. There's a simpler solution: rental of a safe deposit box at any local bank. A **safe deposit box** is a locked storage compartment within the bank's vault. A small one can be rented for about $10 a year.

Financial Advice   Bankers are often a good source of **financial advice** for business and personal finance problems. Loan officers — the bank officials who actually make loans — frequently have ideas on how a business can be run more profitably. This type of advice is often free to the bank's customers. Additionally, many banks have trust departments that offer investment management services for a fee. Many pension funds are managed by bank trust departments, and many individuals have trust departments handle their investments for them.

Automated Teller Machines   Suppose you need cash at 1:30 Saturday morning. Cashing a check could be nearly impossible. Many banks offer a solution to this problem, too: automated teller facilities (also known as remote tellers, cashomats,

and cash dispensers). An **automated teller machine (ATM)** is an electronic machine usually placed outside the bank or in other convenient locations. Most ATMs operate 7 days a week, 24 hours a day. Using a plastic access card, a customer can withdraw cash or make a deposit even though the bank's office isn't open for business. Some ATMs transfer funds between accounts and accept instructions to pay third parties.

THE ROLE OF THE FEDERAL RESERVE SYSTEM

Before 1931 the American financial system operated in fairly chaotic fashion. Although the country prospered during the 1800s, severe economic contractions occurred on several occasions. These depressions were related to numerous bank failures and to a wildly fluctuating money supply. Nor did the federal government have any effective means of moderating wide swings in the economy. (Other countries, such as England, had government-connected central banks that could influence economic cycles.) So in 1913 Congress established the **Federal Reserve System (the Fed).** The original purpose of the Fed was to ensure a viable U.S. money supply, to provide a borrowing source for banks (i.e. a ''banker's banker''), and to improve federal supervision of banking practices. The Fed's activities have since been broadened and today the Fed's policies strongly influence the financial system.

Due to their convenience, automated teller machines continue to grow in popularity and are being offered by more and more banks. Note "Member FDIC" prominently displayed.

Basic Functions of the Fed

The basic concern of the Federal Reserve System is **monetary policy,** which involves the regulation of the money supply and interest rates; these in turn affect the level of economic growth and stability. The Fed is charged with using monetary policy to control inflation, to increase employment levels, and to foster orderly economic growth.

The Federal Reserve System consists of twelve Federal Reserve Banks located across the United States, each with its own board of directors. Most Federal Reserve Banks have a branch bank or two; the total number of these Federal Reserve Branch Banks is 25. Figure 16.2 depicts the geographic breakdown of the Federal Reserve System.

The overall operation of the Federal Reserve System is coordinated nationally by the seven-member **Board of Governors of the Federal Reserve System,** who are headquartered in Washington, D.C. Each member of the Board of Governors is appointed by the president of the United States and confirmed by the Senate for a 14-year term. The Fed is supposed to be a nonpolitical agency; in reality, it often works in concert with the president and Congress in implementing monetary policy. This working relationship was strengthened in 1978 with the passage of the Full Employment and Balanced Growth Act. This law requires the Federal Reserve to report to Congress each year on its up-coming activities and policies.

Defining the Money Supply

The Federal Reserve System is responsible for implementing monetary policy through its control of the money supply. But before analyzing how monetary policy works, we need to define the money supply. It has been variously defined, but to keep it simple: the **money supply** consists of the total amount of currency outstanding (held by the public) and in demand deposits at commercial banks. Demand deposits are the largest component of the money supply.

As of March 1981, the total U.S. money supply (using our definition) was about $365 billion. Of this amount, some $118 billion was currency, with paper money the largest currency component. Coins are minted and paper money is printed by the U.S. Treasury Department and distributed to banks by the Federal Reserve System. Almost all paper money is in the form of Federal Reserve Notes, basically Fed IOUs. If you examine the front side of a dollar bill, you'll see that it's a Federal Reserve Note. The large letter seal on the left indicates which Federal Reserve Bank issued the note. Bills bearing an E seal, for example, are issued by the Federal Reserve Bank of Richmond, while those with an L seal are issued by the Federal Reserve Bank of San Francisco.

Demand deposits, as we have seen, are checking accounts at commercial banks. In March 1981 this component of the money supply totaled $247 billion, or about 68 percent of the money supply. Bank deposits are the most significant portion of the money supply. Basically, the Fed controls the money supply by increasing or decreasing the amount of bank deposits.

Implementing Monetary Policy

The Federal Reserve System uses four tools to implement monetary policy. The four are open market operations, reserve requirements, the discount rate, and selective credit controls. A summary of the effects of each of three of these tools on interest rates and economic activity (inflation, deflation, economic growth) appears in Table 16.2.

Open Market Operations The Federal Reserve System owns a large amount of U.S. Government securities, originally issued by the U.S. Treasury to finance a federal budget deficit. As the Fed buys or sells government securities in its **open market operations,** this causes the money supply to change. When the Fed buys U.S. Government securities, it pays for them with a check. The seller then deposits the check in a bank. This increases the money supply, because the amount of demand deposits in the banking system has increased. As a result, banks have more money to lend, and interest rates fall. In turn, lower interest rates usually stimulate economic activity. The process is reversed if the Fed sells some of its government securities. Fed open market operations are carried on continually, and they are the most frequently used monetary policy tool.

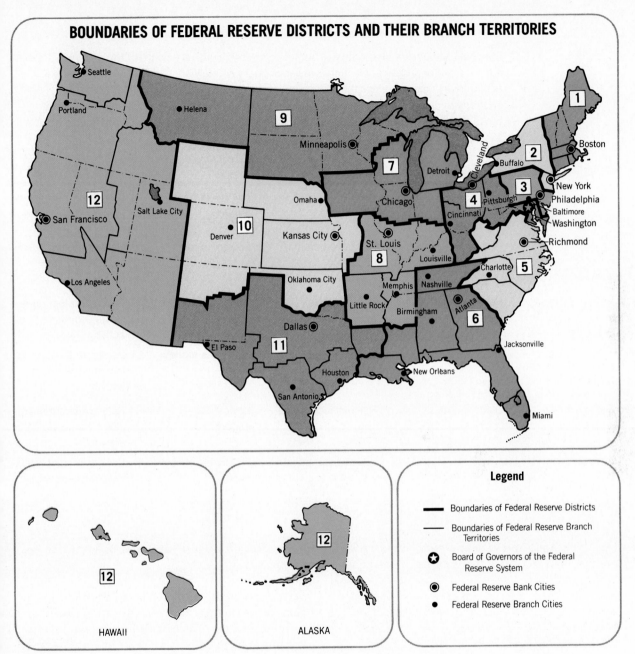

BOUNDARIES OF FEDERAL RESERVE DISTRICTS AND THEIR BRANCH TERRITORIES

Legend

▬ Boundaries of Federal Reserve Districts

— Boundaries of Federal Reserve Branch Territories

★ Board of Governors of the Federal Reserve System

◉ Federal Reserve Bank Cities

• Federal Reserve Branch Cities

FIGURE 16.2

Source: *Federal Reserve Bulletin*, 67 (May 1981) (Washington, D.C.: Board of Governors of the Federal Reserve System, 1981), p. A76.

Reserve Requirements All national banks must belong to the Federal Reserve System; many state banks belong as well. Member banks are obliged to set aside a certain percentage of their deposits in the form of non-interest earning reserves. This percentage is set by the Fed and is called the **reserve requirement.** The reserves must be either member banks' vault cash or in accounts at the Fed. Reserves of this type cannot be invested in loans or in securities.

When the Fed raises the bank reserve requirements, banks have less money to lend because more must be set aside. This causes interest rates to rise and economic activity to diminish. On the other hand, if the Fed lowers reserve requirements, more funds are available to lend. Interest

TABLE 16-2

Major Monetary Policy Tools and Their Short-Run Effect on Economic Activity

Economic activity involves both real output and prices associated with it. Over any period of time either output or prices can be higher, lower, or approximately unchanged. Of most frequent occurrence in the U.S. since the depression of the 1930s is the increase of both real output and prices, with prices increasing faster; thus we get the outcome of creeping inflation. Several times since 1970, however, the creep has been more like a gallop with inflation running at 10 to 15 percent on an annual basis.

Tool	Action	Effect on Money Supply	Short-Run Effect on Economic Activity
Open market operations	Buy government securities	Increases money supply	Lowers interest rates; increases economic activity
	Sell government securities	Lowers money supply	Raises interest rates; slows economic activity
Reserve requirements	Raise reserve requirements	Lowers money supply	Raises interest rates; slows economic activity
	Lower reserve requirements	Increases money supply	Lowers interest rates; increases economic activity
Discount rate	Raise discount rate	Lowers money supply	Raises interest rates; slows economic activity
	Lower discount rate	Increases money supply	Lowers interest rates; increases economic activity

rates then fall, and economic activity usually increases. The Fed uses this tool fairly infrequently because it's difficult for commercial banks to adjust their reserves quickly. A change of reserve requirements has a powerful effect on the economy.

Discount Rate   We've already seen that one of the purposes of the Federal Reserve System is to be a "banker's bank." Banks that belong to the Federal Reserve System can borrow from the Fed; this is often referred to as "going to the window." The interest rate that the Fed charges banks that borrow from it is called the **discount rate.** When the Fed raises the discount rate (considered deflationary), banks usually raise the interest rates on their loans too, thereby slowing economic growth. On the other hand, when the Fed lowers the discount rate (considered inflationary), this tends to lower overall interest rates and to stimulate economic activity.

Selective Credit Controls   In addition to the general monetary controls just described, the Federal Reserve System also has the power to set minimum terms on various types of loans made by banks and others. Examples of these **selective credit controls** include consumer credit rules and margin requirements. Consumer credit rules govern the percentage down payment and period of repayment for car loans, appliance loans, and the like. The Fed hasn't used these powers in recent years.

The margin requirement relates to an investor's purchasing securities on credit; the **margin** is that percentage of the purchase price which must be paid in cash by the investor; the balance can be borrowed from the purchaser's stockbroker or

ON THE FIRING LINE

Is It Time To Limit The Fed's Freedom?

Since the late 1960s the U.S. economy hasn't done as well as it could, or should, some critics argue. Weakened by constant inflation and periodic and severe recessions, it continues to fail. Some blame the Federal Reserve System, particularly its seven-member board and the larger (twelve-member) Open Market Committee, the system's two policy-making bodies. The Fed, they point out, is supposed to monitor and maintain the economy in good health. It does this by controlling (1) interest rates, (2) credit availability, and (3) the money supply. Even with all its power, say the critics, over the last 20 years the Fed has not been able to perform its prescribed role as doctor to the economy. The solution many offer is to give the Fed and its policy-making functions to the president. They back their proposal with several arguments.

First, these critics claim, the Fed has clearly shown itself to be too closely linked to the nation's banking and financial establishment and too much removed from the interests of the people as expressed by Congress. The Fed is obsessed by the desire for stable interest rates, argue many of its critics, who believe that controlling the money supply—and not interest rates—is the key to controlling inflation. The Fed, they complain, has abandoned its money supply growth goals whenever great ups and downs in interest rates have threatened. Over the long term, insist the critics, this excessive concern with interest rates has burdened us with ever greater inflation.

A second argument of those who would give the Fed to the administration is that its power over the economy is too limited to be effective. The administration and Congress decide the nation's fiscal policy—how big the budget and how high the taxes will have to be. Further, the administration has authority to initiate wage and price controls. A healthy economy, say the Fed's critics, is unlikely without coordination in all these areas. Such coordination could best be obtained, they assert, by putting the Fed under the president's thumb.

Others strongly disagree. The Fed, they respond, is not nearly as autonomous as its critics claim. Congress established the Fed, and Congress has ultimate control over the Fed. At least one top official of the system believes Congress would abolish the Fed if it let interest rates see-saw unrestrained.

It may even be, say proponents of a relatively independent Fed, that the administration already has too much power over it. For six months after the Fed began to focus on controlling the money supply in October 1979, it was right on target. However in April 1980, at the request of President Carter, the Fed imposed credit controls. The administration-inspired action resulted in wild fluctuations in both the money supply and interest rates. Perhaps, observe some, the Fed needs more rather than less independence and should remain out of the mainstream of politics and be free to act in the best long-range interests of the economy. Were the Fed to respond to every short-term political, social, or economic problem that arose, as it did in 1980, the economy would be doomed.

Consider, too, that it's the Fed that creates money, advise those against executive control of the Fed. It would be foolish, they say, to give this power to the president. There would then be no end of government spending. The Treasury would make up deficits by simply running the printing presses overtime. If we have learned anything from monetary history, it ought to be that all hyperinflations resulted from an uncontrolled government printing too much money.

Moreover, say the Fed's backers, handing it over to the president would be a sure way to destroy any credibility it might have. People would then have only as much faith in the Fed as they had in the president. History tells us again, however, that presidential popularity (and credibility) is typically short-lived.

bank. For example, if the **margin requirement** were 50 percent and an investor bought $10,000 worth of stock, the investor would have to put up $5000 and could borrow the balance. The Fed does not change margin requirements very often. In fact, the margin requirement has remained at 50 percent for a decade.

Facilitating the Check-Clearing Process

Another very important task of the Federal Reserve System is its assistance to banks in clearing checks. The Fed's **check-clearing system** enables banks to collect quickly on checks drawn even on very distant banks. To illustrate how the system works, we have only to trace a recent transaction. Harry Jones of Key West decided that he wanted to climb Pike's Peak in Colorado Springs. Prior to his trip he decided to buy some cold-weather gear—not easily found in tropical Key West. However, as a regular recipient of the famous L.L. Bean Store's catalog—mailed seasonally from the store's 24-hour-day, 7-day-week operation in Freeport, Maine—Mr. Jones simply placed an order, using the handy form accompanying the catalog. With this order he enclosed a check

FIGURE 16.3

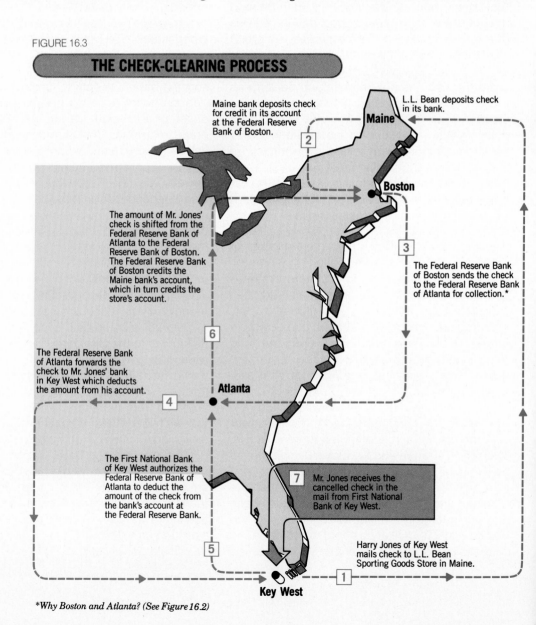

THE CHECK-CLEARING PROCESS

Maine bank deposits check for credit in its account at the Federal Reserve Bank of Boston.

L.L. Bean deposits check in its bank.

The amount of Mr. Jones' check is shifted from the Federal Reserve Bank of Atlanta to the Federal Reserve Bank of Boston. The Federal Reserve Bank of Boston credits the Maine bank's account, which in turn credits the store's account.

The Federal Reserve Bank of Boston sends the check to the Federal Reserve Bank of Atlanta for collection.*

The Federal Reserve Bank of Atlanta forwards the check to Mr. Jones' bank in Key West which deducts the amount from his account.

The First National Bank of Key West authorizes the Federal Reserve Bank of Atlanta to deduct the amount of the check from the bank's account at the Federal Reserve Bank.

Mr. Jones receives the cancelled check in the mail from First National Bank of Key West.

Harry Jones of Key West mails check to L.L. Bean Sporting Goods Store in Maine.

Why Boston and Atlanta? (See Figure 16.2)

drawn on his account with his bank, First National of Key West. Figure 16.3 shows how the check was ultimately cleared. L.L. Bean was paid, and the entire process took only about two weeks. This must be considered fairly swift, given the considerable distances involved. Overall, the Fed's check-clearing services enable banks to process checks quickly.

Providing Deposit Insurance: FDIC

During the Great Depression beginning in 1929, many banks closed their doors and were not able to pay their depositors. As a result, large numbers of people lost substantial sums. To protect depositors from a recurrence of bank failure, Congress established the Federal Deposit Insurance Corporation (FDIC) in 1934, and today almost all banks carry FDIC insurance. A depositor is now protected up to a maximum of $100,000 per-depositor against the risk of loss due to a bank failure. Deposits in mutual savings banks, savings and loan associations, and credit unions are protected by various similar insuring agencies for up to $100,000 per depositor as well. Under each of these arrangements, the insurance premiums are paid by the financial institution.

NEW DIRECTIONS IN BANKING

During the 1970s many new trends hit the banking industry. The electronic revolution, for example, was particularly felt by banks. Many new services resulted from the development of new machines and higher-powered computers. Government regulation of financial institutions is also changing rapidly. As a result, banks now offer interest-bearing checking accounts, and there is much greater competition between financial institutions. Also, banks are broadening their product lines and seeking reforms in state branching laws. What follows is a brief review of these interesting developments.

Electronic Funds Transfer Systems (EFTS)

During a single year, the banking system processes over 30 billion checks. Check processing is expensive, and it involves mountains of paperwork. In addition, billions more transactions are made by paying cash. Is there a simpler way to facilitate transactions? There may be: the cashless society — through the **electronic funds transfer system (EFTS).** EFTS is a centralized and computerized system of paying bills and making purchases that does not require checks or cash. Rather, bank customers make purchases using a coded plastic **debit card,** which is an EFTS-type innovation that is being used in some parts of the country.

A debit card enables a person to pay for purchases on the spot if the merchant has an appropriate **"point-of-sale" (POS) machine,** into which the card is inserted. The POS is hooked into the bank's computer, so that when the purchase is made, funds are automatically taken out of the buyer's bank and transferred into the seller's account. EFTS eliminates the risk of bounced checks and stolen cash receipts. It also eliminates revolving finance charges for credit.

While the traditional Visa credit card has been available for several years, the addition in 1975 of debit cards accessing deposits has provided the customer with greater payment flexibility, as has the issuance of Visa Travelers Cheques.

TALKING BUSINESS

Debit cards. They look like credit cards and act like credit cards, with one big difference—they don't give you credit. When a shopkeeper imprints a receipt with your debit card number and asks you to sign the slip, it's your money you're spending, not the bank's. When the slip is returned to your bank, your checking account is drawn down, or debited.

This arrangement has its advantages. For example, if you have a Visa debit card, you can, in effect, pay by check at any store that accepts the Visa credit card.

So why are there only 1,000,000 Visa debit card holders, compared with the 64,000,000 Visa credit card customers? Because, people figure, why should they use their money to pay now when they can use the bank's money to pay later—and perhaps get a free ride to boot if they settle up before credit card interest starts accruing?

(You can also use Visa debit cards to withdraw money from a Visa-affiliated bank. That really can pay, since there's no grace period on Visa credit card cash advances. However, you may be charged a transaction fee by the bank at which you make the withdrawal.)

Debit cards could get a boost now that many credit card issuers are charging annual fees and otherwise raising the price of their services. But debit cards don't always come free either; banks sometimes levy an annual fee or a transaction charge.

Source: Excerpted from "More Banking Changes to Come," *Changing Times*, November 1980, p. 60. Reprinted with permission from Changing Times Magazine, © Kiplinger Washington Editors, Inc., 1980.

Plastic Money

Since 1960 there's been an explosion in the use of credit cards. Many Americans have one or more **credit cards** including Visa, MasterCard, American Express, Diner's Club, and Carte Blanche. The first two cards are issued by banks and by some savings and loan associations. Credit cards can be used to pay for almost anything (thus the term, **plastic money**). The California state universities, for example, allow students to pay tuition with Visa or MasterCard.

Banks charge merchants fees for redeeming credit card slips. The credit cardholder receives a monthly bill. If the bill is paid promptly, no interest charges are levied. If the cardholder desires to stretch out the payments, finance charges are imposed, usually at an 18 percent annual interest rate. In the past, banks did not impose membership fees on credit cardholders. Now many banks have a yearly membership fee. Bank of America, for example, imposes a $12 yearly fee on Visa and MasterCard holders. Crocker National Bank, a large California institution, follows a slightly different tack: it charges cardholders on a per transaction basis, the fee being twelve cents per transaction. Crocker's Visa and MasterCards could be cheaper to use than Bank of America's if the cardholder does not make more than 100 credit card transactions a year.

Interest Checking

In our earlier discussion of types of deposits, we examined so-called NOW accounts—interest-earning checking accounts. As of January 1, 1981 this service was available from most commercial banks, savings and loan associations, mutual savings banks, and credit unions.

Great Competition and Relaxed Regulations

In March 1980 Congress passed the Depository Institutions Deregulation and Monetary Control Act. This law provides for much greater competition between financial institutions. By the end of the 1980s it should result in many changes in the U.S. financial system. The distinctions between the services offered by commercial banks, savings and loan associations, mutual savings banks, and credit unions will diminish as this law is more fully implemented.

Another aspect of this act is the eventual deregulation of interest rates paid to consumers by financial institutions. The act established March 1986 as the date on which financial institutions would be free to pay any interest rate they wished on savings and time accounts as well as on interest-paying checking accounts. Previously, interest rates were deregulated only for certificates of deposit of $100,000 or more.

Reform of Branching Regulations

Many states do not allow banks or savings and loans associations to have branch offices. Some other states limit branch offices to localities close to the institution's main office. In Illinois, for example, banks are not allowed to have branches; they can only have one office. Louisiana restricts bank branches to only the one parish (county) where the main office is located. In contrast, states such as California, Oregon, Arizona, Nevada, and Hawaii allow statewide branching. The bank can open a branch office anywhere in the state. During the 1980s, it is expected that more states will allow banks to open branches over a wider geographic area.

Another issue that has been raised is nationwide branching. Currently, with one exception (Bank of California), banks can have branches only in their home states. The large commercial banks, such as New York's Citibank and San Francisco's Bank of America, would like to open new branches across the country or acquire other banks through their holding companies. This proposal has met with vehement opposition from many smaller banks, which fear that big banks will force small banks out of the market.

Financial institutions often compete internationally as well as domestically.

PERSPECTIVE ON SMALL BUSINESS

Try to withdraw as little as $500 from Pelham Bank & Trust and the president himself, Louis Fineman, will come out of his office and ask you why.

Tell him your money can get higher interest rates elsewhere, and Mr. Fineman, his hand on your shoulder, will look you in the eye skeptically and ask politely, "How much?" He will hear the figure, roll it around in his mind, furrow his brow and then break into a broad smile. "Why don't you come into my office? We can get you more than that right here," he says.

If Mr. Fineman is persuasive—and he usually is—the customer puts his money right back into the bank and winds up thanking Mr. Fineman profusely. Lou Fineman clasps his own hands together and, sounding more like a country preacher than a banker, intones: "I thank God you came through these doors."

Another thing about Lou Fineman: He is 65 years old and has been a bank executive only 10 years. Before that, he was a local dairy farmer and cattle dealer, and he never took a formal course in banking or finance in his life.

Like many small-town banks, Pelham Bank & Trust—the only bank [in Pelham, New Hampshire]—is in danger of losing its independence. And Mr. Fineman may well become an anachronism. Many little banks across the country are being eyed by bigger institutions in their state,

and, if Congress permits interstate banking, they probably will become takeover targets of big institutions in Boston, New York and other money centers as well. [In 1980,] an estimated 300 banks were acquired, up 50% from 1979.

But although big outside institutions can provide local residents with more banking services, they still can't offer the folksy personal touch that helped make little banks so successful in the first place.

Partly because of the likes of Lou Fineman, most small banks so far have escaped the hazards of a changing banking system—and they are flourishing. Despite the beginning of an anticipated rash of takeovers, the Federal Reserve Board says, the number of banks in the U.S. increased [in 1980] by 129 to 15,201; presumably those formed in growth areas such as the Sun Belt more than made up for those acquired. Moreover, the 12,735 banks classified as small—with assets of $100 million or less—[in 1980] accounted for only 19% of the assets but 29% of the profits in commercial banking, the Fed says.

SOURCE: Excerpted from Mitchell C. Lynch, "Homespun Finance: Personal Touch Helps Pelham, N.H., Banker Keep Money on Hand," *Wall Street Journal*, October 1, 1981, pp. 1, 14. Reprinted by permission of The Wall Street Journal, © Dow Jones & Company, Inc., 1981. All rights reserved.

SUMMARY

Money is anything generally accepted as a means to pay for goods and services. Money has three basic functions: it acts as a medium of exchange, a standard of value, and a store of value. It must have the physical characteristics of durability, portability, and divisibility.

Almost all Americans participate in the US financial system. Households are net savers; they supply more funds to the system than they withdraw. Businesses are net borrowers who use the system to finance expansion. Government, too, is a frequent borrower. The economy, then, contains demanders and suppliers of funds. Sometimes capital suppliers deal directly with demanders; more frequently, financial institutions act as intermediaries between them. Financial institutions include commercial banks, savings and loan associations, mutual savings banks, credit unions, life insurance companies, and pension funds.

Transactions between demanders and suppliers of funds occur in the primary market, where new funds flow to demanders. The securities given in exchange for funds in this market can be resold in the secondary market. The primary market can be divided into (1) the money market—which includes short-term loans—and (2) the long-term securities

more than double the $1.5 billion loss in the first half.

Inflation . . . stagflation . . . recession—all caused by high interest rates, the real culprit. In one of his most memorable statements, shortly before he stepped down from the presidency of the AFL-CIO, the late George Meany condemned Congress for not taking some action to reduce the interest rate. Lane Kirkland, the incumbent president, continues the battle with Congress to act in cutting the interest rates. Paul Volcker, chairman of the Federal Reserve Board, has even been chided by President Reagan for his strict monetary policy, wielded dramatically whenever the money supply increases: the Fed invokes tight controls to discourage further credit extension by raising the discount rate. The big banks stand ready to protect their position by raising the prime rate whenever danger signals appear, and so the economy struggles with recession—despite the plea from almost all quarters: "Somebody should do something about the high interest rate—it's stifling our economy!"

1. Why doesn't Congress do something about the high interest rates?
2. Would not it be a good move on the part of the president to lower the interest rate by executive decree?
3. Who or what can influence changes in the interest rate to improve the economy?

CASE: WHAT IS A BANK . . . TODAY AND TOMORROW?

What kind of business makes loans, provides checking accounts, and offers trust services? That's easy to answer—it's a bank. Wrong! It's stockbrokerage firms. Let's try another. What kind of business assists in buying and selling securities, provides credit to purchase securities on margin, and offers investment advice? Now that has to be a stockbrokerage firm. Right? No, wrong again. It's a savings and loan.

Probably one sure bet for the 1980s is that at its end, financial institutions will look far different from what they did at its beginning. With passage of the *Depository Institution Deregulation and Monetary Control Act in 1980*, changes have taken

place so fast that it's hard to keep up with them. Merrill Lynch now offers a service, called its *cash management account*, that's basically a checking account paying interest on the daily balance. And the interest it pays is at the highest money market rates possible. No wonder billions of dollars have flowed into Merrill Lynch—to the chagrin of commercial bankers, which have lost many deposits.

Not content to sit back and let the flow continue, some financial institutions have counterattacked. Two S&Ls—Coast Federal Savings and Loan of Sarasota and American Federal Savings and Loan of Washington, D.C.—have asked permission from the Federal Home Loan Bank to set up their own brokerage firms. Apparently federal law prohibits banks and S&Ls only from underwriting securities, not from acting as agents in trading them.

The important question for business and individuals is "How do all these changes benefit us?" Answers aren't clear, since the risks are still unknown. Will banks and S&Ls provide the same quality services that stockbrokers now provide? Or will they be better and more accessible to people with low-to-moderate incomes? Can stockbrokers function well as bankers? And what about reserve requirements for them—shouldn't they apply as they do for commercial banks?

1. What arguments can you make to support the view that all financial institutions should be allowed to compete in any area they choose—so long as all play the game by the same rules?
2. But what about the rules of the game; that is, how should regulation take place? For instance, what new roles do you see for the Federal Reserve and the Federal Deposit Insurance Corporation (FDIC)?
3. Sears, Roebuck has become very aggressive in developing its financial services business; for example, in 1980 it acquired Dean-Witter, a large stockbrokerage firm. Of course, it's one of the leaders in insurance with Allstate, and some say it would like to buy a major bank. Do you think a financial supermarket, such as Sears, would appeal to customers? How about safety?
4. Suppose the merchandising end of Sears' business does poorly. How might this affect the financial services end described in question 3?

CHAPTER 17

SECURITIES MARKETS

After studying this chapter you should be able to:

1 Distinguish among the various types and characteristics of securities: common and preferred stocks, corporate and government bonds, mutual funds, futures contracts, and options.

2 Understand the characteristics of organized securities exchanges, securities listed there, the kinds of members, and the role brokers play in executing transactions on these exchanges.

3 Explain how the over-the-counter market operates and how it differs from organized securities exchanges.

4 Describe state and federal regulations pertaining to securities markets.

5 Identify the major sources of economic and financial news and the popular stock averages and indexes that measure market activity.

6 Read and understand the technical data of stocks published in the financial section of most major newspapers.

7 Understand how security transactions are made and how full-service and discount brokers differ in the assistance they provide investors and in the commissions they charge.

William O'Neill moved into the stock market with $1,000 and high hopes. "I wanted to become J. Paul Getty," says the 39-year-old junior-high-school teacher. "My stock portfolio is my empire."

While he's still no tycoon, Mr. O'Neill's empire has grown quickly. His stocks are now valued at $7,000, mostly because he bought a collection of high-risk issues that have, as luck would have it, appreciated quickly. "I wanted to make it or break it fast," he says.

Mr. O'Neill has a lot of company in his visions of financial glory. More than six million new investors have flocked to the stock market since mid-1975. [In 1979 and 1980, they rushed in at the rate of about 4,000 a day.] And many of them aren't the usual crowd.

"The stock market used to be regarded very much as a rich man's game," says Ira Distenfeld, manager of the Miami, Fla., office of Smith Barney, Harris Upham & Co., the big investment firm. "It was in the same category as yachts, the Republican Party and Hotel Pierre."

But that's changing. The newcomers to the market tend to be relatively young and don't have much to invest. But with a gambler's bravado, many are willing to risk their stake in the hope of making money.

"They see the market as Las Vegas East," says Donald Kimsey, senior technical analyst with Dean Witter Reynolds Inc. "They go out and put their money on the table. They're definitely not risk-averse."

And their presence is being felt in the market. Brokerage houses are deluged with new business. Trading volume on the major exchanges, as well as over the counter, hit record levels in 1980, with individuals accounting for an increased share of the trading. Business is booming on the risky options and commodities markets, too.

Source: Excerpted from Patrick O'Donnell, "Taking the Plunge: Many New Investors Have Modest Means but Large Ambitions," *Wall Street Journal*, January 30, 1981, pp. 1, 17. Reprinted by permission of The Wall Street Journal, © Dow Jones & Company, 1981. All rights reserved.

Like William O'Neill, many are fascinated by the stock market; the lure of making a lot of money—fast—is what attracts them. We hear success stories, such as the initial public offering of Genentech's common stock in 1981 that went from $35 a share to almost $80 in 20 minutes after the stock began trading, and we may persuade ourselves that we can find an investment like this. Sometimes we do, many times we do not, and our losses mount. But in the process we begin to learn what the securities markets are all about. We learn the many different kinds of securities available, how to buy and sell them, and some of the government regulations influencing securities markets. This chapter aims at giving the same information that experience provides, but in a more painless way.

BASIC TYPES OF SECURITIES

Securities are essentially pieces of paper issued by governments and corporations. There are two basic types of securities: stocks and bonds. Stocks are ownership interest in a corporation. Bonds are debt obligations (IOUs) issued by corporations and governments. Other securities, such as mutual funds and options, are very similar to stocks and bonds, as we're about to see. First, however, we'll take a closer look at what these securities are.

Common Stock

A corporation is owned by the holders of its **common stock.** If you own 100 common shares of General Motors Corporation, for example, you are a partial owner of GM. Your ownership interest is not large; GM has about 290,000,000 common shares outstanding. But you are an owner just the same—like over 1,219,000 other shareholders in that corporation.

As a shareholder, you're entitled to share in the common stock dividends of General Motors and thus in the net profits of the corporation. Basically, stockholders have a **residual claim** on the firm's assets and profits; that is, they're entitled to what's left after the firm's suppliers, employees, bondholders, and all other creditors have been paid—and after taxes and preferred stock dividends (discussed below) have also been paid. Common stock dividends are paid out of the firm's net profits. Profits that are reinvested in the firm and not paid out as dividends are called *retained earnings.*

As a shareholder, you also have **voting rights,** which shareholders exercise to help decide such matters as mergers and the election of the board of directors at GM's annual meeting. A corporation's board of directors is responsible for hiring and firing management and for setting the basic policies of the firm.

Potential Returns   With common stock, you've two sources of potential returns: **cash dividends** and future stock price increases. After they are declared by the board of directors, cash dividends are usually paid quarterly (four times a year) on a per share basis. For example, Dillon Companies, a large food store operator based in Hutchinson, Kansas, paid a $0.27 per share dividend on January 15, 1981. An investor who owned 100 Dillon common shares would have been mailed a $27 check on that date.

In addition to the dividend income, an investor can also benefit from increases in the stock's price, should they occur. Dillon's common shares, for example, experienced a substantial rise in price between December 1980 and March 1981—from about $13 per share to over $24. (Dillon's stock is listed on the New York Stock Exchange; we'll examine stock listing shortly).

Suppose, then, that you have purchased 100 shares of Dillon in December 1980 and then sold it in March of the following year. You'd have made about an $1100 profit (before commissions) on the trade plus an additional $27 in dividends—an excellent return on your $1300 investment. Unfortunately, stocks don't ordinarily provide such exciting, rapid returns.

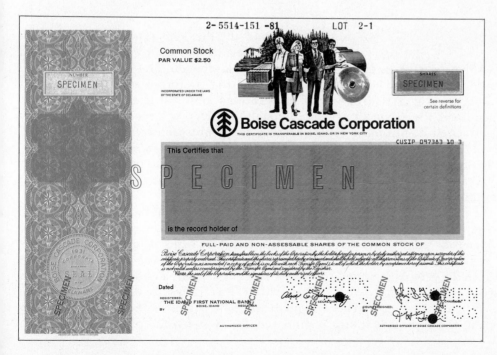

Common stock certificate: Boise Cascade Corporation.

TALKING BUSINESS

Academics and Wall Street practitioners have long debated the effect of dividends on stock prices. During the sluggish market of the late 1970s, some investment advisers argued that high dividend payments by a company attract investors who boost its stock price and thus eventually produce a higher total return. More recent research, however, disputes this. Merton H. Miller, professor of finance at the University of Chicago's graduate school of business, says his computerized studies demonstrate that "high-dividend stocks do not have a greater total return."

In fact, the stocks of some large companies paying no dividend at all have achieved a much higher total return than high-dividend companies of comparable size. Of the 11 companies on the Fortune 500 list that pay no cash dividends at all, seven [National Semiconductor, Teledyne, Tosco, Data General, Penn Central, Digital Equipment, and Lockheed] achieved a total return in the 1971–80 decade that was well above the 9.4% annual median for the 500 companies. The remaining four companies had low returns; they avoided dividends because they had financial problems to begin with.

Many experts contend that big payouts simply signify bad management. Alert executives should have more profitable used for company money than dispensing it as dividends, they argue. A successful company can earn a 20% to 25% return on that money by reinvesting it in new equipment, research or other productive acitivity. The investor gets his reward in the form of capital gains when increased company profits push up stock prices.

Preferred Stock

Preferred stock is called that because its owners receive preferential treatment over the holders of common stock in the distribution of assets (if the corporation is liquidated) and the payment of dividends. All preferred stock dividends must be paid prior to any payment of dividends to holders of common shares. If a company experiences financial difficulties, it can omit payment of both preferred and common stock dividends. However most preferred stocks have a protective cumulative provision, which requires that all past omitted preferred stock dividends be paid before any dividends can be paid to the holders of common shares. Preferred stock with the cumulative provision is called **cumulative preferred stock.**

In return for the preferential dividend treatment, most preferred stocks do not provide voting rights, and the dividend rate is usually fixed—that is, it doesn't increase over time as common stock dividends often do. Preferred stock may also be **participating preferred stock,** which means that it's entitled to its stated dividend and also to additional dividends on a specified basis. It may also be **convertible preferred stock,** which exchanges into common shares at a specific price—a tremendous benefit if the price of the common stock goes up.

Potential Returns Preferred stock investors realize returns primarily from dividend payments; price appreciation realized upon sale isn't likely since dividends don't grow. Price appreciation can occasionally occur, although depreciation is just as likely. Preferred stock dividends are usually paid quarterly. Detroit Edison, for example, has a preferred stock issue that pays dividends at a

$9.32 per share annual rate. A $2.33 per share quarterly dividend is paid on January 15, April 15, July 15, and October 15 each year.

Bonds

A bond is an IOU issued by a corporation or a government. It's a promise to pay the bondholder a specific periodic interest payment, called the *coupon rate*, and to repay the principal, called *par value*, at the bond's maturity date (or due date). For example, American Telephone & Telegraph (AT & T) has an issue of $1000 par value 13 1/4-percent bonds that are due in 1991. The $1000 par value principal amount is to be repaid in 1991. In the meantime, a holder of one $1000 par value bond will be paid $66.25 every six months, or $132.50 per year per $1000 par value (13 1/4 percent of $1000).

Bonds issued by corporations are called **corporate bonds;** they usually have a $1000 par value. Bonds issued by the U.S. Government are called "governments"; par value is usually $10,000. **Municipal bonds** are issued by state and local governments, and their par value is usually $5000. A look at each of these follows.

Corporate Bonds   There are two basic types of corporate bonds: mortgage bonds and debenture bonds. **Mortgage bonds** are secured by a specific asset of the company. **Debenture bonds** are unsecured—that is, they're backed only by the credit worthiness of the issuing corporation and its promise to pay. It might seem that mortgage bonds are safer than debenture bonds, but this isn't always the case. A mortgage bond issued by a financially shaky company (e.g. Chrysler in the later 1970s) is probably less secure than a debenture bond issued by a strong corporation (AT&T, for example).

U.S. Government Bonds   The U.S. Treasury sells three types of IOUs. These are Treasury bills, Treasury notes, and Treasury bonds. Treasury bills bear no interest but are sold at a discount and mature in less that one year (short term). Treasury notes bear interest and mature in one to five years after being issued (medium term). Treasury bonds mature five years or more after first being sold (long term). The Treasury also sells savings bonds to customers through banks. Savings bonds are not resold in the securities markets, however, as are other U.S. obligations. The interest paid on U.S. government IOUs is not subject to state income taxes.

Municipal Bonds   Municipal bonds are issued by states, cities, counties, school boards, and many other state and local government agencies. There are two basic types of municipal bonds: general obligation bonds and revenue bonds. General obligation bonds are backed by the full

11.875% debenture bond certificate: International Minerals & Chemical Corporation.

taxing powers of the issuing government. Revenue bonds, in contrast, are backed only by the income generated by the project being financed. This isn't necessarily bad, because the projects financed—toll roads, bridges, parking structures, power plants, airports, college dormitories, etc.—usually generate enough revenue to pay off the bonds with interest. An announcement—called a **tombstone ad**—for a state housing authority general obligation bond is shown in Figure 17.1.

Municipal bonds have attracted much investor interest in recent years because the interest they pay isn't subject to federal income tax. And if the municipal bonds are issued by governments within the taxpayer's home state, the interest is exempt from state income tax too. In contrast, the interest paid on corporate bonds is fully taxable.

Potential Returns   An investor has two sources of return from a bond investment; the periodic interest income, and any price appreciation that's realized upon maturity, call, or sale. As we saw with preferred stock, price appreciation shouldn't be anticipated. The bond's par value is paid at maturity. Corporations often retain the right to call a bond prior to its maturity. If this happens, the bondholder receives par value plus, in some instances, a small bonus called a *premium*. The amount that an investor receives upon selling the bond depends on the prevailing interest levels when the bond is sold. Usually, if interest rates rise after a bond is bought, its price will subsequently fall. Conversely, if interest rates fall after a bond has been bought, its price should rise. Rising interest rates all during the 1970s meant substantial losses on most bonds sold during that period.

Other Securities

In addition to stocks and bonds, there are other types of securities available for investors. Three of

FIGURE 17.1

Announcement for a housing authority general obligation bond.

Interest exempt, in the opinion of Bond Counsel, according to present Federal laws, regulations, rulings and decisions, from Federal income taxation. (Information regarding requirements as to such exemption is set forth in the Official Statement.)

NEW ISSUE   June 3, 1982

$24,100,000
South Dakota Housing Development Authority
Homeownership Mortgage Bonds, 1982 Series A

Dated: June 1, 1982   Due: May, as shown below

The Series A Bonds are being issued for the purpose of providing the Authority with money to purchase newly originated Mortgage Loans used to finance single family residential housing in the State of South Dakota and to deposit moneys in specified Funds and Accounts, as more fully described in the Official Statement.

The Series A Bonds are general obligations of the Authority, payable out of any of its revenues or moneys, subject only to any agreements with holders of other notes or bonds pledging any particular revenues for the payment thereof, and are further secured as described in the Official Statement.

The Series A Bonds are redeemable prior to maturity, at the option of the Authority, in whole or in part, at any time, on or after May 1, 1992 at a redemption price of 103% of the principal amount thereof and at declining redemption prices thereafter. The Series A Bonds are also subject to redemption at par, at any time, at the option of the Authority, from unexpended Series A Bond proceeds and Mortgage Loan prepayments in excess of the principal then due and payable on Outstanding Bonds. The Series A Bonds maturing May 1, 2013, are subject to mandatory redemption prior to maturity at par from sinking fund installments.

Due May 1	Principal Amount	Interest Rate	Due May 1	Principal Amount	Interest Rate	Due May 1	Principal Amount	Interest Rate
1984	$105,000	8.50%	1988	$150,000	10.35%	1992	$225,000	11.75%
1985	115,000	9.00	1989	165,000	10.70	1993	255,000	12.00
1986	125,000	9.50	1990	185,000	11.00	1994	285,000	12.25
1987	135,000	10.00	1991	205,000	11.40	1995	320,000	12.50

All of the Serial Bonds are priced at 100%

$2,965,000 12¾% Term Bonds due May 1, 2001. Not Reoffered
$18,865,000 13% Term Bonds due May 1, 2013. Price 100%
(Accrued interest to be added on all bonds)

Bonds of particular maturities may or may not be available from the undersigned or others at the above prices on and after the date of this announcement. The offering of the Bonds is made only by the Official Statement, copies of which may be obtained in any State from such of the undersigned as may lawfully offer these securities in such State.

WARBURG PARIBAS BECKER
A.G. BECKER

BLYTH EASTMAN PAINE WEBBER
INCORPORATED

MERRILL LYNCH WHITE WELD CAPITAL MARKETS GROUP
MERRILL LYNCH, PIERCE, FENNER & SMITH INCORPORATED

DAIN BOSWORTH
INCORPORATED

DOUGHERTY, DAWKINS, STRAND & YOUST
INCORPORATED

these are mutual funds, futures contracts, and options. The latter two are generally suitable only for experienced, sophisticated investors, since they're considered very risky investments. We'll examine all three types.

Mutual Funds   Suppose you've $500 that you want to invest. What you may not know is that even with such a relatively small sum of money you can buy a portion of a large portfolio of stocks and/or bonds. Moreover your portfolio can enjoy the benefit of being managed by professionals at very low cost to you. All this is accomplished by investing in **mutual funds,** which are financial intermediaries (see Chapter 16) that pool the funds they raise from investors and then invest these resources in stocks, bonds, and other securities. A mutual fund portfolio consists of all the securities that it owns. Figure 17.2 represents in diagram form how mutual funds operate.

There are many types of mutual funds, all differentiated by the kinds of investment strategy they follow. The **stock fund**, for example, invests primarily in the common stocks of corporations. The municipal bond fund invests in municipal bonds, while the corporate bond fund owns a portfolio of corporate bonds. A balanced fund holds a mix of stocks and bonds. In recent years, a relatively new type of mutual fund has been purchased by millions of investors; the **money market fund,** which invests in short-term money market instruments such as certificates of deposit (CDs), Treasury bills, and commercial paper (including bills, notes, drafts, checks). In January 1982 over $190 billion was invested in money mar-ket mutual funds, up from on $3.8 billion in December 1978.

Futures Contracts   A **futures contract** allows its holder to buy or sell an amount of a specified commodity or other item at a future date at an agreed-upon price. There are futures in cattle, hogs, pork bellies (large slabs of unsliced bacon), eggs, frozen orange juice concentrate, wheat, corn, soybeans, gold, silver, Treasury securities, and many other things. Futures are traded on commodities and other futures exchanges such as the **Chicago Mercantile Exchange (CME)** and the **Chicago Board of Trade. (CBT).**

Options   Options, like futures, are very risky investments because the chance of loss is very high. There are two types of options: call options and put options. A **call option** (or simply *call*) entitles the holder to buy a fixed number of shares (usually 100) at a fixed price within a specified time. The buyer hopes that the value will appreciate within that time. If it does, the buyer can exercise the option and then resell at the appreciated price. If value falls, however, the buyer stands to lose.

A **put option** (or *Put*) is the right to sell a fixed number of shares (again, usually 100) at a fixed price within a specified time. Puts are bought by those who think a stock price will go down. As option holders, they're entitled to sell the stock at the original, fixed price despite any fall—provided the option is exercised within the time specified. Again, if the option isn't exercised, the money paid for it is lost. Options are traded on

FIGURE 17.2

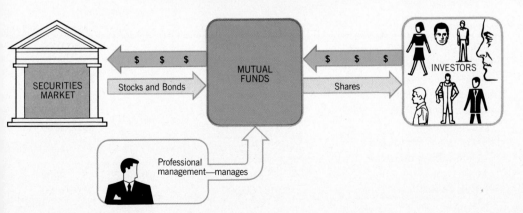

HOW MUTUAL FUNDS WORK

SECURITIES MARKET — Stocks and Bonds → MUTUAL FUNDS — Shares → INVESTORS

Professional management—manages

exchanges including the **Chicago Board Options Exchange (CBOE),** which is a subsidiary of the Chicago Board of Trade.

THE SECURITIES MARKETS

In Chapter 16 we saw that new issues of securities are initially sold to the public in the primary market. Once new issues have been sold, investors can buy and resell them in the secondary market—the resale market for existing securities. The secondary securities market consists of organized exchanges and the over-the-counter market. Each of these is discussed next, followed by a brief discussion of security market regulation.

Organized Securities Exchanges

The principal arenas of secondary trading in stocks and bonds are the organized exchanges. A **stock exchange** is a geographically centralized secondary stock market. By geographically centralized we mean that stockbrokers funnel their customers' orders to a central trading floor, such as the **New York Stock Exchange (NYSE).** (The process of executing customer orders is explained later in this chapter.) The largest United States stock exchange is the New York Stock Exchange; the second largest is the **American Stock Exchange (ASE; Amex).** In addition, there are stock exchanges in Boston, Philadelphia, Cincin-

nati, Chicago, Los Angeles, San Francisco, Spokane, and Salt Lake City. These latter exchanges are called **regional stock exchanges.**

New York Stock Exchange (NYSE) The NYSE is America's oldest and largest stock exchange and perhaps the most prestigious securities exchange in the world. Often called the Exchange or the Big Board, it traces its origins back to the famous Buttonwood Tree Agreement of 1792. This was an arrangement by which stockbrokers met regularly to transact business under an old buttonwood tree just a few blocks from the present site of the NYSE. The NYSE moved indoors in 1817; it's located in downtown New York City at the corner of Wall and Broad Streets.

The NYSE has about 80 percent of the share volume of secondary stock trading done on organized exchanges. Overall, organized exchanges account for about 75 percent of the total share volume traded. Most bond trading is done in the over-the-counter (OTC) market, which we'll examine shortly. Because of its great importance, two important aspects of the New York Stock Exchange are discussed below.

1. Listing requirements For a corporation to have its stocks or bonds traded on an exchange, it must qualify for **listing** on that exchange—that is, the exchange must approve the securities issue for trading on it. Each exchange has certain criteria that must be met by the corporation in order for its securities to be listed. Several of the listing requirements for the NYSE and the American Stock Exchange are presented in Table 17.1.

TABLE 17-1

Listing Requirements of the New York and American Stock Exchanges

Requirement	New York Stock Exchange (NYSE)	American Stock Exchange (Amex)
Publicly held shares	1,000,000	400,000
Pretax income (latest fiscal year)	$ 2,500,000	$ 750,000
Minimum market value of publicly held shares	$16,000,000	$3,000,000
Number of stockholders owning 100 or more shares	2,000	1,200
Tangible assets	$16,000,000	$4,000,000

There are over 1800 corporations whose securities are listed on the Big Board, including Exxon, General Motors, Mobil, IBM, Xerox, Ford Motor, AT&T, DuPont, U.S. Steel, Standard Oil of California, and most other publicly traded large American corporations. Some foreign companies are listed, too, including SONY, Matsushita Electric, Royal/Dutch Shell Group, and British Petroleum. In terms of market value, the common shares of International Business Machines (IBM) were the largest single listed issue at the time this page was written. IBM's 583,806,832 common shares were worth $46.8 billion, based on a market price of $63 per share. Exxon ranked second in terms of market value with its 438,817,644 shares at $70 each, giving a total market value of $30.7 billion. American Telephone & Telegraph (AT&T) has the most shareholders of all NYSE-listed companies. Its common shares are held by approximately 3.0 million shareholders.

2. Exchange membership If you want to buy or sell the stock of a company listed on the NYSE, you must use the services of a stock brokerage firm that's a member of, and owns a seat on, the NYSE. A **seat** is not an article of furniture but rather a license to execute orders on the trading floor of the exchange without having to pay non-member commissions.

The NYSE has a total of 1366 seats, owned by such brokerage firms as Merrill Lynch, Pierce, Fenner & Smith; E.F. Hutton; Blyth Eastman Paine Webber—as well as by other stock trading firms and individuals. Seats have sold for as much as $515,000 (in 1968 and 1969) and as little as $4000 (in 1876 and 1878). About 40 seats change hands every year, and a seat currently costs about $100,000. There are several types of seatholders, as Table 17.2 shows.

Commission brokers are exchange members who execute orders for the public. The firms just mentioned each own a number of seats (Merrill Lynch has more than 20 seats) so that they can handle investors' trades. **Bond brokers** are commission brokers who make only bond transactions for their customers.

Independent brokers (also called "two-dollar brokers") are seatholders who execute orders given to them by commission brokers. If commission brokers get too busy, they give their overflow business to independent brokers. ("Two-dollar"

TABLE 17-2

NYSE Member Activities

Type of Member	Approximate % Total Membership[a]	Primary Activities
A. MAKE TRANSACTIONS FOR CUSTOMERS		
Commission broker	52	Make stock and bond purchase and sale transactions as requested by customers.
Bond broker	2	Commission broker who only makes bond transactions for its customers.
B. MAKE TRANSACTIONS FOR OTHER MEMBERS		
Independent broker ("Two-dollar broker")	10	Executes orders for other brokers who are unable to do so due to excessive market activity.
Specialist	29	Makes a continuous, fair, and orderly market in 6 to 15 assigned issues. Also makes odd-lot (less than 100-share) purchase and sale transactions for members of the exchange.
C. MAKE TRANSACTIONS FOR THEIR OWN ACCOUNT		
Registered trader	4	Purchases and sells securities for own account. Must abide by certain regulations established to protect the public.

SOURCE: From p. 33 in *Fundamentals of Investing* by Lawrence J. Gitman and Michael D. Joehnk. Copyright © 1981 by L. J. G. and M. D. J. Reprinted by permission of Harper & Row, Publishers, Inc.
[a]Because approximately 3 percent of the members are inactive, the percentages given total 97 percent.

Ye first stockbrokers meetings under ye old buttonwood tree: 1792.

refers to the $2 per hundred shares these brokers once received.) **Specialists** are exchange members who make markets in securities. By **"market making"** is meant that they act as dealers in the (rather few) stocks that the exchange assigns to them. A **dealer** is someone who stands ready to buy or sell at specified prices. Just as car dealers buy and sell automobiles, the specialists buy and sell stocks.

The fifth category of seatholders is the **registered traders.** These members buy and sell stocks for their own accounts. Of the five kinds of exchange members, commission brokers are the largest contingent.

American Stock Exchange (ASE or Amex) The Amex, sometimes called the Little Board or the Curb Exchange (it began as an outdoor market where trading took place on the sidewalk or curb), is the second-largest American stock exchange. It accounts for about 10 percent of the share value of trading on all exchanges. Many of the smaller firms in American industry are listed on the Amex. Often as they grow in sales or profits they move their listing from the Amex to the NYSE.

Regional Exchanges　Prior to the development of modern communications equipment, stock exchanges were set up across the country to accommodate the needs of investors in different regions. The largest regional stock exchanges are the Midwest Stock Exchange in Chicago and the Pacific Stock Exchange. The Pacific is unique because it has trading floors in both San Francisco and Los Angeles. Many small, regional corporations list their stock on a regional exchange. In addition, many corporations whose stock is listed on the NYSE or the Amex also list their shares on one or more regional exchanges. These are called *dually listed* issues.

Over-the-Counter Market

Many stocks and most bonds are not listed on any of the regular exchanges but instead are traded in the **over-the-counter (OTC) market.** The OTC market is a geographically decentralized, electronically interconnected secondary securities market consisting of thousands of market-making dealers in stocks and bonds. They're located all across the United States. An OTC dealer need not buy an exchange seat; rather, he or she need only obtain licenses from state and federal securities regulators and meet the requirements of the **National Association of Securities Dealers (NASD).** The NASD is a self-governing body that regulates the OTC market. OTC dealers can electronically communicate with each other by using the National Association of Securities Dealers Automated Quotation (**NASDAQ**) system, which allows OTC dealers to quickly and efficiently execute customers' orders.

About 25,000 stock issues trade in the OTC market, while only about 3000 issues are listed on the organized stock exchanges. However the market value of listed stocks is much greater than OTC stocks. Most of the secondary trading in bonds occurs in the OTC market even though many bonds are listed on an exchange.

Security Market Regulations

The securities markets are heavily regulated by both state and federal regulatory agencies. State securities laws are called **Blue Sky Laws.** ("Blue sky" refers to stock that's of almost no value, "empty" as the sky.) State securities laws vary widely but usually require the registration of secu-

Guerilla activity in Mozambique? Paul Koerner is interested. A blip on the Casablanca stock exchange? He wants to know about that, too. Come evening, Mr. Koerner shuns Dan Rather and picks up the BBC on one of his six short-wave radios.

Being addicted to foreign news presumably makes sense when you are the president of Worldwide Investment Research Ltd., a small (Mr. Koerner and a staff of three) firm dedicated to developing tips for investors seeking to broaden their portfolios beyond the U.S.

Mr. Koerner is a 32-year-old who studied classical languages, economics and history at St. Louis University, Washington University in St. Louis and the University of Toronto. He noted a dearth of material on international investing opportunities, he says, and so he decided to carve out his niche in that field.

His chief service is an eight-page, biweekly newsletter costing $145 a year. It has more than 200 subscribers. He also does consulting and provides, for $1 a page, copies of annual reports of foreign companies not normally available to American investors.

The newsletter takes what one subscriber calls a "rifle approach"; Mr. Koerner picks a subject and goes into it thoroughly. Recent issues have discussed Hongkong Land Co., which posted a 116% profit gain last year; the Tel Aviv stock exchange, which is being used increasingly as an inflation hedge; and Liechtenstein, which is becoming a popular tax haven.

---

rities sold in the state as well as the registration of stockbrokers who do business in the state. In Michigan, for example, the Michigan Corporation Securities Bureau administers the state's securities laws. State securities laws regulate intrastate transactions—that is, those occurring within the borders of the state.

Federal securities laws govern the registration and interstate transaction (i.e. across state lines) of securities and are administered by the **Securities and Exchange Commission (SEC)** in Washington, D.C. The SEC was established after the stock market crash of 1929 by the Securities Acts of 1933 and 1934. These laws require stock exchanges and stockbrokers to register with the SEC; all new issues of securities that are sold in more than one state must also be registered with the SEC. Any company selling securities must file a registration statement with the SEC and must furnish a prospectus to each investor who wants to consider buying the security.

A **prospectus** is a condensed registration statement that contains detailed financial and descriptive information about the issuing company. The SEC requires that the issuing company fully disclose all relevant information about itself and the offering in the registration statement and in the prospectus. (If you're thinking about investing in a new issue of securities, you should read the issue's prospectus very carefully.) SEC rules provide that an investor doesn't have to pay for a new issue of securities until a final (complete) prospectus has been given to him or her.

The SEC administers other securities-related laws too. These require investment advisers and mutual funds to register with the SEC. They also require publicly traded corporations to file periodic financial reports with the SEC. One such report is the **Form 10-K**—a detailed annual report filed by all corporations whose securities are held by the public.

SOURCES OF INVESTMENT INFORMATION

A key to investment success is information. A prospective purchaser should carefully investigate any investment vehicle before buying it. There are many sources of investment information, some of which are available free at a public or university library.

Economic and Financial News

Economic and financial news is communicated by various media, including newspapers, magazines, and other publications. The *Wall Street Journal* is an excellent source of current economic and financial information. It's published weekdays and contains the latest business news. *Barron's*, a weekly newspaper, carries many detailed analyses of companies as well as an extensive statistical section. Both the *Wall Street Journal* and *Barron's* are available to students at very reasonable subscription rates. Your instructor may have a sign-up sheet that will enable you to get cut-rate subscriptions to these publications.

Most libraries carry the Moody's and Standard and Poor's manuals. These contain financial reports of most publicly traded companies. *Money* magazine, an interesting publication for investors, often has investment ideas. Other good financial magazines include *Business Week, Financial World, Fortune,* and *Forbes.* A reference librarian can show you where these publications are located. Other, more specialized publications include the *Financial Analysts Journal* and *Institutional Investor* magazines. These publications are favored by investment professionals.

Market Averages and Indexes

"How's the stock market doing?" This question is a common one. Investors and interested observers like to monitor general stock market movements by watching various broadly based averages and indexes. The most widely followed of these is the **Dow Jones Industrial Average (DJIA or the "Dow").** The DJIA is a regular part of most TV evening news programs, and it's widely publicized. It gauges the relative stock price movements of the 30 large corporations listed in Table 17.3. For example, if the Dow rose 20 points in a day and it had closed previously at 1000.00, that means that the typical price movement of the stocks in the index was about +2.0 percent.

The Standard and Poor's 500 Stock Composite Index (S&P 500) and the NYSE Composite Index are much broader stock market indicators than the "Dow" because many more stock prices are used in compiling these indexes. The **Standard and Poor's 500 Stock Composite Index** utilizes the prices of 500 NYSE-listed stocks—425 industrials, 50 utilities, 25 railroads. All 30 DJIA stocks are included in the S&P 500. The **New York Stock Exchange Composite Index** measures the average movement of all NYSE-listed common stocks—over 1800 issues. It's weighted according to the number of shares listed for each issue.

A variety of financial periodicals are available to investors.

ON THE FIRING LINE

The SEC—An Economic White Elephant?

The Securities and Exchange Commission (SEC) was created in 1934 by an act of Congress. Its purpose was to prevent the kind of abuses that had brought on the 1929 stock market crash and Great Depression. Since its formation, it has become an accepted institution of the American economic scene. Sometimes it's been more, and other times it's been less, aggressive in playing its assigned role. But seldom have its functions and existence been questioned. In the early 1980s, however, public sentiment against costly government regulation and control began to run high. People started to ask what good the SEC really did.

The benefits investors gain from the SEC's activities are not worth their cost in money or freedom, say the commission's critics. In recent years, they claim, enforcement efforts have been directed at relatively minor offenses. Cases are settled with consent agreements—agreements on the part of violators to make restitution and/or behave properly in the future. But, the critics maintain, these consent agreements are nothing more than "slaps on the wrist." In fact, the SEC has neither the money nor the staff to make the wide range of investigations that would really offer investors protection. Furthermore, it has no authority or interest in intervening in some areas where intervention is most needed—in fraudulent private stock placements, for instance. Indeed, the SEC found that some $225 million had been fraudulently obtained in private offerings from 1975 to 1978. Yet when the Government Accounting Office suggested that this was "just the tip of the iceberg" and recommended greater SEC involvement, the commission was unwilling.

Other individuals feel strongly that the SEC is a vital check on deceptive and unfair practices in the securities industry. No regulatory agency, they say in response to the SEC's critics, will ever provide consumers with perfect protection. Imperfect though they may be, the SEC's regulatory and enforcement efforts do offer investors some protection and some recourse in instances of fraud. Brokers and companies issuing securities are less likely to take advantage of consumers if substantial penalties are a possibility. The SEC's mere existence is a strong deterrent to deceptive practices.

Those who stand behind the SEC point to the crusades it has fought and won. It was the SEC that exposed hundreds of undisclosed corporate slush funds and payoffs to officials of foreign governments. The result: a law passed by Congress to make such foreign payments illegal. Also, in the 1970s the commission found that corporate executives were abusing their office by taking millions of dollars in benefits ranging from payment for living quarters, groceries, and home repairs to personal cars, yachts, or planes. This discovery resulted in a ruling that companies must reveal all such payments for personal advantages. In addition, consent decrees are not, say SEC advocates, as weak as the commission's critics insist. Millions of dollars have been returned to investors through these decrees. Sometimes the decrees are designed to stabilize a business that has gone awry. It's no good for investors to have the company whose securities they hold go bankrupt. Those who would replace the SEC's consent decrees with litigation are unrealistic in the extreme. In the backed-up court system, it would take years for investors to be compensated by companies that had defrauded them.

Stockholders' Reports

A good free source of financial and organizational information about a corporation is the reports that it mails to its shareholders. These include the annual report, quarterly reports, and the proxy statement. The **annual report** to shareholders is issued yearly, usually about two months after the end of the company's accounting year. It includes messages to shareholders, a statement of opera-

The 30 Stocks in the Dow Jones Industrial Average

Allied Chemical	International Harvester
Aluminum Company of America	International Paper
American Brands	Johns-Manville
American Can	Merck & Company
American Telephone & Telegraph	Minnesota Mining & Manufacturing
Bethlehem Steel	Owens-Illinois
DuPont	Procter & Gamble
Eastman Kodak	Sears Roebuck
Exxon	Standard Oil of California
General Electric	Texaco
General Foods	Union Carbide
General Motors	U.S. Steel
Goodyear	United Technologies
Inco	Westinghouse Electric
International Business Machines	Woolworth

tions, financial statements, and a report by independent accountants, as well as other information from management.

Stock Price Quotations

Reading the stock price quotations in the *Wall Street Journal*, in other financial media, or in the financial pages of newspapers can sometimes be very confusing for beginning students of the stock market. We shall therefore consider just what the numbers in these quotes mean. A list of the previous day's closing prices for both listed and major OTC stocks usually appears in the last few pages of the *Wall Street Journal*. The stock prices that appear in the *Wall Street Journal* are for the previous day's trading. If you want up-to-the-minute price quotations, you can call or visit a stock brokerage office. Stockbrokers have electronic machines that provide the latest stock price quotes. A visit to a local stock brokerage office can be interesting as well as instructional; brokers are usually available to answer questions and to explain how the stock price quotation machine works.

Listed Stock Prices   Figure 17.3 contains actual stock price quotations as they appeared in the *Wall Street Journal*. The prices listed were for trading on April 29, 1982 and were printed in the April 30, 1982 *Journal*. The top quotations (*A*) show transactions in a number of stocks that are listed on the NYSE. The entry beside the arrow is for General Motors Corporation common stock;

the two lower entries (**pf**) are preferred stock. The first two prices listed under **High** and **Low** are the highest and lowest prices at which GM's common stock traded in the 52 weeks that preceded that day. You can see that GM's stock traded as high as **58** ($58.00 per share) and as low as 33⅞ ($33.875 per share) in the year preceding April 29, 1982. The column labeled **Div.** lists GM's annual dividend rate, which was **$2.40** per share at that time. The small **e** next to the dividend rate means that GM paid an extra cash dividend in addition to its regular $2.40 per share rate.

The column labeled **Yld %** is the stock's current dividend yield—in this case, **5.70**. This is found by dividing the annual dividend rate ($2.40 per share) by the current stock price ($42.00 per share). A stock's **P-E Ratio** is its stock price divided by its earnings per share. GM earned about $0.86 a share in 1981, so it had a P-E ratio of 49. **Sales 100s** lists the trading volume in hundreds of shares in the stock for April 29. There were **652,400** shares of GM traded that day (6524 × 100). The next three columns—**High, Low,** and **Close**—list actual stock price trades of GM on the given day. The highest price that GM's stock traded on April 29 was 42¾ ($42.75 per share). The lowest price at which the stock traded was 41⅞ (41.875 per share). The price at which the last trade in GM's stock occurred that day was **42** ($42.00 per share). This is the close or closing price. GM's stock was down 1 point ($1.00) from the previous day. The **Net Chg.** (net change) column indicates the stock's closing price change as compared to the previous day's closing price.

FIGURE 17.3
Stock Price Quotations
A. Stocks Listed on Organized Security Exchanges

52 Weeks				Yld	P-E	Sales				
High	Low	Stock	Div.	%	Ratio	100s	High	Low	Close	Net Chg.
58	33⅞	GMot	2.40e	5.7	49	6524	42¾	41⅞	42	− 1
33½	27⅛	GMot	pf3.75	13.	..	6	28¾	28⅛	28¼	− ⅛
44⅝	36¾	GMot	pf 5	13.	..	13	38⅜	38	38⅜	+ ⅜
20⅝	8¾	GNC	s .04	.4	17	8	10⅜	10¼	10⅜	+ ⅜
7⅛	4¼	GPU		..	16	397	5⅛	5	5⅛	− ⅛
90⅛	64½	GenRe	2.16	2.5	10	23	88⅜	87⅞	88⅛	− ½
9⅛	2⅜	GnRefr		..	..	32	3¼	3¼	3¼	+ ⅛
50¾	32¼	GnSignl	1.60	4.3	9	453	37½	37	37⅛	− ¼
34¼	26½	GTE	2.84	9.2	7	1848	31⅛	30⅞	30⅞	− ¼

B. Stocks Traded in the Over-The-Counter Market

Stock + Div.	Sales 100s	Bid	Asked	Net Chg.
CBT Corp 1.50	85	23¾	24	...
Cedar Pt 1.52g	12	22½	23¼	− ¼
Cencor Inc .40	9	17	17½	...
CenterrBc 1.80	73	21¼	21½	...
CentrlBcp 1.95	5	17½	17¾	...
CnBkgSys .40g	1	18	18½	...
CentBcsSo .80	13	10	10½	...
CnCaroBT .96	17	16	16¾	− ½
CenFidBk 1.24	1	17⅛	17⅜	...

Source: (A) *Wall Street Journal*, 30 April 1982, p. 48; (B) *Wall Street Journal*, 30 April 1982, p. 44. Reprinted by permission of The Wall Street Journal, © Dow Jones & Company, Inc., 1982. All rights reserved.

Over-the-Counter Quotes The prices of many OTC stocks are also listed in the *Wall Street Journal*. For example, CBT Corporation's common shares as of April 29, 1982 are shown in Figure 17.3 (*B*). You can see that CBTs annual dividend rate is **$1.50** per share and that **8500** shares changed hands that day. The **bid price** listed, **23¾** (or $23.75 per share), is the price that OTC dealers are paying for the stock. The **asked price, 24** ($24 per share), is the price that OTC dealers would charge when selling the stock to investors. In other words, an investor could sell the stock in this case for the $23.75 per share bid price and could buy the stock at the $24 per share ask price. The commission paid to the broker would be added to these prices.

Other Information Sources

Because good information is so important in making investment decisions, many investors gather investment ideas from other sources than those we've been considering. These include stock brokerage firm research studies, investment analyses available by paid subscription, and other investment advisory services. A smart investor is someone who seeks and utilizes as much investment information as he or she can obtain.

Brokerage Firm Research Many stock brokerage firms have extensive investment research departments that furnish up-to-date economic, industry, and individual security analyses. In addition, many will analyze an investor's current holdings and make recommendations for selling securities or for buying different ones.

Subscription Services Several thousand individuals (as well as companies) are licensed by the SEC to sell investment advice through market letters and other publications. A **market letter** is a brief publication offering stock market advice, usually issued on a scheduled basis. The letter usually makes predictions about the stock market in general and offers specific buy or sell recommendations for individual stocks. *Value Line*, for example — a widely used investment service — provides up-to-date analysis of several thousand stocks to subscribers, among whom are many libraries.

MAKING SECURITY TRANSACTIONS

Most novice investors are not familiar with the actual process of buying and selling securities. But even more important than knowledge of the investment process is the establishment of personal investment goals and strategies. A well-planned investment program increases one's chances of success in the securities market.

Establishing Investment Goals

The first question that every investor should consider is: "What do I want to accomplish with my investment program?" It's important to establish *realistic* investment goals. Expectations of "making a killing" on the market and "getting rich quick" are not only unrealistic; they are almost impossible to realize. Instead, one should formulate a strategy that looks at investment risk and potential return.

Any investment has risk, which is basically the

Stocks are increasingly popular with young Americans: In the past five years [1976–81] 6.5 million people bought them for the first time, according to a study sponsored by the New York Stock Exchange. About half of the new shareholders were under 35; nearly 300,000 were between 21 and 25.

No matter how attractive the potential return, however, the stock market can seem frighteningly incomprehensible to a beginner. There are thousands of stocks and brokers to choose from, reams of statistics about possible investments and lots of conflicting advice from self-styled experts. But with a little effort, even the rankest novice can soon demystify the language and business of investing in stocks. For starters, lots of books and financial periodicals can provide basic information. And you don't have to pick out individual stocks yourself; you can buy mutual funds, which have the advantage of being managed by professionals. You can also join an investment club, which will give you a low-cost education in analyzing stocks and choosing investments.

Before investing your first dollar, however, you should think over your investment goals. There are two classic types of investors: those who care chiefly about income, and those who are most concerned about growth of their capital. Most young people belong in the second group. But they must decide how much risk their pocketbooks—and their nerves—can take. The stocks that rise swiftly in prosperous times are often the ones that drop quickly if the economy turns down or the company runs into problems. There is no way that you can avoid risk entirely. Indeed, even cautious, income-oriented investors have lost money on their investments in recent years because of high inflation.

Source: Excerpted from "A Starter Kit for Investors" by Jerry Edgerton, reprinted from the June 1981 issue of *Money* Magazine, pp. 54–56; © Time Inc. All rights reserved.

---

chance that you'll not realize the level of return that you expected, or that you may lose money. Investment returns—such as dividends, interest, and profits realized upon sale—are usually directly related to the level of investment risk.

Making Transactions

Once you're ready to invest, you must choose a stockbroker. There are two types of stockbrokers: full-service brokers and discount brokers, both of which take orders of various kinds.

Full-Service or Discount Brokers   Large, well-known stock brokerage firms, such as Merrill Lynch, Pierce, Fenner, & Smith; E. F. Hutton; Dean Witter Reynolds; and Bache Halsey Stuart Shields are firms that are **full-service brokers.** In addition to executing their clients' trades, they provide investment advice through their research departments, and they offer many other services. Investors pay for these services in the form of much higher commissions on stock trades than discount brokers charge.

Discount brokers usually don't have research departments, and they generally offer a smaller range of services than full-service brokers. However their commission charges are usually much lower than full-service brokers, as Table 17.4 illustrates. Charles Schwab & Company, Source Securities, and Kingsley, Boye & Southwood are leading discount brokerage firms. An ad stating the benefits of a discount broker is shown in Figure 17.4. The question "Which type of broker is best for me?" has no one easy answer. Basically,

TABLE 17-4

Commission Comparisons for Stock Trades: Full-Service vs. Discount Broker (March 1981)

Trade Size	Dollar Amount	Commission Full-Service	Commission Discount	Percent Savings with a Discount Broker
100 shares @ $16	$ 1,600	$ 38.00	$ 24.00	36.8%
200 shares @ $20	4,000	82.00	48.00	41.5
1000 shares @ $6	6,000	102.00	60.00	41.2
500 shares @ $25	12,500	220.00	100.00	54.5
10,000 shares @ $30	30,000	469.00	180.00	61.6

when the services of a full-service broker aren't needed, a discount broker should be used. However many investors seek advice, so their choice of a full-service broker makes good sense.

Opening an Account After choosing a stockbroker, the next step is to actually open an account at the brokerage firm. Two basic types of accounts may be opened: a cash account or a

FIGURE 17.4
Ad for a discount broker.

HOW STOCKBROKERS EXECUTE TRADES

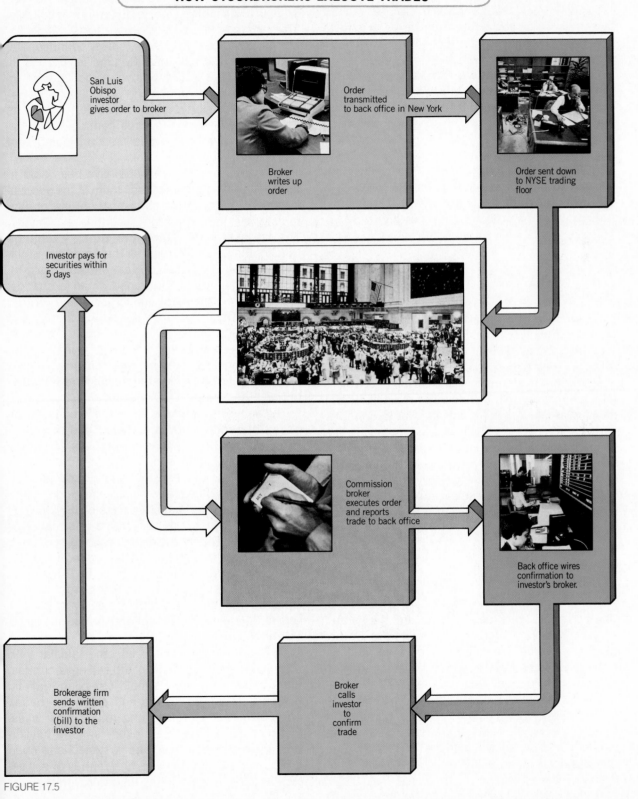

San Luis Obispo investor gives order to broker

Broker writes up order

Order transmitted to back office in New York

Order sent down to NYSE trading floor

Investor pays for securities within 5 days

Commission broker executes order and reports trade to back office

Back office wires confirmation to investor's broker.

Brokerage firm sends written confirmation (bill) to the investor

Broker calls investor to confirm trade

FIGURE 17.5

margin account. In a cash account, securities purchased are paid for in full. In contrast, a margin account enables the buyer to finance part of the purchase by borrowing from his or her stockbroker. (Margin requirements were explained more fully in Chapter 16.)

Opening an account is a very simple process; it can even be done over the telephone. However it's best to meet with one's broker personally. This may provide a better opportunity for discussing investment goals.

The Transactions Process   Once an investor has decided to buy (or sell) securities, the process of executing the trade by the brokerage firm begins. A diagram of the process is shown in Figure 17.5.

Buying Long versus Selling Short

The purchase of a security in anticipation of an increase in its price is called **buying long.** Long purchases are made with the expectation of profiting by "buying low and selling high." It's also possible to sell a security short. **Short selling** is selling a security that one doesn't in fact own. Impossible as it may sound, this kind of selling goes on every day. It's accomplished by borrowing the security from a broker and then selling it. Short sales are predicated on profiting by "selling high and buying low." If, however, the security instead of falling rises, the short seller must cover the difference out of his or her own pocket ("short squeeze").

SUMMARY

The two basic types of securities are stocks and bonds. Stock can be common or preferred. Corporations are owned by their common stockholders. Sources of potential return on this ownership interest are cash dividends and future stock price increases. Owners of preferred stock receive preferential treatment over holders of common stock in the distribution of assets (if the corporation is liquidated) and in the payment of dividends. Preferred stockholders realize returns primarily from dividend payments.

Bonds are IOUs issued by corporations or governments. Two basic types of corporate bonds are mortgage bonds and debenture bonds. The US Treasury sells three types of IOUs—Treasury bills, Treasury notes, and Treasury bonds. Municipal bonds are issued by states, cities, counties, and many other such entities. Returns from bond investments take two forms: periodic interest income and price appreciation.

Other types of securities available to investors include mutual funds, futures contracts, and options. The latter two types are considered very risky.

Once new securities issues have been sold to the public, investors can resell them in the secondary market. The principal arenas of secondary trading are the organized securities exchanges. The largest is the New York Stock Exchange (NYSE); the second largest is the American Stock Exchange (ASE or Amex). There are also many regional exchanges. To be traded on an exchange, stocks and bonds must qualify for listing on that exchange. Once listed on the NYSE, stocks and bonds can be traded only by a stock brokerage firm that is a member of, and owns a seat on, the NYSE. Many stocks and most bonds are not listed on any regular exchange but instead are traded in the over-the-counter (OTC) market.

The securities markets are heavily regulated by both state and federal agencies. State securities laws, called Blue Sky Laws, regulate intrastate transactions. Federal securities laws govern registration of securities as well as interstate transactions in them. These laws are administered by the Securities and Exchange Commission (SEC).

A key to investment success is information— available from many sources, including economic and financial news media, market averages and indexes (the most widely followed is the Dow Jones Industrial Average), and stockholders' reports. Other sources are research studies by stock brokerage firms and investment analyses available by paid subscription.

Novice investors should become familiar with the actual process of buying and selling securities. More importantly, they should establish realistic personal investment goals and strategies based on considerations of risk and return. New investors must also choose a broker—either a full-service or a discount broker. The next step is to open an account at the brokerage firm. To buy or sell securities, the investor enters an order with the broker. The order is then executed. Investors most often buy long in anticipation of price increases, although short sales are sometimes made when a decline in price is forecast.

KEY TERMS

American Stock
    Exchange (ASE,
    Amex)
annual report
Blue Sky Laws
bond broker
buying long
call option
cash dividends
Chicago Board of
    Trade (CBT)
Chicago Board
    Options Exchange
    (CBOE)
Chicago Mercantile
    Exchange (CME)
commission broker
common stock
convertible preferred
    stock
corporate bond
cumulative preferred
    stock
dealer
debenture bond
discount broker
Dow Jones Industrial
    Average (DJIA, or
    the "Dow")
Form 10-K
full-service broker
futures contract
independent broker
listing
market letter
market making
money market fund
mortgage bond
municipal bond
mutual fund
National Association
    of Securities Dealers
    (NASD)
NASDAQ

New York Stock
    Exchange (NYSE)
New York Stock
    Exchange
    Composite Index
over-the-counter
    (OTC) market
participating
    preferred stock
preferred stock
prospectus
put option
regional stock
    exchanges
registered trader
residual claim
seat
Securities and
    Exchange
    Commission (SEC)
short selling
specialist
Standard and Poor's
    500 Stock Composite
    Index
stock exchange
stock fund
tombstone ad
voting rights

REVIEW QUESTIONS

1. How does common stock differ from preferred stock with respect to dividends and distribution of assets in the event the issuing corporation is liquidated?
2. What are bonds? Who issues them? How are investors paid interest on the bonds they own?
3. How safe are corporate and government bonds? What is the main advantage of a municipal bond?
4. What is a mutual fund; what different types are available?
5. Explain call and put options.
6. How do the major stock exchanges differ from the over-the-counter market? What different kinds of brokers hold seats on the New York Stock Exchange?
7. What is a Blue Sky Law? What is the SEC? In what ways does each of these protect investors?

8. Explain the financial data given for GPU in Figure 17.3.
9. How can investors sell what they don't have (which is the case with short sales)? Why would anyone want to make a short sale?

DISCUSSION QUESTIONS

1. What rights do you have as the owner of 100 shares of Xerox Corporation?
2. Are preferred stocks and bonds always "safe" investments? ("Safe" means investors can, at any time, get back what they paid for them plus the dividends or interest they are promised.)
3. What advantages do mutual funds offer small investors?
4. If someone asked "How did the stock market do today?" how would you answer the question?
5. What is meant by establishing investment goals? Aren't all investment goals the same—make a lot of money?
6. Why do full-service brokers charge higher commissions than discount brokers?

CASE: IS LISTENING ENOUGH?

The scene is a big-city restaurant in Dallas buzzing with lunchtime conversation. Two young executives, apparently quite successful, are matching wits over lunch when suddenly all conversation ceases and everyone turns to listen to two senior executives. One has just uttered the magic words: "My broker at E. F. Hutton says the stock to buy is an over-the-counter issue that has just hit the streets at an initial price of $11.50."

The two young executives turn to each other to assess this "inside" information. One says, "I'd like to take advantage of that tip and buy 100 shares to see if I can make a killing in the market." The other replies: "I'd rather put my money in Blue Chips and leave it in for a while to make a long-term gain. Furthermore," he continues, "I can buy a couple a hundred shares on *margin* and cover after closing."

This conversation continues at a rapid pace as the speculator counters with: "My broker will let me work on *margin* too, and I've been quite successful in selling short in this sporadic market." The conservative partner wraps up the conversation with a summary statement: "You can try to beat the market if you like—I'd rather ride a steady course with Blue Chips, drawing dividends on long-term gains. My portfolio also includes some municipals, which help me with income tax and add to my long-range return on investments."

1. Which of these two young investors stands to gain the most with his securities game plan?
2. What are these two men talking about? Can you define all the technical terms they are using?
3. What sound advice could you give to these budding tycoons?

CASE: WHAT WILL IT BE— STOCKS OR BONDS?

Mary Jane Drew had just finished studying a book on the securities market, and she was very excited about making an investment that was sure to bring her a favorable return on her money. Her grandmother was very pleased with Mary's grades last term and gave her a sizable reward for putting forth so much effort in her college studies—$1000.

The way the book explained it, making money on the stock market seemed to be a cinch: all you had to do was buy stock, wait for it to rise in price, and sell for a nice little profit. But Mary Jane was a little cautious. Instead of buying right away, she watched the behavior of the stock market for a couple of weeks. First, the Dow went up a few points, then it went down; then up and down again. It showed very sporadic behavior—nothing to really count on; she couldn't be sure of a rising market and an increase in value of any stock she might have purchased.

Then she remembered the bond market—it was a little more complicated, or so it seemed to Mary Jane. And she didn't like the idea of simply lending money to a company, when all she would get in return would be interest payments. Worse yet, she would have to leave her money with the company for quite a while—maybe two to ten years—before her bonds would be redeemed.

Since Mary Jane always seemed to be in a hurry and wanted things to happen right now, buying stock in a company and following the stock market for a signal when to sell seemed a lot more glamorous than merely lending money to a company and hoping that the company would succeed in whatever it was doing.

1. In light of the recent fluctuations in the stock market, would Mary Jane be wise to invest her $1000 in stock, or would the purchase of a $1000 bond be more advisable? Draw some comparisons for her on the advantages and disadvantages of the purchase of stocks and of bonds.

2. What information about a company should Mary Jane get to help in her decision whether or not to invest in it? What about dividends? Maybe she forgot about them.

3. What about investing in a mutual fund? Would that seem advisable in Mary Jane's case? What about a money market fund?

C H A P T E R   18

FINANCING BUSINESS

After studying this chapter you should be able to:

1 Explain the role and objectives of a firm's financial manager.
2 Understand that good financial planning is crucial to the success of a business.
3 Describe the two important functions in financial planning: forecasting and preparing and approving budgets.
4 Compare two basic types of cash outlays—short-term expenditures and long-term expenditures.
5 Understand two approaches businesses use in raising money—short-term financing and long-term financing.
6 Know the qualifications under which banks and other lenders make unsecured and secured loans.
7 Describe the differences between debt and equity in long-term financing.

Take a poll of Americans or Englishmen or Germans and ask, "What's a Nissan?" and "they're likely to tell you anything from a new kind of radio to a card game," says a business analyst. "You're talking about the second-largest Japanese car company, and nobody outside of Japan ever heard of it."

Exaggerated though that remark may appear, it also reflects the sentiments of Nissan executives as they prepare to abandon the Datsun brand name used on all their cars sold overseas and revert to the name of the company that makes them.

Nissan officials contend it's more than merely a matter of image. They're worried that foreign buyers of Nissan bonds won't recognize the name when it comes time to decide whether to invest in the company.

Although Nissan had no trouble selling $500 million worth of bonds to finance construction of car assembly and engine plants in Britain, a Nissan official said, "our president, Takashi Ishihara, said he wished the company was better known."

"As we are getting into more and more overseas projects," said a Nissan spokesman, "we would like to see our corporate identity well established overseas."

Does the change in name indicate the possibility that Nissan stock may soon be available on the New York Stock Exchange?

"When we have a need we will register on the New York and American exchanges," said a Nissan official.

Nonetheless, Nissan officials left the clear impression that the underlying reason for the name change was to spread the Nissan name abroad with the idea of major expansion, construction—and overseas financing—over the next 10 or 20 years.

Source: Excerpted from Donald Kirk, "Seeking Name Recognition: Datsun-to-Nissan Not Just Image," *Dayton Journal Herald*, July 27, 1981, p. 11. Used by permission of the author.

Of course, Nissan isn't alone in its financing needs. Whether the company is Nissan, Apple Computer—a glamour firm from "silicon valley"—or U.S. Steel (usually considered part of "smokestack America"), each needs to finance itself on an almost perpetual basis. Although radically different in most respects, both Apple and U.S. Steel have demonstrated an amazing ability to raise funds. Investors lined up at their brokers' doors to get a piece of Apple's initial offering of common stock. The company thus raised $100 million almost as easily as many firms its size raise $100 thousand.[1] Raising capital was much harder for U.S. Steel. It had to maneuver by selling off some of its properties, leasing certain assets rather than buying them, arranging 10-year purchase agreements with its customers for a seamless pipe plant, and tap traditional credit sources. When it finished, though, it had accumulated $2 billion of financing that helped considerably when it bought Marathon Oil in 1982 for $6.4 billion.[2]

Both Apple and "Big Steel" ensured their existence, at least for a while, by being able to raise money. That's an important part of the finance function—but not the only part. There's considerably more. Figure 18.1 presents an overview of the total finance function and sets the stage for many of the topics presented in this chapter.

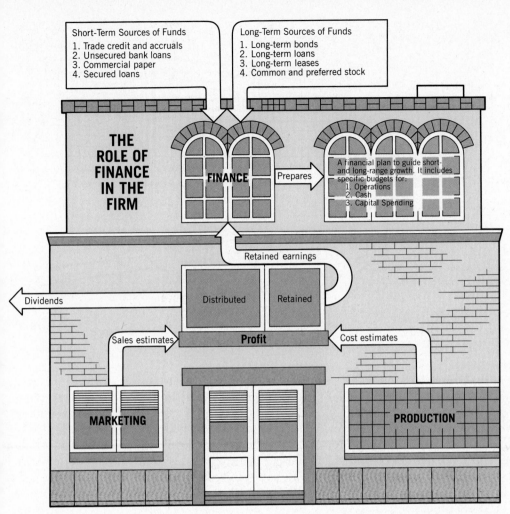

Short-Term Sources of Funds
1. Trade credit and accruals
2. Unsecured bank loans
3. Commercial paper
4. Secured loans

Long-Term Sources of Funds
1. Long-term bonds
2. Long-term loans
3. Long-term leases
4. Common and preferred stock

THE
ROLE OF
FINANCE
IN THE
FIRM

FINANCE → Prepares → A financial plan to guide short- and long-range growth. It includes specific budgets for:
1. Operations
2. Cash
3. Capital Spending

Retained earnings

Distributed   Retained

Dividends

Sales estimates   **Profit**   Cost estimates

MARKETING

PRODUCTION

FIGURE 18.1

THE FINANCIAL MANAGER

A corporate financial manager has a complex job that must be coordinated with the efforts of the other managers of the business. The financial manager, often titled "Vice-President, Finance," uses the information supplied by his or her finance staff and by the production, marketing, and other managers of the business in order to formulate a **financial strategy** for the company. This plan of action, which must be approved by the corporation's board of directors and other top management, is basically the firm's financial blueprint.

Overall Objective of the Financial Manager

The primary objective of a financial manager is to increase the value of the firm. In particular, the firm's entire management strives to maximize the value of the ownership interest (or the price of the common stock in the case of a corporation). That is, the financial manager seeks to develop policies and strategies that will increase the profits and market value of the business. Of course, the financial manager must consider social issues as well, such as equal opportunity employment policies and pollution control. Overall, however, the goal of a financial manager is to

maximize the value of the firm to its owners.

In pursuit of this overall goal, the financial manager must consider the potential impact of future economic conditions on the firm. His or her analysis of changing patterns of product demand, interest rates, and stock market conditions will influence the investment decisions that he or she makes. Thus Ponderosa System, a major steakhouse chain, in 1981 announced that as a result of high interest costs and strained profits, it was significantly reducing its spending program for the coming year.

The Role of the Financial Manager

The financial manager's role in the business is a crucial one, focusing on the central objective of a business—profitable growth. The financial manager's role includes three dynamic functions: financial planning, spending money on investment projects, and raising money to finance projects.

Somewhat like using maps and guidebooks in planning a journey, a business consults and is guided by its plan—a kind of financial roadmap. A financial plan includes estimates of a firm's future revenues, expenses, and future capital needs. It's a projection, then, of the future activities of the business for a given period of time—i.e. the budget period. The financial manager prepares the firm's plan after consulting with other managers as well as with his or her own staff.

A financial manager's also responsible for directing the firm's funds to the most productive investment projects. In the end, the buck stops with the financial manager; it's he (or she) who must decide where the firm's precious (and sometimes scarce) capital resources will be spent. Thus the corporation's future growth and profits may largely depend on the analysis and judgment of its financial manager.

A third important role of the financial manager is raising money for the firm. There are two ways that a company can raise money: internal and external financing. **Internal financing** means that the firm retains and invests a portion of its profits in the business. Profits that aren't distributed to shareholders as dividends but that are reinvested in the business are called **retained earnings**. For many years both Avon Products and IBM financed all their spectacular growth with retained earnings. **External financing** involves the raising of new capital from sources outside the business. External financing is obtained from selling bonds (or borrowing in other ways) or from selling new shares of stock. We'll examine in detail both retained earnings and external financing later in this chapter.

PERSPECTIVE ON SMALL BUSINESS

Business stinks. Sales are slipping, costs are rising, more losses seem inevitable. What's the solution? Many owners are unsure how to get through trying times like these. They don't have a coherent survival plan and do too little, too late. They rarely have a clear understanding of how much trouble their companies face, and they tend to assume things will get better.

But tentative measures and unfounded optimism can be fatal when swift, sure action is called for to save a deteriorating business, says Ian Sharlit, of the Los Angeles consulting firm, Durkee, Sharlit Associates. "Owners should act as if a knife is in their stomachs. They can't sit there and tell themselves things will get better."

For Durkee Sharlit the initial step is to make a worst-case estimate of what will happen to the business in the next 12 months, by making pessimistic forecasts of revenues and expenses. A revenue estimate comes first. "The figure must be lower than you can imagine sales going," Mr. Sharlit says.

After estimating sales, an estimate of expenses for the next 12 months is made. Variable costs are reduced in proportion to the projected decrease in sales or revenue: a 40% drop in sales would cause a 40% decline in sales commissions. Fixed costs, however, are increased to cover continued inflation. Mr. Sharlit uses a 4.5% inflation factor. Then total expenses are subtracted from estimated revenue, producing—in most cases—a sizable loss.

This isn't the extent of the bad news. A business is supposed to make money, so a reasonable profit figure is incorporated into the survival plan. Durkee Sharlit uses a 20% return on owners' equity, but a percentage of sales or revenue could be used instead.

Cutting overhead is distasteful for many owners. They hate to fire people. They don't want to compromise quality or reduce their product lines, even though they need to save money. Some convince themselves they should sit tight and not close factories or sell off idle equipment so they will be ready to meet increased demand when the economy brightens.

That may be suicidal. "Forget about being ready when the market comes back," says Mr. Sharlit. "That's the worst syndrome you can get into. You can start over when the market comes back . . . if you have survived."

SOURCE: Excerpted from Sanford L. Jacobs, "Survival When Business Is Bad Requires a Plan, Lots of Cuts," *Wall Street Journal*, April 5, 1982, p. 27. Reprinted by permission of The Wall Street Journal, © Dow Jones & Company, Inc., 1982. All rights reserved.

FINANCIAL PLANNING

Good financial planning is crucial to the success of a business. A financial manager considers the product lines that the company has or will have, the resources available to produce these products, and the financing needed to provide for modern, productive facilities. The financial manager must then strike a delicate balance between all these variables that produce a winning company—one that maximizes the success of its products, stays out of financial troubles, and—most importantly—causes shareholders (owners) to realize the best results possible.

The game plan of a financial manager incorporates short-run and long-run projections of the sales, expenses, and profits of a business as well as an analysis of the business's needs to spend and to raise money. The ultimate goal of the plan should be to maximize the firm's long-run value.

Making Forecasts

An essential part of a business financial plan is a forecast of future developments. In particular, this forecast is based on economic and other projections of demand for the firm's products.

General Motors, for example, has its central

corporate finance staff develop a forecast of future car and truck sales. The forecast looks at general economic conditions to assess the total market potential and then it makes a specific estimate of its probable market share.

Short-Term Forecasts A **short-term forecast** is basically a projection of immediate and shortly upcoming sales revenues for approximately the next 12 months. At GM, for example, the corporate finance staff projects monthly product sales in order to arrive at an expectation of probable sales levels over the next year. The forecast is developed after consulting with the company's economists and with the staff at each of GM's various operating divisions. Using the short-term forecast, GM's corporate managers then make decisions regarding car production scheduling, building up or lowering inventories of cars, sales promotion scheduling, and other such operating items. A favorable short-term forecast, for example, leads to increased car production and to an increase in GM's inventory of cars. An unfavorable forecast motivates GM's management to cut car production schedules.

A variety of approaches are available for forecasting. One of the easiest and most widely used is **trend projection**. Figure 18.2 illustrates a trend projection. It's assumed here that the trend line was determined by visual inspection of sales from 1978 through 1983; the forecast is for 1984. There are mathematical procedures available for finding the trend line. These are preferred to visual fitting, particularly if there are a large number of data points, or if the data points are scattered widely around the line. However the visual fit in Figure 18.2 would be reasonably close to the estimate provided by the more accurate approach. (Both might be way off in forecasting 1984 sales; that's a risk inherent in forecasting.)

Long-Term Forecasts A **long-term forecast** extends over a long period—often 5 to 10 years into the future. This forecast is a crucial element of a business's long-term strategic plan, which maps out the future financial direction of the company. General Motors' long-term forecast, for example, includes such projections as the level of future car sales, the mix of sales between small and large cars, and the effect of Japanese import sales on the U.S. automakers' market shares. GM suffered much less than Ford or Chrysler during the 1980 car sales slump because it had anticipated a jump in small-car demand well before its competitors.

During the early 1970s, GM's staff forecast that

FIGURE 18.2

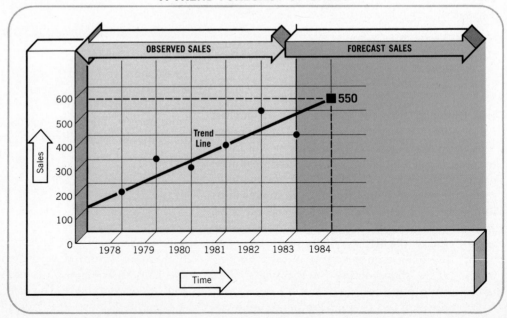

A TREND FORECAST OF SALES

TALKING BUSINESS

In 1972, the average feature film released by a major studio cost $2.5 million to produce. In 1980, the average was $9.4 million. One factor in this increase is the tendency of movies' costs to exceed their budgets.

Says Barry Diller, Paramount Pictures Corporation's chairman and chief executive, "The real problem is the $5 million picture that is costing $17 million, the first-time director shooting a contemporary film in 115 days instead of 34, the stars being paid $2 million to $3 million."

Mr. Diller speaks from experience. Paramount's "Reds" took three years to produce and cost about $33 million; its original budget was $22 million. The cost for "Reds" didn't grow "because someone sat there for hours waiting for the perfect glint of sun off the right wheel of a cannon," Mr. Diller insists. "Like other movies, for better or worse, it evolved in the creative process, and that took time and money."

Nevertheless, Paramount is changing the way it makes film deals in an attempt to avoid future budget overruns. "We have simply told everyone up front that we're going to treat them well, but there aren't going to be any more huge, expensive trailers used as dressing rooms," Mr. Diller says. "We aren't going to pay a leading lady's makeup man five times scale. And we aren't going to take on a director's favorite camera crew for an extra $17,000 a week. We reach an agreement on a realistic shooting schedule, then do everything in our power to make sure they stick to it."

Source: Adapted from Stephen J. Sansweet, "Paramount Manages to Cut Its Movie Costs, but 'Reds' Shows It Can Be a Difficult Task," *Wall Street Journal*, July 20, 1981, p. 15. Adapted by permission of The Wall Street Journal, © Dow Jones & Company, Inc., 1981. All rights reserved.

small cars would be in much greater demand in later years. Acting on this information, GM invested billions of dollars in new factories and machinery to build small cars. GM's X-cars — a new line of fuel-efficient vehicles — were introduced in 1979 with great success giving GM a substantial jump on other domestic automakers. These cars, such as the Chevrolet Citation, sold very well. In contrast, Ford had no new small-car line until the Ford Escort was introduced in 1980.

Further, GM introduced another small-car line — the J-cars — in 1981. These cars enabled GM to weather the financial storm of the 1980–81 new-car sales slowdown better than did Ford and Chrysler. Then, in the summer of 1981, GM announced that it had agreed with two Japanese automakers to cooperate with them on the production and marketing of new "mini-cars" smaller than any GM had ever produced. This venture would yield the technology necessary to produce the tiny and fuel-efficient S-car.

Preparing and Approving Budgets

A **budget** incorporates a forecast of sales into a plan that projects not only future sales revenues but also future operating expenses and cash investment outlays. Every business prepares at least one budget, and most business plans contain three distinct types of budgets: the operating budget, the cash budget, and the capital budget.

An **operating budget** is a projection of the current year's sales revenues and operating expenses. It reflects the financial manager's expectation of sales and the cost of producing the products and services demanded. It doesn't provide for capital items such as plant and equipment purchases.

A **cash budget** incorporates the revenues and expenses of the operating budget but it then goes a step further and projects the firm's future cash needs or possible surpluses. A sample cash budget is shown in Table 18.1.

TABLE 18-1
A Sample Cash Budget for the Year Ended 12/31/84

		Quarters			For the Year as a Whole
	1	2	3	4	
Cash balance, beginning	$ 10,000	$ 15,000	$ 15,000	$ 15,325	$ 10,000
Add receipts:					
Collections from customers	125,000	150,000	160,000	221,000	656,000
(a) Total available before current financing	$135,000	$165,000	$175,000	$236,325	$666,000
Less disbursements:					
For materials	$ 20,000	$ 35,000	$ 35,000	$ 54,200	$144,200
For other costs and expenses	25,000	20,000	20,000	17,000	82,000
For payroll	90,000	95,000	95,000	109,200	389,200
For income tax	5,000	—	—	—	5,000
For machinery purchase	—	—	—	20,000	20,000
(b) Total disbursements	$140,000	$150,000	$150,000	$200,400	$640,400
Minimum cash balance desired	15,000	15,000	15,000	15,000	15,000
Total cash needed	$155,000	$165,000	$165,000	$215,400	$655,400
Excess of total cash available over total cash needed before current financing (deficiency)	$ (20,000)	$ —	$ 10,000	$ 20,925	$ 10,600
Financing:					
Borrowings (at beginning)	$ 20,000	$ —	$ —	$ —	$ 20,000
Repayments (at end)	—	—	(9,000)	(11,000)	(20,000)
Interest (at 10% per annum)	—	—	(675)	(1,100)	(1,775)
(c) Total effects of financing	$ 20,000	$ —	$ (9,675)	$ (12,100)	$ (1,775)
(d) Cash balance, end (a + c − b)	$ 15,000	$ 15,000	$ 15,325	$ 23,825	$ 23,825

SOURCE: Charles T. Horngren, *Cost Accounting: A Managerial Emphasis*, 4th ed., © 1977, p. 135. Adapted by permission of Prentice-Hall, Inc., Englewood Cliffs, New Jersey.

A corporation's **capital budget** is its spending plan for the acquisition of new factories, equipment, and other major long-term investments for the business. The capital budget is based on such things as management's decisions to expand product lines, to move into new product areas, or to sell an existing facility.

Budgets Coordinate Activities Given an estimate of sales revenues, the next step involves the projection of the firm's expenses. Basically, there are two types of operating expenses to be projected. **Fixed costs** are those periodic and continuing expenses that are incurred regardless of the level of sales revenues. Interest paid on long-term debt is an example of a fixed cost. It must be paid on a scheduled basis if sales are $0 or $1 million. **Variable costs** depend on the levels of production and sales. The cost of materials and assembly-line workers' pay are the examples of variable costs for GM. If GM decides not to build a number of cars, the material and labor costs of making these cars don't have to be expended. Both fixed and variable cost forecasts must be made in the budgeting process.

A budget must be balanced. If operating expenses are greater than sales revenues, the company won't be profitable. If the cash budget indicates the need for more money than the company has at hand, arrangements must be made to get new money through borrowing or the sale of ownership interests. We can see, then, how important the budgeting process is: it's a plan to guide the financial operations of the company.

Delegation and Financial Controls Once a company's budget has been approved by the board of directors, it's up to management to monitor the company's actual financial performance. That is, the actual amounts of sales revenues, operating expenditures, capital expenditures, and cash inflows and outflows must be continually compared with the budget projections. Most large corporations require their divisional managers to report actual monthly sales and expenditures to top management so that this comparison can be made. In this way, top management has the opportunity of noting deviations from budget estimates so that corrective action can be taken. Variances from budgeted amounts also serve as a basis for evaluating divisional managers' performances. Someone consistently over budget might be asked for an explanation.

SPENDING MONEY

For a company to grow and prosper, money must be continuously invested in it. There are two basic types of cash outlay: short-term expenditures and long-term expenditures. Short-term expenditures are those incurred in the day-to-day operation of the business. Levi Strauss, for example, has to spend money for blue denim fabric and workers' wages to pay for the manufacture of its jeans. Long-term expenditures are investments made by the company in such things as new factories, new equipment, land, and new businesses. These expenditures are necessary for the company to maintain and expand its operations in order to offer products of the desired quality at a reasonable price.

Short-Term Expenditures

Short-term expenditures, or **operating expenditures,** are related to money tied up in the company's current assets. The current assets of a business consist of all those assets that are held in cash or that can be converted into cash in less than a year. Current assets include short-term investments, marketable securities, inventories, and accounts receivable.

Maintaining Liquidity A prime consideration in the budgeting process and in the actual operation of a business is the need to maintain the firm's **liquidity**—the possession, by the firm, of enough ready cash to pay its bills as they come due. A company's liquidity can be maintained in several ways. One way, of course, is to keep an ample supply of cash in a checking account; but most companies try to keep their checking account balances as low as possible because most business checking accounts either don't pay interest or pay at a very low rate. Instead, companies invest available cash resources in short-term marketable securities, such as Treasury bills and certificates of deposit. These investments are very liquid—that is, they have short maturities and can be quickly converted to cash.

Suppose that a financial manager learns that the company has $10 million in its checking account and that this money isn't needed to pay bills for 30 days. By investing this money in certificates of deposit paying 12 percent annual interest, the manager sees to it that the company gets back its $10 million in 30 days *plus* an additional $100,000 or so in interest earnings. Managing a corporation's liquidity is called **cash management.** The objective of cash management is to maximize the firm's earnings from its liquid investments while at the same time maintaining a level of liquidity that permits the firm to meet its bill payments as they come due.

Inventory Another cash expenditure item is the company's inventories (or, more correctly, the "building up" of the company's inventories after initial inventory levels have been established; conversely, if sales are stable and inventories are reduced, excess cash is generated). These are unsold goods, products still in production, and raw materials. Goods waiting to be sold are called the **finished goods inventory** while goods being built are called **work-in-process inventory**. Whirlpool Corporation, for example, has an inventory of appliances (finished goods); it also has an inventory of units that are being made (work-in-process). Additionally, Whirlpool has bins full of parts that will be assembled into appliances—its **raw materials inventory**.

Three forms of inventory—a major short-term expenditure—for the lumber manufacturing process: top left, raw materials; bottom left, work in progress; right, finished goods.

Retailers such as Sears, Roebuck also have large inventories of merchandise in both their stores and their warehouses. For many of these companies, inventories are their largest single investment.

Accounts Receivable A firm's **accounts receivable** are what it's owed by its customers. Very frequently a company sells its product and isn't immediately paid in cash; instead, the company bills its customer. The bill stands for an account receivable by the seller. Whirlpool, for example, sells many appliances to Sears, which then markets them as Kenmore appliances. When Whirlpool ships goods to Sears stores, it also sends Sears a bill (invoice) for those products. Until that bill is paid, Whirlpool will carry an account receivable from Sears on its books.

Long-Term Expenditures

A firm's long-term expenditures, also called **capital expenditures,** are its investments in long-term assets—items such as land, buildings, machinery, and equipment. Most manufacturing firms have substantial investments in long-term assets; the Boeing Company, for example, invests millions of dollars annually in its airplane manufacturing facilities. Long-term expenditures are also investments in long-lasting assets. Land, for example, is an extremely durable asset with an almost unlimited life. Factory buildings, also called *manufacturing plants*, usually last for 30 to 50 years or more. Equipment and machinery normally has a shorter useful life of 5 to 10 years. Long-term assets tend to be relatively expensive and represent an investment by the company in its future.

ON THE FIRING LINE

Declining Capital Investment: Who's To Blame?

For some years now, American business firms have allowed the level of their investment in plant and equipment to slack off, to fall behind that of competing firms in other Free World countries. As a result, productivity growth has fallen behind as well, and American corporations, critics claim, cannot continue to neglect spending on plant and equipment any longer. If they do not soon earmark large sums for improving their production facilities, they—and the rest of us along with them—will face dire consequences. Obsolete plants and equipment inevitably mean high costs and obsolete products. Yet management hesitates. Why?

Some insist it is the excessive spending of the American consumer that has drained the pool of capital necessary for such investments. Others point the finger at government programs and policies. And still others place the responsibility at corporate management's door.

Are consumers to blame? Those who think so point to several factors. First, credit cards make it easy to buy, whether or not the buyer has cash in hand. Indeed, the credit card "buy now, pay later" syndrome has led many Americans deep into debt. Add to that the constant urging by the media to spend and enjoy, and little money is left for savings.

Inflation is the other reason Americans are consuming goods at record rates. In the 1970s high rates of inflation provided an excellent rationale for buying on time or, in other words, going into debt to make purchases. What, after all, is the point of saving, if the dollars you save merely drop in value over the years? Surely it is far wiser to borrow. You can then pay off your loans in dollars worth less than the dollars you borrowed.

Those critics who find government to blame also have their arguments. They note, government tax policy discourages Americans from adding to the supply of capital by making long-term investments in financial instruments or bonds and stocks. Taxes on interest and dividends make income from such investments unappealing. Furthermore, taxpayers who fill out itemized returns can deduct all interest they pay on debt from their taxable income. This adds up to a powerful antisavings tax bias, which even reductions in tax rates can do little to counteract.

Moreover, how can anyone accuse the American people of overspending when the federal government lives far beyond its means? they ask. Money that industry needs to modernize plants and equipment is being loaned to government. Some speculate that government borrowing reduces the supply of credit available to business firms, and in the process it pushes interest rates up for everybody.

A third group of analysts is convinced that business and industry—not the American people or government—are to blame for current low levels of capital investment.

While European and Japanese executives try to develop and introduce products in advance of consumer demand, American managers seem more cautious. They want to be sure there will be demand for their products before they risk any sizable capital investment. Why? Critics argue that managers, jobs and reputations depend on immediate, short-term returns on investment, which are, right or wrong, the top priority of modern corporate America. Will conditions ever be perfect? While executives wait or go for the short-run profit, corporate plant and equipment in the US continues to age, and the procrastination of timid management, many believe, is doing long-run damage to the US economy.

Perhaps all three views are valid. Perhaps the public, the government, and the business community are all to blame. But if that is the case, is there any hope at all for American business and industry?

Sources of Proposals Within large corporations, proposals for capital expenditures are usually made by divisional managers to the central finance staff at the firm's headquarters. At International Telephone and Telegraph (ITT), a large diversified corporation, capital expenditure proposals from the company's divisions are sent to the firm's headquarters in New York. There the central staff evaluates all proposals and decides which ones should be recommended for approval.

Long-Run Importance The proper budgeting of capital expenditures is crucial to the future success of the firm. Incorrect capital budgeting decisions can lead to future problems, while good decisions can result in sustained future profitability.

A farsighted capital budgeting decision was made by Standard Oil of Ohio (SOHIO) during the 1960s, when, as a small regional oil company, it decided to invest in a risky drilling venture on the North Slope of Alaska. Risky, because oil had not been discovered there. This otherwise costly program paid off handsomely for SOHIO: a huge pool of oil and natural gas was discovered. SOHIO as well as its drilling partners has reaped enormous profits from the project—from $60 million in 1971 to almost $2 billion only ten years later. SOHIO's common stock soared too, reflecting the good news. Over that ten-year period, its stock price increased in excess of 1000 percent. Today SOHIO is an oil industry giant. Much of its success is due to that single decision to invest in the previously undiscovered North Slope oilfields—clearly an excellent capital expenditure program.

RAISING SHORT-TERM MONEY

We've seen the many expenses for which money is needed by businesses; but how do they raise the money? Companies raise money for these needs in three ways: borrowing money, selling ownership interests (common and preferred stock in the case of corporations), and retaining profits. Borrowed funds include short-term and long-term loans. A **short-term loan** is usually repaid in less than one year; a **long-term loan** is repaid over an extended period of time. Short-term sources of funds, which we'll examine here, include both unsecured and secured loans. Long-term sources of funds are analyzed later in this chapter.

Unsecured Short-Term Sources

There are two basic types of short-term financing: unsecured loans and secured loans. An **unsecured loan** or credit doesn't require that the borrower put up any collateral as a condition for receiving the loan; the lender extends credit based solely on the borrower's creditworthiness. (A **secured loan,** in contrast, requires that the borrower put up **collateral,** which is something of value that the lender can seize or sell if the borrower fails to repay the loan.) Unsecured loans include trade credit, accruals, bank loans, and commercial paper.

Trade Credit If Uniroyal sells tires to General Motors, GM isn't required to pay cash on delivery. Rather, Uniroyal periodically bills GM for its tire purchases. Uniroyal is extending credit to GM for the time period between when the tires are delivered and when GM actually pays for them. Recalling our discussion of accounts receivable, we can see that Uniroyal has an account receivable from GM until GM pays. **Trade credit,** then, is basically a loan from the seller to the buyer of goods and services and is a major short-term source of funds for most companies.

Accruals An **accrual** is an expense that's incurred for goods or services that have already been provided and that are paid for in a lump-sum at a future date. Employees, for example, are usually paid on a weekly, biweekly, or monthly basis. The company's obligation to pay them continues over the pay period even though actual payment isn't made until the end of the period. Income taxes are another example of an accrual. Businesses, like individuals, owe income taxes to the government based on ongoing cumulative earnings. Yet actual payments to the government for business income taxes are generally made quarterly (four times a year) instead of continuously.

Bank Loans Unsecured bank loans are a substantial source of short-term funds to business. There are several types of unsecured bank loans, three of them being (1) single-payment notes, (2) lines of credit, and (3) revolving credit agreements.

A **single-payment note** is an IOU that requires the amount borrowed, or principal, to be repaid

Major forms of capital expenditure include plants and equipment. Left, an industrial plant; below, knitting machines used in textile manufacturing.

ing balance equal to 10–20 percent of the amount borrowed.

The **compensating balance** is the minimum (or average) deposit (*at no interest*) in the lending bank that the borrower must maintain. A compensating balance tends to raise the cost of borrowing. For example, if a $100,000 loan is taken out at a prime rate of 15 percent, and the compensating balance to be held on deposit is $20,000, then the $15,000 in interest (15%) is actually being paid on only $80,000 — not $100,000; and the $20,000 required on deposit is meanwhile nonusable. So the interest rate really amounts to 18.75 percent, not 15 percent. (As we'll see below, most companies are charged more than the prime rate.)

A **revolving credit agreement** is similar to a line of credit except that it's generally a two- or three-year agreement, and a commitment fee is commonly charged. Because of the guaranteed availability of funds under this arrangement, the commitment fee, which typically amounts to about 0.5 percent a year on the average amount of unused funds, must be paid by the borrower. Figure 18.3 shows an announcement stating that Worldwide Energy Corporation in July 1981 obtained a $40 million revolving credit agreement from two major banks.

Short-term bank loans are often used to finance the seasonal-inventory and accounts-receivable buildups of businesses. A seasonal business is one whose sales are exceptionally strong during certain times of the year. The seasonal business usually increases its inventory and accounts receivable just before the beginning of the strong sales period.

For example, Frank's Nursery and Craft, based in Detroit, owns a large chain of stores that sell outdoor plants, shrubs, and many other garden and craft items. Most of its stores are in the Great

in a lump sum at the end of the life of the loan. Loans of this type are usually due 90 to 180 days after they're made. Interest accrues immediately after the money is lent and is ordinarily payable either monthly or at maturity.

A **line of credit** is an agreement made by the commercial bank to lend the borrower funds up to a stated maximum amount. The borrower can borrow any amount up to the maximum line of credit as long as the agreement remains in force and the bank has funds available to lend. The terms of a line of credit usually specify that the borrower will repay any funds within one year and that the borrower will maintain a compensat-

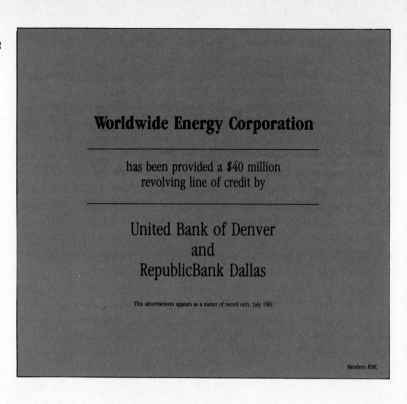
Lakes region whose very seasonal weather results in Frank's gardening business being seasonal. Sales are brisk in the spring and summer, when shrubs and gardens are planted, and very slow in the winter, when Michigan's cold climate makes garden planting impossible. So Frank's builds up its inventory of shrubs and plants prior to the big spring selling season. This seasonal inventory expansion and the increased level of accounts receivable resulting from the heavy sales are usually financed with short-term bank loans. When the goods are sold, a portion of the sales revenue is used to repay the loan.

Commercial Paper **Commercial paper,** is a short-term corporate IOU that's sold in the money market by large corporations to raise short-term funds. General Electric Credit Corporation (GECC), for example, raises millions of dollars of short-term funds by selling commercial paper. GECC finds a ready market for its commercial paper because it's a subsidiary of General Electric. Commercial paper usually is written in amounts between $100,000 and $1 million and matures in 270 days or less. Many commercial paper issuers repay their maturing obligations by selling new issues of commercial paper. The process is often referred to as "rolling over commercial paper."

Secured Short-Term Sources

A secured loan is collateralized by specific assets of the borrower. The lender can seize or sell these assets if the borrower fails to repay the loan. Three popular types of secured short-term loans are those secured by inventory, by accounts receivable, and by money raised through selling accounts receivable.

A firm can pledge inventory as collateral for a short-term loan. **Pledging** means that the asset can be legally taken by the lender if the loan isn't repaid. Inventory loans are very common in the apparel industry. Here the lender can take the borrower's inventory of clothing if the borrower doesn't repay the loan. Many of the new automobiles on dealers' lots are financed with inventory loans extended by commercial banks or other lending institutions; for example, GMAC finances many of the GM cars. This type of lending arrangement is called **floor planning.**

Corporate borrowers can also pledge accounts receivable as collateral for a short-term loan. If the borrower fails to repay the loan, the lender can seize the borrower's accounts receivable and collect them, using the proceeds to repay the loan. Loans of this type are often made under a

TALKING BUSINESS

Deep cuts in federal grant and loan programs have made financing a college education more difficult for many students. While state governments and the colleges themselves offer some aid, banks remain the primary source of loans for college. Interest rates are high—18 percent in mid-1982. However, many banks are devising new kinds of student loan programs to attract customers.

The Citizens Bank of Dallas, Georgia, for example, will lend depositors an amount equal to two and one-half times their savings account balance. A depositor with a savings balance of $15,000 can get a loan of $37,500 over four years at an interest rate of 12 percent a year. However, monthly repayments of $462.96 must start immediately, and the savings balance must not drop below $15,000 during the four-year period.

Source: "Raising Last-Minute Cash for College," by Gail Bronson, adapted from the April 1982 issue of *Money* Magazine, pp. 111–114; © 1982 Time Inc. All rights reserved.

nonnotification plan. This means that the borrower's own customers (debtors) are not told that the company has used its accounts receivable (= customers' debts) as loan collateral.

If a company **factors accounts receivable,** it's actually selling them to a bank or a finance company. Factoring in the textile industry has been popular for many years. It's a very expensive means of financing because the financial institution always pays the company less than the actual amount of the accounts receivable. On the other hand, it assumes all the risks and tasks of collecting on the accounts. When the accounts receivable are sold, the customers (debtors) of the company are notified of this and are instructed to remit their payments directly to the financial institution. This is called a **notification plan.**

Cost of Short-Term Financing

The borrower's cost of short-term financing varies widely, depending on the type of loan. Unsecured bank loans usually have interest rates that are tied to the prime lending rate. The **prime rate** is that short-term interest rate which banks charge their most favored and creditworthy customers. IBM, for example, pays the prime rate on its short-term bank loans. Most companies are charged a higher interest rate than the prime.

For example, if a bank's prime rate were 16 percent, a firm signing a line of credit agreement that specified an interest rate of the prime rate plus 2 percent would be charged at an 18 percent annual interest rate. If the prime rose to 20 percent, this firm's interest rate would be raised to 22 percent. Prime-rate-related bank loans are said to have a **floating interest rate,** which means that each time the prime rate is changed, the loan's interest rate is also adjusted. Illogical as it may seem, secured bank loans usually have *higher* interest rates than unsecured loans. The reason is that most secured bank loans are made to less creditworthy firms where it's felt that there's a greater chance the loan won't be repaid.

RAISING LONG-TERM MONEY

Long-term capital expenditures for items such as factories and machinery are usually financed with long-term money. Long-term sources of capital include long-term debt and equity capital. **Long-term debt** is a loan that is repaid over an extended time period, often 10 to 30 years. **Equity capital** is money invested in the business by the owners—common and preferred stockholders in the case of corporations. This money is raised by selling new ownership interests or by retaining profits. As we saw earlier, retained earnings are

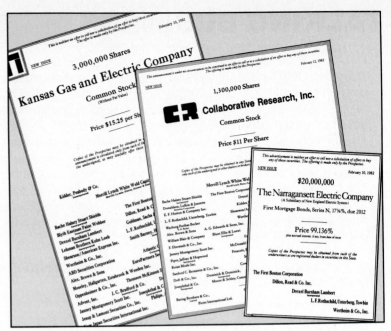

Announcements for a variety of public offerings to raise needed financing.

that portion of profits that's not paid to the shareholders as dividends.

Debt versus Equity

Suppose that General Electric plans to spend $2 billion over the next year to build new factories and buy new machines to make jet engines. GE's top management must decide how to raise this money. They'll probably choose one or more long-term financing sources, including long-term borrowing and equity capital. When making this choice, GE's management must analyze the pros and cons of each alternative, since there are significant differences between these financing methods.

GE's management would carefully consider the key differences between debt and equity capital in deciding how to finance capital projects. Long-term debt has both advantages and disadvantages. Its principal advantage is that interest paid on debt is a tax-deductible business expense. This means that GE's corporate income taxes would be lowered if debt financing were used. In contrast, the dividend payments made to shareholders are not an income-tax deduction to GE. They must be paid from its after-tax income. Thus at a 50 percent corporate tax rate, debt would be twice as expensive as common or preferred stock on an af-

ter-tax basis, even if they were the same on a pre-tax basis.

Debt has a disadvantage, though: interest must be paid at a specified date, and the principal must be repaid at maturity. Failure to make these scheduled payments could result in bankruptcy. If a company goes bankrupt, its affairs are supervised by a bankruptcy court and it could eventually be forced out of business. Debt, then, has the risk of bankruptcy which is called **financial risk.** Equity capital, on the other hand, doesn't involve a contractual obligation to make payments.

The use of borrowed money to finance an investment is known as **trading on the equity,** or simply *leverage.* Leverage can increase the company's return on its investment if it earns profits at a higher rate than the interest rate paid on the borrowed funds. The key to understanding leverage is to remember that leverage always increases the borrower's risk while also increasing the borrower's potential profitability.

Long-Term Loans

There are several types of long-term loans that a corporation can consider. Three of these are long-term bonds, long-term mortgages, and private placement loans. A long-term bond, examined in the last chapter, is a long-term corporate IOU

HOW INVESTMENT BANKING WORKS

CORPORATION — $ $ $ — Securities → INVESTMENT BANKER — $ $ $ ← Securities — INVESTORS

FIGURE 18.4

that's initially sold to the public in the primary market. A long-term mortgage is a loan from a financial institution that's secured by real estate. A private placement loan is a long-term loan obtained from a financial institution.

Long-Term Bonds A **long-term bond** is basically a corporate IOU that's paid off (matures) 20 to 40 years after it's issued. Corporate bonds (described in detail in the previous chapter), as well as new issues of common and preferred stock, are initially sold to the public through investment bankers. An **investment banker**—usually a large stockbrokerage firm, such as EF Hutton—is a financial intermediary that buys a new issue of securities from its corporate issuer and then resells those securities to investors. The process by which investment bankers buy and resell new securities is called *securities underwriting* and is illustrated in Figure 18.4.

Mortgage Loans A mortgage loan, or **long-term mortgage,** is a type of secured loan against which the borrower puts up real estate as collateral. If the borrower fails to repay the loan, the lender can seize the property, sell it, and use the proceeds to satisfy the loan. Long-term mortgage loans are frequently used by corporations to finance new buildings, such as factories and warehouses. An important source of these loans is life insurance companies, which lend billions of dollars each year to corporations in the form of mortgage loans.

Private Placement Loans A **private placement loan** is a long-term loan, often unsecured, that's obtained from a financial institution—typically, a life insurance company or a pension fund. Life insurance companies, such as Prudential, make loans from the premium income they receive; pension funds, such as the Teamsters' fund, make loans from the large pools of money they amass in order to provide retirement benefits to eligible participants. Many corporations finance their long-term expenditures with private placement loans.

Cost of Long-Term Debt Financing Long-term debt financing involves two types of costs. First, the corporation must pay to arrange a loan or to sell bonds to the public. Loan-arranging fees are paid to financial institutions or others for setting up a loan. Publicly sold bonds, for example, have **underwriting costs:** the investment banker is paid a fee for selling the bonds to the public. Mortgage loans usually involve a **loan origination fee** that's paid to the lender—usually about 2 percent of the amount borrowed, paid in addition to interest.

A second, more substantial cost of borrowed funds is the interest that's paid to the lender. Long-term interest rates have soared in recent years. In 1981, for example, many borrowers had to pay over 15 percent interest on long-term bonds compared to only about 6 percent in 1968. In addition to interest, the principal amount must be repaid as well.

Using Long-Term Leases

A lease is a contract to rent a portion (or all) of a building or to rent machinery and equipment for a period of time. The landlord or owner of the building or equipment is called the *lessor* and the business that rents the property the *lessee*. Many corporations lease property and equipment rather than buy it. IBM and Control Data lease many of their computers.

Another example is J. C. Penney, America's third largest nonfood retailing company, which

TALKING BUSINESS

Broadway producers are looking around for new ways of raising money these days. Costs are rising faster than inflation, and money is harder than ever to come by. In 1973, it cost only $650,000 to mount "A Little Night Music." In 1981, it cost at least $1.5 million to produce a musical.

Broadway producers still must rely on private investors, or "angels," for the bulk of the money they need to finance shows; but now they must find other sources as well. In some instances, producers are asking theater owners for money, arguing that the owners need good shows to keep their theaters going. The motion-picture and television industries also need properties that can be turned into motion pictures or TV specials; in recent months, they too have stepped up their interest in Broadway.

The risks of investing in the theater are formidable. However, "people don't invest in the theater to make money," says one Broadway producer. "They do so because it's more fun than the stock market or the bond market."

Source: Adapted from Stephen Grover, "Producers Tap New Backers for Broadway," *Wall Street Journal*, July 30, 1981, p. 21. Adapted by permission of The Wall Street Journal, © Dow Jones & Company, Inc., 1981. All rights reserved.

leases most of its stores in preference to owning them. Penney's would rather have its money invested in merchandise inventories than in real estate. Penney's lessors like this arrangement because the stores are usually rented under a profitable long-term lease. Because they permit firms to obtain the use of property without tying up large sums of money, long-term leases are viewed as a source of long-term funds by business.

Equity Financing

Equity financing involves raising money by selling new issues of common (or preferred) stock or by retaining profits. Selling new stock issues and borrowing money are called external financing. If retained earnings are put to use, this is referred to as internal financing. An advantage of equity financing is its lack of financial risk. As we've seen, borrowed funds have to be repaid, hence the company incurs financial risk.

Selling Common Stock   Corporations use two basic methods of selling new issues of common stock to raise money. The first, a *rights offering*, involves the sale of shares to current holders of common stock. These common shareholders are given the opportunity of subscribing to a new issue of the company's stock in proportion to their current ownership interest.

For example, if a firm having 100,000 shares of common stock outstanding made a rights offering of 10,000 shares, then for each share owned one would receive the right to one-tenth of a new share. A person having a 1 percent interest in the firm (1000 shares) would therefore receive enough rights to buy 100 new shares (1/10 × 1000 shares). After exercising his or her rights, this person would have a total of 1100 shares—still a 1 percent interest in the firm (which would then have 110,000 shares outstanding).

The second method of selling new issues of common stock involves sale to an underwriter (individual or organization), who in turn sells the shares to the public. This is called an *underwritten sale of securities*. For example, Pengo Industries sold 1,000,000 new common shares to the public in March 1981. The issue was sold as a public offering through an underwriter (Eppler, Guerin & Turner) and raised about $25.5 million, from which the investment bankers (underwriters) received a sales commission of $1.25 million. Pengo therefore received about $24.25 million

---

---

from the sale. The first page of the prospectus issued in connection with this offering appears in Figure 18.5. A prospectus (discussed in the last chapter) is a detailed financial document describing the issuer and the bond or stock being offered for sale to the public.

Cost of Equity Financing There are several costs to consider in relation to equity financing. If new shares of stock are sold to the public through investment bankers, an underwriting cost will be incurred. This cost is the investment banker's compensation for arranging the transaction. A second cost of equity financing is the payment of dividends to shareholders. We've already seen that the company doesn't have to pay dividends. However, if investors buy the stock with the expectation of receiving dividends and they're not paid, the investors will likely sell the stock, thereby driving its price downward.

A third cost is known as dilution and is very difficult to measure precisely. **Dilution,** which is not an out-of-pocket cost to the company, refers to the fact that the company has more common shares outstanding after new shares are sold so that each share's percentage claim on earnings and assets is less.

To illustrate how dilution affects each common share's relative portion of a company's profits, consider the sale of 100,000 new common shares to the public by the Phoenix Broadcasting Company. The issue was sold at $50 per share, raising $4.5 million for Phoenix after underwriting costs. Before the sale, Phoenix had 100,000 outstanding shares. During the previous year, Phoenix's net profits were $1 million, or $10 per common share ($1 million/100,000 shares). A corporation's net income per share is called *earnings per share* (EPS). Phoenix's profits improved, reaching $1.3 million the year after the new shares were sold. However, as Table 18.2 reveals, Phoenix's EPS dropped to $6.50 because there were 100,000 more common shares outstanding.

TABLE 18–2

Dilution Effects of the Sale of 100,000 New Shares: Phoenix Broadcasting Company

		Earnings per Share (EPS)	
		Before Sale	After Sale
EPS =	$\dfrac{\text{Net Profits}}{\text{Common Shares Outstanding}}$	$\dfrac{\$1,000,000}{100,000} = \$10.00$	$\dfrac{\$1,300,000}{200,000} = \$6.50$

Thus a financial manager who's considering the sale of new common shares must take into account not only the explicit underwriting and dividend costs but also the potential dilution effects of issuing new shares. Dilution will take place whenever new capital is not invested as profitably as the existing capital. In the case of Phoenix, the new capital must earn a profit of $1 million to avoid dilution.

Retained Earnings Retained earnings are undistributed profits that are reinvested within the business. The company's management and board of directors must decide what proportion of profits will be distributed as shareholder dividends and what proportion will be reinvested in the business. That decision is referred to as the firm's **dividend policy.**

Retained earnings are a source of capital with two major advantages. For one thing, there are no underwriting costs as with the sale of stock. For another, retained earnings don't cause dilution as does the sale of new common shares.

A corporation's dividend policy should strive to balance the proportions of dividends and retained earnings in such a way as to maximize the value of the firm. Often this proportion reflects the nature of the firm and the industry in which it operates. Firms that have only modest growth expectations, such as public utilities, pay a very large proportion of their earnings in dividends. High-growth companies, such as Eli Lilly or Warner Communications, pay a very low proportion. Digital Equipment, a mainframe computer manufacturer, has held to a policy of paying no dividends on its common stock. The attention given to dividend news by the investment community is reflected in the clipping from the *Wall Street Journal* shown in Figure 18.6.

FIGURE 18.6

Dividend news clippings from the *Wall Street Journal*.

Dividend News

Martin Marietta Corp. Raises Dividend Rate And Posts Higher Profit

By a WALL STREET JOURNAL *Staff Reporter*

BETHESDA, Md. — Martin Marietta Corp.'s board raised the quarterly dividend nine cents to 72 cents a share, authorized a 50% stock dividend and posted higher earnings for the second quarter and first half.

The cash dividend is payable Sept. 30, to stock of record Sept. 8. The stock dividend will be paid Oct. 19, to stock of record Oct. 5.

Net income for the quarter rose to $61 million, or $2.45 a share, from $59 million, or $2.36 a share, a year earlier. Sales increased to $880 million from $644 million.

Net income for the six months rose to $101 million, or $4.04 a share, from $93.3 million, or $3.75. Sales increased to $1.6 billion from $1.21 billion.

J. Donald Rauth, chairman and chief executive officer, said aerospace and specialty chemicals businesses made strong contributions to earnings, but said profitability declined in aluminum, cement and aggregate businesses. "In the near term, we find new signs of encouragement in those areas," he said.

* * *

Revco D.S. Inc. said its directors approved a three-for-two stock split and raised the postsplit dividend rate 14%. The operator of disco⋯ ⋯tores also said fiscal ⋯ ⋯

graphics equipment also declared a regular cash dividend of three cents a common share, payable Aug. 21 to stock of record Aug. 7. The company didn't say what its cash dividend will be after the stock split. Kroy's first quarter earnings declined to $1.3 million, or 42 cents a share, from $1.5 million, or 49 cents a share, the year-earlier quarter, despite a 26% increase in sales to $11.2 million from $9 million. The company attributed the earnings decline to heavy advertising costs in the quarter. At the company's annual meeting yesterday, shareholders approved changing its name to Kroy Inc. They also voted to increase authorized common shares to 15 million from 7.5 million. There were about three million shares outstanding as of May 29. Stockholders also voted to change the company's by-laws to require a two-thirds majority vote by holders to approve any sale of the company in cases where the board hasn't approved the transaction. Previously a simple majority had been required.

* * *

Dividends Reported July 23

Company	Period	Amt.	Payable date	Record date
REGULAR				
Acme-Cleveland Corp	Q	.35	8–20–81	8– 6
Alcan Aluminium Ltd	Q	.45	9– 5–81	8– 5
Alexander & Baldwin Inc	Q	.45	9– 3–81	8–13
Alton Packaging Corp	Q	.10	8–10–81	8– 1
American Ship Building	Q	.20	8–28–81	8–14
Bell & Howell Co	Q	.24	9– 1–81	8–15
Block Drug Co Com A	Q	.25	10– 1–81	9– 1
Boston Edison $1.175 pref	Q	.30	9– 1–81	8–10
Boston Edison $1.46 pref	Q	.36½	9– 1–81	8–10
Bruno's Inc	Q	.07½	8–21–81	8– 7
Burlington Industries	Q	.38	9–15–81	8– 3
Canada Permanent Mtg	Q	b.28½	10– 1–81	9– 4
Cedar Point Inc	Q	⋯	9–15–81	8–21
Cluett Peabody & Co	⋯	⋯	9–⋯5–81	9–15
Cluett ⋯				–15

SUMMARY

The primary objective of a financial manager is to increase the value of the firm—in particular, to maximize the value of the ownership interest. The financial manager's role includes three functions: financial planning, spending money on investment projects, and raising money to finance those projects.

Good financial planning is crucial to the success of a business. Essential to financial plans are forecasts. Short-term forecasts project sales revenues for approximately the next year, while long-term forecasts extend over a longer period, often five to ten years.

Budgets incorporate forecasts of sales into

plans that project not only future sales revenues but also future operating expenses and cash investment outlays. Most business plans contain an operating budget, a cash budget, and a capital budget. The budget must balance; if operating expenses are greater than sales revenues, the firm wil not be profitable. Once the budget has been approved by the board of directors, management must monitor the company's actual performance.

Money must be invested in the company to make it grow and prosper. There are two basic types of cash outlay—short-term (or operating) expenditures and long-term (or capital) expenditures. Short-term expenditures include operating expenses and money tied up in current assets, such as short-term marketable securities, inventories, and accounts receivable. Long-term expenditures are investments in long-term assets, such as land, buildings, machinery, and equipment.

Companies raise the money they need by borrowing, by selling ownership interests, and by retaining profits. The first two methods are called external financing; the third, internal financing.

Borrowed funds include short-term and long-term loans. Short-term loans can be unsecured or secured. Types of unsecured short-term loans include trade credit, accruals, bank loans (such as single-payment notes, lines of credit, and revolving credit agreements), and commercial paper. Three popular types of secured short-term financing are loans secured by inventory, loans secured by accounts receivable, and money raised through selling accounts receivable. The borrower's cost of short-term financing varies widely, depending on the type of loan.

Long-term capital expenditures usually are financed with long-term debt or equity capital. The principal advantage of long-term debt is that interest on it is tax-deductible. Its principal disadvantage is that interest must be paid at specified dates and the principal must be repaid at maturity. Using borrowed money for financing is known as trading on the equity or simply leverage. For the borrower, leverage always increases risk while increasing potential profitability.

Types of long-term loans are long-term bonds, long-term mortgages, and private placement loans. Long-term debt financing involves two types of costs—payment to arrange the loan or the sale of bonds to the public and interest on the borrowed funds. Long-term leases are viewed as a source of long-term funds because they permit firms to use property without tying up large sums of money.

Equity financing involves raising money by selling new issues of common or preferred stock. An advantage of equity financing is its lack of financial risk. Corporations use two methods to sell new issues of common stock: the rights offering and the underwritten sale of securities. Costs of equity financing include the underwriting cost, the payment of dividends to shareholders, and the possibility of dilution. Using retained earnings for financing involves no underwriting costs and does not cause dilution.

If a company raises money by selling additional shares of common stock and then fails to earn a suitable return on the cash received, earnings per share of common stock (EPS) will decline. This in turn often leads to a decline in the market price of the common stock.

KEY TERMS

accounts receivable
accrual
budget
capital budget
capital expenditures
cash budget
cash management
collateral
commercial paper
compensating balance
dilution
dividend policy
equity capital
external financing
factor accounts
   receivable
financial risk
financial strategy
finished goods
   inventory
fixed costs
floating interest rate
floor planning
internal financing
investment banker
line of credit
liquidity
loan origination fee
long-term bond

long-term debt
long-term forecast
long-term loan
long-term mortgage
nonnotification plan
notification plan
operating budget
operating
   expenditures
pledging
prime rate
private placement
   loan
raw materials
   inventory
retained earnings
revolving credit
   agreement
secured loan
short-term forecast
short-term loan
single-payment note
trade credit
trading on the equity
trend projection
underwriting costs
unsecured loan
variable costs
work-in-process
   inventory

REVIEW QUESTIONS

1. What are the primary functions of the financial manager?
2. What information is needed in making financial forecasts?
3. Identify three distinct types of budgets utilized in business plans.
4. Explain a capital budget and how management uses it in financial planning.
5. What are the main sources for short-term financing? Discuss both unsecured and secured sources.
6. What are the main sources of long-term financing? Discuss both debt and equity sources.
7. Describe the prime rate and its connection with interest rates charged on bank loans.
8. Explain why J. C. Penney leases most of its stores in preference to owning them?

DISCUSSION QUESTIONS

1. Describe how trend projection is used in forecasting. What advantage is there in forecasting; is there a risk involved?
2. Explain the basic components of a cash budget. (Refer to Table 18.1 for help.)
3. Why is it so important for a company to maintain liquidity? Would a company normally meet all its liquidity needs by holding cash?
4. Describe how businesses finance expenditures by using trade credit and accruals. Are they considered short-term or long-term financing?
5. Discuss the three types of unsecured short-term bank loans—single-payment notes, line of credit, and revolving credit agreements.
6. Summarize how businesses with seasonal activities use secured short-term loans to finance their inventories and accounts receivable.
7. Discuss long-term debt—its advantages and disadvantages. Compare and contrast it to equity financing.
8. What is meant by dilution? Why should financial managers be concerned about it?

CASE: MARY DISCOVERS GOLD

Mary and Seymour Golden saved their money regularly for the past ten years. Each had a good job, and made a fairly good salary. But their dream was to open a dress shop—providing dresses and accessories for young women—while making a profit and a good living. They had both worked in department stores most of their lives and felt that they knew the business well enough to make a go of it on their own. Their dream shop was now not too far from being a reality. With a nest egg of $40,000 to invest, a knowledge of the target market they wanted to reach, and contacts with New York and California clothing manufacturers and distributors—they could move ahead to stage 1. They picked a location in a suburban shopping center surrounded by homes with average incomes of $25,000–$35,000—a perfect setting for their women's dress shop which they cleverly named The Marigold.

They estimated start-up costs to be close to

$100,000, including two months' rent (at $3000 a month), utilities, store furniture and fixtures, a van with a blooming marigold painted on the side, and the same sign in neon lights for the front of the store. They provided for the wages of four people including model-type sales personnel and part-time high school girls. Of course, Mary would be the buyer-manager and Seymour would take care of the books, advertising, and stock control. Both of them would participate in the buying, but Mary had a real feel of the market and of both current and changing styles.

So with Mary and Seymour in charge and in place, the Marigold was about to open in April just before Easter and in time for promotion of its Spring merchandise.

1. Should Mary and Seymour prepare budgets for their business; what kinds do you think are appropriate?
2. Explain how distinguishing between fixed and variable costs will help the Goldens in planning financial activities. Try to pinpoint what you believe will be examples of fixed and variable costs in their type of business.
3. Describe various sources of short-term credit available to the Goldens. Would it be better if they borrow on a secured or unsecured basis? Explain.

CASE: SOMETIMES DENTISTS HURT TOO

Sometimes the role of the dentist is not one of toothsome smiles and eager paying patients. And pain is not always the exclusive feeling of the person reclining in the chair. Sometimes dentists hurt too, and in an even more painful way—in the pocketbook.

Such was the plight of John Butler, a friendly and easygoing dentist who was fond of his patients and enjoyed his work. But somehow things have changed since he decided to start advertising to get a bigger share of the market and to make a little more money.

At first his marketing strategy seemed to be working. He had more patients than he knew what to do with, and he had even added a couple of partners. They too were enjoying an avalanche of clients who wanted to take advantage of lower prices on bridges, fillings, root canals, dentures, etc. Business was booming. Yet somehow the cash was not flowing as freely as the water in the "spit-it-out" bowl.

John had always been generous in allowing patients to pay for their dental work on a monthly basis, and so long as they made partial payments he was happy. He would never press them for payment when they got a little behind. Some of the accounts were extended to 90 or 120 days, others were unpaid even after 12 months. But John had faith in his patients—maybe too much. Usually, they paid—if they didn't lose their jobs or move from the city, which did happen once in a while.

John was very easy in some cases, especially with poor patients who needed dental work but didn't have the funds to pay for the more expensive treatments. He was known to have waived fees for those who couldn't pay and for some of the senior citizens who were trying to live on social security or pensions. They loved John and John loved them all—but somehow something had happened to the cash flow, and John's drilling didn't seem to be turning to geysers.

1. What can this generous dentist do to improve his cash flow?
2. Explain how a financial plan could have helped John *before* he embarked on his strategy to increase business.

CHAPTER 19

RISK AND
INSURANCE

After studying this chapter you should be able to:

1 Define the basic risk and insurance concepts and reasons why individuals and businesses buy insurance.
2 Discuss the four ways of handling risk — avoidance, assumption, loss prevention/reduction, and transference.
3 Understand the terminology of insurance and the criteria of insurable perils.
4 Identify the three major types of insurance and understand their uses and coverage.
5 Explain the differences between property, liability, and health insurance.
6 Identify the three types of life insurance and their advantages or disadvantages.

445

James Moore, a television producer in Troy, N.Y. had been trying to sell his warmly insulated farmhouse for six months. Last Friday, Jack Hope, a 28 year old state worker, made a $50,000 offer.

But Mr. Hope backed out on Tuesday, after a federal agency, citing health concerns, banned use of the urea-formaldehyde foam that insulates the house. "It was something we couldn't live with," Mr. Hope says. Now, Mr. Moore has almost given up on selling, though he says, "I would have bailed out as well."

Owners of some 500,000 foam-insulated homes across the country face substantial losses in the value of their homes as a result of the Consumer Product Safety Commission's ruling Monday. The loss may total $2 billion to $4 billion, based on the $6,000 to $8,000 estimated average cost of ripping out the insulation. Some loss estimates run much higher. Walls must be pulled away from their frames so that the insulation can pop free.

Johnnie L. Roberts and Liz Roman Gallese, "Home Values Hurt by Foam Insulation Ban," *Wall Street Journal*, 26 February 1982, p. 26. Reprinted by permission of the Wall Street Journal, © Dow Jones & Company, Inc., 1981. All rights reserved.

James Moore learned personally the meaning of risk. The energy crisis in 1974 prompted many business firms to search for low-cost, effective insulating material. Urea-formaldehyde foam seemed the perfect answer. Easy to install in existing homes, and at about $1,000 for the average house with part of the cost offset through tax credits, the annual fuel savings could easily recover the homeowner's investment in just a few years. Then came rumors of the health hazard and the industry went into a tailspin: sales in 1980 were a mere $10 million, down from $187 million in the peak year, 1977. For all practical purposes the industry is now "dead," and its members received their lesson in risk.

Risk management is the process of evaluating a firm's (or individual's) total exposure to perils—those that are insurable and those that aren't—and then formulating strategies to minimize losses from them on a cost-effective basis. In an era of increasing litigation and concern for public welfare, risk management plays a vital role in the overall management of the business firm. This is the topic of our present chapter.

BASIC RISK AND INSURANCE CONCEPTS

The primary reason why individuals and busi-

nesses buy insurance—and why insurance companies exist—is to provide protection against the economic effects of various types of risk. **Risk,** in an insurance sense, refers to the chance of financial loss due to a peril. There are many insurable risks, including financial loss due to fire, theft, auto accident, injury or illness, a lawsuit, or death.

Risk

Because risk is such an unavoidable part of life, individuals and businesses use several methods to deal with it. Four ways of handling risk are avoidance, assumption, prevention/reduction, and transference. We shall now analyze each of these methods.

Risk Avoidance One method of dealing with risk is **risk avoidance**—simply stated, this means keeping away from situations that can lead to loss. Certainly one way to avoid the risk of a car accident is not to drive. You could sell your car and take the bus. An airline could avoid the risk of plane crashes by grounding its fleet of jets. Selling your car could put you to real inconvenience, however; and grounding its planes would put the airline out of business. Therefore avoidance, while effective in some circumstances, is not feasible for all risks.

Risk Assumption If you or a business should be willing to bear a risk, this is called **risk assumption**. For example, if someone continues using urea-formaldehyde foam insulation, they must assume the entire risk.

Risk assumption is considered a "practical" way to handle many types of risks. For example, K mart or J. C. Penney may chose not to insure their inventories or buildings and fixtures since their stores are spread out over the entire country. So even if disaster were to strike at one store or even several in a year, the losses would most likely be no greater—and probably less—than the annual insurance premiums on coverage for all their stores. In cases such as this, the company is **self-insuring**.

Loss Prevention/Reduction It's often possible to reduce potential financial loss through a policy of **loss prevention and reduction**. Basically, this is one or another kind of sustained activity calculated either to reduce the chance that a loss will occur or to reduce the loss itself should the unexpected occur. Airlines practice loss prevention by maintaining their aircraft and by thoroughly training their pilots and flight attendants. Installing sprinklers and adequate fire walls in a hotel is another example of loss prevention/reduction. Both Monsanto and DuPont practice good safety procedures and take pride in the low number of lost days due to on-the-job accidents. In many instances, workers are safer in the plants of each of these than they are in their own homes.

Risk Transference There are many risks that can't be assumed or avoided, and for which loss prevention/reduction does not seem enough. For example, a surgeon could conceivably be facing the risk of a large malpractice lawsuit almost every time he or she performed an operation. In such a case **risk transference** to a professional risk bearer—an insurance company, which is paid to bear some or all of the risk of financial loss—is appropriate.

Insurance, then, is the procedure by which those who are concerned about some form of risk contribute to a common fund—usually an insurance company—out of which losses resulting from that risk are compensated (usually up to specified limits). Basically, insurance companies are professional risk bearers.

Terminology and Characteristics of Insurable Perils

It will be helpful to get clear at the outset some of the more important terms relating to insurance. An **insurance policy** is the contract between the person or business that's being covered by insurance—in other words, the insured—and the insurance company that issues the policy—the insurer. The policy specifies which perils the insurance company will bear for the insured and the dollar coverage amount of the policy—the maximum amount that it will pay in the event of a loss. Any payment demanded of an insurance company by the insured to recover for losses under the terms of a policy is called a claim, and the cost to the insured for coverage is the *insurance premium*.

We've seen said that insurance companies are professional risk takers. However insurance companies won't provide coverage against *all* types of risk. Some risks are insurable, some are not. For a risk to be insurable it must meet several criteria, one of which is that the peril in question must be associable with a large group of people or a number of business firms. Another requirement is that the causes of potential loss must be judged accidental. Finally, the cost of insurance relative to the coverage amount must be relatively low.

Large Group Insurance companies must spread out their potential risks of loss by insuring many people and businesses in many locations. This strategy helps to minimize the chance that a calamity in one area will cause huge losses that could lead to financial disaster for the insurance company. Similarly, a company that issues business insurance wouldn't want to insure just one firm; it would prefer to sell policies to many. So a key to successful risk management by insurance companies is the sale of policies to many individuals and businesses in many parts of the country. An insurance company that sells many policies knows for certain that some insureds will suffer losses. Although it cannot predict which ones specifically, the insurance company remains in business by knowing that not all insureds suffer losses—especially at the same time.

Accidental Loss An accidental loss is a financial loss that's judged to have occurred by chance—an unexpected loss that's presumed to have been beyond the insured's control. Insurance companies insure against accidental losses—that is, losses not deliberately caused by the insured. On the other hand, no insurance company will pay for a business's loss if the insured purposely set the store on fire. An insurable risk must therefore be deemed unexpected and beyond the insured's immediate control.

Low Cost   An insurance premium should be relatively low in cost compared to the coverage provided by the policy. This will encourage people and businesses to buy insurance coverage and permit the insurance company to spread out its risk. For example, almost every homeowner buys insurance to cover the perils of fire, theft, vandalism, and other home-related risks. A homeowners policy is usually inexpensive. Annual premiums are equal to about 0.5 percent (or even less) of the value of the home. This low cost encourages almost every homeowner to buy a policy and as a result helps to spread the insurance companies' risks over many homes throughout the country.

Types of Insurance

In this chapter we'll be looking at three basic types of insurance: property and liability insurance, health insurance, and life insurance.

Property insurance covers financial losses due to the damage or destruction of the insured's property as the result of any of a variety of perils. Fire insurance is one kind of property insurance. It protects the insured against financial loss resulting from a fire at the insured's property. **Liability insurance** covers financial losses due to injuries or property losses of others where the insured is considered to be the cause. Automobile liability insurance is an example of this type. It covers financial claims against the insured by others as the result of an auto accident. Property and liability insurance is sold by approximately 2900 insurance companies in the United States today.

Health insurance helps pay for the medical and hospitalization costs of an illness or an injury, which can be very expensive. Wages may be lost owing to inability to work, and there are doctor and hospital bills to be paid. Most Americans have some form of health insurance. It's underwritten by approximately 1200 insurance companies as well as by various Blue Cross/Blue Shield plans across the United States.

Life insurance protects against the financial consequences that could result from a person's death. In addition, some forms of life insurance provide both life insurance protection and a way to accumulate savings. Life insurance is underwritten by about 1900 life insurance companies.

Types of Insurance Companies

There are two basic types of insurance companies: mutually owned companies (mutuals) and stockholder-owned companies. Of the approximately 5000 U.S.-based insurance companies today, the great majority are stockholder owned.

A **mutual insurance company** is owned collectively by its policyholders and is basically an insurance cooperative. The policyholders elect a board of directors who in turn select the company's management. Many of the largest American

There are many insurable risks, such as fire and water damage.

PERSPECTIVE ON SMALL BUSINESS

"Sure we comply with OSHA regulations," says Siegfried Bessler, president of the Shultz Co. in New York City. "But keeping OSHA happy isn't the reason we emphasize safety."

Bessler and Herbert Rodriguez, secretary-controller, know that a more safety-conscious work force means fewer accidents, less downtime, and reduced workers' compensation costs. Between 1978 and 1979, the company reduced accidents by more than 50%, even though its work force was increasing. Its 1979 loss ratio—losses divided by [insurance] premiums—was only 3%. In 1978, it was 100%. Recent accidents are less severe than earlier ones. And if the trend continues, Shultz expects to save close to $25,000 on its insurance premiums. The improvements are the result of a safety program that Bessler and Rodriguez started [in 1979].

Shultz, a manufacturer of supermarket fixtures, employs about 216 workers. In 1978, the company's annual sales were about $4 million, growing at a rate of about 25%. Unfortunately, accidents were also increasing. In 1977, the company had 32 workers' compensation claims. The following year the number was 36. As a result, the company's experience rating slipped from a 13% credit to a 13% debit, costing it $18,000 more for workers' compensation coverage.

The lack of safety awareness was graphically highlighted when a skilled mechanic mangled his hand in a machine. "You can talk all you want about downtime and lost profits," says Rodriguez, "but what's worse is people getting hurt."

Getting employees to think safety is the means to the company's goal of a safer plant. "First we have to get our people to think twice about taking a guard off a machine or leaving a skid in the middle of an aisle," says Rodriguez. "Then we have to get them not to do it."

At least once a month, management and foremen meet to discuss safety, especially those problems that affect the entire plant. They focus on questions such as, "How do we get workers to be more safety conscious? Have there been any notable changes in general safety levels in the plant? Are we properly training workers in how to safely use the machines?"

Special effort is made to insure that meetings aren't just gripe sessions. Solutions, not complaints, are the important issue. "The aim is to recognize potential problems, isolate them, and plan to avoid the damage they may cause," says Rodriguez.

SOURCE: Reprinted with permission of Inc. Magazine. Excerpted from Edwin H. Hittig, "Is Safety Really Worth It?" *Inc.*, October 1980, pp. 65–66. Copyright © 1980 by Inc. Publishing Company, 38 Commercial Wharf, Boston MA 02110.

life insurance companies are mutuals, including five of the top six: Prudential, Metropolitan Life, Equitable Life, New York Life, and John Hancock. These gigantic companies (Prudential's assets exceed $60 billion) were started many years ago as small mutual companies. Even though mutual insurance companies are fewer than stockholder-owned insurance companies, their financial strength and size are larger, out of all proportion to their number.

Stockholder-owned companies are just like all other shareholder-owned corporations. Unlike the policyholder of a mutual company, a person who has a policy issued by a stockholder-owned insurance company need not be a stockholder in the firm. Nor does a stockholder have to be a policyholder of that firm. Aetna Life & Casualty is the largest stockholder-owned insurance company. Its assets are over $30 billion and its stock trades on the New York Stock Exchange. Other recognizable large firms are Allstate Insurance, Home Insurance, Continental Insurance, Kemper Insurance, Fireman's Fund Insurance, and SIGNA Corporation.

TALKING BUSINESS

[Lloyd's of London], almost 300 years old, is not actually an insurance company. You do not insure *with* Lloyd's, but *at* Lloyd's. Really, it is an association, almost a club, of underwriters representing 446 syndicates, whose members, all private individuals, accept insurance business for their own personal profit (or loss) and are individually liable to the full extent of their declared assets to meet the claims. The explanation of this was given by an employee almost a century ago, who told an inquiring woman, "Individually, madam, we are underwriters; collectively, we are Lloyd's."

[Lloyd's underwriters tend to specialize.] One long-established syndicate, De-Rougemont, which started in the late 19th century, covers the transport of diamonds, bullion and works of art. Among 30 syndicates that underwrite personal accident insurance, one offers cover to newly married couples for the extra costs if they should have twins. Another, headed by a jovial fellow named Bert Stratton, has insured not just the lives of Bing Crosby, Bob Hope, Danny Kaye and Frank Sinatra, but such splendid parts of a star's anatomy as Marlene Dietrich's legs (and Betty Grable's), Jimmy Durante's "schnozzle" and Elizabeth Taylor's eyes. Stratton also gamely took a $6,000 premium against a whisky company having to pay a $2.4 million prize to anyone who captured the Loch Ness monster. Stratton stipulated only that the monster had to exceed 20 feet in length.

Source: Excerpted with permission from Timothy Green, "If You Name It, Lloyd's of London May Well Risk It," *Smithsonian* 11 (March 1981), pp. 80–89. First published in the Smithsonian.

PROPERTY AND LIABILITY INSURANCE

Property and liability insurance includes home and building insurance, automobile insurance, business and professional liability insurance, and many other lines. Almost $100 billion was paid by Americans in 1981 to buy this type of insurance. Of this amount, businesses and individuals paid over $36 billion in insurance premiums to insure their cars, buses, trucks, and motorcycles.

Types of Perils

Property and liability insurance provides protection against financial loss due to a variety of perils. The two major types of losses are property loss and liability loss. A *property loss* is a financial loss resulting from damage to personal or business property due to fire, theft, vandalism, windstorm damage, and other potentially destructive perils.

A *liability loss* is a financial loss suffered by a person or a business because that person or business is found to be the cause of property damage or injury to others. An example of a liability loss in business occurred when a cola bottler (Shone Coca-Cola Bottling Company) was sued by a consumer who claimed to suffer emotional shock from consuming part of the contents of a bottle of Squirt that contained a decomposed mouse. The court awarded the consumer $2500 as compensation for the alleged shock. Financial losses of this type can be covered by product liability insurance.

Home and Building Insurance

Home and building insurance is property and liability insurance that protects property owners from financial loss caused by a variety of perils. Homeowners, landlords, and the owners of all types of business property purchase this type of

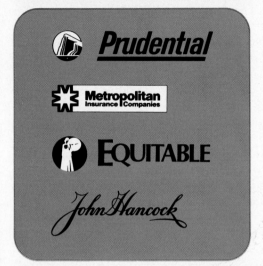

The ownership classifications of some of the major American insurance companies.

insurance. They want to be protected against both property damage losses and liability losses.

Perils Covered Home and building insurance originally covered only fires. Fire insurance societies were set up in the early history of our country to provide fire insurance protection for homeowners and businesses. The coverage of most home and building insurance policies has since been expanded to include losses resulting from such perils as windstorm, lightning, hurricane, robbery, vandalism, riot and other civil disturbance, frozen water pipes, and falling airplanes. However home and building insurance policies do *not* cover losses due to changes in zoning laws and other government policies. Losses caused by flood, war, or nuclear power plant accident are also not covered.

The losses discussed above are basically losses of a property-damage type. The owners of most houses and buildings also buy insurance to protect against financial losses arising from their liability for the injury of others while on the insured's property. This type of liability insurance is usually part of the typical homeowners insurance policy as well as a landlord's or a business's property insurance policy.

Coinsurance Property insurance policies usually contain a coinsurance clause. **Coinsurance** requires the property owner to buy an amount of insurance coverage equal to a specified percentage of the value of the property. If the coinsurance percentage is not met, the insurance company will not provide total compensation in the event of a loss. Most homeowners policies, for example, have an 80 percent coinsurance clause. This means that a homeowner must buy a policy with coverage equal to at least 80 percent of the replacement cost of the house. The value of the building's *site* is not included since it is not insurable. Only the replacement value of the structure can be insured. If the homeowner does not have the required insurance coverage, the insurance company will reimburse the owner for only a portion of any loss.

Insurance companies use the following formula to determine the amount of reimbursement in the event of a loss if the coinsurance clause is violated by the insured:

$$\frac{\text{Amount of Insurance Coverage}}{\text{Amount of Insurance Required}} \times \text{Loss} = \begin{array}{l}\text{Insurance}\\\text{Company's}\\\text{Share of the Loss}\end{array}$$

Suppose, for example, that you own a building worth $600,000 (excluding land), but insure it for only $120,000. In this case the coinsurance clause would require $480,000 (.80 × $600,000) of coverage. Assume that a fire then causes $300,000 of damage. The insurance company will pay you:

$$\frac{\$120,000}{\$480,000} \times \$300,000 = \$75,000$$

The balance of the loss — $225,000 — will be yours. Individuals and businesses should therefore purchase enough building insurance coverage to prevent this kind of financial catastrophe. In periods of rapid inflation, coverage is usually updated annually.

Automobile Insurance

We've already mentioned that Americans spend over $36 billion annually in auto insurance premiums. All 50 states have financial responsibility laws that require drivers to be able to pay for the costs of any accidents that they cause.

Coverages Automobile insurance usually covers financial loss from a number of perils, including accident, theft, fire, and liability lawsuits. Automobile liability insurance pays — up to specified coverage limits — financial compensation to those involved in an accident caused by the insured. There are two types of auto liability insurance: bodily injury and property damage insurance. *Bodily injury (BI) liability insurance* protects against losses due to personal injury lawsuits resulting from an accident. *Property damage (PD) liability insurance* pays for the property losses of others. The maximum BI/PD limits are always stated in the policy. For example, a 50/100/10 policy has a $50,000 per person, $100,000 per occurrence (regardless of the number of people involved) maximum coverage for bodily injury liability and a $10,000 maximum coverage for property damage liability.

Comprehensive automobile insurance covers the insured's losses due to such perils as fire, theft, and windshield breakage. This insurance is particularly expensive in areas such as Boston and New York where there are relatively high numbers of car thefts. And cars that are popular to steal, such as Corvettes, Cadillacs, Mercedes-Benzes, and Porsches, have particularly expensive comprehensive insurance premiums.

Automobile insurance rates for BI/PD and collision coverage usually depend on the driver's age, marital status, sex, home residence, and driving record. The most expensive auto insurance premiums are levied on young male drivers who live in cities and who have had one or more traffic tickets or accidents. The rates are highest for these people because their rating group has historically been involved in a relatively large number of accidents. Table 19.1 shows motor vehicle accident statistics that clearly reveal the

TABLE 19-1

Motor Vehicle Statistics for Various Age Groups

Age Group	Number of Drivers	Percentage of Total	Drivers in All Accidents	Percentage of Total	Drivers in Fatal Accidents	Percentage of Total
Under 20	14,000,000	9.8	5,300,000	17.8	10,700	16.4
20–24	17,100,000	11.9	6,000,000	20.2	13,500	20.7
25–29	17,200,000	12.0	4,200,000	14.1	9,100	14.0
30–34	16,400,000	11.5	3,400,000	11.4	7,800	12.0
35–39	13,600,000	9.5	2,100,000	7.1	4,500	6.9
40–44	11,500,000	8.0	1,800,000	6.1	4,400	6.7
45–49	11,300,000	7.9	1,600,000	5.4	3,500	5.4
50–54	11,500,000	8.0	1,300,000	4.4	2.700	4.1
55–59	9,900,000	6.9	1,300,000	4.4	2.500	3.8
60–64	7,300,000	5.1	900,000	3.0	2.200	3.4
65–69	6,300,000	4.4	1,000,000	3.4	1,700	2.6
70–74	4,200,000	3.0	300,000	1.0	1,200	1.8
75 +	2,800,000	2.0	500,000	1.7	1,400	2.2
TOTAL	143,100,000	100.0	29,700,000	100.0	65,200	100.0

SOURCE: *Accident Facts, 1980* (Chicago: National Safety Council, 1980), p. 54.

"LET'S SEE NOW... THIS IS AN OAK TREE, AND YOUR POLICY COVERS ELM, WALNUT, MAGNOLIA, PINE..."

high incidence of accidents among drivers under 25 years of age.

No-Fault Insurance   No-fault insurance is of fairly recent origin. Basically, **no-fault insurance** provides that the insurance company will pay for the insured's accident losses regardless of who was considered responsible for the accident. No-fault insurance laws also limit the right of the accident victim to sue for damages. The injured can usually sue only if injuries are severe. Currently, 25 states have some form of no-fault auto insurance including Florida, Hawaii, Massachusetts, Kentucky, New Jersey, New York, and Utah. Legislation providing for no-fault has been introduced in many other states including California. You may have already guessed — and rightly — that no-fault is strongly opposed by trial lawyers.

Other Types of Liability Insurance

Businesses and professionals often buy other forms of liability insurance. This insurance protects them against personal financial loss resulting from lawsuits in which they are accused of dam-aging someone else's property or injuring someone else. Popular forms of liability insurance include "umbrella" personal liability insurance, professional liability insurance, and product liability insurance.

Personal injury cases are a large percentage of all liability insurance claims. To illustrate the size of these claims, in 1979 the average judgment for an injured knee was almost $40,000; the average for an accident that caused a death was over $350,000. Since many homeowners policies limit personal injury claims to $100,000, inadequate insurance protection often exists. **Umbrella personal liability insurance** provides liability insurance coverage over and above that provided by a homeowners or automobile policy. It may also afford coverage not offered by the usual liability policies. (The wider coverage is the "umbrella.")

Malpractice-type lawsuits have also been filed in increasing numbers against lawyers, accountants, architects, real estate agents, engineers, and even college professors. To pay the costs of these lawsuits and to cover financial loss due to an adverse verdict, most professionals buy **professional liability insurance**. This pays for legal fees and court-awarded damages up to specific coverage limits.

The suit brought against the Coca-Cola bottler that we saw a few pages back is an example of a product liability lawsuit. A more spectacular example is the many lawsuits filed against McDonnell Douglas Corporation and American Airlines as a result of the DC-10 crash in Chicago in 1979. Those companies have had to pay about $135 million to relatives of the crash victims. **Product liability insurance** protects the producer of a good *or* service against financial loss from court awards to consumers, customers, or next of kin. The cost of this insurance has soared in recent years because of a dramatic increase in product liability lawsuits.

Marine Insurance

Marine insurance protects shippers and their cargoes. The term *marine insurance* is something of a misnomer, since marine insurance protects not only shipments by water but also shipments made over land. **Ocean marine insurance** covers shipowners against damage or loss of a ship or its cargo. **Inland marine insurance** covers damage

TALKING BUSINESS

Judges have reputations as exemplary citizens and sober arbiters of the law, right?

Then why do they need malpractice insurance?

Because, says Complete Equity Markets Inc. of Wheeling, Ill., which introduced the coverage [in September 1981], more people are losing their awe of the bench and filing official complaints against judges. And state judicial review boards are investigating those complaints with greater fervor.

"Judges are given a lot of respect because of their position," says Randall Kleinman, corporate counsel for Complete Equity, which sells insurance to professionals. "But people are starting to realize that judges are human, too."

Just how human is suggested by the brochure Mr. Kleinman wrote to advertise the insurance. Entitled "The Judge on Trial," it lists a dozen or so real life complaints that show judges running the gamut of human frailty: the judge who "totally forgets about a case"; rash remarks and "foul language"; sexual impropriety; financial problems, and "many other areas, including nepotism, drinking, dishonesty, growing marijuana and making obscene phone calls."

Adds Mr. Kleinman: "Every one of those were actual cases. We've even had to turn down a few judges because they were bad risks."

The insurance doesn't protect a judge from censure or suspension. But it does promise to pay the legal costs of a judge's defense—up to $15,000 for each complaint to a maximum of $45,000. The policy costs $200 a year, and Mr. Kleinman says he has sold "close to 100" so far.

or loss of goods shipped by rail, truck, airplane, or inland barge.

Accidents at sea are not limited to ships but also happen with other properties, such as oil-drilling rigs. For example, Ocean Drilling and Exploration Company lost such a rig, the "Ranger" (the pride of its fleet), in early 1982 during a storm off the coast of Newfoundland. In addition to a complete property loss, 84 people died in the tragedy, and the total human and economic loss was substantial.

HEALTH INSURANCE

About 80 percent of all Americans are covered by one or more forms of privately written health insurance, sold by insurance companies and by Blue Cross/Blue Shield. Most other Americans are covered by various governmentally sponsored programs including Medicare and Medicaid.

Importance and Types of Health Insurance Coverage

A serious illness can be financially disastrous for someone uninsured. Consider that a one-to-two-week stay in the hospital can easily result in a bill of $2000–$5000 or more. Surgery, intensive care, and other forms of treatment could total over $10,000 in a matter of days.

Hospital charges are only part of total health care costs. Doctors' fees are rising, as is the cost of various outpatient treatments. Health care can be a huge, unexpected expense, and to help meet it, five basic types of insurance are written: disability

Automobile insurance rates depend on a variety of driver-related factors.

income insurance, hospitalization insurance, surgical and medical payments insurance, major medical insurance, and dental insurance.

Disability Income Insurance The primary source of income for most people consists of earnings from employment. For this reason many people buy disability income insurance and a number of employers provide it as part of an employee benefit package. **Disability income insurance** provides periodic payments to sick or disabled workers. The payments help to offset part or all of the income lost because of inability to work. Disability income insurance is underwritten by many insurance companies. Some states, including California, have state-sponsored disability income insurance programs as well.

Hospitalization Insurance Hospitalization insurance helps to pay hospital bills. These expenses include room fees, operating room charges, and many other hospital-related service charges. However most hospitalization plans don't pay the entire hospital bill. Some plans have a deductible provision by which the insured pays the first $100 (or so) of the bill. Other policies pay a certain percentage of the bill—often 80 per-

cent. Blue Cross is the largest hospitalization insurance provider, but many other insurance companies also sell hospitalization insurance.

Surgical and Medical Payments Insurance Given a major illness, doctors' bills can add up to a sizable expense. Surgical fees, anesthesiologist's fees, doctors' visits in (and out of) the hospital, and consulting doctors' fees can mount quickly. To cover or offset the financial burden of these expenses, **surgical and medical payments insurance** can be bought.

Major Medical Insurance Both hospitalization and surgical and medical payments insurance plans usually have maximum coverage limits, typically $25,000. To protect against the possibility of huge medical bills due to a catastrophic illness, most people buy major medical insurance. First introduced in 1951, **major medical insurance** covers expenses that exceed the coverage of hospitalization and surgical and medical insurance plans. About 150 million Americans own major medical policies, which are available at fairly low cost. They typically have a $250,000 coverage limit, although $1 million coverage limits are becoming more common.

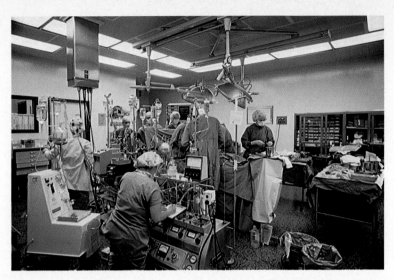

With rising health care costs, health insurance is a necessity.

Dental Insurance **Dental insurance,** a fairly recent arrival on the insurance scene, helps to pay dental bills. Its popularity is rising, particularly because many employers provide it free to their employees. In 1981 it was estimated that about 70 million people had some form of dental insurance. Most of these policies pay a portion of a person's dental bills and have a deductible provision.

Sources of Coverage

There are five primary sources of health-related insurance coverage. These include social security, worker's compensation, group insurance plans, Blue Cross/Blue Shield, and individually purchased coverage. In addition, health maintenance organizations (HMOs) provide services that essentially replace the need for health insurance.

Social Security It's a common misconception that social security provides only retirement income benefits. The official title of the Social Security program is **Old-Age, Survivors, Disability, and Health Insurance (OASDHI).** It provides health insurance benefits under the Medicare program as well as disability income benefits under a related program. **Medicare** is a form of health insurance available to persons 65 years or older and to certain other social security recipients. Medicare does not cover all hospitalization and medical costs, and many Medicare subscribers also buy privately underwritten health care insurance to supplement Medicare coverage. Medicare should not be confused with Medicaid.

Medicaid, (called MediCal in California) is a welfare program to pay the medical bills of the poor. All states except Arizona have Medicaid programs.

Worker's Compensation **Worker's compensation insurance** provides benefits to employees who are injured at work or who contract employment-related illnesses. This insurance pays for job-related medical expenses and provides disability income payments. All states require employers either to buy worker's compensation insurance or to have sufficient resources to pay worker's compensation claims. This insurance is always employer financed.

Group Insurance Plans **Group insurance plans** cover a group of insured persons, usually employees of a business or government. Most companies provide group health insurance coverage for their employees as an employer-paid benefit. Most employer-sponsored group insurance plans have hospitalization, surgical and medical payments, and major medical coverages. Some employers also provide group dental insurance and disability income insurance.

Blue Cross/Blue Shield **Blue Cross/Blue Shield** plans are not insurance in a strict sense; rather, they are **prepaid medical expense plans.** There are about 70 Blue Cross/Blue Shield plans in existence today. Most are in the United States; however they are also in Puerto Rico, Trinidad, and Canada. Premiums paid to Blue Cross/Blue Shield are pooled to pay the health care costs of

TALKING BUSINESS

Should you join an HMO? You ought to consider doing so if you:

- Want to get a variety of prepaid medical services under one roof.
- Aren't satisfied with your present doctors.
- Need a way to find doctors, perhaps because you have just arrived in your community.
- Want unlimited office visits, perhaps because you have a chronic disease.
- Dislike the fuss of making insurance claims.
- Place a high value on preventing illness and staying out of the hospital.

You might object to an HMO if you:

- Are content with your present doctors.
- Dislike making appointments far ahead.
- Learn that the HMO in your area is known for skimping on medical care.

Source: "Medical Care on a Monthly Fee" by Marlys Harris, excerpted from the July 1978 issue of *Money* Magazine, p. 66; © 1978, Time Inc. All rights reserved.

subscribers, and the plans are operated on a non-profit basis. About 90 million Americans belong to Blue Cross hospitalization plans, and approximately 70 million people belong to Blue Shield surgical and medical fee plans. Blue Cross/Blue Shield also provides major medical coverage for about 40 million Americans.

Individual Coverage Those who don't belong to a group health insurance plan can buy individual Blue Cross/Blue Shield coverage, or they can buy a health insurance policy from an insurance company. The cost of individual coverage varies depending on the plan selected, the benefits it pays, and the state in which the insured lives.

Health Maintenance Organizations (HMOs)

Health maintenance organizations (HMOs) are a novelty whose popularity is growing. HMOs are prepaid medical expense plans that allow unlimited use of health care facilities and personnel by their subscribers. In return for a monthly subscription fee, an HMO member can obtain almost any medical service at a nominal charge. HMOs usually also provide health insurance coverage to pay for health care costs incurred by subscribers

who are temporarily away from home. HMOs employ their own doctors, and some even own their own hospitals. Doctors are paid on a salaried basis and are encouraged to keep expenses down wherever possible. HMOs emphasize preventive as well as corrective medicine, and they try to control health care costs by keeping people healthy.

The number of HMOs is growing. By 1981 the number of HMOs had reached 238, up from only 40 in 1971. About 9.5 million Americans belonged to HMOs in 1981. The most successful HMO is probably the Kaiser Foundation Program, which operates in California, Oregon, and Hawaii. It has been found that the Kaiser Program delivers health care services comparable to those of the conventional fee-for-service system, but at a substantially lower cost. Some see the HMO system as the health care system of the future, and government policies are encouraging its growth.

National Health Insurance

National health insurance is basically a federally sponsored universal health insurance plan. This concept has been proposed for the United States, but it has yet to be legislated. Opponents, who are

ON THE FIRING LINE

National Health Insurance—Plague or Panacea?

According to available figures, from 15 to 18 million Americans have no health insurance. Should any of these people need crisis or long-term medical care, the cost could keep them from getting it. On the other hand, they might get it but go broke in the process. Even individuals who do have insurance but only limited coverage can lose their life's savings to serious illness.

The government has introduced programs to help the needy meet their health care expenses. Most, however, do not consider these programs—Medicare for the elderly and Medicaid for the poor—a success. In fact, many believe they have had an ill effect on the provision of health care. It isn't uncommon, for example, for medical and dental providers to refuse to see patients who rely on these government programs. There's added paperwork and red tape, a time lapse before payments are received, and often payment is only for part of the fees. All this is just too much trouble. Patients themselves often have problems unraveling the red tape that ties up these benefit programs. In their confusion, they lose benefits. Fraud and abuse have also drained the programs. According to present estimates, taxpayers are losing $7 billion each year to Medicare and Medicaid fraud and abuse. The time has come, say some, to do away with these piecemeal programs for the needy. What is required, they maintain, is a comprehensive system guaranteeing adequate care to all Americans.

An abundance of plans for national health insurance have been proposed already. They differ in many details. Still, two major approaches have attracted attention. One plan suggested would give each person (or family) a medical credit card. Patients would present their cards on receipt of services of any kind—major or minor.

A second proposal is to limit national health insurance to "catastrophic" coverage. This program would guarantee that no one would have to pay more than, say, $2000 a year for medical expenses. Individuals would thus assume some responsibility for paying for medical care. They would, however, be protected from annual health care debts above $2000. This arrangement, it's said, would discourage frivolous use of providers.

Whatever the plan adopted, say backers of national health insurance, the government would have to regulate rates charged. Such regulation is long overdue, claim these individuals. To date, they say, the market has favored health care providers over consumers. Except where limited by state law, providers have been able to raise fees at will. The reason? Health care is not an item that consumers give up when prices are too high. Most view it as essential, whatever the cost.

Nonetheless many are staunchly opposed to any form of national health insurance. They point to the billions of dollars lost to fraud and abuse in the existing health care programs. Nationalizing health care, they insist, will mean losses many times greater. The cost to the average consumer or taxpayer will soar.

Yet another problem would arise with national health insurance, say its opponents. Giving everyone easy access would increase the demand. One study suggested that unlimited access would result in a 75 percent increase in demand. According to that same study, even a 75 percent coverage would mean a 30 percent increase in demand. Catastrophic health insurance, these same critics say, would be no solution to this problem. It would only encourage doctors and hospitals to raise fees. Thus they'd get past the $2000 mark as fast as possible to make the patient eligible for coverage.

in the majority, argue that the waste and fraud in such a system would undoubtedly be colossal. The Medicaid program provides a good example of why national health insurance legislation hasn't been passed. Billions of taxpayers' dollars have been wasted by Medicaid due to poor cost controls and general mismanagement. The opponents of national health insurance fear a similar result.

Unemployment Insurance

Every state has an **unemployment insurance** program that provides laid-off workers with weekly benefits while they seek new jobs. Unemployment benefits usually start about one week after a worker has lost his or her job and they continue for 26 to 39 weeks. The size of the weekly benefit depends on the worker's previous income and can also vary from state to state. Unemployment insurance is funded by taxes levied on employers. These taxes are discussed in Chapter 23.

LIFE INSURANCE

Life insurance provides for payment of a stipulated sum—the "face amount"—to beneficiaries (or to the insured's estate) upon the death of the insured. Currently, Americans own over $3.2 trillion face amount of life insurance. A life insurance policy's face amount is the dollar amount paid to a beneficiary upon the insured's death. A beneficiary is the recipient of the proceeds (face amount) of the policy. Life insurance is provided to employees through group plans and it is also purchased in individual policies by millions of Americans.

Why Life Insurance?

People buy life insurance because they seek protection against several major risks. These include the financial consequences to a family when the breadwinner prematurely dies and the financial loss to a business that results from a key executive's untimely death. The first reason motivates individuals to buy life insurance, while the second reason persuades many businesses to insure the lives of their key executives.

The recent example of a CPA partnership illustrates this second reason. John Miles, a partner, died suddenly in an auto accident. His partnership interest at his death was worth about $300,000, which became the property of Miles' wife, Susanne. The other two partners, Ed White and Tinsi Wilson, lacked sufficient personal assets to meet this obligation, but fortunately the partners had taken out key executive policies for just such an emergency. As a result, Susanne Miles was paid for her interest, and White and Wilson were able to continue the partnership.

Basic Types of Life Insurance

In order to meet life insurance needs, three basic types of insurance are available to individuals and businesses: term life insurance, whole life insur-

ance, and endowment life insurance. These differ from each other in several ways, including yearly cost and cash surrender value. *Cash surrender value* is the payment received by the policyholder if the policy is canceled and returned to the insurance company prior to the insured's death or termination of the policy's coverage.

Term Life Insurance Term life insurance covers the insured's life for a specific number of years. When the term policy expires, the life insurance protection ceases unless the policy is renewed or a new policy is purchased. Term insurance provides relatively inexpensive coverage for young persons. Table 19.2 shows the term, whole life, and endowment life insurance premiums charged by a major life insurance company. The lower premiums charged on term insurance are clearly reflected in these data. However term insurance does not have any cash surrender value, and its cost increases with the insured's age.

Whole (or "Straight") Life Insurance Whole life insurance provides protection for a person's entire life. Its premiums remain level over the life of a policy. In contrast, term insurance premiums rise as the person ages. Also, whole life insurance has a cash surrender value, which increases over time. However whole life is much more expensive than term insurance.

Endowment Life Insurance Endowment life insurance pays the face amount of the insurance policy if the insured dies *or* lives to a certain age. Endowment life insurance policies are paid by premiums over a fixed time period, usually 20 to 30 years. If the insured dies during that period, the policy's face amount is paid to the beneficiary. If the insured is still alive at the end of the period, the policy "matures." This means that the policy's

TABLE 19–2
Annual Premium Schedule for Males on a $10,000 Life Insurance Policy

Age When Purchased	10-year Term Insurance	Whole Life	20-year Endowment
20	$ 26.50	$132.00	$407.10
30	31.80	177.00	412.15
40	53.60	252.00	440.00
50	117.30	378.00	472.65

Note: Premiums vary extensively between companies.

face amount is paid to the insured or to his/her designee. Endowment life is a relatively expensive form of life insurance because of its maturity feature.

SUMMARY

The primary reason why individuals and businesses buy insurance—and why insurance companies exist—is to provide protection against the economic effect of risk. The chance of loss can be dealt with through risk avoidance, risk assumption, or loss prevention and reduction. When none of these methods is sufficient, risk can be transferred to a professional risk bearer—an insurance company. For a risk to be insurable, it must meet several criteria: It must be associated with a large group; the causes of potential loss must be accidental; and the cost of insurance relative to the coverage must be fairly low.

The three basic types of insurance offered by insurance companies are property and liability insurance, health insurance, and life insurance. Insurance companies can be mutually owned or stockholder-owned.

Property and liability insurance includes home and building insurance, automobile insurance, business and professional liability insurance, and marine insurance. Owners of property purchase home and building insurance for protection against both property damage losses and liability losses. Such policies usually contain a coinsurance clause. People in the United States spend more money on automobile insurance than on any other type of property and liability insurance. A number of variations of coverage are available, including the controversial no-fault insurance.

Health insurance comprises five basic types—disability income insurance, hospitalization insurance, surgical and medical payments insurance, major medical insurance, and dental insurance. Five primary sources of health-related insurance are social security, worker's compensation, group insurance plans, Blue Cross/Blue Shield, and individually purchased coverage. Health maintenance organizations (HMOs) are prepaid medical expense plans that are continuing to grow in popularity. National health insurance programs are government-sponsored health insurance plans. Such

a plan does not now exist in the United States. However each state does provide an unemployment insurance plan.

Life insurance protects not only families but also businesses against the loss of a key executive. Types of life insurance available include term life insurance, whole life insurance, and endowment life insurance. Term insurance is less expensive, at least for younger people; but whole life insurance provides cash surrender value.

KEY TERMS

Blue Cross/Blue
  Shield
coinsurance
dental insurance
disability income
  insurance
endowment life
  insurance
group insurance plans
health insurance
health maintenance
  organizations
  (HMOs)
home and building
  insurance
hospitalization
  insurance
inland marine
  insurance
insurance
insurance policy
liability insurance
life insurance
loss prevention and
  reduction
major medical
  insurance
Medicaid
Medicare
mutual insurance
  company
national health
  insurance
no-fault insurance
ocean marine
  insurance

Old Age, Survivors,
  Disability, and
  Health Insurance
  (OASDHI)
prepaid medical
  expense plans
product liability
  insurance
professional liability
  insurance
property insurance
risk
risk assumption
risk avoidance
risk management
risk transference
self-insuring
stockholder-owned
  companies
surgical and medical
  payments insurance
term life insurance
umbrella personal
  liability insurance
unemployment
  insurance
whole life insurance
worker's
  compensation
  insurance

REVIEW QUESTIONS

1. What is the primary reason businesses and individuals buy insurance?
2. What fair methods are available to individuals and businesses for dealing with risk?
3. What criteria must be met for a peril to be insurable?
4. Briefly explain the three basic types of insurance.
5. List some of the perils commonly covered in home and building insurance. What coverages are available in automobile insurance policies?
6. What are the five primary sources of coverage in health-related insurance? How does a health maintenance organization (HMO) compare?
7. What are the two main reasons for buying life insurance? What are the basic types of life insurance?

DISCUSSION QUESTIONS

1. Discuss how businesses like J. C. Penney use risk assumption to "self-insure."
2. What are the differences between mutually owned insurance companies (mutuals) and stockholder-owned insurance companies? Which has the greater financial strength?
3. Describe how coinsurance works and why it is important for businesses to update their coverage.
4. Mary S. Jones has just purchased a new Pontiac Firebird for $15,000. Briefly describe the automobile insurance she might wish to purchase. Mary is 19 years old; how will her insurance premiums compare to those her father pays?
5. Discuss no-fault insurance advantages and disadvantages. Why do you think that many trial lawyers are opposed to no-fault?
6. Why would a toy manufacturer be particularly interested in product liability insurance?
7. How does term life insurance differ from whole life insurance?
8. Describe a situation where key executive insurance would be important.

CASE: RISK-TAKER AND RISK-SHAKER

Entrepreneurs are defined as *risk-takers*, but the smart ones try to figure out ways to divert risks, or at least make them manageable. Some options: risk avoidance, loss prevention/reduction, and risk transference. Some entrepreneurs can handle the first two; but they're still speculative risks. The recent surge of lawsuits on everything from discrimination to personal injuries on the premises—to safety violations and product liability—puts the entrepreneur in a position similar to that of the medical doctor, who's now subject to malpractice suits, which could readily put him/her out of business.

So many cases of big corporations being sued have been reported that many small entrepreneurs are justifiably scared. There was the telephone company, being sued for wage discrimination; Ford, for its Pinto catching fire in a crash and for one of its cars slipping out of gear. The cost of thousands of recalls for Ford, GM, and Chrysler for alleged faulty parts or systems has been catastrophic and shows the signs of diminishing.

1. Under what conditions should a business firm self-insure?
2. What can an entrepreneur do to protect against such costly suits such as those indicated above? Give several options or actions that can be taken.
3. Spokespersons for the auto industry claim that mandated automatic restraining devices, such as air bags, would add substantially to the cost of a *new car*. However, is it clear that the total of *protection* costs to the consumer would increase? Explain, bringing insurance into your response.

CASE: THREE-WAY TOSS-UP

A lot of good things were happening to Roy Roberts, and he was pleased that at last all his investment in time and energy had begun to materialize. He'd graduated from college just a few short years ago, and after majoring in accounting and preparing for the CPA exam, his study paid off, and he received his CPA certificate.

Roy was in his second year of practice, and with one more year he'd be a full-fledged CPA. Next he got married to a very talented girl, who also had a good job. Together their incomes were providing a good living. But what about the future?

It seemed quite natural that along with planning for a family and settling down, a timely decision was to start putting some money away as an investment for insurance or a nest-egg for future use.

An investment decision can get a little confused when you start talking to "experts." And when the "experts" learned through the grapevine that Roy and Jill were investigating securities, insurance, and other forms of investment and savings, they deluged them with calls. The two finally put a stop to the salespeople and tried to make a decision on their own. The alternatives seemed clear enough: should they buy insurance? If so, what kind—term or whole life? Or should they put their money in stock certificates, or bonds, or other securities? It just takes a little homework and a sharp pencil to figure out the cheapest investments, but there are some real hard questions about the best quality and payoff periods for both insurance and investments.

There were so many things to think about. Anyhow the salespeople had certainly made one lasting impression on them—it isn't easy to make financial decisions about one's life plans.

1. Explain which insurance might be the more suitable for Roy and Jill—term or whole life. How is life insurance similar to an investment? How does it differ?
2. How should a young couple go about planning their investment and insurance future? In relation to your income, does it make sense to have more insurance in the early years of your career and less as you grow older, or vice versa?
3. What other kinds of insurance should Roy and Jill also be concerned with?

CHAPTER 20

REAL ESTATE

After studying this chapter you should be able to:

1 Understand the basic characteristics of real estate.
2 Know the dual role that housing may play both as shelter and as an investment.
3 Describe the various types of mortgage loans available and their comparative benefits.
4 Identify the basic types of residential and commercial income-generating property.
5 Understand some technical real estate terms, such as cash flow depreciation, equity kicker, leverage, and foreclose.
6 Explain the basic activities and goals of land developers.

465

A man and a woman are working at a kitchen table cluttered with columnar workpapers, pens and pencils, books, and two calculators. The woman finishes a calculation, looks up, and explains: "If we can arrange a wrap-around at 16 percent, along with the standing loan of 10 percent, the initial equity outlay will have to be $20,000." The man nods approvingly but wonders, "We're probably expecting too much for any S&L to go for a wrap, but let's hope they don't insist on an equity kicker; at the very least, we should hold our guns on nothing more limiting than a VRM starting at 15 percent." The woman agrees and punches a few more numbers into her calculator and announces, "If we get that, our annual rate of return should be at least 25 percent for the first three years."

This sounds like complicated finance. Obviously, the two are studying and evaluating a very complex investment scheme. They are. They're buying their first home.

If you added up all the assets of American families and businesses, which one would be the largest component of the net worth of all Americans? What's the largest single investment that most American families ever make? Which investment has made (and lost) more money for more people than any other? The answer to all those questions is the same—real estate. Real estate is the most significant American investment as well as being an important component in the production of goods and services in this country.

CHARACTERISTICS OF REAL ESTATE

As we analyze real estate, which includes land and buildings—houses, stores, factories, and the like—we must understand that it has characteristics that differentiate it from financial assets, such as stocks and bonds. These characteristics include the relative scarcity of real estate and its use in the production process. In addition, real estate prices have in recent years increased at a rate exceeding that of inflation. In the next several sections we'll consider these and several other general characteristics of real estate.

Scarce Commodity

Only a given amount of land has been created; the amount of land in existence is fixed and the demand for it is increasing. Adding to this relative scarcity of land is the fact that much of it isn't suitable for development as farms, homes, shopping centers, and plants. Land that is mountainous or situated in flood plains or in very remote dry areas or that is used for parks cannot be developed. The stock of suitable land is therefore becoming more scarce as the population grows and available land is developed.

Uniqueness In addition to the scarcity of total land, it's also important that each individual parcel of land is somewhat unique. No two parcels of land are identical; each has a different location and view relative to other parcels.

Elements of Demand The demand and market prices for property depend on the situation existing in the local marketplace. Factors that affect the demand for property include population growth of the local market, the level of people's income there, and the desire of nonresidents to invest in that area. Areas having strong population influxes tend to experience rising real estate prices, while areas with population outflows may have declining real estate prices.

In recent years, for example, many Sun Belt states have experienced strong population influxes and above-average increases in real estate prices. The **Sun Belt region** of America is basically the southern and southwestern portion of the country as well as California and Hawaii.

High demand for residential properties in certain areas of the sun belt stimulated price increases.

Higher real estate prices are also caused by increasing incomes of local residents. As their incomes rise, people tend to spend more on housing as well as on other items. A generally increasing level of purchasing power should spur the development of new stores and shopping facilities as well as new homes.

An influx of nonresident investors can cause real estate prices to rise. The condominium boom in Florida, for example, was influenced significantly by purchases made by residents of other states, Canadians, and other non-Floridian investors. For example, in some years half of the luxury condominiums sold in Dade County (Miami) are to foreigners.[1] Real estate prices in resort areas such as Aspen, Miami, and Hilton Head have been driven upward as a result of purchases made by nonresident investors. A new development near Aspen, for example, offers plush condos starting at $480,000.[2]

Location "The three determinants of a property's value are location, location, and location" is an overworked saying in real estate. The truth is, though, that a property's location in relation to those things that go to make up demand heavily influences its value. The value of a house, for example, depends on the neighborhood; the incomes of the area's residents; nearness to churches, schools, and places of employment; and nearness to recreational facilities. With commercial properties, a close proximity to cheap power, or a skilled labor pool, or markets in general, will enhance a property's value. A classic example is New York City, where office space in 1981 rented at $75 a square foot, almost twice as much as five years earlier.[3]

Use in the Production Process

Real estate is an important input to the overall production of goods and services. The Sears Tower in Chicago is one example; a cornfield in Nebraska is another. Land is needed on which to locate: factories to produce goods, warehouses to store materials and goods, wholesale and retail stores to sell merchandise, offices in which management is administered and services are provided, and homes and recreational areas where

TALKING BUSINESS

While housing prices stand to rise more slowly on average than in the past, they will spurt in some places and languish in others. That's because they remain closely tied to local economic conditions. In the upper Midwest, for example, where the auto industry's troubles have stalled local economies, home sales have plunged and property values have stopped rising. But in a boomtown like Denver, where jobs have been increasing by 25,000 a year, houses in the most desirable suburbs are appreciating at close to a 20% annual rate.

Over the long run, real estate prices could increase an average of four percentage points a year faster in the strongest markets than in the weakest ones, predicts Michael Carliner, vice president of Regional Data Associates, a New Brunswick, N.J. consulting firm. The places where prices are most likely to surge: fast-growing areas where the supply of houses and condos is also constrained by barriers to new building [such as water shortages in some Western states].

Source: "Location, Location, Location," excerpted from the May 1981 issue of *Money* Magazine, p. 52; © 1981, Time Inc. All rights reserved.

products and services are consumed. As we saw in Chapter 10, land is a very basic element used in the production/consumption process. It works with the other factor inputs of capital, labor, and management expertise.

As An Investment

Real estate investments range in size from small lots to residential buildings to large office buildings to shopping centers. Real estate has attracted widespread investor interest for several reasons. First, the relative scarcity of property coupled with the rising demand for it has driven up real estate prices. This factor has resulted in sizable profits for many real estate investors. Second, there are very favorable income tax laws in relation to real estate profits. Available tax breaks act as an incentive for individuals and businesses to buy real estate.

A prime reason why investors are attracted to real estate is that it can act as an inflation hedge. An **inflation hedge** is an investment whose rate of return is greater than the rate of inflation. The fact is, many real estate investments during the past 20 years have provided such a rate of return.

For example, the coastal community of Los Osos, California had a threefold increase in population between 1970 and 1980—from about 3000 to over 10,000. The level of people's incomes rose as well. One result of these developments was a dramatic increase in real estate prices. The typical home building lot rose in price from $2000 in 1970 to over $30,000 in 1980. Lot prices increased by 1500 percent, while the overall level of inflation doubled during that ten-year period.

Types of Real Estate

There are many categories of property including housing, commercial property, and various forms of "raw" (unimproved) land. Housing includes single-family homes (one house per lot), condominiums, cooperatives, and apartment properties. **Condominiums** are multi-unit structures, with private ownership of individual units and joint ownership of common space such as lawns, lobbies, and swimming pools. **Cooperatives** are apartment buildings in which each tenant owns a proportionate share of the corporation that owns the apartment building. Tenants are in reality stockholders in the building and share the costs of running it.

Commercial property includes shopping cen-

Being located near the labor force and various transportation modes is important for manufacturing operations, such as Boeing's Renton plant in Seattle.

ters, office buildings, and other types of nonresidential property. These rental properties as well as residential rental properties are favored investments because of attractive income tax benefits as well as rapidly increasing property prices. The size of a commercial property investment can range from a corner gas station to a multi milliondollar office building.

Typically, raw (unimproved) land is regarded as the most speculative real estate investment. *Speculative* means that the profits an investor expects to make are relatively uncertain. Unimproved land in the form of building lots and of undeveloped acreage is generally considered a fairly speculative investment. These investments represent a bet that the future demand for the property will rise—and with it, its value.

Somewhat similar to raw land is *farmland*. It differs in that it's developed and improved property, assuming it's used for farming and not left idle. Many nonfarmers have invested in farmland in the anticipation that it will increase in value at a rate greater than the rate of inflation and at the same time provide some current income through sharecropping or sharing arrangements. The price of farmland varies considerably. For example, on February 1, 1980 the average value per acre ranged from $112 in New Mexico to $2400 in New Jersey; the U.S. average for all

states was $640.[4] As an investment, the percentage increase in value per acre from 1970 to 1979 also varied quite a bit: Iowa showed the best nineyear performance with a 317 percent increase; surprisingly, California was the lowest with a 75 percent increase.[5]

HOUSING: SHELTER AND INVESTMENT

Housing is one of the basic necessities of life—but what kind of housing shall it be? An important choice that almost everyone faces at some time is whether to rent or own. The costs and benefits of each must be carefully weighed. An important factor that could influence the decision is the investment nature of home ownership. While renting is easier, the trend is toward ownership. Figure 20.1 illustrates the growing percentage of people who now own their own home—about two-thirds of all American households. Apparently, more Americans prefer owning to renting.

Financing Costs

A big difference between renting and owning is that owning requires a much larger initial cash

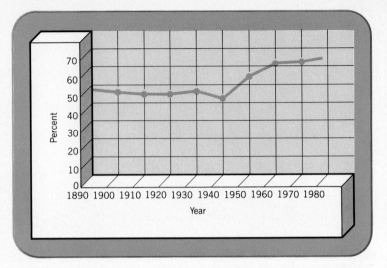

PERCENTAGE
OF
FAMILIES
OWNING
THEIR
HOMES
(1890–1979)

FIGURE 20.1

SOURCE: Bureau of the Census. From *Savings and Loan Sourcebook, 1982* (Washington, D.C.: U.S. League of Savings Associations, 1982). Used by permission.

outlay when the home is purchased. A homebuyer has to make a large downpayment when the home is bought, many times larger than a rental deposit. In addition, monthly mortgage payments must be paid.

Mortgage Payments Most people don't pay cash when they buy a house. Instead they borrow a large portion of the purchase price, using the property as collateral for a mortgage loan. A **mortgage loan agreement** usually specifies what will happen if the borrower defaults—that is, misses payments on the loan. Usually, if a bor-

rower defaults on a mortgage loan, the property is seized by the lender and sold to repay the loan. Any proceeds from the sale in excess of the amount owed would of course be returned to the owner.

There can be any number of mortgages on a property, although one seldom sees more than two. The first recorded is called the **first mortgage,** while the second is the **second mortgage.** If a property is sold, the first mortgage must be paid in full before later mortgages are satisfied. If a second mortgage is arranged as part of a refinancing scheme that leaves the first mortgage in-

"Is that the nice little spot you were telling me about?"

PERSPECTIVE ON SMALL BUSINESS

At first glance it looks like a zoning nightmare; another impression might be motley ghost town.

In fact, it's Tony J. Lozano's used-house lot, and he says business is booming "as if there wasn't any recession."

On a 20-acre spread amid flat farm lands stand two dozen empty houses mounted on timbers or wheels and ranging from a three-bedroom ranch-style to a Victorian bungalow and field-hand shanties. They used to stand in the way of various real-estate developments, but Tony J. Lozano Inc. saved them from the wrecker's ball.

"We buy up these places cheap and move them here for sale," says Mr. Lozano. Potential buyers can browse through the lot, slam doors, inspect woodwork and fixtures, and then dicker about price.

The 58-year-old former roofer says he got the idea for the lot when he was buying, repairing and reselling used houses on a quick turnover basis. In 1960, he found himself facing a removal deadline with no place to store 70 houses he'd purchased from the Alameda Naval Air Station on San Francisco Bay.

Though he eventually sold those houses, the storage problem set him to wondering why he "couldn't run a house business like a used-car lot," he says.

Now he sells about 50 houses a year. They cost him an average of $1,500 each and, depending on size, from $2,000 to $10,000 to move to his lot. Larger houses have to be cut into sections before being moved, then reassembled at the lot, a process that helps keep Mr. Lozano's eight-man crew busy when sales are slow.

Mr. Lozano's customers, most of them blue-collar workers priced out of the conventional real estate market, pay from $6,500 to $29,500 for a house, including moving costs. They get a home usually in reasonable shape, not counting the windows, many of which fall victim to the moving process. All a buyer needs is a site, a foundation and a county building inspector's okay on the setup.

"People who can't buy a house any other way buy from us," Mr. Lozano says. "With a little work, they may end up with a house worth four or five times what they put into it."

SOURCE: Ray Vicker, "The Latest in California Real Estate: Tony J. Lozano's Used-House Lot," *Wall Street Journal*, March 4, 1982, p. 29. Reprinted by permission of The Wall Street Journal, © Dow Jones & Company, Inc., 1982. All rights reserved.

tact (probably because of a favorable interest rate), this is called a **wrap-around.** Creative financing of this type became very popular when interest rates started to soar in the early 1970s.

Mortgage loans may specify a fixed-payment or a variable-payment schedule. With a **fixed-payment mortgage,** the periodic payment stays the same throughout the term of the loan. A **variable-payment mortgage** doesn't have a fixed repayment schedule. Rather, the periodic payments may change over the life of the loan. Examples of variable payment loans include graduated-payment mortgages, variable-interest-rate mortgages, and renegotiated-rate mortgages. A **graduated-payment mortgage (GPM)** provides that payments shall rise after the first year of the loan

and continue to rise gradually each year. After the fifth year that the loan is outstanding, payments usually remain level.

A **variable-interest-rate mortgage (VRM)** allows the lender to adjust the loan's interest rate every six months. This adjustment is designed to reflect changes in financial market conditions. Ordinarily, if the loan's interest rate is altered, the payments change as well. A **renegotiated-rate mortgage (RRM)** allows the lender to change the loan's interest rate every three to five years, and loan payments are adjusted accordingly. Any interest rate adjustments with VRM or RRM loans must be in accordance with state and federal laws. Actual lending policies vary from state to state and are constantly changing.

TABLE 20–1

Loan Payment Table (30-year fixed-payment mortgage)

Amount of Mortgage	Payment					
	@8%	@10%	@12%	@14%	@16%	@18%
$ 40,000	$ 293.50	$ 351.03	$ 411.44	$ 473.95	$ 537.90	$ 602.83
60,000	440.26	526.54	617.17	710.92	806.85	904.25
80,000	587.01	702.06	822.89	947.90	1075.80	1205.67
100,000	733.76	877.57	1028.61	1184.87	1344.75	1507.09
120,000	880.51	1053.08	1234.33	1421.84	1613.75	1808.50
150,000	1100.64	1316.36	1524.93	1777.31	2017.13	2260.63

Table 20.1 shows the monthly payments on fixed-payment 30-year mortgages of various amounts at selected interest rates. As you can see, the monthly payments increase as the loan amount and the interest rate on the loan rise.

The typical American home sold for approximately $75,000 in 1981. To buy this home, you needed a downpayment of about $15,000 and a mortgage loan for the balance of the purchase price, or $60,000. During much of 1981, interest rates for many home mortgage loans were about 16 percent. The monthly mortgage payment on a $60,000, 16 percent, 30-year fixed payment loan is $806.85.

To obtain a mortgage loan from a financial institution, you must qualify under its requirements. One of these is that your monthly income be three to four times the monthly loan payment. So to qualify for the $60,000 loan, you would have had to have a monthly income of at least $2400.

Investment Attributes

In addition to the many pleasures that home ownership provides, it can also act as an excellent investment. Two very positive investment features of home ownership are income tax breaks and the price appreciation potential of the property. Homeowners can lower their income taxes while they own the property and they can often resell their homes at a profit.

Tax Advantages Homeowners enjoy a distinct advantage over renters in income tax deductions. First, a homeowner may deduct property tax. In contrast, a tenant's rent, the level of which is probably affected by the level of property taxes on the building, is not tax deductible. The property tax on an apartment building is paid by the owner, who can deduct it when calculating his or her own income taxes.

TABLE 20–2

Price of Homes versus Inflation during the 1970s

Year	Average Sales Price Existing Homes	Increase in Average Sale Price[a]	Consumer Price Index	Increase in Consumer Price Index[a]	Homes in Relation to Inflation[b]
1970	$25,700	8.4%	116.3	5.9%	+2.5%
1971	28,000	8.9	121.3	4.3	+4.6
1972	30,100	7.5	125.3	3.3	+4.2
1973	32,900	9.3	133.1	6.2	+3.1
1974	35,800	8.8	147.7	11.0	-2.2
1975	39,000	8.9	161.2	9.1	-0.2
1976	42,200	8.2	170.5	5.8	+2.4
1977	47,900	13.5	181.5	6.5	+7.0
1978	55,100	15.0	195.4	7.7	+7.3
1979	65,200	18.3	217.4	11.3	+7.0

SOURCE: *Federal Reserve Bulletins.*
[a]Values represent the percentage change from the immediately preceding year.
[b]Expressed as the difference between increase in home prices and increase in Consumer Price Index.

TALKING BUSINESS

A Las Vegas home builder and a developer from Hawaii have come up with a plan they believe will "HELP" millions more families qualify for mortgages at today's interest rates.

By selling a buyer only 80 percent of the house and renting him the other 20 percent, the two maintain, they can enable nearly twice as many families to afford the payment on a $76,125 house purchased with 10 percent down and a 30-year loan at 14 percent.

The $76,000 is roughly the average price of a new house these days in Las Vegas, where builder Earnest Becker has made about two dozen 80–20 deals and now is ready to tell the world how to go about it.

In a conventional transaction, a buyer who puts 10 percent down on such a house must have an annual income of nearly $39,000 to qualify for a 14 percent, 30-year mortgage. And his payments to principal and interest alone would be $812 a month.

Under Becker's plan, which he and Honolulu developer Dennis Krum call HELP, a buyer needs just $31,000 to qualify for the same loan on the same house. And because he's buying only 80 percent of the house, his monthly payment drops dramatically to $650.

Moreover, according to Becker's and Krum's figures, 16.9 percent of the nation's households have enough income to qualify for a mortgage with their HELP, whereas just 9.2 percent can afford $812 a month. That translates to 14.2 million families as opposed to 7.7 million.

Source: Excerpted from Lew Sichelman, "Mortgages: 'HELP' Is on Its Way," *San Diego Union*, March 15, 1981, p. F-22. Reprinted by permission.

Also, the interest portion of the mortgage payment is a tax deduction. For many homeowners, most of the mortgage payment is interest and is therefore deductible. Thus a homeowner can deduct both property tax and interest payments, which may provide big income tax savings.

Appreciation in Value The decade of the 1970s saw a historically high rate of inflation. During that period consumer prices nearly doubled, while the price of homes tended to appreciate at a rate faster than inflation. Table 20.2 presents average home price as well as Consumer Price Index data for each year during the 1970s. Over that ten-year period the average American home rose in value by about 175 percent, or about 75 percent faster than the rate of inflation. And in every year except 1974 and 1975, the average house value increased at a rate that exceeded the rate of inflation.

INVESTMENT PROPERTY

In addition to home ownership, millions of investors own properties that they don't occupy as residences, including rental houses, condominiums, apartment buildings, shopping centers, office buildings, farmland, and undeveloped land. These investments are made for a variety of reasons including income tax benefits, sources of income, and inflation hedges. In the remainder of this chapter we'll first consider *improved* investment properties—that is, properties with buildings on them. Then we'll look at the property development business.

Income Investment Property

Income properties are those that earn rental income for their owners. The size and scope of in-

A variety of sources of construction and permanent financing is commonly used in commercial property development.

come property investing can vary from a rental condominium to a high-rise office or apartment building. Not only private investors but also large institutional investors own income properties. Many of the major life insurance companies such as Prudential, Metropolitan Life, and Equitable Life have large holdings. As of December 1980, for example, the New York Life Insurance Company had over $239 million invested in rental properties. Pension funds also are increasing their stake in income properties. These large institutional property owners invest in both apartment buildings and commercial properties such as office buildings and shopping centers.

There are two basic types of income property: rental housing and commercial property. **Rental housing** includes rental houses, condominiums (often vacation condos), and apartment buildings. Commercial property as noted earlier includes shopping centers, office buildings, and industrial facilities. Each type of income property has slightly different investment characteristics.

Rental Housing Since about one third of all Americans still rent their homes, there is a substantial market for rental housing. Income property investors choose to own residential rentals for

several familiar reasons: they are a source of income, they provide income tax savings, and they have a price appreciation potential. Investors can choose from a wide variety of rental housing properties depending on their budgets and what properties are on the market. Small investors often start out with a rental house or a condominium. Duplexes and triplexes are also favorites of small investors. Larger multi-unit apartment complexes are often owned by either wealthy investors or property syndicates.

A **property syndicate** is not a form of organized crime; rather, it's an organization in which a group of investors pool their resources to buy a property or properties. By joining a syndicate, each investor owns a portion of the property and derives ownership benefits from the property in proportion to his or her financial contribution.

McNeil Securities Corporation, for example, offers a number of limited partnerships that invest in real estate. One can become a limited partner (which means your loss is limited to the amount you invest) for as small an investment as $5000. This provides a balanced portfolio of garden-style apartments, office buildings, and shopping centers in selected areas of projected economic growth throughout the United States. An

Shopping centers, once the darlings of real estate developers, have lost some of their attraction. Many developers say they'll avoid building them for a while. And when they do go ahead, they'll build mostly smaller centers in smaller cities.

"Shopping centers were so popular just a couple of years ago; they were touted as perpetual money-making machines," says John T. Reed, who writes a real estate investing newsletter. "They still can be good deals, but anything that gets that popular has to go downhill."

What happened, Mr. Reed and others say, is that too many shopping centers were built. The International Council of Shopping Centers figures there were 4,500 shopping centers in 1960, some 12,500 in 1970, and 22,050 in 1980. [In 1980 alone], the council says, 1,650 centers went up.

For [1981], the council forecasts an increase of only 700. Part of the problem is overbuilding; developers saturated many of the country's largest urban areas with giant centers. Meanwhile, high interest rates, tight money and soft retail sales have made shopping center construction financing hard to come by.

"Shopping centers have to compete for dollars," says Daniel Harrison, a spokesman for the shopping center council. "A savvy investor may look at today's market and channel his money elsewhere."

Source: Excerpted from Lawrence Rout, "Shopping-Center Glut Forces Investors to Look Elsewhere," *Wall Street Journal*, August 12, 1981, p. 21. Reprinted by permission of The Wall Street Journal, © Dow Jones & Company, Inc., 1981. All rights reserved.

investor would need a much greater investment than $5000 to achieve this type of diversification on his/her own.

Commercial Property Commercial property includes shopping centers, office buildings, industrial parks, hotels and motels, and other business-related properties. Here again, the size and scope of a commercial property investment ranges widely from a corner gas station to a multimillion-dollar high-rise office building. In recent years foreign investors have increased their ownership of American commercial properties. These purchases include office buildings, several very large shopping centers, as well as many large hotels. San Francisco's commercial property market has seen a substantial influx of foreign investment, particularly from Hong Kong.

Returns

Investors are attracted to income property investments for a variety of reasons, the most important

of which is their favorable profit potential. There are two basic sources of investment return from income properties: cash flow from the rental income and price appreciation realized upon sale.

Cash Flow An income property's **cash flow** is essentially what's left after deducting operating expenses, mortgage payments, and income taxes from rental income. Cash flow is the periodic return that an owner derives from the property. Several important factors affect the size of an owner's cash flow. These include rental income, operating expenses, mortgage payments, depreciation expenses, and income taxes.

Rental Income. A property's rental income will depend on the market in which the property is located, and it's usually set by the prevailing rate of rent in the area. A key indicator of the vitality of a rental property market is the local vacancy factor, which measures the percentage of available rental units that are not occupied by tenants.

Many rental property markets today have a relatively low vacancy factor—around 2 or 3 per-

ON THE FIRING LINE

Foreign Ownership of U.S. Farmland—A Cause for Alarm?

Sizable land purchases by foreign investors have attracted much attention lately. In the fertile San Joaquin Valley of California, for instance, nearly 18,000 acres were bought by foreign investors over a recent two-year period. In Texas, agricultural land that should have sold for $350 an acre was bought by Arab investors for $1000 an acre. The magnitude of these and other such purchases has alarmed some individuals. Certain states have passed laws to restrict or even prohibit foreign land purchases.

Farmers in particular view the foreign purchases with concern. In the world market, American land is a bargain. It's cheap compared to agricultural land in other countries. Foreign buyers are therefore willing to pay inflated prices. When the dollar is weak in the international market, the deal they get is doubly good. This works a hardship on American small farmers in two significant ways. First, it raises property values, and property taxes jump accordingly. Second, small farmers are being deprived of the opportunities they used to have to enlarge their operations. Foreign investments have interfered with the cycles that used to occur in land prices. In the past, the price of farmland dropped in bad years. It was then that small farmers could afford to buy up additional tracts. Currently, though, foreign investments are keeping the prices of farm acreage high.

It's also a concern to some that foreign investments in land may result in future unmanageable immigration. Many Europeans, in particular, are nervous about the political and economic future of their countries. Afraid that they may lose their fortunes at home to political upheaval or socialist regimes, they are buying US land as a hedge. Should their fears be realized, they would probably immigrate to the US since their land holdings would make it easy for them to obtain visas.

Arguments against foreign land purchases are alarmist, nothing more, say others. They are born of an irrational fear of foreign people—xenophobia—and are almost entirely unfounded. For instance, recent anxieties over extensive Arab acquisitions of US land have no basis in fact. Arab world investors do not even rank among the top purchasers. Heading the list are Germans and Italians, followed by British, French, Belgians, Canadians, and Dutch.

It's true that the price of land has been rising sharply in recent years, admit those in favor of foreign investments. They maintain, though, that this is due almost entirely to demand by Americans. Foreign investment in the US real estate market, they say, is not significant enough to establish prices. At the beginning of 1981 agricultural land held all or in part by foreign investors amounted to only 6 percent of all agricultural land in the country. In any case, what little influence foreign purchases have on prices, these same people say, is to the benefit of US landowners. It increases the value of their properties.

Those in the real estate industry maintain, too, that foreign investments in agricultural land (as well as in business and industry) are vital to our economy. We need foreign capital, they say, to spark our GNP's sagging rate of growth. We cannot afford to restrict international trade in order to protect agricultural producers. What we would be protecting is their inefficiency and inability to compete in the world market.

cent. The Empire State Building is 1 percent, while New York City overall is 2.7 percent.[6] That means that only 2 or 3 percent of all available rental units in the market aren't rented out. As a result, many rental property markets are experiencing substantial increases in monthly rents, and income property prices are rising as well.

Operating Expenses. An income property's operating expenses include maintenance costs, property manager's fees, insurance, property

The ease with which commercial property can be rented and the level of rental income depend upon the forces of supply and demand.

taxes, and utility expenses. These costs can vary considerably between properties depending on the age of the buildings, the services that the landlord provides tenants, and the climate of the area. Income property owners generally try to control costs as much as possible by installing energy-saving devices, by fighting excessive property taxes, and by employing professional property managers. Many professional property managers hold a **Certified Property Manager (CPM)** designation—somewhat analogous to the CPA designation for accountants. A CPM is usually a well-trained and experienced property manager.

Mortgage Payments. The largest single periodic expense paid out by an income property's owner is usually the mortgage payment, since almost all income property purchases involve the use of borrowed funds. The terms and interest rate of the mortgage loan can greatly affect the owner's return; favorable terms can substantially increase returns from the property. Mortgage financing of income properties is very similar to that of residential housing, explained earlier.

Depreciation and Income Taxes. One very attractive benefit of income property ownership is the depreciation tax deduction. **Depreciation** is basically a noncash expense incurred by the owner that permits recovery of a portion of his or her investment in the property. Every year, an income property owner can claim depreciation expense. And every year, this tax deduction will lower the owner's income taxes, thereby increasing cash flow. This amounts to a yearly opportunity for the owner to recover a portion of the property's cost.

Price Appreciation   Over the past fifteen years most income properties have appreciated substantially. This appreciation is related to increasing rents and cash flows and also to increases in the value of the land on which these buildings are located. So the combination of rapidly increasing rent levels and rising land prices has pushed up income property prices. Given both the somewhat limited supply of land suitable for income property and the growing population, it's expected that the demand for, and prices of, income properties will continue to rise.

Financing Income Properties

Financing income property is similar to financing residential property. However two factors—equity kickers and leverage—are particularly important here.

Equity Kicker   A recent trend in commercial property lending is the widespread use of "equity kickers." An **equity kicker** in an income property loan means that a lender not only receives interest on the loan but also obtains a portion of the owner's profits from the property. Most loans made by insurance companies for the purpose of financing commercial property investment contain an equity kicker. Essentially, the lender wants to obtain both a good rate of interest on the loan and some of the profits that the owner gets through the use of the lender's funds. Obviously, equity kickers work against the income-property investor.

Leverage Property investments often involve large amounts of borrowed capital. The use of borrowed funds to finance an investment is called **leverage.** So a property that's highly leveraged is one on which the owner has borrowed a substantial percentage of its purchase price.

Technique. Leverage takes place when a buyer makes a downpayment substantially less (10 to 30 percent is common) than the purchase price and borrows the balance from a financial institution or the seller of the property. The use of leverage in purchasing property is inversely related to the size of the downpayment—the smaller the downpayment, the greater the leverage. Leverage magnifies the buyer's property investment; and assuming prices rise, more leverage is considered better than less. Indeed, many "get rich in property" schemes are based on the assumption of almost 100 percent leverage. Needless to say, there are risks.

Risk Factors. Leverage automatically increases a property owner's risk of loss because it carries with it an obligation to make scheduled payments. The owner must repay the loan according to its terms. If an owner defaults, the lender can **foreclose** the property, which means that the property is taken from the owner and sold to satisfy the debt.

A variety of circumstances could lead to financial problems for a property owner. These include an unexpected increase in vacancies or operating expenses. If the property's cash flow is insufficient to repay the loan, the owner must dig into his/her own pocket or face the possibility of foreclosure. But leverage can pay off well if the property's income is greater than the operating and debt repayment expenses. This is called *positive leverage.* The owner's return may also increase if rental income increases and operating expenses are controlled.

Leasing as a Purchase Alternative

Suppose a person needs some space in a building for the conduct of business. This proprietor basically has a single choice: buy the building or lease space from the building's owner. **Leasing** involves renting property. Many businesses, such as retail stores, banks, savings and loan associations, consulting firms—and many professionals such as doctors, dentists, and lawyers—prefer to lease business facilities rather than own them.

Sears, Roebuck, for example, leases a large number of its stores. J. C. Penney, Safeway Stores, K mart, Montgomery Ward, Kroger, and Acme Markets are all substantial leasers of store space. In fact, most retailers lease their stores rather than buy them. Property owners that rent to major retail store chains usually lease their buildings to these companies on long-term (20-to-30-year) leases. A landlord leasing his building to J. C. Penney, for example, would agree to allow Penney's to rent the building for the next 20 years. In return, Penney's would pay the landlord a yearly rental amount.

Many long-term leases of this type will provide that the landlord can raise the rent if the store's retail sales increase. So if the store's dollar sales go up by 10 percent, the landlord's rental income is increased by 10 percent as well. This type of lease offers inflation protection for the landlord because as the store raises its prices with inflation, the landlord's rental income rises as well. In this way it's very similar to an equity kicker.

Large retailing companies, such as Sears, often prefer to rent rather than own their stores because they don't want to tie up capital in property. These firms apparently believe that they can earn greater profits by investing in merchandise inventories and in advertising rather than in real estate. So leasing works out well for both landlord and tenant. The landlord earns a steady rental income, while the tenant doesn't have to tie up large amounts of money in property investments.

Property Development

Because of the ever increasing demand for housing and commercial property, many companies are engaged in the development business. A **land developer** buys land, improves it, puts buildings on it, and resells it as developed property. Property developers with a keen sense of market timing who are attuned to the changing tastes and preferences of consumers can be very successful. A profitable developer usually has strong marketing skills, ample financial resources, and an ability to monitor costs closely.

A good illustration of this occurred in New York with the Bay Club, a twin-tower condominium project in the borough of Queens. The initial developer of this project lacked imagination and market skill to complete it and eventually ran out

There is a large amount of real estate still available for residential or commercial development.

of cash. As a result, the project stood as an unfinished eyesore for over five years. On the verge of being converted to public housing, it was purchased by new developers with a greater flair for marketing and with deeper insights into the ways of the New York homebuyer. After extensive research to determine their particular wants, the new developers featured a high-security alarm system in each rental unit, country club memberships with many sporting activities, and financing at a fixed rate of 13 7/8 percent for 30 years. The turnaround was immediate—over 400 of 1038 units were sold in about four months at prices ranging from $55,000 for a studio apartment to $250,000 for a penthouse unit. Even more incredible, these sales took place from drawings and a scale model, since the project was incomplete and not available for inspection.[7]

SUMMARY

Real estate is differentiated from financial investments, such as stocks and bonds, by its relative scarcity and its use in the production process. It is a popular investment for several reasons. Not only is it scarce relative to demand, but it enables the investor to take advantage of favorable income tax laws and also acts as a hedge against inflation. Categories of real estate include housing, commercial properties, and various forms of raw (unimproved) land. Somewhat similar to raw land is farm land.

Housing is a necessity; people only have the choice of buying or renting. One difference between the two is that buying requires a much larger initial outlay in the form of a downpayment. An important cost is the mortgage payments. Home buyers have traditionally used fixed-payment mortgages, although a number of alternatives have been presented in recent years owing mainly to the prevailing high interest rates. Among these alternatives are graduated-payment mortgages, variable-interest-rate mortgages, and renegotiated-rate mortgages. Buying a home has been a good investment in terms of tax considerations and price appreciation.

Millions of investors own properties they do not occupy as residences. These investments can be classified as either improved properties or undeveloped land. Income properties are those that earn rental income. Two basic types of income property are rental housing and commercial property. The most important returns from income properties are cash flow from the rental income and price appreciation at the time of sale. Factors that affect the size of the cash flow include the rental income, operating expenses, mortgage payments, depreciation expenses, and income taxes.

Equity kickers in addition to scheduled interest payments are commonly required by commercial property lenders today. The use of borrowed funds to finance a property investment—leverage—increases its risk as well as potential return. Many businesses prefer to lease commercial property rather than buy it.

Because of the ever increasing demand for housing and commercial property, many companies are engaged in the business of buying land, improving it, putting buildings on it, and reselling it as developed land.

KEY TERMS

cash flow
Certified Property
    Manager (CPM)
commercial property
condominium
cooperative
depreciation
equity kicker
first mortgage
fixed-payment
    mortgage
foreclose
graduated-payment
    mortgage (GPM)
income properties
inflation hedge
land developer
leasing
leverage
mortgage loan
    agreement
property syndicate
renegotiated-rate
    mortgage (RRM)
rental housing
second mortgage
Sun Belt region
variable-interest-rate
    mortgage (VRM)
variable-payment
    mortgage
wrap-around

REVIEW QUESTIONS

1. Cite some factors that affect the demand for property.
2. Define the term *Sun Belt region*. Why has this area experienced above-average increases in value and volume of real estate?
3. Explain why location is an important determinant of property value. How well has real estate served as an inflation hedge?
4. Discuss the key aspects as well as role of mortgage loans in financing real estate purchases. Describe the three basic types of variable-payment mortgages and compare them to fixed-payment mortgages.
5. Compare and contrast the two basic types of income property—rental housing and commercial property.
6. Describe the two sources of investment return from income properties.
7. What is involved in property development? What does it take to be a profitable developer?

DISCUSSION QUESTIONS

1. Discuss some of the factors that make real estate a scarce commodity.
2. Distinguish between a fixed- and variable-payment mortgage. Which kind would you prefer?
3. What are the two positive investment features of home ownership?
4. What is a property syndicate? Does it offer an investment advantage to the small investor?
5. Explain what is meant by an equity kicker.
6. Discuss the use of leverage and how it is related to the downpayment. Are there risks involved in using high leverage?

CASE: DREAM HOUSE: RENT OR BUY?

Joan and Harry Hansen were faced with a real decision. Finally they had arrived at a time in their short married life when there was a possibility of acquiring their *dreamhouse*.

Both had fairly good jobs—Harry was an insurance claims adjuster earning $18,000 a year; Joan had the prestigious title of personal banker with a salary of $16,000. So together their incomes were sufficient, according to the senior loan officer at the bank, to enable them to buy a house at a cost of around $80,000.

Joan was the one who favored the idea of buying a house. She said that her Dad was willing to put up $16,000 as a downpayment. But Harry argued that he'd rather rent a house for less money and not be "tied to the land" with the monthly obligation of making a mortgage payment. He wanted to be free to move if a really good job opportunity came along. Joan, on the other hand, was ready to settle down and raise a family.

So Joan and Harry got out their scratch pads, sharpened their pencils, and began to figure the costs of renting versus buying a home. They were not about to forget to list the advantages and disadvantages of both.

1. Assume Joan and Harry can negotiate a 30-year, 16% fixed-payment mortgage. Determine their monthly mortgage payment and compare it to, say, a monthly rent of $600 on a comparably appointed house. (Consider income taxes in your answer, but don't make extra calculations.)
2. Do you agree with the loan officer? Can the Hansens afford an $80,000 house?
3. With regard to the current real estate market (as you understand it), would the purchase of a house be a sound investment? Explain.

CASE: THE BROKER HAS GOT TO GO

The real estate business has been in real trouble for the last few years; real estate brokers and agents are dropping out of the market like flies falling off the screen door in a late spring freeze. Everyone is clamoring about interest rates, and it's obvious they're hurting the real estate business. People can no longer afford to buy houses—or at least they're reluctant to buy them at interest rates of 15–17 percent.

In the meantime, the housing market is languishing in the doldrums as people wait for some action to be taken—and almost everyone is pleading that the government do something about the plight of the industry. And cries are often loudest from the real estate people who for years have been complaining about too much government regulation. The day of reckoning is here. What can be done about it? Some of the more creative realtors have proposed plans with variable- or graduated-payment mortgages, wrap-around mortgages, variable-interest-rate mortgages, and second mortgages. Every so often some lucky person announces that he's just bought a home with an assumable mortgage at 9, 10, or 11 percent.

At the risk of oversimplifying the problem, let's explore some possibilities. What if potential sellers—people sitting in homes that they're trying desperately to sell—just decided to sell directly to potential buyers at whatever mortgage rate the seller is sitting on? This would take the buyers back to very attractive interest rates, lowering monthly payments on the mortgage. Of course, most commercial lenders have put a stop to such a practice by including due-on-sale clauses in their mortgage agreements. But there must be a lot of people harboring mortgages at low interest rates—also wanting an appreciation on their property of 100, 200, 300 percent and better.

Why, then, the need to seek government solutions to this problem? Why not let the free marketplace take care of this real estate problem, thereby putting people back into the homes of their dreams?

1. What would such actions on the part of buyers and sellers—avoiding real estate brokers—have on the real estate market?
2. What would this practice do to the savings and loan companies who have been hurt so badly in this real estate recession?

A CAREER IN FINANCE

The world of finance offers many opportunities for people with an interest in money and with basic skills in mathematics. These appear to be simple qualifications, but they become quite complex when put in the perspective of managing the finances of an enterprise—a small business or a huge corporation—and the great variety of financial institutions that serve small and large businesses across the country. These financial institutions include commercial banks, savings and loan associations, investment firms, farm credit banks and production credit associations, credit unions, personal finance companies, and collection agencies. All must be managed and directed, with supervision at many levels and services of all kinds requiring a multitude of talents and technology.

Employment opportunities will be very good in the securities industry, where more than 200,000 people are currently employed with such career titles as stockbroker, securities salesperson, mutual fund salesperson, security analyst, investment advisor, commission and bond broker, and stock specialist. Growing competition among the different financial institutions should increase the demand for graduates with specialized training in finance. In addition, the traditional careers in areas such as real estate and insurance—insurance and real estate salesperson, claims adjustor, property appraiser, and others—should keep pace with the economy in general. Although real estate was extremely depressed during the early 1980s, the pent-up demand for housing is enormous, and improved conditions in credit markets will enhance employment prospects in real estate. A turnaround such as this will offer excellent reward opportunities to graduates willing to assume some risks inherent in this field.

Where the Opportunities Are

1 ■ CORPORATE FINANCIAL MANAGER

There are many positions of financial responsibility in corporations (in manufacturing, trade, service, or financial) ranging from small companies to multinationals. The higher managerial positions carry the titles of finance manager, controller, vice-president for finance, and treasurer. Of course, there are assistant manager positions, or "assistant to" positions, that accompany these top managers.

The person occupying the position at any level in finance is concerned with the source of funds and their allocation throughout the organization. The finance manager is concerned with budgets—specific requirements for funds required at certain times to pay bills or meet obligations for the organization. These financial needs must be forecast and sources for funds made available to finance such activities as payroll, purchase of raw materials, payment of short- and long-term loans, utilities, etc. The manager must also maintain a close relationship with the accounting function to be certain that all funds are accounted for and appropriate records kept. Similar functions are performed by the controller and the vice-president for finance—at high levels of responsibility.

Places of Employment Throughout the country; urban areas offer more opportunities than rural, and the best prospects are in large metropolitan areas.

Skills Required Four-year program. Many employers require an MBA.

Employment Outlook thru 1990 Good; excellent for MBAs.
Salaries Entry level: $15,000; MBA: $20,000.

2 ■ STOCKBROKER OR SECURITIES SALESPERSON

Out of the 200,000 people employed in the securities market, over one half are stockbrokers or securities salespeople. Their responsibilities include handling orders to buy and sell securities, counseling customers on financial matters, supplying the latest bond and stock quotations, and dealing with everyday questions from the general public. Stockbrokers are usually hired by brokerage firms, investment banks, insurance companies, and mutual funds. The smaller firms may hire junior college graduates who are self-motivated, dynamic, and personable. Larger firms usually require college graduates with degrees in finance or business administration.

Most firms offer a trainee program for beginners, preparing them to take standardized examinations (NASD) required for a license. Overall, firms look for personality traits such as savvy, drive, high energy, and confidence.

Places of Employment New York is the nation's primary security trading center. Opportunities can be found, however, in all large cities.

Skills Required Most employers prefer a four-year program.

Employment Outlook thru 1990 Fair.

Salaries Trainee: $13,000; experienced broker: $50,000–$90,000

3 ■ FINANCIAL ANALYST

Security analysts are the experts who study stocks and bonds, usually in specific industries, such as oil, automobiles, or computers. They issue reports on values of securities and predict the overall effect of national economic trends. These are very important investment advisors to general business organizations, brokerage firms, banks, insurance companies, pension funds, foundations, mutual funds, and other financial institutions. The chartered financial analyst (the CFA) represents the highest achievement in this segment of the securities industry. It is on a par with other professional designations (such as the CPA, CMA, or CLU) in both prestige and financial rewards.

Places of Employment Principally New York, although security analysts work for institutions throughout the U.S.

Skills Required Four-year program. An MBA is often required.

Employment Outlook thru 1990 Excellent.

Salaries Junior analyst with MBA: $18,000–20,000.

4 ■ INSURANCE AGENT AND BROKER

Today our population is extremely large and complex, and it is too expensive for people to go unprotected against all the hazardous risks. Instead people share the risks by purchasing insurance policies. Insurance agents and brokers develop programs to fit customers' needs, interview insurance prospects, help with claims on settlements, and collect premiums. Agents are usually employed by a single insurance company, whereas a broker is independent and represents no particular company but can order policies from many. Agents specialize either in life insurance or in property and liability insurance. Others specialize further with one type of property and liability insurance, such as automobile coverage. Certification is designated by the C.L.U. (Certified Life Underwriters), L.U.T.C. (Life Underwriters Training Council), and C.P.C.U. (Chartered Property Casualty Underwriters). These designations are recognized marks of achievement for insurance people who are specialists in their respective fields.

Places of Employment Throughout the country. However, most jobs are in cities where the home offices are located. These include New York, New Jersey, Massachusetts, Connecticut, and Illinois.

Skills Required Two-year program. Some companies prefer a four-year program.

Employment Outlook thru 1990 Good.

Salaries Trainee: $9,000–$12,000; established agent: $17,000–$50,000.

5 ◼ ACTUARY

Actuaries are responsible for determining rates that are charged for different kinds of insurance policies. They deal with statistics, mathematics, and financial calculations in figuring probability for future payments. Actuaries are highly respected and have professional status similar to that of doctors and lawyers.

Places of Employment Home offices of insurance companies (see above).

Skills Required Four-year program or MBA.

Employment Outlook thru 1990 Excellent.

Salaries Beginner: $12,000; MBA: $18,000.

6 ◼ REAL ESTATE AGENT OR BROKER

Selling real estate usually requires the services of a real estate agent or broker, which consist primarily in executing orders from buyers or sellers for the sale of property.

The real estate agent is usually an independent sales worker in the employ of a broker. Some of the agent's duties include meeting with potential buyers and showing them various properties that will fit their needs. Agents must therefore research their potential customers' likes, dislikes, and needs. After finding the right seller/buyer combination, the agent negotiates terms agreeable to both parties. Then the agent draws up a sales contract, after which it's further processed by a lending institution.

Brokers are independent business people with a few years' experience. They are usually involved in several areas besides selling. They make property appraisals, handle rental and building management, and develop new building projects. The broker can also employ several agents to assist him/her.

Many real estate agents and brokers are also certified property managers. In this capacity they act as agents for owners in leasing, collection of rents, payment of operating expenses, and maintaining properties. The owners of these properties are usually investors and don't have the time, knowledge, or desire to manage their property. The property manager usually works for a real estate firm, and fees are based on the gross income of the property.

Places of Employment Throughout the country. Most opportunities are in growth areas such as the Sun Belt. Growth has been dramatic in Texas, Florida, Arizona, California, and Hawaii.

Skills Required Two-year or four-year program.

Employment Outlook thru 1990 Fair.

Salaries Beginner: $10,000; experienced agent: $15,000–$50,000.

7 ◼ CREDIT MANAGER

Over the years, buying on credit has become a customary way of doing business. Consumers use credit to pay for houses, cars, appliances, and travel, as well as day-to-day retail purchases. Most business purchases, such as raw materials used in manufacturing and merchandise to be sold in retail stores, also are on credit.

For most forms of credit, a credit manager has final authority to accept or reject a credit application. In extending credit to a business (commercial credit), the credit manager or an assistant analyzes detailed financial reports submitted by the applicant, interviews a representative of the company about its management, and reviews credit agency reports to determine the firm's record in repaying debts.

Places of Employment Throughout the country. Most jobs are in urban areas.

Skills Required A few jobs for persons with a two-year degree. Most companies prefer a four-year program.

Employment Outlook thou 1990 Fair.

Salaries Trainee: $12,000-$14,000; credit manager: $22,000-$25,000.

8 ■ UNDERWRITER

Insurance companies assume billions of dollars in risks each year by transferring the risk of loss from their policyholders to themselves. Underwriters appraise and select the risks their company will insure. Underwriters decide whether their companies will accept risks after analyzing information in insurance applications, reports from loss control consultants, medical reports, and actuarial studies (reports that describe the probability of insured loss). Their companies may lose business to competitors if they appraise risks too conservatively or may have to pay more claims if their underwriting actions are too liberal.

When deciding that an applicant is an acceptable risk, an underwriter may outline the terms of the contract, including the amount of the premium. Underwriters frequently correspond with policyholders, agents, and managers about policy cancellations and requests for information. In addition they sometimes accompany salespeople on appointments with prospective customers.

Places of Employment Best opportunities are in New York, San Francisco, Chicago, Dallas, Philadelphia, and Hartford.

Skills Required A few two-year programs. Most insurance companies prefer a four-year program.

Employment Outlook thru 1990 Good.

Salaries $17,000-$25,000.

9 ■ CLAIM REPRESENTATIVE

Fast and fair settlement of all claims is essential to any insurance company for meeting its commitments to policyholders and protecting its own financial position. The people who investigate claims, negotiate settlements with policyholders, and authorize payments are known as claim representatives—a group that includes claim adjusters and claim examiners.

When a property-liability (casualty) insurance company receives a claim, the claim adjuster determines whether the policy covers it and the amount of the loss. Adjusters use reports, physical evidence, and testimony of witnesses in investigating a claim. When their company is liable, they negotiate with the claimant and settle the case. Adjusters must make sure that settlements reflect the claimant's actual losses.

In life and health insurance companies, the counterpart of the claim adjuster is the claim examiner, who investigates questionable claims or those exceeding a specified amount. Examiners may check claim applications for completeness and accuracy, interview medical specialists, consult policy files to verify information on a claim, or calculate benefit payments.

Places of Employment Claim adjuster positions can be found throughout the country. Most claim examiner jobs are located in large cities such as New York, San Francisco, Chicago, Dallas, and Philadelphia.

Skills Required Two-year program. A growing number prefer a four-year program.

Employment Outlook thru 1990 Excellent.

Salaries $15,000-$22,000.

10 ■ BANK OFFICERS AND MANAGERS

(See Management Career Appendix).

PART 5

BUSINESS TOOLS

CHAPTER 21

ACCOUNTING

After studying this chapter you should be able to:

1 Understand the importance of the accounting function and accounting systems in business operations.
2 Describe the role of the accountant — both the CPA and the CMA — in business.
3 Understand how internal reporting and external reporting are both vital to a firm's total information system.
4 Identify the three key financial statements used by business firms and explain how the two major ones aid in management decisions.
5 Understand key accounting terms, such as assets, liabilities, owner's equity, revenues, and expenses.
6 Know what ratio analysis means and how ratios are used to identify financial strengths and weaknesses.

489

Not long ago a company was formed that manufactured housing modules. Because the modules, measuring 31 × 12 × 9 feet, were made to order, the company would first negotiate a contract with a buyer, usually a large-scale developer. After the sale, the modules were then produced, delivered to the buyer's building site, and installed by company personnel.

Early on, this firm publicized its approach by erecting a 277-unit project in 36 hours. Such demonstrations attract the attention of the Secretary of HUD and of investors. The company raised roughly $40 million from two public stock offerings and arranged a like amount in loans. Combined with the prospect of large doses of federal money for modular housing, this financing appeared to put the company in good shape. Yet 30 months after going public, the company collapsed.

In brief, the company—Stirling Homex—vastly overstated sales of its modules. At the time of bankruptcy (July 1972) it had an inventory of almost 10,000 finished modules. Although Stirling Homex had already booked the profit on these modules, it appears that only 900 of them had genuinely been sold.

You'd expect such a gap only in the event of deliberate deception of the auditors by company management. Such deception occurred on a large scale. In 1977 five officials of Stirling Homex were convicted of criminal fraud, among other charges.

Source: Adapted from Earl K. Littrell, "Mickey Mouse Files," *Management Accounting* (U.S.A.), November 1980, p. 57. Adapted by permission.

Clearly, an effective accounting process is fundamental to the long-run well-being of the firm—and Stirling Homex illustrates what happens when that process fails to perform as it should. Conversely, there are examples of how effectively designed accounting processes help to improve profitability.

This was the case with Phillips Industries, a large diversified manufacturer of home products for both on-site and modular housing. Confronted in the early 1970s with drastic changes in its major markets and substantial increases in manufacturing costs, the company was on the verge of bankruptcy. However its management addressed these problems head-on and embarked on an ambitious program to restructure product lines and control costs. Phillips' plan demanded a comprehensive and reliable accounting system to provide continuous monitoring of product and market profitability. The company's turnaround didn't come overnight, but by 1981 profits had been restored and a strong financial position

emerged. Accounting didn't cause the changes—management did—but it was helpful in bringing them about.

THE ROLE OF ACCOUNTING

Accounting is the process of collecting, classifying, recording, and reporting information about the transactions of the business firm. Accounting keeps records of the sales, purchases, expenses, and investments that the business makes. It occupies a major place in the decision-making process of the modern business firm since it provides much of the information needed by managers, stockholders, and other interested parties to make intelligent and informed decisions.

To make the process of accounting work, accountants use a set of procedures known as **generally accepted accounting principles (GAAP)**. The GAAP aren't a rigid set of rules but rather

While the specific duties of an accountant may vary, the function exists in all firms regardless of size.

are a set of guidelines that have been adopted by the accounting profession to ensure uniformity in reporting business transactions. Accounting is indeed a business language that's used to communicate information among decision makers.

The Accountant

The role of the accountant differs depending upon the type of work they do. Accountants are generally classified as public or private accountants. The **public accountant** is an independent professional who provides accounting services for other businesses. Public accountants aren't employees of the firms they work for, and they aren't involved with day-to-day activities of the firms. The public accountant is organized as an independent business and provides his or her services to clients on a contract basis. There are several very large public accounting firms, known as the Big Eight. The largest of these is Peat, Marwick, Mitchell and Company; other recognizable names are Arthur Andersen and Company, Arthur

Young and Company, and Price, Waterhouse and Company.

Public accountants offer a wide range of services to their clients. Among these are independent audits of financial records, preparation of tax returns, management advice, consulting on data and information processing problems, assistance in filing loan applications and securities registrations, and design of accounting systems. The public accounting firm serves its clients as a valuable resource in the decision-making process. For a variety of reasons, such as the information explosion, increased government regulation, and greater tax complexity, the demand for public accounting services has grown substantially in the last 25 years.

For example, in 1966 Arthur Andersen and Company (AA) had 73 offices and 4,600 professional staff members. By 1981 these numbers had increased to 137 offices and 17,000 professionals; and by 1986 AA estimates it will need at least 25,000 professionals. Public accounting has been a remarkable career path for young people. In 1981 AA admitted 118 new partners at a starting compensation of about $90,000 a year; impressively, 85 of the 118 were 36 years of age or younger. Moreover the average time that elapses between starting with AA and becoming a partner is only 10 to 12 years. Finally, the average compensation of all partners at AA in 1981 was about $150,000, which compares favorably with most other professions.[1]

The **private accountant** is employed by a specific organization. The role filled by the private accountant is the collection and recording of the day-to-day transactions of the firm that employs him or her. The major responsibility of the private accountant should be to provide financial information to managers in the firm. For example, when requesting phone rate increases, AT&T needs reliable information to support its requests. In addition, AT&T managers need a continuous flow of information to make sound operating decisions. Private accountants are also instrumental in preparing the reports that must be submitted to the firm's shareholders and to government agencies.

The Accounting Profession

The accounting profession is influenced by three major factors. The first, the **Certified Public Accountant (CPA)** certification program, is administered under the laws of the various states. The candidate for the designation is required to pass a standard examination in accounting theory and practice. After passing the examination and complying with other state requirements, the individual is allowed to use the title of Certified Public Accountant and the initials CPA after his or her name. The CPA is principally the one who expresses an opinion as an independent accountant concerning the fairness of the presentation of the data in a client's financial statements.

Certificate in Management Accounting (CMA) was introduced by the **National Association of Accountants (NAA)** in 1972. The CMA program is designed to certify the management (private) accountant's mastery of the body of knowledge relating to accounting for management reporting. The program is intended to give the same status to management accountants that the CPA certification gives to public accountants.

The Financial Accounting Standards Board (FASB) was founded with representatives from business, government, and the accounting profession serving on it. The FASB is charged with formulating and issuing rules or generally accepted accounting principles (GAAP) for use by accountants in recording and reporting the activities of enterprises. FASB issues these GAAP through pronouncements called *accounting standards*.

Accounting in the Business Firm

The accounting function within the business firm usually involves two basic activities. The first of these is to supply management with information that it can use in making decisions. The second is to supply information to be used by people outside the business such as investors, creditors, and regulatory agencies.

The internal reporting of financial information enables operating managers to make judgments about the financial impact of their decisions. If United Airlines is considering dropping one of its flights, it calls on accounting to help keep track of revenues, costs, and investments required by the flight. In addition to financial data, much of the accounting information developed for use by managers carries detail about volume of products, units of production, and other nondollar measures of business activity. Internal reporting is done most often through the use of special reports, ratio analysis, and monthly financial statements.

External reporting is necessary since bankers, investors, financial analysts, and government regulatory agencies all require the business firm to report its activities to them. Accountants must file annual and quarterly reports that summarize the company's income and financial status. These reports are filed with the company's stockholders and with the Securities and Exchange Commission (SEC). When the Bank of America or Prudential Insurance lends money to a company, it needs regular reports in order to be assured that its loan is safe. Investors and financial analysts require information about a company's operations in order to make investment decisions concerning the company. Most of these requirements are met by quarterly and annual reports of financial activity.

TALKING BUSINESS

Some people on Wall Street have their own name for the [1981] tax law. They call it the "Accountants' Relief Act," and they're not far off. [The radical changes in the nation's tax system are translating into big business for accountants.]

"Accounting flourishes when there is change," said Henry Gunders, co-chairman at Price, Waterhouse & Company, which ranks No. 4 among the elite Big Eight firms that dominate the accounting profession. Russell E. Palmer, chairman of Touche Ross & Company, the No. 8 firm, added that "1981 was our best year ever. . . ."

The accounting business is bursting not only in the Park Avenue towers where the leading firms are based, but also in the offices of certified public accountants throughout the land. Greater demands by municipalities, businesses and individuals for more precise information of all types, particularly more accurate financial information, have made the accountant a much sought-out individual. Everybody seems to need accountants. "You have much more complex problems that you are dealing with," explained William L. Raby, chairman of the Federal tax division of the American Institute of Certified Public Accountants. "It's not enough to be somebody who knows a little about taxes. That's becoming dangerous."

As a result, said J. Michael Wrede, director of financial recruiting for the Seattle executive search firm of Murphy, Symonds & Stowell, "the demand for accountants is greater than the supply," even though the supply has soared. In 1960 there were 1,071 United States partners in the Big Eight firms. By 1981, the number had jumped to 7,006.

Because of the demand, accounting firms are one of the most aggressive recruiters on college campuses. Touche Ross claims it hires more graduates from Harvard College, Harvard Business School and Harvard Law School than any other corporation. Peat, Marwick, Mitchell & Company boasts that it is the biggest employer of American college graduates each year, hiring some 2,000 new graduates annually.

Source: Excerpted from Leslie Wayne, "The Year of the Accountant," *New York Times*, sec. 3, January 3, 1982, pp. 1, 15. © 1982 by The New York Times Company. Reprinted by permission.

BASIC ACCOUNTING PROCEDURES

Accounting is a procedural art. The accountant uses a set of classifications in defining and reporting the financial resources of the enterprise. The accountant prepares records and generates reports in a fashion generally consistent and comparable with other enterprises since nearly all accountants use the same definitional procedures. This procedural framework used by accountants to transform data and prepare reports is known as the **accounting process,** or **accounting cycle.**

The accounting process is depicted in Figure 21.1.

The processing of data includes the steps of journalizing, posting, and adjusting. These steps are responsible for recording, classifying, and correcting data entered in the worksheets. The worksheets are known as **trial balances** and are used to display the data. The trial balances are also used to sort data for presentation on the major financial statements.

Three major financial statements are used by business firms. One of these statements is the **balance sheet**, which shows what the company owns and how much it owes others. The second statement is called the income statement. The **income statement** shows the profit or loss of the business. A third financial statement, the **statement of changes in financial position,** summarizes the sources and uses of short - and long-term funds.

In order to understand the nature of recording accounting transactions, the following terms must be defined:

1. Assets **Assets** are anything owned by the business and used in the production of the business's goods and services. Assets are usually classified as current assets and fixed—or long-term—assets. The classes of assets are more fully explained in a later section of this chapter.

2. Liabilities **Liabilities** are the amounts of money that are owed to other people or to other companies. A liability is a claim against the assets of the company. Liabilities usually arise from buying assets and promising to pay for them later, from costs of operations that are not paid immediately, or from borrowing money from a bank or other financial institution, which will be paid back in the future.

3. Owners' Equity The **owners' equity** in the company is measured by subtracting the total liabilities from the total assets of the business. Owners' equity represents the dollar amount of investment the owners have in the business. The owners' investment usually represents the money put into the business—and the profits that were earned and retained within the business—by the owners.

Double-Entry Bookkeeping

The modern accounting system is based on the simple **accounting equation:**

Assets = Liabilities + Owners' Equity

The accounting equation reflects the basic premise that all the assets of a business have the claims of creditors and owners against them. The rights embodied in the assets are equal to the claims of those interests—lenders and owners—whose funds were used to acquire them.

In order to keep these rights equal to the claims and to keep the equation in balance, every trans-

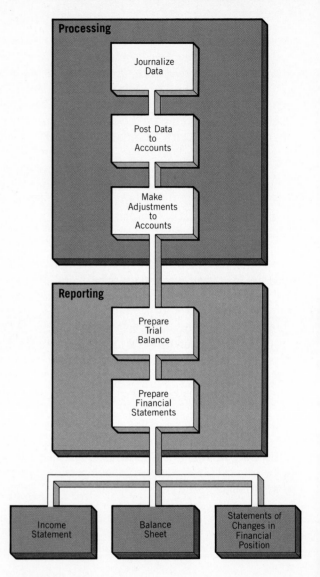

THE ACCOUNTING PROCESS

FIGURE 21.1

action affecting the basic equation requires two entries. This procedure is known as **double-entry bookkeeping.** For example, if the business borrows $10,000 in cash from the bank, the following entry would be needed:

Assets = Liabilities + Owners' Equity
+ $10,000 = + $10,000 + $0

If the company made the scheduled repayment to the bank for a loan of $5000 which was due, this transaction would affect both cash and liabilities, and the following entries would be required:

Auditing a small business is a tricky process. Bookkeeping practices seldom approach the ideals that the American Institute of Certified Public Accountants' rulemakers had in mind when they laid down auditing standards for CPAs. One problem is that an owner has complete control over the books.

In one instance, an owner tried to spruce up the year-end financial statement by hiding a $40,000 bill for a gala company party. "It wouldn't have appeared on the balance sheet as an account payable," says an accountant who knows of the incident and insists on remaining anonymous. "And it wouldn't have appeared as an expense, so the balance sheet and the profit-and-loss statement would have looked a lot better when the owner went to the bank."

Such liberties would be rare in a huge corporation. If they do occur, $40,000, even several million, can't make or break a big company the way keeping $40,000 off the books would enhance a small concern's financial statements. Accountants have to depend on an owner's honesty; they aren't detectives hired to snoop into every corner of the business. "If the owner wants to pull the wool over our eyes," says Sam Derieux, a Richmond, Va., CPA, "it would be difficult or impossible in some instances for the auditor to pick it up."

Accountants prefer owners who exercise good surveillance over record keeping—providing the owner is honest. When a bookkeeper handles all the books and cash transactions, the possibility of embezzlement is great unless the owner is vigilant. In a manufacturing concern, "we like to see the owner keeping track of inventory and the manufacturing process," says Ronald S. Cooper, a partner at the accounting firm of Ernst & Whinney. "In a service business, we like to see an owner with very good control of payroll, someone who actually reviews the payroll register and is the only one who can approve any new entries such as pay changes or new hires."

Paul Allen, a partner at Main, Hurdman & Cranstoun's Wichita, Kan., office, says little companies can cause complex audits. "We have a contractor who owns a trucking company, a landfill, a helicopter service and some oil and gas wells," he says. Ensuring that these operations are properly accounted for requires the time of senior Main Hurdman CPAs. "The audit fee is around $20,000, and the owners are croaking," Mr. Allen says.

$$\text{Assets} = \text{Liabilities} + \text{Owners' Equity}$$
$$-\$5000 = -\$5000 + \$0$$

These bookkeeping entries are referred to as debits and credits. A **debit** entry records:

1. an increase in an asset;
2. a decrease in a liability;
3. a decrease in owners' equity.

A **credit** entry records:

1. a decrease in an asset;
2. an increase in a liability;
3. an increase in owners' equity.

General Journal The initial recording of transactions is made in the general journal. The journal is referred to by accountants as the *book of original entry*. The **general journal** is a financial diary of all business transactions arranged in chronological order. Figure 21.2 illustrates a page from the general journal with the above examples recorded. It can be seen that in the first transaction cash (an asset) is increased (debited) by $10,000 and notes payable (a liability) are increased (credited) by $10,000. In the second transaction notes payable (a liability) are decreased (debited) by $5000 and cash (an asset) is decreased (credited) by $5000.

THE GENERAL JOURNAL

45-602 EYE-EASE
45-702 20/20 BUFF
NATIONAL Made in U.S.A.

	Date	Description	Ref	Debit	Credit	
1	1983					1
2	3 15	Cash	①	10000 —		2
3		Notes Payable – First Bank			10000 —	3
4		To record loan from First Bank				4
5						5
6	3 31	Notes Payable – First Bank	②	5000 —		6
7		Cash			5000 —	7
8		To record the repayment of a loan				8
9						9
10						10
11						11
12						12
13						13
14						14
15						15
16						16
17						17
18						18
19						19
20						20
21						21
22						22
23						23
24						24
25						25
26						26
27						27
28						28
29						29
30						30
31						31
32						32
33						33
34						34
35						35
36						36
37						37
38						38
39						39
40						40

FIGURE 21.2

The accounting activity provides the information used to prepare and file a variety of required forms and statements.

General Ledger The accounts of the business are maintained in the general ledger, which is called the *book of account*. The **general ledger** is a specialized book that collates journal entries into specific accounts. Separate ledger accounts are maintained for such things as cash, sales, salaries, accounts receivable, bank notes, and so on. Recording data in the ledger is called *posting*. Figure 21.3 gives an illustration of the general ledger accounts for the above examples. It can be seen that in the cash account two postings were made. The asset cash increased (debited) by $10,000 and decreased (credited) by $5000. The two notes payable (liability) entries shown were a decrease (debit) of $5000 and an increase (credit) of $10,000.

Electronic Data Processing

The preceding examples illustrate handwritten journal entries and ledger postings. This was done for simplicity, but most well-managed companies, large and small, actually use electronic data processing systems. For example, NCR Corporation, the world's leading manufacturer of electronic cash registers, has developed fully automated ac-

counting systems that require almost no separate accounting effort once an initial transaction is recorded. A salesclerk in a department store rings up the sale of merchandise on an NCR cash register and simultaneously the entry is journalized, held in storage for future posting, and serves as data input to any other part of management's information system. "Do it once" approaches are very much a part of modern accounting.

THE BALANCE SHEET

The classified balance sheet is developed to show the details of the assets, liabilities, and owner equity in the firm. It is arranged in a specific order of presentation. The assets are shown first. Assets are arranged in descending order from the assets most like cash to those least like cash. Another way of describing this arrangement is in terms of liquidity; that is, the most liquid assets occur first and the least liquid last. Liabilities are likewise arranged in a specific order by maturity. The shorter-term liabilities are listed first, with longer-term liabilities listed last. Figure 21.4 shows the 1982 balance sheet for GMF Corporation.

THE GENERAL LEDGER

NATIONAL 45-601 Made in U.S.A

Cash

Date 1983	Reference		Debit	Date 1983	Reference		Credit
	Balance Fwd		8100—				
3 15	GJ-1		10000—	3 31	GJ-2		5000—

Notes Payable—First Bank

Date 1983	Reference		Debit	Date 1983	Reference		Credit
3 31	GJ-2		5000—		Balance		5000—
				3 15	GJ-1		10000—

FIGURE 21.3

Assets

Current Assets:		
Cash	$15,000	
Marketable Securities	4,500	
Accounts Receivable	52,500	
Inventory	25,000	
Total Current Assets		$ 97,000
Fixed Assets:		
Delivery Equipment	$50,500	
Less: Accumulated Depreciation	10,500	$40,000
Furniture and Fixtures	$10,000	
Less: Accumulated Depreciation	4,000	6,000
Total Fixed Assets		46,000
Intangible Assets:		
Patent	$ 7,000	
Total Intangible Assets		7,000
Total Assets		$150,000

Liabilities and Owners' Equity

Current Liabilities:		
Accounts Payable	$30,000	
Notes Payable	15,000	
Accrued Expenses	4,500	
Current Installment of Mortgage Due	5,000	
Total Current Liabilities	$54,500	
Long-Term Liabilities:		
Mortgage on Delivery Equipment	$10,000	
Total Long-Term Liabilities	10,000	
Total Liabilities		$ 64,500
Owners' Equity:		
Common Stock (10,000 shares issued and outstanding)	$30,000	
Retained Earnings	55,500	
Total Owners' Equity		85,500
Total Liabilities and Owners' Equity		$150,000

FIGURE 21.4

Balance sheet for GMF Corporation as of December 31, 1982

Types of Assets

Assets are classified by the length of conversion time, and there are three categories of assets: current assets, fixed assets, and intangible assets.

Current Assets Current assets are those assets which will be converted into cash in the next operating cycle of the business, which for most businesses, is *one year*. The current assets of the firm are important because they are used to meet its currently maturing obligations. Current assets to some degree represent the amount of money that can be raised quickly. The major current assets are:

1. *Cash*, consisting of funds on hand in the bank that are immediately available for use;
2. *Marketable Securities*, representing temporary investments of cash that are not immediately needed in the business;
3. *Accounts Receivable*, consisting of

ON THE FIRING LINE

Forecasting: Art or Artifice in the Annual Report?

Since 1978, the Securities and Exchange Commission has encouraged corporations to include forecasts in their annual reports. Accountants, who conduct the audits and prepare the annual reports, don't all agree that this is a good idea. Corporations, too, are divided in their reaction.

Those who favor forecasting argue that providing estimates of what the future will bring gives investors valuable information. Investors can assume that the accountant's projections match the company's own projections. (If they don't, the company can voice disagreement in its letter to the shareholders.) More likely, though, management would sit down with the auditors and work out any differences that exist. This in turn might well lead to both improved management and more precise forecasts.

Including forecasts in annual reports offers companies another advantage. It makes them less subject to the whims of security analysts, whose job is to advise investors on the value of stocks and other securities. Analysts are viewed as a threat by many companies. A bad rating from them can mean serious financial problems. And their predictions can be disastrously wrong. The best way for management to protect itself against such errors is to include a realistic forecast in its annual report.

Inflation, of course, has made the problem of interpreting financial statements far more complex for investors. Accountants themselves disagree on whether stock prices now correctly reflect corporations' financial status. Some feel investors already take inflation into account; others don't, and they insist on adjusting data in annual reports for inflation. Such adjustments can turn what appear to be excellent earnings into losses. They can make the firms that are most heavily in debt look most attractive. This sort of confusion can be clarified, however, with a forecast.

Accountants and companies opposed to forecasts in annual reports have just as many arguments to support their view. Accountants can't measure the future reliably, they say. Accountants are trained to assess past financial events—which they can do with reasonable accuracy. But forecasting, particularly in a period of mushrooming inflation, is too risky. Many forecasts would be bound to fail. Failures would cause people to lose confidence in accounting and accountants and undermine all financial reporting.

Also, many think that forecasting would be just a name falsely applied to a very different game: stock touting. Companies would not give accurate forecasts, they claim; companies would distort financial data to their own advantage. The record clearly shows that this is the way they play. They already take advantage of accounting techniques that make their profits look good—straight-line rather than accelerated depreciation, for example—even when it costs them more in taxes.

Corporate management also sees pitfalls in forecasting. Little good would come of any forecasts for earnings unless they were high and correct, management insists. A low forecast or a failure to realize a high one would mean a serious loss of investor confidence. Then, too, any predictions in annual reports would probably be short-term (one year) forecasts. In the effort to make short-term forecasts come true, though, management might well neglect important long-term concerns. Construction of a much-needed new plant might be put off, for example, to avoid cutting into earnings.

Whether for the short or long term, forecasting is difficult. One company admitted defeat after including forecasts in its 1977 and 1978 annual reports. None was offered in the 1979 report due to the "problem of making forecasts in an inflationary climate." For all concerned, say opponents, forecasting is touchy and even dangerous. What real protection from liability does the SEC's safe harbor provision provide? What, after all, is a "reasonable, good'faith" estimate? Who decides?

amounts owed to the business by customers to whom sales were made by granting an extension of time in which to pay;

4. *Inventory*, consisting of the stock of items being held for sale by the business or the stocks of items to be used in the production of products for sale;

5. *Prepaid Expenses*, representing assets, such as insurance or office supplies, that were paid for in advance and whose benefit will be received during the operating period.

Fixed Assets Assets used by the business for more than one operating cycle are classified as fixed assets (or long-term assets). These assets are generally used in the production of the products and services that the firm offers for sale. Normally, fixed-asset classifications contain such items as land, buildings, machinery, delivery equipment, and furniture and fixtures. These assets, except for land, are referred to as *depreciable assets*. This is because their cost is assigned to current production by calculating the loss in value resulting from their use in the production period.

Intangible Assets Intangible assets are long-term assets with no physical existence. The value of these assets exists in the rights that they give the business. The most common intangible assets are patents, copyrights, trademarks, and goodwill. Many of these assets convey benefits to the business through their protective nature, e.g. the protection afforded by a copyright.

Types of Liabilities

Liabilities are the financial obligations of the business to other people and to other businesses. They are classified on the balance sheet by the time to maturity.

Current Liabilities Claims that are due in less than one year (the assumed operating cycle) are classified as current liabilities. These short-term claims place the most urgent strain on the current assets of the business. The major current liabilities are:

1. *Accounts Payable*, which are amounts owed to vendors for the purchases of in-

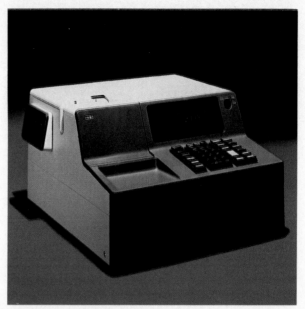

The NCR electronic cash register is a versatile and programmable cash register that, in addition to a variety of other features, allows for direct entry into the general journal.

ventories, supplies, or other assets purchased on credit;

2. *Notes Payable*, which are short-term loans from banks, suppliers, or other people;

3. *Accrued Expenses*, which are obligations that the company has incurred, but on which payment has not been made.

Long-term Liabilities All liabilities that mature in more than one year are classified as long-term liabilities. These include such items as bonds, mortgages, and long-term loans from banks or other lenders.

Owners' Equity

Owners' equity represents the amount of investment that owners have in the business. Owners' equity is made up of two elements—the direct investments of the owners and earnings left in the business.

Direct investment occurs when the owners invest money to start the business or as a subsequent investment later on. For a noncorporate business, the direct investment is recorded in an account called *Capital*. For example, two partners named Steve Brown and John Blank invested $10,000 each in their business. The balance sheet would show the following entries in the owners' equity section:

Steve Brown, Capital	$10,000
John Blank, Capital	10,000
Total Owners' Equity	$20,000

In a corporate business, direct investment by the owners is for purchase of shares of stock in the corporation. The owners' direct investment, both initial and subsequent, are shown collectively on the balance sheet as Common Stock. In Figure 21.4, this amount totals $30,000 for GMF Corporation.

In the noncorporate business, no distinction is made on the balance sheet between initial investment and the earnings retained in the business. The capital accounts of the owners include the totals of the initial direct investment, subsequent direct investment or withdrawals of funds, the addition of the retained profits, and the deduction of losses that may have occurred. For the corporation a separate account is maintained. All earnings retained in the business are accumulated in an account called **retained earnings.** This account is limited to show only the total of all profits and losses since the inception of the business, less any dividends that have been paid to the stockholders. In the balance sheet for GMF Corporation in Figure 21.4, it can be seen that the firm has $55,500 in retained earnings.

THE INCOME STATEMENT

The income statement summarizes revenue and expense activities of the business firm over a specified period of time. An income statement can be developed for any period of time that the managers of the business feel is appropriate. Most large companies develop monthly income statements for internal reporting and prepare quarterly and annual statements for reporting externally. GMF Corporation's income statement for 1982 is shown in Figure 21.5. The elements of the income statement are discussed below.

Revenues and Expenses

Revenues are the receipts that are derived from sales of products, sales of services, and earnings of interest, royalties, rents, and dividends. Revenues reflect the basic flows of cash into the business. An adequate stream of revenues is the life-blood of a successful business firm.

There are two types of **expenses** that are important to accounting. The first is cost of goods sold, which includes expenditures for purchasing merchandise for sale if the firm is a wholesaler or retailer, or the materials, labor, and overhead if the firm manufactures the merchandise it sells. Another part of cost of goods sold is the cost of preparing goods for sale. Such costs as freight for receiving goods and packaging are part of the cost of goods sold. This category of expenditures includes the total direct cost of the merchandise that generates the sales revenue.

The second type of expense is operating expenses, which are incurred in the ordinary course of running the business and are not directly related to the acquisition or production of the goods being sold. Operating expenses include selling and administrative outlays such as sales salaries, advertising, delivery expenses, office salaries, and rent.

Depreciation

Depreciation is the process of assigning the historical cost of a fixed asset to revenues generated

"In the first quarter, we lost $115 million. In the second quarter, we lost $207 million. But in the third quarter, we did very, very well. We only lost $87 million."

Revenues:			
Gross Sales		$250,000	
Less: Sales Discounts		2,500	
Net Sales			$247,500
Cost of Goods Sold:			
Inventory, January 1		$ 28,000	
Purchases		109,500	
Goods Available for Sale		$137,500	
Less: Inventory December 31		25,000	
Cost of Goods Sold			112,500
Gross Profit			$135,000
Operating Expenses:			
Selling Expenses:			
Sales Salaries	$31,000		
Advertising	16,000		
Delivery Expense	18,000		
Total Selling Expenses		$ 65,000	
Administrative Expenses:			
Office Salaries	$18,500		
Depreciation—Delivery Equip-ment, Furniture, and Fixtures	3,000		
Office Supplies	1,000		
Interest	2,500		
Insurance	3,000		
Rent	12,000		
Total Administrative Expenses		40,000	
Total Operating Expenses			105,000
Net Profit Before Taxes			$ 30,000
Less: Income Taxes			6,000
Net Profit After Taxes			$ 24,000

FIGURE 21.5
GMF Corporation Income Statement for the year ended December 31, 1982

through the use of that asset. This cost will continue to be allocated or depreciated in future periods until all of it is applied to operations. The asset is then said to be fully depreciated. The Economic Recovery Act of 1981 replaced the then-existing depreciation methods with the **accelerated cost recovery system (ACRS)**. This new approach provides a choice of two methods for depreciating an asset.

1. *ACRS Depreciation Schedules.* These give specific percentages of the asset's original cost that can be written off each year. The percentages total 100% over the asset's depreciable life, but larger percentages apply in the early years.
2. *Straight-line.* An equal amount of the

original cost of the asset can be written off each year over the asset's depreciable life.

It is important to see that no cash payment actually results from depreciation; and its presence tends to reduce the firm's profits while not increasing its cash outflows.

Net Profit or Loss

Net profit or loss is the amount left after subtracting all allowable costs during the period from sales. These deductions include the cost of goods sold, operating expenses, and taxes on the income earned. Net profit is the balance remaining for the owners of the business. A net loss occurs if

TALKING BUSINESS

Tucked away in the middle of an ordinary-looking press release mailed out by ABC in December [1980] was a line noting that the method of assigning expenses to each showing of prime-time series and movies was being changed. Trivial? Not to an experienced broadcast accountant. That little change could make quite a difference on the bottom line.

The three networks don't really like to tell how they handle the costs of their programs. It won't do much good looking in their annual reports either.

There's no line that describes the networks' annual program expenditures. That number is top secret. When a network buys the rights to show a series or film, that amount goes on the balance sheet under the heading "program rights"—in effect, the network's inventory of shows still to be broadcast. The question is: How much of those costs are charged off on the income statement each time the show is on?

ABC's practice, says Ted James, analyst at Montgomery Securities, had been to charge around 80% of the cost of the show or film the first time it goes on the air. This makes sense. Ad revenues on the first airing are usually higher than later ones, and there's no knowing how long it will run. When the show is broadcast again, that leaves only around 20% of the cost still to be charged off.

What ABC seems to have done is reduce that first-time charge from 80% to around 75% of the show's cost. That doesn't sound like much until you consider the numbers involved. "You're probably looking at around $500 million in first-run programs at ABC during 1980," says James, "so if you start shifting 5% around, you're talking about $25 million, or $12.5 million after taxes. When you realize that it's all being lumped basically into two quarters, it's big."

For ABC, that little switch could well turn a loss into a profit in the first quarter of [1981] and could also boost earnings thereafter.

Source: Excerpted from Thomas Baker, "A Question of Judgment." Reprinted by permission of *Forbes* Magazine from the February 16, 1981, issue, p. 52.

expenditures exceed revenues. While the "arithmetic" is simple enough, very often judgment is involved in determining what is an allowable cost. In theory, the answer is that an allowable cost is one that was incurred in the given period to produce sales in this same period. (This is called the matching principle. Problems arise when a cost produces sales over several (or many) reporting periods. How should these costs be assigned? Depreciation is an obvious judgment item, since it is impossible to know in advance how much of a depreciable asset actually wears out in any given period of time.

Figure 21.5 shows GMF Corporation's net profits are $24,000; these could be paid out in dividends or retained in the business. The portion that is retained is then added to retained earnings on the firm's balance sheet, increasing owners' equity. The retained earnings account therefore acts as the principal link between the income statement and the balance sheet.

RATIO ANALYSIS

An important task of the accountant is to interpret financial data. A tool that the accountant may find useful in helping to interpret financial reports is ratio analysis. **Ratio analysis** is a technique that makes comparisons of selected financial-statement items in percentage terms rather than in dollars. However without a standard with which to compare the calculations, the resulting ratios would not mean much. One way of comparing ratios is to look at their values over time. This is done most conveniently by plotting the values on a piece of graph paper, as shown in Figure 21.6. If the values are then connected by a series of lines (or sometimes a single line is fitted through the points, such as was illustrated for trend analysis, explained in Chapter 18), the result is referred to as a *time series*. Analysis of the series is called *time series analysis*.

For example, if the accountant wants to use time series analysis on the GMF Corporation financial statements, he or she would compare the 1982 ratios to similar ratios for 1977 through 1981. By examining the same ratios over several time periods, the accountant could determine if trends of activity were present in the firm's operations. If such trends were unfavorable, management's attention could be drawn to the problem and corrective action taken. Figure 21.6 illustrates the process.

A second method of using ratios is called *comparative ratio analysis*. In this case one compares the company under analysis with some externally determined standard that's applicable to the company. The most common standard is an industry average that's been developed by a qualified statistical service. (Note the industry average and GMF Corporation's performance relative to it as depicted in Figure 21.6.) Publishers of the most commonly used industry averages are Dun and Bradstreet, Robert Morris Associates, Standard and Poor's, and Prentice-Hall. Each year these publishers release studies of the average ratios of selected industries that are reported to them.

Liquidity Ratios

These ratios measure a company's ability to meet its current cash obligations. A liquid firm is not only free from fear of default but it's also able to avoid the strains and emergencies that might force the company to use high-cost money sources. Being forced to borrow at higher-than-normal rates of interest would be costly both to the company and to its owners. There are two major liquidity ratios.

Current Ratio   The **current ratio** is the ratio of total current assets to total current liabilities. It's used to measure the adequacy of the current assets to meet current obligations. The current ratio is the best-known of all ratios. Traditionally, a 2-to-1 ratio is said to be adequate, but use of this universal rule is not recommended. Because its cash flows are very predictable, a public utility company can function quite well with less than a 2-to-1 ratio. On the other hand, the liquidity of a manufacturing or merchandising company that must carry high inventories and receivables would be dangerously inadequate at 2-to-1.

The formula for the current ratio and the calculation of the current ratio for GMF Corporation is:

$$\text{Current Ratio} = \frac{\text{Total Current Assets}}{\text{Total Current Liabilities}}$$

$$= \frac{\$97,000}{\$54,500}$$

$$= 1.78 \text{ to } 1$$

The 1.78 ratio means little without a basis for comparison. However if the analyst found that the average for the industry in which GMF Corporation competes was 3.22, he or she would probably feel that GMF's current position wasn't sufficiently liquid. All ratios must be treated in

FIGURE 21.6

RATIO ANALYSIS

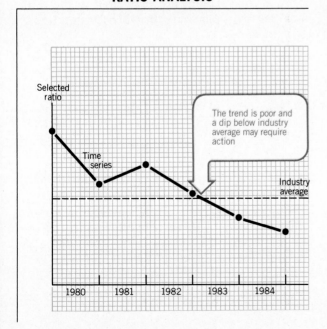

this same manner because a ratio without a basis for comparison is difficult to interpret.

Acid-Test Ratio   The ratio of the most liquid of the current assets to current liabilities is known as the **acid-test ratio** (or quick ratio). For calculation of the acid-test ratio, the inventory is eliminated from current assets. This ratio measures the firm's ability to pay short-term obligations without having to rely on the sale of the inventory. The traditional rule of thumb for adequate acid-test ratios is 1-to-1, though the same cautions apply here as with the current ratio. The calculation for GMF Corporation is:

$$\text{Acid-Test Ratio} = \frac{\text{Current Assets} - \text{Inventory}}{\text{Current Liabilities}}$$

$$= \frac{\$97,000 - \$25,000}{\$54,500}$$

$$= 1.32$$

Profitability Ratios

The profitability ratios measure how productively the firm's resources are being used to generate profits. Many analysts also use profitability ratios to assess how effectively the firm is being managed.

Net Profit Margin   The **net profit margin** measures the after-tax profit relative to the company's sales. The net profit margin is used to assess the adequacy of sales prices, costs, or both, since this ratio gives some indication of a company's practice with respect to its pricing policies and cost control. The net profit margin for GMF Corporation is:

$$\text{Net Profit Margin} = \frac{\text{Net Profit After Taxes}}{\text{Net Sales}}$$

$$= \frac{\$24,000}{\$247,500}$$

$$= .0969, \text{ or } 9.69\%$$

The company is earning 9.7¢ on each sales dollar. We should expect wide variations in this ratio among business firms, usually depending on how frequently they turn over their inventories. The more frequent the turnover, the lower the ratio. For example, Ralston Purina earned only 3.5¢ on

its 1981 sales dollar (its inventories turn over fairly rapidly), whereas Whittaker Corporation, a conglomerate with many activities and a slower inventory turnover, earned almost 6.0¢ on each sales dollar in 1981.

Return on Investment   The **return on investment (ROI)** measures the rate of return stockholders receive from the investment they have made in the firm. The rate of return is important because it reflects the actual earning power—the factor that motivated stockholders to invest their money rather than spend it. If the rate of return becomes too low relative, the return on investment for GMF Corporation's shareholders is:

$$\text{ROI} = \frac{\text{Net Profit After Taxes}}{\text{Total Owners' Equity}}$$

$$= .2807, \text{ or } 28.07\%$$

On the surface, a 28.07 percent return on investment seems quite good. However the riskiness of GMF's business is unknown, and if it's high, then that rate may not represent a substantial return, relative to risk.

Earnings Per Share   The **earnings per share (EPS)** measures the amount of earnings generated on behalf of the owners of the company's common stock. The earnings per share are important to shareholders as an indication of potential dividends and future growth potential which will occur as the earnings are reinvested in the company. Earnings per share for GMF Corporation in 1982 were:

$$\text{EPS} = \frac{\text{Net Profit After Taxes}}{\text{Common Shares Outstanding}}$$

$$= \frac{\$24,000}{10,000 \text{ shares}}$$

$$= \$2.40/\text{share}$$

The concern of the investing public in earnings per share cannot be overemphasized. Indeed, EPS is often regarded as the single most important barometer of financial performance. As we saw in Chapter 18, it's generally conceded that any unexpected incident threatening to dilute EPS—say an offering of more shares of common stock—might depress the market value of the firm's existing shares.

WHOLESALING

Line of Business (and number of concerns reporting)	Quick Ratio	Current Ratio	Current liabilities to net worth	Current liabilities to inventory	Total liabilities to net worth	Fixed assets to net worth	Collection period	Net sales to inventory	Total assets to net sales	Net sales to net working capital	Accounts payable to net sales	Return on net sales	Return on total assets	Return on net worth
	Times	Times	Percent	Percent	Percent	Percent	Days	Times	Percent	Times	Percent	Percent	Percent	Percent
5013 Automotive Parts & Supplies (106)	1.6	4.7	23.5	35.7	27.3	4.3	25.9	5.9	35.4	5.6	5.3	7.7	10.9	17.3
	1.2	3.1	40.4	59.4	49.9	10.7	33.5	4.7	43.4	4.3	6.7	3.7	7.1	13.6
	0.8	2.4	72.2	84.0	94.4	32.9	42.9	3.3	56.1	2.6	9.5	1.7	3.8	8.7
5014 Tires & Tubes (120)	1.3	2.8	43.6	72.4	57.4	14.2	27.3	8.6	34.4	10.8	6.9	3.9	9.2	18.9
	0.8	1.7	105.3	103.3	128.4	23.2	40.8	5.7	42.0	6.5	13.9	2.3	5.1	12.3
	0.6	1.4	170.3	153.0	197.4	51.9	61.6	4.4	56.4	4.9	19.0	1.0	2.4	6.9

RETAILING

Line of Business (and number of concerns reporting)	Quick Ratio	Current Ratio	Current liabilities to net worth	Current liabilities to inventory	Total liabilities to net worth	Fixed assets to net worth	Collection period	Net sales to inventory	Total assets to net sales	Net sales to net working capital	Accounts payable to net sales	Return on net sales	Return on total assets	Return on net worth
	Times	Times	Percent	Percent	Percent	Percent	Days	Times	Percent	Times	Percent	Percent	Percent	Percent
5211 Lumber & Other Building Materials Dealers (105)	2.7	6.7	13.5	27.5	15.8	6.1	28.4	9.2	32.7	6.6	3.1	5.8	12.2	22.1
	1.3	2.8	36.5	73.3	54.3	17.6	40.1	6.2	42.9	4.7	4.9	2.9	8.9	13.6
	0.8	1.9	80.2	119.5	106.7	32.3	54.3	4.0	61.2	2.8	7.8	1.5	4.1	5.6

SERVICES

Line of Business (and number of concerns reporting)	Quick Ratio	Current Ratio	Current liabilities to net worth	Current liabilities to inventory	Total liabilities to net worth	Fixed assets to net worth	Collection period	Net sales to inventory	Total assets to net sales	Net sales to net working capital	Accounts payable to net sales	Return on net sales	Return on total assets	Return on net worth
	Times	Times	Percent	Percent	Percent	Percent	Days	Times	Percent	Times	Percent	Percent	Percent	Percent
7011 Hotels, Motels & Tourist Courts (108)	2.9	4.8	5.0	—	25.6	68.2	—	—	102.1	19.4	2.1	26.5	8.4	23.2
	1.1	2.0	14.7	—	95.5	136.1	—	—	146.8	8.3	3.4	9.0	3.2	11.0
	0.2	0.9	47.9	—	326.7	305.5	—	—	318.3	4.0	6.2	2.6	1.5	3.5
7216 Dry Cleaning Plants, Except Rug Cleaning (118)	4.3	6.9	4.1	—	9.8	40.9	—	—	29.7	15.8	1.0	13.4	15.7	22.3
	1.9	3.5	12.5	—	22.5	74.7	—	—	46.9	9.6	1.8	6.8	10.1	13.9
	1.0	1.6	28.2	—	47.4	94.9	—	—	91.9	4.3	3.0	3.4	6.0	8.2

MANUFACTURING

Line of Business (and number of concerns reporting)	Quick Ratio	Current Ratio	Current liabilities to net worth	Current liabilities to inventory	Total liabilities to net worth	Fixed assets to net worth	Collection period	Net sales to inventory	Total assets to net sales	Net sales to net working capital	Accounts payable to net sales	Return on net sales	Return on total assets	Return on net worth
	Times	Times	Percent	Percent	Percent	Percent	Days	Times	Percent	Times	Percent	Percent	Percent	Percent
2011-2017 Meat Products (113)	2.1	4.2	20.4	89.2	33.3	31.9	12.7	44.2	14.0	31.0	0.9	2.9	11.6	25.7
	1.3	2.2	47.0	144.8	71.8	57.9	17.8	29.0	19.2	15.3	1.8	1.5	6.5	13.9
	0.8	1.6	118.0	221.5	177.2	82.6	24.8	16.3	28.9	11.0	3.2	0.6	2.4	4.8
2021-2026 Dairy Products (125)	1.2	2.0	52.0	133.7	64.3	43.7	18.9	55.0	18.6	41.3	3.7	2.8	9.5	23.1
	1.0	1.4	84.6	228.8	114.7	68.2	26.4	26.9	23.1	19.1	5.6	1.2	5.2	11.1
	0.7	1.2	149.4	434.2	205.0	92.4	32.8	13.9	33.2	12.5	7.7	0.5	1.1	3.1

Dun & Bradstreet's Key Business ratios are a popular source of information for use in comparative ratio analysis. Shown here are excerpts from four selected industry groups.

Debt Ratios

The debt ratios measure the extent to which borrowed funds have been used to finance the firm's operations. If too much borrowed capital is used, the firm faces a problem of meeting interest payments and repaying the principal amount borrowed. Two basic measures of debt use are usually calculated for a company.

Debt-to-Assets Ratio The **debt-to-assets ratio** measures the claims that the creditors (i.e. lenders) have against the assets of the company. For GMF Corporation the debt-to-assets ratio is:

$$\text{Debt-to-Assets} = \frac{\text{Total Liabilities}}{\text{Total Assets}}$$

$$= \frac{\$64,500}{\$150,000}$$

$$= .43, \text{ or } 43\%$$

Interest Coverage Ratio The **interest coverage ratio** reflects the basic ability of the firm's earnings to meet its interest costs. The higher this ratio, the better able the firm is to meet its obligations, and vice versa. For GMF the interest coverage ratio is:

Many annual reports include analyses of financial data and ratios resulting from the most recent year's operation. Shown here is a portion of such a discussion from Bristol-Myers' 1981 annual report.

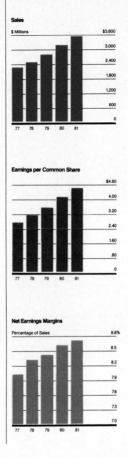

Sales
$ Millions

Earnings per Common Share

Net Earnings Margins
Percentage of Sales

Financial Review

Summary

In 1981, the company again achieved record sales and earnings, with growth across all industry segments of the business. The pharmaceutical and medical products segment achieved significant sales growth; however, unfavorable foreign currency exchange rates limited earnings growth. The non-prescription health care segment turned in another excellent performance this year in both sales and earnings. Sales of the toiletries and beauty aids segment showed a slight increase over 1980 while earnings improved modestly. For the second consecutive year, the household products segment reported improved operating profit margins. The total company's profit margins improved again, for the ninth consecutive year, on the strength of compound annual growth rates of 12% in sales and 15% in net earnings.

The company's strong operating performance in 1981 was achieved in a climate of economic uncertainty, highly competitive marketplaces, and the significant strengthening of the U.S. dollar. As a result of this performance, the company continued to strengthen its financial position. Emphasis on asset management added to the operating performance has improved the cash and securities position to $429 million. In addition, the company continued to finance internally its operating and capital requirements and increased its dividends on common stock for the ninth consecutive year.

Net Sales and Earnings

Net sales in 1981 of $3.5 billion exceeded the prior year by 11%, compared with increases of 15% in 1980 and 12% in 1979. Adjusted for the effects of foreign exchange translation, sales in 1981 would have increased 14%. The effect of fluctuations in foreign exchange rates on sales was not significant in either 1980 or 1979. Selling price increases during the three years were well below the U.S. and world inflation rates, but played a larger part in the sales growth in 1981 and 1980 as compared to 1979.

Net earnings rose 13% in 1981 following increases of 17% and 14% in 1980 and 1979, respectively. The growth in net earnings at a rate faster than sales resulted in the net earnings margin rising to 8.7%, the ninth consecutive year of improvement. Earnings per common share in 1981 were $4.58, up from $4.08 in 1980 and $3.50 in 1979. Foreign exchange losses reduced 1981 earnings by $.63 per share compared to an $.11 loss last year and a $.29 loss in 1979. Since 1979 the effective income tax rate has declined slightly from 45.3% to 44.6%. This decrease is primarily due to a higher proportion of earnings in lower tax jurisdictions and increased investment tax credits, partially offset by the effect of foreign exchange losses.

$$\frac{\text{Interest}}{\text{Coverage}} = \frac{\text{Profit before Interest and Taxes}}{\text{Interest}}$$

$$= \frac{\$24,000 + \$2500 + \$6000}{\$2500}$$

$$= 13 \text{ times}$$

Note that in this calculation the profit before interest and taxes was found by adding the $2500 interest payment and the $6000 in taxes back to the net profit after taxes of $24,000. These "addbacks" are appropriate because (1) interest payments are deductible in calculating income taxes, and (2) we want a measure of profit that doesn't include the item being covered—in this case, interest payments.

SUMMARY

Accounting is the process of collecting, classifying, recording, and reporting information about the transactions of the business firm to provide information needed inside and outside the firm. Accountants are generally classified as either public or private. There are three major influences on the work these accountants do: the Certified Public Accountant (CPA) program; the Certificate in Management Accounting (CMA) program; and the generally accepted accounting principles (GAAP), issued by the Financial Accounting Standards Board (FASB).

The public accountant is an independent professional who provides accounting services for other businesses. Private accountants work for specific firms. Within the firm, accounting has two basic activities: internal reporting to supply information to management and external reporting to supply information to bankers, investors, financial analysts, government regulatory agencies, and other interested parties.

The procedural framework used by accountants is known as the accounting process, or accounting cycle. It includes the steps of journalizing data in the general journal, the book of original entry; posting the data to accounts in the general ledger; and adjusting the data. Worksheets, or trial balances, are prepared from these data to sort them for presentation in the major financial statements.

The accounting system is based on the simple accounting equation (Assets = Liabilities + Owners' Equity). To keep the equation in balance, the accountant uses two entries—a debit and a credit—for every transaction affecting the equation. This system is known as double-entry bookkeeping.

Three major financial statements are used by business firms: the balance sheet, the income statement, and the statement of changes in financial position.

The balance sheet shows the details of the assets, liabilities, and the owners' equity of the firm. There are three categories of assets—current assets, fixed assets, and intangible assets. Major current assets are cash, marketable securities, accounts receivable, inventory, and prepaid expenses. Fixed, or long-term, assets normally include land, buildings, machinery, delivery equipment, and furniture and fixtures. These assets are depreciable. The most common intangible assets are patents, copyrights, trademarks, and goodwill.

Liabilities include current liabilities—accounts payable, notes payable, and accrued expenses—and long-term liabilities—such items ·as bonds, mortgages, and long-term loans. Finally, owners' equity is made up of two elements, the direct investments of the owners (either capital or common stock) and retained earnings.

The income statement summarizes revenue and expense activities of the business over a specified period of time. Two types of expenses important to accountants are cost of goods sold and operating expenses. Another expense—depreciation—is unique in that it doesn't require an outlay of cash. Rather it is the process of assigning the historical cost of a fixed asset to revenues generated through use of the asset. The result of comparing revenues with expenditures—including taxes—is net income or loss.

The accountant can use ratio analysis to help interpret financial reports. Ratios from the financial statements are compared against some standard, either past ratios of the same firm (time series analysis) or industry averages (comparative ratio analysis). One category of ratios deals with liquidity; the two major liquidity ratios are the current ratio and the acid-test ratio. Another category deals with profitability—net profit margin, return on investment, and earnings per share. Debt ratios include the debt-to-assets ratio and the interest coverage ratio.

KEY TERMS

accelerated cost
   recovery system
   (ACRS)
accounting equation
accounting process, or
   accounting cycle
acid-test ratio
assets
balance sheet
Certificate in
   Management
   Accounting (CMA)
Certified Public
   Accountant (CPA)
credits
current ratio
debits
debt-to-assets ratio
depreciation
double-entry
   bookkeeping
earnings per share
   (EPS)
expenses
Financial Accounting
   Standards Board
   (FASB)
general journal
general ledger
generally accepted
   accounting
   principles (GAAP)
income statement
interest coverage ratio
liabilities
National Association
   of Accountants
   (NAA)
net profit
net profit margin
owners' equity
private accountant

public accountant
ratio analysis
retained earnings
return on investment
   (ROI)
revenues
statement of changes
   in financial
   position
trial balances

REVIEW QUESTIONS

1. Describe the duties of the public and the private accountant. Which one is an independent professional?
2. Briefly summarize the procedures involved in *internal reporting* and *external reporting*.
3. What is the "accounting equation"? Explain, using the terms *debits* and *credits* in your answer.
4. List the major items included in the balance sheet and the income statement. What role does liquidity play in arranging items on the balance sheet?
5. Distinguish between current and fixed assets and between current and long-term liabilities.
6. Name and interpret two ratios used to measure a company's liquidity.
7. What is the difference between the net profit margin and the return on investment?
8. A firm's interest coverage ratio is 6.3; explain what that means.

DISCUSSION QUESTIONS

1. Explain the significance and use of generally accepted accounting principles (GAAP) in accounting work. Who (or what) formulates GAAP?
2. How do the roles differ for public and private accountants?
3. Explain what is meant by double-entry bookkeeping and how the accounting equation is related to it.
4. How does the balance sheet differ from the income statement?
5. Distinguish between time-series and comparative ratio analyses. In what way is each of these used?

6. How important is return on investment (ROI) to the business owner/operator and stockholder?
7. How is earnings per share (EPS) calculated and what does it measure?

CASE: THE AMBITIOUS ACCOUNTANT WITH ANEMIA AND AMNESIA

Last week, the county attorney's office issued a warrant for the arrest of the disappearing fraternity treasurer whose bank account had just turned up a $10,000 deficit in the fraternity accounts.

There followed accusations of embezzlement, and many of Dan Daniel's fraternity brothers were ready to describe how their treasurer had been very loose with their funds. Several of the accounting students told the county attorney that Dan was responsible for handling all of the fraternity funds and paying all the bills. He was authorized to sign checks and was in charge of deposits of both membership payments and monthly payments for rent and utilities. They also pointed out that the accounting system was very poor and that they were continually under scrutiny from the national office for the way they did business. Dan had taken it upon himself to try to keep the fraternity in good standing with the national headquarters, and at the same time accommodate late-paying members and still meet current bills.

Not long after a related article appeared in a newspaper, Dan called the editor to report that it was completely unfounded; he hadn't embezzled any funds. He had left town because he was sick and went home to recuperate. He'd be back in a couple of days to clear up the whole mess. When Dan got back he explained that there was no shortage of funds: the fraternity was actually in debt $10,000. He had tried desperately to meet bills, but the revenues just didn't offset the current expenses. In some cases he himself had written checks on his own bank to cover expenses so as not to reflect on the fraternity, but when things got out of hand he just had no way to cover for the deficiencies caused by poor financial control and a general shortage of funds. Unfortunately, Dan didn't have a good set of books or documents to substantiate his story. Consequently, his future, as well as that of the local fraternity, would rest with the judgment of the university auditors, the alumni, and the county attorney's office.

1. Describe how an appropriate accounting system might have avoided the problems cited above.
2. What recommendations should be made to the fraternity in this financial mess?
3. Do you think the fraternity should insist upon having a CPA audit its financial records? Explain.

CASE: MARY JEAN'S GENTRY FASHIONS

Mary Jean's Gentry Fashions is a women's clothing store located in a medium-sized Southern city. Mary Jean Rewing founded the business in the early 1960s and operated it as a sole proprietorship until 1976. Wanting more free time, Rewing took on a partner, Donna Hall, in that year. The business was eventually incorporated, with each woman receiving 5000 shares of common stock. Rewing then assumed an inactive managerial role, placing all operating functions in Hall's hands. She insisted, though, on a large dividend payout each year.

Much to her surprise, the dividend was actually cut in 1983 to $3.86 a share from $10.55 in the previous year. On top of that, she learned that some of her suppliers were complaining about late payments. The store had recently gone through an extensive renovation, and Rewing felt the business was in good shape. Her confidence shaken, she planned to discuss the situation with Hall. Prior to a discussion, though, she'd have to put together and review some selected data from previous financial reports (shown below).

1. Using the ratios presented in this chapter, use time series analysis to analyze the three-years of financial data and discuss the financial strengths and weaknesses of the business.
2. What additional information is needed in order to perform comparative ratio analysis? Explain how such data might prove useful.

MARY JEAN'S GENTRY FASHIONS
Condensed Financial Statements
1983, 1982, 1981

Balance Sheet Data:	1983	1982	1981
Cash	$ 27,300	$ 36,800	$ 40,200
Accounts receivable	78,600	75,200	68,400
Inventories	112,800	83,600	74,500
Building, furniture, fixtures (at cost)	223,000	160,000	140,000
Accumulated depreciation	(132,000)	(86,000)	(46,000)
Total assets	$ 309,700	$ 269,600	$ 277,100
Accounts payable	$ 63,800	$ 55,100	$ 43,400
Current portion of 15% mortgage loan	20,000	16,000	16,000
15% mortgage loan	160,000	130,000	146,000
Common stock issued (10,000 shares)	60,000	60,000	60,000
Retained earnings	5,900	8,500	11,700
Total liabilities and owners' equity	$ 309,700	$ 269,600	$ 277,100
Income Statement Data:			
Sales (all on credit)	$1,650,000	$1,820,000	$1,780,000
Cost of goods sold	(870,000)	(930,000)	(910,000)
Operating expenses	(688,000)	(680,000)	670,000)
Interest expense	(26,500)	(24,300)	(26,700)
Income taxes	(29,500)	(83,500)	(77,900)
Net profit after taxes	$ 36,000	$ 102,200	$ 95,400
Dividends paid on common stock	$ (38,600)	$ (105,400)	$ (90,000)

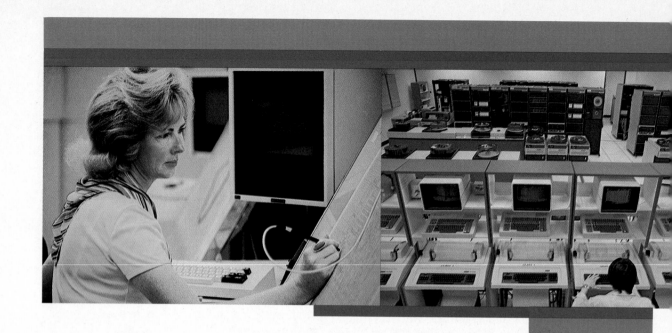

CHAPTER 22

COMPUTERS AND DATA PROCESSING

After studying this chapter you should be able to:

1 Describe a computer and give its basic functions.
2 Understand the development and current phase of computer technology.
3 Identify a computer system and explain the difference between hardware and software.
4 Describe the three basic processing modes and the four common output devices used with computers.
5 Explain an operating system and how the central processing unit (CPU) and binary number system are related to it.
6 Identify the key types of programs and languages used to communicate with computers.
7 Discuss data processing and the considerations that a systems designer must address to make a management information system work effectively.
8 List some important business applications of the computer in the areas of management, marketing, and finance/accounting.
9 Understand what the computer of the future will be like.

513

It is no secret, of course, that the engine driving today's computer and data-communications revolution is the remarkable little microprocessor—or computer on a chip. By now, the prices of microprocessors have plunged so low—and their capability has increased so dramatically—that actual computing power is virtually free. As computer people like to point out, an advanced microprocessor chip costing $20 today has the power of a computer that cost $15 million years ago.

Moreover, computer technology can be expected to become continually more cost-effective as microprocessor designers find ways to cram more and more information on a single chip. Earlier, . . . Hewlett-Packard Co.'s desktop computer division used optical lithography to make a computer chip that has a staggering 450,000 transistors built into it. And at AT&T's Bell Laboratories, materials scientists are now working with photoresist coating materials that, they believe, will permit the production of an integrated circuit that contains 1 million components or more.

For business, the most important result of the dramatic change in the price/performance ratio of computing power has been the spread of computer-based applications to virtually every nook and cranny of the office. Howard Frank, a well-known data-communications expert who is president of Network Analysis Corp., describes it as a kind of chain reaction, with one trend leading to another.

Source: Reprinted from p. 66 of "Technology: A Price/Performance Game," with the special permission of *Dun's Review*, August 1981, Copyright 1981, Dun & Bradstreet Publications Corporation.

"What hath Babbage wrought?" This quotation is seen on the walls of many computer rooms; and there was a time when some people wondered if the technological marvels called computers, which sprang from years of improvements on Charles Babbage's crude "analytical engines," were indeed a boon or a curse to mankind. As we've just seen, today computers are an important part in the lives of most of us. There are computers ranging in size from small hand-held models to those large enough to fill a complete floor of a large office building. And their price tags go from a few hundred to several million dollars. They're used in almost all aspects of business and government; wherever large amounts of data and information must be handled, a computer will generally be found doing the work.

WHAT IS A COMPUTER?

A simple definition of a **computer** is that it's an electronic machine that can assemble and store

data, perform arithmetic functions on data, and manipulate and report data for use in making decisions. It does all this by virtue of being told to do so—that is, by being programmed. Perhaps most amazingly, a computer can perform only two arithmetic procedures: addition and subtraction. No matter what the computer is instructed to do, it accomplishes the task with these two basic arithmetic operations. For example, in deciding which number in a series comes first, the computer uses subtraction and tests the result for positive or negative signs and then orders the numbers accordingly.

Basic Computer Functions

Despite the major role computers play in today's business world, the functions they perform are extremely simple. Whether the computer is actively involved with controlling the space shuttle at NASA, writing stockholders' dividend checks at AT&T, or keeping track of airline reservations for

Micro chip technology has revolutionized the computer industry. This dime sized 32 bit chip contains almost 150,000 transistors.

American Airlines, it performs only four simple functions: (1) arithmetic computation, (2) logical transfer, (3) program control, and (4) storage.

Arithmetic Computations The computer has the capability of performing the **arithmetic operations** of addition, subtraction, multiplication, and division. All these computations are accomplished by adding and subtracting data even though the user's instructions might be to multiply or divide. These computations are done by the central processing unit of the computer using the binary number system, which is explained more fully in a later section of this chapter.

Logical Transfers The computer can perform logical tests, and in this sense it's a decision-making tool. By using sets of instructions, the computer can compare pieces of data and "decide" what's required. The computer processes this decision by using its arithmetic computing power, and if the sign of the result is positive, it takes one course of action; if the sign is negative, another course is taken. This selection process is known as **logical transfer** of activity.

Program Control The computer is controlled by a predefined set of instructions called a *program*. The computer cannot perform any activity until the operator tells it what to do. The program performs this function.

Storage Capacity: Memory Computers are capable of storing large amounts of data until they're needed for processing. Two types of storage exist with most computers. The **main memory** is called **core** and is a part of the central processing unit of the computer. **Auxiliary storage** or **secondary storage** is used for data to be utilized at a later time. The most common secondary storage devices are magnetic tapes and magnetic disks. For example, your transcript of grades at college is updated at the end of each semester. If all students' transcripts were stored in the main memory, much of the processing space would be wasted. Since transcript records are needed only occasionally, it's more economical to store them on tape or disk until they're needed, at which time they are brought back into the central processing unit. This kind of procedure is used by Federated Department Stores and similar retailers in preparing customer bills and updating their current status.

Phases of Current Computer Technology

The computers used by business today are the result of major evolutionary stages in hardware design called *generations*. Most computer authorities identify four generations of computer development.

The First Generation The time period for the first generation of computers extended from the introduction of UNIVAC I (1951) to the late 1950s. The UNIVAC I was the first commercially

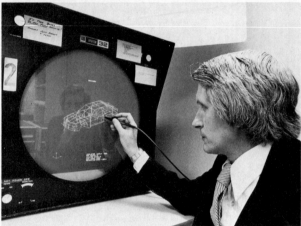

The use of computers is commonplace in many aspects of business today. The few shown here are (top left) airline reservations, (top right) stock trading, (bottom left) textile manufacturing, and (bottom right) automobile design.

produced electronic computer. The technology of these computers featured vacuum tube circuitry, limited main storage, and slow input-output response. The machines were large, and the heat generated by the vacuum tubes caused many problems with maintenance. Programming was done in machine language, and very little applications software was available. Computers in use during this time were machines like the UNIVAC I and IBM's RAMAC 305 and 650.

The Second Generation   Lasting from the late 1950s to the mid-1960s, the second generation of computers introduced solid-state components using transistors and diodes to replace the heat-producing vacuum tubes. The processing speeds increased along with input and output response times. Both the size of the units and the amount of generated heat were reduced by the solid-state circuitry. These improvements led to greater reli-

ability and fewer maintenance problems. High-level programming languages such as FORTRAN and COBOL emerged, and vendors began to supply useful software packages. A prime example of a second-generation machine was the IBM 1401.

The Third Generation   The third generation of computers came into existence on April 7, 1964 with the announcement of the IBM 360 computer system. The computers of the third generation feature greater speed, versatility, reliability, and performance. The technology of these computers uses integrated circuitry and results in much smaller physical size. The period has seen the development of computer "families" that consist of many different hardware devices allowing a business to customize its computer design exactly to its needs. Widespread development and use of applications software packages and time-sharing computer applications have taken place.

TALKING BUSINESS

With this console I thee wed, or so it goes in California's Silicon Valley, where for $6 the Rev. Apple, the electronic pastor, will join a young couple in programmed matrimony.

A Universal Life Minister, Ron Jaenisch, came up with the idea for a computer wedding program for deaf people and discovered that the Universal Life Church would ordain a computer "the same way they ordain anything else." The ceremony has become somewhat of a novelty for couples who met through their work with computers, and six of them have exchanged electronic vows in the last eight months [March–October 1981].

"The first couple had nothing to do with computers," the Rev. Mr. Jaenisch said. "He drove a tow-truck and was an hour late for the ceremony because he wanted to work overtime. But the second couple was very involved with computers. They even asked for a printout of the ceremony."

The ceremony differs very little from the traditional wedding. The computer, a model made by Apple Computer Inc., does not understand the concept "I do" so the couple must type "yes" in response to the vows.

The most recent computer nuptials were last weekend for Ernie and Nickie Lunsford (he services the power supply for the computers in her company). "We just thought it was unique," Mr. Lunsford said. "And we were used to dealing with machines all the time. It was nice with our friends all gathered around the console, and someone brought champagne." Mr. Lunsford insists that his life is not all chips and disks.

"Part of our vow was never to buy a home computer," he said. "We have to get away from machines sometime."

Source: "In the Silicon Valley, a Computer Ties the Knot," *New York Times,* October 11, 1981, p. 23. © 1981 by The New York Times Company. Reprinted by permission.

A Fourth Generation? Many people believe a fourth generation of computer systems has begun. They feel that the mid-1970s marked the beginning of the fourth generation, although no major computer technology was announced at that time, unlike the beginning of the other generations. However certain changes have occurred that cause observers to feel a fourth generation is evolving.

For one thing, many computer systems are using large-scale circuitry, resulting in far better performance of the storage and processing functions. The age of microelectronics that allows tiny silicon chips to contain thousands of circuits has led to lowered cost and widespread use of minicomputers and microcomputers. Secondly, the period has also seen more user involvement with computer systems through the use of terminals and on-line processing. As Steve Jobs, one of the founders of Apple Computer, likes to point out, this new era is characterized by a personal relationship between a user and his or her computer. Indeed, since prices of personal computers have fallen so drastically, there's a good likelihood that in the future each of us will have our own computer as we now might have our own radio or television set.

WHAT IS A COMPUTER SYSTEM?

A computer system consists of components that perform five basic functions: (1) input of data, (2)

ON THE FIRING LINE

Privacy—Victim of Computerized Progress?

Not long ago, computers were so huge and costly that only a few of the richest public and private agencies could afford them. Now almost everybody can. Legally or illegally, almost everybody can gain access to large computer data banks too. We must act quickly, some people insist, to make laws preventing government and private enterprise from gaining too much access to our private lives.

Others believe that information gathering and sharing is vital to our progress and security. They say we must be willing to give up some privacy to improve the quality of our life and live in relative peace and harmony. A look at three spheres of activity—education, medicine, and security and law enforcement—quickly reveals the dilemma that modern techniques of data storage create.

Education. In a school system of any size, a computer offers great savings in time and money. Student profiles and academic records are easily stored in computers. So, too, are test results. Computerization provides swift access to these records when needed to chart student progress and map out future programs. Computerized records also aid educational research by making it easy to identify student populations with certain common characteristics. Research of this sort is the basis for developing new and better ways to teach.

Yet as more and more data on students are stored, students' rights—to privacy and individuality as well as to learn—are more gravely endangered. The results of achievement, attitudinal, psychological, and personality tests may be made available without their knowledge to potential employers, government officers, or researchers. Mistakes they've made, academic failures they've overcome, and ideas, activities, and attitudes they've long since given up may be attributed to them for the rest of their lives.

Medicine. In medicine, too, banking data in massive computer systems is problematic. Access to personal medical histories is considered essential to research, but requiring patient consent to gain access to records could make most research impossible. Research is often historical. It takes place when the patients have long since left the area where they were treated. In many cases, consent can no longer be obtained. Yet people suffer when their medical records aren't kept confidential. Notations in them are often speculative, not fact. Moreover one recent survey indicates an error rate of over 20 percent in complex hospital charts.

As a recent government report states, access to medical records—which may include intimate personal and family histories—is less controlled than ever before. Government agencies obtain personal medical records in order to determine appropriate welfare benefits and as an aid in law enforcement. Personnel managers, too, frequently make decisions based in part on medical records. And just about anyone can obtain medical records simply by impersonating a doctor or nurse—an all-too-common practice.

Security and Law Enforcement. Through computers, police and other security officers have instant access to arrest and conviction records, state crime reports, and auto registration information. In hundreds of ways, law enforcement and intelligence officials use computers to give us the best possible protection. To keep their files confidential, they establish codes for access to specific types of information.

Still, there's growing concern that these massive files will be subject to misuse. Private enterprises are pressuring for access to them. They want to use them in hiring decisions and in resolving more run-of-the-mill problems such as plant parking-lot infractions.

Others object, noting first of all that the information stored is not 100 percent accurate. Serious mistakes could be made, they say—mistakes bad enough to ruin innocent people's lives. They also observe that once access to one portion of a system is granted, little stands between the sophisticated user and the other data stored in the system. There are numerous ways to sabotage security measures, break control codes, and gain entry to these systems.

storage of data, (3) control of processing, (4) processing, and (5) output of information. The basic elements of a computer system are hardware and software. Both are essential to operating the computer, but each is a distinct entity.

Computer **hardware** relates to the basic equipment needed to operate the computer system. Hardware includes input devices such as card readers and terminals, processor units, auxiliary storage devices such as tape drives and disk units, and output devices such as printers and terminals. Hardware is the visible part of the computer system and is what one visualizes as an IBM 360/165 or an Amdahl 470.

Software is the set of instructions giving the computer system its capability to perform operations. Software consists of the set of computer programs that direct the computer system, the instructions or **documentation** for the programs, and the machine language appropriate to the particular computer system. The widespread use of video games, such as Warner Communications' Atari or Mattel's Intellivision, are the result of ex-

"IT'S ANALYZED OUR SITUATION THOROUGHLY, AND HAS CONCLUDED THAT OUR BUSINESS DOESN'T NEED A COMPUTER."

tensive software development. While you probably see Pac Man as a fun game to play, a programmer sees it as the application of genius in his or her trade.

Processing Modes

In order to understand better the function of input and output devices, it's necessary to understand how data are submitted for processing. There are three basic processing modes used in data processing: batch mode, on-line mode, and time-sharing.

Batch Mode Processing **Batch processing** is the process of collecting data in similar groups and processing the groups of data. The set of programs that are used to process the data are executed and completed before the programs for another group of data are started. For example, a local building contractor's accounts payable program may call for the submission of payment vouchers in groups of 100 invoices before any processing of the accounts payable system begins. Once started, all 100 invoices then will be processed before another program is begun.

On-Line Mode When a direct link to the computer exists and each transaction is entered as it is received or occurs, the system is operating in an **on-line mode**. On-line processing gives users instant input and retrieval capability. An example of an on-line processing system is an airline reservation system used by American, Delta, and most other carriers. As each call for space on a flight is received, a reservationist enters the data required to book a seat, determines if space is available, and immediately issues a confirmation of the reservation or explains that the flight is full and offers to make alternative travel arrangements. The on-line system gives the reservationist up-to-the-second information and saves the traveler time and worry.

Time-Sharing **Time-sharing** occurs when many users are connected to the same computer; each user pays only for the time used. The unique feature of time-sharing is that the user terminals may be hundreds of miles from the main computer, but through time-sharing many users can share the cost of an expensive computer system.

You most likely have access to your university's computer through time-sharing arrangements.

Input-Output Devices

Several basic input and output media are used by computer systems. The most common input devices are card readers, magnetic tape, magnetic disk, and terminals.

Card Readers The **card reader** is a device used for interpreting the data recorded on punched cards. Punched cards with holes representing data are passed through the reader and automatically read by the electronic impulses caused by the holes in the card. The data recorded in the cards are then put into the main storage unit of the computer. Cards may be used to input data and programs into the computer's memory unit.

Magnetic Tape The **magnetic tape unit** for a computer system works on the same principle as a cassette tape recorder that records music or a lecture in class. Standard data tape for computer-system use is a 1/2-inch-wide strip of mylar with a magnetic coated surface on which data are encoded. Data are recorded onto the tape as magnetic spots, and the tape may be stored for future use. When data are needed for processing, the computer operator uses the read function of the tape drive unit to enter the data into the computer's memory for processing. Magnetic tape may also be used as storage for output information, but this application is less common than its use for inputting data. Many of our tax returns are stored on magnetic tapes and held in the archives of the Internal Revenue Service.

Magnetic Disk The **magnetic disk** is a flat circular plate that has a magnetic surface where data are stored. The data are recorded on the

Magnetic tape and magnetic disks are the most common computer input-output and secondary storage devices.

disk in concentric circles called *tracks*. The disk reader is used for data manipulation on the disk. Magnetic disk units usually employ several disks mounted on a common spindle, and these multiple disk units are called *disk packs*.

Terminals   Terminals are the key to on-line and time-sharing processing systems. A **terminal** is a keyboard device that transmits data to the computer. Two types of terminals are used in computer systems. First is the **hardcopy terminal**, which is essentially a typewriter with ability to communicate with a computer. As data are entered, the terminal types out on paper what's being sent to the computer. The **CRT (cathode ray tube) terminal** performs the same function, but the data being put into the computer are displayed on a screen similar to a television screen. Terminals in an on-line processing mode are also used as output devices that print or display information requested by the user.

The output media used by various computer systems depend heavily on how information being returned by the processing unit will be used. Many of the same devices used as input devices are also used as output devices. These input-output devices are punched cards, magnetic tapes, magnetic disks, and terminals—all of which we've already examined.

However one device that's used exclusively for producing output is the printer. Printers produce printed copies of reports, forms, and schedules containing information developed by processing a particular computer program. Reports generated by the computer system printer might include financial statements, accounts receivable listings, vendor checks, and W-2 forms for employees. Some modern computer system printers are extremely fast. For example the IBM 3800 Laser printer uses an image-producing technology allowing it to produce up to 20,040 lines per minute!

Operating System

The **operating system** is a group of programs that the computer system uses to supervise its own operations. The operating system is used because many applications require the ability to run more than one program at a time. The operating system uses three types of programs: control programs, compiler programs, and data management programs.

Control programs supervise and schedule the computer resources used in processing. They provide the automatic control of the computer system and allow for handling of multiple programs without intervention by a computer operator. **Compiler programs** are used to translate the program codes of the programming languages into machine language. The machine language is transferred to the main memory of the computer for use in processing data. The organization and the access of data used in processing are controlled by **data management programs,** which open, update, and close files that store data and processing programs. These programs prevent the computer from having to develop the file structure for every data entry.

Central Processing Unit (CPU)   The **central processing unit (CPU)** is the controller of the computer system. The CPU is part of the computer hardware that stores data and does computational processing. It decodes instructions and performs calculations and logical transfers of data according to the program. The CPU contains the **arithmetic logic unit (ALU)** and the main memory. The ALU is the electronic circuitry of the central processor that performs arithmetic operations of addition, subtraction, multiplication, and division. The ALU also performs the logical comparisons used in sorting and ordering the numbers.

The *main memory* is the part of the CPU where data and instructions are stored. The main memory can store letters, numbers, and special characters. Memory is passive and is used by the CPU to process data. Everything that enters or is retrieved from memory is under the control of the CPU. Both programs and data must be in main memory before data processing can take place. Figure 22.1 shows a diagram of the components of a computer system.

The basic storage unit is called a **bit**, and computer designers have developed a coding scheme of grouping bits into units called **bytes** that are used to represent numbers and letters.

The power of a computer is often measured by the amount of storage space in the main memory. The letter K, which symbolizes the basic storage unit, consists of 1,024 bytes. The expression "256K memory" would therefore mean a storage

COMPONENTS OF A COMPUTER SYSTEM

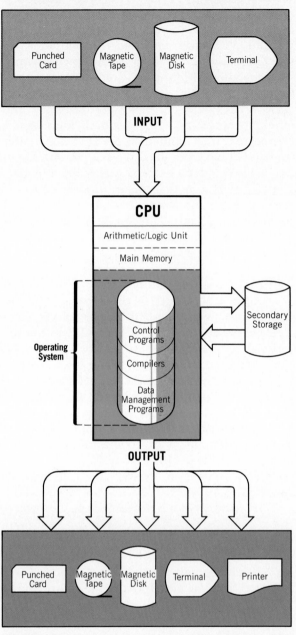

FIGURE 22.1

Decimal Number	Binary Number
1	00001
2	00010
4	00100
8	01000
16	10000
•	•
•	•

and so forth

To form other numbers:

3	00011 which is 2 + 1
5	00101 which is 4 + 1
14	01110 which is 8 + 4 + 2

FIGURE 22.2
The Binary Number System

to form whatever number we want. For example, the number 106 is simply (10 × 10) plus 6. Since the electronic circuit of a computer can have only two positions—*on* or *off*—the computer uses a counting system that's a combination of only two numbers: 1 (*on*) and 0 (*off*). Figure 22.2 shows how this two-number or **binary number system** is used to form all other numbers. Notice carefully that moving the number 1 one place to the left increases the previous value by a multiple of two.

Communicating with the Computer

Communicating with a computer is accomplished through coded instructions called *programs*. The computer requires two types of programs in order to process data: **Job control programs** and **applications programs**. Both of these program types require coding in symbols and characters that the computer can understand. These sets of symbols are called **programming languages**.

Job Control Language (JCL) Job control language (JCL) is the instructions linking the operating system to the applications programs. JCL defines the order and the procedure for processing jobs submitted to the computer system. JCL will differ from one computer system to another since each computer manufacturer generally has some unique features in the operating system used on its computers. Nevertheless JCL has the same basic purpose in all operating systems: it permits the computer to be automatic in its execution of jobs.

capacity of 262,144 bytes. A small personal computer might have as little as 8K capacity, while Cray Research's supercomputer, the CRAY 1, has 5000K (referred to as 5 megabytes).

The Binary Number System Computers count differently than we do. Our counting system—the decimal system—combines ten different numbers

Applications Programming Languages Applications programming languages are problem oriented and are called **high-level languages**. In high-level languages a single statement may be equivalent to several machine instructions. The programming languages increase the efficiency and productivity of computer programmers. The most common high-level languages are FORTRAN, COBOL, BASIC, PL/1, and APL. Certain other new high-level languages are also evolving. A brief description of each of the major high-level languages is given in Table 22.1.

Unquestionably, the single most important factor bringing use of the computer to the individual is the development of **"friendly" languages**— that is, having a system of communicating with the computer that can be learned in a very short period of time. The creation of business application programs by Visicorp (developers of Visi-Calc) that were adaptable to the Apple computer gave Apple an important early edge in the small computer market segment. Eventually, VisiCalc programs were made adaptable to other small computers, but by then, Apple was a market leader.

DATA PROCESSING

Data processing activity is an essential element of the management information system. The simple accumulation of data is of little use to a business. For data to be useful to the managers of the business, it must be assembled, classified, and reported in a way that provides assistance in the decision-making process.

TABLE 22–1
The Major High-Level Programming Languages

FORTRAN   The FORTRAN language was introduced by IBM in 1957 and is short for *FOR*mula *TRAN*slation. The language allows programmers to write processing instructions in formula format. FORTRAN was introduced primarily as a scientific language for use by scientists, mathematicians, and engineers; but it gained fairly wide acceptance for use in business.

COBOL   COBOL means *CO*mmon *B*usiness *O*riented *L*anguage and was designed for use in solving problems common to business. COBOL is a user-developed language introduced in 1960. It relies on the use of an English-like format and eliminates much of the troublesome algebraic notation on which FORTRAN is based.

BASIC   BASIC language is the standard language of time-sharing applications and the microcomputers like the Apple and the TRS-80. BASIC is an acronym for *B*eginners *A*ll-purpose *S*ymbolic *I*nstruction *C*ode and was developed at Dartmouth College for use in academic computing applications. The language is easily learned and widely used for on-line interactive computer applications.

PL/1   This language was developed by IBM for use as a general purpose language with applications to both business and scientific programming. PL/1 is an extremely powerful and flexible language but hasn't been readily accepted by the business community since it doesn't have many advantages over COBOL.

APL   A language developed in the 1970s that combines the needs of both scientific and business applications is *A P*rogrammer's *L*anguage (APL). APL is a simple language with many features that make it extremely useful for terminal input and output applications. The language hasn't gained widespread use in business but has been used mainly for its power and brevity in scientific applications.

New Languages   Two new languages that were developed in the late 1970s are PASCAL and ADA. PASCAL was named for the French mathematician Blaise Pascal. The language was developed for scientific applications and has gained much acceptance in computer science. PASCAL has limited input/output capability but handles complex data quite easily. PASCAL's suitability for business problems has yet to be evaluated. ADA is a derivation of PASCAL and is named for Lady Ada Augusta Lovelace, an important 19th-century computing pioneer. ADA was developed under contracts issued by the Defense Department and went into use in early 1980. ADA is more flexible in its input/output capability and some observers feel ADA will gain more acceptance in business than has PASCAL.

PERSPECTIVE ON SMALL BUSINESS

One of Dan Bricklin's Harvard professors scoffed at his idea for a new microcomputer program. And when his partner and longtime friend, Bob Frankston, tried to sell it to a couple of experts at the National Computer Conference in 1979, they walked away. But industry analyst Ben Rosen thought the program, called Visi-Calc—for "visible calculator"—had potential. It would allow business executives to work up complicated budget forecasts with comparative ease. In his widely read "Electronics Letter," Rosen wrote, "VisiCalc could someday be the software tail that wags (and sells) the personal-computer dog."

Rosen was never more right. Bricklin, 30, and Frankston, 32, have adapted VisiCalc to every major personal computer on the market—and in two years they have sold more than 200,000 copies. Their program pushed computers out of the realm of hobbyists and onto office desks, and their Cambridge, Mass., company, Software Arts, now has more than $3 million in annual sales. Its success has inspired a host of competing products, dubbed "visiclones" and "calcalikes."

Bricklin's idea for an electronic "spreadsheet" came to him in 1978 as he gazed at a blackboard during a class at Harvard Business School. His professors had sketched out columns of mock budget variables, and each time they changed a figure they had to laboriously recalculate several others. Bricklin, an MIT graduate, decided he could design a computer program that would do all the work instantly. He coaxed Frankston, another MIT man

who was doing some work for a tiny software-publishing company run by Daniel Fylstra, into tinkering with his rough draft. Frankston mentioned the project to Fylstra.

Fylstra's only big seller in 1978 was a chess game. Envisioning a home-budget system that would expand his catalog, he agreed to market VisiCalc. "VisiCalc didn't sound too great," Frankston recalls, but it seemed superior to their other ideas, such as Electropage and Calculedger. And in fact, the name has proved to be a stroke of genius. Fylstra now sells programs called VisiPlot, VisiFile and VisiDex, and [in February 1981] he changed the name of his company, now located in San Jose, Calif., from Personal Software, Inc., to VisiCorp.

Bricklin and Frankston are planning an expansion of their own. This summer they will move into bigger quarters in an old chocolate factory, and they are debugging a new program they hope to market later this year. All they will say about the new product is that it might be useful in education, as well as business. Skeptics are already wondering if they can repeat their success—or, for that matter, if they can manage the huge business they now have on their hands. But such questions may miss the mark: with VisiCalc, Bricklin and Frankston have already secured a niche in the folklore of the microcomputer industry.

SOURCE: Frank Gibney, Jr., "The Tail That Wags the Dog," *Newsweek*, February 22, 1982, p. 55. Copyright 1982 by Newsweek, Inc. All rights reserved. Reprinted by permission.

Designing the System

To use the computer effectively, a business must design and install a system that employs the computer and other resources at its disposal. A **system** is a collection of equipment, people, and methods used to perform a specific task. As an illustration, both IBM and Xerox believe there's enormous po-

tential for an **executive work station.** This refers to a system that enables a manager to perform a wide variety of tasks through the use of a desktop terminal linked to a computer. For example, by using a joy-stick, a manager can move a pointer to a file folder on the screen, then move the file folder to a file cabinet (also shown on the screen), and then execute a command that will file the

The Xerox 8010 Star information system is a type of executive work station that allows business professionals to create, modify, store and retrieve text, graphics and records.

folder.[1] There are many other tasks managers can perform without ever leaving their desks.

Desired Output The primary concern of the systems designer must be with who uses the system. The system must be designed with the user's needs in mind, and the designer must ask the user what information is needed to do the job effectively. Outputs are then developed to meet those requirements.

Necessary Inputs Once output requirements are developed, the designer must determine the input data needed to generate the desired output information. The designer must also decide how input will be entered into the system. The time requirement of the user will help the designer to decide if batch or on-line processing is needed. After the input requirements are defined, the collection procedures, collection forms, and input devices are determined and designed.

Computational Requirements Defining the computational requirements involves the designer in developing the way in which data will be stored by the computer and what the processing procedures will be. The **file design** is a critical step in the system design. This step tells the computer where to put data for processing. The file design determines what data will be stored in main memory and which auxiliary storage devices will be used.

Processing is controlled by applications programs. The necessary programs for making required computations are designed, usually by using flowcharts. A **flowchart** is a diagram that graphically shows the steps needed to complete the required processing. The programs controlling the computation by the computer are coded into a programming language by following the steps shown on the flowcharts. The programs are stored in the computer's memory until they are required to process information needed by various users.

A College Registration System Illustrated

A typical application of the computer is the college registration process. Because it is repeated many times during the enrollment period and the registrar needs up-to-date information about student status and closed classes, a computer-based system is ideal. The procedure is described below and in the flowchart shown in Figure 22.3.

The student begins the process by checking the schedule of classes for the semester and filling out a trial schedule. The trial schedule is then reviewed for completeness and accuracy and eventually given to a terminal operator.

The operator keys the student number into the CPU, which accesses the student identification file and compares the student number with the student's status record. If the student's status isn't current, the operator instructs the student what action must be taken to establish current enrollment status. If the student's status is current, the operator enters the trial schedule. The computer accesses the class records for each class and sends a message back to the operator's terminal as to whether or not the classes are open and the student can be accepted. If any classes are closed, the student is instructed to choose replacements for the closed classes.

When the student's course schedule is complete, the operator enters any changes to the stu-

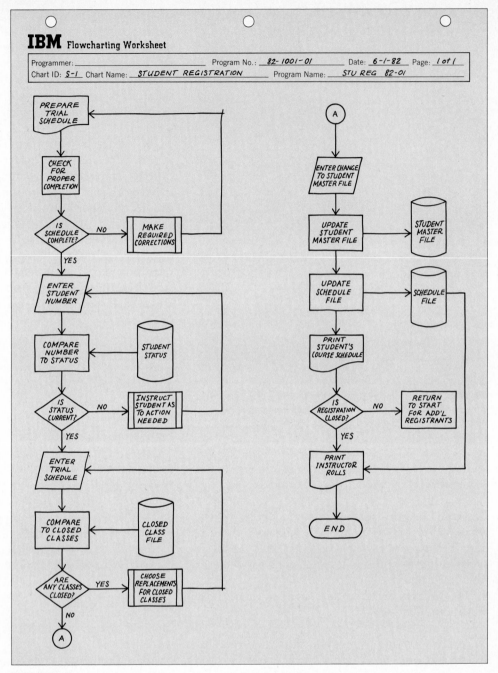

FIGURE 22.3

dent's master file so that a new master file will be correct when enrollment for the next semester begins. Also, the student schedule file is updated in order to reflect the student's enrollment in each of his or her classes. After all corrections and the course schedule are entered, the computer pro-

gram instructs the printer to print out the course schedule for the student. At the close of registration, the program instructs the printer to print class rolls for both instructors and other administrators who need them. The registration process is then terminated.

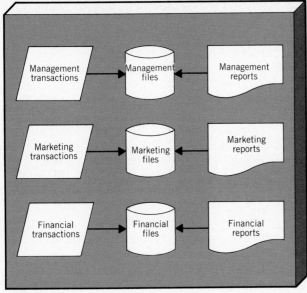

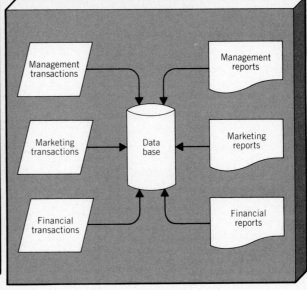

FIGURE 22.4

BUSINESS USE OF COMPUTERS AND DATA PROCESSING

Computers have been instrumental in improving the managerial control of business operations. The computer's capacity for storing and manipulating large amounts of data about business transactions permits managers to receive more information in the areas under their control. Instead of a slow, out-of-date, manually prepared report, the computer can be programmed to produce up-to-the-minute reports showing not only those specific activities they are responsible for, but indicating also the indirect consequences of their decisions. For example, if the credit manager of a local department store increases customer requirements for credit acceptance, this action would lead most likely to fewer credit customers and so to lower credit sales. While the credit manager can reduce bad debts in this way, the reduced profit resulting from fewer sales may be much greater than the reduction in bad debts. By seeing the overall impact of decisions such as this, management gains more effective control of the business.

The computer and its auxiliary storage devices have the ability to perform file maintenance by storing, locating, and retrieving large amounts of information about business transactions. For example, a BASF 1253 disk pack contains 11 disks and is capable of storing 300 million characters of data—and it costs only $1100. With low-cost auxiliary storage, a company can maintain more extensive files covering its operations. The company can also obtain rapid data access, allowing it to prepare analytical reports quickly and economically. File maintenance has led to a concept known as **data base management,** which means that the various functional areas of a business all have access to the same basic sources of data. Figure 22.4 shows a simplified representation of the traditional file structure and the alternative data base file structure.

The business applications of computers and data processing can be described best as they relate to key functional areas of the firm—manage-

TALKING BUSINESS

It's annual meeting season—the time of year for companies to show off their skills in handling shareholders and staying out of trouble.

At American Telephone & Telegraph Co., that's done partly with a computerized system called "Oz." It helps the chairman rattle off the most obscure statistics to answer annual meeting questions. Shareholders entering special phone booths to pose questions are asked in advance what they have on their minds. Then three "wizards"—technicians who operate Oz—call up pertinent information on a computer and flash it on a screen in front of the chairman. They can now call up any of about 200 pages of information in half a second—down from three and a half seconds three years ago [in 1979].

Sometimes even Oz is stumped. The wizards then flash "no answer available" on the screen.

ment, marketing, finance/accounting. Some of these applications are discussed below.

Management Applications

The computer has proved to be a powerful tool for aiding the managerial decision process. It has enabled managers to use sophisticated decision processes without the need for long and tedious clerical activity.

Personnel One of the first computer applications made by a company is in personnel: the payroll system is generally the first procedure to be computerized. This payroll system is used to produce payroll checks, keep payroll records, prepare payroll reports for the Internal Revenue Service, and issue W-2 forms to employees. Most payroll systems can accomplish these tasks quickly, privately, and accurately. Another personnel application is the human resources inventory, which keeps a record of the skills, training, experience, and development of all company employees. This inventory aids the manager in making promotion and compensation decisions.

Production and Inventory Control Computers have been used by companies to control produc-

tion processes and operations. Many manufacturing operations have been put under computer control, with the computer programmed to monitor production and correct machine settings, thereby avoiding delays in the production process.

General Electric has perhaps the most advanced version of automation in the workplace with its "Factory of the Future." This concept is an attempt to link separate islands of automation in the factory into an integrated network, thus producing a truly automated factory. GE believes the linchpin to the whole scheme is a "data highway" that will tie together the various parts through process control, numeric control, and other controls. Of course, computers play a crucial role in the "data highway."

Inventory control systems have been developed to provide an evaluation of inventory levels. By using on-line computer processing, inventory managers can control inventory more effectively. They can make sure that customer orders are quickly and correctly filled and that inventory cost is minimized by eliminating excess or unnecessary purchases that lead to excessive inventories.

Scheduling Operations-research techniques employing computers help managers control resources at their disposal. Scheduling techniques,

The growing importance of computerized inventory control is highlighted in the text of this Sperry-Univac ad.

as described in Chapter 10, determine where and when workers, materials, and machines are needed and in what quantities. Sophisticated scheduling techniques such as PERT or CPM (described in Chapter 10) depend almost exclusively on computer availability since they deal with many variables and huge amounts of data.

Marketing Applications

Marketing information systems provide the information needed for servicing customers in the most effective manner. These systems provide data for decisions about prices, promotion, and distribution.

Pricing While prices are determined by the market forces of supply and demand, nevertheless in the long run a company must establish prices that cover costs and make an adequate profit. So the marketing information system must report the total costs of selling each product. The pricing program must take note of sales volume, competition in various sales territories, and production costs. The marketing manager then uses these data to make decisions about the product price, promotion, and distribution channels. Considering that many companies produce and sell hundreds — and even thousands — of products in markets throughout the world, the usefulness of the computer in making profit evaluations for each product, or market, can be greatly appreciated. In fact, in its absence managers more often than

not guess at which products (or markets) produce profit and which ones do not.

Promotion and Distribution The computer has become a priceless tool in evaluating promotional activities and distribution channels. With respect to the former, management must be in a position to decide whether its advertising media mix is optimal: are maximum sales being generated from the advertising budget? Testing various media combinations and evaluating the results require substantial data analysis that would be almost impossible without computer assistance.

In addition to evaluating promotional activities, other computer models have been developed to aid in the selection of new products or expansion into new market areas. Most of these models are based on statistical analysis of data provided by the marketing information system. Market research models are used to develop mailing lists and to perform statistical surveys for new product introduction. Many products are introduced using a mailing scheme developed through a computer analysis of large data bases such as zip code listings.

Finance/Accounting Applications

Financial applications of the computer are used to assist in the processing of accounting data and the development of planning data. Common applications are available for recording data and preparing financial statements.

TALKING BUSINESS

Computer jobs are going begging because not enough people have the necessary skills, and the demand for those with training is expected to increase 50% by 1990.

Beyond all the jobs in manufacturing, programming, operating and servicing computers, the need is great for people who can sell the machines and teach others to use them. Computer salesmen typically earn $40,000 compared with an average of $34,000 for salesmen who sell other products to industry. Out-of-work schoolteachers, after some retooling, are finding jobs training employees at companies that use computers, while publishers and computer makers are hiring writers to turn technical gibberish into readable instruction manuals.

Opportunities abound for entrepreneurs too. For instance, two salesmen of electronic office equipment, noting how noisy computer printers are, started a company that makes soundproofing cabinets. The firm, Vitech of Hopkins, Minn., posted sales of $1 million in 1981, its first year.

Paying Bills Automatic processing of vendor invoices and check writing are commonly one of the first computer applications made by the firm. The accounts payable system is designed to help maintain good relationships with suppliers, pay bills on time, take discounts for prompt payment, and maintain appropriate financial controls.

Collections The accounts receivable application of the computer involves preparing invoices to bill customers for sales made on credit. The system also provides information for use in collecting outstanding debts. For example, a report called an *accounts receivable aging schedule* is developed from billing and collections data. This report shows the amount due from each account classified by the length of time the debt has been outstanding. Often linked to this procedure is a program that produces statements and reminder letters that are sent to customers.

Budgeting Budgeting and planning systems are usually based on models that simulate future operations of the company. These models use simple equations to represent product demand, production, sales, operating costs, and other facts about the company. Company managers make different assumptions about each of these segments and then enter data into the computer model. The computer model processes the data and reports possible outcomes from the various alternative actions.

The big advantage of computer simulation is its ability to examine a wide variety of assumptions and to make sure all parts of the corporate model are integrated logically with each other. For example, if the sales manager believes (assumes) sales will increase 10 percent in the next period, then areas such as inventory control and production must respond accordingly, or the sales target may not be reached. Many corporations use company models and simulation; for example, Dayton Power and Light Company (a public utility in southwestern Ohio) has an extensive corporate model that assists its management in planning output capacity to satisfy customer demand. The very long lead times required in constructing generating capacity make effective planning all the more crucial.

THE FUTURE OF COMPUTERS

The business computer industry is, by most standards, an infant industry. Born in 1951, it has made remarkable technological advances. Computer hardware costs have declined significantly and productivity has increased many fold. A *Computerworld* magazine advertisement expresses it best: "If the auto industry had done what the computer industry has done in the last 30 years, a Rolls-Royce would cost $2.50 and get 2,000,000 miles per gallon."[2] According to leading market research firms, the computer industry will continue to grow, and shipments should top $42 billion by 1984. In addition, certain segments of the market should grow even faster. For example, the expected annual growth rate for computer graphics will be a healthy 35 percent through 1987; and the use of data communications terminals should grow sixfold by 1990. These observations by leading market analysts are representative of the enthusiasm generally felt about the future of the computer industry. What will the fifth generation of computers bring? Some trends seem to be emerging.

Computers of the future will most likely move away from the large mainframe central processing units. Computers will be smaller, more compact, yet more powerful and versatile. As we noted earlier, the smaller computers will be distributed throughout the company and tied together with data communication linkages, such as GE's "data highway." These smaller computers will be more user oriented, and users will be able to program their own applications. The systems are likely to provide on-line processing with input and output occurring on CRT terminals.

Advances in electronic components technology that lead to smaller size will also lead to lower cost of computer power. Large markets for smaller, lower-cost systems will induce computer manufacturers to meet the demand for lower-cost systems by developing appropriate technology, which, if the future is like the last 30 years, will not be at the expense of productivity but rather will be accompanied by productivity gains.

For example, a new technology called **cryoelectronic memories** is currently in the development stage and seems very promising for the future. These memories would operate at temperatures close to absolute zero ($-269°$ Celsius) and use up to 1000 times less power than semiconductor units. Heat problems are almost eliminated, and circuits can be further compacted to reduce size while speed is increased enormously in comparison to existing systems.

Perhaps even more intriguing than cryoelectronics is the effort of some researchers to use genetic engineering to produce strains of bacteria that actually could be used as memories. If this succeeds, the cost of memory would fall drastically and be virtually free.

SUMMARY

Defined simply, a computer is an electronic machine that can assemble and store data, perform arithmetic functions on data, and manipulate and report data for use in decision making. Interestingly, it can perform only two arithmetic procedures—addition and subtraction.

Although the functions computers perform are simple, they are carried out at extremely high speed. All computerized applications are accomplished by use of four basic functions—arithmetic computation, logical transfer, program control, and storage capacity.

The first commercially produced electronic computer was the UNIVAC I. Most computer authorities identify four generations of computer development since the UNIVAC I was introduced in 1951.

A computer system's components perform five basic functions: input of data, storage of data, control of processing, processing, and output of information. The basic elements of a computer system are hardware and software. Data are submitted to the computer for processing in three ways: through the batch mode, the on-line mode, and time-sharing. The most common input devices are card readers, magnetic tapes, magnetic disks, and terminals. Many of the same devices are used for output—punched cards, magnetic tapes, magnetic disks, and terminals. One device that's used only to produce output is the printer.

The operating system is a group of programs the computer system uses to supervise its own operations. This sytem utilizes three types of programs—control programs, compiler programs, and data management programs.

The central processing unit (CPU), the controller of the computer system, contains the arithmetic logic unit (ALU) and the main memory. To store data electronically, the memories of most modern computer systems use the binary number system.

Communicating with a computer is accomplished through programs. Two types of programs are required—job control programs and applications programs. Job control language (JCL) links the operating system to the applications programs, which usually are written in high-level, problem oriented programming languages. Major high-level languages include FORTRAN, COBOL, BASIC, PL/1, APL, PASCAL, and ADA.

The role of the computer system in data processing is to receive data from input devices, process it, and report the results as useful information in the output form the user wants. Thus the designer of such a system must be concerned with desired output, necessary inputs, and computational requirements.

Computers and data processing systems can be applied to all the key functional areas of the firm. In management, applications include personnel, production and inventory control, and scheduling. In marketing, information on pricing, promotion, and distribution, and market research can be provided. Finance and accounting applications include uses in paying bills, making collections, and budgeting.

The business computer industry has made remarkable technological advances and is expected to continue to grow. Computers of the future will probably be smaller, more powerful, more versatile, less expensive, and more user oriented. In addition, many further interesting technological innovations seem likely.

KEY TERMS

applications program
arithmetic logic unit
  (ALU)
arithmetic operations
auxiliary storage
batch processing
binary number system
bit
byte
card reader
central processing
  unit (CPU)
compiler program
computer
control program
core
CRT (cathode ray
  tube) terminal
cryoelectronic
  memories

data base management
data management
  program
data processing
documentation
executive work station
file design
flowchart
"friendly" languages
hardcopy terminal
hardware
high-level languages
job control language
  (JCL)
job control program
logical transfer
magnetic disk
magnetic tape unit
main memory
on-line mode
operating system
programming
  language
secondary storage
software
system
terminal
time-sharing

REVIEW QUESTIONS

1. Describe a computer and list its four basic functions.
2. Briefly describe the evolution of the four generations of computers.
3. What are the five basic functions of a computer system's components?
4. What do the terms *hardware*, *software*, *time-sharing*, and *CRT* mean in computer terminology?
5. Describe the various input and output devices used in computer systems.
6. How does the binary number system differ from a decimal system? Illustrate how the number 209 would be written in the binary system.
7. What languages do programmers and operators use to communicate with computers? What is meant by a "friendly" language?
8. Describe at least two applications of com-

puters for each of the following areas: management, marketing, and finance/accounting.

DISCUSSION QUESTIONS

1. Do you think computers will replace middle managers?
2. What can computers do that people can't do, and vice versa?
3. Would it be practical for a large retailer, such as J.C. Penney, to have all its customer information stored in the core of its central processing unit? Explain.
4. Describe important considerations that go into the design of a management information system.
5. Why all the interest in computers? What can computers do for business?
6. What will the "factory of the future" be like?
7. How is the computer changing the modern office and business operations? What is the future outlook for computer technology?

CASE: YOUR FRIENDLY COMPUTER

According to Steve Jobs, one of the founders of the now famous Apple Computer, the new generation of computers is characterized by a personal relationship between a user and his or her computer. And since prices of personal computers have fallen so drastically, there's a good likelihood that each of us will have our own computer just as we now have our own radio or television set.

The term "friendly" used with respect to the computer has to do with the development of a simple language system allowing users to communicate with the computer. This "job control language" (JCL) has to do with the instructions linking the operating system to the applications programs, which were adapted to the Apple Computer and gave it an important early edge in the small computer market. Not only have computers been instrumental in improving the managerial control of business operations, but the Apple people have vowed that they're going to put a computer in every home to be used for budgeting, bill paying, keeping the checkbook in balance, electronic funds transfer, and even for computer-assisted instruction providing advanced education at home.

The latest breakthrough is Sears' daring move to place its catalog on video discs, capable of storing up to 54,000 pictures on a side, enabling the customer to go "video disc shopping."

1. Why have prices of personal computers fallen so much? Do you think they'll continue to fall in the future? Explain.
2. If you were to buy a small computer (maybe you already have one) in what ways would you (do you) use it?
3. Discuss some advantages of "Video disc shopping" in comparison to the traditional Sears catalog. What other types of retailers might use this new shopping device?

CASE: COMPUTER BUDDY CHANGES GRADES

The administration now has something more to worry about with its new computerized student records. Students are always trying to beat the system, and this action tops them all.

One of the computer "whiz kids" rigged up a portable computer in his dorm room and then proceeded to break the code to the computer grade bank in the Registrar's office, all by remote control and a Dataphone.

When this student figured out what he had done, he set about to change grades for his friends. What a position to be in: Computer King for a day, with all the power to manipulate the university computer bank.

But the computer didn't come to his rescue when he was arrested and charged with tampering with Government records—which just happens to be a felony. Where was his computer "buddy" now, as he spent the night in jail? No, the jail lock was not on the computer system.

Some say that computers will be taking over our lives before long; still, computers need the help of the bright men and women who love to play computer games.

1. What implications does this incident hold for the use of computers in business?
2. How can a university guard against violations of its computer system by such "whiz kids"?
3. Can computer companies do anything to prevent people from misusing their products?

CAREERS IN ACCOUNTING, COMPUTERS, AND DATA PROCESSING

The accounting function used to occupy a very definite and readily definable position in most businesses, large and small. When the computer revolution began to invade business enterprises, the accountants were quick to assume the responsibility for the computer operations, often located in a computer center; and the accountants used the computers mainly for storing and utilizing accounting information. As computers became more sophisticated, and the accountants proceeded to analyze their services, they discovered that to be cost effective, computers had to encompass more functions if they were to justify their existence. So the accountants reached out to adopt a more comprehensive approach, which they identified as "management information systems."

Management information systems is a very convenient term used to identify the tools for management decision making. This is a functional approach in combining the basic operations of accounting, data processing, and financial controls in a central location to serve related operations for the total organization. This may be called a *computer center*, which may be used to retrieve and store information from many operations for the benefit of managers who need specific information to make decisions.

This total information approach has changed the job descriptions and career categories for many managers and executives. The computer revolution brought about this change in business, and the original thrust of the computers was toward very expensive large computers serving total operations with access of managers through the use of remote terminals and data-phone hookups. It became obvious that only the large corporations could afford such luxuries as these million-dollar computers and strategic computer centers.

Thus only large corporations were able to afford this kind of organizational centralization.

This trend in business and industry was dominated by the large computer manufacturers—IBM, Burroughs, Honeywell, and Sperry Rand, Univac. But other companies decided not to drop out of competiton; and they started another computer revolution that challenged the direction and magnitude of the dominating computer manufacturers. Of course, developments in technology brought about this second revolution, and smaller computers began to pop up in the marketplace. These were indentified as *minicomputers*, and *microcomputers*. Meeting the challenge, even IBM changed its direction and moved back into the small computer competition. Thus these changes in technology and strategy have affected the jobs and careers of managers and executives in most businesses. With the introduction of the smaller computer, small businesses are now able to utilize the information that can be stored in compact computers to be used in the managerial decision-making process. The functions and duties of managers and supervisors at all levels have been affected by this new revolution, and new knowledge and skills are required to handle the complexity of the computerized business organization.

Where the Opportunities Are

1 ◼ ACCOUNTANT

There are over a million accountants working in various positions in the United States and the field is still growing. The Bureau of Labor Statistics predicts that in the next decade, job openings will increase by almost 30 percent. These accountants work in four segments: about 60 percent in industrial accounting, 25 percent in public accounting, 12 percent in government, and 3 percent in education.

Industrial accounting includes management, corporate or internal accounting with positions located in small businesses, large corporations, and multinational corporations. They may have such titles as managerial accountant, which may carry the license designation of Certificate in Management Accounting (CMA); Certified Public Accountant (CPA); internal auditor; tax accountant; staff accountant; controller; vice-president—accounting; treasurer; etc. Another designation for accountants is the Certified Internal Auditor (CIA). These accountants may occupy positions in industry, CPA firms, or governments.

Public accounting offers the most lucrative opportunities. There are over 250,000 CPAs in the U.S., working in the "Big Eight" and other accounting firms located throughout the U.S., and some with international operations. The "Big Eight" firms are Price, Waterhouse & Co.; Arthur Andersen & Co.; Coopers & Lybrand; Haskins & Sells; Peat, Marwick, Mitchell & Co.; Arthur Young & Co.; Ernst & Whinney; and Touche, Ross & Co.

Government accounting positions are available at all levels of government from cities, counties, states, and federal offices. In most cases, these positions carry civil service rank, and advancement in dependent on education and experience.

Accountants may establish businesses of their own, hanging out their shingles as CPAs, tax accountants, or accounting consultants. They may be so successful as to follow the pattern set by Henry Block, who captured a large share of the tax business as H&R Block Income Tax Specialists, with offices all across America.

Minorities, including women, have excellent opportunities for entry into positions as accountants, in public accounting firms, in corporate businesses, and in government jobs. Opportunities do exist; however competition is very keen. Survival is dependent on ability and production—regardless of status, race, sex, etc.

Places of Employment Throughout the country; however most opportunities are in large urban areas.

Skills Required Four-year program. Large accounting firms prefer MBAs.

Employment Outlook thru 1990 Excellent.

Salaries Beginning: $15,000–$19,000; partner in CPA firm: $100,000–$300,000; government accountants: $15,000–$50,000.

2 ■ PROGRAMMER

Programmers usually work from problem descriptions prepared by systems analysts who have carefully studied the task that the computer system is going to perform—perhaps organizing data collected in a survey or estimating the stress on portions of a building during a hurricane. These descriptions contain a detailed list of the steps the computer must follow, such as retrieving data stored in another computer, organizing them in a certain way, and performing the necessary calculations. An applications programmer then writes the specific program for the problem by breaking down each step into a series of coded instructions using one of the languages developed especially for computers.

A business applications programmer developing instructions for billing customers would first take the company records the computer would need and then specify a solution by showing the steps the computer must follow to obtain old balances, add new charges, calculate finance charges, and deduct payments before determining a customer's bill. The programmer then codes the actual instructions the computer will follow in a high-level programming language, such as COBOL.

Next, the programmer tests the operation of the program to be sure the instructions are correct and will produce the desired information. The programmer tries a sample of the data with the program and reviews the results to see if any errors were made. If errors did occur, the program must be changed and rechecked until it produces the correct results. This is called "debugging" the program. Finally, an instruction sheet is prepared for the computer operator who will run the program.

Places of Employment   Throughout the United States.

Skills Required   Two-year program. Some employers require a four-year college program.

Employment Outlook thru 1990   Excellent.

Salaries   Beginning programmer: $15,000; experienced system programmer: $25,000–$30,000.

3 ■ SYSTEMS ANALYST

Analysts begin an assignment by discussing the data processing problem with managers or specialists to determine the exact nature of the problem and to break it down into its component parts. If a new inventory system is desired, for example, systems analysts must determine what new data must be collected, the equipment needed for computation, and the steps to be followed in processing the information.

Analysts use various techniques, such as cost accounting, sampling, and mathematical model building to analyze a problem and devise a new system. Once a system has been developed, they prepare charts and diagrams that describe its operation in terms that managers or customers can understand. They also may prepare a cost-benefit analysis to help the client decide whether the proposed system is satisfactory.

If the system is accepted, systems analysts translate the logical requirements of the system into the capabilities of the computer machinery or "hardware." They also prepare specifications for programmers to follow and work with them to "debug" or eliminate errors from the system.

Prior work experience is important. Nearly half of all persons entering this occupation have transferred from other occupations, especially from computer programmer. In many industries, systems analysts begin as programmers and are promoted to analyst positions after gaining experience.

Places of Employment   Most opportunities are in the Midwest and the northeastern portion of the United States. Positions are also available in other large urban areas.

Skills Required   Four-year program. Many positions require MBAs or advanced degrees in computer science.

Employment Outlook thru 1990   Excellent.

Salaries   Beginning systems analyst: $15,000–$20,000; systems analyst: $30,000—$35,000.

PART 6

FURTHER
DIMENSIONS AND
OPPORTUNITIES

CHAPTER   **23**

THE LEGAL AND TAX ENVIRONMENT

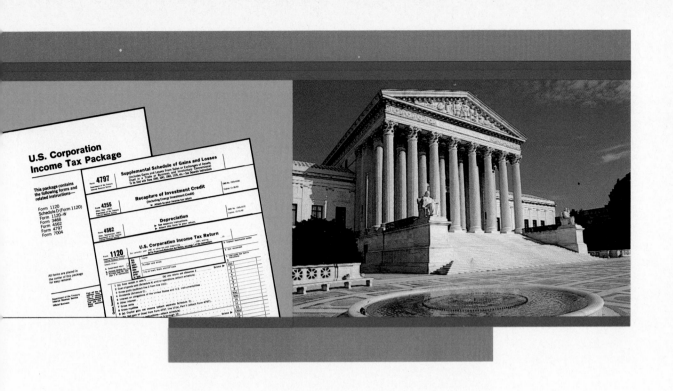

After studying this chapter you should be able to:

1 Give the definition of law, differentiate between public and private law, and describe the Uniform Commercial Code (UCC).
2 Explain what is a legally enforceable contract (in particular, the sales contract) and then discuss the meaning of breach of contract and possible remedies—damages, punitive damages, specific performance, and restitution.
3 Understand the rights and obligations relating to ownership, use, and sale of property, with application to business law.
4 Discuss the use of agency law, tort law, and bankruptcy law and how they affect business practices.
5 Understand and fully appreciate the nature of government's role in regulating business competition, marketing activity, and credits and collections.
6 Explain the taxation of business income and how government uses taxation to pay for the services it provides as well as to regulate economic activity.
7 Understand the major types of non-income taxes—*sales tax*, *property tax*, and *payroll tax*.

Spurred by recent court decisions against giant computer makers, more and more small firms are suing computer vendors on charges ranging from fraud and misrepresentation to failure to meet warranty and service obligations.

Three recent court cases have found the vendors to be at least partly liable. In July [1981], a federal district court in New York ruled against Detroit-based Burroughs Corp., finding it guilty of fraud and three other charges, and awarding the plaintiff, a vitamin distributor in Farmingdale, N.Y., $250,000 in damages. In June [1981], a wholesale floral company in Mobile, Ala., won $500,000 in a misrepresentation case, also against Burroughs.

Last spring, Steven Depper, vice-president of a wholesale suede and leather cleaning company in Oakland, Calif., was awarded $2.3 million by a San Francisco jury. The court concluded that NCR Corp., of Dayton, Ohio, had sold Depper a minicomputer that NCR knew wouldn't work.

It took Depper four years to decide to file suit against NCR. "We couldn't afford to buy a new system," he says. "They didn't leave us any alternative. When the NCR regional manager said, 'You can sue us,' that was the last straw, I don't think he'll ever forget those words."

The decision to sue led to a costly search for people who would testify against NCR. "One of the problems I had initially was finding people to say something in court," says Depper's attorney, Richard Perez. "Most of them still had service contracts with that vendor."

NCR has appealed the case and is confident that the verdict will be overturned. That leaves open the possibility of protracted litigation, adding to the more than $60,000 in legal fees Depper has already spent, but he vows to stick it out.

"The chances of obtaining successful remedy through the courts seem to have improved over the past 5 to 10 years," says Richard Raysman, chairman of the New York State Bar Association's computer law subcommittee. "The courts are getting more and more sophisticated with regard to the technical aspects of computer cases."

According to industry sources, several hundred small firms have sued computer vendors as a result of data processing problems. *MIS Week*, a trade journal, reports that court cases against the Burroughs Corp. alone could easily reach 100.

When Steven Depper was unable to gain satisfaction from NCR, his last recourse was an appeal to the law. His case is but one of many thousands resolved in courts of law each year. It's obviously important to him, and perhaps it's also important in establishing precedent in future litigation against computer manufacturers, but by many standards it's a minor case. Depper spent $60,000 in legal fees; by contrast, IBM has spent many millions defending itself against antitrust charges by the Justice Department. In what's been referred to as "the case of the century," 13 years after it was begun—and after some 66 million pages of testimony—the case was dismissed in early 1982 by Attorney-General William Baxter for being "without merit."[1]

Whether the case is a collossus, such as IBM's, or one for less than $500 in a small claims court, or something in between, such as Steven Depper's, the principle is the same—protection under the law.

The existence and enforcement of laws is vital to business as well as other participants in our society. Cities, counties, states, and the federal government are all involved with the regulation of our activities, and each has authority to impose taxes on us. In this chapter we describe legal and tax systems so that students of business can understand and more fully appreciate the nature of government's role in society.

LAW: THE RULES OF SOCIETY

The laws and the legal system of the United States are the result of a long-term evolutionary process that continues to take place. The laws that govern our society were developed as society advanced and its needs changed. Laws generally develop in response to a specific social need for controlling behavior. **Law** is the set of principles that govern the conduct and activities of society. It is based on what society believes standards for behavior should be.

For example, the rise of the American legal system can be traced to the growth and expansion of modern American society. As it developed, laws

and regulations were passed to solve problems threatening society. For instance, the **Sherman Antitrust Act (1890)** was passed in order to curb monopoly powers of large companies that undermined the existence of smaller companies and reduced competition. Also, no one worried much about the environment at that time; but 80 years later Congress passed the **National Environmental Protection Act (1970)** in response to a public outcry to clean up—and maintain the cleanliness of—our environment. So the legal system in the United States evolves to meet the changing needs of people, property, and business. Table 23.1 summarizes the four basic types of law—natural, common, statutory, and administrative—that illustrate the evolutionary nature of law.

Public vs. Private Law

Public law is concerned with standards and protection of society in general. It deals with the development and maintenance of welfare and is concerned with the interests of all members of society. Such matters as treason, civil disturbance, forgery, counterfeiting, bribery, homicide, arson, robbery, and kidnapping are dramatic examples of the subjects of public law. Less dramatic, but equally relevant to businesses, are laws such as the

TABLE 23-1

The Four Basic Types of Law

Natural Law   The belief that most people would act morally, even in the absence of society-made laws, constitutes natural law. The **natural laws** of a society are based on its religious or moral standards, which are present in all societies. Even the most primitive societies had taboos that were forbidden by the "gods". The origin of these natural rules of order cannot always be specifically identified, but it's clear that all members of the society know them.

Common Law   The set of principles that reflect the customs of society and that are found in court decisions is called **common law.** Common law is considered to be unwritten law because it was not developed by a legislative body. Much of the common law of a society finds its roots in the natural law. The common law may likewise form the basis for statutory law.

Statutory Law   **Statutory laws** are developed and enacted by the legislative branches of various government units. In the United States, statutory law is passed by city, state, and federal governments. Statutory laws that are developed by cities are called *ordinances.* Each level of government has a court system that helps enforce the provisions of statutory law.

Administrative Law   A type of law that is growing in importance is administrative law. **Administrative law** is a set of administrative rules and regulations used to implement the provisions of statutory law. Administrative law is made by the various government agencies and carries full force of law. The Federal Trade Commission (FTC), the Occupational Safety and Health Administration (OSHA), and the Environmental Protection Agency (EPA) are examples of agencies that have developed extensive bodies of administrative law.

Foreign Corrupt Practices Act of 1977. This law prohibits the offering of bribes to public officials in foreign countries for the purpose of obtaining economic advantages there. Thus large corporations such as Gulf Oil or GTE must abide by this law in establishing and maintaining business contacts abroad, even though in some instances the paying of bribes or "gratuities" might pose as a common business practice. Moreover large companies are also required to establish adequate internal controls in their accounting system in order to detect bribes of this sort.[2]

Private law is a set of principles that relate to individual members and organizations within the society. Private law deals with the rights and concerns of these individuals from the viewpoint of both common and statutory law. Such matters as consumers' rights, damages from failure to yield at a stop sign, windows broken by errant golf shots, and breaches of contractual obligations are examples of the concerns of private law.

Uniform Commercial Code (UCC)

Laws that cover many aspects of business are based on a set of uniform model statutes adopted by the 50 states. This set of uniform statutes is called the **Uniform Commercial Code (UCC).** The UCC deals with commercial transactions of businesses and individuals. Developers of the model statutes for the UCC wanted to establish a commercial code that would eliminate some of the legal problems of doing business on an interstate basis. The UCC contains regulations for sales, personal property, financial transactions, bills of lading, and investment securities.

CONTRACT LAW

You are looking at a new car with a sticker price of $12,000, but you think that the dealer will come down if you bargain a bit. The sales representative writes up a contract and quotes a price of $11,000. But you think an even lower price is possible, so you counter by saying, "I'll give you $10,000." If the representative agrees, have you bought the car for $10,000? The answer is yes since all the characteristics required for a legally enforceable contract appear to have been met. In order for a contract to exist and be legally en-

forceable, it must possess specific characteristics—mutual acceptance, consideration, capacity, and legal form. Table 23.2 briefly defines each of these characteristics.

Breach of Contract

When a party to a contract doesn't fulfill the obligations imposed by the contract, the contract is breached. **Breach of contract** means that the contract was broken. When this violation of the contract provisions occurs, the other party or parties have a right to seek remedy for the breach through the courts. These remedies include damages, specific performance, and restitution.

Damages The money that's awarded to the person who was harmed by the breach of contract is called **damages.** Damages are generally awarded for loss(es) incurred because the contract wasn't fulfilled. Assume that Ajax Roofing enters a contract to repair the roof of Mr. Wells' house after a severe hailstorm. Ajax agrees to complete the project in one day and schedules the project on

"FRANKLY, I'M DUBIOUS ABOUT AMALGAMATED SMELTING AND REFINING PLEADING INNOCENT TO THEIR ANTI-TRUST VIOLATION DUE TO INSANITY."

TABLE 23–2
Required Characteristics of a Legally Enforceable Contract

Mutual Acceptance   Each party to the contract must have entered into the agreement freely and by genuine assent. The agreement covered in the contract results from an offer and an acceptance of the offer. One person, called the offeror, makes a proposal to perform some action of value for another person. The second person, the offeree, accepts the offer by his/her own free will. The agreement must have *both* offer and acceptance of the offer before a contract can exist.

Consideration   For a contract to exist, consideration must be present. Consideration is the legal price agreed on for the acceptance of the offer. Consideration is an inducement for the parties to enter into a contract. Consideration must be agreed to through the bargaining process. Consideration is a value that the offeror receives for the offer to obligate himself to perform. Consideration may be in the form of money, goods, services, or a legal right given up.

Capacity   Contracts can be entered into only by parties defined by the state statutes as competent. Certain individuals are not allowed by the laws of most states to enter into legally binding contracts. These individuals are minors, insane persons, intoxicated persons, convicts, and aliens.

Legal Form   Valid contracts may be either oral or written. Written agreements are preferable. If a contract is written, both parties can see what's being agreed to. A written agreement lessens the danger of disagreement in the future, and it provides evidence of the contract. Written evidence of the agreement keeps one party from denying that a contract was made. Certain types of contracts must be in writing in order to be enforced. Such contracts are: contracts for more than one year of time, sale of real estate, assuming debts of others, and promises made in consideration of marriage. The statute that requires these contracts to be in writing is called the *statute of frauds*.

Tuesday. The Ajax repair crew doesn't come to do the work, and on Tuesday an all-night downpour causes $10,000 worth of water damage to the inside of Wells' house and to its contents. Wells may sue for all damages that occurred because Ajax breached the contract. If Wells can prove that Ajax never intended to do the work and deceived him into signing the contract, Mr. Wells may also sue for punitive damages. **Punitive damages** punish the wrongdoer for intentional acts.

Specific Performance   The victim of a breach of contract may ask for **specific performance,** under which the court will require the provisions of the contract to be carried out. If there'd been no rain damage, Wells might have asked the court to direct Ajax to fix the roof at the price and under the conditions agreed upon. Generally, specific performance and full damages will not be awarded for the same breach of contract.

Restitution   In restitution, the contract is in effect canceled. **Restitution** seeks to return the parties to their positions before the contract was signed. The parties return what they received before entering the contract. Both restitution and damages cannot be awarded for the same breach of contract.

Sales Contracts

The most common contract in American business is the **sales contract.** It's entered into millions of times each day in the ordinary course of business. Steven Depper's case was most likely built around interpretation of the sales contract. The sales contract in modern business is governed by the evolutionary elements of the English merchant law, common law, and statutory law. These three elements were the basis for the sales law that's included in Article 2 of the Uniform Commercial Code.

Sale/Purchase   Sales law defines the considerations for selling goods to a customer. The provisions of the law relate to sales for both money or credit. Sales law covers the sale of goods only; it

TALKING BUSINESS

Gladys Fields has been waiting a long time for her day in court—more than five years.

She charges that she suffered severe burns when a robe she was wearing ignited and failed to resist flames. In 1976, she filed a federal court suit seeking $3.4 million from three companies that variously made or sold the garment.

No trial date has been set. Settlement talks have been unproductive. In the interim, Miss Fields moved from a Boston suburb to Phoenix. The long wait for resolution of the suit, she says, "has left me very, very frustrated."

Her lawsuit, like thousands of others, is caught in the mounting backlog of cases in the nation's courts. Despite efforts by judges, lawyers and lawmakers in some places to speed the process, civil suits frequently take more than a year, and often two to three years or even longer, to be completed. As a result, legal costs skyrocket, witnesses' memories fade and the parties involved must endure the anxiety of waiting.

"Delay and expense in the resolution of lawsuits are increasing at an alarming rate," Supreme Court Justice Byron White said in a speech at the recent American Bar Association convention in New Orleans. "They have become urgent matters."

Source: Excerpted from Stephen Wermiel, "Delays in Civil Suits Mount As Courts Struggle with Backlogs, Attorneys," *Wall Street Journal*, 28 October, 1981, p. 25. Reprinted by permission of The Wall Street Journal, ©Dow Jones & Company, Inc., 1981. All rights reserved.

excludes the sale of securities, personal services, or real estate. The UCC defines a sale as a transaction in which title to goods is transferred. The sale must have both transfer of title and passage of consideration in the form of the price for the goods.

The law of contracts is applicable to sales. Businesses that sell goods must consider the consequences of both sales law and contract law when they draw up sales agreements with their customers. The sales contract doesn't have to be in writing in order to be valid. There are certain instances where the UCC does require written sales contracts for the contract to be enforceable. For example, a sales contract for more than $500 must be in writing.

In enforcing the sales contract, a written agreement is always best, but the courts will interpret the intent of the buyer and seller when a written agreement isn't available or is unclear. Also, the courts will consider partial performance, past dealings between buyer and seller, and methods of doing business within the industry. These fac-

tors are examined in assessing damages and establishing remedies.

Warranties A **warranty** is a representation made regarding the quality and performance of goods. An express warranty is stated specifically by the seller as a fact or promise. The express warranty is generally considered by sales law to be a part of the basis of the bargain and is an influence on the action of the buyer. Express warranties are in the form of statements that can be interpreted as fact. "This machine will process 1000 gallons of paint per hour" is an example of an express warranty.

An implied warrant is a warranty imposed on a sales transaction by statute or court decision. Article 2 of the UCC covers three types of implied warranties. These are warranty of "merchantibility"—fitness of goods for ordinary purposes; warranty of fitness for a particular purpose; and warranty of title. Implied warranties can be excluded or modified by the seller only prior to sale and in writing. For example, Whirlwind Pump Company manufactures a submersible pump designed to pump oil and heavy liquids quickly and cleanly. The pump isn't designed internally to pump lighter liquids such as water or gasoline, although a customer who doesn't know about the design of the pump might assume it would move any kind of liquid product. If Whirlwind Pump doesn't want to warranty the pump for use with light liquids, it must state in writing before the sale that the pump isn't intended for use with water or light liquids.

PROPERTY LAW

One of the basic rights of the free-enterprise system is the right to own and use property. Property is used by businesses to produce and sell goods and services in order to make a profit. The rights and obligations relating to ownership, use, and sale of property are an essential element of business law.

Types of Property

Two types of property are used by businesses: real property and personal property. Land, buildings, and rights in the land of another are defined as **real property.** Real property may be purchased or leased. The lease of property doesn't convey ownership rights to renters, but it does give them the right to use the property as if it were their own.

Personal property is property that's movable. It also includes rights and claims to personal property. Business assets such as inventory, furniture, automobiles, and machinery are personal property of the business. Personal property consists of two classifications of property: tangible personal property and intangible personal property. **Tangible personal property** refers to property that can be seen, touched, and physically relocated. Tangible personal property includes inventory, machines, trucks, and so on. **Intangible personal property** consists of rights and claims owned by the business or individual. Examples of intangible personal property are accounts receivable, patents, and copyrights. These items represent rights or claims owned by a business or an individual.

Transferring Property

Most transfers of property result from the normal course of business activity. The sale of goods represents a transfer of ownership to the purchaser of goods held in inventory by a business. But there are also transfers of property that occur less frequently. For example, a mechanic who has changed positions and has become a shop supervisor may want to sell his tools since he no longer needs them.

Real Property A contract for sale of real estate must be in writing. The evidence of transfer of ownership and acceptance of the contract terms is the deed. The transfer of ownership may occur by selling the property or by giving it as a gift to another. Either type of transaction is evidenced by a deed of title. The deed must be signed by the person making the transfer, and the signature must be witnessed by two or more people. The deed of title that evidences the transfer of real property is usually recorded in the office of the county official where the property is located.

Real property can be transferred in ways besides sale or gift. One way is by adverse possession. In order to acquire real property through this method, it must be held by someone other than the owner for the time period specified by law. The usual time period is 21 years, but some state statutes define the time from 10 to 20 years. This type of acquisition was referred to in the past as "squatter's rights."

Another method of transfer is by will. The will is a formal document that directs the transfer of a person's property at the time of death. The will generally covers all property, both real and personal.

Personal Property As we've seen, personal property transfers usually result from ordinary business dealings, although transfers of personal property are made also by gift, by will, or by creation. The first three methods are the more common ways to transfer or acquire ownership of personal property. The last method—by creation—refers to acquisition of personal property rights by creating something that's patentable or copyrightable (this textbook, for example). Trademarks and servicemarks can also be included in this category. A **patent** gives an inventor exclusive right to manufacture, use, and sell an invention for 17 years. A patent may be obtained on any new and useful device. The physical process, machine, or formula is what's patented, and the patent rights are personal property.

A **copyright** is an exclusive right given to a writer, artist, composer, or playwright to use, produce, and sell his or her creation. The copyright is issued for the life of the creator of the work and 50 years after the creator's death.

A **trademark** is an identifying symbol, work, or design for a product. A **servicemark** is a symbol, work, or design that identifies a service. These marks are valuable rights for companies because they create uniqueness in the minds of their customers. Sometimes a trademark becomes so well known that it's used to describe all similar types of products. For example, Coke is often used to refer to any cola drink—not just to those produced by the Coca-Cola Company. Reference is often made to an "IBM machine" even when the computer was actually made by some other company such as Control Data, Sperry, or Cray Research. The same fate sometimes befalls such well-known names as Scotch tape and Xerox.

Evidence of the transfer of personal property is made by use of the bill of sale. The bill of sale is somewhat similar to a deed and evidences substantial transfers of personal property.

OTHER TYPES OF LAW

Contract and property law are the major types of law that business firms encounter, but there are other types that also influence business activities. These are agency law, tort law, and bankruptcy law.

Agency Law

Agency is a common relationship in business. Businesses often employ others to act in their behalf. Some agency relationships exist of necessity, such as employing an attorney to represent the company in a complex merger negotiation. Other agency relationships are for convenience or efficient business practices such as hiring people to negotiate sales contracts in various areas of the company's market.

Agency is the legal relationship in which one person authorizes, expressly or by implication, another person to act or represent him or her. The person giving the authorization is called the principal and the person who acts in the place of the principal is called the agent. Businesses use agency relationships extensively in real estate, insurance, advertising, and travel.

Some of the well-known trademarks that are often used to describe similar types of products.

PERSPECTIVE ON SMALL BUSINESS

To take on Standard Oil Co. back in the old days would have marked any small businessman as a probable half-wit and a sure loser. Lo, how the mighty have fallen.

When Jersey Standard's successor, Exxon Corp., with $108 billion a year in revenue, sued half-pint $1 million-a-year Exxene Corp., the result was an upset. Exxene won a lengthy trial, partly with the reluctant assistance of Exxon's own lawyers and executives, and in doing so invalidated 18 of Exxon's zealously guarded trademark registrations.

Exxon had sued for trademark infringement shortly after Exxene was formed in Wayne, Ill., in 1976. Exxene, now in Corpus Christi, Texas, makes antifog coatings for plastics and says its name is a contraction of "excellent scene," the view you get through, say, ski goggles coated with Exxene's stuff. "If they'd been gentlemanly, I would have changed my name," says William Warmack, the 56-year-old inventor who owns and runs Exxene. "But they acted like God, and like I'm some little guy."

He hit back with a countersuit challenging Exxon's own trademark registrations. In court, Exxene played its mom-and-pop, underdog role to the fullest. Exxene attorney Thomas Juettner called Mr. Warmack and his wife by their first names so often that an Exxon lawyer irritably exclaimed, "This isn't a lawsuit, this is the Bill and Marilyn Show."

When Exxene couldn't manage an expert witness of its own, it got an *Exxon* lawyer to testify that trademarks unused for more than two years become invalid. Then Exxene got some of Exxon's executives to testify that many of the questioned labels had fallen into disuse.

Exxon conceded it hired a private investigator to snoop around. Mr. Warmack had spotted him. "He looked just like Peter Falk, with a cigar and everything. He said he was a race-car driver who wanted an antifogger, but he kept asking about how the company got its name." Meanwhile, Exxene lawyers presented evidence of fabrication of consumer surveys commissioned by Exxon that purported to show confusion about the two names.

A court order that Exxon had won back in 1979 to keep the proceedings unpublicized was lifted only [in December 1981]. U.S. District Judge Stanley J. Roszkowski ordered Exxon to pay Exxene $250,000 in damages after a jury in August [1981] found against Exxon. But Mr. Warmack, who feels "poor and tired" after five years of litigation, says the money won't cover his legal fees.

Exxon appealed and won't discuss the case.

SOURCE: Meg Cox, "Exxon, Schmexxon, Says the Jury, Score This Round for the Little Guy," *Wall Street Journal*, 14 December, 1981, p. 21. Reprinted by permission of The Wall Street Journal, © Dow Jones & Company, Inc., 1981. All rights reserved.

Tort Law

In the late 1970s Three Mile Island and Love Canal became almost as familiar (and dreaded) events as Hiroshima and Nagasaki. The total environmental damages from these two incidents has yet to be assessed fully, but they will certainly run into the many millions, perhaps billions. A large part of these damages will result from private cases dealing with torts. To most people *tort* is an unfamiliar term; yet when actions regarded as torts are described, they generally recognize that such actions are damaging.

What is a Tort? A **tort** is a civil or private wrongful act to another person or another's property. A tort is a private-law concept and is different from a crime. It concerns acts of one or more persons to another individual. For example, Mrs. O'Shea, owner of O'Shea's Irish Pub and Restaurant, experienced a decline in business. One afternoon, a regular customer stopped by the restaurant and gave her a copy of a letter he had received form one of O'Shea's competitors, Mr. Grady. The letter stated that O'Shea used inferior foods in preparation of her menu items and that the restaurant had been reprimanded by the Health Department for unclean kitchen and food-handling conditions. None of the accusations in the letter was true; moreover O'Shea had recently received the renewal of her operating permit by the Health Department and had received excellent ratings for her operations. Since O'Shea can prove that the statements are false, and if the statements were intentionally made by the competitor to hurt O'Shea's business, Grady has committed the tort of libel, and O'Shea may seek damages from him in court.

A well-noted tort was the series of wrongful-death suits arising from the tragic 1980 fire at the MGM Grand Hotel in Las Vegas, Nevada, which killed 84 persons and injured hundreds of others. The wrongful-death act in Nevada allows heirs of the victims to sue for compensatory and punitive damages based on wrongful death and also for grief and sorrow caused by the wrongful death of the victims. Other types of torts are slander, defamation of character, assault, battery, infringement, and conspiracy to restrict competition. These are defined in the next section.

Crime and Negligence **A crime** is a wrong resulting from the violation of public law. An act may be both a tort and a crime. The burglary of a home is such an example. The burglar can be tried for burglary, and the homeowner may sue the burglar for a tort to property and seek damages resulting from the tort. A tort is separate from breach of contract. A tort is sometimes alternatively defined as a civil wrong that's noncontractual. Tort law does not cover contracts and is not a part of the UCC. To recover damages from a tort, one of two elements must be proved to exist.

First, the damage must have resulted from *negligence*. Negligence occurs when a person fails to exercise due care in his or her actions. Due care refers to the caution and responsibility that can reasonably be expected under the circumstances. Thus Layne, while making a delivery on her cosmetics route, doesn't secure her car adequately and it rolls forward, injuring Smith. Smith can bring charges against Layne arguing negligence on her part. The second element is *deliberate intent*. In a previous example, it appears Mr. Grady deliberately intended to cause harm to Mrs.

O'Shea. This element relates to the intention to cause the harm. The person who files suit must prove the act resulting from either element caused actual damages or injury.

Bankruptcy Law

The Congress of the United States has provided a means for the financially distressed company or individual to begin a new economic existence. Under **bankruptcy law,** the debt-burdened party can petition the courts for relief from debts by allowing the court to distribute owned assets to the creditors. In return, the bankrupt party is cleared of most of the debts. Bankruptcy may be initiated on either a voluntary or an involuntary basis. A *voluntary bankruptcy* case begins with the debtor's filing an application with the court alleging that debts exceed assets. This application is called a petition in bankruptcy: it asks the court to declare the party bankrupt. Creditors of a business or individual may file the bankruptcy petition. When this happens, it's known as *involuntary bankruptcy*. An involuntary bankruptcy petition can be filed against a debtor if one of the following three conditions is met:

1. The firm has past-due debts of $5,000 or more.
2. Three or more creditors can prove that they have aggregate unpaid claims of $5000 against the firm. If the firm has fewer than 12 creditors, any creditor owed more than $5000 can file the petition.
3. The firm is *insolvent*, which means that (a) it's not paying its debts as they come due, or (b) within the immediately preceding 120 days a custodian (a third party) was appointed or took possession of the debtors property.

The dominant bankruptcy legislation today is the **Bankruptcy Reform Act (1978)** which provides for the quick and efficient resolution of bankruptcy cases. Its two key sections are Chapters 7 and 11. Chapter 7 details the procedures to be followed when liquidating the failed firm. Chapter 11 of the act outlines the procedures for reorganizing the failed firm whether its petition is filed voluntarily or involuntarily. If under this chapter a workable plan for reorganization can't be developed, the firm will be liquidated under Chapter 7.

Braniff Files Bankruptcy Petition; Other Airlines Seeking Its Routes

By AGIS SALPUKAS

The Braniff International Corporation yesterday filed for protection under the bankruptcy laws, the first major United States airline to do so.

The filing, which came a few hours after Braniff had suspended all its domestic and international flights, set off a scramble by other airlines to handle hundreds of stranded passengers and to pick up some of Braniff's business and routes.

Most of Braniff 9,500 employees jobless

attempt to reorganize, probably as a much smaller airline.

There had been a sharp decline in passenger traffic in recent weeks, they said, as the public lost confidence in the money-losing airline. The decline squeezed cash reserves severely. There also was a problem, they said, in meeting the bimonthly payroll, due this week. Braniff's monthly salary outlay is estimated at $25 million.

Finally, the executives said, there concern that if Braniff did not file

GOVERNMENT REGULATION OF BUSINESS

Government regulation of business has been a focal point of controversy for decades. Some observers maintain that there should be less government regulation and that government is smothering business with red tape and paperwork. Others feel that regulation hasn't gone far enough and that business is often unethical and must be kept in line through strict government control. The scope of the impact of government regulation in one instance is shown by Figure 23.1. This illustration summarizes a study done at Colorado State University on the regulations affecting the average hamburger sold by fast-food restaurants in the United States. The study indicates that 200 laws and 111,000 court cases lead to 41,000 regula-

tions at the federal and state levels that will directly or indirectly touch the hamburger.

Regulation of Competition

Competitive regulations are concerned with keeping the marketplace free from restrictive competitive influences. Regulation of competition has focused on three major areas. The first of these is antitrust regulation that prohibits companies from entering agreements to control trade through monopoly actions in the marketplace. Most of the antitrust action is initiated by the U.S. Department of Justice. The major regulatory acts concerned with competition are the Sherman Antitrust Act (1890), **the Clayton Act (1914),**

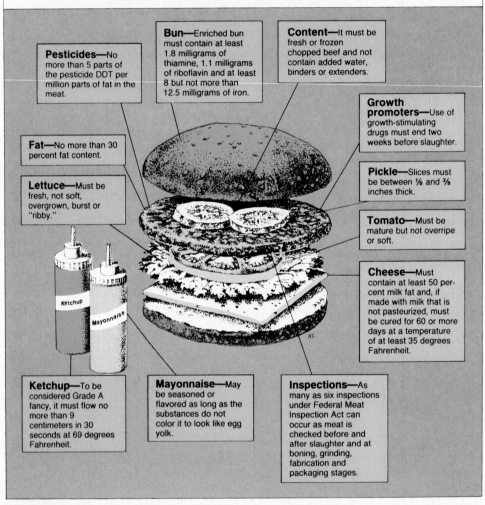

Your Hamburger: 41,000 Regulations

The hamburger, staple of the quick, inexpensive meal, is the subject of 41,000 federal and state regulations, many of those stemming from 200 laws and 111,000 precedent-setting court cases.

These rules, cited in a three-volume study by Colorado State University, touch on everything involved in meat production—grazing practices of cattle, conditions in slaughterhouses and methods used to process meat for sale to supermarkets, restaurants and fast-food outlets. Together, they add an estimated 8 to 11 cents per pound to the cost of hamburger.

The chart on this page gives just a sampling of the rules and regulations governing the burger you buy at the corner sandwich stand.

Pesticides—No more than 5 parts of the pesticide DDT per million parts of fat in the meat.

Bun—Enriched bun must contain at least 1.8 milligrams of thiamine, 1.1 milligrams of riboflavin and at least 8 but not more than 12.5 milligrams of iron.

Content—It must be fresh or frozen chopped beef and not contain added water, binders or extenders.

Growth promoters—Use of growth-stimulating drugs must end two weeks before slaughter.

Fat—No more than 30 percent fat content.

Lettuce—Must be fresh, not soft, overgrown, burst or "ribby."

Pickle—Slices must be between ⅛ and ⅜ inches thick.

Tomato—Must be mature but not overripe or soft.

Cheese—Must contain at least 50 per-cent milk fat and, if made with milk that is not pasteurized, must be cured for 60 or more days at a temperature of at least 35 degrees Fahrenheit.

Ketchup—To be considered Grade A fancy, it must flow no more than 9 centimeters in 30 seconds at 69 degrees Fahrenheit.

Mayonnaise—May be seasoned or flavored as long as the substances do not color it to look like egg yolk.

Inspections—As many as six inspections under Federal Meat Inspection Act can occur as meat is checked before and after slaughter and at boning, grinding, fabrication and packaging stages.

FIGURE 23.1
Regulatory impact.
Source: U.S. News & World Report, February 11, 1980, page 64.

and the Federal Trade Commission Act (1914). The Federal Trade Commission was created by the act and is responsible for monitoring unfair trade practices. The **Celler-Kefauver Act (1950)** focused on merger activity. This act amended the Clayton Act and prohibits the purchase of one company by another if such a transaction will result in a decrease of competition in the given industry.

Many suits have been filed by the Justice Department under these acts. A recent and rather novel one had to do with alleged price-fixing activities by three dominant grocery chains in the Cleveland area—First National Supermarkets,

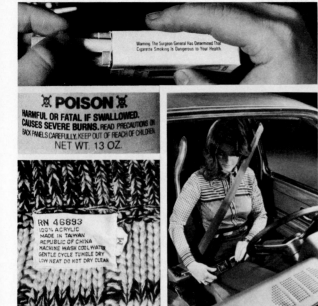

Inc., Fisher Foods, Inc., and the Association of Stop-N-Shop Supermarkets. The Justice Department charged that representatives of the three met clandestinely in parking lots, motels, and apartments and used post office box numbers and code names to coordinate their plans. One interesting aspect of the case was its settlement: the judge ordered $30 million returned to area residents in the form of scrip that could be used in the stores involved; each household in a seven-county area was to receive $20 worth of scrip.[3]

Regulation of Marketing Activity

Even though competitive regulation relates to marketing, there's a group of regulations that directly impact the marketing activities of the firm as they relate to the product, its promotion, and its price. A product's package must be clearly labeled for contents, ingredients, and quantity of product contained within it. The label must show the ingredients in descending order of their importance in the product. The package must also contain warnings of hazards to health. If the product is poisonous or dangerous to children, it must have a lid that can't be opened by a child.

Advertising is regulated by several government agencies. The focus of regulation is to keep companies from becoming overly enthusiastic about their products and making false or misleading claims about them. The effect of advertising on consumers' purchases has become a concern of consumer product legislation as well.

Pricing policies can't be discriminatory to the customers of the company. The Robinson-Patman Act of 1936 prohibits differential pricing practices that are based on customers and not on the quality and quantity of the goods that customers buy. For example, a firm can't offer a customer a discount simply because the customer buys exclusively from the firm. However it *can* offer the customer a discount if the discount is based on the quantity the customer buys. Moreover that same quantity discount must be available to all customers ordering like amounts.

Credit and Collection Regulation

The focus of credit regulation is on disclosure and fairness. Credit regulation requires that a lender fully disclose the loan terms and costs of borrowing. The regulations require that any customer to whom credit is denied on the basis of a report from a credit reporting agency be informed of the name and address of the agency. The company must also advise the customer of his or her rights in the case of an incorrect billing.

The **Equal Credit Opportunity Act (1975)** prohibits credit discrimination on the basis of sex, marital status, race, religion, age, and national origin. The act also requires that credit be reported in both the husband's and wife's names if they request it. The **Fair Debt Collection Practices Act (1978)** prohibits abusive and unfair practices by debt collectors. The act establishes procedures for use by collectors in contacting a credit user and restricts their contacts with people other than the debtor. For example, a debt collector can't contact a debtor at inconvenient hours, use false identification (such as being a representative of an attorney or a credit bureau), threaten to take property, contact the debtor at work without the employer's permission, make the debtor accept collect calls, or tell anyone else that the debtor is behind in his or her bills.

TAXATION OF BUSINESS

Paying taxes is sometimes seen as the price we pay for an opportunity to live in a civilized society. Taxes are assessed on individuals and businesses by all levels of government and are used by those governments to pay for the services that they provide. Taxing authority is also used by governments to regulate economic activity. While many items have been used as a tax base (medieval kings were fond of taxing salt), the most common taxes collected by governments today are based on income.

"You're going to meet an intelligent, inquisitive, beautiful girl....she's an auditor for the IRS."

From *The Wall Street Journal*, by permission of Cartoon Features Syndicate.

TABLE 23-3
Corporation Tax Rates

Income (in dollars)	Tax Rate (in percentages)
0–25,000	15
25,001–50,000	18
50,001–75,000	30
75,001–100,000	40
Over 100,000	46

Income Taxes

Income taxes are taxes based on income received by individuals and businesses. The income taxes that individuals and business pay to the federal government are regulated by the **Internal Revenue Code.** Tax rates are set by Congress and taxes are collected by the Internal Revenue Service (IRS).

Individual Versus Corporate Taxes   A dual system of tax rates exists for U.S. businesses. Nonincorporated businesses aren't actually taxed as such since the tax laws make no distinction between the sole proprietorship, or partnership, and the owners of these types of businesses. Thus the income of these firms is taxed at individual rates ranging from 10 percent to 50 percent depending on the amount and type of income reported.

In contrast, incorporated businesses pay taxes on their income at the corporate tax rate. The owner and the corporation are separate taxable entities; therefore the corporation pays its own taxes. The corporate tax structure is much simpler than the multiple tax rate structure for individuals. The federal income tax rates for corporations established by the Economic Recovery Act of 1981 are shown in Table 23.3.

In 1983 Central Services, Inc. had taxable income of $137,650. The company therefore owes $43,069 in federal corporate income taxes. The tax computation for Central Services is:

$$\$25,000 \times 15\% = \$\ 3,750$$
$$\$25,000 \times 18\% = \$\ 4,500$$
$$\$25,000 \times 30\% = \$\ 7,500$$
$$\$25,000 \times 40\% = \$10,000$$
$$\$37,650 \times 46\% = \underline{\$17,319}$$
$$\text{Total tax} \quad \underline{\underline{\$43,069}}$$

ON THE FIRING LINE

The VAT—More or Less Painful than Income Tax?

The apparent inadequacies of the present tax system in the US have led some to suggest use of a value-added tax (VAT). A VAT, already in use in most European and some Latin American countries, is much like the state and local sales taxes we pay. However it's imposed at each stage of production rather than only on retail sales.

Suppose, for example, a VAT of 10 percent were levied. We can see how the tax would work in the following hypothetical example of the manufacture and sale of a wool coat. At the first stage of production, the raw product, wool, is sold to a mill for $30 plus VAT. With a 10 percent VAT, the mill will pay $30 + $3 = $33. The $3 tax is collected from the mill and paid to the government by the seller of the raw wool. At the second stage, the mill then sells the finished cloth to a coat manufacturer at a price of $50 + $5 (VAT) = $55. The mill has added a value of $20 to the unfinished product ($50 − $30). It has collected $5 VAT, but in buying the raw wool it already paid $3 VAT. The mill, therefore, must give the government only $2 of the $5 VAT it collected. This $2 is, of course, exactly 10 percent of the value the mill added to the product.

The tax is paid in this way throughout the chain of production. Assume that finally a retail store sells the coat to a customer for $140 + $14 VAT = $154. Since the consumer does not sell the coat there is no way of collecting the tax from someone else. He or she must bear the entire burden of the $14 VAT on the product. Clearly then, the VAT is essentially a retail sales tax. It differs from the sales taxes we are familiar with only in its method of collection.

Many believe a VAT should replace some portion of our income tax. In several crucial ways, they say, it would bolster our sagging productivity. Applying a tax to spending by means of a VAT would encourage consumers to save and invest their money. The result, these individuals claim, would be growth in investment capital, expansion in business and industry, and increased productivity.

Another point in the VAT's favor is what some call its "neutrality." Unlike the income tax, it does not favor certain types of businesses or methods of financing over others.* The VAT is imposed equally on all products and services.

In addition, the VAT would lead to greater efficiency, some think. The income tax, they say, discourages firms from seeking greater and greater profits. The more profits there are, the more taxes a firm pays. This situation doesn't tend to promote cost control. The VAT, though, is imposed on all transactions without regard to profits. Logically, then, the VAT would encourage firms to cut costs in order to increase profits. Finally, VAT backers maintain, their tax is easy to administer—while the income tax clearly is not.

There are three main arguments against the VAT. The one most often cited is that it is regressive. That is to say, it distributes the burden of paying taxes unfairly. People whose income is small must pay almost all of it out for day-to-day living expenses. They cannot easily absorb an across-the-board, fixed-rate tax on purchases.

Another fault people find with the VAT is its impact on inflation. If it should be introduced all at once, it would mean a one-time, dramatic rise in prices. With a 10 percent VAT, the cost of all goods would immediately go up by 10 percent. If the annual rate of inflation happened to be about 10 percent as well, prices could rise by 20 percent in one year. Public reaction in the face of such a sudden increase could play havoc with the economy, even if the income tax were reduced accordingly.

Finally, some consider the VAT dangerous because it is a hidden tax. People would pay it bit by bit as they buy. They would not see how much of their income was consumed by taxes. Consequently they would be less likely to hold government responsible for keeping taxes down. When they felt pinched, they would blame business rather than government.

*Currently, for example, allowable tax deductions encourage firms to finance with debt rather than equity. Similarly, poor depreciation allowances favor businesses that don't require heavy capital investments.

TALKING BUSINESS

[As of May 15, 1981,] a lot of people were still waiting for their tax-refund checks from Uncle Sam. But Ford Motor Co. didn't have to wait.

The company got its refund—all $695 million of it—on April 15, two days after filing its tax return.

As soon as the money was ready, a Ford man flew [from Detroit] to Chicago to pick it up. He arrived at the Internal Revenue Service office at about 2 p.m. By close of business, the money was on deposit in a nearby bank, earning interest. Within days, the money had trickled into the pool of cash Ford uses to pay bills and salaries to keep its operations going.

"We were anxious for it," says a Ford spokesman. Because car sales have been weak, the money-losing No. 2 auto maker has been scrambling for cash.

Normally, Ford is more relaxed about tax time. In a typical year, Ford's accounting people get extensions from the standard filing deadline of March 15, waiting until the last possible day (Sept. 15) to file. But normally, Ford doesn't get a big tax refund.

Like other companies, Ford pays estimated federal income taxes quarterly. Once a year, like millions of other taxpayers, Ford files an annual return. Usually it comes pretty close to squaring with the quarterly ones.

[In 1981,] the difference was Ford's huge 1980 loss—$1.54 billion from all its operations. A good portion of that was from U.S. operations. Under U.S. tax law, companies can "carry back" those losses for three years, or forward for seven years [in 1981; 15 years beginning in 1982], to lower the average tax payments. When they do that, they can get refunds of taxes paid in other years. So [in 1981] the rush was on at Ford to get the money the IRS owed the company.

Source: Excerpted from Amanda Bennett, "How Ford Got Its Tax Refund without Delay," *Wall Street Journal*, May 15, 1981, p. 29. Reprinted by permission of The Wall Street Journal, © Dow Jones & Company, Inc., 1981. All rights reserved.

By way of comparison, if Central Services had been a proprietorship and had had the same taxable income, assuming the owner was married with no other dependents and filed a joint return, his or her tax liability would have been $38,702 plus 50 percent of all income over $109,400 for a total tax bill of $52,827. Filing as a corporation has saved $9758 ($52,827 minus $43,069) in taxes.

Ordinary Income Versus Capital Gains The gross income of a business may consist of both ordinary income that's earned in the normal and usual course of business activities and capital gains. **Ordinary income** results from sale of merchandise or performance of services for which the business was organized. Ordinary income is taxable at the full individual or corporate tax rate, whichever is applicable.

A **capital gain** occurs when a business sells assets such as machinery, equipment, real estate, or security investments for more than their original purchase prices. Capital gains are then classified as long-term or short-term. *Long-term capital gains* occur when the assets sold were held for longer than one year. Long-term capital gains receive preferential tax treatment. The long-term capital gains tax rate is only 40 percent of the individual rate on ordinary income, and for corporations it's a maximum rate of 28 percent. Gains on assets held one year or less are called *short-term capital gains*. There is no preferential tax treatment given short-term gains, so these gains are taxed at ordinary income tax rates for both nonincorporated and incorporated businesses.

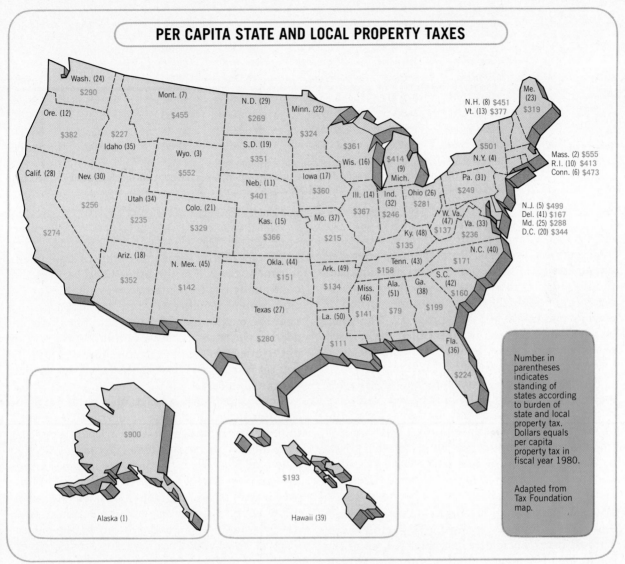

PER CAPITA STATE AND LOCAL PROPERTY TAXES

Wash. (24) $290
Ore. (12) $382
Idaho (35) $227
Mont. (7) $455
N.D. (29) $269
Minn. (22) $324
Wis. (16) $361
Mich. (9) $414
N.H. (8) $451
Vt. (13) $377
Me. (23) $319
N.Y. (4) $501
Mass. (2) $555
R.I. (10) $413
Conn. (6) $473
Calif. (28) $274
Nev. (30) $256
Utah (34) $235
Wyo. (3) $552
S.D. (19) $351
Iowa (17) $360
Neb. (11) $401
Ill. (14) $367
Ind. (32) $246
Ohio (26) $281
Pa. (31) $249
N.J. (5) $499
Del. (41) $167
Md. (25) $288
D.C. (20) $344
Ariz. (18) $352
Colo. (21) $329
Kas. (15) $366
Mo. (37) $215
Ky. (48) $135
W. Va. (47) $137
Va. (33) $236
N.C. (40) $171
N. Mex. (45) $142
Okla. (44) $151
Ark. (49) $134
Tenn. (43) $158
Miss. (46) $141
Ala. (51) $79
Ga. (38) $199
S.C. (42) $160
Texas (27) $280
La. (50) $111
Fla. (36) $224

Number in parentheses indicates standing of states according to burden of state and local property tax. Dollars equals per capita property tax in fiscal year 1980.

Adapted from Tax Foundation map.

Alaska (1) $900

Hawaii (39) $193

FIGURE 23.2

Source: *Monthly Tax Features*, vol. 26, no. 1, January 1982 (Washington, D.C.: Tax Foundation, Inc.), pp. 1, 4.

Other Types of Taxes

The business firm must also pay other types of taxes. The major classes of these others are sales taxes, property taxes, and payroll taxes.

Sales Taxes   **Sales taxes** are taxes levied on the purchasers of products, based on the sale prices. Sales taxes are generally imposed by state and city governments on retail sales. Both tax rates and requirements for paying sales taxes vary from one locality to another. Some states, such as Alaska, Delaware, Montana, New Hampshire, and Ore-

gon, don't have a state sales tax, while other areas have both a state and a city sales tax. For instance, a resident of San Francisco pays a 4.75 percent California sales tax and a 1.75 percent city sales tax.

Property Taxes   **Property taxes** are taxes assessed on real and personal property and are often referred to as **ad valorem taxes.** They raise a substantial amount of revenue for state and local governments, whereas the federal government collects no taxes based on property valuation of land, buildings, equipment, inventories, and

TABLE 23-4

Employer's Payroll Taxes

Employee Number	Earnings Year-to-Date	Earnings Current Period	Social Security (6.65%)	Federal Unempl. (.7%)	State Unempl. (2.7%)	Total Payroll Taxes
1001	$7200	$ 900	$59.85	$ -0-	$ -0-	$59.85
1002	$4800	$ 600[a]	$39.90	$4.20	$16.20	$60.30
1006	$6000	$1000	$66.50	$ -0-	$ -0-	$66.50
1010	$5600	$ 800[b]	$53.20	$2.80	$10.80	$66.80

[a]Federal and state unemployment taxes apply to the entire $600.
[b]First $6000, so the period's federal and state unemployment taxes are applicable only to $400; i.e., $6000 − $5600 = $400 × .007 and $400 × .027, respectively.

other personal property. Property taxes are based on some value of the property. Certain taxing authorities use fair market value, others use replacement value, and still others use some portion of the fair market value of the property. The value on which the taxes are based is called the assessed value. The tax rate is applied to the assessed value to determine the taxes due.

For example, the city commission has set a tax rate of $7.655 per $100 of assessed valuation based on 60 percent of fair market value of the property. Alpha Corporation owns real property worth $100,000 and its tax bill is ($60,000/$100) × $7.655 = $4593. Figure 23.2 shows per capita state and local property taxes for the 50 states.

Payroll Taxes If a business employs personnel and meets a payroll, it must pay payroll taxes. **Payroll taxes** include the employer's share of the social security taxes, federal unemployment taxes, and state unemployment taxes. The payroll taxes must be paid on wages, salaries, and commissions that are paid to the employees of the business. In 1981 a social security tax rate of 6.65 percent on the first $29,700 of earnings was in effect for all employers. The unemployment taxes are levied on the first $6000 of cash wages at a maximum rate of 3.4 percent. The 3.4 percent rate is composed of a Federal unemployment tax of 0.7 percent and a maximum state unemployment tax rate of 2.7 percent. The state unemployment tax rate varies from 0 to 2.7 percent, and its application depends on the company's experience with discharged employees who collect unemployment benefits.

For instance, a company that has never had an employee eligible for unemployment benefits will pay a very low (or even a zero) rate of state unemployment taxes. On the other hand, a firm that continually has former employees eligible for unemployment benefits will have to pay a rate very near the maximum of 2.7 percent. The credit for good experience applies only to the state portion of the unemployment taxes and doesn't affect the federal rate. Table 23.4 shows how payroll taxes are calculated.

The total dollar impact of payroll taxes on business firms should not be overlooked or minimized. For example, in 1980 corporations paid $161 billion in payroll taxes. By contrast, they paid only $65 billion in corporate income taxes—the tax most people believe is the largest.[4] Moreover payroll taxes also act as a barrier to hiring more people, since the amount business firms pay depends directly, and only, on employment—whether or not that employment produces more profit.

SUMMARY

The laws and the legal system of the United States are the result of a long-term evolutionary process that continues to take place as society's needs change. This evolutionary process is illustrated by four basic types of law—natural, common, statutory, and administrative.

Public law is concerned with society in general, while private law relates to individual members and organizations in society. Laws that cover many aspects of business are based on the Uniform Commercial Code (UCC).

The types of law most important to business are contract law and property law. Contract law specifies that for a contract to exist and be legally enforceable, it must be characterized by mutual acceptance, consideration, capacity, and legal form. When breach of contract occurs, the party harmed by the breach can seek damages, specific performance, or restitution. The most common contract in US business is the sales contract. Businesses that sell goods must consider both sales law and contract law as they draw up sales agreements with their customers.

Rights and obligations relating to ownership, use, and sale of property are covered by property law. Two types of property used by businesses are real property and personal property. Real property can be transferred by sale, gift, adverse possession, or will. Personal property can be transferred through ordinary business dealings, by gift, by will, or by creation.

Other types of law business firms may encounter are agency law, tort law, and bankruptcy law. Damage from a tort must have resulted from negligence or deliberate intent. Bankruptcy may be initiated either on a voluntary or on an involuntary basis. The dominant bankruptcy legislation today is the Bankruptcy Reform Act of 1978.

Government regulation of business has been a focal point of controversy for decades. Important types of regulation include regulation of competition, of marketing activity, and of credit and collection activities.

All levels of government tax individuals and businesses to pay for the services they provide. The most common taxes collected by governments today are based on income. Nonincorporated businesses are taxed at individual rates, while incorporated businesses are taxed at the corporate tax rate. Ordinary income is taxed differently from capital gains. Other major types of taxes include sales taxes, property taxes, and payroll taxes.

KEY TERMS

ad valorem tax
administrative law
agency
bankruptcy law
Bankruptcy Reform
   Act (1978)
breach of contract
capital gain

Celler-Kefauver Act
   (1950)
Clayton Act (1914)
common law
copyright
crime
damages
Equal Credit
   Opportunity Act
   (1975)
Fair Debt Collection
   Practices Act (1978)
intangible personal
   property
Internal Revenue
   Code
law
National
   Environmental
   Protection Act (1970)
natural law
ordinary income
patent
payroll tax
personal property
private law
property tax
public law
punitive damages
real property
restitution
sales contract
sales tax
servicemark
Sherman Antitrust
   Act (1890)
specific performance
statutory law
tangible personal
   property
tort
trademark
Uniform Commercial
   Code (UCC)
warranty

REVIEW QUESTIONS

1. What is *law*? What is the difference between public and private law? What is uniform commercial code (UCC)?

2. List specific characteristics that make a contract enforceable. Must all contracts be in writing?

3. What is meant by *breach of contract*? What remedies are available to a party who is a victim of a breach?

4. What are the two types of property recognized by law? Define the terms deed, lease, tangible personal property, and intangible personal property.

5. What is the meaning of *tort*? Is a tort a crime? Are torts covered under contract law?

6. Describe the process of voluntary and involuntary bankruptcy. Give the name of the act that is the dominant bankruptcy law.

7. How does the government regulate marketing and credit and collection activities? Give at least two examples relative to each.

8. What is the difference between individual and corporate income taxes? How much corporate income tax would be due if the corporation's taxable income was $165,000?

9. What is a *payroll tax*? In what sense is it more important than the corporate income tax?

DISCUSSION QUESTIONS

1. Discuss the growth and expansion of American society in relation to the legal system.

2. Why were the Sherman Antitrust Act and the National Environmental Protection Act made law?

3. Discuss the difference between public law and private law, and how they affect the consumer and businesses.

4. Discuss the various ways that real property can be transferred.

5. How is unfair competition regulated in the free marketplace? List the three methods used.

6. What is the focus of credit and collection regulations? Why was the *Equal Credit Opportunity Act of 1975* established?

7. Discuss ordinary income and capital gains. When are capital gains considered short-term and long-term?

8. Briefly summarize how sales tax, property tax, and payroll taxes are assessed.

CASE: DEADBEATS— MY SPECIALTY

Guy Tuffe had a rather obnoxious personality, and he decided to capitalize on his "talents." He considered himself a natural for the job of bill collector. The name he selected for his enterprise was "Deadbeats—My Specialty" with the subtitle "Bill Collecting at Large"—quite accurate since Guy was six feet, three inches tall and weighed 225 lbs. He had been an offensive tackle on the varsity team, and he had played the role offensively.

Guy started his business in a small way—with a bicycle. He attached his sign to the frame and pedaled down the street to meet his first "deadbeat." Guy's strategy was not to beat down the door of the unsuspecting delinquent customer but instead simply to park his bicycle conspicuously at the curb or near the door and just sit, eat his lunch, or read a book, until the unsuspecting debtor came home from work.

Of course, Guy got lots of attention, and these first attempts at bill collecting were very successful. Business was so good in fact that Guy moved up to a van, on which he had painted the same sign in very colorful letters with an illustration of a gorilla flailing the air. Then he went happily down the streets to the addresses of his newly chosen delinquent accounts. The first one, after a harsh exchange of words and a few threats by Guy, paid up his bill, threw up his arms, and retreated into his home.

In the second client, however, Guy met his match. After sitting out in front of this home for a couple of hours playing loud Rock music on his car radio, Guy looked up to behold a veritable monster of a man emerging from the door and coming right toward him.

The "monster" turned out to be a professional wrestler with an unenviable record of delinquent accounts—but with not too many creditors brave enough to try to get a hold on him. Interestingly, there was no violence in the scene that ensued: the wrestler read from a sheaf of papers he had in hand, sounding more like a frequent courtroom participant than a Masked Marvel. Included were sections from what were obviously the Equal Credit Opportunity Act of 1975 and the Fair Debt Collection Practices Act of 1978. With that done, it quickly appeared that Guy Tuffe was headed out of business—at least as he knew it.

1. What might have been some of the things that the Wrestler pointed out to Guy about his debt collection practices?
2. Are these fairly recent pieces of legislation a real benefit to customers who are delinquent in their payments?
3. What rights do business people have in collecting legitimate debts from people who take advantage of lenient credit practices?

CASE: TAX LIMIT— ALMOST THERE?

"Only the wealthy and politicians can afford to be philosophical about taxes. Politicians have a knack for projecting revenue curves (which means taxation!) that'll rise to meet all the government services these big *spenders of other people's money* can offer."

This is the kind of talk you hear daily in conservative circles—if you can stay awake long enough. But people—especially taxpayers—are getting fed up with all the philosophizing, and instead they want *action*—action in reducing taxes and increasing take-home pay.

There's been no end to the increases that politicians have made in imposing a variety of taxes: property tax, income tax, sales tax, and excise tax. And not coincidentally a new economy has come into being—the "Underground Economy": those

who've decided to defraud the system and not report their incomes, or in some cases report only part of their incomes. Some business people have joined the ranks of the Underground Economy: they don't report some of their sales. In fact, some have very defiantly turned off their cash registers for a certain period of time each day to take in revenues just for their own use. They say, in effect, "To heck with the government—I've given all I can give to help other people; now I'm going to look out for my own welfare."

Some politicians have been haranguing about the Underground Economy, claiming that billions of dollars are being lost by those who would rip-off the government for their own personal gain. The IRS has threatened to crack down on these offenders—and it will, too, unless curbed by Congress.

1. In mid-1982, people began talking seriously about a flat-rate income tax as a substitute for the existing complex tax structure. If passed, it would do away with all exemptions and deductions that are a part of the current tax law. Discuss what you believe are some advantages and disadvantages of the flat-rate income tax.
2. Would an extensive "Underground Economy" return us to the barter system? Discuss.
3. It's not uncommon for workers to turn down overtime work at substantial premium pay. Explain if you think the tax law has something to do with this behavior. (Hint: The expression "bracket creep" is often used in discussing this issue.)

CHAPTER 24

INTERNATIONAL BUSINESS

After studying this chapter you should be able to:

1   Understand the importance of international trade in the world economy.
2   Discuss the position of the United States in the world market.
3   Explain why countries concentrate on manufacturing and exporting certain goods and services.
4   Understand the barriers to international trade.
5   Discuss the need to expand international trade and distinguish the various obstacles to expansion.
6   Specify various ways for a business to enter into foreign trade.
7   Clarify the role of the multinational corporation in world trade.

Japan: restaurant capital of the world. Hard to believe? But it's true: there's one eating establishment for every 81 people—not that all 81 dine out the same night. Understandably, there are many proprietors eager for the diner's patronage. Rather a stiff market.

One outfit which has been able to penetrate that market is Kentucky Fried Chicken. In this scenario, Commodore Perry steps aside for Colonel Sanders. But whereas the Commodore came unbidden on a gunboat, the Colonel was actually invited by the giant Mitsubishi conglomerate to participate in a joint fast-food venture.

The invite was not merely a hands-across-the-sea gesture; it was solid business: Mitsubishi happens to be Japan's largest chicken grower. And, suh, the Colonel, why he wasn't at all offended! Without Mitsubishi, he would have had a heap of trouble rounding up enough fryers to keep the Japanese lickin' their chopsticks; and they say that you can't import the birds, because they develop skin disease.

Things American have long been of interest—often a vogue—with the Japanese. So no "Bluegrass Teriyaki" for them—they want the real thing! And they get it. But while the product is the same as in the United States, just about everything else is not. Kentucky Fried Chicken is positioned differently in the market, appealing to a higher-paying customer. The familiar restaurant design is altered to fit a limited space. Outside, the restaurant displays the typical Japanese plastic models of the food available inside. Two pieces; three pieces; a bucket of pieces. And a cup of the Colonel's best green tea.

The Mitsubishi-KFC partnership has proved mutually rewarding. The tough conglomerate provides the tender chickens, at the same time escorting the Colonel through the maze of Japanese governmental bureaucracy. As for KFC, it grosses $200 million a year and nets a solid profit.

Source: Adapted with the permission of WGBH, Boston, Massachusetts, from the article "The Colonel Comes to Japan," published in *A Guide to Enterprise*, Copyright © 1981, WGBH Educational Foundation.

THE IMPORTANCE OF TRADE

International trade is extremely important to KFC and to thousands of other American businesses. Moreover trade is of major importance to most nations of the world. The value of world trade is over $1300 billion a year and has been growing at a rate of almost 20 percent a year.[1] Trade helps bolster a country's economy, improves relationships between friends and allies, helps to ease strains and tensions between nations, uplifts people's standards of living, and in the end improves the quality of life.

Exports and Imports

The developed nations of the world account for more than 66 percent of the world's exports. Developed countries are also the major customers (71.6%) for almost every conceivable good and service. Countries that are geographically close together tend to be major trading partners. For example, about half of all the exports in Europe are to other European countries. The United States takes about 70 percent of Canadian exports and supplies the Canadians with about the same percentage of their imports. Also, the level and

volume of trade between the United States and Mexico is growing dramatically, with America importing gas and oil and exporting finished goods.

The 10 countries in Table 24.1 account for 65 percent of the world's exports. However the dominance of the largest exporters has declined since 1970, when the 10 largest were responsible for over 70 percent of the world's exports. Also, Saudi Arabia became the ninth largest exporter in the world during the decade of the 1970s. Many developing nations, such as Spain, Korea, and Nige-

ria, are growing exporters. Generally, a **developing nation** is one that is not highly industrialized and has not achieved a high standard of living.

The United States exports an increasing percentage of its food, feeds, and beverage products. And it imports a greater percentage of its industrial supplies (such as steel) and capital goods. It's also a major exporter of engineering products and other high-technology items (capital goods). Despite its impressive list of resources and great variety of both consumer and industrial products, America's sheer volume of imports is constantly

TABLE 24-1

The Largest Exporters in 1978

	Merchandise Exports (billions U.S. $)	Exports of Goods and Services as Percentage of Gross Domestic Product	Percentage of World Trade
United States	141.2	8	11.1
Germany	142.1	25	11.2
Japan	97.5	11	7.7
France	76.6	21	6.0
United Kingdom	71.7	30	5.7
USSR	52.2	n.a.[a]	4.1
Italy	56.0	25	4.4
Netherlands	50.2	47	4.0
Saudi Arabia	40.7	62	3.2
Canada	46.1	26	3.6
World Total	1,269.2	—	70.0

[a]Not available.

SOURCE: World Bank, *World Development Report 1980* (New York: Oxford University Press, 1980), Annex Tables 5 and 8; reprinted by permission.

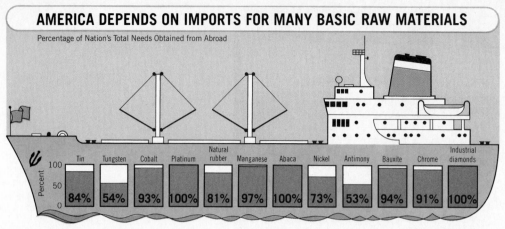

AMERICA DEPENDS ON IMPORTS FOR MANY BASIC RAW MATERIALS

Percentage of Nation's Total Needs Obtained from Abroad

Tin	Tungsten	Cobalt	Platinum	Natural rubber	Manganese	Abaca	Nickel	Antimony	Bauxite	Chrome	Industrial diamonds
84%	54%	93%	100%	81%	97%	100%	73%	53%	94%	91%	100%

FIGURE 24.1

Source: Data from Walter Emery, ed., *Commodity Yearbook 1981* (New York: Commodity Research Bureau, 1981).

growing. Some of our imports are critical raw materials not available from domestic sources. For example, we get over 90 percent of our bauxite (to make aluminum), chromium (to make stainless steel), and all of our diamonds from abroad (see Figure 24.1). Most of our favorite hot beverages are imported — coffee, tea, and cocoa. While these are not critical to our country's needs, they do improve the quality of life. We also import Scotch whisky, English bicycles, German and Japanese automobiles, Italian and Spanish shoes, Central American bananas, Philippine plywood, Hong Kong textiles, and French wines.

WHY NATIONS TRADE

Principle of Comparative Advantage

Developing a trade relationship with another country usually makes both countries better off. Why? Because the distribution of resources, both natural and human, varies from country to country. Some countries have more natural resources (tin, rice, iron, etc.). Since resources are unevenly distributed, some countries end up with an over-abundance of some resources (America usually produces a surplus of wheat) and critical shortages in others. By exchanging natural resources and manufactured goods, countries can usually improve their quality of life.

The great variety of goods and services marketed worldwide demands a corresponding variety of resources and technology. A given product or service usually results from a favorable combination of resource and technological factors. This should create an advantage for the producer and in turn make for a profitable operation. For example, Japan has a shortage of land but a rich supply of skilled labor. Japan's advantage therefore lies in combining these two factors, and the result is a profitable electronics (and related) industry. This involves minimal use of land and maximal use of skilled labor. On the one hand, an obstacle is overcome; on the other, an asset is exploited.

Argentina is the opposite of Japan in these respects. It has vasts amounts of land, petroleum, a mild climate, and a relatively unskilled (but improving) labor force. These resources don't lend themselves to the production of high-technology electronics or automobiles but rather to the growing of cattle and the exporting of oil. So trade takes place because nations need to buy goods and services that they can't efficiently produce at home.

The nature of what's exported and imported by a country depends on many things — as you'll discover later in the chapter. To return to the Japan/Argentina example of transistors and cattle raising: if each produces both, inefficiency results. It's much wiser for the two nations to engage in trade. This trade would be based on the comparative advantage that Japan has in transistors and Argentina in cattle. Argentina would specialize in raising cattle and import transistors from Japan. The result of trade based on comparative advantage would be that both countries were better off. In summary, the **principle of comparative advantage** says that if each nation specializes in goods that it can produce most readily and

Comparative advantage works equally well for Japan and Argentina.

cheaply, and trades those goods for others that foreign countries can produce most cheaply, there will be more goods available at lower prices.

Balance of Trade

The concept of comparative advantage shows us why trade occurs between two nations. The **balance of trade** for a country is a measure of its exports and imports of goods and services. When a nation exports more goods than it imports, it's said to have a *favorable balance of trade*. On the other hand, if it imports more products than it exports, it has an *unfavorable balance of trade*. Nations strive for a favorable balance of trade because, especially in the past, unfavorable balances of trade had to be paid off in gold—and promptly.

Although the importance of gold has been played down to some degree in today's international finance, nations still don't like to give up their gold reserves—and have more time in which to do so. When imports exceed exports, more money flows out of the country than into it. In 1980 the United States had an unfavorable balance of trade of approximately $20 billion.[2] When a country has a favorable balance of trade, then gold or money (or other forms of currency) flow into that country.

Balance of Payments

The balance of payments is a broader concept that includes all the transactions involving imports and exports (balance of trade), as well as other types of financial transactions between nations. These include long-term overseas investments in plants and equipment by businesses, loans made by governments to each other, gifts and foreign aid between nations, military expenditures made in foreign nations, and money deposits and withdrawals in foreign banks. The balance of payments, then, includes the balance of trade and all the above transactions. The **balance of payments** is the difference between a nation's total payments to foreign countries and its receipts from foreign countries.

Since the beginning of this century the United States had a favorable balance of trade until 1970. However the other items listed above — making up the balance of payments — were bigger than the additional funds coming from the favorable balance of trade (i.e. from imports being less than exports). Therefore since 1950 America has had an unfavorable balance of payments for almost every year. Unfortunately, since 1970 we've had both an unfavorable balance of trade and an unfavorable balance of payments.

This long-term shift in the balance of trade and balance of payments had been due to many factors. After World War II the United States assisted in the industrial development of Japan and Western Europe to repair their war-devastated economies. Such industrial bases as iron and steel manufacturing, cement plants, and automobile factories were completely rebuilt after World War II. Thus their capital was more modern than that of the United States. Highly productive capital goods plus low labor rates made Japan and Western Europe very strong competitors. New industrial plants and lower labor costs make it possible for many countries to produce quality products at lower prices and sell them in the United States as well as abroad.

Since the mid-1970s the huge increase in the price of oil has further hurt the balance of payments. Because our oil payments quadrupled in one year, we were no longer able to repay our deficits in gold. At that point, the United States decided that it could no longer redeem dollars for gold at the low price of $35 an ounce. Because the dollar had a fixed value based on gold, the dollar had been the standard world currency, against which all other currencies were valued and traded.

However in today's international finance, the foreign currencies of any country must now be sold in the open market, where prices are subject to daily change. The new system is called **floating currency** which means that the price or the value of a currency depends on the supply and demand, much like a stock listed on the New York Stock Exchange. If a nation doesn't want to sell large quantities of dollars at the current market rate, it can hold them in the hope that the value of the dollar will appreciate. This means that there's a continually changing foreign exchange rate — the number of yen or pounds or francs (or any other form of currency) that can be exchanged for one dollar. In the early summer of 1981 a Japanese businessperson could exchange about 218 yen for $1. In recent years the trading ratio has been over 300 yen to $1.

The value of a nation's currency is a very complicated concept; it depends on how the international financial market evaluates that country's economic health and its stability. Some of the considerations in valuing a nation's currency include the attitudes of its dominant political party and the powers-that-be toward business; its ability to control inflation; its balance of payments and trade; its wage rates; and the productivity of its factories.

BARRIERS TO INTERNATIONAL TRADE

International trade is carried out both by private business firms and by governments. Sometimes trade barriers can affect the willingness and ability of firms to sell to one another in foreign markets. Generally speaking, there are three major obstacles that restrict trade among nations. These are (1) natural barriers, (2) tariff barriers, and (3) nontariff barriers.

Natural Barriers

Even though it may be cheaper to grow beef on the plains of Argentina than in the bitter cold of Siberia, the cost of shipping the beef to Siberia might make the price prohibitive. Distance is a natural barrier to international trade. Although jet airplanes help reduce the time lag of shipping between two countries, their cargo is limited to products with a high unit value. For example, it would not make sense to ship coal or gravel on an airplane. On the other hand, orchids, computers, and critical replacement parts are commonly moved by airfreight. Improvements in technology

ON THE FIRING LINE

Trade with the Soviet Union—How Great a Threat?

For years the US, bearing the standard of democracy, has led the battle against the form of tyranny now referred to as communism. The leadership role for the other side long ago fell to the USSR. The two nations have directly or indirectly engaged each other with almost every kind of weapon. They've tried armed force, propaganda, culture and education, politics, and trade.

Just how effective any of these weapons may be is debatable. Recently, for example, US trade with the communist bloc, particularly the USSR, has come under fire. People voice concern at pro-trade policies for two main reasons. First, they say, by cutting off all trade we can discourage the USSR from acts of aggression such as the invasion of Afghanistan. Thus they advocate economic warfare. Second, they believe that by trading we actually bolster the military might of the Soviet Union. Through trade, they insist, we jeopardize our own national security and the security of many other, small, nonaligned nations.

To wage an effective economic war against the USSR, these same individuals feel, the US must gain the cooperation of the entire Western bloc and Japan. We can hope to do this only if we eliminate all US–USSR trade. Other nations can't be expected to show total commitment unless we do, they say. To date, the Soviets have taken advantage of competition between West-bloc businesses. They play them off against each other to get advanced technological information.

The proponents of embargo go on to observe that the last decade has seen the Soviet Union purchase $50 billion of goods from the West. The nature of these purchases, they say, is ominous. Included are machine tools; power lines; technology needed for missiles, tanks, command control and communications systems, spy satellites, and radar. Many purchases present a threat less obvious but just as real. These include dual-use items that have poten-

tial military applications. Trucks, for example, can be converted for military use. Indeed, trucks purchased from the West were used in the invasion of Afghanistan.

Those who favor trade with the USSR also point out that trade is only one of many means the Soviets have for extracting strategic technology from us. Spying, of course, is another technique. Often, though, not even that much effort is required. The Freedom of Information Act guarantees access to much data contained in federal government files. These include, for instance, patents—a key resource on the latest technology. The Soviets have yet another strategy: they buy controlling interests in Western companies and thus obtain access to technology that they're not allowed to purchase directly. There are over 25 such communist-controlled companies in the US now.

Still another argument in favor of trade with the Soviet bloc is that it contributes to détente. Economic ties, in this view, form the foundation for cultural, educational, and political exchange. These in turn can be instrumental in promoting desirable internal changes (for instance, in the area of human rights) in the otherwise closed communist countries. They can also promote cooperation in solving long-term global problems such as population explosion, food supplies, diminishing natural resources, and environmental protection.

Finally, assert advocates of trade with the Soviet Union, the US and its allies badly need the communist market. Indeed, it's unlikely that all our NATO allies and Japan would ever accept a total embargo on trade with the East. West Germany, for instance, is already involved in a swap of technology for Soviet natural gas, a commodity in short supply in the West. The Soviets have made much of their need for help in developing their natural gas and oil resources. If help is provided, they claim, they won't have to venture into the Persian Gulf.

have made it possible to transport liquefied natural gas, asphalt, and other products by ship or barge—something not feasible some 15 years ago. Continued improvements in technology may help lower natural barriers.

Language is another natural barrier. Inability to properly translate what someone is saying hinders the establishment of mutual understanding. Language difficulties sometimes result in the wrong merchandise being shipped after trade is established.

Tariff Barriers

A **tariff** is a tax or customs duty levied by a nation on imported goods. It may be a **specific tariff** assessed per unit of imported good or an *ad valorem tax* based on the value of the imports, or it may be a combination of the two. Regardless of the type, the effects of a tariff are to make imported items more expensive and to reduce their ability to compete with domestic products. A tariff designed to discourage imports is called a **protective tariff.** It's set high enough to make the product less attractive to potential buyers. Our government, for example, imposes protective tariffs on certain types of imported steel, poultry, textiles, and shoes.

A second purpose of tariffs is to raise money through tax revenue. Such a tariff is called a **revenue tariff.** Since it is not the purpose of a revenue tariff to restrict imports, it's usually quite low. Revenue tariffs were important in the United States before 1900, when we had a limited manufacturing capacity. By taxing the many manufactured products coming from Europe and other countries, our government raised revenue. Although the United States no longer relies on revenue tariffs, many developing nations continue to use them as a means of raising funds.

Arguments for and against Tariffs Congress has been debating the wisdom and necessity of tariffs since 1789. There's basically only one argument against tariffs. It is that the abolition (or prevention) of all tariffs most encourages free trade, and free trade allows the principle of comparative advantage to work most efficiently.

Other people argue for "protection" in the form of tariffs. One of the oldest arguments for a tariff is called the **infant industry argument.** Advocates of this position say that tariffs are needed to protect new domestic industries from well-established foreign competitors. Accordingly, a tariff should be imposed until the struggling industry can reach its ultimate level of technical superiority and become an effective competitor. History has shown, however, that after the infant industry grows up, it lobbies very strongly to retain the high protective tariff.

A second argument for tariffs is the **home industry argument.** This holds that American markets should be reserved for American industry by building "tariff walls" around domestic industries, regardless of their maturity. Supporters of this position would protect, for example, the American automobile, clothing, and semiconductor industries without regard to comparative advantages held by other countries.

A third argument for tariffs is often heard in connection with the automobile industry. Unions claim that tariffs should be used to keep foreign labor from taking American jobs. This, they say, is what happens when low-wage countries sell products in America at lower prices than American manufacturers can afford to charge. (The higher prices help pay America's higher wages.) Advocates of this position tend to be especially vocal during periods of high unemployment.

Members of the military as well as defense suppliers often advance the **defense preparedness argument** for tariffs. They say that we should protect industries and technology that are vital to maintaining a high level of defense preparedness. Military planners feel that in case of war, these industries will be needed; they must therefore be protected during peacetime. Our shipbuilding industry, manufacturers of gunpowder, and textile producers who manufacture uniforms are beneficiaries of this tariff.

Nontariff Barriers

There are a number of other tools that can be used by governments to restrict trade. Many of them have been applied by the United States and other trading nations over the years. They include import quotas, embargos, exchange controls, "buy national" regulations, and dumping.

Import Quotas An **import quota** is a control on the quantity of merchandise imported over a period of time. The objective of an import quota is

PERSPECTIVE ON SMALL BUSINESS

Exporting saved Jim Blau's company. Snow-Way International, Inc., Milwaukee, had a wonderful product that nobody needed in 1979: a $1,300 snowplow designed to be attached to subcompact, front-wheel-drive cars like the Volkswagen Rabbit. It was a dry winter, and inventory piled up. "We had to have a broader marketing base. So I took a $10,000 gamble," recalls the 50-year-old Blau. "I flew to a trade show in Germany, taking a plow with me. I spent $2,000 for a booth. I didn't know what to expect."

He wasn't in doubt for long. Blau's patented design, which does not require remodeling of a car's front end, was an instant success. "The reception was wild," he says. "The plow was perfect for the European market, fitting in with the narrow streets. They had never seen anything like it." After he took $150,000 in orders, and even sold the plow on display, local auto dealers flocked to his hotel room. Blau, a Subaru and Volvo dealer himself, signed up 11 distributors.

Unfortunately, Blau returned to the US without the vaguest idea of how to ship those orders. "I started picking brains," he says. He called friends who had export experience, called the local Commerce Department office for advice and recommendations and rang up several freight forwarders. They all helped.

Today Blau's snowplows are sold from Australia, where they clear mudslides, to Saudi Arabia, where they are used to clear sand from driveways. Foreign sales were such a snap—"Using containers, it is as easy and inexpensive [$100] to ship a plow to Switzerland as to Portland," says Blau—that he now prefers the overseas business. About 75% of Snow-Way's estimated $2 million in 1981 revenues will come as a result of exports.

He has little time to tinker these days. A recent free ad in a Commerce Department magazine produced an 8-inch stack of inquiries. Snow-Way's 6 employees (25 subcontractors produce parts for the plow) are hard pressed to handle the volume of incoming mail and outgoing shipments. "I'm keeping 200 to 300 people busy," says Blau, still a little awed at the profitable results of that desperation trip to Germany.

SOURCE: Larry Marion, "Exporting without Tears: Snowplows to Saudis," *Forbes*, 13 April 1981, p. 64. Reprinted by permission of Forbes Magazine from the April 13, 1981, issue.

---

to permit a country to determine the maximum amount of a given product that it considers advantageous to import. The Japanese agreed to a voluntary quota on American importation of their automobiles in the spring of 1981. The voluntary agreement was preceded by threats of a strict import quota. The effects of a protective tariff and an import quota are essentially the same. However a protective tariff generates revenue for the government; a quota creates profits for the importer that holds the import license.

Embargos   An **embargo,** or boycott, prohibits the importing of certain products into a country or—in some cases—exporting materials to a country. Often, embargos are established for military purposes. Thus we don't allow exportation of high-technology computer products or oil drilling equipment to the Soviet Union. Sometimes embargos are established for health reasons. Certain breeds of parrots, for example, cannot be imported into the United States because they're common carriers of diseases. Also, the importation of piranha is prohibited in the state of Florida because the many warm fresh-water canals might become populated with schools of piranha.

Embargos are also used for political reasons. Coca Cola and Ford were boycotted by some Arab countries because of their operations in Israel. In fact the Arab nations developed a lengthy list of companies with which they wouldn't conduct business because of the companies' dealings or sympathy with Israel.

Exchange (currency) Controls   Exchange controls are another major tool for regulation of foreign trade. **Exchange control** is a government monopoly of all dealings in foreign exchange. This means that a company earning foreign exchange (such as yen or pounds) from its exports must sell the foreign exchange to the control agency, usually a central bank. A company that wants to buy merchandise from abroad must buy its foreign exchange from the control agency rather than from the free market. Exchange control typically means that foreign exchange is in scarce supply and therefore the government is rationing it based on its own priorities such as limiting the importation of luxury goods. When foreign exchange is limited, government must use what little is available to purchase necessities and capital goods. Capital goods, such as basic machinery, help a country to produce goods domestically and therefore reduce the demand for imports. Firms producing merchandise within the country but using foreign parts or supplies must be on the government's favored list to get exchange to pay for these imported supplies. Otherwise they have to develop local suppliers, which may lead to higher costs and poorer quality. Sears' ability to expand its operations in several Latin American countries has been limited by exchange controls. Sears in, say, Lima cannot obtain enough dollars through Peruvian exchange controls to bring in quality manufactured products from the United States. Locally produced goods haven't met Sears' standards or were simply unavailable.

"Buy National" Regulations   **"Buy national" regulations** give special priority and privileges to domestic manufacturers. One of America's regulations, for example, prohibits the use of foreign steel in the construction of our highways. In addition to buy-national regulations, other so-called *invisible tariffs* exist. These include customs documentation requirements, mark of origin (a mark specifying where the merchandise comes from),

food and drug legislation, and label laws. Invisible tariffs are quite diverse and vary from country to country. Yet their impact is still the same: all of them restrict foreign trade.

Dumping   Sometimes, trade restriction is justified, particularly in the case of **dumping.** This is a form of international price discrimination in which a company charges lower prices (or even below cost) in foreign markets than it does for the same merchandise in its home market. The company might be trying to win customers away from the same kind of goods manufactured in the foreign markets; or it might merely be seeking to get rid of surplus goods. To aid in creating exports, some governments will subsidize certain industries so that they can sell at lower prices in the international market. Two examples are the Japanese steel industry and Air France (the French national airlines). Where the variation in price can't be explained by differences in the cost of serving the two markets (home and foreign), dumping is considered to have occurred. European steel producers have been accused of dumping by American steelmakers. Conversely, American producers of synthetic fibers have been accused of dumping by the European textile industry.

Most industrialized countries have antidumping regulations that are intended to control possible excesses stemming from the practice. Governments are particularly concerned about "predatory" dumping. This is the attempt to gain control of a market by systematically destroying competitors through artificially low prices. Under the Antidumping Act of 1974 the U.S. Treasury Department decides whether imports are sold at "less than fair value." If it's determined that domestic industry is being hurt, extra duties can be imposed, calculated to be the difference between the price here and in the country of origin. In the 1970s a dumping duty was placed on steel imported from Japan. Imports priced below the predetermined Japanese delivery price of steel resulted in a duty that gave quick relief to our domestic steel industry.

A low price is not in itself sufficient reason to warrant an antidumping duty. There must be injury to a local industry as well. The reason that injury is a necessary condition is that consumers tend to benefit from low prices coming from *any* source. Thus unless a domestic industry is negatively affected, the price should be allowed to stand. Developing nations where mature industries are nonexistent usually do not have anti-dumping regulations.

ATTEMPTS TO INCREASE WORLD TRADE

Up to this point it might almost seem that governments acted to restrain trade! Appearances to the contrary, governments in fact often do try to *increase* trade. The movement to liberalize trade gained momentum after World War II, culminating in the **General Agreement on Tariffs and Trade (GATT)** in 1947. GATT is perhaps the single most effective mechanism for worldwide trade liberalization and tariff concessions. Its goal is to eliminate tariff barriers to worldwide trade. GATT has a basic set of rules under which trade negotiations take place. It also has an administrative organization for overseeing and implementing the rules. GATT provides a means for negotiating trade concessions and issues rules governing nondiscrimination in trade relations. The member countries of GATT meet annually to review recommendations, settle disputes, and study new ways to reduce tariffs.

The Trade Expansion Act

In 1962 the United States **Trade Expansion Act** was passed. It granted the president a major increase in authority to make important tariff concessions and to expand U.S. economic adjustment to new import competition. Specifically, it gave the president authority to negotiate further tariff reductions, eliminate or reduce tariffs on European Common Market goods, and reduce tariffs on the basis of reciprocal trade agreements. In other words, the act recognized the principle of comparative advantage and also that some domestic industries could not compete against more efficient imported merchandise. The president could thus somewhat withdraw protection from these industries in order to negotiate tariff structures and trade arrangements more favorable to more competitive American industries. The relocation of capital to these industries was seen as increasing America's economic growth in the long run.

The Kennedy Round

The Trade Expansion Act of 1962 served as a background for the Kennedy Round of tariff negotiations undertaken two years later by the 50 member nations of GATT. The negotiations were called the **Kennedy Round** because they were initiated by President John Kennedy when tariff duties were cut on 60,000 items. Tariffs were reduced by an average of 40 percent.

As tariffs were negotiated downward on a product-by-product basis, the relative importance of nontariff barriers grew. An attempt was made during the Kennedy Round to reduce certain nontariff barriers, but this largely failed. To avoid backsliding into protectionism, the United States took steps to further liberalize trade. It made proposals to reduce tariffs on industrial products. It also began to relax restraints on agricultural trade. The proposals were continued in the Trade Act of 1974, on which a new round of trade negotiations was established, generally called the Tokyo Round. These discussions began in Geneva in 1975 and lasted until 1979. The Tokyo Round cut tariffs by an average of one third. It also yielded many new agreements to liberalize nontariff barriers. Attempts were made, for example, to ensure the availability of foreign exchange, to liberalize licensing problems for importers and exporters, and to reduce "buy-national" agreements.

The Ottawa Economic "Summit"

In 1981 representatives of the United States, France, West Germany, Italy, Britain, Canada, and Japan met at an international economic "summit" conference in Ottawa. Their objective was to halt the dangerous trend toward trade barriers among industrialized countries. Two weeks earlier, the Reagan administration had set forth the American position in a policy statement. This pledged strong government resistance to growing trade barriers, declaring that free trade is essential in securing a strong U.S. economy. The attack on import restrictions was coupled with a pledge to challenge subsidized competition, such as Air France. The statement also warned that the United States would strictly enforce its trade laws and international agreements relating to dumping and subsidized exports.

TABLE 24–2
Regional Economic Associations

Name	Membership	Date of Origin
ANCOM: Andean Development Corporation (also called the Andean Common Market)	Bolivia, Colombia, Ecuador, Peru, Venezuela	1967
Arab Economic Unity Agreement	Iraq, Jordan, Kuwait, Syria, Egypt, Sudan, Yemen	1964
ASEAN: Association of Southeast Asian Nations	Indonesia, Malaysia, Philippines, Singapore, Thailand	1967
Benelux	Belgium, Luxembourg, the Netherlands	1947
CACM: Central American Common Market	Costa Rica, El Salvador, Guatemala, Honduras, Nicaragua	1960
CARICOM: Caribbean Common Market	Antigua, Barbados, Dominica, Grenada, Guyana, Jamaica, Montserrat, St. Christopher-Nevis-Anguilla, St. Lucia, St. Vincent, Trinidad, and Tobago	1966
CMEA: Council for Mutual Economic Assistance (also called COMECON)	Bulgaria, Czechoslovakia, East Germany, Hungary, Mongolian People's Republic, Poland, Romania, USSR, Cuba, Yugoslavia (partial participant)	1949
East African Community	Kenya, Tanzania, Uganda	1967
EEC: European Economic Community	Belgium, France, West Germany, Italy, Luxembourg, the Netherlands, Denmark, Ireland, United Kingdom	1958
EFTA: European Free Trade Area	Austria, Norway, Portugal, Sweden, Switzerland, Iceland, Finland (associate member)	1960
LAFTA: Latin American Free Trade Association (also called ALALC)	Argentina, Bolivia, Brazil, Chile, Colombia, Ecuador, Mexico, Paraguay, Peru, Uruguay, Venezuela	1960
The Nordic Council	Denmark, Finland, Iceland, Norway, Sweden	1953
OCAM: Organisation Commune Africaine et Malgache	Central African Republic, Dahomey, Gabon, Ivory Coast, Mauritius, Niger, Rwanda, Senegal, Togo, Upper Volta	1965

SOURCE: From *International Marketing*, rev. ed., p. 42, by Vern Terpstra. Copyright © 1978 by Dryden Press, a division of Holt, Rinehart and Winston, Inc. Reprinted by permission of Holt, Rinehart and Winston, CBS College Publishing.

Economic Integration

When governments meet and agree on a common economic policy, the result is called **economic integration.** Some nations may agree on a **preferential tariff,** which specially advantages one nation (or several nations) over others. In this case, tariffs on the same commodity (e.g. spring wheat) differ according to the source of the commodity. Members of the British Commonwealth have preferential tariff treatment when they trade with Great Britain. In other cases, nations form free trade associations and establish free trade zones — areas where there are few, if any, export and import duties or other regulations that would act as barriers to trade. The largest trade association is called the European Economic Community (EEC); and one of the major organizations in this group is the European Free Trade Association (see Table 24.2). Nations may integrate further by creating a customs union. In this arrangement not only are tariffs and nontariff barriers reduced among themselves, but also common policies are established regarding trade outside the union.

The Common Market The European Economic Community, also called the **Common Market,** began as a European coal and steel community in 1950. Initial members were the "Inner Six": Belgium, France, West Germany, Italy, Luxembourg, and the Netherlands. In 1957 these countries signed the Treaty of Rome, in which they agreed to set up the Common Market, expand its membership, and create a customs union. The Common Market was expanded in 1973 to include Great Britain, Denmark, and Ireland. In 1975 many countries of Africa and the Caribbean became members. More recently Greece, Portugal, and Spain have applied for full membership. The Common Market has established common import duties for its members; it has also abolished tariff barriers between them. Goods imported from nonmember nations, however, face stiff tariffs. The Common Market is thus a kind of United States of Europe, where trade can take place freely within the community but outsiders must pay to get in.

As differences in markets declined in the Common Market, there developed greater uniformity in the approach of international firms to member countries. For example, a manufacturer of home care products closed down eight national production offices in Europe soon after the Common Market was formed. It concentrated its continental European production in the Netherlands to gain the economies of mass production (low unit cost associated with large quantity of output) possible within the free trade area. The firm also standardized its packages, designs, and color. However advertising copy was continued in different national languages.

WAYS OF ENTERING THE INTERNATIONAL MARKET

Unlike the big conglomerates many small firms are reluctant to enter the international market. Usually, international operations are characterized by greater uncertainty than domestic operations. Most small organizations lack the necessary knowledge concerning tariffs, quotas, and demand for their product in international markets. Without adequate information, a small firm can have a hard time making the right decisions in the international marketplace. Also, many small firms don't want to deal in foreign currencies because of the complexities involved.

Exporting

If a firm decides to take the international plunge, it will probably begin with simple exporting. This is the least complicated way to enter the international marketplace. In fact there's actually little mechanical difference between export sales and domestic sales—with the exception of dealing in a foreign currency. One approach to exporting is to sell the company's wares to an export agency. The firm may sell the merchandise outright at a specified price or offer it to the export agency on a consignment basis. When it is sold on consignment, it's shipped by the export agency to the foreign importer and sold for whatever price it may bring. The American company is then reimbursed by the export agency when the agency receives payment from the (foreign) importer. When an American company sells outright to an export agency, the agency buys the goods for its own account and sells the products at a markup in international trade. In addition, the American firm wishing to export directly might rely on one of a variety of forms of federal assistance available to American exporters (see Table 24.3).

Licensing

A firm wanting to take a more aggressive stance in international trade may use **licensing,** which can often minimize risk and yet increase the domestic firm's income. The firm (as "licensor") agrees to let a foreign firm (the "licensee") use its patents, trademarks, production processes, brands, products, or company name. The licensee in turn agrees to pay the licensor royalty fees or a fixed amount agreed on by both parties. A license may be exclusive or nonexclusive. That is, the licensee may have the exclusive right to use a trademark in a particular country or group of countries. Most license agreements are usually for a five- or ten-year period, with a royalty fee of between 5 and 10 percent of sales.

There are number of advantages for the firm offering a license. During the licensing period, goodwill generated for a product may pave the way for the firm's decision to do its own production in the foreign country later on. Licensing

TABLE 24–3

Examples of Government Assistance to International Business

Institution	Purpose
1. Foreign Trade Zones	1. The Foreign Trade Zones Act of 1934 permits the creation of foreign trade zones in the United States. These are areas into which goods can be imported without being subject to customs duties or quotas. Often, the imported materials are manufactured into finished products that are re-exported or enter into domestic commerce. If re-exported, they are not subject to any tariffs. If they enter into domestic commerce, they are subject to regular tariffs.
2. The Export-Import Bank (Eximbank)	2. This agency was created in 1934 by the U.S. government to reduce domestic unemployment. It makes loans to exporters who cannot secure financing through private sources. It also makes loans to foreign countries who use the funds to buy American-made goods.
3. The Foreign Credit Insurance Association (FCIA)	3. Eximbank and the private American insurance industry created the FCIA in 1961. A firm can buy insurance from FCIA to cover political risk (such as expropriation and loss due to war). Comprehensive coverage can be bought to cover business risks (such as credit default). The exporter can also buy insurance coverage on credit sales to foreign customers. FCIA places American exporters on a more equal footing with exporters whose governments provide financial assistance to them.
4. The International Bank for Reconstruction and Development (World Bank)	4. The World Bank began operations in 1946 to advance the economic development of member nations by making loans to them. These loans are made either directly by the World Bank using its own funds, or indirectly by the World Bank's borrowing from member countries.
5. The International Monetary Fund (IMF)	5. The IMF began operations in 1947 to promote trade among member countries by eliminating trade barriers and promoting financial cooperation among them. It enables members to cope better with balance of payments problems. Thus, if firms in Peru wish to buy from American firms but Peru lacks enough American dollars, Peru can borrow American dollars from the IMF. It pays the loan back in gold or the currency it receives through its dealing with other countries.
6. The General Agreement on Tariffs and Trade (GATT)	6. GATT was negotiated in 1947 by member nations to improve trade relations through reductions and elimination of tariffs. GATT has resulted in tariff reductions on thousands of products.
7. The International Development Association (IDA)	7. The IDA began operations in 1960 and is affiliated with the World Bank. It makes loans to private businesses and to member countries of the World Bank. In addition to the IDA, there are similar organizations that make loans to governments and firms in certain country groupings. The Inter-American Development Association, for example, is for countries belonging to the Organization of American States.
8. The International Finance Corporation (IFC)	8. The IFC began operations in 1956 and is also affiliated with the World Bank. It makes loans to private businesses when they cannot obtain loans from more conventional sources.
9. Domestic International Sales Corporation (DISC)	9. In December 1971 Congress authorized American firms to form tax-shelter subsidiaries (DISCs) to handle their export sales. The purpose is to spur exports and encourage American firms to enter the export market. A firm can defer some of its taxes on export earnings by establishing a DISC.

SOURCE: John A. Reinecke and William F. Schoell, *Introduction to Business: A Contemporary View*, 3d ed. (Boston: Allyn and Bacon, 1980), pp. 560–61. Reprinted by permission.

As worldwide economic and political conditions continue to churn, more and more corporate managers are turning to political risk analysts for advice. Large oil companies and banks have always had in-house analysts to weigh the stability of nations and regions. But a survey [in 1980] by the Conference Board, a New York business study group, found that smaller and less wealthy firms are now beginning to seek out specialists as well.

The analysis ranges from assigning junior executives to keep watch over a potential foreign hot spot, to the elaborate computerized system that American Can Co. set up in 1978 to rank investment risks in some 70 different countries. Many smaller companies hire outside consultants like Chicago's Associated Consultants International and Boston's Arthur Little Inc. to provide political risk assessments. . . .

Businessmen realize that such advice is now a vital part of making deals in a politically unstable world.

Source: Excerpted from "In Search of Stable Markets," *Time*, 25 May 1981, p. 69. Copyright 1981 Time Inc. All rights reserved. Reprinted by permission.

also avoids the need to make large expenditures of capital abroad and/or to assign important personnel to a foreign country.

Contract Manufacturing

Firms that don't want to become heavily involved in licensing agreements or that want to pursue the international market more directly may decide to contract for the manufacture of their products by established foreign manufacturers. This is simply private label manufacturing by a foreign company, called **contract manufacturing.** The foreign company produces a predetermined volume of products to specifications, and the domestic firm's brand name is attached to the goods. Marketing may be handled by either the domestic company or the foreign manufacturer.

Contract manufacturing enables a company to "test the water" by trying to build market position and developing brand loyalty without a large investment in equipment. After a solid base has been established, the company can switch to direct investment or a joint venture.

Joint Venture

A **joint venture** is an enterprise in which two or more firms or investors share ownership and control over operations and property rights. These owners may share patents, trademarks, or control over manufacturing and marketing. Many joint ventures come about because of necessity; that is, no single firm is willing to assume the financial risk involved. Large, capital-intensive, long-term investments are natural candidates for joint ventures. The building of factories abroad and the extraction of resource deposits—such as petroleum, bauxite, and iron ore—are often accomplished through joint ventures. In the latter case, one firm may do the actual mining, another provide the transportation, and yet another provide the refining and extraction.

Direct Investment

Direct investment is the purchase of active ownership in a foreign company. Direct investors have a controlling (or else large minority) interest, and

TALKING BUSINESS

Here's how Procter & Gamble describes cultural differences within its detergent market:

> There is no such thing as one best detergent for the whole world. For example, people in the Philippines mainly wash their clothes by hand. But, Germans prefer machine washing with scalding water. Canadians also use machines, but like their water warm. In each situation, a different detergent formula is preferred.

> Of course, P & G could produce a single detergent that would work reasonably well in almost any country. But, it wouldn't do the best job for everyone. So we go the extra step and produce more than 100 different laundry cleaning formulas to match various uses and circumstances around the world.

> This means that consumers in Latin America, Canada, Europe, the Far East or anywhere else, are getting the type of detergent that will work best for them.

Source: The Procter & Gamble Company, *People and Products* (Cincinnati: Procter & Gamble, 1980), p. 9. © 1980 The Procter & Gamble Company. Quoted material reprinted by permission.

---

this arrangement offers the greatest potential reward. Naturally, the possibility of substantial rewards means greater risk. Sometimes direct investments are made because no suitable local partners can be found. Potential problems of communication and conflict of interests that may arise with a joint venture partner are eliminated.

An organization may make a foreign direct investment by acquiring an interest in an existing company or by constructing new facilities. A firm may seek an acquisition because it's difficult either to transfer some resource to a foreign operation or to acquire that resource locally for a new facility. One such resource is personnel, particularly if the local managerial labor market is tight. Instead of paying higher salaries than competitors, the domestic firm may simply buy an entire organization and obtain all the personnel intact.

THE CULTURAL AND POLITICAL ENVIRONMENT IN INTERNATIONAL MARKETS

Regardless of whether a domestic firm is considering simple export or direct foreign investment, it should understand the political and cultural nature of the country with which it plans to do busi-

ness. Often political and cultural factors are more important in completing a sale than the price or even the product itself. If two companies are selling essentially the same product (e.g. agricultural commodities), the company with the greater insight into the foreign culture is likelier to make the sale.

Political Considerations

Government policies run the gamut from the prohibition of private ownership and the suppression of individual freedom to minimum central government and maximum personal freedom. As the rights of private property increase, government-owned industries and centralized planning tend to decrease. In addition to the basic political structure of a country, nationalism is also a concern of the international businessperson. **Nationalism** is a sense of national consciousness that boosts the culture and interests of one country over all others. Countries with strong nationalistic tendencies often tend to discourage investment by foreign companies.

Stability is another consideration for companies thinking about exporting or investing in for-

Johnson & Johnson is a multinational company.

eign countries. Rapid political changes can sometimes upset what might otherwise be a good, long-range plan. One clue to instability is frequent changes in a regime. Changes in the ruling party may mean major changes in the political environment of business. This is particularly true if there has been a violent overthrow or coup d'etat. Some African nations, Poland, Nicaragua, and Iran were relatively unstable during the early 1980s.

Culture

Without understanding a country's culture, a firm has little opportunity of effectively penetrating the market. Culture is that set of beliefs, values, and social norms shared by members of a society which determines what's socially acceptable. Culture forms the basis of social organization, such as the family, the educational system, or the social class system.

The history of product failures in international business reflects many examples of the incompatibility of a product and a country's culture. Fluffy frosted cake mixes were introduced by American companies in the United Kingdom, where cake is eaten at teatime with the fingers rather than as a

"IT'S NOT SURPRISING. THE PRODUCTION DEPARTMENT IS IN SPAIN, THE WAREHOUSE IS IN KOREA, THE ACCOUNTING DIVISION IS IN BOLIVIA, THE BOARD OF DIRECTORS IS IN CANADA..."

TABLE 24–4

The World's 25 Largest Industrial Corporations

Rank '80	Company	Headquarters	Sales ($000)	Net Income ($000)
1	Exxon	New York	103,142,834	5,650,090
2	Royal Dutch/Shell Group	The Hague/London	77,114,243	5,174,282
3	Mobil	New York	59,510,000	3,272,000
4	General Motors	Detroit	57,728,500	(762,500)
5	Texaco	Harrison, N.Y.	51,195,830	2,642,542
6	British Petroleum	London	48,035,941	3,337,121
7	Standard Oil of California	San Francisco	40,479,000	2,401,000
8	Ford Motor	Dearborn, Mich.	37,085,000	(1,543,000)
9	ENI	Rome	27,186,939	98,046
10	Gulf Oil	Pittsburgh	26,483,000*	1,407,000
11	International Business Machines	Armonk, N.Y.	26,213,000	3,562,000
12	Standard Oil (Ind.)	Chicago	26,133,080	1,915,314
13	Fiat	Turin (Italy)	25,155,000	N.A.
14	General Electric	Fairfield, Conn.	24,959,000	1,514,000
15	Francaise des Pétroles	Paris	23,940,355	946,772
16	Atlantic Richfield	Los Angeles	23,744,302	1,651,423
17	Unilever	London/Rotterdam	23,607,516	658,820
18	Shell Oil	Houston	19,830,000	1,542,000
19	Renault	Paris	18,979,278	160,165
20	Petróleos de Venezuela	Caracas	18,818,931	3,450,921
21	International Telephone & Tel.	New York	18,529,655	894,326
22	Elf Aquitaine	Paris	18,430,074	1,378,222
23	Philips' Gloeilampenfabrieken	Eindhoven (Netherlands)	18,402,818	165,210
24	Volkswagenwerk	Wolfsburg (Germany)	18,339,046	170,964
25	Conoco	Stamford, Conn.	18,325,400	1,026,195

SOURCE: "The 50 Largest Industrial Companies in the World," *Fortune*, 10 August 1981, p. 205. © 1981 Time Inc. Courtesy of Fortune Magazine.

dessert and with a fork. The result was lack of sales and failure. The Renault Dauphine was introduced into the United States in 1959 to a market that subjected cars to driving conditions far more harsh than those found in France. The results were breakdown and failure. Green Giant tried to market corn in Europe, where the prevailing attitude is that corn is a grain fed to hogs, not people. The result was a lack of sales and severe losses on investments in European corn production. Hellmann's Real Mayonnaise, a product of CPC International, wasn't selling in U.S.-sized jars in Central America. The company then placed the mayonnaise in small plastic packets, and sales increased immediately. The plastic packets were within the food budgets of the local consumers and required no refrigeration.[3]

THE IMPACT OF MULTINATIONAL CORPORATIONS

Successful multinational corporations are aware of cultural differences between countries and regions, for they're heavily engaged in international trade. A **multinational corporation** is one that moves resources, goods, services, and skills across national boundaries without regard to the country in which its headqarters office is located. A multinational is more than a business entity; as one scholar puts it:

The multinational corporation is, among other things, a private 'government,' often richer in assets and more populous in stockholders and employees than are some of the nation-states in which it carries on its business. It is simultaneously a citizen of sev-

eral nation-states, owing obedience to their laws and paying them taxes, yet having its own objectives and being responsive to a management located in a foreign nation. Small wonder that some critics see an irresponsible instrument of private economic power or economic 'imperialism' by its home country. Others view it as an international carrier of advanced management science and technology, an agent for the global transmission of cultures bringing closer the day when a common set of ideals will unite mankind. [4]

A nation has control over only that portion of a firm that's within its borders. While that nation's government may be able to influence decisions taken by the firm in other countries, influence is often remote. A multinational can shift resources from one subsidiary to another, based on forecasting profitability and risks. Unlike a purely national firm, it can resist the pressures of any single government by threatening to withdraw or by cutting back on its activities.

Yet the multinational corporation is widely recognized as a valuable agent of economic modernization and industrial development. This is because it assists in the international transfer of technology and resources. Many countries recognize the positive role that multinationals play in the process of economic development. For that reason governments continue to encourage direct investment in their countries. They also press the corporations to create more jobs, perform more in-country research and development, generate more exports, and contribute more revenue— that is, to increase the benefits that they provide to the countries in which they operate.

A number of the multinationals are huge corporations, as shown in Table 24.4. To put the matter in some perspective: in 1980 the sales of Exxon, Royal Dutch/Shell Group, and Mobil were larger than the GNP of most nations in the world. [5] Today more than half of the earnings of such well-known American companies as Colgate-Palmolive, Heinz, Hoover, Mobil, National Cash Register, and Exxon come from abroad.

SUMMARY

International trade is extremely important to most nations of the world. The distribution of resources, both natural and human, varies from country to country. The principle of comparative advantage says that if each nation specializes in goods it can produce most readily and cheaply, and trades for goods that foreign countries can produce most cheaply, more goods at lower prices will be available for everyone involved.

When a nation exports more goods than it imports, it has a favorable balance of trade. If it imports more than it exports, it has an unfavorable balance of trade. When imports exceed exports, more money flows out of the country than into it. The balance of payments includes the balance of trade and a number of other financial transactions; it is the difference between a nation's total payments to and receipts from foreign countries. In today's system of "floating currency," the value of a nation's currency depends on supply and demand.

Three major obstacles restrict trade among nations: natural barriers, tariff barriers, and nontariff barriers. Natural barriers include distance and language differences. Tariffs, levied by nations on imported goods, may be either specific tariffs or ad valorem taxes. Tariffs designed to discourage imports are protective tariffs; tariffs designed to raise money are revenue tariffs. Nontariff barriers include import quotas, embargos, exchange controls, "buy national" policies, and antidumping regulations.

Governments can also work to increase world trade as well as to place restrictions on it. The movement to liberalize trade gained momentum after World War II, culminating in 1947 in the General Agreement on Tariffs and Trade (GATT). In 1962 the US Trade Expansion Act was passed to facilitate world trade; this act served as a background for the Kennedy Round of tariff negotiations undertaken by GATT two years later. After passage of the Trade Act of 1974, a new round of trade negotiations, the Tokyo Round (1975–1979) was established. It reduced not only tariffs but also nontariff barriers. In 1981 representatives of the United States and a number of other nations met in the Ottawa Economic "Summit" to discourage establishment of trade barriers.

When governments meet and agree on a common economic policy for their nations, the result is called economic integration. Types of agreements may include provisions for preferential tariffs, free trade associations, and customs unions. The largest trade association is the European Economic Community (EEC), or Common Market.

Firms can enter the international market in a number of ways. A firm may simply sell its goods to an export agency, either at a specified price or on a consignment basis. To export directly, the firm may use a foreign freight forwarder. A more aggressive stance involves the use of licensing, in which the firm agrees to let a foreign firm use its patents, trademarks, production processes, brands, products, or company name in exchange for a royalty fee or a contractually agreed-upon amount. One form of licensing is international franchising. In contract manufacturing, firms contract for the manufacture of their products by established foreign manufacturers. Firms may decide to enter a joint venture, in which two or more firms or investors share ownership and control over operations and property rights. They may share patents, trademarks, or control over manufacturing and marketing. Finally, the firm may decide to become a direct investor by purchasing active ownership interests in a foreign company. To be successful, firms that engage in international trade must understand the political and cultural environments in the countries with which it hopes to trade.

A multinational corporation moves resources, goods, services, and skills across national boundaries without regard to the country in which its headquarters is located. A multinational corporation is more than a business entity; it is a "private government" and a valuable agent of economic modernization and industrial development.

KEY TERMS

balance of payments
balance of trade
"buy national"
    regulations
Common Market
contract
    manufacturing
defense preparedness
    argument
developing nation
direct investment
dumping
economic integration
embargo
exchange control
floating currency

General Agreement
    on Tariffs and
    Trade (GATT)
home industry
    argument
import quota
infant industry
    argument
joint venture
Kennedy Round
licensing
multinational
    corporation
nationalism
preferential tariff
principle of
    comparative
    advantage
protective tariff
revenue tariff
specific tariff
tariff
Trade Expansion Act

REVIEW QUESTIONS

1. What are the major benefits a country can expect from participating in international trade?
2. Explain the concept of comparative advantage.
3. What is the difference between *balance of trade* and *balance of payments*?
4. Explain each of the three major obstacles that restrict foreign trade.
5. List and describe the different tariff and nontariff barriers to trade that governments can impose.
6. Describe briefly at least three important international approaches to increasing world trade.
7. Outline and describe five ways for business to enter into foreign trade.
8. Distinguish between a multinational corporation and a business that exports products to three or four different countries.

DISCUSSION QUESTIONS

1. Study the case of Kentucky Fried Chicken in Japan. What benefits are there for the U.S. and Japan from this venture?

2. What techniques can a small developing nation use in order to participate more fully in international trade?
3. List some of the natural barriers to international trade and explain how you feel they can be minimized or eliminated.
4. Should the U.S. protect businesses in this country from foreign businesses that produce useful goods at a lower cost?
5. List and explain at least three reasons why the U.S. has had a negative balance of trade since 1970. How can this be changed?

CASE: EASTWARD HO!

Clark Copy International, a manufacturer of small copy machines, developed a unit employing the latest in solid-state electronics. Especially unique was the fact that the copier could be sold on the world market for under $25. But even with this low price the market in the US looked too complex and competitive to Otto Clark, the company president, so he turned to the international market. He found a ready customer in China.

Clark worked out a long-term contract with the Chinese government where in the first phase he would sell them over $5 million in machines and parts. The next phase would include his training Chinese workers to assemble the machines, which would be marketed by China. Profits would be shared.

In addition to new technology lowering the price of solid-state component parts, Clark attributed his success to the reluctance of Japan to share technology with China and the big American manufacturers' reluctance to take on smaller markets.

1. What advantages and disadvantages do you see in Clark's arrangements?
2. Do you think that Clark's opportunity is just a chance happening—or can similar opportunities arise in international business for other small businesses?

CASE: WHEAT FOR THE SOVIETS—C.O.D.

A venturesome midwestern bank for cooperatives decided to "make hay while the sun shines" and do something with the grain that had been piling up in the elevators over the past several years waiting for a price increase and some customers.

The bank's international representative had just come back from a trip to Moscow—via Washington—and had reported that the Russians were ready to do business with us. The government meanwhile had left the trade door ajar, citing a federal law permitting export loans by banks in the nationwide Farm Credit System.

The Russians, still cringing from the last US grain embargo, were stretching a pleading hand to the US market because of a disastrous Soviet crop year (and because its Argentinian benefactor was in trouble with the British).

The president of the bank for cooperatives was eager to make the first export loan in the fifty-year history of the bank, the forerunner of similar deals that would help clear US grain elevators of record harvests. He was confident that the Russians would repay the obligation at interest rates of 16 percent. It's also obvious that US commercial banks had turned their backs on Russia, and the possibility of a $6.5 million loan for the grain would be a real stimulus to the farming community. The condition for payment discussed with the Soviets was that they could pay for grain when it was delivered in the Soviet Union rather than the usual payment for purchases at Port of Houston, where the grain would be loaded.

In a statesman-like comment the bank president said that he hoped the Russian consumers became dependent on US agriculture to the point where their government would be pressured to spend on US grain instead of on armaments, a worthy objective.

1. In the light of US-Soviet relations, do you consider this a viable trade arrangement for this midwestern bank for cooperatives?
2. Do you think the farmers are ready to deal with the Russians? What other options do they have?
3. Would the bank be taking a chance requesting payment on delivery at a Soviet port rather than Port of Houston?

CHAPTER 25

OPPORTUNITIES FOR YOU IN TOMORROW'S WORLD

After studying this chapter you should be able to:

1 Discuss different possible trends that affect American business.
2 Recognize various economic, social, and political factors and their impact on future business.
3 Begin a process of evaluation to consider the possibility of a career in business.
4 Learn the means and techniques of applying for a job.

In the late 1960s and early 1970s, Boise Cascade Corporation, one of America's largest forest products companies, diversified into the land development business. It acquired U.S. Land Company of Indianapolis, a major developer of lake-oriented resort properties. Boise, with its management policies of loose control and maximum decentralization, let U.S. Land run itself. The Land Company tended to follow old ways of thinking—cut it up, develop it, sell it, and move on. If property owners later experienced a problem, the Land Company management was long gone.

The marketing tactics of Boise and its subsidiaries led to numerous lawsuits against the company. Boise failed to recognize the impact of consumerism on public attitudes and policies. High-pressure sales tactics that might have gone unchallenged in the past were fast becoming targets of public outcry and impetus for new government regulation. Boise also overlooked the growing ecology movement in America. Public opinion was against planned projects on a Puget Sound shoreline, a Hawaiian beach, and other locations. In projects underway, ecologist pressure meant more green open spaces, underground utilities, and more stringent sewer treatment standards. Naturally, these improvements meant higher costs which Boise attempted to pass forward to the prospective buyer. As lot prices rose, demand tended to decline rapidly.

Despite major efforts by Boise to clean up the marketing practices of its land development subsidiary and to meet the demands of the ecologists, the damage had been done. Sales were dismal and future prospects seemed no brighter. Getting out of the land development business proved to be a very expensive proposition. The company took writeoffs and losses of approximately $300 million. Some projects were sold to other companies.

Adapted by permission from *Marketing Mistakes*, 2d ed., ed. Robert F. Hartley (Columbus: Grid Publishing Co., 1981), pp. 207–13.

THE ACCELERATING RATE OF CHANGE

The **Boise Cascade** example strengthens the idea that it's important for business managers to properly forecast the future. Failure to foresee trends can be extremely costly to the firm. For example, the rapid increase of new products during the years 1970–1977 yielded very few with substantial sales. Of 6695 introductions of dry/frozen/refrigerated human and pet food, only 93 products reached sales of $15 million or more.[1] This level of sales may be only break-even for a large company geared up for national production and distribution.

Future Shock

One reason for the lack of new product success is that as the rate of change in our society increases, the ability to accurately predict and control the future tends to decline. The term **future shock** means a disorientation brought on by rapid social change. Sometimes we may find ourselves asking the question "What is going on—where are we going from here?" It became apparent in the late 1970s and the early 1980s that the future was becoming harder and harder to keep under control. There were growing pressures to plan and think further ahead. An example could be cited in the radioactive waste from the nation's growing nuclear research and utility efforts. This is thought to pose a potential danger not only for several hundred years but in some cases for the next 50,000.

Where Does America Go from Here?

Predicting where America will go from here is risky at best. One approach, however, might be to present several scenarios without estimating the probability of any of them. The following scenarios were developed by the center for the Study of Social Policy at Stanford Research Institute.

Hitting the Jackpot All goes well. There is abundant energy, widespread prosperity, highly responsible business leadership, worldwide environmental cooperation, and a scientific community able to deal with most of the earth's technical problems. There's even favorable climate and plenty of food. America meets the challenge of vigorous competition from abroad as well as problems posed by the near doubling of the world's population. It also rises to the challenges of pressure on natural resources, shifts in the global political balance, and the problems of economic development in the Third World. Rural populations decline even further and the process of urbanization continues. Birthrates and rural immigration are reduced throughout the world. Huge investments in housing, sewage systems, and other public utilities—plus the expansion of health, fire, and public services—aid in the solution of urban problems. A lower birthrate makes child care and education a less pressing issue for society. America can then concentrate on the provision of health and welfare services for the growing older-age group. America's great corporations continue to grow and become an even more dominant factor in the world market. The Japanese model of lifetime employment becomes increasingly acceptable in the United States.

Doomsday Specter A second scenario is not quite as cheerful as the first. A decline in the energy supply, worsening climate, and food shortages combine to create a major depression in the late 1980s. Yet we struggle, and our social and economic institutions survive without becoming a highly centralized, authoritarian system. There's

economic recovery in the 1990s, although Americans are less well-off than in previous recoveries. The first years of the next century are characterized by a resource-conserving behavior. Americans become increasingly concerned about conservation, backyard gardening, and other "technologies of scarcity." The late 1980s, according to this scenario, is a period when everything malfunctions, even the weather. Power outages, transportation breakdowns, crop failures, and shortages of raw materials and spare parts are characteristic of the economy. But after 1990 there's gradual improvement. Demands on the system are no longer so great—nor are expectations.

The Center Holds A third scenario has it that despite energy shortages, a bad climate, an eroding living standard, and increases in political terrorism during the 1980s, the established order of big business, agriculture, and government is able to retain its power and control. A major depression is avoided. Good weather and technological breakthroughs on the energy front enable the big powers to hold on to the world sociopolitical system of the early 1980s through the remainder of the century. But the system is now more highly regulated and authoritarian. Loyalty to the nation and to the family unit as well as striving for more education and higher job and income status remain the context in which most people expect to live their lives and through which they will gain their rewards. Big cities, big industry, and big government—all relying on complex science and technology—remain the major institutions through the rest of the century.

The Industrial Renaissance Although there are as many potential scenarios as there are forecasters, let's end on a relatively positive note. Our final scenario holds that the failure of America's leaders to control energy consumption touched off the recession in the early 1980s. A rich new energy technology comes on line during the middle or late 1980s, and rapid growth becomes the order of the day. The scientists, engineers, and planners who rescued society gain new power, credibility, and income. By the year 2000 this technological elite corps has created a nonwasteful, nonpolluting America with a purposeful goal of slow growth. The social system of the United States and the rest of the industrial nations pass through the remainder of this century with easy, smooth, continuous change. Major break-throughs in nonnuclear energy technology—coal gasification and oil processing—are coupled with the exploration of new offshore oil fields. This triggers a resumption of economic growth and our society once more finds its direction.

The old system of controls and restraints is eliminated. Multinational corporations, which had declined during the period of energy short-ages, find themselves being courted by the strug-gling new industries of the OPEC countries. Even during this period of renewed expansion, Ameri-cans don't return to the old, unbridled emphasis on growth. For one thing, the evidence appears to be that the new resources are no more infinite than the old had been. For another, they accept the warnings of scientists about the environmen-tal hazards of the industrial process. The tradi-tional American family with two or fewer children becomes the norm. Population stabilizes and even begins to decline. Industrialization continues, but better-planned satellite cities of manageable size tend to replace sprawling, uncontrolled growth. Apartment houses and condominiums replace de-tached single-family houses, but parks, municipal gardens, and community workshops enhance the quality of life.[2]

An ad emphasizing the "age of me."

Will any of these scenarios come to pass? It's doubtful that America will be transformed pre-cisely into any one of them. Predicting the world of tomorrow, as we have said, is difficult at best. And there are always the "unk-unks," the *unk*nown *unk*nowns—i.e. those "unknowns" that aren't even suspected.

General Electric collected 1556 predictions made publicly by Americans (inventors, writers, industrialists, etc.) in the years 1890–1940 and sorted them into four classes: fulfilled; in progress (the development is evident but not fully estab-lished); not proved (but not proved impossible, ei-ther); and refuted. The results of this study found that less than half of the predictions had been ful-filled or were in the process of being fulfilled. A full third have been refuted.[3]

FACTORS IMPACTING ON THE FUTURE OF BUSINESS

One technique to aid in predicting the future is to consider those factors that will impact on busi-ness. These include social considerations, eco-nomic factors, natural resource shortages, com-petition, political and legal factors, technology, and demographic factors. We'll look at each of these in the sections that follow.

Social Considerations

America's values and lifestyles have changed sig-nificantly during this century. **Values** are goals or principles to which individuals subscribe as being desirable. A lifestyle is a distinctive yet typical mode of living, such as the "family man," the "ca-reer woman," or the "single swinger."

The Protestant Ethic   Perhaps the most funda-mental change in values has been the decline of the so-called Protestant ethic. The **Protestant ethic** is the belief that all people should engage in some productive activity.[4] It stresses work, thrift, self-discipline, building for the future as opposed to living only for today, and service to others. And it accounts in part for the emphasis we place on "doing one's best."

However social observers have for some time noted changes in the work atmosphere related to a decline in the Protestant ethic, even in its modern form. "While many young people are socialized to value Protestant-ethic based principles of hard work and frugality, they are bombarded with encouragement to spend, use credit, get high, and the like. The emphasis is on consumption rather than production."[5]

Emphasis on Self In addition to the declining Protestant ethic, there's been a growth of new lifestyles that emphasize the *self*. One such lifestyle theme might be characterized as "my life, my way"—a self-centered outlook with emphasis on "doing one's own thing" and looking out for number one. You've probably heard it expressed as "you owe it to yourself," "you deserve it," and "you've earned it." This lifestyle emphasized self-gratification. For example, parents "lead their own lives" rather than live for their children. It also means fewer children, less emphasis on obligations and—in some cases—actually shirking responsibility. This lifestyle finds workers willing to switch jobs if they can find one that's more enjoy-

able and satisfying. And company loyalty is little emphasized.

Besides the "self" orientation, America will see greater value placed on leisure. We'll become even more willing to trade higher income for more leisure time, and pressure for a reduced work load will increase. People will make time to pursue leisure-oriented lifestyles rather than working the traditional 40-hour week.

Changing Role of Families Another significant social factor that will impact on business is the changing role of families. The decline of the Protestant ethic has meant a tremendous growth in the number of women in the work force. And not only are women moving into the work force; they're also moving into middle and upper management. The heightened status of women has many implications for business. Ads that depict women in menial or subservient roles are ineffective today. Women are issued credit cards in their own names based on *their* earning potential rather than on their husband's. Time is a precious commodity, and consumers want uncluttered stores, well-marked shelves, and rapid checkout.

Finally, combined incomes mean that luxury goods, formerly out of reach for many, can now be had.

Economic Factors

Besides social change, economic factors will also have a major impact on the future of business. Perhaps the most important economic variable is inflation. The consumer, historically the most reliable brake on a runaway economy, has been infected with so-called inflation psychology: "Buy it today, because it'll cost more tomorrow. Borrow to buy—you can repay with cheaper dollars." Often this rationale has been unfortunately true. Although rates of inflation will probably be lower in the second half of the 1980s than in the first, they bear a good chance of remaining at a moderately high level.

Inflation acts like suggestion and bad advice, pushing comsumers beyond good judgment in managing personal debt. It also forces government to make national and international public policy decisions that may not be in our best long-term interest. Inflation discourages investment that could improve production efficiency and create new job opportunities.

Natural Resource Shortages

Part of the inflationary problem is caused by shortage or unavailability of natural resources. This was illustrated most dramatically in the quadruple price increase of oil in 1974 by the OPEC nations. We may continue to experience a shortage not only of certain energy-related resources through the remainder of the decade, but also of many strategic metals, such as platinum and cobalt. As worldwide demand for strategic minerals and metals continues to grow, there is the danger that new cartels may create an even greater rate of inflation.

In the area of energy there are still a number of laws that mandate or restrict the use of coal, oil, or natural gas. Many of these regulations have become—or soon will become—obsolete, since demand, supply and cost are continually changing.

The shortage of natural resources may ultimately lead to a "conserver" society, one that does more with less. It could be characterized as a

People today pursue many leisure oriented lifestyles.

"waste-not, want-not" society. So technological development may play a greater role in emphasizing products that are more durable, require less service, and need less energy.

Competition

Competition isn't likely to decrease during the remainder of the decade but in fact will probably intensify. One important determinant of competition is the number and size of the competitors. If there's only one firm in the industry (one supplier), it has control over supply and therefore over prices. A music star, for example, can command high wages for a performance because there's no direct substitute. There's only one Barbra Streisand, Kenny Rogers, Willy Nelson, and Olivia Newton-John. As the number of competitors increases, the availability of potential substitute goods and services increases, thereby increasing the degree of competition.

Some markets are dominated by the giants in sales and market share, yet a number of small competitors have been able to carve out their own niches. For example, in the late 1970s the aircraft manufacturers (dominated by Boeing, General Dynamics, and McDonnell Douglas) still faced competition from over 140 independent manufacturers in the United States. There are more than 70 manufacturers of sewing machines, 250 luggage manufacturers, and 135 manufacturers of elevators in the United States. Of course, some of these are little more than cottage ("ma and pa") operations almost unknown outside their own industries. Yet some are large enough to be continuously hacking away at the major competitors.

Political and Legal Factors

Regulation Federal regulations have been called irritating, costly, and inflationary by many business people. Some add that the worst that can be said of federal regulations is that often they don't work. The regulatory agencies have spent billions of dollars and they have caused billions more to be spent. Yet there is surprisingly little evidence that society is any better off than it would have been without federal regulation.

Dr. Sam Peltzman, a University of Chicago economist, found that new drug rules were costing American consumers three to four times as much as the economic benefits they produced.[6] It has also been suggested that a too cautious approach to approval of new drugs might rule out or delay life-saving advances in pharmaceutical technology.

In other areas, it seems that agencies have tried to feather their own nests through growth. The Federal Trade Commission (FTC) was criticized severely during the early 1980s for being arbitrary and for pushing the law well beyond its outer limits in antitrust and consumer protection cases. David Stockman, Budget Director during the Reagan Administration, said in 1981, "In recent years, the FTC has served the public interest very poorly, in major part because it has sought to expand its power and influence beyond that envisioned by the Congress.[7]

Deregulation While the FTC has tried to expand, other federal agencies—such as the Federal

Mobil is a business which speaks out against excessive regulation.

Aeronautics Association, the Interstate Commerce Commission, and the Federal Communication Commission—are currently being cut back. **Deregulation**—a lessening of government regulation and restriction of private enterprise—will probably continue to grow during the remainder of the decade. Of course, there will be long arguments, both pro and con, any time an industry faces the prospect of deregulation. The Civil Aeronautics Board, for example, under 1978 legislation is gradually losing its regulatory powers and is to be abolished by 1985. The smaller regional carriers for the most part viewed airline deregulation as a major opportunity for growth and expansion. On the other hand, a number of trunk carriers (Delta, Eastern, American, United) were very uneasy about the prospects of deregulation.

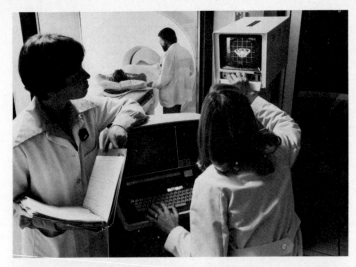

New technology will impact on our lives in many ways. Shown here are just a few of the "hot" technology areas: solar energy, medical diagnostic equipment, and satellite communications.

Technology

Just as predictable as the growth of deregulation is the growth of America's high-technology industries. The "hot" areas for the remainder of the decade will include satellite communications, sophisticated diagnostic equipment for hospitals, biotechnology, semiconductors, and personal computers. There will also be an expansion in the use of industrial robots by 1985. Robots save money, boost productive efficiency, and help the firm increase its market share against domestic and international competition.

The improvement in technology in the semiconductor industry drove the cost of storing one bit of information down 98 percent between 1971 and 1981[8]—from two cents to less than three hundredths of a cent. The new generation of semiconductor chips will cram a million "transis-

tors" on a chip, up from the 100,000-transistor content now considered state of the art. With each successive improvement and increase in performance, further opportunities are created for applying microelectronic technology. More electromechanical components can be replaced by chips, and greater "intelligence" can be built into machinery of all kinds. This will lead to a further merger of computers and telecommunications that will transform much of society by the end of the decade.

Demographic Factors

Perhaps the change that can be forecasted most accurately lies in demographics, providing an important economic stimulant during the remain-

PERSPECTIVE ON SMALL BUSINESS

James Ward has traded the hurly burly of Manhattan for an electronic cottage.

He used to be a managing director in charge of bond trading at Dillon Read & Co. Now he is on his own; his bond-trading room is perched atop a secluded hilltop in suburban New Jersey, surrounded by trees, mossy rocks and blissful quiet.

The room, of course, is in his home. Computer technology made it possible to set up his four-man firm, Ward Brittany & Co., at a comfortable remove from Manhattan's financial enclave. Using electronic facilities, Mr. Ward and his associates trade municipal and corporate bonds and government securities.

"It gives you a greater reward for your time," he says. He has gotten tired of 90-minute commutes, jostling with New York crowds and getting home at night after his children had gone to bed. Mr. Ward got the notion of moving after reading about electronic cottages in Alvin Toffler's book "The Third Wave." Mr. Ward believes that the securities business is tailor-made for the dispersion of big, centralized work places into small operations connected by computers.

SOURCE: Excerpted from Tim Carrington, "Computer Linkups Letting Traders Start Up Securities Firms at Home," *Wall Street Journal*, 9 December 1981, p. 25. Reprinted by permission of The Wall Street Journal, ©Dow Jones & Company, Inc., 1981. All rights reserved.

---

der of the 1980s. There will be a bulge in the big-spending 35–44 age group—slated to grow from 28 to 40 million people during the 1980s. The 45–64 age group will grow much wealthier. There will be about 27 million people over 65 by 1990.

People in the 25–40 age bracket will increase to about 60 million by 1990 (almost 53 percent of the labor force). The promotion rate will fall dramatically, since the number of candidates for jobs will expand to its highest rate ever. With a decline of inflation during the latter half of the 1980s, greater incentive for early retirement can be expected, and the promotion problem won't be particularly acute. Nor will middle managers in expanding industries like electronics be hurt, because new positions will constantly be created.

Not only will the average age of the population continue to rise, but people will also continue their migration to the Sun Belt. Between 1980 and 1990, approximately 3.3 million people will move from the Northeast and the Midwest to the South and West. By the end of the decade, the South and the West will account for 54 percent of the nation's total population. Moreover growth in manufacturing jobs advanced three times faster in the South and the West than in the Northeast and the Midwest during the 1970s. Other demographic trends that will shape business during the

remainder of the decade are:

- A population growing at a slower rate.
- Legal and illegal immigration accounting for a greater portion of population growth.
- Hispanics outnumbering blacks by 1990.
- Nearly one half of all children living with only one parent much of the time before they are 18, due to the increasing divorce rate.
- The number of single-parent households continuing to increase dramatically.

YOUR CAREER IN BUSINESS

Who Am I?

Now that we've examined where the future might take us, let's look at your opportunities in tomorrow's business world. Preparing for your first job requires a logical sequence of events, as shown in Figure 25.1. As you prepare for career development, step number one is to ask the question "Who am I?" This leads to a **self-assessment.** You should examine your likes and dislikes. Do you enjoy working indoors or outdoors? Do you like to meet new people, or do you prefer to work alone?

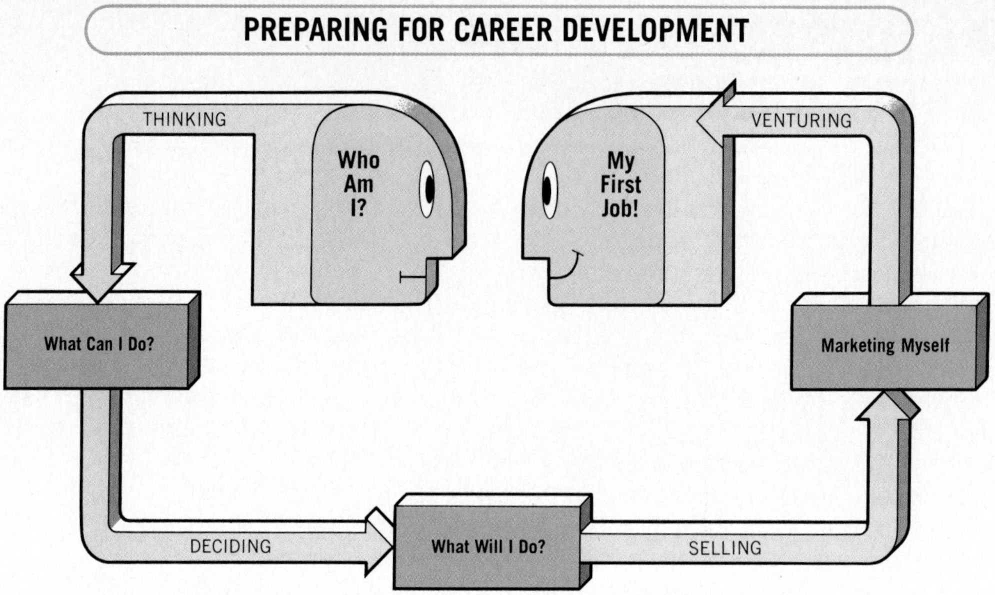

PREPARING FOR CAREER DEVELOPMENT

THINKING

Who Am I?

What Can I Do?

VENTURING

My First Job!

Marketing Myself

DECIDING

What Will I Do?

SELLING

FIGURE 25.1
Source: Data from Walter Emery, ed., *Commodity Yearbook 1981* (New York: Commodity Research Bureau, 1981).

What are your basic values? Do you want to help society? Do you want to contribute to the betterment of the world? Do you want to help other people directly? Is it important to be recognized as a member of a major corporation? By answering these and similar questions, you can develop insights into your basic value patterns.

What Can I Do?

After determining what is important to you, the second step in the career development path is to ask the question "What can I do?" (**skill assessment**). This means that you must assess your bank of skills, which will market you to an employer. Your skills represent your key abilities and the characteristics that give you the greatest value in successfully dealing with problems, tasks, and interactions with people. Many skills aren't limited to being useful within a single kind of occupation but instead are valued across a wide range of occupations. For example, the ability to speak clearly and strongly will help you in almost any work you wish to take on.

In addition to examining your transferable skills, you should also look at your leisure-time skills and the things that you enjoy. For example, are you good at golf? sailing? Do you enjoy tennis? racquet ball? Often business transactions are

made during leisure hours. Being able to play a skillful game of golf can be an important asset in some careers.

You should also consider your work experience, such as part-time jobs while going to school, summer jobs, volunteer jobs, and intern positions that you have had. Any of these may give you valuable work experience that increases your attractiveness to a potential employer. It's never too early or too late to consider a part-time job in the field where you ultimately hope to gain a position. For example, if you feel that a career in accounting is for you, it would be good to try to get a part-time job with a CPA firm.

What Will I Do?

Just a reminder, in case you haven't noticed, that you will find a personal career appendix for each of the following areas covered in this book:

Management (after Chapter 10)
Marketing (after Chapter 15)
Finance (after Chapter 20)
Business Tools (after Chapter 23)

And a career appendix for Legal, Tax, Small Business, and International Management follows this chapter.

The third step in planning for your career development is to ask the question "What will I do?" This question involves not only the choice of a general type of work but also consideration of your lifestyle and leisure objectives. If you enjoy being outdoors most of the time, a career that requires you to be in an office eight hours a day may not be for you. If you like living in small towns, going to work for a major corporation with headquarters in cities like New York and Chicago may not suit your lifestyle. Answering the question "What will I do?" might also mean a detailed library search and a thorough examination of the *Career Employment Opportunities Directory—Business Administration*. The directory lists several hundred up-to-date sources of career employment offered by businesses, government agencies, and professional organizations.

Another important secondary source for you to examine is the *Occupational Outlook Handbook*, published yearly by the U.S. Department of Labor. The introductory material in the *Handbook* projects tomorrow's job opportunities, such as the growth in service-producing industries, and the distribution of employment by industry in 1990.

The *Occupational Outlook Handbook* is divided into 13 occupational clusters such as education, sales, transportation, health, and social services. In addition to discussing hundreds of individual occupations and future employment opportunities, the *Handbook* also describes work in several industries. If you're interested in an industry, or if an industry is a major employer in your area, you may find it useful to read about that industry. Over 35 industries are described in the *Handbook*, grouped according to major divisions in the economy. Each job description follows a standard format beginning with the nature of the work, working conditions, training, other qualifications, advancement, employment outlook, earnings, related occupations, and sources of additional information.

As you begin to narrow down your career choices, you may want more information about a particular type of occupation. We've projected a number of different positions available to business graduates and their average annual salaries for the years 1985–1987 (see Table 25.1). This information may help you determine whether a particular career will meet your financial needs.

TABLE 25–1
Average Annual Salaries, 1985–1987

	1985[a]	*1986*	*1987*
Accounting manager	$42,356	46,592	51,251
Auditing manager	43,806	48,187	53,005
Cost accounting manager	39,135	43,049	47,353
Payroll supervisor	29,633	32,596	35,856
Credit and collection manager	36,398	40,038	44,042
Personnel director	46,383	51,021	56,123
Employment manager	35,592	39,151	43,066
Customer service manager	37,203	40,923	45,016
Compensation manager	43,001	47,301	52,031
Manager—administrative services	39,619	43,581	47,939
Manager—electronic data processing	47,188	51,907	57,097
Branch manager	37,364	41,100	45,210
Sales manager	47,993	52,792	58,072
Advertising manager	43,967	48,364	53,200
Warehouse manager	35,592	39,151	43,066
Plant manager	51,053	56,158	61,774
Supervisor	34,304	37,734	41,508
General supervisor	39,619	43,581	47,939
Purchasing agent	40,263	44,289	48,718
Buyer	32,532	35,785	39,364

NOTE: Projections assume a 10 percent rate of inflation.
[a]Projections for 1985 based on the 1981 Administrative Management Society's *1981 AMS Guide to Management Compensation*, (Willow Grove, Penn.: AMS, 1981). Reprinted by permission.

Another important consideration is the employment outlook for professional business occupations. The fields with the greatest growth may give you the widest array of employers from which to choose. Also, salaries tend to rise at a faster rate in high-growth occupations than in those with slower growth. Table 25.2 shows you where the "action will be" in 1990 for many types of business positions, and where it has been in recent years.

Your Major As you enter business school, you begin to answer the question "What will I do" by selecting a major course of study or a field of concentration. If you decide to concentrate in **accounting,** for example, you'll find job opportunities with public accounting firms, industrial companies, and various government organizations. The world of accounting includes developing financial statements, analyzing investment opportunities, and determining tax liabilities. It generally centers on analytical processes and the reporting of financial results.

If you choose to major in **economics,** the subject matter will take in not only the principles underlying the pricing, production, wage, and investment decisions of private enterprise. It will also include the principles that guide public policy and matters of taxation, regulation, money, and international trade and exchange. A degree in economics provides a foundation for direct entry into many business careers. However employment as an economist usually requires several years of advanced graduate study.

If you decide that **finance** is your basic field of interest, you may become a financial manager upon graduation. The financial manager is involved with the question of which assets to buy — and how to pay for them.

Another popular area of study is **management.** A concentration in management is designed to prepare students for managerial roles in a wide variety of organizations, from privately owned small businesses to large, multinational corporations. Modern management has become more and more the profession where those who wish to enter must be well educated and skilled in the task of "working through others." Upon graduation, students may choose to take entry-level management positions in a wide variety of different organizations.

Marketing Yourself

By selecting a major, you are beginning to narrow your focus of job opportunities. When graduation nears, you'll need to prepare to market yourself to prospective employers. The first step might be to visit your placement office. Most campuses have established an office to assist students with the formulation and advancement of their career plans. It may be called the placement office, the office of career planning, student services, etc. The size and scope of these offices will vary from campus to campus. They'll include some or all of the following functions: testing, counseling, part-time employment, summer employment, college recruiting, and financial aid. The placement office can help you narrow your employment objectives and, most importantly, prepare you for marketing yourself.

Letters Three important tools for self-marketing include letters to potential employers, your résumé, and knowing how to make a positive impression during a job interview. A **cover letter** to a prospective employer should open with a paragraph that will arouse interest. You should say why you're writing the letter and let the employer know why you're interested in the company. The middle paragraph should create desire. What in your background makes you a potential candidate? State what you want in a job. Point out those items in your résumé that you want the potential employer to notice. The final paragraph should suggest something you may do next or ask what you can do to follow up. You should be specific about your plans for follow-up. Are you requesting an application form and appointment for an interview? Will you call or drop by for a visit? Are you going to wait to hear from them? The last is the weakest form of follow-up.

A sample letter is shown in Figure 25.2.

Résumés The objective of an employment letter is to get the potential employer to examine your **résumé.** A résumé is a summary account of a job-applicant's education, career, relevant activities, achievements, and goals. It is designed to both interest and inform a prospective employer. A well-developed and visually appealing résumé is necessary for an efficient and effective job search. Careful thought should always be given to its con-

TABLE 25-2
Professional Business Occupation Employment Outlook for 1990

Occupation	Employment (× 1,000) 1990	Percent change, 1978-90
Computer specialists	754	93.94
Computer programmers	361	77.22
Computer systems analysts	392	112.38
Social scientists	248	41.26
Economists	42	56.30
Accountants and auditors	1,055	35.83
Appraisers, real estate	48	49.79
Assessors	38	28.26
Buyers, retail and wholesale trade	298	25.13
Cost estimators	108	34.94
Personnel and labor relations specialists	208	22.86
Purchasing agents and buyers	202	23.69
Tax examiners, collectors, and revenue agents	60	19.61
Tax preparers	51	77.93
Travel agents and accommodations appraisers	70	56.06
Underwriters	90	28.98
Managers, officials, and proprietors	10,677	21.31
Auto parts department managers	59	23.28
Construction inspectors, public administration	61	37.62
Inspectors, excluding construction, public administration	125	20.82
Restaurant, cafe, and bar managers	650	30.27
Sales managers, retail trade	323	23.93
Store managers	1,107	19.52
Wholesalers	284	21.42
Salesworkers	8,079	25.40
Real estate brokers	49	44.47
Sales agents and representatives, real estate	400	56.74
Sales agents and representatives, insurance	405	30.81
Sales agents and representatives, security	88	60.70
Clerical workers	22,519	26.37
Bank tellers	606	37.51
New accounts tellers	66	36.57
Tellers	540	37.62
Bookkeepers and accounting clerks	2,014	23.72
Accounting clerks	845	20.74
Claims examiners, insurance	58	52.29
Clerical supervisors	526	30.81
Collectors, bill and account	113	32.26

SOURCE: From Max L. Carey, "Occupational Employment Growth through 1990," *Monthly Labor Review*, August 1981, pp. 48-53.

P.O. Box 20222
Brazos House
Arlington, Texas 76019

December 25, 19___

Mr. James L. Dwyer
Labor Relations Manager
Dynamics Corporation
Chicago, Illinois

Dear Mr. Dwyer:

Dr. Randall Powell, Professor of Business Administration at the University of Texas at Arlington, recently suggested that I write you concerning your opening and my interest in a labor relations assistant position. I have a B.A. degree in management and courses in labor economics, collective bargaining, labor law, and personnel. I am confident that I could make a positive contribution to your company. The part played by Dynamics Corporation in the development of the Tycho III rocket booster, and the series of articles on your company in The Wall Street Journal and Fortune, have been of great interest to me.

During the last two summers, I worked as a general laborer on a production line, once in a unionized shop, and once in an unorganized plant. My ability to appreciate several points of view on labor problems should prove to be a major asset in my future career performance. Before I left my last summer job, my supervisor had recommended that I be hired as a first-line foreman after graduation. Although I am enthusiastic about the foreman's position, I think my energies and resourcefulness might be better suited to handling union-management problems as a third party in the grievance steps. This has been a four-year college goal for me.

I would very much like to talk with you because I know I can show you why I am a strong candidate for the position. Any Friday or Monday should be ideal for an interview appointment. I will call you in three days to see if your schedule might be open. I look forward to meeting with you.

Thank you for your time and consideration.

Sincerely,

Joan L. Herzing

FIGURE 25.2

tent, since the résumé usually creates the first detailed impression an employer forms about an applicant before ever seeing him or her. The objective of the résumé is not to get a job but to obtain an interview. The employer wants to know who you are, what you want to do, and what you *can* do. The employer prefers a concise and relatively brief summary of your qualifications rather than a comprehensive life history. Your goal is to attract and inspire sufficient interest to create an opportunity to be interviewed. Only positive information about skills and accomplishments should be included in the résumé. It should present well-organized facts concerning your past and present accomplishments—personal, academic, and occupational.

There is no "right" résumé format. You must select the one that best reflects what you want to express to a potential employer. Almost all résumés begin with your name, address, and tele-

```
                              Jane Smith
                             102 Elm St.
                         Arlington, Texas   76015
                            (817) 467-2090


OBJECTIVE:
        I am seeking a position that would let me utilize skills in
        public relations, copywriting, preparing news releases, organ-
        izing, and coordinating and promoting events.

EDUCATION:
        I am a graduate of the University of Texas at Arlington with a
        bachelor of arts degree in journalism and a minor in business.
        My GPA in journalism is 3.7 and my overall GPA is 3.5.

EXPERIENCE:

PUBLIC RELATIONS
        As a public relations director for Junior Achievement of Tarrant
        County, I have increased publicity for the organization in area
        newspapers, in-house publications of local businesses, high school
        newspapers, radio, and television by making good media contacts.

COPYWRITING, NEWS RELEASES AND PHOTOGRAPHY
        I have published articles in the newspapers of the colleges I
        attended and have also written Junior Achievement press releases
        for area newspapers.  I have had training in photography and own
        a 35mm camera.

ORGANIZING
        My duties as membership chairman for a newcomers club included
        organizing and directing a committee that contacted about 100
        new residents each month.  I maintained all records of contacts
        with prospective members and 250 active members.  I have been
        active in Girl Scouts, church, school, federated women's clubs,
        and a hospital auxiliary.

COORDINATING AND PROMOTING EVENTS
        I coordinated the efforts of Junior Achievement members and the
        Clean City Commission of Fort Worth to mount a clean-up campaign
        in downtown Fort Worth.  This was done in preparation for the
        20th World Gymnastics Championships.  Three television stations
        covered the event as did a Fort Worth newspaper.

PERSONAL INFORMATION:
        Designing and sewing my own clothes is a special interest of mine.
        I also enjoy tennis and swimming.

        My health is excellent.

REFERENCES:
        References will be submitted upon request.
```

FIGURE 25.3

Source: *Occupational Outlook Handbook, 1980–1981* (Washington, D.C.: Bureau of Labor Statistics, 1980), Bulletin 2075, p. 20.

phone number. This is followed by a clear statement of the applicant's objective, which tells the potential employer what the applicant wants to do in terms of job titles and responsibilities, or functional areas within the firm. If you decide to search in two or three widely separated fields, you may need to develop several résumés, each one geared to fit a specific goal.

The résumé shown in Figure 25.3 emphasizes experience rather than education. Note that Jane's experiences are organized around functions that she's performed. This is an excellent approach for highlighting the nature of your work activity.

The Interview Sending out a "good" résumé will hopefully lead to a series of interviews. The purpose of the interview is an exchange of information, not one person "grilling" another. You should view it as an opportunity of describing

TABLE 25-3

Questions Commonly Asked by Recruiters and Applicants

BY RECRUITERS:

1. What do you really want to do in life?
2. What are your long-range career objectives?
3. How do you plan to achieve your career goals?
4. What are the most important rewards you expect in your business career?
5. What do you expect to be earning in five years?
6. Why did you choose the career for which you are preparing?
7. Which is more important to you, the money or the type of job?
8. What do you consider to be your greatest strengths and weaknesses?
9. What do you think it takes to be successful in a company like ours?
10. In what ways do you think you can make a contribution to our company?
11. What qualities should a successful manager possess?
12. Describe the relationship that should exist between a supervisor and subordinates.
13. What two or three accomplishments have given you the most satisfaction? Why?
14. Describe your most rewarding college experience.
15. If you were hiring a graduate for this position, what qualities would you look for?
16. Why did you select your college or university?

BY APPLICANTS:

1. Please describe a typical workday (after I've completed training).
2. Do you have an organization chart showing the company/division/department structure? If I'm seriously considered for employment, where would I be on the organization chart?
3. What are your expectations for travel? For mobility?
4. How can a person improve his/her skills while working for you? Do you have a formal training program? On-the-job training? Do you have training manuals? Do you encourage employees to attend special classes or to work on an advanced degree at a local university?
5. Please describe the type of supervision I'd receive during my first 3 months, 6 months, and 12 months on the job.
6. How and when do you evaluate employee performance? How will I know when I'm doing well, or where I may need to improve?
7. What resources are available to me? Do you have a professional library? What types of equipment would I have to work with? Have you computerized certain processes?

SOURCE: Northwestern Endicott Report published by the Placement Center, Northwestern University, Evanston, Illinois 60201. Reprinted by permission.

your knowledge and skills and interpreting them to the interviewer in terms of specific jobs or needs of the employer. Sometimes an initial screening interview is used to form an impression of the applicant, which then leads to in-depth interviews or perhaps a job offer.

Interviews generally have three parts. First comes ice-breaking time (about five minutes) to make you feel comfortable. Then comes a period of questions by the interviewer to elicit information. The third part is your opportunity to ask questions concerning the company. There's the **directive interview,** which is used to get specific information about knowledge, skills, type of academic work, and specific job experience. A second form is the **nondirective interview,** which avoids direct questioning and prompts the person being interviewed to talk freely and informally. Nondirective interviews often lead to discussions of interests, ideas, values, priorities, and personal traits. A single interview may combine both directive and nondirective aspects. Generally, however, there's a focus on one of the types.

There are several things that you should do to prepare for your interview. First, you should plan to arrive about 10 to 15 minutes early. This will allow spare time for any unexpected delay. Second, do your homework: research the company interviewing you and find out everything you can about it. It will be helpful to know the company's history, its product line, and the like. This will help you understand the kind of person the company is looking for and enable you to ask appropriate questions during the interview.

Appearance is also important in the interview. Impressions can sometimes be lasting. As a general rule, you should dress conservatively. You should also be aware that communication takes many forms. Body language is thought to make up much of our total communication. Facial and eye expressions should reinforce verbal messages. Good eye contact with an interviewer doesn't necessarily mean a fixed stare, but it does mean looking at the interviewer's face at least half of the time. It also means that you should smile and try to be relaxed and at ease. Use of the hands, placement of the feet, and your posture during the interview are all part of body language.

Since the purpose of the interview is for the employer to find out about you, the interviewer will ask a series of questions. A list of common questions asked by recruiters is shown in Table 25.3. The second half of the table provides sample questions that applicants should consider asking the recruiter.

If you favorably impress the recruiter in a **screening interview** (about 30 minutes), you'll be invited for a second interview. The second interview is offered to about 20 percent of those initially interviewed. It begins with the personnel department, where an itinerary is developed for the day. You talk with many managers in different departments, usually for about 30 minutes to an hour each. At the end of this second interview, the personnel department again talks with you to discuss completion of the application materials, and to indicate when a letter of acceptance or rejection will be sent. You should remember that most employers eventually hire only 10 percent of the people they originally interview; therefore rejections are commonplace. And sometimes a number of weeks—perhaps even months—may elapse before final word is received.

Beginning A New Job

When you accept a full-time job, whether it's your first or a change of careers, no period is more crucial and potentially nerve-racking than the first few months. It's during this breaking-in period that the employer decides whether you're valuable enough to keep and in what capacity. Sometimes the whole future of employment with a company rides on the first few weeks or months. So it's very important to make a positive impression on your new employer.

In most corporations some degree of formal orientation will be given. Generally speaking, however, the employer expects you to quickly learn (1) the goals of the organization, (2) the organization chart, including your place in the organization and your chain of authority and responsibility, (3) basic personnel policies, such as coffee breaks, reporting illness, overtime, parking, dress, and appearance, and (4) the nature of interpersonal relations—the necessary degree of familiarity and formality, social expectations, etc.

So there you have it—our forecast for the rest of the 1980s and some tips on beginning a career. Business is an exciting and challenging world; and remember: there are millions of opportunities out there for the remainder of this century and beyond.

SUMMARY

It is important for business managers to properly forecast the future. Failure to anticipate trends can be extremely costly. However, as the rate of change in our society increases, the ability to accurately predict and control the future tends to decline.

One technique businesses can use to help them predict the future is to consider the factors that will have the most impact on them. These factors include social considerations, economic factors, and demographic factors. Social considerations include the decline of the Protestant ethic, the growth of new lifestyles that emphasize the self, and the changing role of families. Perhaps the most important economic variable is inflation. In turn, part of the inflationary problem is caused by shortages of natural resources. Competition, especially for smaller firms, will probably intensify, in part because of rising costs, further resource shortages, slower population growth, and increasing foreign competition. Political and legal factors to be considered include the issue of regulation; deregulation will probably continue to grow during the remainder of the 1980s. Growth is also likely in US high-technology industries, such as those dealing in satellite communications, sophisticated diagnostic equipment for hospitals, biotechnology, semiconductors, and personal computers. Finally, the change that can be most accurately forecast involves demographics; important demographic features include the aging of the US population and continued migration to the Sun Belt.

Preparing for a career in tomorrow's business world requires that you follow a logical sequence of activities. Step one involves self-assessment to develop insights into your basic value patterns. The second step requires a skill assessment, which should include consideration of your key abilities and the characteristics that give you the greatest value in successfully dealing with problems, tasks, and people; your leisure-time skills and the things you enjoy; and your work experience. The third step involves not only the choice of a general type of work but also consideration of your lifestyle and leisure objectives. Selecting a major course of study or field of concentration in school is part of this third step. When graduation nears, you must prepare for the fourth step—marketing yourself to prospective employers. You might begin by visiting your school's placement office. Three important tools for self-marketing are letters to potential employers, résumés, and job interviews.

When you accept a job, no period is more crucial than the first few months. In most organizations, you will be expected to learn the goals of the organization, the organization chart and your place on it, basic personnel policies, and the nature of interpersonal relations in the firm.

KEY TERMS

cover letter
deregulation
directive interview
future shock
maintenance of self
nondirective
   interview
Protestant ethic
résumé
screening
self-assessment
skill assessment
structured interview
unstructured
   interview
values

REVIEW QUESTIONS

1. What are the alternative scenarios developed for the US for the remainder of this century?
2. In what way do self-assessment skills aid you in assessing a possible career for yourself?
3. What is meant by "marketing yourself"?
4. Review the first set of questions in Table 25.5. Briefly answer every one that you can. Develop an answer for every one that you find difficult.

DISCUSSION QUESTIONS

1. Considering your own career objectives at this time, which of the four scenarios of trends presented do you feel would give you the best opportunities?
2. Looking at the seven factors that will affect the future of business, how would you rank them in order of importance? Explain your approach.

CASE: A SAFE WALK OR A BIG SPLASH?

Most students would have gladly traded places with Joe Maxwell, who appeared to be sitting comfortably in a position with a big architectural engineering firm. He had an internship that paid him $4 an hour while he learned the business, and he was working directly under the head of the Contracting Department, which negotiated contracts with clients as well as suppliers.

The decision process was very sophisticated, tied as it was to computer systems with data input for costs and revenue forecasts that actually utilized the information Joe had gained in his Decision Science classes. He was amazed at the practical application of much of what he'd learned in college, especially in his computer, statistics, and quantitative methods courses. The most abstract were his economics courses, which didn't have much application to this particular job. Economics had been his major, and his minor was statistics. At times he wished it had been the other way around.

Joe had been in the internship for two semesters, and even though it was quite a compliment to have the internship extended by the company, he was getting a little restless. He had been on a fast track ever since high school, with only a few breaks for vacation, during which he usually worked at various jobs to earn money for his education. He did have a lot of stamina and determination, which he had acquired as an athlete: in high school he had been a track star, and he earned letters in football as a wide receiver. He was also captain of the football team. However he never neglected his studies in college preparatory courses. He graduated with a high average as a member of the National Honor Society.

Joe tolds his friend Chuck Barnes of his restlessness and his desire to get into something a little more exciting. Chuck gave him a ready answer, inviting Joe to join him in his new business. He had made a real financial killing selling insulation and taking advantage of the federal subsidies offered people who remodeled their homes to save energy. Chuck had made over a $100,000 the year before, and this looked very enticing to Joe, who had been plodding along at $4 an hour. (Joe was not sure whether that $100,000 was gross or net profit; Chuck did not make that clear). Then Chuck threw out a more dazzling lure: he was adding a new product to his line—"solar panels," one of the hottest selling products in the construction market. He pointed out that a competitor on the West Coast had made over $500,000 the past year without having to invest much money in advertising and promotion.

The life of the entrepreneur was the way to go, according to Chuck, and he was eager to have his bright and energetic friend to join the firm. This could be a real winning combination.

1. What would be the best choice for Joe Maxwell to make in planning his future career?
2. Does Joe have the qualities of the entrepreneur or should he stick with the more secure position in the architectural engineering firm?

CASE: PATHWAY OR TREADMILL?

Christine Peters was faced with a dilemma of sorts and a big decision: which one of two job opportunities to go for. Of course she felt very fortunate. But she had played her cards right, had interviewed early, and had some good practical experience behind her.

Of the two possibilities, one was a managerial position with a personal finance company similar to the well-known Beneficial Finance. She would be supervisor of four loan counselors, deciding whether or not to make loans to applicants, then following up with penalty assessments for late payments and collections.

The prospect didn't frighten her, however, because she'd worked as a secretary in a fairly large corporation her first two years of college. From there she'd moved into a bank-teller position with a large savings institution, progressing in her senior year to "personal banker," the title the bank used for a loan counselor. She'd also had the opportunity of working with the bank during its changeover to a computerized checking department, on-line from the main bank.

Finally, the job with the personal loan company would pay very well: $15,000 a year to start, with advancement to $18,000 in six months if Peters' work was satisfactory.

As for the other job: it was more challenging, probably a lot more work, and considerably less pay—only $13,000 to start, with no guarantee of advancement. This second job carried the title of "administrative assistant," which usually meant she'd have to do anything that the supervising administrator designated as her duties and tasks. The supervisor was a "systems analyst," and the nature of the job was to install a new computer system that combined word processing and computer operations. It was apparent there would be much detailed work coordinating efforts with computer programmers, the manufacturer's systems people, and other computer analysts.

This was Peters' final year, and she would graduate in the spring with a degree in Business Administration—a major in Finance with a strong minor in Computer Science. Her ultimate objective was to be a financial officer in a corporation.

1. Which job do you think Chris Peters should accept?
2. Could you plot the future for each of these jobs as they relate to her objectives?

A CAREER IN INTERNATIONAL BUSINESS

A career in the international field can be one of the most stimulating and challenging opportunities in business. More than 4 million people in the U.S. are involved in some business related to foreign trade. It's estimated by the Department of Labor that there are some 25,000 Americans employed by U.S. private industry abroad. Travel to distant places, absorbing new cultures, and learning new languages are often requisites for the international business person. On the other hand, you can have a career in international business and never leave the United States. You might work in the international division of a corporation in Kansas City and rarely venture abroad. Knowing a second or third language is not always a prerequisite to obtaining an international position. However you can often expect to be placed in an intensive language training program after accepting a position.

If you think that international business is the place to be, you might first consider summer work abroad. Although potentially very rewarding, these jobs are difficult to get. One important source of summer employment information is published by the Council on International Educational Exchange (777 UN Plaza, New York, NY 10017). Another possibility is to obtain a summer internship. Pay is often low to nil, but the organization may provide transportation and an allowance for food and lodging. Several sources of internships include the United Nations, the U.S. Department of State, Bank of America, Citibank, Exxon, Mobil, and the Associated Press. The latter is primarily limited to students seeking a career in international journalism.

Where the Opportunities Are

1 ■ INTERNATIONAL BANKING

A variety of functions are carried out in the international department of large banks. These include attracting deposits, making loans, and providing other financial services to promote trade and investment. Those working as lending officers in branches located on foreign soil provide international banking services to U.S. and foreign customers; they also travel to various parts of the world to sell bank services to corporations and government entities. This requires working knowledge of various countries' financial systems, trade relations, and economic conditions.

Places of Employment Throughout the world. Most entry-level positions are in New York, San Francisco, Chicago, and Los Angeles.

Skills Required Four-year program but M.B.A. usually preferred.

Employment Outlook thru 1990 Excellent.

Salaries Entry level: $16,000–$28,000.

2 ■ INTERNATIONAL DEPARTMENT OF MULTINATIONAL CORPORATION

Most positions are in the fields of marketing, finance, and accounting. A manager in a foreign subsidiary would be responsible for developing and implementing plans for marketing strategies and investments.

Places of Employment   Throughout the world.
Skills Required   Four-year program or M.B.A.
Employment Outlook thru 1990   Good.
Salaries $15,000–$30,000 entry-level positions.

APPENDIX

BUSINESS
RESEARCH
METHODS

WHY STUDY RESEARCH AND STATISTICS?

Understanding statistics is vital for anyone in today's environment—business or nonbusiness. We live in a world of numbers and use statistics every day, although we usually don't think much about it. For example, the weather forecast is given as a probability; the expression "There is an 80 percent chance of rain this afternoon" is a statistic that helps us decide if we should take an umbrella with us.

In business, managers gather data about things such as sales volume, competitor's prices, costs per unit, production per man-hour, and debt-to-equity ratios. These numbers are also statistics; some come directly from the company's financial statements, while others come from outside sources. They all serve one basic purpose: to provide management data and information for making decisions.

Statistics

Statistics are used for many purposes—for example to make a point in a speech or to show essential relationships among various factors. We often hear that "with statistics you can prove anything" or that "statistics don't lie, but statisticians do." There's an element of truth in each of these overstatements. You can prove a point by gathering only those statistics supporting your position, carefully ignoring all those that don't. Or a statistic can be posed in such a way as to create an image different from what the statistic really says. Some years ago a well-known coffee manufacturer advertised that its instant coffee was so delicious that it was preferred even over fresh-brewed coffee by the majority of those taking a taste test—*and who had also expressed a preference for instant coffee*. Needless to say, this last bit of information was mentioned very quickly in the commercial. But what did the test actually show? Only that people who liked instant coffee to begin with, continued to like it!

While statistics themselves are merely numbers, there's a field of study in mathematics called *statistics* that includes gathering and analyzing data and making decisions based on the analysis. There are two types of statistical studies.

Descriptive Statistics Statistics of this type describe a situation or a problem. Here data are developed and displayed in a format that makes understanding the problem easier.

Inductive Statistics This branch of statistics has to do with the scientific method of making inferences about a population based on samples taken from it. For example, Westinghouse might try to determine the reliability of one of its new light bulbs. To do so it selects a sample of perhaps 100 bulbs and leaves them on until they burn out. Statistical observations are then made—for example, perhaps 22 of the 100 burned for over 200 hours—and inferences drawn concerning the entire output (probably millions) of the new bulb.

To illustrate the use of this information: suppose it was determined that almost all the bulbs burned out at about the same time—say within a two-hour span. Westinghouse might use this reliability factor in promoting the new bulb because it's usually much cheaper (in terms of labor costs) to replace all bulbs in an office or factory at one time than to replace them individually as they burn out. But if their lives varied considerably, mass replacement would mean throwing out bulbs that have life remaining—and that also could be expensive.

Sampling Procedures

Sampling procedures rest on the fundamental proposition that the sample must be enough like the population from which it is drawn so that it adequately represents it. This assumption allows the researcher to infer that attributes of the sample adequately reflect attributes of the population.

OBTAINING DATA

Data for business decisions exist in both the internal and the external environment of the firm. Both types of data are needed in order to make successful business decisions.

Internal Data Sources

Internal data are generated from the company's own records. The data are recorded in the company's accounting journals and ledgers, and in special records. Internal data are facts about the actual performance results of the company. Examples of data developed internally are sales receipts, sales volume, man-hours worked, production labor costs, inventory levels, and accounts-payable balances. These and other data are recorded in, or are directly available from, the company's information system.

External Data

External data are developed from sources other than the company's records. They're used to evaluate markets, competitor activity, and economic conditions. External data are classified as secondary or primary types. *Secondary data* are those that have been derived from other sources. They have some advantages that favor their use, including:

1. They can be found quickly and inexpensively.
2. They provide the expertise of others who have investigated similar research questions.
3. They may cover a much wider range of data than that which the company can develop on its own. For example, the company's trade association has access to more companies' data than does an individual firm.

However, secondary data have limitations, some of which are:

1. They are prepared by someone else for some other purpose. This purpose may be different from that of the current investigation and may lead to biased results.
2. They may be obsolete before they're made available to others for general use.

Data developed specifically for the problem currently under investigation are called *primary data*. Primary data are usually developed by observation or survey and relate directly to the research question at hand. For example, a personnel manager may want to determine whether employees are satisfied with the company's fringe benefits program. Her only course of action is to interview employees about their attitudes toward the fringe benefits. The results are primary data since they're unique to the fringe benefit study.

Sources of Secondary Data Secondary data come from a variety of sources, one of the principal ones being federal government agencies. The U.S. Bureau of the Census develops many data sources for various segments of the United States economy. A major statistical data source published by the federal government is the *Census of Population*, taken every ten years. Census information develops detailed data about the population of the United States including social, economic, ethnic, and occupational characteristics. There are several other major sources of government statistical data produced at regular intervals. These sources are:

1. *Statistical Abstract of the United States*
2. *County and City Data Book*
3. *Survey of Current Business*
4. *Census of Manufacturing*
5. *Census of Housing*
6. *Federal Reserve Bulletin*
7. *Monthly Labor Review*
8. *Business Conditions Digest*
9. *Census of Business*

Sources of Primary Data Primary data are generally developed from observation, survey, or experiment. Data collection by *observation* is visually or mechanically measured and recorded. For example, counting traffic at an intersection may be accomplished by stationing people to count the cars going by or, alternatively, by employing a traffic count meter.

The observation method of gathering data is limited in its ability to obtain information. The *survey* method gathers information by asking questions of persons who possess desired experience or knowledge in the survey area. Surveys pose a list of specific questions called a *questionnaire*, which is used in several ways. The most common is to mail the questionnaire to the desired person, asking that it be completed and returned to the researcher. People to be questioned can also be contacted by telephone, in which case the researcher reads each question and records responses. Finally, questioning may be done by asking the questions in person. In this—the personal interview—the researcher records responses and comments made by those interviewed.

The usefulness of the survey method depends on the accuracy of the answers it yields. A person responding to a questionnaire might give misleading or false answers, thereby distorting the results, and care must be taken that the questionnaire is answered completely and with reasonable accuracy. The basic rules for questionnaire construction are:

1. Keep the questionnaire short.
2. Use the questionnaire with people who have the desired information.
3. Don't let the form of the question influence the answer.
4. Avoid asking questions in ways that can be interpreted differently.
5. Ask only questions essential to the research effort; avoid extraneous or redundant questions.

An *experiment* is a research method that obtains data through manipulation of key variables under carefully controlled conditions. The purpose of an experiment is to determine how variables in a situation are related to each other. Experiments may be conducted in laboratories, classrooms, offices, work settings, or any other place where a researcher is able to control changes in variables. This control is needed so that the relationships among the factors under study can be measured and evaluated.

STATISTICAL ANALYSIS

Statistical analysis is a method of summarizing data in order to present their major characteristics. We've seen that statistics can be used to describe a situation (descriptive statistics) in more detail, or it can be used to test hypotheses (inductive statistics). Either way, certain statistical properties are often examined. Four of these are (1) averages, (2) correlation analysis, (3) time series analysis, and (4) index numbers.

Averages

Statistical measures called *averages* are used to summarize the general behavior of a large number of observations. The average reduces a large number of separate values to a single number and produces a common denominator that can be used in making comparisons. The most common averages are the arithmetic mean, the median, and the mode. The data shown in Table A.1 will be used for calculation of each average discussed below.

TABLE A–1

Sales and Newspaper Advertising for Grimmer Tire Company, 1983

Week (observations)	Sales (thousands)	Grimmer's Newspaper Advertising (thousands)
1	$ 100	$ 6.0
2	93	6.5
3	90	6.5
4	90	6.0
5	86	5.0
6	86	5.5
7	83	5.0
8	82	5.0
9	80	4.5
10	78	4.5
11	78	5.0
12	78	4.0
13	78	3.5
14	76	3.5
15	76	2.5
16	74	2.5
17	70	3.0
18	66	1.5
19	58	2.0
20	56	1.5
21	52	1.5

Mean: The Average   When the term *average* is used it generally refers to the arithmetic mean. The mean of any series of numbers is found by adding them together and dividing the total by the number of values in the sum. It is probably the most widely used average in statistics because it's an easy measure to calculate and easy to understand.

The mean for sales presented in Table A.1 is calculated as follows:

1. Find the total of the weekly sales by adding all the values in column 2. The total is $1630.
2. Divide the total by the number of weeks (observations), which is 21.
3. Dividing 1630 by 21 gives the result of $77.6; therefore the mean of the sales shown in Table 23.1 is $77.6. Grimmer's average weekly sales is $77.6 thousand.

The Median: The Midpoint   The middle value of any set of data is called the *median*. In order to calculate the median, the data must be arranged in ascending or descending order. The middle value of an odd-numbered group of data is the median. (For an even-numbered group, the average of the two middle values is used.) In Table A.1 the median is the eleventh week's sales of $78.0 thousand.

The median is better than the mean as an average when a few very large or a very few small data values exist in the observations. This is so because the median reflects more clearly the central tendency of the data, which would be distorted by the mean.

The Mode: The Most Frequent The *mode* is the most frequent value to occur in the set of data. The mode gives the value around which most results tend to cluster, and it's the most appropriate average to use when the most frequent value is of major concern. The mode of the sales given in Table A.1 is $78.0 thousand.

Correlation Analysis

If an analyst suspects that changes in one variable are associated with changes in another, he or she can use correlation analysis to examine that relationship. The example in Table A.1 illustrates a need for correlation analysis. It's fairly obvious that sales increase as the advertising variable increases; this is an example of *positive correlation*. Conversely, if two variables move in opposite directions, *negative correlation* exists. There are several ways to measure correlations. A statistic that you might have heard of—the *coefficient of correlation, r*—can be calculated arithmetically and it answers the question: How does the behavior of one variable relate to changes in the other? (This doesn't necessarily imply that one "causes" changes in the other.) Formal courses in statistics cover this area in considerable depth.

Time Series Analysis

The analysis of changes in data over time is called *time series analysis.* The major components of time series are secular trend, seasonal variation, cyclical variation, and random variation. The *secular trend* refers to the general direction of change in the data. *Seasonal variation* refers to changes in data that result from seasonal levels of activity, while *cyclical variation* is the change resulting from periodic changes in economic activity, often referred to as the *business cycle. Random variations* are data that cannot be effectively identified as being part of the trend, seasonal, or cyclical movements. Time series data are usually used to develop long-range and short-range forecasts. By isolating time series patterns in historical data related to company activities, the manager can use this information to develop effective forecasts for future company actions. Figure A.1 illustrates a hypothetical time series showing trend, cyclical, and seasonal variations.

Index Numbers

Index numbers measure changes in the value of a variable with respect to some predetermined base, usually time. The index number is stated as a percentage change in value, and it compares the present value of the variable with the past value that was chosen as a base. The base value is usually set equal to 100, and all subsequent data are stated in terms of that value. For example, a company may choose 1975 as its base year for sales; say sales were then $200 thousand. Any changes in sales from the sales amount in 1975 will be reflected as a percentage of 1975 sales. An index number of 160 for 1981 indicates that sales in 1981 are 60 percent above the 1975 sales, or $320 thousand.

Index numbers are commonly used in reporting government statistics. Perhaps the most common index number is the Consumer Price Index; each month it's calculated by economists to keep track of the rate of inflation. Other frequently watched index numbers are the New York Stock Exchange Index, the Wholesale Price Index, and the Federal Reserve Board Index of Industrial Production.

DATA PRESENTATION

Data presentation is concerned with displaying data in a useful form once they've been collected and analyzed. Most research studies produce large amounts of data that would be meaningless without effective presentation. The method of reporting data must be clear, concise, and understandable.

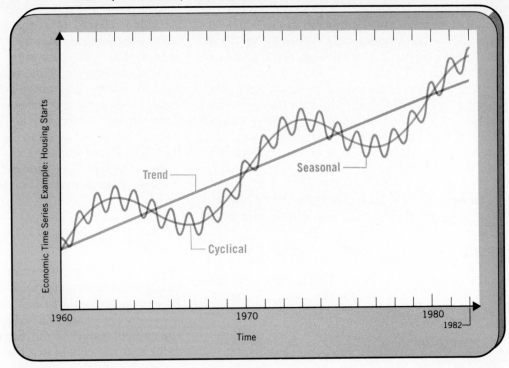

FIGURE A.1

Using Tables

Tables are used when there's a large number of values to be presented in the report. Tables can be used for various reasons. *Reference tables* present information used as a reference for other purposes. *Summary tables* are the type most often used in business research reports. Such a table must be clearly labeled for contents and the purpose for which the data are intended. The table should also include the sources of any secondary data that are used. The rows and columns must be clearly titled so that users can understand ex-

actly what the research study found. The basis of the numeric values, and whether they represent actual numbers, indexes, or abbreviations, must be shown. Table A.2 presents a time series data table developed in order to study a company's operating results over the period 1977–1982.

Using Graphs and Charts

It's often said that "a picture is worth a thousand words." This observation forms the basis for the use of graphs and charts in data presentation.

TABLE A–2
Tabular Presentation of Time Series Data for Bison Production Company (all numbers in thousands)

Year	Units Sold	Gross Receipts	Total Costs	Net Profit
1977	3.7	$ 3,600.1	$ 2,736.1	$ 396.0
1978	4.9	4,300.2	3,268.2	473.9
1979	6.9	8,001.1	6,080.0	880.1
1980	8.7	11,610.9	8,823.6	1,277.2
1981	10.5	13,208.0	10,038.1	1,452.9
1982	13.2	16,400.1	12,464.1	1,804.0

Graphs and charts are ways of pictorially representing data. Technically, a graph or a chart is defined as an illustration of the relationship of one set of data to another set. The many types of graphs and charts include bar charts, line graphs, pie charts, and statistical maps—both two- and three-dimensional. These are illustrated in Figures A.2 through A.6.

VERTICAL FORMAT BAR CHART

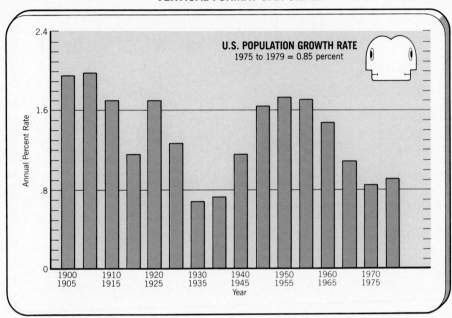

FIGURE A.2

Source: Board of Governors of the Federal Reserve System, *1980 Historical Chart Book*, p. 23.

FIGURE A.3

LINE GRAPH

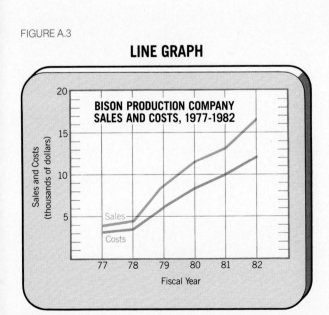

FIGURE A.4

PIE CHART

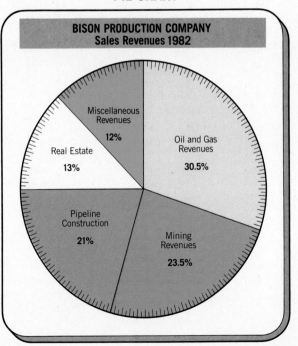

TWO-DIMENSIONAL STATISTICAL MAP

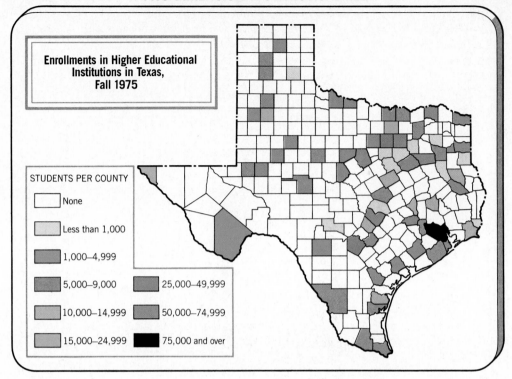

Enrollments in Higher Educational Institutions in Texas, Fall 1975

STUDENTS PER COUNTY

- None
- Less than 1,000
- 1,000–4,999
- 5,000–9,000
- 10,000–14,999
- 15,000–24,999
- 25,000–49,999
- 50,000–74,999
- 75,000 and over

FIGURE A.5

Source: Reprinted from *Atlas of Texas* (1976) by permission of the Bureau of Business Research, University of Texas at Austin.

FIGURE A.6

Source: Aspex Program, Harvard Laboratory for Computer Graphics and Spatial Analysis Mapping Service.

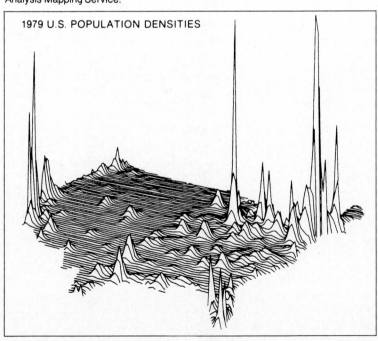

1979 U.S. POPULATION DENSITIES

GLOSSARY

The numbers that appear in parentheses after the terms indicate the chapters in which the terms are defined.

Accelerated cost recovery system (ACRS) (21) A new approach to depreciating an asset, allowing the use of either the ACRS depreciation schedule or the straight-line method.

Accessories (12) Capital goods that are usually less expensive and more standardized than installations and that have no important long-run consequences for the firm. *See also* **Installations**.

Accounting (25) A business major that includes learning to develop financial statements, to analyze investment opportunities, and to determine tax liabilities.

Accounting equation (21) The theory that the modern accounting system is based on: Assets = Liabilities + Owners' Equity.

Accounting process (21) The procedural framework used by accountants to transform data and prepare reports. Also called accounting cycle.

Accounts receivable (18) An account of the money owed to a corporation by its customers.

Achievement motive (7) The desire to accomplish or reach personal goals.

Acid-test ratio (21) The ratio of the most liquid of the current assets to current liabilities. Also called quick ratio.

Ad volorem tax (23, 24) A tariff based on the value of imports. Also a tax assessed on real and personal property.

Administrative law (23) A set of administrative rules and regulations used to implement the provisions of statutory law.

Advertising (11) Any paid form of nonpersonal presentation of goods and services by an identified sponsor.

See also individual entries, such as **Informative advertising; Reminder advertising**.

Advocacy advertising (13) The aspect of institutional advertising that involves taking a stand on certain issues and proposals of a controversial, social, or economic nature.

Affirmative action (8) The effort by employers to significantly expand the number of minority applicants for positions with their firms.

Ageism (2) The unfair treatment of individuals merely because of their age.

Agency (23) The legal relationship in which one person authorizes, expressly or by implication, another person to act for or represent him or her.

Agency shop (9) A union security clause under which a person is not required to join a union but must pay a fee to cover the union's expenses in representing the nonunion employee.

Altered workweek (8) A work plan that does not follow the standard 8-hour day, 5-day week schedule.

American Federation of Labor (AFL) (1) A major national labor union in the United States.

American Stock Exchange (ASE; Amex) (17) The second largest stock exchange in the United States.

Analytic process (10) A production process in which the basic input is broken down into component parts.

Annual report (17) A yearly corporation report to shareholders including a statement of operations, financial statements, and other information from management.

Anti-Injunction Act *See* **Norris-LaGuardia Act**.

Applications program (22) One of the two types of programs required in order for a computer to process data. The other is called a job control program.

Arbitration *See* **Grievance arbitration**.

Arithmetic logic unit (ALU) (22)   The electronic circuitry of the central processor that performs the arithmetic operations and the logical comparisons used in sorting and ordering the numbers.

Arithmetic operations (22)   The addition, subtraction, multiplication, and division functions that a computer performs.

Aspiration, level of   *See* **Level of aspiration**.

Assembly line (10)   An arrangement of tools, machinery, and workers through which the product is mechanically conveyed on its way to completion.

Assessment center (8)   A method of identifying employees with managerial potential; during an intensive one day to a week, a group of candidates is rated by a team of personnel assessors.

Assets (21)   Anything owned by the business and used in the production of the business's goods and services.

Authority (6)   The power of an individual to make decisions and give orders—a power designated by formal arrangement and approval.

Autocratic decision style (5)   A decision style in which the manager solves a problem and issues a related order to employees.

Automated teller machine (ATM) (16)   An electronic banking machine, usually placed outside the bank or in other convenient locations, that provides twenty-four hour banking for customers.

Automation (10)   The replacement of human effort by automatic machines used to control production processes.

Auxiliary storage (22)   Storage of data to be utilized at a later time. Also called secondary storage.

Bait-and-switch pricing (15)   An unethical and illegal pricing strategy that lures customers into a store by advertising an item for an unusually low price (the bait); once the customer is in the store an aggressive personal effort is applied to get the customer to buy a more expensive item (the switch).

Balance of payments (24)   The difference between a nation's total payments to foreign countries and its receipts from foreign countries.

Balance of trade (24)   A measure of a country's exports and imports of goods and services.

Balance sheet (21)   A statement that shows what the company owns and how much it owes others.

Balanced fund (17)   A mutual fund that holds a mix of stocks and bonds.

Bank charter (16)   A license to operate a bank.

Bankruptcy law (23)   A law under which a debt-ridden party can petition the court for relief from debts by allowing the court to distribute owned assets to the creditors.

Bankruptcy Reform Act (23)   An act that provides for the quick and efficient resolution of bankruptcy cases.

Bargaining   *See* **Collective bargaining; Zone of bargaining**.

Batch processing (22)   The process of collecting data in similar groups and processing the groups.

Binary number system (22)   The counting system, used by computers, that is a combination of only two numbers: 1 and 0.

Bit (22)   The basic storage unit of a computer system.

Blacklist (9)   A list that contains the names of workers involved with unions, used to keep such workers from being hired.

Blue Cross/Blue Shield (19)   A prepaid medical expense plan under which premiums are pooled to pay the health care costs of subscribers; operated on a nonprofit basis.

Blue Sky Laws (17)   A name given to state laws that regulate the securities markets.

Board of Governors of the Federal Reserve System (16)   The seven-member board that coordinates the overall operation of the Federal Reserve System.

Bond broker (17)   A commission broker who makes only bond transactions for customers.

Bonds (17)   *See individual entries, such as* **Corporate bond; Mortgage bond**.

Boundaries (6)   Points of contact with other organizations or interested groups in the environment.

Boundary spanner (6)   A person who comes into contact with others outside the firm, thus linking the firm with the environment.

Brainstorming (7)   A decision-making approach used if a problem is very unstructured; group members discuss the problem and then offer all the ideas and solutions that they can possibly think up.

Brand (12)   A term used to identify a product or service by word, name, symbol, design, or a combination of these things. *See also* **Dealer brands; Family branding; Manufacturers' brands; Private brands**.

Brand loyal (11)   A characteristic marked by habitual purchase of the same brand product.

Breach of contract (23)   A violation of the obligations imposed by a contract.

Breaking bulk (14)   The breaking down by a wholesaler of a boxcarload or truckload shipment into smaller, more usable quantities to be sold to retailers.

Broker (14)   A person who brings a buyer and a seller together.

Budget (18)   A projection of future sales revenues, future operating expenses, and cash investment outlays.

Business (1)   A social process involving the assembly and utilization of productive resources to produce products and services capable of satisfying society's needs and wants. *See individual entries, such as* **Manufacturing businesses; Service businesses.**

Buy national regulations (24)   Regulations giving special priority and privileges to domestic manufacturers.

Buying long (17)   The purchase of a security in anticipation of an increase in its price.

Bytes (22)   Units of grouped bits used to represent numbers and letters.

Call option (17)   An option that entitles the holder to buy a fixed number of shares at a fixed price within a specified time.

Canned presentation (13)   A memorized presentation that is sometimes used to sell products to final consumers.

Capital budget (18)   The spending plan for the acquisition of new factories, equipment, and other major long-term investments of the business.

Capital expenditures (18)   Investments in long-term assets such as land, buildings, machinery, and equipment.

Capital gain (23)   Income that results when a business sells assets such as machinery, equipment, real estate, or security investments for more than their original purchase price.

Capital market   *See* **Long-term securities market.**

Capitalism (1)   An economic system under which individuals can participate in business through investments in new and existing businesses that are relatively free from government control.

Card reader (22)   A device used for interpreting the data recorded on punched cards.

Career (8)   A series of jobs, roles, and statuses through which a person progresses until retirement.

Cash budget (18)   A projection incorporating the revenues and expenses of the operating budget and the firm's future cash needs or possible surpluses.

Cash discount (15)   A price reduction given to a buyer for paying a bill within a specified period of time or for an immediate cash payment.

Cash dividends (17)   Returns on the stockholder's investment usually paid quarterly on a per share basis.

Cash flow (20)   What is left from rental income after deducting operating expenses, mortgage payments, and income taxes.

Cash management (18)   The process of managing a corporation's liquidity.

Catalog showroom (14)   A catalog store that has many cost advantages over other retailers because of lower sales cost, display cost, and service cost.

Cathode ray tube   *See* **CRT (cathode ray tube) terminal.**

Celler-Kefauver Act (23)   An act that focuses on merger activity and prohibits the purchase of one company by another if such a transaction will result in a decrease of competition in the given industry.

Central processing unit (CPU) (22)   The controller of the computer system, which stores data and does computational processing.

Centralization (6)   A situation where only a limited amount of authority in an organization is assigned downward.

Certificate in Management Accounting (CMA) (21)   A certification program designed to ensure the management accountant's mastery of the body of knowledge relating to accounting for management reporting.

Certificates of Deposit (CDs) (16)   IOUs issued by banks, savings and loan associations, and credit unions; they pay interest at a stated rate and have a specified maturity.

Certified Property Manager (CPM) (20)   A well-trained and experienced property manager hired to help the income property owner control costs and manage the property.

Certified Public Accountant (CPA) (21)   A person who has passed a standard examination in accounting theory and practice.

Chain of command (6)   The series of unbroken one-to-one authority and reporting relationships that begins with the lowest level of the organization and progresses to the top level.

Channel of distribution (14)   The sequence of marketing institutions through which a product passes on its way from the producer to the final user.

Check-clearing system (16)   The assistance of the Federal Reserve System that enables banks to clear checks quickly.

Chicago Board of Trade (CBT) (17)   One of the commodities and futures exchanges where futures are traded.

Chicago Board Options Exchange (CBOE) (17)   An exchange on which options are traded; a subsidiary of the Chicago Board of Trade.

Chicago Mercantile Exchange (CME) (17) One of the commodities and futures exchanges where futures are traded.

CIO See **Congress of Industrial Organizations (CIO).**

Clayton Act (23) One of the major regulatory acts concerned with competition.

Closed shop (9) A union security clause under which a person must be a union member in good standing before being hired as an employee; now illegal under the Taft-Hartley Act.

Cohesiveness (7) People's sense of solidarity and desire to remain in a group, as well as their tendency to resist outside influences.

Coinsurance (19) A clause that requires the property owner to buy an amount of insurance coverage equal to a specified percentage of the value of the property.

Collateral (18) Something of value that a lender can seize or sell if a borrower fails to repay a loan.

Collective bargaining (9) The process of negotiating, administering, and interpreting the labor agreement.

Commercial banks (16) Institutions that offer the widest range of financial services to their customers.

Commercial paper (18) A short-term corporate IOU that is sold in the money market by large corporations to raise short-term funds.

Commercial property (20) Property that includes shopping centers, office buildings, and other types of nonresidential property.

Commission broker (17) A member of the stock exchange who executes orders for the public.

Commitment (4) One requirement of a business owner—to stay with a business long enough for it to become successful.

Common law (23) The set of principles that reflect the customs of society and that are found in court decisions.

Common Market (24) The European Economic Community, which has established common import duties for its members and abolished tariff barriers between them; goods imported from nonmember nations face stiff tariffs.

Common stock (17) Stock that enables holders to own a portion of a corporation.

Communication (13) The process by which messages, such as attitudes, emotions, and feelings, are exchanged between people through a common system of symbols.

Communism (1) An economic system under which a classless society owns all productive resources collectively rather than individually.

Comparative advantage See **Principle of comparative advantage.**

Comparative advertising (13) Product advertising in which two or more specific products, mentioned by name, are compared in terms of product/service features.

Compensating balance (18) The minimum or average deposit (at no interest) that the borrower must maintain in the lending bank.

Compiler program (22) A program used to translate the program codes of the programming languages into machine language.

Component parts and materials (12) Humanly put together components, either custom-made or standardized, that are incorporated into the end product of a firm.

Compressed workweek (8) A plan scheduling 40 hours of normal work into less than 5 days or working less than 40 hours a week but receiving 40 hours of pay.

Computer (22) An electronic machine that can assemble and store data, perform arithmetic functions on data, and manipulate and report data for use in making decisions.

Conceptual skills (5) Skills that enable a manager to view the business as a whole, understand how its various parts fit together, and see how it relates to other organizations.

Conciliation (9) A process in a labor dispute in which a third-party neutral tries to keep the parties to the dispute on the issues of disagreement.

Condominium (20) A multi-unit structure with private ownership of individual units and joint ownership of common space such as lawns, lobbies, and swimming pools.

Congress of Industrial Organizations (CIO) (1) One of the major national labor unions in the United States.

Construction businesses (4) Businesses that build houses, offices, factories, highways, and other facilities needed by society.

Consultative decision style (5) A decision style in which the manager shares a problem with employees and asks for their suggestions.

Consumer behavior (11) Any or the total of the decision processes and acts of people who are involved in buying and using products.

Consumer goods (12) Goods and services purchased and used by the ultimate buyer.

Consumer orientation (11) The process of identifying the groups of people who are most likely to buy a company's products and then determining how best to meet their needs.

Consumerism (2) The organized effort by independent groups (and by groups within government and business) to protect the consumer from undesirable effects resulting from the manufacture and sale of goods and services.

Containerization (14) A method of rail service in which the trailer portion of a truck is placed on a railroad flatcar and shipped to a distant city, where it is unloaded and re-attached to a truck tractor. Also called piggy-back service.

Continuous process (6,10) The process of continuously feeding raw materials into the manufacture of large quantities of standardized products. Also called mass production.

Contract manufacturing (24) Manufacturing by a foreign country of a predetermined volume of products to specifications of a domestic firm and then putting the domestic firm's brand name on the goods.

Control (5) A process that ensures that what is being done agrees with the plans developed.

Control program (22) A program that supervises and schedules the computer resources used in processing.

Convenience goods (12) Goods that are relatively inexpensive and require little shopping effort.

Conversion process (10) The process of converting inputs into final outputs.

Conversion system (10) The running of a conversion process either continuously or intermittently.

Convertible preferred stock (17) Preferred stock that exchanges into common shares at a specified price.

Co-op sampling (13) A method of sampling in which several different products are delivered in the same container at the same time.

Cooperative (3, 20) An organization set up to provide the opportunity for businesses or individuals with like products, services, or interests to act in concert in carrying out their business missions. Also an apartment building in which each tenant owns a proportionate share of the corporation that owns the building.

Copyright (23) An exclusive right given to a writer, artist, composer, or playwright to use, produce, and sell his or her creation.

Core *See* **Main memory**.

Corporate bond (17) A bond issued by a corporation.

Corporate bond fund (17) A mutual fund that owns a portfolio of corporate bonds.

Corporation (3) A "legal person" established by the laws of the state in which it is formed enabling it to operate as a business.

Cost of holding (10) The investment, storage, handling, insurance, and shrinkage costs associated with holding inventories.

Cost-of-living adjustment (COLA) (9) A union contract clause that requires automatic wage increases as the cost of living advances.

Cover letter (25) A letter accompanying a résumé that attempts to attract a prospective employer's interest.

Craft union (9) A union that organizes and represents workers in a single craft or occupation.

Credit (21) A bookkeeping entry that records (1) a decrease in an asset, (2) an increase in a liability, and (3) an increase in owners' equity.

Credit cards (16) Cards that can be used to pay for almost anything. Also called plastic money.

Credit union (16) A savings cooperative whose members have something in common, such as the same employer or church membership.

Crime (23) A wrong resulting from the violation of public law.

Critical Path Method (CPM) (10) A network model in which a single time-estimate is developed for each activity.

CRT (cathode ray tube) terminal (22) A terminal that displays the data being put into the computer on a screen similar to a television screen.

Cryoelectronic memories (22) New technology memories that would operate at temperatures close to absolute zero and use up to 1000 times less power than semiconductor units.

Cumulative discount (15) A quantity discount that can be added up over a period of time.

Cumulative preferred stock (17) Stock with a protective cumulative provision that requires that all past omitted preferred stock dividends be paid before any dividends can be paid to the holders of common shares.

Current ratio (21) The ratio of total current assets to total current liabilities.

Damages (23) Money awarded to a person harmed by a breach of contract.

Data base management (22) A computer storage concept that the various functional areas of a business all have access to the same basic sources of data.

Data management program (22) A program that opens, updates, and closes files that store data and processing programs.

Data processing (22) The assembling, classifying, and reporting of data in a way that provides assistance in the decision-making process.

Dealer (17) Someone who buys and sells stocks for his or her own account.

Dealer brands (12) The brands of wholesalers and retailers that tie a consumer to the retailer or wholesaler. Also called private brands.

Debenture bond (17) An unsecured corporate bond—that is, one backed only by the credit worthiness of the issuing corporation.

Debit (21) A bookkeeping entry that records (1) an increase in an asset, (2) a decrease in a liability, and (3) a decrease in owner's equity.

Debit card (16) A coded plastic card that enables a person to pay for purchases on the spot if the merchant has a point-of-sale (POS) machine. *See also* **Point-of-sale (POS) machine.**

Debt-to-assets ratio (21) A measure of the claims that the creditors have against the assets of the company.

Decentralization (6) A situation where considerable authority and decision-making freedom are delegated to lower-level managers.

Decision style (5) The way in which a manager interacts with employees to solve a problem.

Decline stage (12) The fourth stage of a product life cycle, characterized by permanently falling sales due to changes in consumer taste and the introduction of new and better products.

Defense preparedness argument (24) A belief that tariffs should be used to protect industries and technologies that are vital to maintaining a high level of defense preparedness.

Deferred pay increase (9) A pay increase that becomes effective later in the contract period.

Delegation (6) The downward distribution of job duties and corresponding authority to the people in the organization.

Demand (1) A negative relationship between quantity and price; more is demanded at low prices and less at high prices.

Demand deposits (16) Checking accounts established with a financial institution.

Dental insurance (19) Insurance to help pay dental bills.

Department store (14) A store with many departments located in one building to achieve more effective promotion, buying, service to the customer, and control.

Departmentation (6) The process of grouping people, products, and various resources into departments.

Depreciation (20, 21) A noncash expense incurred by the owner that permits recovery of a portion of his or her investment in the property. Also the process of assigning the historical cost of a fixed asset to revenues generated through the use of that asset.

Deregulation (25) A lessening of government regulation and restriction of private enterprise.

Developing nation (24) A nation that is not highly industrialized and has not achieved a high standard of living.

Dilution (18) The lessening of each share's percentage claim on a corporation's earnings and assets after the sale of new common shares.

Direct investment (24) The purchase of active ownership of an existing company or new facilities in a foreign country.

Direct retailing (14) Selling to the consumer in his or her home, using a catalog, telephone, or direct-mail piece.

Directing (5) Guiding and motivating employees in order to help the firm move toward its goals.

Directive interview (25) An interview technique used to get specific information about knowledge, skills, type of academic work, and specific job experience.

Disability income insurance (19) Insurance that provides periodic payments to sick or disabled workers.

Discount broker (17) A broker who executes clients' trades but does not supply the full range of services that a full-service broker does.

Discount rate (16) The interest rate that the Fed charges banks that borrow from it.

Discount store (14) A store that carries lines of merchandise that enable it to sell a high volume at a low price.

Distribution *See individual entries, such as* **Channel of distribution; Exclusive distribution; Selective distribution.**

Dividend policy (18) A decision on what proportion of profits will be distributed as shareholder dividends and what proportion will be reinvested in the business.

Divisibility (16) A characteristic of suitable money that allows for the money to be easily divided into smaller parts.

Documentation (22) The instructions for the programs that direct the computer system.

Dollar votes (15) The "votes" for (purchases of) a product when people believe that the retailer or other merchant has established a fair price for it.

Double-entry bookkeeping (21) The two-entry style of bookkeeping that keeps the accounting equation in balance.

Dow Jones Industrial Average (DJIA; the Dow) (17) The most widely followed index used to monitor general stock market movements.

Dues checkoff (9) A clause under which union members annually authorize the employer to automatically deduct the amount of union dues and assessments from their paychecks; the funds are then given to the union in a lump sum at the end of the pay period.

Dumping (24) A form of international price discrimination in which a company charges lower prices in foreign markets than it does for the same merchandise in its home market.

Durability (16) A characteristic of suitable money that requires that the money last a long time and be replaceable.

Earnings per share (EPS) (21) The amount of earnings generated on behalf of the owners of the company's common stock.

Ecology (2) The interrelationship of living things and their environments, including the interaction between different kinds of living things.

Economic integration (24) The result of governments meeting and agreeing on a common economic policy.

Economic risk (14) The possibility that a purchase decision will greatly reduce the consumer's budget and not yield substantial satisfaction.

Economics (25) A business major that includes learning the principles underlying pricing, production, wage, and investment decisions and the principles that guide public policy and matters of taxation, regulation, money, and international trade and exchange.

Economies of scale (15) The tendency for the average cost per unit to decline when a firm produces large quantities of a single item.

Efficiency (1) The ability of a firm to produce its output at the lowest possible cost.

Electronic funds transfer system (EFTS) (16) A centralized and computerized system of paying bills and making purchases that does not require checks or cash.

Embargo (24) A boycott that prohibits the importing of certain products into a country or, in some cases, exporting materials to a country.

Employee-centered leader (5) A leader who shows concern for followers by understanding their personal needs, developing meaningful work-related relationships with them, and expanding their capabilities.

Employee services (8) Activities and services offered to employees to improve morale and working conditions.

Employer unfair labor practices (9) A provision of the Wagner Act intended to help protect employees' rights.

Employment agency (8) An agency that helps job applicants and employers by coming up with an acceptable employment match.

Endowment life insurance (19) Insurance that pays the face amount of the insurance policy if the insured dies or lives to a certain age.

Entrepreneur (1) A person willing to take financial risk to achieve personal goals.

Equal Credit Opportunity Act (23) An act that prohibits credit discrimination on the basis of sex, marital status, race, religion, age, and national origin.

Equal Employment Opportunity Commission (EEOC) (8) A commission created by the 1964 Civil Rights Act and authorized to investigate and resolve charges of employment discrimination.

Equipment costs (10) Major cost items for mass-production industries.

Equity capital (18) Money invested in the business by the owners—common and preferred stockholders in the case of corporations.

Equity kicker (20) A clause in an income property loan that means that a lender not only receives interest on the loan but also obtains a portion of the owner's profits from the property.

Esteem needs (7) The fourth level of human needs, reflected in a person's self-worth (ego) and reputation.

Ethics (2) The set of criteria or standards for judging the rightness or wrongness of human conduct.

European Economic Community See **Common Market**.

Exchange control (24) A government monopoly of all dealings in foreign exchange.

Exclusive distribution (14) Distribution in which a manufacturer selects one or two dealers per area.

Exclusive jurisdiction (9) In terms of the early AFL, giving a member union of the AFL free rein to organize all workers within a skilled trade or craft.

Executive search firm (8) An agency that works almost

exclusively with employers to recruit people for middle management or executive-level positions.

Executive work station (22) A computer system that enables a manager to perform a wide variety of tasks through the use of a desktop terminal linked to a computer.

Expectancy (7) The employee's estimate of his or her chances of accomplishing some goal (outcome) and receiving an award.

Expenses (21) The costs of running a business, including two main types: costs of goods sold and operating expenses.

Experience (4) One requirement of a business owner— to have a working knowledge of the kinds of decisions that are needed in operating a business.

Explicit communication (13) The use of language as a symbol to establish common understandings between people.

External financing (18) The firm's raising of new capital from sources outside the business.

External labor market (8) A job-applicant pool outside the organization where qualified persons can be found.

Factoring accounts receivable (18) Selling accounts receivable to a bank or finance company in order to raise money.

Factors of production (10) The inputs that are used in the production process.

Factory outlet (14) An outlet that sells merchandise from the factory directly to the consumer, usually at far below the average retail price because both the wholesaler and the retailer are bypassed.

Factory system (1) A system of commercial production featuring work specialization that grew out of individual family enterprises.

Fair Debt Collection Practices Act (23) An act that prohibits abusive and unfair practices by debt collectors.

Family branding (12) Using a brand name on a number of different products.

Federal Deposit Insurance Corporation (FDIC) (16) A government agency, established in 1934, that protects depositors against the risk of loss due to bank failure.

Federal Reserve System (the˙Fed) (16) An agency established by Congress in 1913 to ensure a viable U.S. money supply, to provide a borrowing source for banks, and to improve federal supervision of banking practices.

Field service company (11) An organization hired by custom research firms and corporate market research departments to conduct the actual interviewing for marketing research.

File design (22) A step in system design that determines what data will be stored in main memory and what auxiliary storage devices will be used.

Finance (25) A business major that allows students to learn about the question of which assets to buy and how to pay for them.

Financial Accounting Standards Board (FASB) (21) An organization whose purpose is to formulate and issue rules or generally accepted accounting principles for use by accountants in recording and reporting the activities of enterprises.

Financial advice (16) Advice concerning business and personal financial problems, often offered by bankers to their depositors.

Financial institutions (16) *See individual entries, such as* **Commercial banks; Savings and loan associations**.

Financial intermediation (16) The process by which financial institutions take money that savers entrust to them and invest it in the securities that capital demanders issue to them.

Financial markets *See individual entries, such as* **Money market; Primary market; Secondary market**.

Financial risk (18) The risk of bankruptcy that debt incurs.

Financial strategy (18) A corporate financial blueprint formulated by the corporate financial manager with the help of production, marketing, and other managers.

Finished goods inventory (10, 18) The inventory of the completed production that is stored to meet customer demand.

First mortgage (20) The first recorded loan on a property.

Fixed costs (18) Periodic and continued expenses that are incurred regardless of the level of sales revenues.

Fixed-payment mortgage (20) A mortgage under which the periodic payment stays the same throughout the term of the loan.

Flat structure (6) In a managerial hierarchy, a wide span of control that usually implies few managerial levels.

Flexitime (8) A plan specifying that all employees be present and working during a core (high-volume) work period of the day; the remaining hours are completed whenever the employee wants.

Floating currency (24) A system where the price or value of a currency depends on the supply and demand.

Floating interest rate (18) A loan's interest rate that is adjusted each time the prime rate is changed.

Floor planning (18) Pledging of inventory as collateral for a short-term loan.

Flowchart (22) A diagram that graphically shows the steps needed to complete the required processing in a computer system.

FOB (15) "Free on board," meaning the seller will place the merchandise free on board the truck or other carrier and the buyer will pay the shipping charges.

Focus group (11) A form of personal interview in which individuals are recruited for participation in a group discussion.

Foreclose (20) To take property from an owner who defaults on a loan and to sell it to satisfy the debt.

Form 10–K (17) A detailed annual report filed by all corporations whose securities are held by the public.

Formal study (1) Information about the role of business and its operations obtained from degree programs offered by colleges and universities and from programs from business schools.

Forward buying (10) The buying of materials to meet production standards for an extended period of time.

Franchise agreement (4) A contract between a franchisor and franchisee that spells out the conditions of their franchising arrangement.

Franchisee (4) The person who handles products or services for a franchisor.

Franchisor (4) A supplier who allows a franchisee to handle his or her product or service.

Free enterprise (1, 15) A system under which individuals rather than government determine what goods and services to produce, how to produce them, and who gets the rewards from their production. Also the right to engage in any economic endeavor that one wishes to engage in.

Freight absorption pricing (15) A form of geographic pricing where the seller absorbs all or part of the freight charges.

Friendly languages (22) Systems of communicating with computers that can be learned in a very short period of time.

Fringe benefit (8) A form of pay in addition to the wage or salary.

Full-bodied money (16) A commodity with an intrinsic value of its own that is used for money; the most familiar type is gold.

Full-service broker (17) A broker who executes clients' trades, provides investment advice, and offers many other financial services.

Functional authority (6) A combination of line and staff authority in which a specialist is delegated direct authority for supervising some specialized area of activity.

Functional discount (15) A payment made to members of a channel of distribution for performing their functions. Also called a trade discount.

Functional organization (4) A formal framework through which the practice of business management is carried out.

Future shock (25) A disorientation brought on by rapid social change.

Futures contract (17) A contract that allows its holder to buy or sell an amount of a specified commodity or other item at a future date at an agreed-upon price.

Gantt charts (10) Charts that graphically measure the relationship between scheduling and actual performance.

General Agreement on Tariffs and Trade (GATT) (24) The organization of many countries that is considered the most effective mechanism for worldwide trade liberalization and tariff concessions; its goal is to eliminate tariff barriers to worldwide trade.

General journal (21) A financial diary of all business transactions arranged in chronological order.

General ledger (21) A specialized book that collates journal entries into specified accounts.

General partnership (3) The standard form of partnership referred to by the Uniform Partnership Act.

Generally accepted accounting principles (GAAP) (21) A set of guidelines that have been adopted by the accounting profession to ensure uniformity in reporting business transactions.

Generic product (12) A no-frill, low-cost product that simply has the name of the type of merchandise on the box; no brand name is associated with it.

Goal (5) A desired future condition or state of affairs.

Goal orientation (11) Keeping the company's own goals, both financial and nonfinancial, clearly in mind.

Graduated-payment mortgage (GPM) (20) A plan under which payments rise after the first year of the loan and continue to rise gradually each year; payments usually remain level after the fifth year.

Grapevine (6) A term used to describe the informal information network of a firm.

Grievance (9) A problem that develops because a

worker feels that management has violated some provision of the collective bargaining agreement.

Grievance arbitration (9) The final step in the grievance procedure, using an impartial third party (arbitrator) to settle the dispute.

Group (7) A social unit consisting of two or more people who share the same goal and who cooperate to achieve it.

Group-centered decision style (5) A decision style in which the manager and employees meet as a group to discuss the problem, to generate alternative solutions, and to come up with a solution by mutual agreement.

Group insurance plans (19) Insurance that covers a group of insured persons, usually employees of a business or government.

Growth stage (12) The second stage of a product life cycle, characterized by rapidly increasing sales.

Hardcopy terminal (22) A terminal that is essentially a typewriter with the ability to communicate with a computer.

Hard-core unemployed (2) Disadvantaged workers who do not meet normal company selection standards for even the lowest-level jobs.

Hardware (22) The basic equipment needed to operate a computer system.

Health insurance (19) Insurance that helps pay for the medical and hospitalization costs of an illness or injury.

Health maintenance organizations (HMOs) (19) Prepaid medical expense plans that allow unlimited use of health care facilities and personnel by their subscribers.

Hierarchy (6) The number of levels of management within the business, arranged by degree of authority.

Hierarchy of motivations (7) A theoretical model, pioneered by Abraham Maslow, of five categories of human needs: physiological, safety, social, esteem, and self-actualization.

High-level languages (22) The problem-oriented programming languages used by computer programmers to increase efficiency and productivity.

Home and building insurance (19) Property and liability insurance that protects property owners from financial loss caused by a variety of perils.

Home industry argument (24) A belief that the American market should be reserved for American industry by building "tariff walls" around domestic industries, regardless of their maturity.

Hospitalization insurance (19) Insurance to help pay hospital bills.

Human relations (7) The study of the importance of individuals as they interact on the job.

Human resources management (8) A method of maximizing worker satisfaction and improving worker efficiency.

Human skills (5) Skills used in working with people to accomplish organizational goals.

Implicit communication (13) Nonverbal communication that involves "intuitive interpretation" of symbols and gestures.

Import quota (24) A control on the quantity of merchandise imported over a period of time.

Income properties (20) Properties that earn rental income for their owners.

Income statement (21) A statement that shows the profit or loss of the business.

Independent brokers (17) Seatholders on the stock exchange who execute orders given to them by commission brokers.

Industrial distributor (14) A distributor somewhat like an industrial department store that serves a particular industry.

Industrial goods (12) Goods or services bought by businesses or institutions for use in making other goods or rendering services.

Industrial Revolution (1) A period in American business history characterized by major changes in production technology and the development of large-scale factories.

Industrial union (9) A union that serves a single industry regardless of its members' occupations and levels of skill.

Infant industry argument (24) A belief that tariffs are needed to protect new domestic industries from well-established foreign competitors.

Inflation hedge (20) An investment whose rate of return is greater than the rate of inflation.

Informal structure or organization (6) Relationships between people at the same organizational level and between people at different levels in different departments that constitute an informal information network outside the formal organization chart.

Informal study (1) Information about the role of business and its operations gathered by reading business books, magazines, and newspapers and by talking to other people at meetings and parties.

Informative advertising (13) A type of advertising that explains the product's merits to potential buyers; used in the early stage of a product's life cycle.

Injunction (9)   A court order that restricts a union from interfering with a plant's production.

Inland marine insurance (19)   Coverage against damage or loss of goods shipped by rail, truck, airplane, or inland barge.

Input mix (10)   A specific combination of inputs used in production.

Installations (12)   Large, expensive capital items that have a long life span and that get special tax treatment. *See also* **Accessories**.

Institutional advertising (13)   Advertising that tries to improve the image of a firm by creating a favorable picture of the firm, its ideals, services, role in community affairs, and the like.

Insurance (19)   The procedure by which those who are concerned about some form of risk contribute to a common fund—usually an insurance company—out of which losses resulting from that risk are compensated. *See also individual entries, such as* **Health insurance; Property insurance**.

Insurance policy (19)   The contract between the person or business being covered by insurance (the insured) and the insurance company that issues the policy (the insurer).

Intangible personal property (23)   Personal property consisting of the rights and claims owned by a business or individual.

Intelligence network (6)   The informal information network of a firm.

Intensive distribution (14)   Wide distribution that strives for maximum market coverage.

Interactive-based technology (6)   Technology in which information feedback is frequently a critical element.

Interactive control (5)   A control that operates while work is being performed.

Interest coverage ratio (21)   A ratio that reflects the basic ability of a firm's earnings to meet its interest costs.

Intermittent process (10)   A production process in which the product is in process of completion over an extended period of time; general purpose machines are used, but not continuously.

Internal financing (18)   A firm's retaining and investing a portion of its profits in the business.

Internal labor market (8)   A job-applicant pool within the organization where qualified persons can be found.

Internal Revenue Code (23)   The set of laws that regulates the income taxes that individuals and businesses pay to the federal government.

Interview   *See individual entries, such as* **Directive interview; Nondirective interview; Screening interview; Selection interview**.

Introductory stage (12)   The first stage of a product life cycle, characterized by little competition, frequent product modifications, limited distribution, and a high failure rate.

Inventory (10)   *See individual entries, such as* **Raw materials inventory; Work in process inventory**.

Inventory, producing to (10)   Taking a product from storage or inventory when it is needed or ordered.

Investment banker (18)   A financial intermediary that buys a new issue of securities from its corporate issuer and then resells those securities to investors.

Job (8)   A collection of tasks and responsibilities, making up a unit of work, that may be performed by one or more people.

Job analysis (8)   A systematic study of a unit of work, or job, in terms of its tasks and processes.

Job-centered leader (5)   One whose efforts are largely directed toward doing those things necessary for completing a specified task, such as planning the workplace, assigning duties, and inspecting output.

Job control language (JCL) (22)   The language that defines the order and procedure for processing jobs submitted to the computer system and that links the operating system to the applications programs.

Job control program (22)   One of the two types of programs required in order for a computer to process data. The other is called an applications program.

Job description (8)   A listing of the tasks and responsibilities of a job—including the authorizations, limits, conditions, and other elements built into it.

Job enlargement (6)   Expansion of the scope and responsibilities of a job so that a worker experiences greater satisfaction and interest and thus increased productivity.

Job enrichment (6)   Provision of greater authority, new responsibilities, more challenge, and the opportunity of increased personal achievement and recognition to boost job productivity and interest.

Job maintenance factors (7)   Those things required to keep a worker on the job, such as good working conditions.

Job satisfaction (7)   Pleasure experienced from good work attitudes and job performance.

Job satisfiers (7)   Factors that affect one's work motivation and degree of job satisfaction.

Job-shop operation (6) An operation in which each finished product is unique and requires different skills, materials, and equipment. Also called small batch operation.

Job specification (8) A form that records the skills, knowledge, and abilities necessary for a job.

Joint venture (3, 24) An enterprise in which two or more firms or investors share ownership and control over operations and property rights. Also a special type of partnership that is established to undertake a specific project or to operate for a specific amount of time.

Jurisdiction (9) The scope of a national union and its affiliated local units.

Kennedy Round (24) Tariff negotiations, initiated by President Kennedy, with 50 member nations of the GATT that reduced tariffs by an average of 40 percent.

Knights of Labor (9) One of the first major national labor organizations.

Labor boycott (9) A boycott that occurs when union members and others are urged by the union to stop doing business with an employer with whom the union has a dispute.

Labor force (9) All of the people who have chosen to work, including those looking for work and those temporarily absent from work.

Labor-Management Relations Act *See* **Taft-Hartley Act**.

Labor-Management Reporting and Disclosure Act *See* **Landrum-Griffin Act**.

Labor market *See* **External labor market; Internal labor market**.

Labor union (9) An organization of workers formed to deal with the employer on a group basis in order to pursue common goals.

Land developer (20) A person who buys land, improves it, puts buildings on it, and resells it as developed property.

Landrum-Griffin Act (9) An act that deals primarily with the internal affairs of labor unions. Also called the Labor-Management Reporting and Disclosure Act.

Law (23) The set of principles that govern the conduct and activities of society. *See also individual entries, such as* **Common law; Private law**.

Lead time (10) The time that is expected to elapse between the placement of an order and the receipt of the materials.

Leader pricing (15) Pricing merchandise below the normal markup or even below cost in order to increase sales volume and profits.

Leadership (5) The exercise of influence of one person over another for the purpose of attaining some specified goal.

Leadership style (5) The way in which a leader succeeds in encouraging followers to accomplish a productive activity.

Leasing (20) Renting a facility instead of buying it.

Level of aspiration (7) The standard of performance by which one measures whether or not goals have been reached.

Leverage (18, 20) The use of borrowed funds to finance an investment. *See also* **Trading on the equity**.

Liabilities (21) The amounts of money that are owed to other people or to other companies.

Liability insurance (19) Insurance that covers financial losses due to injuries or property losses of others where the insured is considered to be the cause.

Licensing (24) A process, intended to increase international trade, under which a firm (licensor) agrees to let a foreign firm (licensee) use its patents, trademarks, production processes, brands, products, or company name in return for royalty fees or a fixed sum.

Life insurance (19) Insurance that protects against the financial consequences that could result from a person's death.

Life insurance company (16) A type of company with large investments in the financial markets.

Lifestyle (11) A distinctive mode of living, analyzed by looking at a person's typical activities, interests, and opinions.

Limited liability (3) Limiting stockholders' liability for corporate debts to the actual amount invested in the corporation for the shares of stock the stockholder owns.

Limited partnership (3) An association of one or more general partners who have unlimited liability and one or more (usually many more) limited partners whose liability is limited to their capital contributions.

Line authority (6) The right to issue decisions and orders concerning production, marketing, finance, and other line functions.

Line of credit (18) An agreement by a commercial bank to lend a borrower funds up to a stated maximum amount.

Line organization (6) An organization in which there are direct, clearly understood lines of authority and communication flowing from the top of the firm downward, with employees reporting to only one supervisor.

Line-staff conflict (6) Conflict that arises when line

managers and staff specialists fail to recognize each other's value in making the organization successful.

Linking pin (7)   A lower-level manager who links the work group he or she manages with the employee group immediately above it.

Liquidity (18)   The need to possess enough ready cash to pay bills as they come due.

Listing (17)   Approval by a stock exchange for a corporation to have its stocks and bonds traded on that exchange.

Loan origination fee (18)   A fee on mortgage loans, usually about 2 percent of the amount borrowed, paid to the lender in addition to the interest.

Lockout (9)   A situation in which a firm shuts the business down and forces the workers off the job in order to get the union to change its position on some crucial issue.

Logical transfer (22)   The selection process a computer uses to determine a course of action.

Long-term bond (18)   A corporate IOU that matures twenty to forty years after it is issued.

Long-term debt (18)   A loan that is repaid over an extended time period, often ten to thirty years.

Long-term forecast (18)   A projection of the future business climate; a crucial element of a business's long-term strategic planning.

Long-term loan (18)   A loan that is repaid over an extended period of time.

Long-term mortgage (18)   A type of secured loan against which the borrower puts up real estate as collateral.

Long-term securities market (16)   A subdivision of the primary market where only long-term bonds, mortgages, and stocks are sold. Also called a capital market.

Loss prevention and reduction (19)   A sustained activity calculated either to reduce the chance that a loss will occur or to reduce the loss itself should the unexpected occur.

Magnetic disk (22)   A flat or circular plate that has a magnetic surface where data are stored.

Magnetic tape unit (22)   The recording unit for a computer system consisting of mylar tape with a magnetic coated surface on which data are recorded and stored as magnetic spots.

Main memory (22)   Part of the central processing unit of the computer. Also called core.

Maintenance roles (7)   Roles that help develop and sustain good relationships within a group.

Major medical insurance (19)   Insurance that covers the expenses of catastrophic illnesses that exceed the coverage of hospitalization and surgical and medical insurance policies.

Majors, college   *See individual entries, such as* **Accounting; Economics; Finance; Management**.

Management (5, 25)   The act of bringing about improvement in organizations by setting goals and then integrating human, material, and information resources toward the accomplishment of those goals. Also a business major designed to prepare students for managerial roles in a wide variety of organizations.

Management and organization audit (5)   A periodic examination of the entire organization, including objectives, strategies, functions, and processes.

Management by objectives (MBO) (5)   An approach to management by which goals or objectives are set for managers, whose performance is then evaluated on attainment of those objectives.

Management decision support system (MDSS) (5)   A computer-based system that categorizes, stores, and analyzes information from many sources to support the planning, controlling, and operations functions of the firm by generating timely information for many routine decisions.

Managerial hierarchy   *See* **Hierarchy**.

Mandatory item (9)   A collective bargaining provision relating to wages, hours, and working conditions; employers must discuss and respond to mandatory items.

Manufacturers' brands (12)   Brand names that are well-known in a wide geographical area. Also called national brands.

Manufacturer's representative (14)   A salesperson who functions as an independent agent rather than as a salaried employee of the company. Also called a manufacturer's agent.

Manufacturer's sales branch (14)   A wholesaler that performs the same functions as a full-service merchant wholesaler except that it is managed, owned, and completely controlled by a manufacturer. *See also* **Merchant wholesaler**.

Manufacturing businesses (4)   Businesses engaged in the conversion of raw materials and labor into products needed by society.

Margin (16)   The percentage of the purchase price of a security that must be paid in cash by the investor.

Margin requirement (16)   The rule that relates to an investor's purchase of securities on credit.

Market letter (17) A brief publication issued by an individual or company licensed to sell investment advice.

Market making (17) Specialists acting as dealers in the stocks that the exchange assigns to them.

Market segmentation (11) A process of separating, identifying, and evaluating various strata or layers of a market.

Market share (15) A company's percentage of the industry's total sales.

Marketing (11) The performance of those business activities directed at satisfying needs and wants through the exchange process.

Marketing concept (11) The theory that satisfying needs and wants is the principal function of business.

Marketing mix (11) A unique blend of (1) product and service offerings, (2) a distribution system created to reach a specific group of consumers called the target market, (3) pricing, and (4) promotion.

Marketing research (11) The planning for, collection, recording, and analysis of data relative to the marketing of goods and services, and the communication of those results to management.

Mass-merchandising shopping chain (14) A group of stores similar to department stores in many ways but having huge sales volumes, promotional budgets, store brands, and numbers of stores.

Mass production *See* **Continuous process**.

Matrix organization (6) A structure having vertical and horizontal authority relationships that helps an organization manage several projects over a period of time.

Maturity stage (12) The third stage of a product life cycle, characterized by still mounting sales but at a decreasing rate from the growth stage.

Mediation (9) An intervention process in a labor dispute in which a neutral third party engages in substantive discussions with union and management negotiators in separate meetings and in joint sessions.

Medicaid (19) A welfare program to pay the medical bills of the poor.

Medicare (19) A form of health insurance available to persons 65 years or older and to certain other social security recipients.

Medium of exchange (16) A function of money that allows for the exchange of goods and services in an easy, simple process.

Meeting competition (15) Determining what competitors are charging and then pricing at approximately the same level.

Merchant wholesaler (14) A wholesaler with two major characteristics: (1) it buys manufacturers' products for its own account and resells them to other businesses, and (2) it operates one or more warehouses where it receives merchandise, takes title to it, stores it, and later ships it to the buyer.

Middlemen (11) The institutions that help move the product from the manufacturer to the ultimate buyer.

Minimization of cost (10) The process of increasing profit by reducing cost.

Minority Enterprise Small Business Investment Company (MESBIC) (4) A loan program of the SBA that makes loans to companies that are organized to supply capital to minority-owned small businesses.

Mission (5) An organization's general purpose or reason for existence.

Mixed economies (1) Economic systems characterized by public ownership of some basic industries and private ownership of others. Also called social welfare economies.

Mixed union (9) A union that tries to organize and bargain for a wide variety of workers.

Monetary Control Act of 1980 (16) An act that allows most financial institutions to pay interest on certain types of checking accounts.

Monetary policy (16) A policy that involves the regulation of the money supply and interest rates; these in turn affect the level of economic growth and stability.

Money (16) Anything that is generally accepted as a means to pay for goods and services.

Money market (16) A subdivision of the primary market where only short-term securities are sold.

Money market fund (17) A mutual fund that invests in short-term money market instruments such as certificates of deposit, Treasury bills, and commercial paper.

Money supply (16) The total amount of currency outstanding (held by the public) and in demand deposits at commercial banks.

Monopolistic competition (1) Competition characterized by product differentiation; a large number of sellers sell products that are generally the same but that are differentiated by minor changes in product design, style, or technology.

Monopoly (1) An industry with only one firm, such as electric utilities and telephone companies; in the United States monopolies exist under strong government regulations.

Mortgage bond (17) A corporate bond secured by a specific asset of the company.

Mortgage loan agreement (20) An agreement that specifies what will happen to the property if the borrower defaults on the loan.

Motivation (5) An internal state that causes people to behave in a particular way.

Multinational corporation (24) A corporation that moves resources, goods, services, and skills across national boundaries without regard to the country in which its headquarters office is located.

Municipal bond (17) A bond issued by state and local governments.

Municipal bond fund (17) A mutual fund that invests in municipal bonds.

Mutual funds (17) Financial intermediaries that pool the funds from investors and then invest these resources in stocks, bonds, and other resources.

Mutual insurance company (19) A company owned collectively by its policyholders; an insurance cooperative.

Mutual savings bank (16) A savings oriented institution that distributes its profits to depositors.

NASDAQ (17) The National Association of Securities Dealers Automated Quotation system, which allows OTC dealers to quickly and efficiently execute customers' orders.

National Association of Accountants (NAA) (21) The national organization of accountants.

National Association of Securities Dealers (NASD) (17) A self-governing body that regulates the OTC market.

National brands *See* **Manufacturers' brands**.

National union (9) A group of many local unions in a particular industry, skilled trade, or geographic area.

Nationalism (24) A sense of national consciousness that boosts the culture and interests of one country over all others.

National health insurance (19) A federally sponsored universal health insurance plan proposed for the United States but not yet legislated.

National Labor Relations Board (NLRB) (9) The board that enforces the Wagner and Taft-Hartley acts by investigating charges of unfair labor practices and supervising union representation elections.

National emergency strike procedures (9) Procedures passed by Congress as part of the Taft-Hartley Act to give the president of the United States the right to declare a national emergency if a strike creates major health or safety problems and to halt the strike through legal action.

National Environmental Protection Act (23) An act passed in response to a public outcry to clean up—and maintain the cleanliness of—the environment.

Natural law (23) The belief that most people would act morally, even in the absence of society-made laws.

Need (7) A want of something requisite, desirable, or useful.

Needs theory (7) A theory of motivation that proposes that people act in order to satisfy or fulfill various needs.

Negotiating function (14) The buying and selling of the merchandise and the transference of title of ownership from one institution to another.

Net profit (21) The amount left after subtracting all allowable costs from sales.

Net profit margin (21) A margin that measures the after-tax profit relative to the company's sales.

Network models (10) Models drawn to show the order of priorities of the various events and activities of a project, making it possible to plan for effective completion of the project.

New York Stock Exchange (NYSE) (17) The oldest, largest, and most prestigious stock exchange in the United States.

New York Stock Exchange Composite Index (17) An index that uses all NYSE-listed common stocks to monitor the average movement of the stock market.

No-fault insurance (19) Coverage that provides that the insurance company will pay for the insured's accident losses regardless of who is considered responsible for the accident.

Noise level (13) In advertising, anything that makes comprehension of the message more difficult.

Noncumulative discount (15) A once-only quantity discount based exclusively on the number of units bought at a single time.

Nondirective interview (25) An interview technique that avoids direct questioning and prompts the person being interviewed to talk freely and informally.

Nonnotification plan (18) A form of using accounts receivable as collateral for a short-term loan when the borrower's own customers (debtors) are not told that the company has used its accounts receivable as loan collateral.

Norm (7) A standard of behavior or performance used for determining if the actions of a member of a specified group are acceptable or unacceptable.

Norris-LaGuardia Act (9) The act that largely ended the use of injunctions by employers and prohibited their use to avoid strikes. Also called the Anti-Injunction Act.

Notification plan (18) After a company has sold its accounts receivable, a plan under which its customers (debtors) are notified and instructed to remit their payments directly to the financial institution.

NOW (negotiable order of withdrawal) accounts (16) The name given to checking accounts that earn interest.

Objectives (5) Specific, hoped-for results that can be expressed in quantitative and measurable terms with timetables set for achievement and that can be expressed in broad terms when addressed to the general public as part of the company's public relations effort.

Ocean marine insurance (19) Insurance that covers ship owners against damage or loss of ships or their cargo.

Odd-even pricing (15) A psychological pricing strategy that says that consumers prefer odd prices over even ones for most products—for example, $499.95 instead of $500.

Office of Federal Contract Compliance Programs (OFCCP) (8) An organization created by Executive Order 11246 to police firms under government contract to make sure that applicants and employees get fair treatment under affirmative action plans and programs.

Office of Minority Business Enterprise (OMBE) (4) An agency established to encourage and assist minority business to enter industries other than service and retail trade.

Old-Age, Survivors, Disability, and Health Insurance (OASDHI) (19) The official title of the Social Security program, providing both health insurance and disability income benefits.

Oligopoly (1) An industry characterized by a few large firms, many entry barriers, and strong control over price.

On-line mode (22) A method of computer system operating when a direct link to the computer exists and each transaction is entered as it occurs or is received.

Open market operations (16) The process of the Fed buying or selling government securities; the most frequently used monetary policy tool of the Fed.

Open system (6) A system under which a firm continuously engages in exchange transactions with the external environment.

Operating budget (18) A projection of the current year's sales revenue and operating expenses.

Operating expenditures (18) The money tied up in the company's current assets, which include cash or anything that can be quickly converted into cash.

Operating system (22) A group of programs that the computer system uses to supervise its own operations.

Opportunity exploration (12) Searching for and getting new ideas or concepts for products.

Order, producing to (10) Producing a product when it is needed or ordered.

Order cost (10) The cost of placing orders to increase inventories.

Order cycle time (14) The elapsed time between placing an order and the customer receiving the merchandise in good condition.

Ordinary income (23) The business income that results from sale of merchandise or performance of services for which the business was organized.

Organization (5) A group of people deliberately assembled to set, plan, and accomplish specific goals.

Organization structure (4, 6) The order and design of relationships among employees, jobs, and departments within a firm. Also a plan to identify areas of responsibility of owners, managers, and employees.

Organizing (5) The process of creating structure, relationships, and other orderly arrangements in order to make the best use of a firm's assets.

Over-the-counter (OTC) market (17) A geographically decentralized, electronically interconnected secondary securities market consisting of thousands of market-making dealers in stocks and bonds that are not listed on any regular exchange.

Owners' equity (21) The dollar amount of the owners' investments and profits measured by subtracting the total liabilities from the total assets of the company.

Participating preferred stock (17) Preferred stock that is entitled to its stated dividend and to additional dividends on a specified basis.

Participative approach to managing people (4) A managerial method that allows employees to participate in business goal setting and decision making.

Partnership (3) An association of two or more persons to carry on as co-owners a business for profit. *See also* **General partnership; Joint venture; Limited partnership.**

Partnership agreement (3) An agreement that specifies the contributions of the partners to the business, the roles each partner will play, and the major points of agreement among the partners.

Patent (23) An official document giving an inventor exclusive right to manufacture, use, and sell an invention for seventeen years.

Payroll tax (23) The tax that includes the employer's share of the social security taxes, federal unemployment taxes, and state unemployment taxes.

Penetration pricing (15) Initially selling a good or service at a low, mass-market price in the hope of having a large sales volume. *See also* **Price skimming**.

Pension fund (16) A large pool of money that a company or government sets aside for paying pension benefits to its employees.

Performance (5) The manner in which an action or task is carried out.

Performance appraisal (8) Comparing of actual and expected employee performance.

Performance standard (5) A level or amount of performance to be attained, usually expressed in concrete, quantitative terms.

Perpetual inventory (10) A system that keeps continuous track of all major inventory items and identifies orders, sales, and receipts as they occur.

Personal property (23) Property that is movable, including inventory, furniture, machinery, and automobiles.

Personnel planning (8) Planning that helps a firm have the correct number of people with the appropriate skills at the right places and at the right times.

Persuasive advertising (13) A type of advertising that attempts to persuade people to buy one product over another; used mainly in the growth stage of a product's life cycle.

Physical distribution (14) The process of getting the finished products through the channel of distribution.

Physiological needs (7) The most basic human needs, which are bodily in nature.

Piggy-back service *See* **Containerization**.

Pioneering advertising (13) Product advertising that is used to stimulate demand for a new good or service.

Planning (5) A future oriented activity that requires setting objectives and designing the strategies, policies, and methods necessary for achieving them.

Plastic money *See* **Credit cards**.

Pledging (18) Permitting a lender to legally take over an asset if a loan is not repaid.

Point-of-purchase advertising (POP) (13) Promotional material (displays, printed material, and so on) placed inside retail stores next to the advertiser's goods.

Point-of-sale (POS) machine (16) A machine hooked into a bank's computer that enables funds to be automatically taken out of the buyer's bank and transferred into the seller's account after a purchase is made.

Policy (5) A standing decision that serves as a guideline for making subsequent decisions in particular situations.

Pollution (2) The contamination of the environment with the byproducts and effects of human activity.

Portability (16) A characteristic of suitable money that allows it to be easily carried and conveyed.

Positioning (11) The strategic placement of a product in the market.

Postage stamp pricing *See* **Uniform delivered pricing**.

Postcontrols (5) Controls based on delayed feedback with information directed back to the manager after an operation has been completed.

Power (6) The ability to exercise control over others.

Precontrol device (5) A control device established before any work is performed.

Preferential tariff (24) A tariff in which nations agree to give special advantages to one country or group of countries over others.

Preferred stock (17) Stock on which owners receive preferential treatment over the holders of common stock in the distribution of assets and the payment of dividends.

Preliminary profit plan (12) The development of financial statements that project potential profits over a period of time for a new product concept.

Prepaid medical expense plans (19) Plans under which premiums are pooled to pay the health care costs of subscribers.

Prestige pricing (15) A form of psychological pricing in which it is believed that a product will be perceived as having greater value or higher quality if its price is raised.

Pricing lining (15) A form of base pricing where a retailer or manufacturer sets a limited number of prices for a line of merchandise.

Price skimming (15) Skimming off the top or cream of a market by charging a high introductory price and then successively lowering it as the product moves through its life cycle in an effort to get all the trade the market will bear at each level. *See also* **Penetration pricing**.

Pricing *See individual entries, such as* **Freight absorption pricing; Penetration pricing**.

Primary data (11) Data that are collected for the first time directly from the original source for the purpose of solving a problem under investigation.

Primary market (16) The market where new funds flow in transactions between demanders and suppliers of funds.

Prime rate (18) The short-term interest rate that banks charge their most favored and creditworthy customers.

Principle of comparative advantage (24) A principle that states that if each nation specializes in goods that it can produce most readily and cheaply and trades those goods for others that foreign countries can produce most cheaply, there will be more goods available at lower prices.

Private accountant (21) A person who collects and records the day-to-day transactions of the firm that employs him or her.

Private brands (12) Brands of products distributed only in the retailer's or wholesaler's own distribution channels. Also called dealer brands.

Private law (23) A set of principles that relates to individual members and organizations within the society.

Private placement loan (18) A long-term, often unsecured, loan that is obtained from a financial institution such as a life insurance company or a pension fund.

Procedure (5) An ordered series of steps to be followed in accomplishing something.

Product (1, 12) Any want-satisfying good or service, as well as its perceived tangible and intangible attributes and the benefits that people attribute to it.

Product differentiation (11) The distinguishing of one firm's goods or services from another's.

Product liability insurance (19) Insurance that protects the producer of a good or service against financial loss from court awards to consumers, customers, or next of kin.

Product life cycle (12) The total sales of a product, typically going through four stages: introduction, growth, maturity, and decline and death.

Production function (10) The conversion of inputs or factors of production into outputs.

Production orientation (11) A company's concentration on having an efficient and economical production system—one that produces what the company can manufacture best.

Professional liability insurance (19) Insurance to provide coverage for expenses related to malpractice lawsuits and verdicts against professional people.

Professional salesperson (13) A salesperson with three primary characteristics: (1) complete product knowledge, (2) creativity, and (3) knowledge of the customer's needs.

Profit (1) The amount remaining from sales revenues after all production and selling costs are deducted.

Profit maximization (15) A firm's production of units of an output that will yield the largest possible profit on a product or service.

Profit motive (1) The desire to make a profit in business ventures.

Program Evaluation and Review Technique (PERT) (10) A network model in which three time-estimates are developed for each activity in order to take into account time variability.

Programming languages (22) Sets of symbols and characters that the computer can understand.

Project management (6) The pulling together of people from several departments to work on a special project.

Promotion (11) The mix of personal selling, advertising, sales promotion, and publicity.

Promotional allowance (15) A cash or merchandise payment to a retailer for performing a promotional task for the manufacturer.

Promotional mix (13) The unique combination of advertising, personal selling, sales promotion, and public relations (publicity) used to achieve behavior modification or reinforcement of existing behavior.

Property (23) *See individual entries, such as* **Personal property; Real property.**

Property insurance (19) An insurance that covers financial losses due to the damage or destruction of the insured's property as the result of any of a variety of perils.

Property syndicate (20) An organization in which a group of investors pool their resources to buy property or properties.

Property tax (23) A tax assessed on real and personal property. Also called an ad valorem tax.

Prospecting (13) The process of identifying those firms and persons most likely to buy the seller's offerings.

Prospectus (17) A condensed registration statement that contains detailed financial and descriptive information about the issuing company.

Protective tariff (24) A high tariff designed to discourage imports.

Protestant ethic (25) The belief that all people should engage in some productive activity.

Proxy (3) A document a shareholder signs to assign his or her voting right in a corporation to someone else.

Proxy battle (3) A struggle waged at a corporation's annual meeting when a group seeks to unseat existing management by getting proxies from shareholders.

Psychographics (11) The development of psychological profiles of consumers and their lifestyles.

Psychological contract (7) The unwritten expectations between worker and company.

Public accountant (21) An independent professional who provides accounting services for other businesses.

Public law (23) Law concerned with standards and protection of society in general.

Public relations (13) Any communication or activity that tries to increase the prestige or create a favorable public image of a product, an individual, or an organization.

Publicity (11, 13) Information about a product, person, or company featured by the media.

Punitive damages (23) Damages that can be collected if it can be proved that a person involved in a breach of contract is guilty of intentional wrongdoing.

Purchase planning (10) The efficient planning of material purchases to ensure optimal materials inventory.

Pure barter system (16) The direct exchange of goods and services.

Pure competition (1) A market structure consisting of so many buyers and sellers that no individual buyer or seller has any influence on either the price of the product or the amount traded over some period of time.

Put option (17) An option that entitles the holder to sell a fixed number of shares at a fixed price within a specified time.

Quality circle (7) A small group of workers who meet periodically to find solutions to production problems.

Quality control (10) Regulation of the inputs to a productive process to ensure that the finished product conforms to a preselected standard.

Quality Control (QC) Circle (10) A group of workers and managers who periodically meet to study methods for improving quality.

Quantity discount (15) Price reduction based on the number of units purchased; the more units bought, the lower the price per unit.

Quasi-public organizations (3) Business organizations in which some level of government has an active role in their operations.

Quick ratio *See* **Acid-test ratio**.

Racism (2) The unfair treatment of individuals because of their race.

Ratio analysis (21) A technique that makes comparisons of selected financial statement items in percentage terms rather than in dollars.

Raw materials (12) Those natural resources—for example, forest products, minerals, and farm products—from which finished goods are made.

Raw materials inventory (10, 18) An inventory of materials that will be used in the manufacturing process.

Real property (23) Land, buildings, and rights in the land of another.

Recruiting (8) An attempt to find and attract qualified and compatible applicants from the external labor market.

Regional stock exchanges (17) Stock exchanges, smaller than the NYSE or ASE, located in various United States cities.

Registered traders (17) Stock exchange seatholders who buy and sell stocks for their own account.

Remedy (9) An order that is issued if the NLRB finds an employer or union guilty of an unfair labor practice.

Reminder advertising (13) A type of advertising that attempts to maintain "top-of-the-mind" awareness; used mainly in the mature stage of a product's life cycle.

Renegotiated-rate mortgage (RRM) (20) A mortgage that allows the lender to change the loan's interest rate every three to five years, with the loan payments adjusted accordingly.

Rental housing (20) Housing that includes rental houses, condominiums, and apartment buildings.

Repositioning (12) Changing the image or perceived use of a product to initiate a new growth phase.

Reserve requirement (16) A certain percentage, set by the Fed, of a national bank's deposits that are set aside in the form of non-interest earning reserves.

Residual claim (17) A stockholder's right to the firm's assets and profits after all creditors, taxes, and preferred stock dividends have been paid.

Responsibility (6) Acceptance and accountability for job duties and authority assigned. *See also* **Social responsibility**.

Responsible consumption (2) The rational and efficient use of resources by consumers and business with a view to the present and future condition of society.

Restitution (23) Seeking to return parties involved in a breach of contract to their positions before the contract was signed.

Résumé (25) A summary account of a job applicant's education, career, relevant activities, achievements, and goals.

Retail and wholesale businesses (4) Businesses that provide merchandising activities.

Retained earnings (18, 21) Undistributed profits that are reinvested within the business.

Return on investment (ROI) (21) The rate of return stockholders receive from the investment they have made in the firm.

Revenue tariff (24) A low tariff designed to raise money, not to restrict imports.

Revenues (21) The receipts derived from sales of products, sales of services, and earnings of interest, royalties, rents, and dividends.

Revolving credit agreement (18) An agreement similar to a line of credit except that it is generally written for two or three years and a commitment fee is charged.

Risk (14, 19) In an insurance sense, the chance of financial loss due to a peril. *See also* **Economic risk; Social risk.**

Risk assumption (19) The willingness of an individual or business to bear a risk without having insurance.

Risk avoidance (19) Keeping away from situations that can lead to a loss.

Risk management (19) The policy of insurance companies spreading out the risk of potential losses by selling policies to many individuals and businesses in many parts of the country.

Risk transference (19) The transferring of risk to an insurance company—a professional risk bearer.

Role (7) A set of expectations about what an individual can and cannot do when holding a particular work position; also the actual behavior displayed by the occupant of the role. *See also* **Maintenance roles; Task roles.**

Routing (10) The process by which the manager specifies the machines and their sequence of operation as an order progresses from start to finish.

Rules (5) Very narrow and specific plans for carrying out a policy; they also prescribe regularity in behavior.

Rumor mill (6) A description of the informal information network of a firm.

Sacrifice (4) One requirement of a business owner—to be able to devote enough time, money, and effort to operate a successful business.

Safe deposit box (16) A locked storage compartment within a bank's vault.

Safety needs (7) The second level of human needs, which is exhibited in a need for protection from work hazards and loss of job.

Saleable sample (13) A method of sampling in which a manufacturer offers a "trial size" container for sale.

Sales contract (23) An agreement entered into by buyers and sellers for the transfer of goods.

Sales promotion (11) A marketing element that includes trade shows, catalogues, premiums, coupons, games, and so on.

Sales tax (23) A tax based on the sale price levied on the purchasers of products.

Savings and loan associations (16) Institutions that offer both savings and checking accounts and have a heavy dependence on home mortgage loans for their income.

Savings deposits (16) Savings accounts established with a financial institution.

Scheduling (10) The process that specifies and controls the time it takes for each task to begin and end.

Screening interview (25) A type of short questioning used by a recruiter to decide if the individual should be considered for further in-depth interviews.

Seasonal discount (15) A price reduction offered to a retailer or wholesaler when goods are bought out of season.

Seat (17) A license to execute orders on the trading floor of the exchange without having to pay nonmember commissions.

Second mortgage (20) The second loan taken out on a property.

Secondary data (11) Data that can be obtained from "middle" sources such as government agencies, trade associations, research bureaus, universities, and commercial publications for the purpose of solving a problem under investigation.

Secondary market (16) The market where securities that have already been issued are bought and sold.

Secondary storage *See* **Auxiliary storage.**

Secured loan (18) A loan that requires that the borrower put up collateral as a condition for receiving the loan.

Securities and Exchange Commission (SEC) (17) The commission that administers the federal securities laws that govern the registration and interstate transactions securities.

Selection interview (8) A method of interviewing that gathers in-depth information about the applicant's work experiences and training, communication skills, and personal mannerisms; widely used for making the actual hiring decision.

Selective credit controls (16) Controls set by the Federal Reserve System that govern consumer credit rules and margin requirements.

Selective distribution (14) Distribution in which dealers are screened to exclude all but a few outlets in one area.

Self-actualization (7) The highest level of human needs—living up to one's potential and capabilities.

Self-assessment (25) The process of asking questions of oneself to develop insight into one's basic value patterns.

Self-insuring (19) A form of risk assumption under which a company or individual does not buy insurance and absorbs any losses alone.

Seniority (9) The length of continuous service with a firm; it is used for several purposes in collective bargaining.

Sequencing of production (10) Determining the most efficient sequence of machines necessary to manufacture a product.

Service (1) An output of a firm, such as services rendered by beauticians, attorneys, hotels, and accountants.

Service businesses (4) Businesses engaged in providing essential or special services to their customers.

Servicemark (23) A symbol, work, or design that identifies a service.

Services (12) Special skills hired from outside organizations to help plan, facilitate, or support company operations.

Sexism (2) The unfair treatment of individuals merely because they are males or females.

Sherman Antitrust Act (23) An act passed in order to curb monopoly powers of large companies that undermined the existence of smaller companies and reduced competition.

Shopping goods (12) Goods that are usually more expensive than convenience goods, are found in fewer stores, and require more preplanned shopping; included in this category are furniture, automobiles, and appliances.

Short selling (17) Selling a security one does not in fact own by borrowing the security from a broker and then selling it.

Short-term forecast (18) A projection of immediate and shortly upcoming sales revenues for approximately the next twelve months.

Short-term loan(18) A loan that is usually repaid in less than one year.

Shortage cost (10) The cost of maintaining an inadequate level of inventory.

Single-payment note (18) An IOU that requires that the amount borrowed be repaid in a lump sum at the end of the life of the loan.

Skill assessment (25) The process of determing one's marketable skills or key abilities and characteristics.

Small batch operation *See* **Job-shop operation**.

Small Business Administration (SBA) (4) An agency designed to provide broad assistance exclusively for small businesses.

Small Business Investment Company (SBIC) (4) Any company licensed by the SBA to provide capital to small enterprises.

Social audit (2) A systematic assessment of, and report on, company activities that have social impact.

Social needs (7) The third category of human needs, shown in the need to interact with others and to affiliate with work groups.

Social responsibility (2) Those obligations that a corporation has for the welfare of society that go beyond those provided for by law or union contracts.

Social risk (14) A perceived risk that assumes that what a person buys—or where he or she buys it—affects how other people view that person.

Social welfare economies *See* **Mixed economies**.

Socialism (1) An economic system under which basic industries are owned and operated by the government.

Software (22) The set of instructions giving the computer system its capability to perform operations.

Sole proprietorship (3) A business owned by one person, who receives all the profit earned and is responsible for all the liabilities incurred.

Source credibility (13) The trust that the consumer places in the media.

Span of control (6) The number of employees reporting directly to a manager.

Span of management (5) Number of people directly reporting to a manager or supervisor.

Specialist (17) A member of the stock exchange who makes markets in securities.

Specialization of labor (10) Having a worker perform one or several tasks, rather than performing all the tasks, in the manufacture of an item.

Specialty goods (12) Goods for which consumers search long and hard and will accept no substitutes.

Specialty store (14) A store that sells a single line of merchandise, such as women's clothing or sporting goods, and that usually carries a greater variety of the merchandise than would a chain or department store.

Specific performance (23) Requiring a person found guilty of breach of contract to fulfill the provisions of the contract.

Specific tariff (24) A tariff assessed per unit of imported goods.

Staff authority (6) The right to advise, assist, or support line managers and other staff personnel.

Staff organization (6) An organization in which people, working by themselves or in small groups, provide advice, recommendations, and specialized support services to line managers.

Stagflation (1) An economic situation characterized by high unemployment coupled with inflation and stagnant economic growth.

Standard and Poor's 500 Stock Composite Index (17) An index that uses 500 NYSE-listed stocks to monitor general stock market movements.

Standard of value (16) A function of money that provides a measure of the relative value of goods and services.

Statement of changes in financial position (21) A report that summarizes the sources and uses of short- and long-term funds.

Status (7) An individual's power and social position that come from the job and nature of the job that he or she holds.

Statutory law (23) Laws developed and enacted by the legislative branches of various government units.

Stewards (9) Local union members who represent workers to management when trying to resolve worker complaints.

Stock (17) *See individual entries, such as* **Common stock; Convertible preferred stock; Preferred stock**.

Stock exchange (17) A geographically centralized secondary stock market. *See individual entries, such as* **American Stock Exchange; New York Stock Exchange**.

Stock fund (17) A mutual fund that invests primarily in the common stocks of corporations.

Stockholder-owned company (19) An insurance company owned by its shareholders.

Store of value (16) A function of money that allows a person to hold wealth by keeping money in preference to other assets.

Strategic planning (5) Planning that is long-range and comprehensive and that takes into account the firm's environment as well as the organization itself.

Strike *See individual entries, such as* **National emergency strike procedures; Sympathy strike**.

Strikebreakers (9) New employees who are hired to replace striking union workers.

Subchapter S corporation (3) A tax-option corporation authorized by the Internal Revenue Code under which the corporation's shareholders may elect to be taxed as a partnership.

Sun Belt region (20) The southern and southwestern portion of the country as well as California and Hawaii.

Supplementary unemployment benefits (9) Benefits paid from a fund, established by the employer, to workers on temporary layoff; these benefits are in addition to state unemployment compensation benefits.

Supplies (12) Items bought routinely in large quantities that are set aside, available for use, and dispensed at need; they do not become part of the final product.

Supply (1) A positive relationship between quantity and price; sellers offer more for sale at higher prices than they do at lower prices.

Surgical and medical payments insurance (19) Insurance to cover or offset the financial burden of a major illness.

Sympathy strike (9) A strike mounted by workers not directly involved in a collective bargaining dispute to support the strikers directly involved.

Syndicated research service (11) A service that compiles a standard set of specialized marketing research data on a continuing basis and distributes it to subscribers.

Synthetic process (10) A production process in which the basic inputs are combined to produce the final product.

System (22) A collection of computer equipment, people, and methods used to perform a specific task.

Tactical planning (5) Planning that is short-range and more detailed than strategic planning, that is based on central planning decisions, and that is focused on current operations of the business.

Taft-Hartley Act (9) The act amending the Wagner Act, which was viewed by many as pro-labor. Also called the Labor-Management Relations Act.

Tall structure (6) In a managerial hierarchy, a narrow span of control that usually implies many managerial levels.

Tangible personal property (23) Personal property that can be seen, touched, and physically relocated.

Target return on investment (15) A company's desired profitability in terms of a return on investment or sales.

Tariff (24) A tax or customs duty levied by a nation on imported goods.

Task interdependency (6)   The necessity of performing various tasks in the correct order or sequence.

Task roles (7)   The activities aimed at getting a job done.

Technical skills (5)   Specialized knowledge, procedures, processes, and methods that a person has at his or her command and brings to the job.

Term life insurance (19)   Insurance that covers the insured's life for a specific number of years.

Terminal (22)   A keyboard device that transmits data to the computer.

Test marketing (12)   Placing a new product in the stores of one to several cities that are typical of the market for the product, advertising in the local media, and measuring sales results.

Theory X (7)   An authoritarian management approach that suggests that managers must constantly prod workers to perform and must closely control their on-the-job behavior.

Theory Y (7)   A management approach in which managers recognize individual worker differences and continually encourage worker learning and self-development, thereby building on the idea that worker and organization interests are the same.

Theory Z (7)   From the Japanese, a management approach that depends on trust, subtlety, and intimacy and that ideally contributes to both organizational performance and individual emotional well-being.

Time deposits   *See* **Certificates of Deposit (CDs).**

Time-sharing (22)   Sharing a computer by having many users connected to the same computer; each user pays only for the time used.

Timing flexibility (13)   The amount of freedom and flexibility an advertiser has in altering an advertising message to meet changing marketing conditions.

Tombstone ad (17)   An announcement for a municipal bond.

Tort (23)   A civil or private wrongful act to another person or another's property.

Trade credit (18)   Credit that functions as a loan from the seller to the buyer of goods and services; a major short-term source of funds for most companies.

Trade discount   *See* **Functional discount.**

Trade Expansion Act (24)   The act that granted the president a major increase in authority to make important tariff concessions and to expand U.S. economic adjustment to new import competition.

Trademark (12, 23)   A legally protected design, name, or other identifying mark associated with a company or its product.

Trading on the equity (18)   The use of borrowed money to finance an investment. Also call leverage.

Training and development program (8)   A program that attempts to increase the knowledge and skills of employees, making them more productive and efficient.

Trend projection (18)   A corporate forecasting approach using a visual or mathematical procedure to determine the trend line.

Trial balances (21)   The worksheets that are used to display the processing of data and to sort data for presentation on major financial statements.

Umbrella personal liability insurance (19)   Liability insurance coverage over and above that provided by a homeowner or automobile policy; may also provide coverage not offered by the usual liability policies.

Underwriting costs (18)   The fees paid to an investment banker for selling bonds to the public.

Unemployment benefits   *See* **Supplementary unemployment benefits**.

Unemployment insurance (19)   A program that provides laid-off workers with weekly benefits while they seek new jobs.

Unfair labor practices   *See* **Employer unfair labor practices; Union unfair labor practices**.

Uniform Commercial Code (UCC) (23)   A set of uniform model statutes adopted by all fifty states that eliminates some of the legal problems of doing business on an interstate basis.

Uniform delivered pricing (15)   A form of pricing where the manufacturer computes the average cost of transportation and charges this fee to every buyer; thus the total cost is the same for each buyer regardless of location. Also called postage stamp pricing.

Union   *See* **Labor union**.

Union penetration rate (9)   Union membership expressed in terms of its percentage of the total labor force.

Union shop (9)   A union security clause under which a person does not have to be a union member to be hired but must join the union within a specified period.

Union unfair labor practices (9)   A provision of the Taft-Hartley Act prohibiting the union from doing certain things, such as charging excessive dues and having too many members picketing at strike sites.

Unity of command (6)   The authority and responsibility relationship that exists between a superior and an employee.

Unsecured loan (18) A loan that does not require that the borrower put up any collateral as a condition for receiving the loan.

Value analysis (10) The process by which a product is completely analyzed in terms of its cost and intended use in order to determine the least costly (but still satisfactory) specification for the product.

Values (25) Desirable goals or principles to which individuals subscribe.

Variable costs (18) Costs that depend on the levels of production and sales.

Variable-interest-rate mortgage (VRM) (20) A mortgage that allows the lender to adjust the loan's interest rate every six months, which usually results in a payment change.

Variable-payment mortgage (20) A mortgage under which the periodic payments vary according to the type of agreement.

Venture capital (16) Long-term investment in high-risk, high-growth potential enterprises.

Venture capitalist (4) One who puts up money to enable an entrepreneur to begin a new business.

Voting right (17) The right of a shareholder to vote on such matters as mergers and the board of directors.

Wagner Act (9) An act whose basic purpose was to encourage the creation of unions and more collective bargaining.

Warranty (23) A representation made regarding the quality and performance of goods.

Whole life insurance (19) Insurance that provides protection for a person's entire life.

Wholesale businesses See **Retail and wholesale businesses**.

Wholesaler (14) A "middleman" positioned between the manufacturer and the retailer.

Wildcat strike (9) A strike by a group of union employees or the entire local union while the contract is in effect, thereby violating it.

Wiring funds (16) A transfer of funds from one bank to another by means of a money-wiring facility.

Work ethic (7) The placing of a high value on working and the enjoyment of work.

Work group (7) A group that has been created to accomplish a specific task.

Work-in-process inventory (10, 18) The intermediate inventory, including products at any of the various stages of production prior to completion.

Worker's compensation insurance (19) Insurance to provide benefits to employees who are injured at work or who contract employment-related illnesses.

Workweek See **Altered workweek; Compressed workweek**.

Wrap-around (20) A refinancing scheme whereby a second mortgage on a property is arranged, leaving the first mortgage intact.

Yellow dog contract (9) An agreement by an employee that, as a condition of being hired, he or she will not join a labor union.

Zone of bargaining (9) In the bargaining process, the starting positions of labor and management.

Zone pricing (15) A form of geographic pricing where a marketing manager computes the average freight charges within a given zone and charges everyone within that zone the average rate.

SOURCE NOTES

Chapter 2

[1] D. S. McNaughton, "Managing Social Responsiveness," *Business Horizons* 19 (December 1976): p. 19.
[2] Brad Knickerbocker, "Progress on Air Pollution: Is It Cost-Effective?" *Christian Science Monitor*, 28 July 1981, p. 3.
[3] Peter F. Drucker, "The Function of Profits," *Fortune*, March 1949, p. 110.
[4] Milton Friedman, "Milton Friedman Responds," pp. 6–7. Reprinted by permission from the *Business and Society Review*, Spring 1972, Number 1, Copyright © 1972, Warren, Gorham, and Lamont Inc., 210 South St., Boston, Mass. All rights reserved.
[5] George Fisk, *Marketing and the Ecological Crisis* (New York: Harper & Row, 1972), p. 43.
[6] Upton Sinclair, *The Jungle* (1906; reprint ed., Cambridge, Mass.: R. Bentley, 1972), p. 135.
[7] Frederick Webster Jr., "Does Business Misunderstand Consumerism?" *Harvard Business Review* 51 (September–October 1973): p. 89–97.
[8] Allen R. Andreasen and Arthur Best, "Consumers Complain—Does Business Respond?" *Harvard Business Review* 55 (July–August 1977): p. 93–101.
[9] Vernon E. Jordan, "Human Resource Perspectives for the 80's," *The Personnel Administrator* 24 (October 1979): p. 75.
[10] Stephen N. Brenner and Earl A. Molander, "Is the Ethics of Business Changing?" *Harvard Business Review* 55 (January–February 1977).
[11] Brenner and Molander, op. cit., p. 54.

Chapter 3

[1] Robert Townsend, *Up the Organization*. Greenwich, Conn.: Fawcett Book Group, 1970, p. 161.
[2] Laurence J. Peter, "Popular Incompetents," *Human Behavior*, April 1979, p. 171.
[3] *Wall Street Journal*, 22 December 1981, p. 5.

[4] Boris Emmet and John E. Jeuck, *Catalogues and Counters: A History of Sears, Roebuck, and Company* (Chicago: University of Chicago Press, 1950), pp. 23–46.
[5] *Wall Street Journal*, 22 December 1981, p. 2.
[6] Marlys Harris, "How to Be Your Own Boss Without Having a Fool for an Employer," *Money*, June 1977, p. 53.
[7] *Wall Street Journal*, 1 December 1981, p. 40.
[8] Harris, "How To Be Your Own Boss," p. 54.
[9] *Wall Street Journal*, 30 December 1981, p. 6.
[10] *Wall Street Journal*, 31 December 1981, p. 1.
[11] *Wall Street Journal*, 22 December 1981, p. 1.
[12] Ford S. Worthy, "The 500: The Fortune Directory of the Largest U.S. Industrial Corporations," *Fortune*, 4 May 1981, p. 324; *Statistical Abstract of the United States 1980* (Washington, D.C.: Government Printing Office, 1980), pp. 897–907.
[13] *Wall Street Journal*, 16 December 1981, p. 12.

Chapter 4

[1] "Small Business Column," *Management Accounting*, September 1981, p. 22.
[2] "3rd Annual Venture Capital Directory," *Venture*, January 1982.
[3] "What's Going to Happen in 1982?" *Inc.*, January 1982, p. 40.
[4] Frederick C. Klein, "Manageable Size," *Wall Street Journal*, 5 February 1982, p. 1.
[5] "Going Public Backfired for MAPI, Inc.," *Dayton Journal Herald*, 7 August 1981, p. 12.
[6] "Cod-Cake Rebellion: Arthur Treacher's Unit Verges on Bankruptcy," *Wall Street Journal*, 23 December 1981, p. 1.

Chapter 5

[1] "Why Griffiths is Out as RCA Chairman," *Business Week*, 9 February 1981, p. 72.

[2] Rensis Likert, *New Patterns of Management* (New York: McGraw-Hill, 1961), pp. 5–25.

[3] Robert J. Thierauf, Robert C. Klekamp, and Daniel W. Geeding, *Management Principles and Practices* (New York: John Wiley & Sons, 1977), pp. 56–68.

[4] Robert L. Katz, "Skills of an Effective Administrator," *Harvard Business Review* 52 (September–October 1974): 90–102.

[5] Peter F. Drucker, *The Practice of Management* (New York: Harper & Row, 1954).

Chapter 6

[1] Howard Aldrich and Diane Herker, "Boundary Spanning Roles and Organization Structure," *Academy of Management Review* 2 (April 1977): 217–29; and Richard Leifer and Andre Delbecq, "Organizational/Environmental Interchange: A Model of Boundary Spanning Activity," *Academy of Management Review* 3 (January 1978): 40–50.

[2] See Frederick Herzberg, "One More Time: How Do You Motivate Employees?" *Harvard Business Review* 46 (January–February 1968): 53–62.

Chapter 7

[1] Douglas McGregor, *The Human Side of Enterprise* (New York: McGraw-Hill, 1960), pp. 33–35.

[2] Frederick W. Taylor, *The Principles of Scientific Management* (New York: Harper, 1911).

[3] McGregor, op. cit., pp. 47–49.

[4] David C. McClelland, *The Achieving Society* (Princeton, N.J.: Van Nostrand, 1961).

[5] Frederick Herzberg, *Work and the Nature of Man* (Cleveland, Ohio: World Publishing, 1966).

[6] Victor Vroom, *Work and Motivation* (New York: John Wiley & Sons, 1964).

[7] Edward E. Lawler, *Pay and Organizational Effectiveness: A Psychological View* (New York: McGraw-Hill, 1971).

[8] William J. Kearney, "Pay for Performance? Not Always," *MSU Business Topics* 27 (Spring 1979): 5–16.

[9] Fritz J. Roethlisberger and William J. Dickson, *Management and the Worker* (Cambridge, Mass.: Harvard University Press, 1939).

Chapter 8

[1] Allen R. Janger, *The Personnel Function: Changing Objectives and Organization* (New York: The Conference Board, 1977), pp. 1–32.

[2] Ruth W. Stidger, "Looking for Competent Employees," *Sky*, March 1981, p. 80.

[3] Bernard M. Bass and James A. Vaughan, *Training in Industry: The Management of Learning* (Belmont, Calif.: Brooks/Cole, 1969), p. 8.

[4] Robert Kirk Mueller, *Buzzwords: A Guide to the Language of Leadership* (New York: Van Nostrand Reinhold, 1974), pp. 54, 55. *See also* George W. Hettenhouse, "Compensation Cafeteria for Top Executives," *Harvard Business Review* 49 (September–October 1971).

Chapter 9

[1] Leonard R. Sayles and George Strauss, *The Local Union* (New York: Harcourt, Brace & World, 1967), pp. 97–98.

[2] Russell A. Smith, Leroy S. Menifield, and Theodore J. St. Antoine, *Labor Relations Law* (Indianapolis, Ind.: Bobbs-Merrill, 1974), pp. 2–7.

[3] U.S. Department of Labor, Bureau of Labor Statistics, *Brief History of the American Labor Market* (1964), pp. 11–13.

[4] Bureau of National Affairs, *Basic Patterns in Union Contracts* (Washington, D.C.: Bureau of National Affairs, Inc., 1979), pp. 73–77.

Chapter 10

[1] "K-Cars—Chrysler's Bid for a Future," *Production Engineering*, January 1981, p. 35.

[2] "Inventory Control by Computer," *New York Times*, Business Section, 5 April 1981, p. 28.

Chapter 11

[1] "Procter & Gamble's Profit Problem—Food," *Business Week*, 26 January 1980, p. 56.

[2] "Learning to Think about Today's Mature Market," *Marketing Times*, May–June 1979, pp. 27–29.

Chapter 12

[1] "Survey Finds 67% of New Products Succeed," *Marketing News*, 8 February 1980, p. 1.

[2] "Disastrous Debuts—Despite High Hopes, Many New Products Flop in the Market," *Wall Street Journal*, 23 March 1976, p. 1.

[3] Joseph T. Joyce, "How to Select and Protect a Trademark," *Product Marketing*, May 1977, p. 26.

[4] "No-Frills Food—New Power for the Supermarkets," *Business Week*, 23 March 1981, p. 70.

[5] "Consumers Winning Improvements in Packaging, Industry Is Advised," *Marketing News*, 17 November 1978, p. 7.

[6] Harold S. Gorschman, "New Dimensions in Unhidden Persuasion," in Harold W. Berkman, ed., *Marketing Up-*

date (Dubuque, Iowa: Kendall Hunt Publishing Co., The Academy of Marketing Science, 1977), p. 331.

[7] Arnold A. Bennigson, "Product Liability—Producers and Manufacturers Beware," *Research Management* 18 (March 1975): 16.

Chapter 13

[1] "How Good Are Advocacy Ads?" *Dun's Review*, June 1980, pp. 76–77.

[2] Stanley I. Tannenbaum, "For Comparative Advertising," *Advertising Age*, 5 July 1976 pp. 26–27.

[3] Bernice Kanner, "Prime Time 30 at $342,000 Seen by 1990," *Advertising Age*, 10 March 1980, p. 16.

[4] Nancy Millman, "Record $1.4 Billion Changed Hands in '81," *Advertising Age*, 1 February 1982, p. 3 ff.

[5] "Business Bulletin," *Wall Street Journal*, 21 February 1980, p. 1.

[6] "Clip, Clip," *Fortune*, January 1977, p. 26.

[7] William A. Robinson, "Match Wits: Rate Promos," *Advertising Age*, 16 February 1981, p. 56.

Chapter 14

[1] "Centralized Ad Staff, Promotion of Discount Prices, Helped K-Mart Hit $14 Billion in Sales," *Marketing News*, 3 April 1981, p. 10.

[2] Walter McQuade, "There's a Lot of Satisfaction (Guaranteed) in Direct Marketing," *Fortune*, 21 April 1980, p. 12.

Chapter 15

[1] Milton Moskowitz, "Social Responsibility at ARCO: A Critique," in *Participation II* (Los Angeles: Atlantic Richfield Co., 1977).

[2] Robert Buzzell, Bradley T. Gale, and Ralph G. M. Sultan, "Market Share—A Key to Profitability," *Harvard Business Review* 53 (January–February 1975): pp. 97–106.

[3] "Sears Denies FTC Charge of Using Bait and Switch Ad," *Advertising Age*, 15 July 1974, p. 7.

Chapter 16

[1] *The VNR Dictionary of Business and Finance*, s.v. "money supply" (New York: Van Nostrand Reinhold Company, 1980).

Chapter 18

[1] "To Market, to Market—More Firms Go Public," *U.S. News and World Report*, 16 March 1981, p. 75.

[2] "U.S. Steel Corporation: Loaded with Cash and Innovative Financing Techniques," *Dun's Review*, July 1981, pp. 28–32.

Chapter 20

[1] "Getting Burned on the Beach," *Forbes*, 16 March 1981, pp. 91–94.

[2] "The Best Buys in Second Homes," *Business Week*, June, 22, 1981, pp. 116–18.

[3] "Condominium Rents: The Sky's the Limit," *Dun's Review*, June 1981, pp. 42–50.

[4] "The Yen to Own a Place in the Country," *Changing Times*, July 1980, pp. 40–46.

[5] Ibid.

[6] "Condominium Rents: The Sky's the Limit," *op. cit.*

[7] "Condominium Market Slows, Prompting New Sales Ploy," *Wall Street Journal*, 30 September 1981, p. 27.

Chapter 21

[1] Information about Arthur Andersen was provided by James W. Blain, managing partner of the Dayton, Ohio office of Arthur Andersen and Company.

Chapter 22

[1] "Will the Boss Go Electronic, Too?" *Business Week*, 11 May 1981, pp. 106–8.

[2] Advertisement of CW Communications, Newton, Mass. in *Advertising and Publishing News*, September 1979.

Chapter 23

[1] *Wall Street Journal*, 11 January 1982, p. 3.

[2] Robert K. Mautz and Alan G. Merten, "Business Diversity and Government Regulation," *Financial Executives*, November 1981, p. 20.

[3] *Wall Street Journal*, 23 February 1982, p. 35.

[4] "News From The Front," *Forbes*, 13 April 1981, p. 115.

Chapter 24

[1] Hal Mason, Robert Miller, and Dale Weigel, *International Business*, 2d ed. (New York: John Wiley & Sons, 1981), p. 9.

[2] U.S., Department of Commerce, Bureau of the Census, "Highlights of U.S. Export and Import Trade," FT 990 (December 1980), p. 11.

[3] Some of these examples are taken from Warren Keegan, *Multinational Marketing Management*, 2d ed. (Englewood Cliffs, N.J.: Prentice-Hall, 1980), p. 84.

[4] Neil Jacoby, "The Multinational Corporation," *Center Magazine* 3 (May 1975): p. 37. Reprinted with permission from *Center Magazine*, a publication of the Robert Maynard Hutchins Center for the Study of Democratic Institutions, Santa Barbara, California.

[5] Robert Stauffer, *Nation Building in a Global Economy: The Role of the Multinational Corporation* (Beverly Hills: Sage Publications, 1973), p. 13.

Chapter 25

[1] "The Marketing Process: Painful Lessons of the 70's," *Advertising Age*, August 1980, p. 16.

[2] These scenarios are taken from *Alternative Futures for Environmental Policy Planning: 1975–2000*, Document EPA-540/9-75-027 (Washington, D.C.: The Environmental Protection Agency); and Paul Dickson, *The Future File* (New York: Rawson Associates Publishers, 1977), pp. 108–21.

[3] Dickson, *Future File*, p. 21.

[4] Thomas J. Sullivan et al., *Social Problems: Divergent Perspectives* (New York: John Wiley & Sons, 1980), p. 702.

[5] Ibid., pp. 670–71.

[6] Barry Crickmer, "Regulation: How Much Is Enough?" *Nation's Business*, March 1980, pp. 26–32.

[7] "Can Reagan Rope the Regulators?" *Dun's Review*, May 1981, pp. 41–48.

[8] "The Lure of High Tech for Cutting Costs," *Business Week*, 1 June 1981, p. 96.

[9] Phillip W. Dunphy, Sidney F. Austin, and Thomas J. McEneaney, *Career Development for the College Student*, 4th ed. (Cranston, R.I.: Carroll Press, 1976), p. 106.

Acknowledgments for Part-end Career Appendixes
Part 4: Finance

"Actuaries," *The Encyclopedia of Careers and Vocational Guidance*, vol. 2 (Chicago: J. C. Ferguson Publishing, 1978), pp. 10–13.

"Bank and Thrift Institution Officers," *The Encyclopedia of Careers and Vocational Guidance*, vol. 2 (Chicago: J. C. Ferguson Publishing, 1978), pp. 37–41.

John L. De Jong and Alfred O. Stromquist, "Banking," *The Encyclopedia of Careers and Vocational Guidance*, vol. 1 (Chicago: J. C. Ferguson Publishing, 1978), pp. 139–46.

Rolf Kaltenborn, "Brokerage and Investments," *The Encyclopedia of Careers and Vocational Guidance*, vol. 1 (Chicago: J. C. Ferguson Publishing, 1978), pp. 165–79.

"Life Insurance Agents and Brokers," *The Encyclopedia of Careers and Vocational Guidance*, vol. 2 (Chicago: J. C. Ferguson Publishing, 1978), pp. 417–23.

Robert H. Pease, "Real Estate," *The Encyclopedia of Careers and Vocational Guidance*, vol. 1 (Chicago: J. C. Ferguson Publishing, 1978), pp. 569–75.

"Property and Casualty Insurance Agents and Brokers," *The Encyclopedia of Careers and Vocational Guidance*, vol. 2 (Chicago: J. C. Ferguson Publishing, 1978), pp. 427–30.

"Real Estate Agents and Brokers," *The Encyclopedia of Careers and Vocational Guidance*, vol. 2 (Chicago: J. C. Ferguson Publishing, 1978), pp. 431–35.

"Securities Sales Workers," *The Encyclopedia of Careers and Vocational Guidance*, vol. 2 (Chicago: J. C. Ferguson Publishing, 1978), pp. 447–49.

Mitchell Thomas, "Insurance," *The Encyclopedia of Careers and Vocational Guidance*, vol. 1 (Chicago: J. C. Ferguson Publishing, 1978), pp. 283–90.

U.S. Department of Labor, *Occupational Outlook Handbook*, 1980–81 ed. (Washington, D.C.: Government Printing Office, 1980), pp. 102–105, 107, 108, 194, 195, 199, 200.

John W. Wright, *The American Almanac of Jobs and Salaries* (New York: Avon Publishing, 1982), pp. 519–28, 524–34, 683–87.

Part 5: Business Tools

"Employment Statistics Job Outlook '82," *National Business Employment Weekly*, 10 January 1982, pp. 15, 16.

U.S. Department of Labor, *Occupational Outlook Handbook*, 1980–81 ed. (Washington, D.C.: Government Printing Office, 1980), pp. 100, 101, 113–15.

U.S. Department of Labor, *Occupational Outlook Quarterly* (Washington, D.C.: Government Printing Office, Summer 1981), pp. 3–31.

John W. Wright, *The American Almanac of Jobs and Salaries* (New York: Avon Publishing, 1982), pp. 349–61.

Acknowledgments for Chapter-end Cases

Chapter 9: *Ford's New Model Management/Labor Contract*: adapted from several news stories distributed by the Associated Press, March 1, 1982. Used by permission.

Chapter 13: *Would You Believe Fish Farms?*: adapted with the permission of WGBH, Boston, Massachusetts, from the article "Catfish Fever" published in *A Guide to Enterprise*, copyright © 1981, WGBH Educational Foundation.

The "On the Firing Line" boxes appearing in each chapter were written by Judith Lynn Bleicher, who used a variety of sources for their composition.

PHOTO CREDITS

Chapter 1

4: Left, Charles Harbutt/Archive Pictures; right, Cary Wolinsky/Stock, Boston. 5: Left, Charles Harbutt/Archive Pictures; right, Gilles Peress/Magnum. 8: Left, Peter Menzel/Stock, Boston; center, Eastern Photo Service/de Wys; right, Leonard Speier. 9: Left, Bruce Roberts/Photo Researchers; center, Michael Hayman/Stock, Boston; right, Peter Vandermark/Stock, Boston. 10: Left, Everett C. Johnson/de Wys; right, Janice Fullman/The Picture Cube. 15: Culver Pictures. 16: The Bettmann Archive. 19: Sidney Harris.

Chapter 2

24: Left, Ann McQueen/Stock, Boston; right, Michael O'Brien/Archive Pictures. 25: Left, Donald Dietz/Stock, Boston; right, Michael O'Brien/Archive Pictures. 27: Sidney Harris. 28, Figure 2.1: Courtesy Gannett. 32: Top, H. Gloaguen/VIVA/Woodfin Camp; bottom, Sygma. 35: Courtesy Joseph E. Seagrams & Sons. 37: Top left, Dick Durrance/Woodfin Camp; buttom right, Courtesy of International Telephone & Telegraph Corporation. 41, Figure 2.3: Courtesy of Whirlpool Corporation.

Chapter 3

46: Left, Hiroyuki Matsumoto/Black Star; right, Steve Proehl/Photo Researchers. 47: Left, Frank Wing/Stock, Boston; right, Catherine Ursillo/Photo Researchers. 49: Alan Carey/The Image Works. 52: Eric Roth/The Picture Cube. 55: Michael Rizza/Stock, Boston. 57: Owen Franken/Stock, Boston. 59: Courtesy of Fortune Magazine. 61: Sidney Harris. 63, Figure 3.2: Courtesy of Hammermill Paper Company.

Chapter 4

68: Left, Joel Gordon; right Richard Hutchings/Photo Researchers. 69: Left, Mike Mazzaschi/Stock, Boston; right, Bruce Roberts/Rapho-Photo Researchers. 73: Top left, Marilyn L. Schrut; top right, Alan Carey/The Image Works; bottom left, Joel Gordon; bottom right, Rick Smolan/de Wys. 79: Left, Marilyn L. Schrut; right, courtesy of Fotomat Corporation. 84: Van Bucher/Photo Researchers. 85: Courtesy of Business Data Service. 88: Top, Catherine Ursillo/Photo Researchers; bottom, courtesy of The First Women's Bank.

Chapter 5

96: Left, Michael O'Brien/Archive Pictures; right Charles Harbutt/Archive Pictures. 97: Left, Bonnie Freer/Photo Researchers; right, Joel Gordon. 100: Joel Gordon. 105, Figure 5.4: Courtesy Dow Chemical Company. 112: Sepp Seitz/Woodfin Camp.

Chapter 6

122: Left, Jim Cartier/Photo Researchers; right, Lowell J. Georgia/Photo Researchers. 123: Left, Charles Harbutt/Archive Pictures; right, courtesy of TRW. 132: Alan Carey/The Image Works. 135: Left, Joel Gordon; right Craig Aurness/Woodfin Camp. 137: Top, Ken Karp; Figure 6.9, Daniel D. Sullivan/Photo Researchers. 139: Top, Bohdan Hrynewych/Stock, Boston; center, Craig Aurness/Woodfin Camp; bottom, Michael Heron/Woodfin Camp.

Chapter 7

150: Left, Dick Durrance II/Woodfin Camp; right, Michal Heron/Woodfin Camp. 151: Left, Michal Heron/Woodfin Camp; right, Charles Harbutt/Archive Pictures. 156: Courtesy Ingersoll Rand. 160: Jeff Jacobson/Archive Pictures. 163: Charles Harbutt/Archive Pictures. 166: Michael Hayman/Stock, Boston.

Chapter 8

174: Left, courtesy of TRW; right, Lincoln Russell/Stock, Boston. 175: Left, Guy Gillette/Photo Researchers; right, Dennis Purse/Photo Researchers. 183: Lincoln Russell/Stock, Boston. 184: Sidney Harris. 185, Figure 8.6: Courtesy of Johnson & Johnson. 187, Figure 8.8: Courtesy of General Electric. 188, Figure 8.9: Courtesy of E. F. Wonderlic, Northfield, Illinois; © E. F. Wonderlic. 191: Al Stephenson/Woodfin Camp.

Chapter 9

200: Left, Eric Kroll/Taurus; right, Michael Abramson/Black Star. 201: Left, Cary Wolinsky/Stock, Boston; right, Martin Adler Levick/Black Star. 214: Michael Hayman/Photo Researchers. 219: Arnold Zann/Black Star. 220: Michelle Bogre/Sygma.

Chapter 10

224: Left, Joel Gordon; right, Mark Godfrey/Archive Pictures. 225: Left, Charles Harbutt/Archive Pictures; right, Georg Gerster/Photo Researchers. 228: Top, Sepp Seitz/Woodfin Camp; bottom, Peter Southwick/Stock, Boston. 230, Figure 10.3: Courtesy of Chrysler Corporation. 233: Left, Bruce Roberts/Photo Researchers; right, John Blaustein/Woodfin Camp. 234, Figure 10.5: Courtesy of the Arkansas Industrial Development Commission. 237: Left, Courtesy Goodyear; right, Mark Antman/The Image Works. 238: Dick Durrance/Woodfin Camp. 241: Sidney Harris.

Chapter 11

252: Left, Leo de Wys; right, Clifford W. Hausner/de Wys. 253: Left, Christopher Springmann/Black Star; right, Alan Becker/Photo Researchers. 260, Figure 11.2: Courtesy of Business Committee for the Arts. 263: Top left, courtesy of American Honda Motor Company; bottom left, Courtesy of Colgate-Palmolive Company; bottom center, Courtesy of Bristol-Myers; right, Courtesy of Bonne Bell, Lakewood, Ohio. 264: Courtesy of Levi Strauss & Company. 266, Figure 11.5; Left, courtesy of United Airlines; right, courtesy of Hanes Hosiery. 267, Figure 11.7: Left, and right, courtesy of Philip Morris Incorporated; center, courtesy of Brown & Williamson. 271: Courtesy of North American Philips Consumer Electronics Corporation.

Chapter 12

276: Left, Stacy Pick/Stock, Boston; right, Geoff Gilbert/Photo Researchers. 277: Left, Mark Antman/The Image Works; right, Marilyn L. Schrut. 281: Left, Sepp Seitz/Woodfin Camp; top right, Michael Collier/Stock, Boston; bottom right, Joel Gordon. 284: Top, Daniel S. Brody/Stock, Boston; bottom left, Peter Menzel/Stock, Boston; bottom right, Peter Southwick/Stock, Boston. 288: Courtesy of Johnson & Johnson. 289, Figure 12.6: Courtesy of The Coca-Cola Company. 292: Peter Lerman.

Chapter 13

298: Left, courtesy of The Procter & Gamble Company, Colgate-Palmolive Company, © 1980 Kellogg Company (Tony the Tiger is a registered trademark of Kellogg Company) and the Pillsbury Company, Minneapolis, Mn.; right, J. P. Laffont/Sygma. 299: Left, Peter Vandermark/Stock, Boston; right, courtesy of Ted Bates Advertising Agency. 301, Figure 13.1: Left, courtesy of Gerber Products Company; center, courtesy of Thomasville®; right, courtesy of American Telephone and Telegraph Company, Long Lines Department. 304, Figure 13.3: Courtesy of International Paper Company. 305, Figure 13.4: Courtesy of U.S. Steel. 306: Courtesy of Bristol-Myers. 308: Courtesy of Scientific American Magazine. 310, Figure 13.5: Marilyn L. Schrut. 314, Figure 13.8: Courtesy of The Harris Trust & Savings Bank, Chicago; bottom, Ray Ellis/Photo Researchers. 316: Joel Gordon. 318, Figure 13.9: K. Bendo.

Chapter 14

322: Left, James Foote; right, Peter Menzel/Stock, Boston. 323: Left, Steve Proehl/Photo Researchers; right, Bill Gallery/Stock, Boston. 327: George Malave/Stock, Boston. 329: G. Zimbel/Monkmeyer. 331: Left, courtesy of Bloomingdale's; right, courtesy of K-mart. 335: Top, Donald Dietz/Stock, Boston; bottom, John Blaustein/Woodfin Camp. 340: Top left, Omikron/Photo Researchers; bottom left, Ken Robert Buck/Stock, Boston; right, Peter Southwick/Stock, Boston.

Chapter 15

344: Left, Barbara Pfeffer/Peter Arnold; right, Bart Bartholomew/Black Star. 345: Left, Eric Kroll/Taurus; right, Edith G. Haun/Stock, Boston. 349, Figure 15.1: Courtesy of A. C. Nielsen Company. 354: Joel Gordon. 356: Courtesy of The Great Atlantic & Pacific Tea Company. 358: Left, courtesy of Sears Roebuck and Company; right, Courtesy of Tiffany & Company. 365: Harvey Wilks/Stock, Boston.

Chapter 16

372: Left, Joel Gordon; right, Alex Webb/Magnum. 373: Left, Ann McQueen/Stock, Boston; right, Len Speier. 378: Shelly Katz/Black Star. 383: Joel Gordon. 389: Courtesy of VISA. 391: Courtesy of Manufacturers Hanover and Edwin Bird Wilson Advertising Agency; art director, Marty Giuriceo; photographer, Marvin Koner.

Chapter 17

396: Left, Catherine Ursillo/Photo Researchers; right, Richard Laird. 397: Left, Alex Webb/Magnum; right, Roger Malloch/Magnum. 399: Courtesy Boise Cascade Corporation. 401: Courtesy International Minerals & Chemical Corporation. 402, Figure 17.1: Courtesy South Dakota Housing Development Authority. 406: Courtesy of the New York Stock Exchange. 408: Peter Lerman. 412: Courtesy E. F. Hutton & Company, and Henderson & Friedlich Advertising Agency. 414, Figure 17.4: Reproduced with permission of Charles Schwab & Company. 415, Figure 17.5: Top left, Sylvia Johnson/Woodfin Camp; top right, Robert Eckert/Stock, Boston; center, Edward C. Topple, New York Stock Exchange; bottom left, Mark Antman/The Image Works; bottom right, Christopher Morrow/Stock, Boston.

Chapter 18

420: Left, Everett C. Johnson/de Wys; right, Michael Melford/Peter Arnold. 421: Left, Bill Gallery/Stock, Boston; right, James Foote. 424: Henry Martin. 430: Top left, Susan McCartney/Photo Researchers; bottom left, Paolo Koch/Photo Researchers; right, Joe Rychetnik/Black Star. 433: Top, Robert A. Isaacs/Photo Researchers; bottom, Courtesy of Burlington Industries. 434, Figure 18.3: Courtesy of Worldwide Energy Corporation. 439, Figure 18.5: Courtesy of Pengo Industries. 440, Figure 18.6: Reprinted by permission of The Wall Street Journal © Dow Jones & Company.

Chapter 19

444: Left, John Storkey/Black Star; right, Joel Gordon. 445: Left, John Running/Stock, Boston; right, Cecil Simpson/de Wys. 448: Joel Gordon. 453: Sidney Harris. 455: Courtesy of Aetna Life & Casualty. 456: Milton Feinberg/Stock, Boston. 459: Courtesy of The Travelers Insurance Companies.

Chapter 20

464: Left, Joel Gordon; right, Jim Ayres/Black Star. 465: Left, Bohdan Hrynewych/Stock, Boston; right, Jock Pottle/Design Conceptions. 467: Courtesy of Adams & McGuire, Inc., Jockey Club. 469: Georg Gerster/Rapho-Photo Researchers. 470: From Field & Stream Magazine. 474: Bohdan Hrynewych/Stock, Boston. 477: Werner Wolff/Black Star. 479: Daniel S. Brody/Stock, Boston.

Chapter 21

488: Left, Mimi Forsyth/Monkmeyer; right, Everett C. Johnson/de Wys. 489: Left, Marilyn L. Schrut. 491: Left, Richard Wood/Taurus; right, Mark Antman/The Image Works. 497: Left, Peter Lerman. 501: Courtesy of NCR. 502: Sidney Harris. 507: Courtesy of Dun & Bradstreet. 508: Courtesy of Bristol-Myers Company.

Chapter 22

512: Left, Frank Wing/Stock, Boston; right, Costa Manos/Magnum. 513: Left, Michael O'Brien/Archive Pictures; right, courtesy of Bell Labs. 515: Courtesy of Bell Labs. 516: Top left, courtesy of Delta Air Lines; top right, Christopher Morrow/Stock, Boston; bottom left, Bruce Roberts/Photo Researchers; bottom right, Jean-Pierre Laffont/Sygma. 519: Sidney Harris. 520: Left, C. B. Jones/Taurus; right, James Foote. 525: Courtesy of Xerox Corporation. 529: Courtesy of Sperry-Univac.

Chapter 23

540: Left, courtesy of the Securities and Exchange Commission; right, Joel Gordon. 541: Right, S. Vidler/de Wys. 544: Sidney Harris. 548: Peter Lerman. 551: Top, Shelly Katz/Black Star. 552, Figure 23.1: Courtesy of *U.S. News and World Report*, February 11, 1980, p. 64. 553: K. Bendo and seat belt photo courtesy of General Motors Corporation.

Chapter 24

562: Left, Larry Reynolds; right, Guy Gillette/Photo Researchers. 563: Left, Charles Harbutt/Archive Pictures; right, Frank Wing/Stock, Boston. 565: J. P. Laffont/Sygma. 567: Top, Grey Davis/Sygma; bottom, Diego Goldberg/Sygma. 579: Top, courtesy of Johnson & Johnson; bottom, Sidney Harris.

Chapter 25

584: Left, Kenneth Karp; right, John Marmara; Woodfin Camp. 585: Left Abigail Heyman/Archive Pictures; right, courtesy of General Electric. 588: Courtesy of Adidas, USA. 590: Stan Goldblatt/Photo Researchers. 591: Courtesy of Mobil Oil Corporation. 592: Top left, John Blaustein/Woodfin Camp; bottom left, Kent & Donna Dannen/Photo Researchers; right, courtesy of Sandia Laboratories.

NAME INDEX

CORPORATE NAME INDEX

SUBJECT INDEX

Key terms and their page numbers appear in **boldface** type for ease in locating them.

dental, 456
disability income, 455
group insurance plans for, 456
and health maintenance organizations, 457
and hospitalization coverage, 455
and individual coverage, 457
and major medical coverage, 455
national program for, 457–459
prepaid medical expense plans for, 456–457
Social Security providing, 456
sources of coverage for, 456–457
surgical and medical payments by, 455
and workmen's compensation coverage, 456
Health maintenance organizations, 457
Hidden tax, 13
Hierarchy (management), 125, 127–128
Hierarchy of motivation, 158–159
Hierarchy of needs, 158–160
High-level languages, 523
Home and building insurance, 450
coinsurance clause for, 451–452
perils covered by, 451
Home industry argument, 570
Horizontal channel of communication, 111
Hospitalization insurance, 455
Housing:
financing costs of, 469–472
investment attributes of, 472–473
price appreciation of, 472, 473
tax advantages of ownership of, 472–473
rental, 474
types of mortgages for, 470–472
see also Real estate
Human relations, 152, 153–170
in Japanese industry, 152, 157
management of, for small businesses, 83
Theories X and Y of, 154, 156, 161
Theory Z of, 155
and work attitudes, 153–156
see also Groups
Human resources demand forecast, 180

Human resources management, 176, 177–196. *See also* specific personnel entries
Human resources planning, 180–183
Human skills, 119

Implicit communication, 300–301
Import quotas, 570–571
Imports, 564–566
Income property, *see* Investment property
Income statement, 493–494, 502–508
Income taxes, 554, 556. *See also* Taxation
Incorporators, 55
Independent brokers, 405–406
Index numbers, 610
Inductive statistics, 607
Industrial distributor, 326
Industrial goods, 283
accessories as, 283
component parts and materials as, 284
distribution channels for, 325, 326
installations as, 382
promotional mix for, 302
raw materials as, 283–284
services as, 8, 285
supplies as, 284–285
Industrial revolution, 14
Industrial robots, 231
Industrial union, 205. *See also* Labor unions
Industry average, 505
Infant industry argument, 570
Inflation affecting business, 17
Inflation hedge, 468
Influence, 141
Influencer, 272
Informal organization, 81, 83, 131–132
Informal structure, 131–132
Informal study of business, 19
Information distributor, manager as, **100**
Information seeker, manager as, **100**
Informative advertising, 301
Initial screening, 184
Injunction, 219
Inland marine insurance, 453–454

Input mix for production process, **229**
Installations, 283
Insurable perils, 447–448
Insurance, 447
cost of, relative to coverage, 448
large group principle of, 447
types of, 448
see also Automobile insurance; Health insurance; Home and building insurance; Life insurance; Property and liability insurance; Property insurance
Insurance companies, 448–450
Insurance policy, 447
Insurance premium, 447
Intangible assets, 501
Intangible personal property, 547
Intelligence network, 132
Intensive distribution, 327
Interactive-based technology, 138, 139, 140
Interactive control, 115
Interest coverage ratio, 507–508
Interest rates, 394–395, 435
Intermittent process, 228
Internal data sources, 607–608
Internal financing, 424, 435–436, 440
Internal labor market, 183
Internal Revenue Code, 554
International business, 564–581
careers in, 584–585
contract manufacturing in, 577
cultural considerations for, 579–580
direct investment in, 577–578
entry into, 573–578
exporting, 574–575
government assistance to, 576
impact of nationalism on, 579
joint ventures in, 577
licensing, 575, 577
and multinational corporations, 580–581
political considerations of, 578–579
see also Trade
Interpersonal communication, 111
and group behavior, 164–168
Introductory stage of product life cycle, **287**
Inventory:
cost of holding, 238